MW00427018

GTK+ PROGRAMMING IN C

ISBN 0-13-014264-6

90000

9 780130 142641

Editorial/Production Supervision: *Argosy*
Acquisitions Editor: *Gregory Doench*
Editorial Assistant: *Brandt Kenna*
Marketing Manager: *Debby vanDijk*
Cover Design Director: *Jerry Votta*
Cover Designer: *Talar Agasyan-Boorujy*
Art Director: *Gail Cocker-Bogusz*
Project Coordinator: *Anne R. Garcia*
Manufacturing Manager: *Alexis Heydt-Long*

Prentice-Hall, Inc.
Upper Saddle River, NJ 07458

The publisher offers discounts on this book when ordered in bulk quantities. For more information contact: Corporate Sales Department, Prentice Hall PTR, One Lake Street, Upper Saddle River, NJ 07458. Phone: 800-382-3419; FAX: 201-236-7141; E-mail: corpsales@prenhall.com

Printed in the United States of America

10 9 8 7 6 5 4 3 2 1

ISBN 0-13-014264-6

Pearson Education Ltd.
Pearson Education Australia PTY, Ltd.
Pearson Education Singapore, Pte. Ltd.
Pearson Education North Asia Ltd.
Pearson Education Canada, Ltd.
Pearson Educación de Mexico, S.A. de C.V.
Pearson Education -- Japan
Pearson Education Malaysia, Pte. Ltd.
Pearson Education, Upper Saddle River, New Jersey

GTK+ PROGRAMMING IN C

SYD LOGAN

PH PTR

Prentice Hall PTR
Upper Saddle River, New Jersey 07458
www.phptr.com

Library of Congress Cataloging-in-Publication Data

Logan, Syd.
Gtk+ programming in C / by Syd Logan.
p. cm.
ISBN 0-13-014264-6 (pbk.)
1. C (Computer programming language) 2. GTK+. 3. Graphical user interfaces (Computer systems)
I. Title.

QA76.73.C15 L63 2001
005.2'84--dc21 2001032173

TABLE OF CONTENTS

CHAPTER 3

SIGNALS, EVENTS, OBJECTS, AND TYPES . . . 47

CHAPTER 4

CHAPTER 6

CHAPTER 7

CHAPTER 8

SEPARATORS, ARROWS, IMAGES, PIXMAPS, AND ENTRY WIDGETS . . . 319

CHAPTER 10

CONTAINER AND BIN CLASSES 417

CHAPTER 13

RANGE WIDGETS AND ADJUSTMENT OBJECTS 665

CHAPTER 14

CHAPTER 15

MISCELLANEOUS WIDGETS 725

APPENDIX

INTRODUCTION

Gtk+ was originally developed by two University of California at Berkeley students, Spencer Kimball and Peter Mattis. They had developed, as a part of a school project, an image manipulation called The GNU Image Manipulation Program (The GIMP, *www.gimp.org*). Originally it was written in Motif, but due to the (at the time) closed-source nature of Motif and, as a result, its scarcity on freely available open-source UNIX platforms, they decided to come up with an open-source toolkit, inspired by Motif, to which The GIMP could then be ported. The goal was not to develop a general-purpose toolkit for the X Window System, although that is what Gtk+ has become. Hundreds if not thousands of programs have been written using Gtk+ to date, ensuring that Gtk+ will be around for some time to come. More information on the history of Gtk+ (and The GIMP) can be found at *www.gimp.org/~sjburges/gimp-history.html.*

About This Book

This book covers the 1.2 version of the GIMP Toolkit (Gtk+) and was written with the following goals in mind:

- To provide a general introduction to programming applications with Gtk+ 1.2
- To provide a detailed description of the Gtk+ 1.2 widget set
- To provide a quick reference to the Gtk+ 1.2 widget set for those programmers already familiar with Gtk+

For those of you looking for an introduction to Gtk+ programming, I suggest reading Chapters 1 through 4 first, followed by Chapter 10, "Container and Bin Classes." The first few chapters (Chapters 1, 2, and 3) describe the architecture of Gtk+ and provide information needed to program and build a simple Gtk+ application. Most readers will want to skim through Chapter 4, "Widgets," which describes GtkWidget. GtkWidget is the parent class from which the remaining widgets in the Gtk+ class hierarchy inherit much of their functionality. Container widgets are used to organize the layout of other widgets in a window (or within other containers). The concept of container widgets is described in the first few sections of Chapter 10. The GtkBox widgets are by far the most versatile of the container widgets implemented by Gtk+ 1.2 and, as a result, are the most commonly used. GtkBox, GtkHBox, and GtkVBox are all described in Chapter 10 of this book.

The remaining chapters provide detailed descriptions of the bulk of the widget classes implemented in Gtk+ 1.2. I have made every effort to describe in detail the application-level programming interfaces exposed by the Gtk+ widget sets covered in this book. I have included most of the code I wrote while investigating the Gtk+ widget set. In some cases, the source code consists of a full-size (although functionally limited) application. In all other cases, I simply present short code snippets that help to illustrate points made in the surrounding text. Complete source-code examples for the book can be found on my Web site at *www.cts.com/crash/s/slogan/gtkbook.html.*

I have placed Gtk+ widget reference material directly in the main body of the text (as opposed to placing it at the end of the book in an appendix). The reference material provides function prototypes for each of the application-level functions that have been exposed by the widgets described in the book and a one-line sentence describing the purpose of each of these functions. In the reference section, I also enumerate all of the object attributes that can be set and/or retrieved on the widget (see the "Object Attributes" section in Chapter 3, "Signals, Events, Objects, and Types"). I also list the signals that can be generated by the widget, if any. For each signal, I supply the function prototype of the application-level signal handler invoked when the signal fires (see the "Signals" section in Chapter 3). The reference material provides an introduction to the widget for first-time programmers and can serve as a quick reference for programmers who are already familiar with widgets. More information about the structure of the reference section is spelled out in Chapter 4 (see the reference section for the GtkWidget widget).

This book focuses on describing the Gtk+ widget set. This book does not cover the Gtk+ Drawing Kit (GDK), or the G Library (Glib), or widget writing in any detail (except where unavoidable). For GDK and GLib, I refer you to one or both of the following books: *Developing Linux Applications with GTK+ and GDK* by Eric Harlow and *GTK+/Gnome Application Development* by Havoc Pennington. You can also find reference material on these topics at *www.gtk.org*. I do plan to provide an additional chapter on Gtk+ widget development on my Web site; it should be available shortly after this book goes to press. Hopefully, this material will be included in a subsequent edition of this book.

Source Code

I have placed source code throughout the book to provide illustrative examples of the concepts discussed. In some cases, line numbers are prefixed to each line of source code, like this:

```
static void
ClickedCallback(GtkWidget *widget, GtkWidget *dialog_window)
{
   GtkWidget *window, *labelFrame, *labelTest, *vbox;

   window = gtk_window_new( GTK_WINDOW_TOPLEVEL );
   gtk_window_position (GTK_WINDOW (window), GTK_WIN_POS_MOUSE);
   gtk_widget_set_usize( window, 320, -1 );
```

```
    vbox = gtk_vbox_new (FALSE, 0);
    gtk_container_add (GTK_CONTAINER (window), vbox);
```

For code that is simple to read or relatively short (a few lines or so in length), I will often omit the line numbers. Full (and, in some cases, incomplete but long) listings of example code are prefixed with a listing number and title as follows:

Listing 1.1 GtkLabel Attribute Sample Code

```
#include <gtk/gtk.h
#include <stdio.h>

static GtkWidget *leftButton, *rightButton, *centerButton;
static GtkWidget *trueButton, *falseButton;

static void
QuitCallback(GtkWidget *widget, GtkWidget *dialog_window)
{
   gtk_main_quit();
   exit( 0 );
```

I plan to make the source code for this book available online. Please go to *www.users.cts.com/crash/s/slogan/gtkbook.html* for further details.

Onward . . .

By purchasing this book, you have decided to develop an application for Linux/UNIX, and you have also decided to develop this application using Gtk+. In addition to learning about Gtk+, you should take some time to learn more about the desktop environment(s) within which users will be executing your application. If you are targeting GNOME—and some of you are—you should learn about developing for the GNOME environment using the books and Internet resources available. This book covers the Gtk+ toolkit, upon which all GNOME applications are based, but I do not cover GNOME application development specifically within these covers.

Acknowledgments

I'd like to thank several people for their help in the development of this book. First of all, I'd like to thank Greg Doench at Prentice Hall for taking the time to discuss this project with me when it was just an idea, for consenting to read my proposal, and for making this project possible. I'd also like to thank Jim Markham, also at Prentice Hall, for guiding me through the bulk of the editorial work. Amy Lepore applied her substantial copy editing skills to the manuscript, and somehow turned my gibberish into something that hopefully appeals to software developers and English teachers alike. Caroline Roop coordinated the copy edit process and helped to shape the format of the book which you now hold in your hands. To my reviewers, Ariel Rios (GNOME project) and Rob Flynn (maintainer of GAIM), I extend my thanks for a job well done. Any errors that may remain in the text are, of course, my responsibility alone. Joe Hewitt produced the nonscreenshot figures for this book, and for this I am most thankful. I would like to thank the people who contributed ideas and suggestions for the book, including Ramiro Estrugo (formerly of Eazel), who pointed out the possibility of including reference material within the main body of the text. Finally, I'd like to thank the vast number of people who made Gtk+ and GNOME possible. It is through efforts like theirs that desktop Linux is becoming a reality for more and more users.

Each and every line of the original manuscript was written on a GNU/Linux system using the VIM editor (an open-source vi clone that is available, usually by default, on GNU/Linux systems and by download for Win32, Mac, and other platforms; see *www.vim.org*). Screen shots were grabbed using The GIMP *(www.gimp.org)*, a freely available image-editing program that was, in fact, the first Gtk+ application ever written. Sample programs were also created in VIM, compiled using gcc, and in some cases, debugged with gdb. The gdb debugger was also used to inspect Gtk+ internals during its execution in order to learn more about the operation of certain widgets.

During the review process, a Hypertext Markup Language (HTML) version of the book was developed using the Gtk+-based Bluefish editor *(http://bluefish.openoffice.nl/)*. The output from Bluefish, prior to being uploaded to reviewers, was proofed using a development version of Netscape 6 *(www.netscape.com)*, which in turn was derived from the open-source browser Mozilla *(www.mozilla.org)*. All of this work was done, of course, on a GNU/Linux system.

CHAPTER

1

GTK+ IN CONTEXT

Gtk+ is a toolkit designed for use in the development of applications for the X Window System. It is just a part of the overall picture, however. To fully appreciate Gtk+, you need to have a basic understanding of the X Window System. For those of you already familiar with the X Window System and its components, feel free to skip to Chapter 2, "Hello Gtk+!," where I provide an overview of Gtk+.

The X Window System

The X Window System (called X, X11, or sometimes X Windows) is a network-based, client-server user interface technology developed by the MIT X Consortium in the mid 1980s. The architect of the X11 system was Robert Schiefler. He, along with a small team of developers at MIT, formed the nucleus of what was known as the MIT X Consortium. Their job was to oversee and guide the development of the X Window System and to develop and release a sample implementation of the X server and the core client libraries (Xlib, Xt, and so forth) to member companies of the consortium.

The member companies of the X Consortium each had a business interest in ensuring that a vendor-neutral, interoperable user interface for the UNIX operating system flourished. These companies contributed source code to the sample implementation, created products that were based on it, or did a little of both. I was very fortunate to work for one of these member companies during this time. AGE Logic, founded in the late 1980s, initially focused on taking the MIT sample implementation and using it to develop the software portion of several X terminals developed during this period of time. In the early 1990s, an X terminal was the least expensive way to run X-based applications on a desktop. The alternative was to dedicate a workstation (e.g., a Sun, HP, or RS/6000) to each user; such a solution could easily decrease the bank account of a company given the cost of workstations (tens of thousands of dollars) as well as increase the workload of system administrators. The alternative, X terminals, cost one or two thousand dollars, were easier to maintain, were much less expensive to own, and since X terminals could be optimized for running an X server, often improved the overall performance of X-based applications because they were able to execute X faster.

Once Microsoft Windows 3.0 became available, the industry focus shifted away from X terminals toward PC-based X server software. This software allowed users to access X client applications executing on workstations from their personal computer desktops and further reduced the cost of accessing X-based applications.

All along, the major workstation vendors pumped large amounts of money and resources into X11 on both sides of the X Protocol pipe (client and server). When MS Windows 3.0 arrived, it was clearly seen as a threat to their market share. MS Windows was maturing, PC-based systems were becoming more capable in terms of their performance, and graphical user interfaces (as opposed to command-line interfaces) were being demanded by more and more end users, thus making UNIX a less attractive alternative. Efforts were made to develop desktop environments such as CDE (discussed later in this chapter) in an attempt to answer the threat. These efforts came up short, and as a result of this and other (perhaps more influential) factors, MS Windows and MacOS dominated desktops during the 1990s, and they continue to do so today.

To those involved, the early to mid 1990s were fertile times for the X Window System and the industry it supported. Numerous products were on the market, there were magazines dedicated specifically to X11-based software development, and there were even yearly major industry trade shows and developer conferences, such as Xhibition and X World, that attracted dozens of vendors and hundred of attendees.

The X Consortium made its last major release, X11R6, in 1994 and disbanded shortly thereafter. Since then, energy has shifted from the X Consortium to a collaborative effort of X.org *(www.x.org),* an organization of the Open Group, and XFree86 *(www.xfree86.org).* This shift has neatly coincided with an explosion in the availability of free UNIX-like operating systems such as GNU/Linux, FreeBSD, and NetBSD, each of which is capable of executing on consumer-level PC hardware. The X servers available today continue to expand on the X11R6 sample implementation, perhaps most notably by providing extensive support for PC-based video drivers. The combination of freely available PC-based UNIX and X software has, for the most part, made X terminals and PC-based X server software things of the past, and desktop X is a reality for everyone who desires it, including home users. But the promise of a Linux-based desktop has yet to be fully realized. Microsoft still dominates the end-user marketplace, although a few open-source efforts show promise in advancing Linux on the desktop. One of them, GNOME, has its roots in Gtk+, the topic of this book. I will have more to say on this issue later in this chapter.

Architecture of X

Now that we know something about the history of the X Window System, let's take a look at its architecture. X consists of three components: a client, a server, and the protocol that exists between them. The following sections describe each in detail, starting with a look at the X Protocol.

The X Protocol

The X Protocol forms the basis of any X-based software system. It is an application-level protocol that exists between the X server and X client applications, both of which are described in the following sections. The protocol consists of requests, which are sent by the client to the server, as well as events and errors, which are sent by the server to a client. A request initiates an action to be performed by the X server. Examples include the creation of a window (CreateWindow) and the drawing of a line (DrawLine). Events, sent by the server, tell the client about state changes within the server, such as the pressing of a key or mouse button by the user or the resizing of a window. Errors are sent by the server in response to invalid or unexecutable protocol requests sent by the client. For example, a BadDrawable error is sent by the X server to the client if the client specifies an invalid window as part of a DrawLine protocol request.

Two attributes of the X Protocol are worth mentioning. The first is that the protocol was designed in such a way that the client and server can execute either on the same host or on separate hosts connected by a network (usually communicating over the Transmission Control Protocol/Internet Protocol [TCP/IP]). For PC UNIX users, most of the time, the client and server are executing on the same machine. Certainly, the X server is always executing on the desktop machine, be it PC UNIX or an X terminal. In some installations, a user may need to telnet into a host on a remote system to execute a specific client; this might be the case for commercial or custom software running on a proprietary UNIX system for which the user has obtained a license to execute. To tell the client which X server to connect to, the user specifies the IP address of the server on his desktop by setting his or her DISPLAY variable, as in the following:

```
$ typeset -x DISPLAY=156.27.60.4:0
```

This will cause the client running on the remote system to display its windows and to draw its graphics on the X server running on the desktop machine with the IP address of 156.27.60.4. Mouse and keyboard events that occur on the machine running the X server will be sent to the machine on which the client is executing.

The second attribute of fundamental interest is the lack of policy imposed by the X Protocol on user interface look and feel. The X protocol was designed to support only the most fundamental tasks required of a Graphical User Interface (GUI), such as the capability to create a window, draw a line, and report keyboard presses and mouse button presses and movement. How the user interface looks is outside the scope of the X Protocol. There is no such thing as a menu, a list box, or a push button in X. All of these things are abstractions provided by toolkits, and they are implemented by combining X Protocol requests in a way that achieves the abstraction desired, as I will discuss later in this chapter. The end result is rather remarkable. Because the protocol does not enforce a policy, X supports any policy that a toolkit designer can dream up, provided it is consistent with the core architecture of X. Hence, we see the prolific number of toolkits in existence today: Gtk+, Xt/Motif, Xt/Xaw, Qt, XView, and so on.

The X Server

An X server is the program that manages the screen and its input devices (usually a mouse and keyboard). The X server always runs on the machine in front of which the user interacting with the application (or client) sits. Using TCP/IP, the client software connects to the server and sends requests to it using the X Protocol. The X server, once it has been started, listens for incoming TCP/IP client connections on a well-known port. Assume that a client has connected to the server and that the client wants to create a window and draw a line inside of it. To do so, the client sends a CreateWindow request to the server to create the window. To draw a line in the window, the client then sends a DrawLine request to the X server. More protocol requests than these are actually required for a real client to operate, but hopefully you get the idea. Upon receiving a DrawLine request, the X server validates the request, making sure that the window to which the line is to be drawn actually exists. Then it either performs the request if valid or, if there was an error of some kind, sends an error message back to the client. As another example, if the user moves the mouse, the X server will respond by sending a MotionNotify event (if it was solicited) to the client to tell it about the change made to the position of the mouse.

The Client (Xlib)

By now, I think I have adequately defined the role of the client in the X Window System. To summarize, it connects to a server and then sends requests to the server to create windows, draw graphics, and perform other operations involving the user interface of a client. The client also receives and responds to events sent from the X server to report any state changes made by the user to the mouse, the keyboard, or other input devices supported by the server and of interest to the client application.

One aspect of the client I have not mentioned is the interface library used by client developers. With few exceptions, all client applications ultimately make calls to a library of functions known as Xlib. Xlib was developed by the X Consortium, dating back to the early years of X. Xlib is a fairly simple Application Programming Interface (API), providing little more than a layer above the X Protocol. To draw a line in a window, for example, you issue a call to XDrawLine(). Arguments to XDrawLine() identify the server to which the request should be sent, the window within which the line is to be drawn, and the endpoints of line. Xlib applications are typically difficult to program because the level of abstraction is too low; Xlib, as I described, does not provide controls like menus, buttons, or dialogs, which are essential to modern GUI applications. Applications that need such features must either program them themselves or use a toolkit. Programming these abstractions is not an option because it is difficult, error prone, and inefficient. X applications, therefore, are for the most part written using a toolkit.

Toolkits

A toolkit is code that forms an abstraction layer directly above Xlib. The toolkit we are studying in this book is Gtk+. Toolkits provide two major benefits to application developers. First, they abstract the X Protocol, providing meaningful objects with which applications can be more easily developed. Implementing menus in Xlib is difficult because Xlib does not support the notion of a menu. To implement a menu in Xlib, you would have to write code that draws the menu as a series of windows containing text, appropriately positioned on the user's desktop. Drawing the window is perhaps the easy part; responding to mouse movement as it occurs over the menu items, popping up and down the menu, supporting accelerators, and so forth, could easily make the task more difficult than writing the rest of the application. Similar arguments can be made for other user interface abstractions such as buttons, scrollbars, lists, toolbars, and so forth. Instead of writing all this code yourself, you link to a toolkit library and use the API it provides instead of Xlib.

The second benefit provided by the use of a toolkit is user interface consistency. Simply put, if each and every application on a system were written using a single toolkit, the user, in theory, could learn one application and then be instantly comfortable using other applications. This is because the abstractions he or she encountered in the first application (buttons, menus, scrollbars) would be the same in all other applications, making the second and subsequent applications easier to learn and use. In practice, this is not always true. A toolkit almost never enforces the labels used on dialog buttons; one application might label buttons in a dialog "OK" and "Cancel" while another uses "Yes" and "No" or changes the order of button placement. A "style guide" is one strategy that helps toolkit applications be more consistent. Style guides define rules or suggestions for the design of menus, the placement of buttons, and the behavior of dialogs, among other things. In practice, not all toolkits define style guides, and when they are defined, not all programmers follow them. The other strategy a toolkit can use to promote GUI consistency is to provide higher abstractions that remove the ability of programmers to make choices. For example, to display a message to a user, the toolkit might require an application to use a "message" widget. The "message" widget would create the "OK" button that the user presses to dismiss the dialog, removing from the programmer the choice of what label is displayed by that button. For the most part, toolkits that have been developed for use in X-based clients do not specify style guidelines and tend to not provide abstractions such as the "message" widget I just described. Motif is one toolkit that has taken a multifaceted approach to the problem. The core set of widgets provided in Motif gives the programmer the flexibility he or she may need as well as abstractions that promote consistency among Motif applications, if used. Motif also has a published style guide for use by application developers.

I've used the word "widget" often thus far, so perhaps it is time I defined it. Simply put, a widget is the source code that implements a user interface abstraction. In Gtk+, the widget that implements a push button is known as GtkButton. The term "widget" will be used time and again in this book, and you will no doubt become accustomed to its use as you read the chapters that follow.

Historically, toolkit programming in X has, for the most part, been achieved via Xt Intrinsics (referred to as Xt from this point on). Xt is another technology developed by the X Consortium. Xt is a set of functions and a widget hierarchy. The widget hierarchy is minimal, and only the highest level widget classes are provided. A widget set such as the Athena Widget Set (Xaw) or Motif provides the remaining levels of the widget class hierarchy, and it is from these widgets that an application can construct a user interface.

There are many books on Xt and Motif, so I will not go into any significant details here. There are some points, however, that I would like to make about Xt. First of all, Xt, in a way similar to the X Protocol, is independent of any user interface look-and-feel policy. Xt only provides a core set of three widget classes; the widget set (e.g., Motif) that you link to provides all of the look-and-feel policy. The open-source community can and has developed open-source widget sets for use with Xt. One such widget set, LessTif *(www.lesstif.org)*, was designed as a freely available, open-source version of OSF Motif. In theory, someone could even write an Xt-based version of Gtk+ or Qt or design a completely new widget set that has its own look and feel. Second, programmers that learn how to develop to the Xt

Intrinsics can transfer their knowledge from one widget set to another. Most of the calls in an Xt-based application are made to functions in the Xt API; the arguments passed to these functions define the widget set used. To create a button widget in Motif, for example, one can call XtVaCreateManagedWidget(), as follows:

```
Widget button;

button = XtVaCreateManagedWidget( "button", xmPushButtonWidgetClass,
        parent, NULL);
```

The argument xmPushButtonWidgetClass tells Xt to create an instance of the XmPushButtonWidget class. Assume that a Gtk+ widget set for Xt was implemented and that the widget class for push buttons was called GtkButtonWidgetClass. Then we might see the following code in a port of the application from Xt/Motif to Xt/Gtk+:

```
Widget button;

button = XtVaCreateManagedWidget( "button", gtkButtonWidgetClass,
        parent, NULL );
```

As you can see, the changes necessary (on this line) to perform a port from Motif to the Gtk-like widget set were minimal. It is really never quite this easy; the application developer has responsibilities that can drastically affect widget set portability. However, like no other toolkit I know of, Xt was designed with the portability of an application from one widget set to another in mind. The decisions made by the designers of Xt to ensure the portability of widget sets also resulted in a dramatically reduced API size as well. Thus, only a small set of functions must be learned by application developers to create, configure, and destroy widgets; this knowledge is completely reusable as the developer switches from one widget set to another.

Window Managers

A window manager is a specialized client that is responsible for bringing order to the user's desktop. Window managers control the initial placement of windows on the desktop; without a window manager, windows likely would all be placed on top of each other at location 0, 0 (unless otherwise specified by the client application, which is not commonly done). The title bar of a window is actually created by the window manager, not by the client application. To set the title of a window, the application sends a hint in the form of a property on the X server for the window; this hint is read by the window manager application, which uses it to draw the title text in the title bar window that it manages.

The window manager is also responsible for providing controls that enable the user to move, resize, minimize, and iconify windows on the desktop. Without these controls, each application would need to provide some mechanism for its users, which is highly impractical.

Many window managers, especially the more recently developed ones, add features such as virtual desktops, taskbars, and command menus. Since a window manager is an application, it is relatively easy to add such features.

There are numerous window managers in existence. Some are older and date back to the early days of X. Many are newer and are open-ourced. Although in some cases there may be some indirect benefit for users to run a window manager that has been designed with a specific toolkit in mind (Motif applications and the mwm window manager come to mind), it is impossible to predict what window manager the user will be running. For that reason, it is not practical to write an application that assumes a given window manager will be present.

Generally, Gtk+ will handle any interaction your application must have with the window manager. An example is setting the text of the window title bar label. As previously mentioned, the title bar is a window created by the window manager, not your application. Therefore, your application cannot (easily) draw text in this window. Instead, your application must set a property on the X window that specifies the window title. The window manager will be notified when this property changes, will retrieve the text it contains, and then will draw the text specified by the client in the title bar of the window. All that your application needs to do is call the Gtk+ function gtk_window_set_title() (see Chapter 7, "Windows and Dialogs"), passing it a reference to the window and a string that specifies the desired window title.

Desktop Environments

A desktop environment is one step beyond the window manager. To understand why a desktop environment is important, let's take a look at mainstream desktop environments like MS Windows and MacOS. Both of these environments have more control over the look and feel of applications, the desktop, and the set of applications that comes with default installations than does X11, which is, in contrast, indifferent to these issues by definition. While this indifference certainly makes X flexible and resilient to constantly changing requirements, it does have the undesirable side effect of promoting inconsistency for the end user.

Without control over the environment, a user is faced with running applications developed with different toolkits, minimizing the advantage of past experience with a given application. While the claim that a MacOS user only has to learn one application and then instantly knows the rest is taking things a bit far, there is some truth to the claim. Anyone who has used Motif scrollbars in one application and Xaw scrollbars in another certainly can attest to the vast differences that can exist among X-based toolkits. Lists in Motif work very differently than those in Gtk+. Gtk+ supports tree widgets, while tree widgets are not a part of the core Motif widget set. The examples are numerous.

Users may find themselves running one window manager at work and another window manager at home. Contrast this to MS Windows users; regardless of where they may be, Windows 98 behaves more or less the same.

Any given X installation may have applications that are not present in another. The early X distributions provided sample applications like xcalc and xclock, and generally speaking, you can expect these applications to be present. Historically, however, X has not provided consistent access to default applications (or accessories, as they are sometimes called).

A desktop environment attempts to correct these inconsistencies. A desktop environment is all of the following:

- A toolkit that promotes a consistent look and feel among applications that execute within the environment.
- A set of applications, written using the preceding toolkit, preferably written to some set of standards enforced by the toolkit or described by a published style guide. These applications must give the user the capability to control and configure the environment and perform any basic tasks that may be needed. Clocks, calculators, text editors, games, and other "accessory" applications fall into this category. The style guide (or toolkit) ensures that applications have consistently named menus, consistently placed and labeled buttons in pop-up dialogs, and so forth.
- A window manager that gives the desktop a consistent look and feel from one system to another. In the best of worlds, the window manager is written using the same toolkit used to write the applications provided by the environment and adheres to the same user interface guidelines established for applications.

The following sections describe a few of the major desktop environments.

CDE

The first major desktop environment for X was the Common Desktop Environment (CDE), developed as part of the Common Open Software Environment (COSE) initiative back in the 1990s. CDE uses Motif as its toolkit, expands the widget set with some CDE-specific widgets, and provides a number of accessory applications, a file manager, and a window manager (dtwm). CDE has been the desktop for major workstation vendors such as IBM (AIX) and HP (HP/UX) for some time now and has enjoyed relative success. It is available for GNU-based systems as well. Although it has done well in the workstation marketplace, it suffers in open-source environments such as Linux due to its closed source. (Motif has since gone "open source" but perhaps too late for the trend toward other toolkits and desktop environments to be reversed.) You can find out more about CDE at *www.opennc.org/tech/desktop/cde/cde.data.sheet.htm.*

GNOME

GNOME *(www.gnome.org)* is one of the two desktop environments currently gaining widespread adoption in the open-source community (the other is KDE). It is the standard desktop environment of the GNU project. The toolkit for GNOME is Gtk+ 1.2, which is described in this book. GNOME also expands the Gtk+ widget set with a set of GNOME-specific widgets that attempt to strengthen the consistency of applications that execute within the environment. At this point in time, there is no published set of user interface style guidelines, though my expectation is that one will evolve over time. A rich set of applications exists, but it is not clear to me that consistency has been fully achieved in the presentation of these applications. Consider, for example, Red Hat 6.2 configured to use the GNOME desktop. Two calculator programs can be launched from the GNOME system menu; one brings up a Gtk+-based calculator, while the other brings up xcalc, which was written with the Athena widgets. The

File menu in the GNOME calculator has an Exit menu item, while the File menu in Midnight Commander, which is a file system browser, does not have an Exit menu item. It is this kind of inconsistency that needs to be overcome for mainstream users to fully adopt an environment like GNOME as their desktop of choice.

In contrast to CDE, GNOME does not provide or standardize on a window manager. The major strengths of GNOME are its adoption by the open-source community, an extremely aggressive amount of application development (again, based on Gtk+), and its inclusion as a desktop option by most of the Linux distributions.

KDE

The K Desktop Environment (KDE, see *www.kde.org*) is another open-source desktop environment. The toolkit for KDE is Qt *(www.trolltech.com)*, developed by Trolltech. The Qt toolkit is C++ based, in contrast to Gtk+ which is based on C. Qt has also been the center of controversy in the open-source community, given that it is maintained by a business (Trolltech) as opposed to an open-source effort. KDE provides a window manager (kwm), a Web browser, a suite of office applications, and an assortment of accessory applications. Some feel that KDE is a more solid and self-consistent environment as compared to GNOME (which may be true), and over time, this could lead it to dominate the desktop market. However, its dependency on a single company for the Qt toolkit and the requirement that applications be developed in C++ seem to be holding it back from widespread domination.

Summary

In this chapter, I introduced the X Window System. At the lowest level, X consists of a protocol that exists between a client and a server. The X server is software that responds to requests sent by the client and represents the desktop that users interact with. Requests allow the client to create windows and draw text and graphics, all of which are displayed on the server. The X server notifies the client whenever the user moves the mouse, presses a key on the keyboard, or clicks a mouse button by sending the client an event. The X Protocol supports only basic primitives that are required by all GUI applications. The application programming interface to the X Protocol, Xlib, provides a very thin layer above the X Protocol itself. It is via the API provided by Xlib that clients issue requests to the X server and receive errors and events from the X server. The client and X server can either exist on the same machine, or they can be running on different machines separated by a network. Communication between the client and server always occurs over TCP/IP.

Sitting on top of Xlib are toolkits such as Xt/Motif, GDK/Gtk+, and Qt. These toolkits provide higher-level widgets than abstract user interface components that are commonly found in GUI applications. Menus, buttons, scrollbars, and lists are examples of widgets found in all of the major toolkits. Each of the toolkits ultimately uses Xlib to implement these abstractions in software on the client side of the X Protocol. The toolkits themselves vary in terms of look and feel, and their API. These variations are based upon decisions that were made by the toolkit designer. Gtk+ is the toolkit described by this book.

A window manager is an application that allows the user to organize applications that are executing on the desktop. Window placement and iconification are the principle features provided by a window manager. Window managers are generally written to be independent of the client applications that they manage, but some, like the Motif Window Manager, are designed to take advantage of certain simple features made available by the toolkit for which they were designed.

A desktop environment combines a window manager with a set of applications that were written using a single toolkit. The Common Desktop Environment (CDE), GNOME, and KDE are familiar desktop environments. Desktop environments typically provide a suite of simple desktop applications like calendars, clocks, simple text editors, and calculators. In many ways, a desktop environment strives to provide a workspace to UNIX users that is similar to that provided by commodity PC operating systems such as MacOS and Microsoft Windows. In order for a desktop environment to be successful, it must provide applications that are self-consistent in terms of user interface and interoperability. Such consistency is provided by the use of a single toolkit (e.g., Gtk+), or it can be obtained by adhering to conventions described in a style guide designed specifically for the toolkit or desktop environment.

CHAPTER

2

HELLO GTK+!

In this chapter, we'll take our first look at what it is like to develop a Gtk+ application. First I will introduce the basic structure of a Gtk+ application. Then I'll go on to describe how to build and debug a Gtk+ application using tools such as gmake(1), gcc(1), and gdb(1). We'll also take a look at Gtk+ functions that must be called in order to initialize Gtk+ upon startup and tear down Gtk+ at application exit. As you'll see, most of the action in a Gtk+ application happens once main() makes a call to a routine named gtk_main().

In this chapter, we also look at several routines that allow a Gtk+ application to modify the behavior of the main loop. For example, an application can arrange for gtk_main() to call application code at idle time or whenever a timeout has been triggered.

Beginnings

Learning a lower-level user interface API such as Win32, Xlib, or MacOS Toolbox becomes easier, I believe, when the programmer is presented a basic skeleton application from which more complicated, real-life applications can be constructed. One of the reasons that a template or skeleton is helpful is that each of the preceding APIs requires the application programmer to code an event loop. In this event loop, events received from the user interface API (e.g., Win32, Xlib, or MacOS Toolbox) are dispatched to other portions of the application for processing. The details associated with programming the event loop can be overwhelming for the uninitiated.

However, Gtk+ is not that kind of programming environment. If there did exist a skeleton application for Gtk+, it would be a very minimal one, along the lines of the following code snippet:

```
#include <gtk/gtk.h>

...

int
main( int argc, char *argv[] )
{
        ...

        /* Initialize Gtk+ */
```

```
        gtk_set_locale ();
        gtk_init (&argc, &argv);

        ...

        /* Create basic user interface here and arrange for Gtk+
           to call your application when something interesting
           happens. The code here will vary from one application
           to the next. */

        ...

        /* Call into Gtk+. Gtk_main() will process events and call
           your application as prearranged by the code above. */

        gtk_main();
        return( 0 );
}
```

As you can see, our main() makes two calls to allow Gtk+ to initialize itself. This initialization code is always followed by application-specific code that will instantiate widgets and arrange for Gtk+ to make calls back to the application whenever something interesting happens in the user interface. Finally, main() disappears into a routine called gtk_main(), which does not return until the application is ready to exit. The event processing that an Xlib programmer typically needs to provide is handled within gtk_main(). Therefore, when you program in Gtk+, a skeleton application is not really needed because Gtk+ has implemented the basic skeleton of your application for you.

Readers experienced with the Xt Intrinsics will find Gtk+ to be a very natural and familiar paradigm. This is because the structure of a Gtk+/GDK application shares much in common with its Xt/Xlib counterpart. Programmers with experience programming to APIs such as Xlib, MacOS Toolbox, or Win32 will find that Gtk+ provides a welcome level of abstraction above the details these APIs expose, as was hinted to in the preceding discussion. However, knowledge of any of these APIs, especially Xlib, is never a bad thing in my opinion and will help when it comes time to understand GDK, which is the thin layer of code that sits directly above Xlib in the UNIX implementation.

For those of you totally new to GUI programming, don't worry. We'll start from very humble beginnings, namely with character-based console applications, and work forward from there.

The bulk of this chapter consists of a discussion of how to build a simple Gtk+ application using make(1) and gcc(1). I will also discuss how to use a debugger (gdb(1)) to discover and fix those pesky crash bugs that will inevitably occur during the course of program development. Let's get started.

A Simple Example: Hello Gtk+!

Programmers who know the C language will no doubt be familiar with the following code:

Listing 2.1 Hello World!, Console I/O Version

```
#include <stdio.h>

int
main( int argc, char *argv[] )
{
        printf( "Hello World!\n" );
}
```

Obviously, what this program does is print to stdout (i.e., the console) the string "Hello World!". To build the application, we make use of gcc(1):

```
$ gcc foo.c
$
```

Assuming we received no compiler errors, we can now run the executable as follows:

```
$ a.out
Hello World!
$
```

Note that gcc(1) generates an a.out by default. Use -o to specify some other name for the generated executable.

Adding Interactive Features to a Console Application

To make things interesting, let's modify this simple application just a little bit. Instead of assuming that the person wants to see "Hello World!" each time, we are going to change the program so that it prompts the user for the string to be displayed. If the user responds by hitting the Enter key, the application will exit without printing anything. If the user types in a string with a nonzero length, however, that string will be displayed to the console, followed by application exit. In essence, this program does exactly what echo(1) does: print whatever the user types (including nothing).

Here is Hello World!, version 2.0:

Listing 2.2 Hello World, Console I/O Version, Interactive

```
#include <stdio.h>

int
main( int argc, char *argv[] )
{
        char    buf[BUFSIZE];      /* should be enough */

        fgets( buf, BUFSIZ, stdin );
        if ( strlen( buf ) )
```

```
                printf( "%s\n", buf );
}
```

This application is also built using gcc(1) in the same way that was done for Hello World! version 1. The following example illustrates what the user might see when the above code is executed:

```
$ a.out
Hello Big World          <---- the user types this...
Hello Big World          <---- and Hello World! version 2 prints this
$
```

A Paradigm Shift

You must be wondering at this point, "Why is he talking so much about console applications? This book is supposed to be teaching me how to develop GUI-based applications in Gtk+!" The reason is simple: For those of you new to GUI applications, you are about to face a major paradigm shift, and understanding the difference is critical to understanding how to program a GUI application with Gtk+.

In non-GUI console applications, flow of control goes from one statement to the next. Thus, in Hello World! versions 1 and 2, each line is executed in sequence, one after another. If the program must wait for user input, as is done when fgets(3) in Hello World! version 2 is called, the program will block and only resume execution after the input request has been satisfied. Even control structures such as while and for loops impose a serial, one-after-another flow of control on the application. Execution starts at the top of the loop with the first statement in the body of the loop and then goes to the second statement, and so forth. When at the bottom, control returns to the top of the loop, and the process starts all over again.

In Gtk+, things are different. To see how, let's dive right in and look at Hello World! version 3, written using the Gtk+ toolkit:

Listing 2.3 Hello World!, Gtk+ Version

```
#include <stdio.h>
#include <gtk/gtk.h>

static GtkWidget *entry;

void
PrintAndExit (GtkWidget *widget, GtkWidget *window)
{
    char     *str;

    str = gtk_entry_get_text( GTK_ENTRY(entry) );
    if ( str != (char *) NULL )
            printf( "%s\n", str );

    gtk_widget_destroy (window);
```

```
    gtk_main_quit ();
}

void
PrintByeAndExit (GtkWidget *widget, gpointer data)
{
    printf( "Goodbye, world!\n" );
    gtk_exit(0);
}

int
main( int argc, char *argv[] )
{
    GtkWidget *window, *label, *vbox, *hbox, *button, *separator;

    gtk_set_locale ();

    gtk_init (&argc, &argv);

    window = gtk_window_new (GTK_WINDOW_TOPLEVEL);
    gtk_window_set_policy( GTK_WINDOW( window ), FALSE, FALSE, FALSE );

    gtk_signal_connect (GTK_OBJECT(window), "destroy",
            GTK_SIGNAL_FUNC(PrintByeAndExit), NULL);

    gtk_window_set_title (GTK_WINDOW (window), "Hello Gtk+!");
    gtk_container_border_width (GTK_CONTAINER (window), 0);

    vbox = gtk_vbox_new (FALSE, 0);
    gtk_container_add (GTK_CONTAINER (window), vbox);

    hbox = gtk_hbox_new (FALSE, 0);
    gtk_box_pack_start (GTK_BOX (vbox), hbox, FALSE, FALSE, 0);

    label = gtk_label_new( "Enter a message:" );
    gtk_box_pack_start (GTK_BOX (hbox), label, FALSE, FALSE, 0);
    entry = gtk_entry_new ();
    gtk_entry_set_text (GTK_ENTRY (entry), "");
    gtk_editable_select_region (GTK_EDITABLE (entry), 0, -1);
    gtk_box_pack_start (GTK_BOX (hbox), entry, FALSE, FALSE, 0);

    separator = gtk_hseparator_new ();
    gtk_box_pack_start (GTK_BOX (vbox), separator, FALSE, FALSE, 0);

    button = gtk_button_new_with_label ("Print");
    gtk_signal_connect_object (GTK_OBJECT (button), "clicked",
            GTK_SIGNAL_FUNC(PrintAndExit), GTK_OBJECT (window));
    gtk_box_pack_start (GTK_BOX (vbox), button, FALSE, FALSE, 0);
    GTK_WIDGET_SET_FLAGS (button, GTK_CAN_DEFAULT);
    gtk_widget_grab_default (button);

```

```
067      gtk_widget_show_all (window);
068
069      gtk_main ();
070
071      return( 0 );
072  }
```

As you can see, Gtk+ Hello World! applications can be rather lengthy compared to the length of the console version. Before we take a look at the code, let's first understand what the application is designed to do.

Understanding the Gtk+ Hello World Sample

The premise of this example is similar to that of Hello World! version 2: to echo a string supplied by the user (or nothing should the user not type in a string). The application starts out as shown in Figure 2.1. The dialog displayed contains a text edit field, below which is a button labeled Print. When the user presses the Print button, the application prints the text entered by the user in the text field to stdout and exits. If the user does not enter any text, nothing is printed.

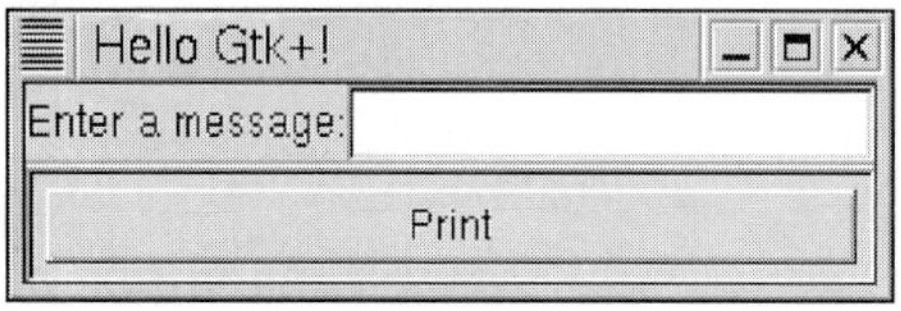

Figure 2.1 Hello World!

Lines 001 and 002 identify the include files required by the source code. We include *<stdio.h>* because we will use printf() to display the text entered by the user. *<gtk/gtk.h>* is required because this is a Gtk+ application. The Gtk+ includes should be located in */usr/include/gtk* on your system. If the compiler has problems finding *gtk.h,* it might be located somewhere else; check with your systems administrator if you can't locate them and need help.

The include file *gtk.h* includes the remaining include files found in */usr/include/gtk.* Including *<gtk/gtk.h>* is all you need to do to bring in the types, constants, and macros needed by your source code. This is in contrast to the Motif development environment, where typically programmers are required to individually include header files corresponding to widgets needed by the application, one by one.

Our main routine starts on line 027. On line 029, several variables of type GtkWidget * are declared. A GtkWidget is roughly analogous to the Widget type in Motif. For readers not familiar with widgets (I will use the term "widget" to describe the object represented by the GtkWidget type), for now think of a widget as an opaque data type representing a window or a control that the user sees on the display and interacts with. We'll spend a lot of time talking about widgets in this book because learning Gtk+ largely amounts to learning about the widgets that the toolkit provides and how to make good use of them when constructing an application user interface.

On line 031, gtk_set_locale() is called. This is actually a wrapper function that calls gdk_set_locale(), which in turn calls setlocale(3).

Line 033 introduces our first major Gtk+ routine, gtk_init(). All Gtk+ clients must call gtk_init() at the beginning of the application before creating any widgets. gtk_init() takes as arguments the argc and argv arguments that were passed to main() by the runtime environment. gtk_init() will inspect each argument that was passed to the application on the command line, processing and removing those arguments that are recognized. A modified argc, argv will be returned to the application if any arguments were processed by gtk_init(), with the processed arguments removed from argv and the value of argc decremented accordingly. Later in this chapter, we will look at some of the command-line arguments handled by gtk_init(). Other tasks performed by gtk_init() include signal initialization, getting the system default colormap and visual, and registering an exit function so that cleanup can be performed should the application not exit in a clean manner.

Our user interface definition starts with line 035, where we create a top-level window. For us, the top-level window represents a place within which the text edit field and Print button will be placed. As we will see, it is a bit more complicated than this because the top-level window is actually a container not only for the text field and the button, but for other widgets that are not visible to the user but are needed by the application to help manage the placement of the visual controls (the text field and the button) within the top-level window.

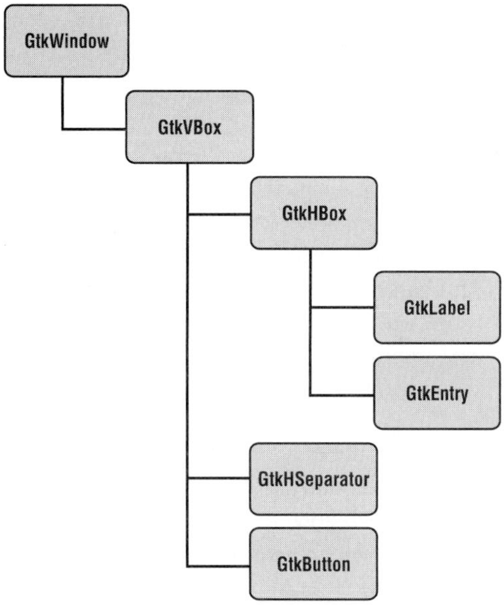

Figure 2.2 Widget Instance Hierarchy Tree

Figures 2.2 and 2.3 should help to make this clear. Figure 2.2 illustrates the widget instance hierarchy for our example application. Widgets that are higher in the hierarchy (e.g., closer to the top widget, or the root of the inverted tree) are parent widgets to widgets residing lower in the hierarchy. A widget residing immediately below a given widget in the tree is the child widget of the widget above it in the hierarchy.

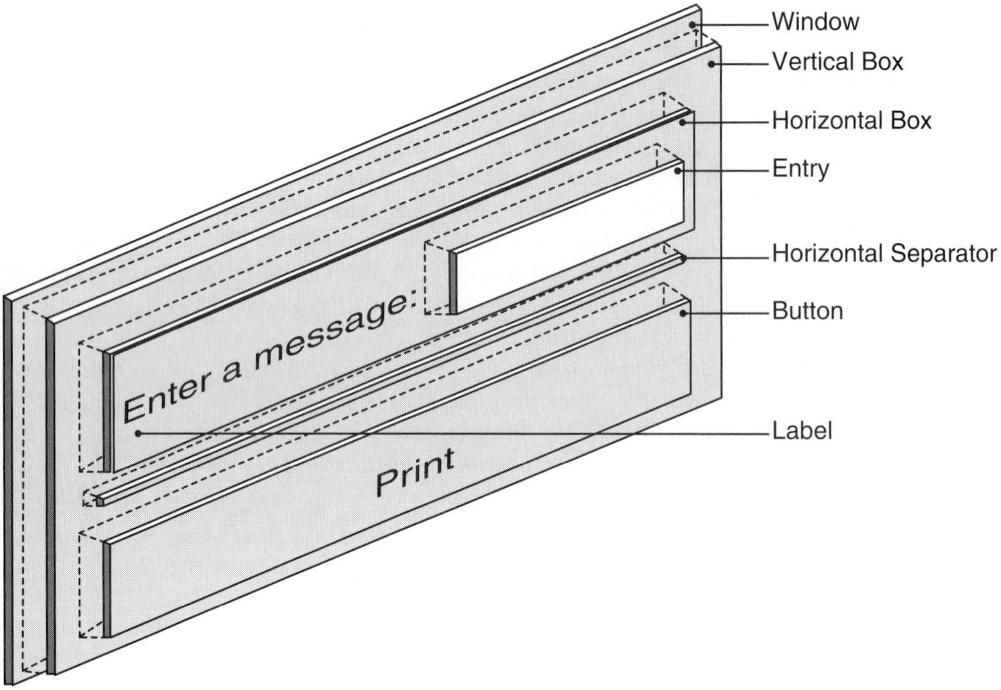

Figure 2.3 Widget Instance Hierarchy, GUI Perspective

Figure 2.3 illustrates the same instance hierarchy in a different way. Items on the left side of the drawing are higher in the widget instance hierarchy than widgets on the right side of the drawing. Note that it is clear in this figure that some of the widgets are visible to the user of the application, while, as we shall see, there are nonvisible widgets used to control how the visible widgets are laid out and organized.

The top-level widget in our application then is a window that will hold the components making up our application's user interface. This window will be a target for the decorations and menus placed around it by the window manager application (e.g., twm, MWM, fvwm, sawfish) that will allow the user to move, resize, iconify, and close the application, as desired.

Note that we save the return value of gtk_window_new() in a variable named window, which is of type GtkWidget *. We do this for two reasons. First, the window is going to be used as the parent widget of widgets lower than it in the instance hierarchy. So we need a handle to the widget to pass to the functions used to create the child widgets in order to identify the window as their parent. Second, there are functions we will call to modify attributes of the window, and we need to tell these functions for which window they must perform their task.

The next several lines of source illustrate this. On lines 038 and 039, we register a signal handler, or callback, with Gtk+. Without going into much detail, what we are doing here is telling Gtk+ that when the window is destroyed (meaning when it is closed by the user via the window manager or when the application exits normally), we would like Gtk+ to call our function PrintByeAndExit(). We might use PrintByeAndExit() to perform any cleanup chores necessary, such as saving user input, before the application exits. In our example, there is nothing to clean up, however, so we simply print the string "Goodbye, world!" and exit.

```
038              gtk_signal_connect (GTK_OBJECT (window), "destroy",
039                   GTK_SIGNAL_FUNC(PrintByeAndExit), &window);
```

Notice the use of the macros GTK_OBJECT and GTK_SIGNAL_FUNCTION. These macros coerce variables of a given type to some other type. If coercion is needed but not used, warnings will be generated at compile time. To illustrate this, I removed the GTK_OBJECT and GTK_SIGNAL_FUNC macros from the preceding lines and recompiled with the following result:

```
bash$ gmake
gcc -g `gtk-config --cflags` -c hellogtk+.c -o hellogtk+.o
hellogtk+.c: In function 'main':
hellogtk+.c:41: warning: passing arg 1 of 'gtk_signal_connect' from
incompatible pointer type
hellogtk+.c:41: warning: passing arg 3 of 'gtk_signal_connect' from
incompatible pointer type
gcc -g `gtk-config --libs` hellogtk+.o -o hellogtk+
```

The use of signals is an example of how a Gtk+ application differs greatly from a console application such as Hello World! version 2.0. In a console application, flow is predictable. The program spends its time executing one statement after another, falling into and returning from function calls, or waiting, blocked until an I/O request has finished. In a Gtk+ application, there are plenty of times when the application will be executing code in a serial fashion but will find itself inside of a routine, such as PrintByeAndExit(), as if by magic.

This "we'll call you later" paradigm is used extensively in Gtk+ applications. It is the mechanism by which an application can find out that it is going to close. It is also the mechanism by which Gtk+ makes an application aware that a push button has been clicked by the user, that a menu item has been selected, or even that a window has been resized or exposed and we need to redraw its contents.

Writing a Gtk+ application, then, amounts to developing code that creates the user interface, defining functions that will get executed as the user interacts with your application, and connecting the user interface components to these functions so that Gtk+ can call the application when something of interest has happened. We'll see examples of this paradigm time and time again in this book, so if the concept isn't clear now, don't worry too much about it. Before long, it will seem like second nature.

Line 041 calls the function gtk_window_set_title() to set the window title of our top-level window to "Hello Gtk+". Line 042 calls the function gtk_container_border_width() to set the width of the window's border to zero pixels. At this point, you may have noticed a trend in the naming convention used for Gtk+ functions. Generally, the convention is the string "gtk" followed by the name of the class to which the function belongs (or the class of the object that is being operated upon by the function), followed by something that describes what the function does. Underscore characters separate all of these components. For the function gtk_window_set_title(), then, the class being operated on is window, and the functionality performed is described by set_title. Note that the class component of the function name will identify, usually, the type of the first argument. As you can see, the first argument to gtk_window_set_title() is cast to GTK_WINDOW, and the first argument to gtk_container_border_width() is cast to GTK_CONTAINER. Note that this convention does not always hold. For example, the first argument to the function gtk_signal_connect() is of type GTK_OBJECT, as we saw on line 037.

```
041         gtk_window_set_title (GTK_WINDOW (window), "Hello Gtk+!");
042         gtk_container_border_width (GTK_CONTAINER (window), 0);
```

Now that we have created our main window, let's turn our attention to code that will create and arrange the user interface components with which the user will interact. In our case, these include a text edit field and a push button. We'll also add a separator widget to the user interface to visually separate the text edit field from the push button in the dialog. A label is used to give some context to the text edit field.

Before we create the label, text field, separator, and button, we first create a container within which these widgets will reside. This is done on lines 044 and 045. The routine gtk_vbox_new() allocates a vertical box widget. On line 045, we add this widget to the window. Note on line 045 that the window is being cast to the container widget class using the macro GTK_CONTAINER. Because the window class is a subclass of the container class, such an operation is permissible. A window can act as a container (but not the other way around). A vertical box widget is another form of container but with special behavior. As widgets are added by a program to a vertical box, they are placed vertically below the previously added widget by the vertical box widget. If the client prefers, widgets can be packed into a vertical box in the opposite direction, with newly added widgets placed above previously added widgets. The vertical box widget enables the application to control some aspects of how its widget children (the items added to the vertical box) are placed. For example, the client can specify whether widgets are to be expanded to fill the entire area of the vertical box. The client can also control such things as right and left justification and centering of child widgets. We'll spend time discussing the box widgets in a later chapter. Box widgets are pretty much the mechanism by which widget layout in a dialog or window is achieved in Gtk+ applications.

```
044         box = gtk_vbox_new (FALSE, 0);
045         gtk_container_add (GTK_CONTAINER (window), box);
```

The next widget created is a horizontal box widget; this is done on lines 047 and 048. The horizontal box widget will hold the text edit field and its label. On line 050, a label widget is created and then is added to the horizontal box on line 051. Following this, the text edit, or entry, widget is created on line 052 and is added to the horizontal box on line 053. Because entry widgets are used to implement text edit fields in Gtk+, I will try to use the term "entry" whenever I am talking about text edit fields from now on.

On line 053, we initialize the text displayed by the entry widget to the empty string " ", and on line 054, we make the entry widget editable, allowing a user to click in the entry widget and modify the text displayed using the keyboard. On line 055, we add the widget as a child to the horizontal box widget. The first argument to gtk_box_pack_start() is the horizontal box widget, and the second argument is the entry widget being added. The third argument, which is a boolean that is set in this case to FALSE, directs (if set to TRUE) the box widget to expand the entry field so that it fits its entire allocated area. The fourth argument, which is ignored unless the third argument is set to TRUE, determines whether, during expansion, extra space is allocated around the child widget (FALSE) to fill the area into which the child is expanding, or the child grows horizontally to consume the entire area being filled (TRUE).

On lines 057 and 058, we create and add to the vertical box container widget a separator widget. Separator widgets come in two types: horizontal and vertical. We use a horizontal separator because we want the line to run left to right and visually separate the work area of our dialog (consisting of the entry widget) from the action or button area of our dialog (consisting of the Print button). Most (if not all) of the dialogs in this book will be designed with two areas: a work area consisting of widgets that allow the user to input data or perform a task, and an action area containing buttons that allow the user to commit or cancel changes made in the work area and to dismiss the dialog. These two areas will always be separated by a horizontal separator widget.

```
057     separator = gtk_hseparator_new ();
058     gtk_box_pack_start (GTK_BOX (box), separator, TRUE, TRUE, 0);
```

Now it is time to create our action area. We only have one button in the action area, labeled Print. It is created and then added to the dialog on lines 060 through 063.

On line 060, the widget is created. Using gtk_button_new_with_label() enables us to create the widget and assign its label in one function call. On line 061, we again make use of the signal/callback facility of Gtk+. This time, we register a signal function with Gtk+ that will be invoked when Gtk+ detects that the user has pressed our button. The first argument specifies the widget we want Gtk+ to monitor, which is the button created on line 060. The second argument tells Gtk+ which event or signal to monitor. Here, the string "clicked" represents just what you think, a button press. The third argument to gtk_signal_connect_object() is the address of the function we want to have called by Gtk+ when the button press occurs. The final argument is simply data that we want Gtk+ to pass to PrintAndExit() when it is invoked. We will see later how important this final argument can be to the design of a Gtk+ application that supports multiple, simultaneously open dialogs, each of which corresponds to a specific instance of user data (much like a word processor that has multiple documents open at the same time).

On line 063, we add the button to the vertical box widget, just as was done for the preceding horizontal box and separator widgets.

```
060     button = gtk_button_new_with_label ("Print");
061     gtk_signal_connect_object (GTK_OBJECT (button), "clicked",
062             GTK_SIGNAL_FUNC(PrintAndExit), GTK_OBJECT (window));
063     gtk_box_pack_start (GTK_BOX (vbox), button, FALSE, FALSE, 0);
```

Now that all of the user interface widgets have been created, we must make them eligible for drawing by calling gtk_widget_show_all(), passing the window widget as an argument.

The routine gtk_widget_show_all() will make visible the widget passed in as an argument and all of its children, visible. The routine gtk_widget_show() also takes a widget as an argument, but only that widget, not its children (if any), will be eligible for drawing. We could have added a gtk_widget_show() for each widget in the application, and you will see Gtk+ code on the Internet that does just that, but in this case, it seems cleaner to just do it all at the end with a single function call.

```
067            gtk_widget_show_all (window);
```

Finally, on line 069, we go into the black hole known as gtk_main(). As long as our application is running, we will not return from gtk_main(). In concert with widget code that you need not be concerned with (we will design our own widget later in this book), gtk_main() is where all of the power in a Gtk+ application resides.

```
069            gtk_main ();
070
071            return( 0 );
072  }
```

Well, we've certainly covered a lot in the last several pages. Maybe it is time to catch your breath, perhaps take the dog for a walk or take a well-deserved nap. Once you are back, refreshed, and ready to go, fire up an editor, type in the source code for hellogtk+, compile it, and give it a try. The remainder of this chapter will show you how to build, execute, and (gasp!) debug the hellogtk+ application.

Building the Sample Client

To build our example client, we invoke the following command line:

```
$ gcc hellogtk+.c -o hellogtk+ `gtk-config --cflags` `gtk-config --libs`
```

The `gtk-config --cflags` and `gtk-config --libs` portions of the command line are used to derive compiler and linker flags and arguments needed to compile a Gtk+ application in your environment. On my Red Hat system, executing

```
$ gtk-config --cflags
```

results in the following output:

```
-I/usr/X11R6/include -I/usr/lib/glib/include
```

Executing

```
$ gtk-config --libs
```

results in the following:

```
-L/usr/lib -L/usr/X11R6/lib -lgtk -lgdk -rdynamic -lgmodule -lglib -ldl \
-lXext -lX11 -lm
```

This output will be pasted into the command line and passed to the compiler.

Assuming the build is successful, we will be left with a binary named hellogtk+, which we can then execute:

```
$ hellogtk+
```

To simplify the addition of multiple source files, provide support for maintaining include file dependencies, and eliminate the need to type difficult command lines to build a project, the use of gmake(1) is recommended. Here is a makefile that can be used to build hellogtk+:

```
CC = gcc -g -I/usr/include/gdk

all: hellogtk+

hellogtk+: hellogtk+.o
        $(CC) `gtk-config --libs` hellogtk+.o -o hellogtk+

hellogtk+.o: hellogtk+.c
        $(CC) `gtk-config --cflags` -c hellogtk+.c -o hellogtk+.o

clean:
        rm -f *.o hellogtk+
```

The gtk-config command used in the command line corresponding to the hellogtk+ dependency is passed the --libs argument. When building hellogtk+.o, it is passed the --cflags argument. This is because, in the first case, we are linking, so we only need to pass linker flags. In the second case, we are building the .o, and in this case, we need to pass compiler flags.

To remove all binaries and do a clean build, type the following:

```
$ gmake clean
```

Once all of the binaries have been removed, you can build hellogtk+ by typing the following:

```
$ gmake
```

Debugging the Sample Client

You may have noticed that when the Print button is pressed, nothing is printed to the console, and hellogtk+ exits without doing anything (or it prints garbage to the screen or even crashes). For me, it was printing garbage.

You may be able to figure out what is causing this bug simply by inspecting the code. However, it is more often the case that a bug cannot be figured out by code inspection. Here's where a debugger like gdb(1) comes in handy.

To use gdb, make sure to add a -g flag and remove any optimization flags from the compiler build line, as was done in the CC macro in the preceding makefile. Once you have built with -g and have a debug binary, invoke gdb using the following command line:

```
$ gdb hellogtk+
```

Doing so, you should see the following output from gdb:

```
GNU gdb 4.17
Copyright 1998 Free Software Foundation, Inc.
GDB is free software, covered by the GNU General Public License, and
you are welcome to change it and/or distribute copies of it under
certain conditions.
Type "show copying" to see the conditions.
```

```
There is absolutely no warranty for GDB.  Type "show warranty" for
details. This GDB was configured as "i386-redhat-linux"...(no
debugging symbols found)...
(gdb)
```

Once gdb loads your binary, it will display a prompt and wait for a command. To debug our problem, we first take a guess as to where the problem is most likely to be. Since the routine PrintAndExit() is responsible for printing the output to the screen, it seems reasonable to start our search there. To do this, we will set a breakpoint on the routine PrintAndExit() by typing the following command:

```
(gdb) b PrintAndExit
Breakpoint 1 at 0x8048c06
(gdb)
```

Once we hit the breakpoint, we will single step the routine, one line at a time, in an attempt to discover what is going wrong.

To start execution of the application, we type in the following:

```
(gdb) run
Starting program: /home/syd/book/src/chapter3/hellogtk+
```

Once hellogtk+ starts, type the string "Hello gdb" into the text edit field and hit the Print button. Once you've done this, hellogtk+ should stop executing. Return to the console window in which gdb is executing. You should see the following printed by gdb:

```
Breakpoint 1, PrintAndExit (widget=0x8061f90, window=0x8061f90) at
        hellogtk+.c:11
11              gtk_entry_get_text( GTK_ENTRY(entry) );
(gdb)
```

This indicates that gdb is stopped in PrintAndExit() on the line that is currently being displayed (line 11). We can tell that the widget and window arguments are both pointing to address 0x8061f90. We can print out what they are pointing to with the print command:

```
(gdb) print *widget
$1 = {object = {klass = 0x8061ff8, flags = 264144, ref_count = 1,
    object_data = 0x8067268}, private_flags = 0, state = 0 '\000',
  saved_state = 0 '\000', name = 0x0, style = 0x8065a80,
    requisition = {width = 178, height = 97}, allocation = {x = 0, y = 0,
  width = 178, height = 97}, window = 0x8069db0, parent = 0x0}
(gdb) print *window
$2 = {object = {klass = 0x8061ff8, flags = 264144, ref_count = 1,
    object_data = 0x8067268}, private_flags = 0, state = 0 '\000',
  saved_state = 0 '\000', name = 0x0, style = 0x8065a80, requisition = {width
        = 178,
    height = 97}, allocation = {x = 0, y = 0, width = 178, height = 97},
  window = 0x8069db0, parent = 0x0}
```

These seem normal enough, so the arguments coming into PrintAndExit() appear to be fine. Let's single step a few instructions and see what happens:

```
(gdb) n
12              if ( str != (char *) NULL )
(gdb) n
13                      printf( "%s\n", str );
```

Because, for me, garbage was being printed, I was fairly certain that the printf statement was being reached, and the debugger has confirmed this. I know from experience that the printf statement is well formed, so what I want to know is the value of str. It should be "Hello gdb". First let's use "print" to determine the value of the string and the value it is pointing to:

```
(gdb) print str
$3 = 0xbffff380 "à'\n@¨óÿ¿d_\006@\220\037\006\b"
(gdb)
```

Well, it certainly looks like str is pointing to garbage. Notice that the value of str is 0xbfff380. That looks a little odd, given that widget and window have a value of 0x8061f90 and we see other pointers in widget and window that are nearby, such as klass = 0x8061ff8 and style = 0x8065a80. Perhaps str is pointing to bad memory, but we can't be sure. So let's take a look at the code again and see how str is being assigned:

```
006  void
007  PrintAndExit (GtkWidget *widget, GtkWidget *window)
008  {
009          char    *str;
010
011          gtk_entry_get_text( GTK_ENTRY(entry) );
012          if ( str != (char *) NULL )
013                  printf( "%s\n", str );
014
015          gtk_widget_destroy (window);
016          gtk_main_quit ();
017  }
```

As you can see, we declare str on line 009, and we use it on lines 012 and 013, but we never give it a value. Oops! The prototype for gtk_entry_get_text(), found in gtkentry.h, is as follows:

```
gchar *
gtk_entry_get_text(GtkEntry *entry);
```

To fix our code, we need to assign the return value from gtk_entry_get_text() to the variable str. So quit out of the debugger, fire up an editor, and change line 011 to the following:

```
011  str = gtk_entry_get_text( GTK_ENTRY(entry) );
```

Recompiling and executing hellogtk+ should show that the preceding change was what was needed to fix our bug.

I will have more to say in the next section about debugging when I discuss the various debug command-line arguments supported by Gtk+.

Application Startup, Termination, and Main Loop Functions

This section takes a look at the functions that must be called by an application to initialize Gtk+/GDK at startup, as well as routines that should be called by an application to tear down Gtk+ cleanly prior to application exit.

Application Startup

The first routine we'll look at is gtk_set_locale():

```
gchar*
gtk_set_locale (void)
```

gtk_set_locale() must be called before gtk_init(), if your application decides to call it at all. gtk_set_locale() is a wrapper that calls gdk_set_locale(), which in turn calls setlocale(LC_ALL,""), causing the localization database to be read in for the locale defined by the LANG environment variable set in the user's environment. For details on internationalizing your application, refer to the man page for setlocale(1) and the locale(7) man page. If you don't call gtk_set_locale(), the locale defaults to the portable "C" locale.

In addition to setlocale(), two Xlib routines are called by gtk_set_locale(): XSupportsLocale() and XSetLocaleModifiers(). If XSupportsLocale() fails, then X does not support the locale defined by the LANG environment variable, and the application reverts to the portable "C" locale. XSetLocaleModifiers() reads the XMODIFIERS environment variable, which consists of a series of "@category=value" strings. A locale modifier is an X extension to the LANG variable processed by setlocale(). The only standard modifier category defined as of R6 is "im", which is used to specify the input method to be used for internationalized text input for the locale. Refer to XSetLocaleModifiers(7) for more information.

gtk_set_locale() will generate one or more warning messages should setlocale(), XSupportsLocale(), or XSetLocaleModifiers() fail. Regardless of success or failure, the current locale string will be returned. To ensure that the user's locale choice has been honored, you should compare the returned string to the LANG environment variable and exit if they don't match, as follows:

```
gchar *envlang, *lang;

envlang = getenv( "LANG" );
lang = gtk_set_locale();

if ( envlang != (char *) NULL && strcmp( lang, envlang ) ) {
        fprintf( stderr, "Unable to set locale to %s\n", envlang );
        exit( 1 );
}
```

The next optional function we'll look at is gtk_check_version():

```
gchar *
gtk_check_version(guint major, guint minor, guint micro)
```

gtk_check_version() takes three arguments: a major, minor, and micro number. Calling this routine enables your application to ensure that the version of Gtk+ to which your application is bound at runtime, if built as a shared executable, meets minimum version requirements that you have set. If the major number of the Gtk+ lib is greater than major, or the major number is equal to major and the minor number is greater than minor, or the major number and minor number are equal to major and minor, respectively, and the micro number is greater than or equal to micro, then NULL is returned, indicating that the shared Gtk+ library linked to the application meets the version requirements set by the application. Otherwise, a pointer to a nonlocalized error string is returned. For example, if the major number is too small, the following string is returned:

```
"Gtk+ version too old (major mismatch)"
```

The next routine, gtk_init(), must be called by all Gtk+ applications:

```
void
gtk_init (int *argc, char ***argv)
```

The purpose of gtk_init() is to initialize the GDK and Gtk+ libraries for use by your application. A Gtk+ application cannot run unless Gtk+ and GDK have been initialized by calling gtk_init() early in main() before any widgets are instantiated. If gtk_init() fails (for example, a connection to the X server cannot be established), your application will exit.

gtk_init() searches argv for runtime arguments that it recognizes. Each argument that is recognized is processed and removed from the argv vector. Upon return, argv contains those arguments that were not recognized by Gtk+, and argc holds the number of arguments that remain in argv. The arguments listed in Table 2.1 are all recognized by the 1.2 version of Gtk+.

Table 2.1 Command-Line Arguments Recognized by Gtk+

Argument Name	*Description*
--gtk-module module	Load the specified module at startup. Modules are described in a later section.
--g-fatal-warnings	Warnings and errors generated by Gtk+/GDK will cause the offending application to exit.
--gtk-debug flags	Turn on specific Gtk+ trace/debug messages. I will describe trace and debug messages for Gtk+ and GDK later in this chapter.
--gtk-no-debug flags	Turn off specific Gtk+ trace/debug messages.
--gdk-debug flags	Turn on GDK trace/debug messages.
--gdk-no-debug flags	Turn off specific Gtk+ trace/debug messages.

Table 2.1 Command-Line Arguments Recognized by Gtk+ (Continued)

Argument Name	*Description*
--display h:s.d	Connect to the specified X server, where "h" is the hostname, "s" is the server number (usually 0), and "d" is the display number (typically omitted). If --display is not specified, the DISPLAY environment variable is used.
--sync	Call XSynchronize (display, True) after the X server connection has been established. This makes debugging X protocol errors easier because X request buffering will be disabled and X errors will be received immediately after the protocol request that generated the error has been processed by the X server.
--no-xshm	Disable use of the X Shared Memory Extension.
--name progname	Set program name to "progname". If not specified, program name will be set to argv[0].
--class classname	Following Xt conventions, the class of a program is the program name with the initial character capitalized. For example, the class name for gimp is "Gimp". If --class is specified, the class of the program will be set to "classname".

The --gtk-module argument, as well as the arguments --gtk-debug, --gtk-no-debug, --gdk-debug, and --gdk-no-debug, all need further explanation. These are covered in the next few sections.

Modules

Gtk+ (via Glib) allows applications to load shared library code at runtime and execute routines that the shared library exports. The mechanism that Glib provides is essentially that of a wrapper to the routines described by the dlopen(3) man page. Now might be a good time to look at the man page for dlopen(3) if you are not familiar with this facility. Gtk+ requires the shared library to export a function named gtk_module_init(), which will be called by Gtk+ once the module has been loaded. The function gtk_module_init() is required to conform to the following function prototype:

```
G_MODULE_EXPORT void
gtk_module_init (gint *argc, gchar ***argv);
```

In Windows, G_MODULE_EXPORT is a #define for __declspec(dllexport). In UNIX, this defines to nothing. The arguments argc and argv are pointers to the command-line arguments that were passed to the application at startup. This allows the shared library code to inspect the command-line arguments, processing and removing any arguments that are specific to the module.

The module facility can be used to add plug-in support to an application. We will look more at modules when I discuss Glib, but for now, all you need to be aware of is that --gtk-module is one of the ways of specifying a shared library (or plug-in) to be loaded by your application at runtime.

If --gtk-module is required by a shipping product, it would be better to wrap its use in a script, presenting a simpler interface to users. For example, say your application is a word processor, and you provide a spell checker plug-in module in a shared library called libspell.so. Instead of forcing the user to type

```
$ myedit --gtk-module spell myfile
```

it would be easier for the user to provide a shell script named runedit that accepts a -s argument, for example

```
$ runedit -s myfile
```

and let the script construct the preceding myedit command line and execute it on behalf of the user. Or, perhaps better, place all of the options the user wants in a preference file and have your script read that file and create the appropriate command line.

An alternate way to specify any modules to be loaded by Gtk+ at application startup is to use the GTK_MODULES environment variable. Each component in this variable consists of a module name, separated by the ':' character. For example, to load the modules libfoo.so, libfee.so, and libbar.so, you would set GTK_MODULES as follows:

```
$ typeset -x GTK_MODULES=foo:fee:bar
```

Debug Arguments

The remaining command-line arguments (--gtk-debug, --gtk-no-debug, --gdk-debug, and --gdk-no-debug) all control the amount of debug information displayed by Gtk+, GDK, and Glib at application runtime. Some of the debug output will be of interest to application designers; other information is really only important to those working on specific portions of Gtk+, GDK, or Glib. In this section, I'll try to cover all aspects of debug support, both at compile time and at runtime, in addition to the command-line arguments listed here.

Compile Time. At compile time, there are four defines that can be used to control the amount of debug information supplied by an application at runtime.

- **G_ENABLE_DEBUG** This compile-time flag is recognized by Gtk+, GDK, and Glib code. If defined, the only area that is impacted in Glib, as of Glib 1.2.0, is the gdate module, which will generate informational messages in a few places should any abnormal circumstances occur. Gtk+ must be built with G_ENABLE_DEBUG in order for the --gtk-debug, --gtk-no-debug, --gdk-debug, and --gdk-no-debug command-line arguments to be parsed at startup and for the GDK_DEBUG and GTK_DEBUG environment variables (discussed in the next section) to be recognized. Various Gtk+ and GDK modules must be built with G_ENABLE_DEBUG in order for debugging support that they provide to be enabled. For example, building GDK with G_ENABLE_DEBUG enables debugging support in the drag-and-drop, X Input Method (XIM), visual, and color-context modules. Whether or not a module actually generates debug output is controlled by the debug command-line arguments and/or the GDK_DEBUG flag, as we will see in the next section.

- **G_DISABLE_ASSERT** If enabled, Glib's g_assert() and g_assert_not_reached() macros are defined to do nothing. Otherwise, the g_assert() and g_assert_not_reached() macros, used extensively throughout Gtk+, Glib, and GDK, will be enabled.
- **G_DISABLE_CHECKS** If enabled, Glib's g_return_if_fail() and g_return_val_if_fail() macros are defined to do nothing. Like g_assert() and g_assert_not_reached(), these macros are used throughout Glib, GDK, and Gtk+.
- **GTK_NO_CHECK_CASTS** If enabled, checking is not performed when casts occur between different object types. In Chapter 3, "Signals, Events, Objects, and Types," I'll introduce objects and casting. Macros such as GTK_OBJECT, GTK_WINDOW, and GTK_BUTTON, which are used to cast a widget or an object variable to another widget or object class, will execute extra code to verify that the cast is valid. Enabling GTK_NO_CHECK_CASTS disables this check.

You can enable or disable G_ENABLE_DEBUG, G_DISABLE_ASSERT, G_DISABLE_CHECKS, and GTK_NO_CHECK_CASTS at the time Gtk+ is configured. The configure script accepts an --enable-debug option. If set to "minimum", which is the default, only inexpensive sanity checking will be performed, and GTK_NO_CHECK_CASTS will be set, disabling object casting checks. If set to "yes", then G_ENABLE debug is set. If set to "no" or if the configure script option --disable-debug is specified, then all debugging support is disabled by setting G_DISABLE_ASSERT, G_DISABLE_CHECKS, and GTK_NO_CHECK_CASTS.

Runtime. If Gtk+ was compiled with debugging enabled (i.e., G_ENABLE_DEBUG was defined), then various debug information will be printed out as conditions warrant it. As stated earlier, the output of debug information at runtime is controlled on a module-by-module basis with the GTK_DEBUG and GDK_DEBUG environment variables as well as the --gtk-debug, --gdk-debug, --gtk-no-debug, and --gdk-no-debug command-line arguments supported by Gtk+. The environment variables are applied first, if present, followed by the command-line arguments. The values assigned to the environment variables and command-line arguments share the same syntax, which consists of a colon-separated list of modules. The value "all" is used to denote all modules that allow their debug output to be controlled via the debug environment variables and command-line arguments. Table 2.2 lists the supported modules and indicates how the command-line arguments and environment variables affect each.

Table 2.2 Arguments and Variables Affecting Debug at Runtime

Module	*Environment*	*Command Line*	*Comment*
objects	GTK_DEBUG	--gtk-*	Traces creation and destruction of objects and prints a summary when program terminates

Table 2.2 Arguments and Variables Affecting Debug at Runtime (Continued)

Module	*Environment*	*Command Line*	*Comment*
misc	Both	All	Miscellaneous messages/debug
signals	GTK_DEBUG	--gtk-*	Traces emission of signals
dnd		All	Drag-and-drop messages/debug
events	GDK_DEBUG[(a)]	--gdk-*	Traces X event reception
plugsocket	GTK_DEBUG	--gtk-*	GtkSocket messages
color-context	GDK_DEBUG	--gdk-*	Color-context module messages
xim	GDK_DEBUG	--gdk-*	X Input Method module messages

(a) *Can also be enabled or disabled at runtime by calling gdk_set_show_events()*

Of the preceding, only objects, events, and signals are likely to be of interest to application developers. The rest are mostly in place for the maintainers of the modules.

For example, say you have linked an application, foo, to Gtk+/GDK libraries that were built with G_ENABLE_DEBUG, and you would like to trace signal emission and event reception. The following are all ways to accomplish this:

```
$ setenv GDK_DEBUG all; setenv GTK_DEBUG all; foo

$ setenv GDK_DEBUG events; setenv GTK_DEBUG signals; foo

$ foo --gdk-debug=events --gtk-debug=signals
```

In the preceding, we turned on all messages for Gtk+ and GDK, including signals and events.

Error messages are generated to stdout or stderr depending on the error level set for the individual message, as listed in Table 2.3.

Table 2.3 Debug Output Error Levels

Error Level	*Comment*
G_LOG_LEVEL_ERROR	Always fatal
G_LOG_LEVEL_CRITICAL	Fatal if --g-fatal-warnings
G_LOG_LEVEL_WARNING	Fatal if --g-fatal-warnings
G_LOG_LEVEL_MESSAGE	
G_LOG_LEVEL_INFO	

Table 2.3 Debug Output Error Levels (Continued)

Error Level	*Comment*
G_LOG_LEVEL_DEBUG	

Error levels lower in the table are smaller in value. Messages with error levels greater than or equal to G_LOG_LEVEL_MESSAGE will go to stderr, while the rest of the messages will go to stdout.

Recall the --g-fatal-warnings flag previously mentioned. Specifying this flag causes your application to exit should any of the debug messages you have enabled generate a message that has an error level greater than or equal to G_LOG_LEVEL_WARNING.

Application Termination

To exit a Gtk+ application, call gtk_exit():

```
void
gtk_exit (int errorcode)
```

gtk_exit() is, in Gtk+ 1.2, a wrapper for gdk_exit(), which just calls exit(1), passing errorcode as its argument. Generally, a value of zero indicates success, and a nonzero error code indicates failure.

Try to avoid calling exit(1) in place of gtk_exit(). It is unclear what, if any, additional functionality may be placed in gtk_exit() in future versions. Also, as Gtk+ is ported to new environments, the implementation of gtk_exit() and/or gdk_exit() is subject to change.

Gtk+ and GDK register exit functions, using g_atexit(), at initialization time. Modules (or widget implementations) may also register an exit function in the same manner. An exit function is called by the system when the exit(1) system call is invoked. GtkObject is an example of a widget that makes use of this functionality, registering a routine called gtk_object_debug(). At exit time, if "object" debugging has been enabled, a list of objects still active in the application will be displayed to the screen by the exit function. The exit functions registered by Gtk+ and GDK are used mainly to clean up the application and X environments at exit. You can register your own exit handlers using the Glib function g_atexit():

```
void
g_atexit (GVoidFunc func)
```

GVoidFunc is simply a pointer to a function that takes a void argument, for example:

```
void
MyExitFunc( void )
{
        ...
}
```

g_atexit() is a wrapper of the UNIX function atexit(3).

Gtk+ Main Loop Functions

Earlier in this chapter, I introduced the function gtk_main():

```
void
gtk_main (void)
```

We've seen that once a Gtk+ application calls gtk_main(), Gtk+ takes control. gtk_main() is essentially a loop, endlessly waiting for user input such as key presses and mouse movement and making calls to signal functions registered with widgets by your application in response to whatever input is received. It is within these signal functions that the logic of your application resides, and other than the code in main leading up to gtk_main(), the bulk of the code in your application resides within the context of a signal function. Of course, there are exceptions to this rule that we will look at later in the book: UNIX signal functions, X error handlers, and such, are among these exceptions.

Terminating the Main Loop

To leave gtk_main(), your application must make a call to gtk_main_quit():

```
void
gtk_main_quit (void)
```

gtk_main_quit() basically causes gtk_main() to break out of its loop and return. Most applications will make the call to gtk_main_quit() from within a signal function associated with a Quit or Exit button or menu item.

Gtk+ allows nesting of gtk_main(), which is helpful since there may be times when you will need to call gtk_main() from inside a signal function. I'll cover the use of nested calls to gtk_main() later when I discuss dialogs. Note that each call to gtk_main() should be matched with a call to gtk_main_quit().

An application can determine the current level of gtk_main() nesting by calling gtk_main_level():

```
guint
gtk_main_level (void)
```

A return value of zero means your application is not currently executing within the context of gtk_main(). A value of 1 indicates that a single call to gtk_main() is in effect, and so forth.

Controlling the Main Loop

In situations similar to those that would require nesting of gtk_main(), an application might instead call gtk_main_iteration(). gtk_main_iteration() causes Gtk+ to make a single pass through the main loop, processing the next available event and allowing widgets to invoke signal functions, and so forth. Init and quit functions, described later in this chapter, are not invoked, however; these are only invoked via a call to gtk_main(). The following is the function prototype for gtk_main_iteration().

```
gint
gtk_main_iteration (void)
```

The advantage of using gtk_main() is that gtk_main() executes a loop that will run indefinitely until the application calls gtk_main_exit() from inside signal function. If your program has registered init and quit functions, these will be called each time the loop is entered. If these init and/or quit functions are vital to your application, meaning they need to be called frequently, then use gtk_main(). If they do not need to be called or are somehow harmful to the application if called in the context in which nested main loop iteration is being performed, then use gtk_main_iteration() instead because neither init nor quit functions are invoked from within gtk_main_iteration().

It is unlikely that a single call to gtk_main_iteration() will accomplish what your application needs to accomplish. Typically, your application will need to go into a loop, calling gtk_main_iteration() until some flag is set from within a signal function. For example:

```
flag = 0;
while ( !flag )
         gtk_main_iteration();
```

In this case, the expectation is that flag will eventually be set in a signal function that is triggered from within gtk_main_iteration().

Checking for Pending Events

Applications can determine if any events are pending in the event queue by calling gtk_events_pending():

```
gint
gtk_events_pending (void)
```

gtk_events_pending() will return FALSE if there are no events to process at the time of the call; otherwise, it returns TRUE. gtk_events_pending() will not block, nor will it process, events that might be waiting in the event queue. We can modify the preceding loop to perform application-specific tasks when there are no events waiting to be processed, as follows:

```
flag = 0;
while ( !flag )
         if ( gtk_events_pending() == TRUE )
                  gtk_main_iteration();
         else
                  do_something();
```

Here, if gtk_events_pending() returns TRUE, there is an event to dispatch, and this is handled by calling gtk_main_iteration(). Otherwise, do_something() is called to do whatever it is that do_something() does. Timeout or idle functions, described later in this chapter, are another and perhaps better way to organize such a loop, with Gtk+ calling your code periodically as opposed to your code calling Gtk+.

Init and Quit Functions

You can register init functions with Gtk+ that will be called the next time your application makes a call to gtk_main(). Any number of functions can be registered, but each must have the following prototype:

```
void
function( gpointer data );
```

To add a function, call gtk_init_add():

```
void
gtk_init_add (GtkFunction function, gpointer data)
```

The first argument is a pointer to the function you want called; the second can be any value cast to a gpointer. If you need to pass more than one value to the init function, store these values in a struct and pass a pointer to the struct. You must ensure that data is valid at the time the init function is called by Gtk+.

Each time gtk_init_add() is called, the function and data passed are added to a list maintained by Gtk+. The next time gtk_main() is called, before Gtk+ enters its event loop, it will call each function, removing the function and data from the list once the function returns.

Quit functions are analogous to init functions but are called after gtk_main() has left its event loop, which is triggered by a call to gtk_main_quit(). The function prototype for a quit function is mostly the same as that of an init function, except it must return a gint status. This status return is explained later in this section. A quit function can be registered with Gtk+ by calling gtk_quit_add():

```
guint
gtk_quit_add (guint main_level, GtkFunction function, gpointer data)
```

The arguments to gtk_quit_add() are the same as those for gtk_init_add(), except that gtk_quit_add() requires an additional argument, main_level, which tells Gtk+ to which nesting level of gtk_main() the quit function pertains. If zero, the quit function will be executed every time gtk_main_quit() is invoked. If nonzero and greater than or equal to 1, the function will only be executed when gtk_main_quit() for that nesting level has been called.

Your quit function, as previously mentioned, must return a status value. If the return value is zero, the quit function will be removed from the list of quit functions maintained by Gtk+, never to be called again unless it is returned to the list via a call to gtk_quit_add(). If nonzero, the quit function is subject to further invocation, according to the main_level value originally passed to gtk_quit_add(). That is, if your application in the future reaches a nesting level of gtk_main() equal to main_level, then each call to gtk_main_quit() that corresponds to that nesting level will cause the quit function to be invoked, assuming that the function continues to return a nonzero return value. If, on the other hand, the quit function was added with a main_level equal to zero, returning zero from the quit function will guarantee that it is invoked each time gtk_main_quit() is called, unless of course it returns nonzero, which will cause the quit function to be removed from Gtk+'s list.

gtk_quit_add() returns a guint ID value. This ID value can then be passed to gtk_quit_remove() to remove the quit function from Gtk+'s list:

```
void
gtk_quit_remove (guint id)
```

If there is no quit function on the list that can be identified by the passed ID, the call to gtk_quit_remove() is a no-op.

Your application can also remove a quit function that is identified by the data Gtk+ will pass to it when invoked. The routine capable of performing this task is gtk_quit_remove_by_data():

```
void
gtk_quit_remove_by_data (gpointer data)
```

The argument data is the same data that was passed to gtk_quit_add(). Note that only the first quit function found on the quit list that corresponds to data will be removed. If you have registered more than one quit function that accepts the same data argument, you will need to invoke gtk_quit_remove_by_data() once for each such quit function. Because gtk_quit_remove_by_data() does not return a value, there is no way to know if the routine found and removed a quit function or not, so it is up to your application to remember how many such quit functions there are that would need to be removed. An improvement to gtk_quit_remove_by_data() would be for it to return a status that indicates whether the remove was performed or not. By checking this status, an application would know whether there are additional quit functions to remove that correspond to the data value. Additionally, a function that removes all quit functions associated with a given data value would seem to me to be a reasonable addition to the Gtk+ API.

Destroying Objects When a Main Loop Exits

Gtk+ allows applications to register objects for automatic destruction whenever the application leaves a main loop (i.e., gtk_main_exit() has been called). For applications that have a single main loop and exit the application upon returning from gtk_main(), there is no need for this because the environment will ensure that destruction of objects occurs at application exit. However, gtk_quit_add_destroy() provides a convenient way for objects to be destroyed automatically by those applications that make use of nested main loops.

```
void
gtk_quit_add_destroy(guint main_level, GtkObject *object)
```

The argument main_level is the level of the (nested) main loop that, when left by a call to gtk_main_exit(), will cause the object to be destroyed. main_level must be greater than zero in value. object is the object ID of the object to be destroyed.

Timeouts and Idle Processing

An application may need to perform a task that has some uncertainty involved with regard to the amount of time it will take for the task to complete, whether or not the task will complete at all, or both. Also, some applications must perform one or more tasks at some predefined interval (e.g., once every 30 seconds). Both of these issues can be addressed through the use of timeouts.

An e-mail package like Mozilla, Z-Mail, or MUSH provides an excellent example of an application potentially well-suited for the use of timeouts. Most mail user agents are designed to poll for new mail from the mail server or local mailbox at a user-specified interval. When it comes time for the mail user agent to check for mail on a mail server, the mail user agent will send a command to the mail server, requesting information that can be used to determine whether new mail has arrived, and will wait for a response from the server. In short, the following steps are involved in polling for new mail:

1. Waiting for the duration of the polling interval (e.g., 2 minutes) to transpire
2. Sending a command to the mail server, requesting mailbox information (e.g., how many messages are in the mailbox), and waiting for a response from the mail server

As I will illustrate, both of these tasks can be implemented in part by using a timeout facility such as the one provided by Gtk+.

There are two routines in Gtk+ that provide timeout support: gtk_timeout_add() and gtk_timeout_remove(). The function prototypes are

```
guint
gtk_timeout_add (guint32 interval, GtkFunction function, gpointer
data)
```

and

```
void
gtk_timeout_remove (guint tag)
```

Adding a Timeout

The first argument to gtk_timeout_add(), interval, is an unsigned 32-bit value, indicating the amount of time (in milliseconds) that Gtk+ must wait before the timer expires. Once the timeout interval has expired, the routine specified by the function argument to gtk_timeout_add() is invoked, with the value specified by the data argument passed by Gtk+ to the function as its single argument. The prototype for the timeout function is as follows:

```
gint
function( gpointer data )
```

If the timeout function returns a nonzero value, Gtk+ will restart the interval timer, and your timer function will be invoked once again when the timeout interval has expired. If zero is returned by your timeout function, the timeout will be unregistered by Gtk+ and will no longer be triggered.

Removing a Timeout

gtk_timeout_add() returns a unique handle of type guint. This handle may be passed to gtk_timeout_remove() to unregister the timeout it references before the timeout is triggered. Calling gtk_timeout_remove() is equivalent to returning zero from the timeout function when called. gtk_timeout_remove() is needed by applications that use timeouts as a way to ensure that some operation completes during a specified period of time. If the timed operation completes before the timeout is triggered, the timeout is no longer needed and should be removed by the application with a call to gtk_timeout_remove().

Timeout Example

Let's revisit the e-mail application and see how Gtk+ timeouts might be applied. To enable a mail polling feature that triggers every *n* seconds, a Gtk+ e-mail application would call gtk_timeout_add() to specify the polling interval and to register with Gtk+ the function that will be called each time the polling interval transpires. This routine, when called, will contact the mail server to determine whether new mail has arrived and perhaps to read the mail headers and ensure that the user interface is updated in case new mail has arrived. The timeout routine should return a nonzero value; this will cause Gtk+ to reset the interval timer and call the timeout function the next time the specified interval has transpired. The user might at any time want to disable polling for new mail; this can be implemented easily by calling gtk_timeout_remove(). The user might also want to change the polling interval itself; this can be done by removing the timeout and reregistering it with a call to gtk_timeout_add(), specifying the same function and the new polling interval as arguments.

Inside the timeout function, we will need to establish a network connection to the mail server, assuming mail is being read from a POP or IMAP4 mail server, and then send a command requesting the status of the remote mailbox. In both of these instances (i.e., when connecting and when sending the status request), we should register a timeout function that will be triggered in the event that the connection cannot be established or the server does not respond to the status command that we send. Should the connection occur or we receive a response to the status command before the timeout expires, we need to remove the timeout with a call to gtk_timeout_remove(). The timeout function, if it is triggered, might perform cleanup chores associated with the failed connection or command and let the user know that there was a failure by displaying a message. The timeout function should always return zero to ensure that it will not be called again by Gtk+.

Timeout Precision

It is important to realize that the timeouts themselves are what I would call low-precision, in the sense that Gtk+ is traversing the list of registered timeouts once during each iteration of the main loop, comparing the current time with the time at which a timeout is due to trigger and firing those timeouts for which the timeout interval has expired since the last time the list was checked. Thus, there is the potential for a latency associated with the triggering of a given timeout should Gtk+ not get through an iteration of the main loop in time to handle a timeout that has just expired. For example, at time t0, Gtk+ might invoke an application callback in response to an event. If a timeout is due to expire at time t1 and the callback function does not return or give control back to the main loop until after time t1, then Gtk+ cannot dispatch the timeout function at time t1 as was intended. There are two ways to deal with this.

The first way would be to ensure that cycles are being given to the main loop during operations that are of a duration that is long enough to potentially impact the timely processing of timeouts by Gtk+. This can be done by making frequent calls to gtk_main_iteration(), as previously described. Each call to gtk_main_iteration() will cause Gtk+ to make a single pass through the main loop and process any timeouts that may have triggered.

The second way would be to not use Gtk+ timeouts at all and instead use the UNIX alarm(2) system call to implement timeouts in your application. Although the use of alarms will eliminate any latency issues, your application cannot enjoy the benefit associated with Gtk+ passing user data to your timeout function because alarms do not provide this facility.

Idle Functions

Idle functions differ from timeouts in that idle functions are called each pass through the Gtk+ main loop. Because of this, there is a latency involved. Just as Gtk+ cannot guarantee the frequency with which timeouts are evaluated and their associated functions invoked, Gtk+ cannot guarantee that an application's idle functions will be invoked at a fixed, reliable rate. This is something that for idle functions is much less of a concern, however, due to the sort of processing that an application would tend to perform in an idle function.

So, what would one do in an idle function? The general answer is, anything that takes a long time to accomplish. Such time-consuming tasks could be just about anything: rendering a fractal image, reading a file from a network server, or computing prime numbers. Performing tasks that take a long time to complete should, in general, not impede a user's ability to interact with an application, nor should it impede the application's ability to respond to system events. A program such as Netscape Communicator would be very unfriendly if it did not allow its users to perform other tasks during a lengthy file download, such as surfing the Web or reading newly arrived mail messages. A program performing a file transfer will usually provide the user with a way to cancel the operation; in a GUI program, this is usually in the form of a Cancel button. Gtk+ must get cycles in its main loop in order to process the user event associated with clicking the Cancel button. Gtk+ also needs to be given time to process system events such as window exposures. A well-written GUI application will redraw exposed portions of its user interface soon after the exposure occurs, not after the file transfer it has been performing has completed. This can only be achieved if time is being shared between processing being performed by the application and the Gtk+ main loop. Idle functions are one way to allow this to happen.

Adding an Idle Function

Adding an idle function is just like adding a timeout except there is no need to specify an interval. The routine to call to register an idle function with Gtk+ is gtk_idle_add():

```
guint
gtk_idle_add (GtkFunction function, gpointer data)
```

The argument function is the idle function that will be invoked by Gtk+, and data is the argument of type gpointer that the function will be passed. A handle of type guint is returned; this handle can be used to remove the idle function, as I will discuss later in this chapter. The idle function provided by your application must adhere to the following function prototype:

```
gint
function( gpointer data );
```

An idle function returning a value of zero will be destroyed by Gtk+ and will no longer be called unless reregistered by the application. A nonzero return value will ensure that the idle function remains to be invoked during the next iteration of the gtk main loop.

Idle Function Priorities

Idle functions can be assigned a priority value by the application at the time they are added by calling gtk_idle_add_priority():

```
guint
gtk_idle_add_priority (gint priority, GtkFunction function,
       gpointer data)
```

Functionally, gtk_idle_add_priority() is the same as gtk_idle_add() except for an extra argument, priority. The Gtk+ and Glib headers define the priority values in Table 2.4.

Table 2.4 Priority Levels

Priority	*Value*
G_PRIORITY_HIGH	–100
G_PRIORITY_DEFAULT	0
G_PRIORITY_HIGH_IDLE	100
G_PRIORITY_DEFAULT_IDLE	200
G_PRIORITY_LOW	300
GTK_PRIORITY_REDRAW	G_PRIORITY_HIGH_IDLE + 20
GTK_PRIORITY_RESIZE	G_PRIORITY_HIGH_IDLE + 10
GTK_PRIORITY_HIGH	G_PRIORITY_HIGH
GTK_PRIORITY_INTERNAL	GTK_PRIORITY_REDRAW
GTK_PRIORITY_DEFAULT	G_PRIORITY_DEFAULT_IDLE
GTK_PRIORITY_LOW	G_PRIORITY_LOW

The default priority, assigned by Gtk+ when an idle function is registered by a call to gtk_idle_add(), is GTK_PRIORITY_DEFAULT. Smaller values are higher in priority; greater values are lower. It is perfectly reasonable for applications to register idle functions at GTK_PRIORITY_DEFAULT + 30, for example, if they so choose.

Idle functions at the same priority level are executed in a round-robin fashion. Gtk+ will only execute those idle functions having the highest priority of all idle functions currently registered. Idle functions that are lower in priority are not eligible to be invoked until all higher priority idle functions have been destroyed. Because of this, an application must be careful when using idle functions. Idle functions that are lower in priority will experience starvation if one or more idle functions have been registered by the application at a higher priority, and these higher priority idle functions are never destroyed. Gtk+, Glib, or GDK may register idle functions for internal purposes; for these idle functions to receive cycles, applications must ensure that no application-registered idle functions of a higher priority exist.

Basically, it is safest to register idle functions with gtk_idle_add(), or with gtk_idle_add_priority() with a priority of GTK_PRIORITY_DEFAULT. If you must add an idle function at priorities other than GTK_PRIORITY_DEFAULT, the best way to ensure that the idle function is not starved by higher-priority idle functions, and in turn that it does not starve idle functions lower in priority, would be to return zero from all idle functions, ensuring that that they are destroyed after they are executed. Idle functions that need to be executed multiple times should be given lower priority or be utilized in a way that ensures that other idle functions are not being starved.

Destroying Idle Functions

As previously mentioned, an idle function can be destroyed or unregistered by returning 0 from within the idle function, once it has been called. Another way to destroy an idle function is to call gtk_idle_remove(), passing the guint value returned by gtk_idle_add_priority() or gtk_idle_add():

```
void
gtk_idle_remove (guint tag)
```

Idle functions can also be removed based on the user data that was registered with the idle function at the time of its creation. This can be done by calling gtk_idle_remove_by_data() and passing as an argument the gpointer argument that was passed to gtk_idle_add*() at the time of the idle function's creation. The function prototype for gtk_idle_remove_by_data() is as follows:

```
void
gtk_idle_remove_by_data (gpointer data)
```

Snooping Key Presses

The final main loop routines that I'd like to discuss in this chapter include gtk_key_snooper_install() and gtk_key_snooper_remove(). The function prototypes for these routines are as follows:

```
guint
gtk_key_snooper_install (GtkKeySnoopFunc snooper, gpointer func_data)

void
gtk_key_snooper_remove (guint snooper_id)
```

gtk_key_snooper_install() accepts as arguments a pointer to a snooper function (described later in this chapter) and user data in the form of a gpointer that will be passed to the snooper function each time it is invoked by Gtk+. A unique ID or tag value is returned by gtk_key_snooper_install(). This ID can be used by the application to identify the "key snooper" when attempting to remove it with a call to gtk_key_snooper_remove().

The function prototype for the snooper function is as follows:

```
gint
function( GtkWidget *widget, GdkEventKey *event, gpointer data )
```

The argument widget is the widget receiving the key event. The argument event describes the key event in detail. GdkEventKey is defined as follows:

```
typedef struct _GdkEventKey
{
  GdkEventType type;
  GdkWindow *window;
  gint8 send_event;
  guint32 time;
  guint state;
  guint keyval;
  gint length;
  gchar *string;
} GdkEventKey;
```

Perhaps the fields of most interest to snooper functions include the type field, which will be set to GDK_KEY_PRESS, and keyval, which is the ASCII code for the key that was pressed. The time value might be of interest to game developers who support keyboard input, when reaction to the key press is based in part on how frequently a key is being pressed. In the following source code, we make use of the keyval and string fields to implement a password input dialog. Events in general are described in more detail in Chapter 3.

Multiple snooper functions may be registered with Gtk+ by an application. As a key is pressed, each snooper function registered by the application is invoked until one of the snooper functions returns a nonzero value, indicating that the snooper function has swallowed the key press event or there are no further snooper functions to invoke. When a snooper function returns 0, this is basically telling Gtk+ to continue processing the key press as though the snooper function were never called in the first place. If some snooper function returns 0, then Gtk+ does not process the key press event further, and the key press event is discarded.

An application might do several interesting things using a key snooper. One of them, as previously mentioned, is a password-entry dialog. To provide some measure of security, a password-entry dialog should not echo the characters being typed by the user. This reduces the ability of a person (or a camera) to monitor the dialog and discover the password being typed. The following snooper function implements this feature:

```
gint
foo( GtkWidget *widget, GdkEventKey *event, gpointer data )
{
   static char tmp[2];
   static char password[1024] = "";
   char c;

   if ( (c = (char) event->keyval) == '\n' || c == '\r' ) {
           printf( "Password is '%s'\n", password );
           gtk_exit( 0 );
   }

   tmp[0] = c;
   tmp[1] = '\0';
```

```
018     strcat( password, tmp );
019     event->keyval = event->string[0] = '*';
020     return( 0 );
021  }
```

The function foo() maintains a statically allocated buffer of characters, named password, to hold the characters typed by the user, up to the carriage return or newline character that signifies the end of data entry. On line 011, the keyval field of the key press event is retrieved and stored for later use. If the character corresponding to the key press is a newline or carriage return, the password that was accumulated by the snooper function is printed to the console, and the application is terminated. (This is just an example application. In an actual application, the password would be stored somewhere accessible to the rest of the application, and the dialog used to obtain the password would be torn down.)

Otherwise, the snooper function creates a character string on lines 016 and 017, using the character retrieved from the key press event, and then concatenates this string to the password string being constructed by the snooper function.

On line 019, the keyval and string fields of the key event are changed so that the key event indicates a pressing of the asterisk (*) key (Shift+8). On line 020 we return a 0, which tells Gtk+ to continue processing the event. Assuming that no other snooper function exists to claim the key press event, Gtk+ will dispatch the key press event to the widget that has keyboard focus. In the case of the GtkEntry widget, this will result in the display of an asterisk, effectively hiding the password being typed by the user from any prying eyes.

There is one problem with the preceding algorithm; it does not correctly deal with backspace and delete characters typed by the user. It is a simple matter to fix this problem; I leave this as an exercise to the reader. The complete code for the sample password entry application is as follows:

Listing 2.4 Password Entry Sample

```
001  #include <stdio.h>
002  #include <gtk/gtk.h>
003
004  gint
005  foo( GtkWidget *widget, GdkEventKey *event, gpointer data )
006  {
007     static char tmp[2];
008     static char password[1024] = "";
009     char c;
010
011     if ( (c = (char) event->keyval) == '\n' || c == '\r' ) {
012             printf( "Password is '%s'\n", password );
013             gtk_exit( 0 );
014     }
015
016     tmp[0] = c;
017     tmp[1] = '\0';
018     strcat( password, tmp );
019     event->keyval = event->string[0] = '*';
020     return( 0 );
```

```
021 }
022
023 int
024 main( int argc, char *argv[] )
025 {
026    GtkWidget *window, *box, *entry;
027
028    gtk_set_locale ();
029
030    gtk_init (&argc, &argv);
031
032    window = gtk_window_new (GTK_WINDOW_TOPLEVEL);
033    gtk_window_set_title( GTK_WINDOW( window ), "Enter Password" );
034
035    box = gtk_vbox_new (FALSE, 0);
036    gtk_container_add (GTK_CONTAINER (window), box);
037
038    entry = gtk_entry_new ();
039    gtk_entry_set_text (GTK_ENTRY (entry), "");
040    gtk_editable_select_region (GTK_EDITABLE (entry), 0, -1);
041    gtk_box_pack_start (GTK_BOX (box), entry, TRUE, TRUE, 0);
042
043    gtk_key_snooper_install( foo, (gpointer) NULL );
044
045    gtk_widget_show_all( window );
046
047    gtk_main ();
048
049    return( 0 );
050 }
```

Our main() basically consists of three sections. The first of these, on lines 028 through 030, initializes Gtk+ as described earlier in this chapter. The second section, on lines 032 through 041, creates the user interface for the application, which is essentially just a window (lines 032 and 033) and a GtkEntry widget (lines 038 and 041). A vertical box widget is used to provide a container in the window for the GtkEntry widget. The final section consists of lines 045 through the end of main(). The structure of our main(), as we have seen, is a fairly typical one for a Gtk+ application. Between section 2 and section 3, we make a call to gtk_key_snooper_install() to register the key snooper function that will be called when the user types in the GtkEntry widget. For this example, it really did not matter where we registered the key snooper as long as it occurred after section 1 and before the call to gtk_main() in section 3. In a real-life Gtk+ application, however, the key snooper should be registered just prior to the display of the password entry dialog and should be removed once the dialog is dismissed with a call to gtk_key_snooper_remove(). The snooper function should also take care to ensure that the key event it is processing actually occurred inside of the GtkEntry field, especially if the password entry dialog is nonmodal or if there are other widgets (entry or otherwise) that could obtain keyboard focus while the password entry field is accessible to the user. A fairly simple way to accomplish this would be to pass the widget handle of the GtkEntry field as the func_data argument to gtk_key_snooper_install(). Gtk+ will then pass this data as the third argument to the snooper function. A slight modification to the snooper function would be for it to compare its data and widget arguments for equality and immediately return 0 if they are not the same because this is an indication that the key press was not made in the password entry field.

Summary

In contrast to console applications, Gtk+ applications are event driven. A Gtk+ program creates a user interface and then enters a main loop, gtk_main(). User interaction with buttons, menu items, and other widgets in the user interface results in the invocation of signal functions, or callbacks, implemented by the application and registered with the controls or widgets that invoke them. It is within the context of a signal function that the application responds to user input and performs meaningful work. Time was spent analyzing a simple Gtk+ application, and we also took a look at how to compile and debug a Gtk+ application. The rest of the chapter focused on functions related to the main loop of a Gtk+ application, and this included a discussion of the use of timeout and idle functions.

CHAPTER

3

SIGNALS, EVENTS, OBJECTS, AND TYPES

This chapter begins with a discussion of signals and signal handling. The topic of signals is an important one. A typical Gtk+ application will perform all of its useful work within the context of a signal handler, as we will see time and again throughout the course of this book. In addition to signals, we'll also cover Gtk+ events and objects, defining what they are and how they can be used and manipulated by an application. The chapter will close with a short discussion on Gtk+ types.

Signals

Signals provide the mechanism by which a widget communicates useful information to a client about some change in its state.

In Chapter 2, "Hello Gtk+!," we developed and discussed three "Hello World!" applications. Two of these were console-based, using standard I/O to display output to the screen and retrieve input from the user. We saw that flow of control in these programs was synchronous, meaning that statements were executed one after another, and when I/O was needed, the program would block in a routine such as fgets() until the input data needed by the application was entered by the user. The third of our "Hello World!" applications was also our first Gtk+ application. Two signal functions or callbacks were implemented in hellogtk+. Neither of these functions was called directly by hellogtk+. Instead, one of these functions was invoked by Gtk+ in response to the user pressing the "Print" button. The other was invoked in response to the application being closed (via a window manager control, for example).

An Example: GtkButton Signals

To better understand the functionality provided by signals, let's take a closer look at how signals are used by the GtkButton widget class.

GtkButton, the widget class that implements push button in Gtk+, generates a signal whenever one of the following events is detected:

- The pointer enters the rectangular region occupied by the button.
- The pointer leaves the rectangular region occupied by the button.
- The pointer is positioned over the button, and a mouse button is pressed.

- The pointer is positioned over the button, and a mouse button is released.
- The user clicks the button (a combination of pressing and releasing a mouse button while the pointer is positioned over the button).

Each widget class implements signals needed to make that widget class useful to application designers. In addition, widget classes inherit signals from classes higher in the Gtk+ class hierarchy. For example, a signal is emitted when a push button is destroyed. This signal is actually generated by a superclass of GtkButton. The signals implemented by a superclass represent functionality needed by many classes of widget. It is better to implement this functionality once in a superclass, allowing child classes to inherit the behavior, than it is to replicate the same functionality in each of the widget classes that need it.

Gtk+ does not force clients to use any of the signals that a class implements. However, in order to be useful, most applications will need to make use of at least one of the signals provided so that the widget can communicate useful information back to the client.

Handling Signals

Handling a signal in a Gtk+ application involves two steps. First, the application must implement a signal handler; this is the function that will be invoked by the widget when the signal triggers. Second, the client must register the signal handler with the widget. Registering a signal handler with a widget occurs after the application has created or instantiated the widget, by calling the Gtk+ routine gtk_signal_connect(). The prototype for this function is:

```
gint
gtk_signal_connect(
        GtkObject *object,          /* the widget */
        gchar *name,                /* the signal */
        GtkSignalFunc func,         /* the signal handler */
        gpointer func_data );       /* application-private data */
```

The first argument, object, tells Gtk+ from which widget instance we would like the signal to be generated. This widget pointer is returned by a call to one of the gtk_*_new functions. For example, if the widget we are registering the signal handler with is a GtkButton, then the object argument is the return value from the function gtk_button_new() or gtk_button_new_with_label(). Because both of these functions return a variable of type GtkWidget *, we must use one of the casting macros provided by Gtk+ to coerce the GtkWidget * variable holding the widget instance pointer to the type GtkObject *. For example:

```
GtkWidget *button;

...

button = gtk_button_new_with_label( "Print" );
gtk_signal_connect( GTK_OBJECT( button ), ... );
```

The second argument to gtk_signal_connect() is the name of the signal we would like to associate with the signal handler. For those signals implemented by GtkButton, this will be one of the following strings:

- **enter** The pointer entered the rectangular region occupied by the button.
- **leave** The pointer left the rectangular region occupied by the button.
- **pressed** The pointer was positioned over the button, and a mouse button was pressed.
- **released** The pointer was positioned over the button, and a mouse button was released.
- **clicked** The user clicked the button (a combination of pressing and releasing the mouse button while the pointer was positioned over the button).

The third argument to gtk_signal_connect() is a pointer to the function that should be invoked by the widget when the signal specified by argument two, name, is triggered. The final argument to gtk_signal_connect() is a pointer to private data that will be passed to the signal handler by the widget when the signal handler is invoked.

Unfortunately, signal functions do not adhere to a single function prototype. The arguments passed to a signal handler will vary based on the widget generating the signal. The general form of a Gtk+ signal handler is as follows:

```
void
callback_func( GtkWidget *widget, gpointer callback_data );
```

I will describe the function prototypes for signal handlers in later chapters, along with the widgets that generate them. However, at this point, I can say a couple of things about callback function arguments that hold true regardless of the widget class involved:

- The first argument of the signal handler will always be a pointer to the widget that generated the signal.
- The callback_data argument will always be the last argument passed to the signal handler.
- Any arguments that are specific to the widget or to the signal will occur between the first and last arguments of the signal handler.

The final argument passed to the callback function, callback_data, contains a pointer to data that is private to the application and has no meaning whatsoever to the widget. The use of private callback data is a practice that Gtk+ borrowed from Xt/Motif, and it has powerful implications for application design.

Client Callback Data Example

To illustrate the use of client data, let's design a simple application. Here's the code:

Listing 3.1 Passing Client Data to a Callback

```
#include <stdio.h>
#include <time.h>
#include <gtk/gtk.h>

void
Update (GtkWidget *widget, char *timestr)
```

```
{
        time_t timeval;

        timeval = time( NULL );
        strcpy( timestr, ctime( &timeval ) );
}

void
PrintAndExit (GtkWidget *widget, char timestr[][26])
{
        int     i;

        for ( i = 0; i < 4; i++ )
                printf( "timestr[ %d ] is %s", i, timestr[ i ] );
        gtk_main_quit ();
}

int
main( int argc, char *argv[] )
{
        GtkWidget *window, *box, *button;

        static char times[ 4 ][ 26 ] =
                { "Unset\n", "Unset\n", "Unset\n", "Unset\n" };

        gtk_set_locale ();

        gtk_init (&argc, &argv);

        window = gtk_window_new (GTK_WINDOW_TOPLEVEL);

        gtk_signal_connect (GTK_OBJECT(window), "destroy",
        GTK_SIGNAL_FUNC(PrintAndExit), times);

        gtk_window_set_title (GTK_WINDOW (window), "Signals 1");
        gtk_container_border_width (GTK_CONTAINER (window), 0);

        box = gtk_vbox_new (FALSE, 0);
        gtk_container_add (GTK_CONTAINER (window), box);

        button = gtk_button_new_with_label ("Update 0");
        gtk_signal_connect (GTK_OBJECT (button), "clicked",
                GTK_SIGNAL_FUNC(Update), &times[0]);
        gtk_box_pack_start (GTK_BOX (box), button, TRUE, TRUE, 0);

        button = gtk_button_new_with_label ("Update 1");
        gtk_signal_connect (GTK_OBJECT (button), "clicked",
                GTK_SIGNAL_FUNC(Update), &times[1]);
        gtk_box_pack_start (GTK_BOX (box), button, TRUE, TRUE, 0);

        button = gtk_button_new_with_label ("Update 2");
        gtk_signal_connect (GTK_OBJECT (button), "clicked",
```

```
059                         GTK_SIGNAL_FUNC(Update), &times[2]);
060             gtk_box_pack_start (GTK_BOX (box), button, TRUE, TRUE, 0);
061
062             button = gtk_button_new_with_label ("Update 3");
063             gtk_signal_connect (GTK_OBJECT (button), "clicked",
064                     GTK_SIGNAL_FUNC(Update), &times[3]);
065             gtk_box_pack_start (GTK_BOX (box), button, TRUE, TRUE, 0);
066
067             gtk_widget_show_all (window);
068
069             gtk_main ();
070
071             return( 0 );
072     }
```

The purpose of this example is to illustrate how private data can be passed to a callback routine. On lines 029 and 030, we declare an array of four 26-character strings, 26 characters being what is needed to hold the value returned by the ctime(3) function. These strings are initialized to the value "Unset\n" so that the callback routine that will be invoked when we exit, PrintAndExit(), has something sensible to print should the user not change one or more of the string's values. On lines 048, 053, 058, and 083, we register the signal function Update() with the GtkButton that was created a line or two earlier, using gtk_signal_connect(). Each of these calls to gtk_signal_connect() is passed a different func_data argument; the first call is passed the address of the first cell in the array of times, the second call is passed the address of the second cell of times, and so forth.

Whenever the user clicks one of the buttons labeled "Update 0", "Update 1", "Update 2", or "Update 3", Update() will be invoked. The timestr argument will be set by Gtk+ to the private data assigned when the callback or signal function was registered.

This may be a silly example, but it illustrates a very important technique. Note that we have no logic inside of Update() that concerns itself with the button pressed by the user; we simply don't need to know this. All we need to know is that the callback function is being passed a pointer to a string presumed to be big enough to hold the ctime(3) result that is going to be stuffed into it.

It is easy to extend this example to a real-life application such as a word processor or to any application that allows a user to manipulate more than one document at a time, such as a spreadsheet or a photo manipulation program like xv or GIMP. Whenever a callback is designed to manipulate data of some kind, try to make that data available to the callback function via the func_data argument. This will enable reuse of callbacks and minimize the need for maintaining global data.

Events

Events are similar to signals in that they are a method by which Gtk+ can tell an application that something has happened. Events and signals differ mainly in what it is they provide notification of. Signals make applications aware of somewhat abstract, high-level changes, such as GUI (not mouse) button presses, toggle button state changes, or the selection of a row in a list widget. Events mainly provide a way for Gtk+ to pass along to the client any X11 events that have been received over the X server connection in which the client has expressed an interest.

Events and signals share the same Gtk+ APIs. To register a callback function for an event, use gtk_signal_connect(). The APIs involved will be discussed later in this chapter.

Event Callback Function Prototypes

The function prototype for event callbacks is slightly different than for signals:

```
gint
callback_func( GtkWidget *widget, GdkEvent *event,
        gpointer callback_data );
```

widget is the Gtk+ widget to which the event pertains, event is a GDK data structure that contains information about the event, and callback_data is the application-specific data that was registered with the handler by the client at the time that gtk_signal_connect() was called.

Most event callbacks adhere to the preceding prototype, but there are variations. In the following section where individual events are described, I will provide the callback function prototype that is most appropriate for each event.

Table 3.1 defines each of the events supported by Gtk+ 1.2. Note that the names all start with GDK_ because the events all originate from within GDK code.

Table 3.1 GDK Events

Event Name	*Description*
GDK_NOTHING	No event. (You should never see this value.)
GDK_DELETE	This is a client message, likely from a window manager, requesting that a window be deleted.
GDK_DESTROY	Maps to the X11 DestroyNotify event. A window has been destroyed.
GDK_EXPOSE	Maps to an X11 Expose or GraphicsExpose event. If Expose, some portion of a window was exposed and is in need of a redraw. If GraphicsExpose, then X protocol was CopyArea or CopyPlane, and the destination area could not be completely drawn because some portion of the source was obscured or unmapped.
GDK_NO_EXPOSE	Maps to an X11 NoExpose event. X protocol was CopyArea or CopyPlane, and the destination area was completely drawn because all of source was available.

Table 3.1 GDK Events (Continued)

Event Name	*Description*
GDK_MOTION_NOTIFY	Maps to an X11 MotionNotify event. The pointer (controlled by mouse, keyboard, touchpad, or client via X protocol) was moved.
GDK_BUTTON_PRESS	Maps to an X11 ButtonPress event. A mouse button was pressed.
GDK_2BUTTON_PRESS	GDK detected a mouse double-click while processing an X11 ButtonPress event.
GDK_3BUTTON_PRESS	GDK detected a mouse triple-click while processing an X11 ButtonPress event.
GDK_BUTTON_RELEASE	Maps to an X11 ButtonRelease event.
GDK_KEY_PRESS	Maps to an X11 KeyPress event. Reports all keys, including Shift and Ctrl.
GDK_KEY_RELEASE	Maps to an X11 KeyRelease event. Reports all keys, including Shift and Ctrl.
GDK_ENTER_NOTIFY	Maps to an X11 EnterNotify event. The pointer has entered a window.
GDK_LEAVE_NOTIFY	Maps to an X11 LeaveNotify event. The pointer has left a window.
GDK_FOCUS_CHANGE	Maps to an X11 FocusIn or FocusOut event. A field in the event structure is used to indicate which. A window has obtained or lost server focus.
GDK_CONFIGURE	Maps to an X11 ConfigureNotify event. Some change in the size, location, border, or stacking order of a window is being announced.
GDK_MAP	Maps to an X11 MapNotify event. A window's state has changed to mapped.
GDK_UNMAP	Maps to an X11 UnmapNotify event. A window's state has changed to unmapped.
GDK_PROPERTY_NOTIFY	Maps to an X11 PropertyNotify event. A property on a window has been changed or deleted.
GDK_SELECTION_CLEAR	Maps to an X11 SelectionClear event. See the following discussion.
GDK_SELECTION_REQUEST	Maps to an X11 SelectionRequest event. See the following discussion.

Table 3.1 GDK Events (Continued)

Event Name	*Description*
GDK_SELECTION_NOTIFY	Maps to an X11 SelectionNotify event. See the following discussion.
GDK_PROXIMITY_IN	Used by X Input Extension-aware programs that draw their own cursors.
GDK_PROXIMITY_OUT	Used by X Input Extension-aware programs that draw their own cursors.
GDK_DRAG_ENTER	Motif Drag and Drop top-level enter.
GDK_DRAG_LEAVE	Motif Drag and Drop top-level leave.
GDK_DRAG_MOTION	Motif Drag and Drop motion.
GDK_DRAG_STATUS	Motif Drag and Drop status message.
GDK_DROP_START	Motif Drag and Drop start.
GDK_DROP_FINISHED	Motif Drag and Drop finished.
GDK_CLIENT_EVENT	Maps to an X11 ClientMessage event which is a message or event that was sent by a client.
GDK_VISIBILITY_NOTIFY	Maps to an X11 VisibilityNotify event. A window has become fully or partially obscured, or it has become completely unobscured.

Note that there are X11 events that are not passed on to your Gtk+ application. For example, MappingNotify events are responded to by GDK by calling XRefreshKeyboardMapping(), which is the standard way for Xlib clients to handle the reception of this event. Unless you take extraordinary means to look for it, your application will never see a MappingNotify event.

In X11, clients must tell the server which events the client is interested in receiving by soliciting the events. If an event is not solicited by a client, it will not be sent. There are a few exceptions, however: MappingNotify, ClientMessage, and the Selection* events are all nonmaskable and will always be sent to the client.

In Gtk+/GDK, clients must also solicit the events in which they have interest. This is done on a per-widget basis, using a technique that is very similar to calling XSelectInput() from an Xlib program. In Gtk+, the routine to call is gtk_widget_set_events(). Here is its prototype:

```
void
gtk_widget_set_events (GtkWidget *widget, gint events)
```

The argument events is a bitmask used to indicate the types of events the client would like to receive notification of from Gtk+, and widget is the handle of the Gtk+ widget to which the event notification pertains. The X server will only send events specified in the events mask that belong to the window defined by the widget. This implies that widgets that do not create a window cannot receive events (we'll return to this issue later in this book). Events that are not solicited for a window are not transmitted to the client by the X server.

Unless you plan to handle a specific event in your application, there is really no need for you to call this routine. This does not mean that events will not be solicited for the widget; it is very likely that one or more events will be solicited by the widget implementation.

The events bitmask can be constructed by OR'ing together one or more of the constants defined by GDK (see Table 3.2).

Table 3.2 GDK Event Masks

Mask	*Event(s) Solicited*
GDK_EXPOSURE_MASK	Expose event (but not GraphicsExpose or NoExpose)
GDK_POINTER_MOTION_MASK	Fewer pointer motion events
GDK_POINTER_MOTION_HINT_MASK	All pointer motion events
GDK_BUTTON_MOTION_MASK	Pointer motion while any mouse button down
GDK_BUTTON1_MOTION_MASK	Pointer motion while mouse button 1 down
GDK_BUTTON2_MOTION_MASK	Pointer motion while mouse button 2 down
GDK_BUTTON3_MOTION_MASK	Pointer motion while mouse button 3 down
GDK_BUTTON_PRESS_MASK	Pointer button down events
GDK_BUTTON_RELEASE_MASK	Pointer button up events
GDK_KEY_PRESS_MASK	Key down events
GDK_KEY_RELEASE_MASK	Key up events
GDK_ENTER_NOTIFY_MASK	Pointer window entry events
GDK_LEAVE_NOTIFY_MASK	Pointer window leave events
GDK_FOCUS_CHANGE_MASK	Any change in keyboard focus
GDK_STRUCTURE_MASK	Any change in window configuration
GDK_PROPERTY_CHANGE_MASK	Any change in property
GDK_VISIBILITY_NOTIFY_MASK	Any change in visibility
GDK_PROXIMITY_IN_MASK	Used by X Input Extension programs
GDK_PROXIMITY_OUT_MASK	Used by X Input Extension programs
GDK_SUBSTRUCTURE_MASK	Notify about reconfiguration of children
GDK_ALL_EVENTS_MASK	All of the above

The masks in the preceding table are not one-to-one with the events listed in Table 3.1. Some of the masks will lead to the reception of more than one event, and your callback function may have to check to see which event was received, depending on the application. Table 3.3 should clarify the mapping that exists between masks and events.

Table 3.3 Event Mask-to-Event Mappings

Mask	*Event(s) Solicited*
GDK_EXPOSURE_MASK	GDK_EXPOSE
GDK_POINTER_MOTION_MASK	GDK_MOTION_NOTIFY
GDK_POINTER_MOTION_HINT_MASK	GDK_MOTION_NOTIFY
GDK_BUTTON_MOTION_MASK	GDK_MOTION_NOTIFY
GDK_BUTTON1_MOTION_MASK	GDK_MOTION_NOTIFY
GDK_BUTTON2_MOTION_MASK	GDK_MOTION_NOTIFY
GDK_BUTTON3_MOTION_MASK	GDK_MOTION_NOTIFY
GDK_BUTTON_PRESS_MASK	GDK_BUTTON_PRESS GDK_2BUTTON_PRESS GDK_3BUTTON_PRESS
GDK_BUTTON_RELEASE_MASK	GDK_BUTTON_RELEASE
GDK_KEY_PRESS_MASK	GDK_KEY_PRESS
GDK_KEY_RELEASE_MASK	GDK_KEY_RELEASE
GDK_ENTER_NOTIFY_MASK	GDK_ENTER_NOTIFY
GDK_BUTTON_RELEASE_MASK	GDK_BUTTON_RELEASE
GDK_LEAVE_NOTIFY_MASK	GDK_LEAVE_NOTIFY
GDK_FOCUS_CHANGE_MASK	GDK_FOCUS_CHANGE
GDK_STRUCTURE_MASK	GDK_DESTROY GDK_CONFIGURE GDK_MAP GDK_UNMAP
GDK_PROPERTY_CHANGE_MASK	GDK_PROPERTY_NOTIFY
GDK_VISIBILITY_NOTIFY_MASK	GDK_VISIBILITY_NOTIFY
GDK_PROXIMITY_IN_MASK	GDK_PROXIMITY_IN
GDK_PROXIMITY_OUT_MASK	GDK_PROXIMITY_OUT

Table 3.3 Event Mask-to-Event Mappings (Continued)

Mask	*Event(s) Solicited*
GDK_SUBSTRUCTURE_MASK	GDK_DESTROY GDK_CONFIGURE GDK_MAP GDK_UNMAP
GDK_ALL_EVENTS_MASK	All of the above

What happens if you specify a mask that does not contain bits set by the widget? For example, the GtkButton widget selects GDK_BUTTON_PRESS_MASK for its window when the buttons' window is created. Let's say your client calls gtk_set_widget_events(), and the mask you supply does not have the GDK_BUTTON_PRESS_MASK bit set, as in the following code:

```
button = gtk_button_new_with_label ("Print");
gtk_signal_connect_object (GTK_OBJECT (button), "clicked",
       GTK_SIGNAL_FUNC(PrintString), GTK_OBJECT (window));

gtk_widget_set_events (button, GDK_POINTER_MOTION_MASK);
gtk_signal_connect (GTK_OBJECT (button), "motion_notify_event",
       GTK_SIGNAL_FUNC(MotionNotifyCallback), NULL);
```

In this case, button press events will be sent to the client and processed by the GtkButton widget, in addition to MotionNotify events that will be handled by the client in MotionNotifyCallback().

What about selecting an event that has already been selected by a widget? For example:

```
button = gtk_button_new_with_label ("Print");
gtk_signal_connect_object (GTK_OBJECT (button), "clicked",
       GTK_SIGNAL_FUNC(PrintString), GTK_OBJECT (window));

gtk_widget_set_events (button, GDK_BUTTON_PRESS_MASK);
gtk_signal_connect (GTK_OBJECT (button), "button_press_event",
       GTK_SIGNAL_FUNC(ButtonPressCallback), NULL);
```

This too will not affect the widget. When a button press occurs, Gtk+ will first call ButtonPressCallback() and then call PrintString(). Note that we really did not need to call gtk_widget_set_events() to select GDK_BUTTON_PRESS_MASK for the GtkButton widget because that event was already selected by the widget itself, but it didn't hurt.

Event Types

Earlier we introduced the function prototype for the callback function invoked by Gtk+ upon reception of a signal that the client has solicited and for which a signal function has been registered. The prototype, once again, is as follows:

```
gint
callback_func( GtkWidget *widget, GdkEvent *event,
        gpointer callback_data );
```

GdkEvent is actually a C union of structures, one structure for each signal type listed in Table 3.1:

```
union _GdkEvent
{
  GdkEventType              type;
  GdkEventAny               any;
  GdkEventExpose            expose;
  GdkEventNoExpose          no_expose;
  GdkEventVisibility        visibility;
  GdkEventMotion            motion;
  GdkEventButton            button;
  GdkEventKey               key;
  GdkEventCrossing          crossing;
  GdkEventFocus             focus_change;
  GdkEventConfigure         configure;
  GdkEventProperty          property;
  GdkEventSelection         selection;
  GdkEventProximity         proximity;
  GdkEventClient            client;
  GdkEventDND               dnd;
};
```

The following describes each of the structures encapsulated within the GdkEvent union (with the only exceptions being GdkEventProximity, which is not covered, and GdkEventDND, which is an internal event type used in the implementation of Drag and Drop, also not discussed in this book). Each of the preceding names is a typedef for a struct that has the same name but is prefixed with '_'. For example:

```
typedef struct _GdkEventExpose GdkEventExpose;
```

In each of the following structures, as well as in the preceding GdkEvent, GdkEventType is an enum that defines the events in Table 3.1. Thus, in a callback function that is supposed to process LeaveNotify events, the event type can be verified using code similar to the following:

```
void
LeaveFunc( GtkWidget *widget, GdkEvent *event, gpointer callback_data )
{
        if (event==(GdkEvent *)NULL || event->type!=GDK_LEAVE_NOTIFY) {
                ErrorFunction( "LeaveFunc: NULL event or wrong type\n" );
                return;           /* bogus event */
        }

        /* event is good */

        ...
}
```

In the preceding routine, we leave the signal function if the event pointer is NULL or if the type of the event is not GDK_LEAVE_NOTIFY.

GdkEventExpose

```
struct _GdkEventExpose
{
  GdkEventType type;     /* GDK_EXPOSE */
  GdkWindow *window;
  gint8 send_event;
  GdkRectangle area;
  gint count;            /* If non-zero, how many more events follow */
};
```

Event Name String

expose_event

Callback Function Prototype

```
gint
func(GtkWidget *widget, GdkEventExpose *event, gpointer arg);
```

Description

Expose events are identified by a type field set to GDK_EXPOSE. Window identifies the window that needs repainting, and area defines the region that this expose event describes. If more than one region in a window becomes exposed, multiple expose events will be sent by the X server. The number of events pending for the window is identified by count. If your code ignores the area field and redraws the entire window in the expose signal function, then your code should wait until it receives an expose event with a count field equal to zero.

GdkEventNoExpose

```
struct _GdkEventNoExpose
{
  GdkEventType type;                /* GDK_NO_EXPOSE */
  GdkWindow *window;
  gint8 send_event;
};
```

Event Name String

no_expose_event

Callback Function Prototype

```
gint
func(GtkWidget *widget, GdkEventAny *event, gpointer arg);
```

Description

NoExpose events are received if CopyArea or CopyPlane X protocol is performed successfully. This will happen only if all values in the source image were able to be copied by the

X server, with no portions of the source window obscured, and if the graphics_exposures flag in the X GC used in the CopyArea or CopyPlane request was set to True.

XCopyArea is invoked by both gdk_draw_pixmap() and gdk_window_copy_area().

GdkEventVisibility

```
struct _GdkEventVisibility
{
  GdkEventType type;                    /* GDK_VISIBILITY_NOTIFY */
  GdkWindow *window;
  gint8 send_event;
  GdkVisibilityState state;
};
```

Event Name String

visibility_notify_event

Callback Function Prototype

```
gint
func(GtkWidget *widget, GdkEventVisibility *event, gpointer arg);
```

Description

Visibility events are sent when the visibility of a window has changed. The state field of the event describes the nature of the change and can be one of the following values in Table 3.4.

Table 3.4 Visibility Event States

Value	*Meaning*
GDK_VISIBILITY_UNOBSCURED	Window was partially obscured, fully obscured, or not viewable, and became viewable and completely unobscured.
GDK_VISIBILITY_PARTIAL	Window was viewable and completely unobscured, or not viewable, and became viewable and partially unobscured.
GDK_VISIBILITY_FULLY_OBSCURED	Window was viewable and completely unobscured, or viewable and partially unobscured, or not viewable, and became viewable and fully unobscured.

GdkEventMotion

```
struct _GdkEventMotion
{
  GdkEventType type;                    /* GDK_MOTION_NOTIFY */
  GdkWindow *window;
  gint8 send_event;
```

```
    guint32 time;
    gdouble x;
    gdouble y;
    gdouble pressure;
    gdouble xtilt;
    gdouble ytilt;
    guint state;
    gint16 is_hint;
    GdkInputSource source;
    guint32 deviceid;
    gdouble x_root, y_root;
};
```

Event Name String
motion_notify_event

Callback Function Prototype

```
gint
func(GtkWidget *widget, GdkEventMotion *event, gpointer arg);
```

Description
Motion notify events indicate that the pointer has moved from one location of the screen to another. The time field indicates the time of the event in server-relative time (milliseconds since the last server reset). If the window is on the same screen as the root (which is usually the case), then x and y are the pointer coordinates relative to the origin of the window; otherwise, they are both set to 0. x_root and y_root are the coordinates relative to the root window. Pressure is always set to the value 0.5, and xtilt and ytilt are always set to the value 0. Source is always set to GDK_SOURCE_MOUSE, and deviceid is always set to the value GDK_CORE_POINTER. Is_hint is set to 1 if the mask used to select the event was GDK_POINTER_MOTION_HINT_MASK; otherwise, it will be 0. If is_hint is 1e, then the current position information needs to be obtained by calling gdk_window_get_pointer(). State is used to specify the state of the mouse buttons and modifier keys just before the event. The values possible for state are constructed by OR'ing any of the following bits in Table 3.5.

Table 3.5 Motion Event States

Value	*Meaning*
GDK_SHIFT_MASK	shift key is pressed.
GDK_LOCK_MASK	lock key is pressed.
GDK_CONTROL_MASK	control key is pressed.
GDK_MOD1_MASK	mod1 is pressed (typically Alt_L or Alt_R).
GDK_MOD2_MASK	mod2 is pressed (typically Num_Lock).

Table 3.5 Motion Event States (Continued)

Value	*Meaning*
GDK_MOD3_MASK	mod3 is pressed.
GDK_MOD4_MASK	mod4 is pressed.
GDK_MOD5_MASK	mod5 is pressed.
GDK_BUTTON1_MASK	Button1 is pressed (typically the left button).
GDK_BUTTON2_MASK	Button2 is pressed (typically the right button).
GDK_BUTTON3_MASK	Button3 is pressed (typically the middle button).
GDK_BUTTON4_MASK	Button4 is pressed.
GDK_BUTTON5_MASK	Button5 is pressed.

shift, lock, control, mod1 through mod5, and Button1 through Button5 are logical names in X11 and are subject to remapping by the user. The X11 user command for performing this remapping is xmodmap(1). The xmodmap(1) command can also be used to view the current logical name to keysym mapping, for example:

```
bash$ xmodmap -pm
xmodmap:  up to 2 keys per modifier, (keycodes in parentheses):

shift       Shift_L (0x32),  Shift_R (0x3e)
lock        Caps_Lock (0x42)
control     Control_L (0x25),  Control_R (0x6d)
mod1        Alt_L (0x40),  Alt_R (0x71)
mod2        Num_Lock (0x4d)
mod3
mod4
mod5        Scroll_Lock (0x4e)
```

GdkEventButton

```
struct _GdkEventButton
{
  GdkEventType type;         /* GDK_BUTTON_PRESS, GDK_2BUTTON_PRESS,
                                GDK_3BUTTON_PRESS, GDK_BUTTON_RELEASE */
  GdkWindow *window;
  gint8 send_event;
  guint32 time;
  gdouble x;
  gdouble y;
  gdouble pressure;
  gdouble xtilt;
  gdouble ytilt;
  guint state;
  guint button;
```

```
  GdkInputSource source;
  guint32 deviceid;
  gdouble x_root, y_root;
};
```

Event Name Strings
button_press_event
button_release_event

Callback Function Prototype

```
gint
func(GtkWidget *widget, GdkEventButton *event, gpointer arg);
```

Description
Button events indicate that a mouse button press or release has occurred. The time field indicates the time of the event in server-relative time (milliseconds since server reset). If the window receiving the button press or release is on the same screen as the root (which is usually the case), then x and y are the pointer coordinates relative to the origin of window; otherwise, they are both set to zero. X_root and y_root are the coordinates of the press or release relative to the root window. Pressure is always set to the value 0.5, and xtilt and ytilt are always set to the value zero. Source is always GDK_SOURCE_MOUSE, and deviceid is always set to the value GDK_CORE_POINTER. State is used to specify the state of the mouse buttons and modifier keys just before the event. The values possible for state are the same values as those previously described for GdkEventMotion. Button indicates which button the event is for, with 1 indicating button 1, 2 indicating button 2, and so on.

GdkEventKey

```
struct _GdkEventKey
{
  GdkEventType type;                /* GDK_KEY_PRESS GDK_KEY_RELEASE */
  GdkWindow *window;
  gint8 send_event;
  guint32 time;
  guint state;
  guint keyval;
  gint length;
  gchar *string;
};
```

Event Name Strings
key_press_event
key_release_event

Callback Function Prototype

```
gint
func(GtkWidget *widget, GdkEventKey *event, gpointer arg);
```

Description

Key events indicate that a keyboard key press or key release has occurred. The time field indicates the time of the event in server-relative time (milliseconds since server reset). State is used to specify the state of the mouse buttons and modifier keys just before the event. The values possible for state are the same as those previously described for GdkEventMotion. Keyval indicates which key was pressed or released. Keyval is the keysym value that corresponds to the key pressed or released. Keysyms values are symbolic values that represent the keys on the keyboard. Keyboards generate hardware-dependent values that are mapped by Xlib to keysyms using a table provided by the X server. For example, the hardware code generated when the user presses the key labeled "A" is converted to the keysym value XK_A. It is this value (e.g., XK_A) that is stored inside the keyval field. String contains a string of ASCII characters that were obtained by GDK by calling the Xlib function XLookupString(). Usually, the string will be of length 1 and will correspond directly to the glyph or symbol displayed on the key that was pressed or released (e.g., for XK_A, the string will be "A"). However, clients can associate an arbitrarily long string with a key using XRebindKeysym(). The length of this string, which is limited to 16 characters by GDK, is stored in length, and string contains the value of the string (truncated if necessary to 16 characters) returned by XLookupString().

GdkEventCrossing

```
struct _GdkEventCrossing
{
  GdkEventType type;              /* GDK_ENTER_NOTIFY GDK_LEAVE_NOTIFY */
  GdkWindow *window;
  gint8 send_event;
  GdkWindow *subwindow;
  guint32 time;
  gdouble x;
  gdouble y;
  gdouble x_root;
  gdouble y_root;
  GdkCrossingMode mode;
  GdkNotifyType detail;
  gboolean focus;
  guint state;
};
```

Event Name Strings

enter_notify_event
leave_notify_event

Callback Function Prototype

```
gint
func(GtkWidget *widget, GdkEventCrossing *event, gpointer arg);
```

Description

Crossing events indicate that the mouse pointer has entered or left a window. The window into which the pointer has entered, or from which it has left, is indicated by window. If the event type is GDK_LEAVE_NOTIFY and the pointer began in a child window of window, then subwindow will be set to the GDK ID of the child window, or else it will be set to the value NULL. If the event type is GDK_ENTER_NOTIFY and the pointer ends up in a child window of window, then subwindow will be set to the GDK ID of the child window, or else it will be set to the value NULL. The time field indicates the time of the event in server-relative time (milliseconds since server reset). If window is on the same screen as the root (which is usually the case), then x and y specify the pointer coordinates relative to the origin of window; otherwise, they are both set to zero. X_root and y_root are the coordinates of the pointer relative to the root window. If the enter or leave event was caused by normal mouse movement or if it was caused by a pointer warp (that is, the client has explicitly moved the mouse), then mode will be set to GDK_CROSSING_NORMAL. Or, if the crossing event was caused by a pointer grab, mode will be set to GDK_CROSSING_GRAB. Finally, if the crossing event was caused by a pointer ungrab, then mode will be set to the value GDK_CROSSING_UNGRAB. If the receiving window is the focus window or is a descendant of the focus window (subwindow is not NULL), then focus will be set to TRUE; otherwise, it will be set to FALSE. State specifies the state of the mouse buttons and modifier keys just before the event. The values possible for state are the same as those previously described for GdkEventMotion.

The final field, detail, is a bit complicated to describe. Here we'll simply list the GDK values that can be stored in this field and the X11 values to which they map. In practice, X11 client applications (and, by extension, Gtk+ applications) rarely, if ever, will make use of the data in this field (see Table 3.6).

Table 3.6 Event Crossing Event Detail Field

X11 Value	*GDK Value*
NotifyInferior	GDK_NOTIFY_INFERIOR
NotifyAncestor	GDK_NOTIFY_ANCESTOR
NotifyVirtual	GDK_NOTIFY_VIRTUAL
NotifyNonlinear	GDK_NOTIFY_NONLINEAR
NotifyNonlinearVirtual	GDK_NOTIFY_NONLINEAR_VIRTUAL

GdkEventFocus

```
struct _GdkEventFocus
{
  GdkEventType type;                    /* GDK_FOCUS_CHANGE */
  GdkWindow *window;
  gint8 send_event;
  gint16 in;
};
```

Event Name Strings
focus_in_event
focus_out_event

Callback Function Prototype

```
gint
func(GtkWidget *widget, GdkEventFocus *event, gpointer arg);
```

Description
Focus events indicate a change in keyboard focus from one window to another. When keyboard focus changes, two events are sent. One event is sent for the window that had the keyboard focus just prior to the focus change. The other is sent for the window that just obtained the keyboard focus. The in field is used to define the type of focus change. If the X11 event type is FocusIn, then the window identified by window received focus, and in will be set to TRUE. Otherwise, the X11 event type was FocusOut, the window identified by window lost input focus, and in will be set to FALSE.

GdkEventConfigure

```
struct _GdkEventConfigure
{
  GdkEventType type;                    /* GDK_CONFIGURE */
  GdkWindow *window;
  gint8 send_event;
  gint16 x, y;
  gint16 width;
  gint16 height;
};
```

Event Name String
configure_event

Callback Function Prototype

```
gint
func(GtkWidget *widget, GdkEventConfigure *event, gpointer arg);
```

Description
Configure events indicate a change in the size and/or location of a window. The window field identifies the window that was moved or resized. The x and y fields identify the new x and y locations of the window in the root window coordinate space. Width and height identify the width and the height of the window.

GdkEventProperty

```
struct _GdkEventProperty
{
  GdkEventType type;                    /* GDK_PROPERTY_NOTIFY */
```

```
  GdkWindow *window;
  gint8 send_event;
  GdkAtom atom;
  guint32 time;
  guint state;
};
```

Event Name String
property_notify_event

Callback Function Prototype

```
gint
func(GtkWidget *widget, GdkEventProperty *event, gpointer arg);
```

Description
Property events indicate a change of a property. Properties are named data associated with a window. This data is stored on the X server to which your Gtk+ client is connected. Properties have a unique ID that either is predefined or is assigned by the X server at the time the property is installed. This ID is identified by the atom field in the preceding event struct. Several standard properties are used to help the window manager do its job. For example, when you call gtk_set_window_title(), GDK will set the XA_WM_NAME atom of the window to the character string that was passed to gtk_set_window_title(). The window manager will be notified of this property change by the X server via a PropertyNotify event. Upon receiving the event, the window manager will redraw the title displayed in the window title bar decoration that the window manager has placed around your application's top-level window.

While the major use of properties is in satisfying window manager protocols (such as specifying window titles and icon pixmaps) or client notification of window deletion, properties can also be used as a form of interprocess communication among cooperating clients. GDK provides routines that allow you to create, modify, and destroy properties.

The time field stores the time that the event occurred in server-relative time (milliseconds since server reset). State identifies the type of change that has occurred. PropertyNewValue indicates that the value of the property identified by atom has changed. PropertyDelete indicates that the property identified by atom no longer exists on the server.

GdkEventSelection

```
struct _GdkEventSelection
{
  GdkEventType type;       /* GDK_SELECTION_CLEAR GDK_SELECTION_REQUEST
                              GDK_SELECTION_NOTIFY */
  GdkWindow *window;
  gint8 send_event;
  GdkAtom selection;
  GdkAtom target;
  GdkAtom property;
  guint32 requestor;
  guint32 time;
};
```

Event Name Strings

selection_clear_event
selection_request_event
selection_notify_event

Callback Function Prototype

```
gint
func(GtkWidget *widget, GdkEventSelection *event, gpointer arg);
```

Selections are an important form of interprocess communication available to all X clients, including those written in Gtk+. Selections provide the mechanism by which copy and paste operations among clients are performed. The classic example of such an operation is highlighting text in an xterm(1) and using mouse button 2 to paste the highlighted text in another xterm window. The xterm in which the text is highlighted is referred to as the owner client, and the xterm into which the text is pasted is referred to as the requestor client. Owner clients have data currently selected, and requestor clients want that data. Selections allow the requestor to become aware that data is available and provide the mechanism by which the owner can convert the data into a form that is useful by the requestor. A client (or a widget) can either be an owner or a requestor, as the need arises.

Selection Protocol. Basically, the protocol between the owner and requestor is as follows. In this example, we'll assume we are performing copy and paste between text edit (entry) widgets in two different clients. We'll refer to the text edit widget in client 1 as entry-1 and the text edit widget in client 2 as entry-2.

When the user selects text in entry-1 (we ignore here how that is done), client 1 will call gtk_selection_owner_set() to obtain ownership of the selection atom named GDK_SELECTION_PRIMARY (XA_PRIMARY). If successful and client 1 did not already own the selection, a SelectionClear (GDK_SELECTION_CLEAR) event will be sent to the previous owner (perhaps client 2, but this could be any X11 client connected to the X server, written using Xlib, Motif, or any other X11 toolkit). The client receiving the SelectionClear event will respond by unhighlighting the previously selected text. Notice that all we have done so far is switch the ownership of the primary selection atom from one client to another. No data has been transferred at this point.

Assume now that the text edit widget in client 2 (entry-2) obtains focus, and the user initiates a paste operation in some application-specific way. Client 2 now takes on the role of requestor and calls gtk_selection_convert() to obtain the data. Gtk_selection_convert() will call gdk_selection_convert(), which in turn will call XConvertSelection(). XConvertSelection() is passed a window ID, the GDK_SELECTION_PRIMARY atom, and a target atom. The target atom is used to indicate the data type to which the requestor would like the selected data to be converted, if necessary or even possible, by the owner prior to transferring the selected data to the X server. A base set of targets is predefined by X11's Inter-Client Communication Conventions Manual (ICCCM). Table 3.7 illustrates some predefined target atoms in X11.

Table 3.7 Predefined Target Atoms in X11

Atom	*X11 Data Type*
XA_ARC	XArc
XA_POINT	XPoint
XA_ATOM	Atom
XA_RGB_COLOR_MAP	Atom (standard colormap)
XA_BITMAP	Pixmap (depth 1)
XA_RECTANGLE	XRectangle
XA_CARDINAL	int
XA_STRING	char *
XA_COLORMAP	Colormap
XA_VISUALID	VisualID
XA_CURSOR	Cursor
XA_WINDOW	Window
XA_DRAWABLE	Drawable
XA_WM_HINTS	XWMHints
XA_FONT	Font
XA_INTEGER	int
XA_WM_SIZE_HINTS	XSizeHints
XA_PIXMAP	Pixmap (depth 1)

After the requestor has successfully called gtk_selection_convert(), the owner receives a SelectionRequest (GDK_SELECTION_REQUEST) event. Selection identifies the selection to which the request pertains. Usually, selection will be GDK_SELECTION_PRIMARY unless the owner is supporting multiple selections. Target is the target atom (for example, one of the atoms listed in Table 3.7). Property identifies the atom or property where the selected data should be placed. Requestor identifies the window of the client that is making the request.

Now that the owner has received the GDK_SELECTION_REQUEST event, it attempts to convert the selection it owns to the requested type. If the owner is unable to perform the conversion (for example, the data associated with the selection is text and the requestor wants it converted to a colormap), then the owner creates and sends to the requestor a GDK_SELECTION_NOTIFY event with the property field set to GDK_NONE. If the conversion was successful, the owner also sends a GDK_SELECTION_NOTIFY event but with the property field set to the same value received by the owner in the GDK_SELECTION_REQUEST event. The selection and target fields in any GDK_SELECTION_NOTIFY event should be the same values as those received in the GDK_SELECTION_REQUEST event.

The final major portion of the selection protocol happens back on the requestor. The requestor will receive a GDK_SELECTION_NOTIFY event. If the property field is GDK_NONE, then the requestor knows that the selection failed. Otherwise, the selection was successful, and the requestor then reads the property specified in the property field for the converted data.

GdkEventClient

```
struct _GdkEventClient
{
  GdkEventType type;                    /* GDK_CLIENT_EVENT */
  GdkWindow *window;
  gint8 send_event;
  GdkAtom message_type;
  gushort data_format;
  union {
    char b[20];
    short s[10];
    long l[5];
  } data;
};
```

Event Name String
client_event

Callback Function Prototype

```
gint
func(GtkWidget *widget,  GdkEventClient *event, gpointer arg);
```

Client events provide a mechanism by which one client can send an event to some other client executing on the same X server. An example of this was illustrated when we discussed selections. The owner of a selection, in response to a GDK_SELECTION_REQUEST event, will send a GDK_SELECTION_NOTIFY event to the requestor client to indicate the result of the request.

Any event type can be sent by a client to another client using this mechanism. In practice, however, use of client events is generally restricted to selections, where it is needed to satisfy the selection protocol, or to window managers which use them to notify clients of some pending event, such as the destruction of a window.

Client events are never selected by the receiving client; they will always be sent to the receiving client regardless of the event mask associated with the receiving clients' window.

Message_type is an atom that is used to identify the type of the message sent. It is up to the clients that send and receive messages of this type to agree on the value of this field. Data_format specifies the format of the message sent in the event and must have one of these values: 8, 16, or 32. This is necessary so that the X server can do the necessary swapping of bytes. Data contains the actual data sent in the message, either 20 8-bit chars, 10 16-bit shorts, or 5 32-bit longs.

GdkEventAny

```
struct _GdkEventAny
{
  GdkEventType type;              /* any event type is possible here */
  GdkWindow *window;
  gint8 send_event;
};
```

Event Name Strings

destroy_event
delete_event
map_event
unmap_event
no_expose_event

Callback Function Prototype

```
gint
func(GtkWidget *widget,  GdkEventAny *event, gpointer arg);
```

GdkEventAny is a convenient, event-independent means by which the type, window, and send_event fields of any event can be accessed. Generally, your signal functions will map to a specific type of event, and you will never make use of this type. However, several events only communicate type and window information, and so they make use of GdkEventAny to pass event information into a callback function, perhaps at the cost of decreased code clarity. Event types that have GdkEventAny * in their callback prototypes include GDK_DESTROY, GDK_DELETE, GDK_UNMAP, GDK_MAP, and GDK_NO_EXPOSE.

Signal and Event APIs

Each widget in Gtk+ supports signals that, when triggered, represent a change in the state of the widget. Signal functions, or callbacks, are the way that the logic of your application is connected to the occurrence of these events.

As a programmer, you are free to register none, one, or multiple callbacks for any signal supported by an object. Gtk+ will invoke each of the signal functions registered for an object in the order they were registered by the programmer. In addition, a "class function" associated with the signal is also invoked by Gtk+. This class function is what would normally be executed by Gtk+ for that widget. Unless you are overriding the behavior of the widget, you generally need not be concerned with the class function. But there are times when you might, and I will present an example in this chapter. You can control whether or not your callback function is called after all the class functions by registering your callback with gtk_signal_connect_after(). It is up to the widget designer to determine what the default is for a given widget; the choices include calling the class function before, after, or both before and after your callbacks for the widget have been called.

Let's look at the functions that are available to application programmers for use in creating, controlling, and destroying signals. In doing so, we will discuss a few interesting tidbits about signals not covered so far.

Signal Lookup

The first function is gtk_signal_lookup(). The prototype for this function is as follows:

```
gint
gtk_signal_lookup (gchar *name, gint object_type)
```

What gtk_signal_lookup() does is search the widget hierarchy for the signal identified by name, starting with the object type specified by object_type and searching recursively higher to include the object type's parents if needed. If the search is successful, then the signal identifier, a unique number that identifies the signal, will be returned. If the search is not successful, then gtk_signal_lookup() returns 0.

To use this function, you need to know what object types and signal names are. Let's start with object types. Each widget class in Gtk+ has an object type, defined by the widget programmer. The naming convention for object types seems to be GTK_OBJECT_*, where * is replaced with the name of the widget class. For example, the object type that corresponds to the GtkButton widget class is GTK_OBJECT_BUTTON. The object type is defined in the header file for the widget class, usually gtk.h, where type is the name of the widget class. Again, using GtkButton as our example, the header file in which the GTK_OBJECT_BUTTON macro is defined is named gtkbutton.h. The object macro is defined to be a call to a function also defined by the widget writer. There is a convention for the naming of this function, too; in this case it is gtk_*_get_type(), which for the GtkButton class would be gtk_button_get_type().

Now let's turn to signal names. In the example code presented earlier in this chapter, we connected a callback routine to the "destroy" signal of the window object that represented our application's main window with the following code:

```
        gtk_signal_connect (GTK_OBJECT(window), "destroy",
                GTK_SIGNAL_FUNC(PrintAndExit), times);
```

Here, destroy is an example of a signal name. Another signal that we connected to our application was the "clicked" signal, defined by the GtkButton widget class. Each widget class defines some number of signals that are specific to the widget class. Signals that are common to more than one class will be defined in a parent class, from which the widget classes that share that signal can inherit.

When I introduce a widget class in the chapters that follow, I will specify the name of the object type macro that corresponds to the widget class as well as the name and behavior of each signal supported by the widget class.

Let's now take a quick look at how gtk_signal_lookup() might be called. To make the example familiar, we'll simply modify the earlier example to use gtk_signal_lookup() to validate the signal name we pass to gtk_signal_connect(). Note that this is sort of a contrived example, but it does illustrate how to call gtk_signal_lookup().

```
if ( gtk_signal_lookup( "destroy", GTK_OBJECT_WINDOW ) )

/* The "destroy" signal is implemented, go ahead and register the
   signal function with the widget */

         gtk_signal_connect (GTK_OBJECT(window), "destroy",
                   GTK_SIGNAL_FUNC(PrintAndExit), times);
else
         fprintf( stderr, "'destroy' is not implemented\n" );
```

The following is another way to make the call to gtk_signal_lookup():

```
GtkObject *object;

object = GTK_OBJECT(window);
if ( gtk_signal_lookup( "destroy", GTK_OBJECT_TYPE(object) ) )
```

The GTK_OBJECT_TYPE macro takes a GtkObject * argument. I'll discuss objects in detail later in this chapter. Notice that the preceding code promotes reusability. We can use this strategy to define a function that can be called to search for support for a given signal name in an arbitrary widget:

```
/* Returns 0 if signal name is not defined, otherwise 1 */

gint
HasSignal( GtkWidget *widget, char *name )
{
         GtkObject *object;
         int       retval = 0;

         object = GTK_OBJECT(widget);
         if ( object != (GtkObject *) NULL )
                 retval = gtk_signal_lookup( name,
                         GTK_OBJECT_TYPE( object ) );
         return( retval );
}
```

Gtk+ also defines a function that takes a signal number and returns that signal's character string name. Here is its prototype:

```
gchar*
gtk_signal_name (gint signal_num)
```

Gtk+ maintains a global table of signal names. A signal number in Gtk+ is merely an index into this table, so what this function really does is return the string that is stored in the table indexed by signal_num (or 0 if signal_num is not a valid index into the table).

Emitting Signals

Although in practice this may not be a very common thing to do, Gtk+ does give a client the ability to cause events and signals to trigger. This can be done by calling one of the gtk_signal_emit* functions:

```
void
gtk_signal_emit (GtkObject *object, gint signal_type, ...)

void
gtk_signal_emit_by_name (GtkObject *object, gchar *name, ...)
```

The first argument to either function is the object from which the signal or the event will be generated. The second argument to gtk_signal_emit() is the type of the signal. This can be found by calling gtk_signal_lookup(), as previously described (or the function HasSignal(), as previously developed). The second argument to gtk_signal_emit_by_name() is the event name; gtk_signal_emit_by_name() will do the lookup operation itself. If you already have the signal type value, it is more efficient to call gtk_signal_emit() to avoid the overhead incurred by gtk_signal_emit_by_name() to look up the event name string and convert to the signal type value accepted by gtk_signal_emit().

The remaining arguments to the gtk_signal_emit* functions will vary in type and number based on the signal being emitted. For example, the prototype for the map_event (GDK_MAP) callback function is as follows:

```
gint
func(GtkWidget *widget,  GdkEventAny *event, gpointer arg);
```

The call to gtk_signal_emit_by_name() would then be as follows:

```
GdkEventAny event;
gint retval;

...

gtk_signal_emit_by_name( GDK_OBJECT(window), "map_event", &event,
          &retval );
```

The third argument to gtk_signal_emit_by_name() is a pointer to a GdkEventAny struct, and it is passed as the second argument to the signal callback function. The fourth parameter is a pointer to hold the value returned by the callback function, which is of type gint. If the callback function being invoked is void, we would simply omit the final argument to the gtk_signal_emit* function (as in the example that follows).

Note that the application making the preceding call would need to fill in the fields of event, including the event type, the window ID, and the send_event fields. The third and final argument to the callback is the application-specific pointer or data that was passed to gtk_signal_connect().

As a second example, the callback function for the GtkButton widget "pressed" signal has the following function prototype:

```
void
func(GtkWidget *button, gpointer data);
```

To invoke this handler, we would call gtk_signal_emit_by_name() as follows:

```
gtk_signal_emit_by_name (GTK_OBJECT (button), "pressed");
```

Since there is no return value from the callback (the function is void), we need not pass a pointer to hold the return value, and so we pass NULL instead. Also, the callback function has no arguments (except for the obligatory widget pointer and application-private data that all callback functions are passed), so we pass no additional arguments to the gtk_signal_emit* function.

Some widget signal functions do take arguments. For example, the callback function invoked by the GtkCList widget (which we will talk about in detail later in this book) when a row is selected by the user has the following function prototype:

```
void
select_row_callback(GtkWidget *widget, gint row, gint column,
        GdkEventButton *event, gpointer data);
```

The function select_row_callback() takes three arguments—row, column, and event—in addition to the widget and data arguments that are passed to every signal function. The call to gtk_signal_emit_by_name() in this case would be as follows:

```
GtkWidget *clist;
int       row, column;

...

gtk_signal_emit_by_name (GTK_OBJECT (clist), "select_row", row,
          column, NULL);
```

The value NULL will be passed as the "event" argument to select_row_callback().

Emitting Signals—An Example

Now might be a good time to provide some example code. This example creates a top-level window with a GtkDrawingArea widget child. Every second, the application generates and handles a synthetic mouse motion event. It also handles actual mouse motion events that occur in the same window when the user moves the mouse over the window.

```
#include <stdio.h>
#include <time.h>
#include <gtk/gtk.h>
#include <unistd.h>
#include <signal.h>

static GtkWidget *drawing;

void
AlarmFunc( int foo )
{
    GdkEvent event;
    gint retval;
```

```

    gtk_signal_emit( GTK_OBJECT(drawing),
            gtk_signal_lookup( "motion_notify_event",
            GTK_OBJECT_TYPE(drawing) ), &event, &retval );

    alarm(1L);
}

static void
motion_notify_callback( GtkWidget *w, GdkEventMotion *event, char *arg )
{
    static int count = 1;

 fprintf( stderr, "In motion_notify_callback %s %03d\n", arg, count++ );
    fflush( stderr );
}

void
Exit (GtkWidget *widget, gpointer arg)
{
    gtk_main_quit ();
}

int
main( int argc, char *argv[] )
{
    GtkWidget *window, *box;
    struct sigaction old, act;

    gtk_set_locale ();

    gtk_init (&argc, &argv);

    window = gtk_window_new (GTK_WINDOW_TOPLEVEL);

    gtk_signal_connect (GTK_OBJECT(window), "destroy",
            GTK_SIGNAL_FUNC(Exit), NULL);

    gtk_window_set_title (GTK_WINDOW (window), "Events 3");
    gtk_container_border_width (GTK_CONTAINER (window), 0);

    box = gtk_vbox_new (FALSE, 0);
    gtk_container_add (GTK_CONTAINER (window), box);

    drawing = gtk_drawing_area_new ();
    gtk_widget_set_events (drawing,
            GDK_POINTER_MOTION_MASK);
    gtk_signal_connect( GTK_OBJECT(drawing), "motion_notify_event",
            GTK_SIGNAL_FUNC(motion_notify_callback), "Hello World" );
    gtk_box_pack_start (GTK_BOX (box), drawing, TRUE, TRUE, 0);

    gtk_widget_show_all (window);
```

```
066
067     act.sa_handler = AlarmFunc;
068     act.sa_flags = 0;
069     sigaction( SIGALRM, &act, &old );
070     alarm( 1L );
071
072     gtk_main ();
073
074     sigaction( SIGALRM, &old, NULL );
075     return( 0 );
076 }
```

Analysis of the Sample

On line 058, a GtkDrawingArea widget is created, and then on lines 059 and 060, the event mask for the GtkDrawingArea widget is set to GDK_POINTER_MOTION_MASK, enabling motion_notify event notification for the widget. On lines 061 and 062, the signal callback function motion_notify_callback(), implemented on lines 023 through 029, is registered with Gtk+ to be invoked when motion_notify_events in the GtkDrawingArea widget are received.

```
058 drawing = gtk_drawing_area_new ();
059 gtk_widget_set_events (drawing,
060           GDK_POINTER_MOTION_MASK);
061 gtk_signal_connect( GTK_OBJECT(drawing), "motion_notify_event",
062           GTK_SIGNAL_FUNC(motion_notify_callback), "Hello World" );
```

On lines 067 through 070, we use POSIX signal function sigaction(2) to register a SIGALRM signal handler named AlarmFunc(), which is implemented on lines 009 through 020. Then, on line 070, we call alarm(2) to cause the SIGALRM signal to fire one second later. When SIGALRM is triggered, AlarmFunc() is entered.

```
009 void
010 AlarmFunc( int foo )
011 {
012     GdkEvent event;
013     gint retval;
014
015     gtk_signal_emit( GTK_OBJECT(drawing),
016               gtk_signal_lookup( "motion_notify_event",
017               GTK_OBJECT_TYPE(drawing) ), &event, &retval );
018
019     alarm(1L);
020 }
```

In AlarmFunc(), we call gtk_signal_emit() to generate a motion_notify_event on the window associated with the GtkDrawingArea widget named drawing. Doing this will cause our signal callback function, motion_notify_callback(), to be called by Gtk+. Motion_notify_callback() simply prints a message that includes a serial number and the application-dependent data that was registered with the signal callback function, the string "Hello World".

There are two reasons why I made use of alarm(2) in this example. The first is that alarm() provides a convenient method by which an asynchronous event can be generated at a fixed interval, giving me an opportunity to generate the motion_notify_events needed to illustrate the main idea of this example. The second reason for using alarm() is to point out a possible point of confusion with regards to terminology. It is important to note that signals in Gtk+/GDK are not the same thing as UNIX signals, as described in signal(7) and handled by UNIX functions such as signal(2) and sigaction(2).

There are certainly times when sending a signal to yourself is appropriate. I will give one such example when I discuss the GtkDrawingArea later in this book.

Controlling Signals

Gtk+ provides a few functions that allow applications to control signals in a variety of ways. The first of these functions is gtk_signal_emit_stop():

```
void
gtk_signal_emit_stop (GtkObject *object, gint signal_type)
```

The function gtk_signal_emit_stop() stops the emission of a signal. A signal emission is defined as the invocation of all signal callback functions that have been registered with a widget for a given signal type. For example, should an application register with a widget a dozen callback functions for an event or signal, the emission of that signal will begin once the event occurs and will continue until each of the callback functions registered by the application has been called. The argument signal_type is obtained in the same way as the argument of the same name passed to gtk_signal_emit(). If you'd rather identify the signal by name instead of by signal_type, call gtk_signal_emit_stop_by_name():

```
void
gtk_signal_emit_stop_by_name (GtkObject *object, char *name)
```

An example should make this clear. I modified the preceding example slightly so that five different signal callback functions are registered with the GtkDrawingAreaWidget:

```
gtk_signal_connect( GTK_OBJECT(drawing), "motion_notify_event",
        GTK_SIGNAL_FUNC(motion_notify_callback1), "Hello World1" );
gtk_signal_connect( GTK_OBJECT(drawing), "motion_notify_event",
        GTK_SIGNAL_FUNC(motion_notify_callback2), "Hello World2" );
gtk_signal_connect( GTK_OBJECT(drawing), "motion_notify_event",
        GTK_SIGNAL_FUNC(motion_notify_callback3), "Hello World3" );
gtk_signal_connect( GTK_OBJECT(drawing), "motion_notify_event",
        GTK_SIGNAL_FUNC(motion_notify_callback4), "Hello World4" );
gtk_signal_connect( GTK_OBJECT(drawing), "motion_notify_event",
        GTK_SIGNAL_FUNC(motion_notify_callback5), "Hello World5" );
```

Each signal callback function (motion_notify_callback1(), etc.) will be invoked by the GtkDrawingArea widget after AlarmFunc() calls gtk_signal_emit(). I then modified each callback function slightly to generate a random number in the range [0,100]. If the random number falls below 50, then the signal callback function makes a call to gtk_signal_emit_stop_by_name() to stop the emission of the signal. For example:

```
#define RAND( value ) ( ((float) random() / RAND_MAX) * value )

...

static void
motion_notify_callback1(GtkWidget *widget, GdkEventMotion *event, char
    *arg )
{
  static int count = 1;

 fprintf( stderr, "In motion_notify_callback1 %s %03d\n", arg, count++ );
  fflush( stderr );
  if ( RAND( 100 ) <50 )
          gtk_signal_emit_stop_by_name (GTK_OBJECT(drawing),
                 "motion_notify_event");
}
```

The effect of this change is that, should one of the signal callback functions generate a random number below 50, the remaining signal callback functions will not be invoked for the signal emission because signal emission will be stopped. In testing this function, motion_notify_callback2() was called approximately half as often as motion_notify_callback1(), motion_notify_callback3() was called approximately half as often as motion_notify_callback2(), and so on. At least this demonstrates that my random number macro was performing approximately as it should have been.

Note that we do not need to reconnect the signal callback functions after an emission is stopped. The next time the signal is generated, all functions are once again eligible for invocation. Also, calling gtk_signal_emit_stop*() for a signal that is not being emitted is a no-op.

I mentioned that connecting a signal with gtk_signal_connect() will cause the registered signal function to be invoked after all signal functions previously registered with the widget for that signal and prior to the default class signal function implemented for the widget. However, applications can arrange to have signal callback functions invoked after the class signal callback function by registering the callback with gtk_signal_connect_after():

```
gint
gtk_signal_connect_after (GtkObject *object, gchar *name,
        GtkSignalFunc func, gpointer func_data)
```

A slightly different way to connect a signal to a signal callback function is to call gtk_signal_connect_object(), which has the following prototype:

```
gint
gtk_signal_connect_object (GtkObject *object, gchar *name,
        GtkSignalFunc func, GtkObject *slot_object)
```

The major difference between gtk_signal_connect_object() and the other signal connection functions—gtk_signal_connect() and gtk_signal_connect_after()—is reflected in the function prototypes of the gtk_signal_connect* functions and in the function prototypes of the signal callback functions that are invoked.

The final argument to gtk_signal_connect() and gtk_signal_connect_after() is application private data. The first argument to a callback function registered using gtk_signal_connect() and gtk_signal_connect_after() is the widget or object with which the signal callback function was registered. In contrast, gtk_signal_connect_object() takes as its final argument a GtkObject pointer, which is the first (and only) argument passed to the signal callback function when the signal or event is triggered. The effect is that an event happening in the widget with which the signal callback function was registered will cause a callback function to be invoked as though the event or signal happened in some other object.

The function gtk_signal_connect_object_after()is analogous to gtk_signal_connect_after() in that the signal callback function will be invoked after the default widget class signal function for the widget has been invoked:

```
gint
gtk_signal_connect_object_after (GtkObject *object, gchar *name,
        GtkSignalFunc func, GtkObject *slot_object)
```

The classic example of gtk_signal_connect_object() is in tying together the press of a Quit, Cancel, or Dismiss GtkButton object with the destruction of the dialog or window in which the button is being displayed. The following code fragment taken from testgtk.c, an example application that is a part of the Gtk+ distribution, illustrates how this can be done:

```
GtkWidget *button, *box2;

...

button = gtk_button_new_with_label("Close");
gtk_box_pack_start(GTK_BOX(box2), button, TRUE, TRUE, 0);
gtk_signal_connect_object (GTK_OBJECT (button), "clicked",
     GTK_SIGNAL_FUNC(gtk_widget_destroy), GTK_OBJECT (window));
```

Here, the clicked signal supported by the GtkButton class is registered with the GtkButton instance defined by button. When the "clicked" signal is triggered, the function gtk_widget_destroy() will be invoked. The function prototype for gtk_widget_destroy() is as follows:

```
void
gtk_widget_destroy (GtkWidget *widget);
```

Note that gtk_widget_destroy() takes only one argument, which in this case is a widget to destroy. The widget argument passed to gtk_widget_destroy() is the same object that was passed as the last argument to gtk_signal_connect_object().

It is likely that the only time you will ever use this technique is when handling the destruction of simple dialogs such as those used to display an error or warning message to the user. There is little need for an application signal callback function to deal with the cancellation or dismissal of such a dialog, and so the preceding technique works well. However, if you have a dialog that allows users to make changes to data, you'll want to register an application-specific signal callback function with the "clicked" signal of "Cancel" or "Dismiss" button so that your application will have the opportunity to verify the cancellation operation.

Gtk+ supplies two functions that can be used by an application to disconnect a previously registered signal callback function from a signal or event. The first of these is gtk_signal_disconnect():

```
void
gtk_signal_disconnect (GtkObject *object, gint id);
```

The argument object is the object with which the signal was registered, corresponding to the first argument that was passed to the gtk_signal_connect* family of functions. As I pointed out earlier, more than one signal callback function can be registered with a given signal, so the id argument to gtk_signal_disconnect() is needed to identify which of the registered signal callback functions is to be disconnected. The argument id is the value returned by the gtk_signal_connect* function used to connect the signal callback function to the signal. In the following example, a signal callback function is connected to a clicked signal, and then is immediately disconnected, to illustrate the techniques involved:

```
GtkWidget *button;
gint id;
...

button = gtk_button_new_with_label("Close");
id = gtk_signal_connect_object (GTK_OBJECT (button), "clicked",
        GTK_SIGNAL_FUNC(gtk_widget_destroy), GTK_OBJECT (window));
gtk_signal_disconnect (GTK_OBJECT (button), id);
```

gtk_disconnect_by_data() performs the same operation as gtk_signal_disconnect(), but instead of identifying the signal callback function by its id, the signal function is identified by the application data passed as the func_data argument to gtk_signal_connect() or gtk_signal_connect_after(), or by the slot_object argument passed to either gtk_signal_connect_object() or gtk_signal_connect_object_after(). Here is the function prototype:

```
void
gtk_signal_disconnect_by_data (GtkObject *object, gpointer data);
```

Note that multiple signal callback functions can be disconnected with a call to gtk_signal_disconnect_by_data(), as every signal callback function registered with the object or application data to which data pertains will be disconnected by this function.

Gtk+ also allows an application to temporarily block the invocation of a signal callback function. This can be done by calling gtk_signal_handler_block():

```
void
gtk_signal_handler_block (GtkObject *object, gint id);
```

The arguments passed to gtk_signal_handler_block() are analogous to those passed to gtk_signal_disconnect(). The first argument, object, is the object with which the signal being blocked was registered by calling one of the gtk_signal_connect* functions. The argument id is the value returned by the gtk_signal_connect* function that registered the signal callback function with the object.

A similar function, gtk_signal_handler_block_by_data(), performs the same task as gtk_signal_handler_block(), but the data argument is used to identify the signal callback function(s) to be blocked. This is similar to how the data argument gtk_signal_disconnect_by_data() is used to identify the signal callback functions to be disconnected. Here is the function prototype for gtk_signal_handler_block_by_data():

```
void
gtk_signal_handler_block_by_data (GtkObject *object, gint data);
```

The argument blocking a signal handler function is not the same as stopping signal emission by calling gtk_signal_emit_stop(). When signal emission is stopped, it is only for the emissions corresponding to the triggering of a single event. The next time the event or signal is triggered, each and every signal callback function is once again eligible for invocation. When a signal callback function is blocked, it will not be invoked until it has been unblocked, no matter how many times the signal or event is triggered.

Each signal callback function registered with an object maintains a "blocked" count that starts at 0 and is incremented each time the signal is blocked by a call to a gtk_signal_handler_block* function.

Signal callback functions that are blocked can be unblocked at any time by a call to gtk_signal_handler_unblock():

```
void
gtk_signal_handler_unblock (GtkObject *object, gint id);
```

This decrements an object's blocked count by one. When the blocked count goes to zero, the signal callback function for the specified object, identified by id, will become eligible for invocation the next time the signal or event is triggered. The function

```
void
gtk_signal_handler_unblock_by_data (GtkObject *object, gint data);
```

is analogous to gtk_signal_disconnect_by_data() in that it has the ability to unblock more than one blocked signal callback function.

The final function that operates on signals that I will discuss in this section is gtk_signal_handlers_destroy():

```
void
gtk_signal_handlers_destroy (GtkObject *object);
```

gtk_signal_handlers_destroy() destroys all signal callback functions that have been registered with the specified object. This will not, however, destroy the class signal and event functions that are implemented by the object or widget.

Objects

The very first argument passed to gtk_signal_connect() is a pointer to variables of type GtkObject. Example code in the preceding section made use of a macro named GTK_OBJECT to coerce variables that were declared as GtkWidget * to GtkObject * so that the code would conform to the function prototype of the routine being called. Objects have played a part in nearly every function that has been discussed so far in this chapter. However, until now, I've not really defined yet what an object is. Obtaining a basic understanding of objects is the main idea behind this section.

Many of you will no doubt have some previous experience with C++, Smalltalk, or some other object-oriented language or programming paradigm. Perhaps you have heard about object-oriented programming but have no actual experience in its use. Or perhaps you have no idea at all what I am talking about when I use the terms "object" and "object-oriented programming."

It is not within the scope of this book to present an in-depth look at object-oriented systems or design. Gtk+ is a C-based toolkit, and C is not considered to be an object-oriented language, although object-oriented designs can in fact be implemented in C.

For us, a widget is the practical manifestation of what it is that we talk about when we refer to objects in Gtk+. Widgets, as we will come to see in the chapters that follow, are characterized by both visual representation and functionality. Visual representation defines how the widget appears in the user interface of the application. A widget's functionality defines how that widget will respond to input events directed towards it by Gtk+.

Button Widgets as Objects

The GtkButton widget can be used to illustrate both of these widget attributes. Visually, buttons are simply rectangular areas in a window that have labels that identify the action that the application will perform when the button is clicked. The button's label can be a text string, which is usually the case, or it can be in the form of a pixmap that graphically represents the operation that will be performed by the application when the button is clicked. Figure 3.1 illustrates instances of the GtkButton widget.

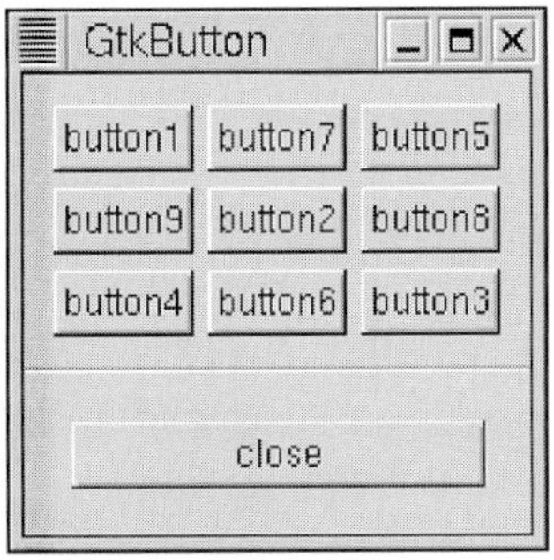

Figure 3.1 Button Widgets

Functionally speaking, a GtkButton widget will invoke an application-registered callback function when any one of the following events occur (these events were mentioned earlier in this chapter but are repeated here for convenience):

- The pointer enters the rectangular region occupied by the button.
- The pointer leaves the rectangular region occupied by the button.
- The pointer is positioned over the button, and a mouse button is pressed.
- The pointer is positioned over the button, and a mouse button is released.

- The user clicks the button (a combination of pressing and releasing a mouse button while the pointer is positioned over the button).

The behavior of a widget often corresponds to visual change, as is the case with the GtkButton widget, which will change its appearance after one of the preceding events has occurred. For example, as the pointer enters the rectangular region occupied by the button, the widget will redraw the button in a different color (a lighter shade of gray) to provide visual feedback to the user that the pointer is in a region owned by the button (see Figure 3.2). Should the user press mouse button 1 while the pointer is positioned over a GtkButton widget, the widget will redraw itself as shown in Figure 3.3.

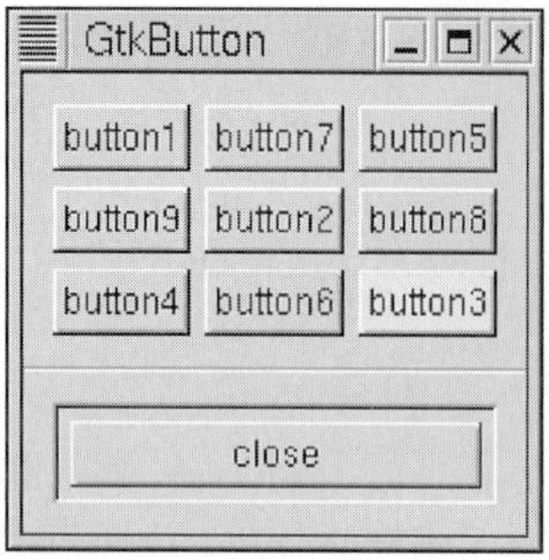

Figure 3.2 Pointer Positioned Over Button 3

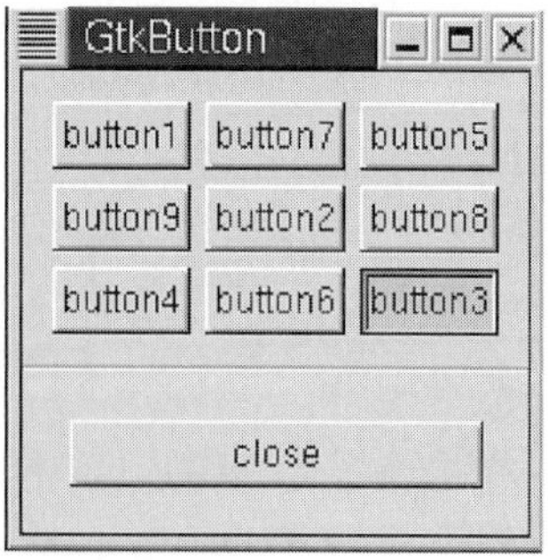

Figure 3.3 Button 3 Clicked

Let's now take a look at another Gtk+ widget, the GtkToggleButton, and see how it compares to the GtkButton widget.

Toggle buttons are used by an application to represent a value that can have one of two states. Examples include On or Off, Up or Down, and Left or Right.

In the nontoggled state, a GtkToggleButton widget has an appearance much like that of a GtkButton widget (see Figure 3.4). GtkToggleButton widgets are rectangular in shape and have a label. Like GtkButton, a GtkToggleButton widget's label can be either a text string or a pixmap. Visually, a user would be hard-pressed to tell a button from a toggle button in a user interface at first glance.

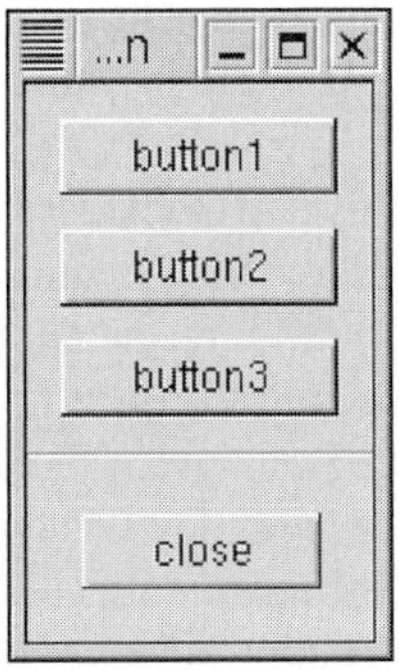

Figure 3.4 GtkToggleButton Widgets

Functionally, GtkToggleButton and GtkButton are closely related. Both respond basically the same way to the pointer entering or leaving the region occupied by a widget instance. The GtkToggleButton widget supports the same signals as GtkButton, plus a new signal, "toggled." The GtkToggleButton widget will emit this signal after the user positions the pointer over a toggle button and presses mouse button 1, the same condition that leads GtkButton to emit a "clicked" signal. In fact, a GtkToggleButton widget can also emit a "clicked" signal if the application so desires.

As the pointer enters the area occupied by a GtkToggleButton widget, the widget will redraw itself in a lighter shade of gray, just as a GtkButton widget does. However, GtkToggleButton's visual response to presses and releases is different. In the toggled state, a toggle button will appear as in Figure 3.5, which corresponds to the pressed state of GtkButton. In the untoggled state, a toggle button will appear as in Figure 3.4, corresponding to the unpressed state of GtkButton. The transition between the toggled and untoggled state occurs at the time of the button release (assuming the pointer is still within the area of the button at the time of release; otherwise, the toggle button widget will revert to its prior state).

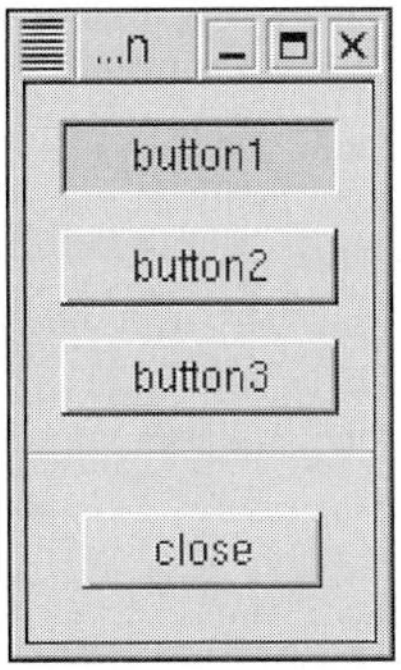

Figure 3.5 GtkToggleButton Widget in Toggled State

We've now established that GtkButton and GtkToggleButton share much in terms of look, feel, and functionality. So, how does this relate to objects?

Widgets in Gtk+ are organized as a hierarchy of classes. Each class in the Gtk+ widget class hierarchy is ultimately a descendant of the class named GtkObject. Refer to the appendix for a listing of the Gtk+ class hierarchy as of Gtk+ 1.2.

The GtkObject class represents a parent class from which all classes in the widget hierarchy inherit basic behavior. GtkObjects' contribution is minimal but important. Among the functionality provided by GtkObject is the signal mechanism. As one descends the hierarchy, visual representation (if any) and functionality become increasingly specialized. Each node in the class hierarchy diagram that has descendants provides a base class from which those descendants can, if they choose, inherit their look and feel or functionality. A child class will always replace some (perhaps all) of the look and feel or functionality of its parent class or introduce new look and feel or functionality that was not present in the parent class.

Such is the case with GtkButton (the parent) and GtkToggleButton (the child). Much of the implementation of GtkToggleButton is inherited from GtkButton. GtkToggleButton overrides the semantics of button presses and button releases and introduces the "toggled" signal, but essentially, a toggle button is really a button for the most part.

Object API

GtkObject implements an API that can be used by widget implementations and client developers. Here I just focus on a few of the application-level functions in this API so we can obtain a better understanding of what objects are from the perspective of an application. The first routine is gtk_object_destroy():

```
void
gtk_object_destroy( GtkObject *object )
```

gtk_object_destroy() takes an object as a parameter and destroys it. This routine can be called from any place that gtk_widget_destroy() is called. We saw one example of the use of gtk_widget_destroy() earlier in this chapter when I discussed gtk_signal_connect_object().

For example, let's say you have a GtkButton widget that you need to destroy. You can perform the destruction using either of the following techniques:

```
GtkButton *button;

...

gtk_widget_destroy( GTK_WIDGET( button ) );
```

or

```
GtkButton *button;

...

gtk_object_destroy( GTK_OBJECT( button ) );
```

To be complete, you could declare the button as GtkObject, in which case:

```
GtkObject *button;

...

gtk_widget_destroy( GTK_WIDGET( button ) );
```

or

```
GtkObject *button;

...

/* No cast needed, it is already an object */

gtk_object_destroy( button );
```

Finally, we could declare the button as GtkWidget, and then it would be:

```
GtkWidget *button;

...

/* No cast needed, it is already a widget */

gtk_widget_destroy( button );
```

or

```
GtkWidget *button;

...

gtk_object_destroy( GTK_OBJECT( button ) );
```

Regardless of how it's done, in the end, the button will be destroyed. Notice the use of the casting macros. If a routine expects an object and you have a widget, use GTK_OBJECT to convert the widget to an object. And, going the other way, use GTK_WIDGET to cast an object to a widget when a widget is needed.

These casting macros are not restricted to just GtkWidget and GtkObject. All widget classes in the widget hierarchy implement a macro that can be used to convert from one widget class to another. In later chapters, I will point out the macro name when I discuss the corresponding widget class, but as a general rule of thumb, the name of the macro can be formed by taking the widget class name, converting it to all uppercase, and inserting an underscore (_) after the initial GTK. For example, the casting macro for GtkButton is GTK_BUTTON. It is not actually this easy; additional underscores are added in some cases in which the class name is formed by a concatenation of words. For example, the casting macro for the class GtkDrawingArea is GTK_DRAWING_AREA.

These "casting" macros do not perform just a simple C-style cast. They also make sure that the item being cast is non-NULL and that the class to which the object is being cast either is of the same class (making the cast a no-op) or is a super-class in the widget instance hierarchy. Thus, a cast from any widget class (e.g., GtkButton) to GtkWidget will be successful because all buttons inherit from GtkWidget. A cast from GtkList to GtkText will fail because GtkList does not inherit from GtkText. The casting macros generate warning output if, for whatever reason, the cast being performed is illegal.

As you become moderately experienced as a Gtk+ programmer, deciding when and when not to use the casting macros will become somewhat second nature.

Here is a source code snippet that illustrates casting at a few different levels:

Listing 3.2 Object/Widget Casting Example

```
#include <gtk/gtk.h>

void
PrintAndExit (GtkWidget *widget, char *foo)
{
    if ( foo )
             printf( "%s\n", foo );
}

int
main( int argc, char *argv[] )
{
    GtkWidget *widget;
    GtkButton *button;
    GtkObject *object;

    gtk_set_locale ();

    gtk_init (&argc, &argv);

    ...

    /* button */

    button = (GtkButton *) gtk_button_new_with_label ("foo");

    gtk_signal_connect (GTK_OBJECT(button), "destroy",
           GTK_SIGNAL_FUNC(PrintAndExit), "button, object destroy");

    gtk_object_destroy( GTK_OBJECT( button ) );

    button = (GtkButton *) gtk_button_new_with_label ("foo");

    gtk_signal_connect (GTK_OBJECT(button), "destroy",
           GTK_SIGNAL_FUNC(PrintAndExit), "button, widget destroy");

    gtk_widget_destroy( GTK_WIDGET( button ) );

    ...
```

```
069        return( 0 );
070    }
```

The application basically creates and destroys six buttons. Here, I only show the lines pertaining to creating the button and storing its handle in a variable of GtkButton *. The full application contains code that creates and destroys instances of GtkButton, storing them as GtkObject * and as GtkWidget *. Our first need for a cast occurs on line 039. Here, the return value from gtk_button_new_with_label() is GtkWidget *, and I am required to cast this result to (GtkButton *) to eliminate a compile-time warning from gcc(1). Note that all gtk_*_new() functions return a handle of type GtkWidget * because buttons, scrollbars, labels, toggle buttons, and so on, are all widgets. I personally feel that using "GtkButton *button;" to declare a variable that is going to hold a widget handle to a GtkButton to be better style, but adding the casts is annoying, so I suggest all widgets be declared as GtkWidget *. There are other good reasons for doing this, but avoiding the need for adding casts all over the place is reason enough.

On lines 041 and 042, we register a signal callback function with Gtk+ for the "destroy" signal. The user data argument is a string that identifies the operation; in this case, "button, object destroy" means we have stored the widget in a "button" variable (i.e., a variable of type GtkButton *) and we are going to call gtk_object_destroy() as opposed to gtk_widget_destroy() to destroy the widget. On line 044, we destroy the widget by making a call to gtk_object_destroy(). Note that the argument is cast by the GTK_OBJECT macro because the widget instance was stored in a GtkButton * variable, but gtk_object_destroy() requires a variable of GtkObject *.

The same basic logic prevails on lines 046 through 051, except this time, the button is destroyed with a call to gtk_widget_destroy(), requiring us to cast the button variable from a GtkButton to a GtkWidget using GTK_WIDGET.

Object Attributes

In Gtk+, objects have attributes. When you instantiate a GtkButton widget with a call to gtk_button_new_with_label(), for example, you are setting the button widget's label to the string that was passed in as an argument. Actually, there is more going on than just this, but from an application's perspective, this is effectively what happens.

Usually, perhaps ideally, applications will not make use of the following functions. However, it is worthwhile to look at them because it will strengthen your concept of what an object is in Gtk+.

The first function we'll look at is gtk_object_query_args():

```
GtkArg *
gtk_object_query_args (GtkType type, guint32 **flags, guint *nargs);
```

The function gtk_object_query_args() can be used to obtain the list of attributes supported by a widget class. This can only be done after the application has instantiated at least one instance of the class being queried. The argument type defines the class to be queried. The best way to obtain the value of type is to call a routine provided by the class implementation. For the GtkButton class, this is gtk_button_get_type(). For other classes, it will be named gtk_*_get_type() by convention (the actual names are documented along with the widget classes as they are discussed later in this book).

The second argument, flags, is a pointer to an array of unallocated guint32 (or guint) values. You can pass (gunit32 **) NULL here or the address of a variable of type guint32 *:

```
type = gtk_button_get_type();

args = gtk_object_query_args (type, (guint32 **) NULL, ... );
```

or

```
guint32 *flags;

args = gtk_object_query_args (type, &flags, ... );
```

The second argument is ignored if NULL. If non-NULL, gtk_object_query_args() will allocate an array of 32-bit unsigned ints, each corresponding to an attribute supported by the widget class. The number of elements in this array is stored in the value returned in nargs, a pointer to an unsigned int, which is the third and final argument to gtk_object_query_args(). Once you are done with the flags array, you must free it by calling g_free():

```
g_free( flags );
```

The flags in Table 3.8 are supported by Gtk+.

Table 3.8 Flags Supported by gtk_object_query_args()

Flag	*Meaning*
GTK_ARG_READABLE	Attribute's value can be read
GTK_ARG_WRITABLE	Attribute's value can be written
GTK_ARG_CONSTRUCT	Can be specified at object construction time
GTK_ARG_CONSTRUCT_ONLY	Must be specified at object construction time
GTK_ARG_CHILD_ARG	Attribute applies to children of widget (used by containers)
GTK_ARG_READWRITE	Same as GTK_ARG_READABLE | GTK_ARG_WRITABLE

The flags relevant to applications include GTK_ARG_READABLE, GTK_ARG_WRITABLE, and GTK_ARG_READWRITE. These flags specify whether an application can query the value of an argument, change its value, or do either, respectively. The remaining flags are relevant to the widget writer and do not concern us here.

gtk_object_query_args() returns a pointer to an array of type GtkArg. The array will have nargs entries in it. Once you are finished with the array, it must also be freed with a quick call to g_free().

If you are curious about the contents of GtkArg, the structure is defined in gtktypeutils.h. However, you can, and should, access the fields in this structure using accessor macros defined by Gtk+. Table 3.9 lists the possible simple data types that an attribute can have, along with the accessor macros that can be used to obtain the data for each type.

Table 3.9 Nonaggregate Accessor Macros

Type	*Accessor Macro*
gchar	GTK_VALUE_CHAR(a)
guchar	GTK_VALUE_UCHAR(a)
gboolean	GTK_VALUE_BOOL(a)
gint	GTK_VALUE_INT(a)
guint	GTK_VALUE_UINT(a)
glong	GTK_VALUE_LONG(a)
gulong	GTK_VALUE_ULONG(a)
gfloat	GTK_VALUE_FLOAT(a)
gdouble	GTK_VALUE_DOUBLE(a)
gchar *	GTK_VALUE_STRING(a)
gint	GTK_VALUE_ENUM(a)
guint	GTK_VALUE_FLAGS(a)
gpointer	GTK_VALUE_BOXED(a)
gpointer	GTK_VALUE_POINTER(a)
GtkObject *	GTK_VALUE_OBJECT(a)

Accessor macros are also defined for the following aggregate types in Table 3.10.

Table 3.10 Aggregate Accessor Macros

Accessor Macro	*Type*
GTK_VALUE_SIGNAL(a)	`struct { GtkSignalFunc f; gpointer d; } signal_data;`

Table 3.10 Aggregate Accessor Macros (Continued)

Accessor Macro	*Type*

GTK_VALUE_ARGS(a)	`struct {`
	`gint n_args;`
	`GtkArg *args;`
	`} args_data;`

GTK_VALUE_CALLBACK(a)	`struct {`
	`GtkCallbackMarshal marshal;`
	`gpointer data;`
	`GtkDestroyNotify notify;`
	`} callback_data;`

GTK_VALUE_C_CALLBACK(a)	`struct {`
	`GtkFunction func;`
	`gpointer func_data;`
	`} c_callback_data;`

GTK_VALUE_FOREIGN(a)	`struct {`
	`gpointer data;`
	`GtkDestroyNotify notify;`
	`} foreign_data;`

To determine the type of an attribute, use the macro GTK_FUNDAMENTAL_TYPE(), passing the type field of the GtkArg struct from which data is to be accessed:

```
GTK_FUNDAMENTAL_TYPE( a.type );
```

The following code snippet illustrates how to call gtk_object_query_args().

Lines 008, 009, and 010 declare the variables needed for the call to gtk_object_query_args().

```
008     GtkArg *args;
009     guint nArgs;
010     guint32 *flags = (guint32 *) NULL;

...

020     args = gtk_object_query_args( gtk_button_get_type(), &flags, &nArgs );
021
022     if ( args == (GtkArg *) NULL ) {
023             fprintf( stderr, "Unable to query widget's args\n" );
024             exit( 1 );
025     }
```

On line 020, we call gtk_object_query_args(). Then, on lines 029 through 080, we iterate through the array of GtkArg structs returned. For each arg, we determine its type using GTK_FUNDAMENTAL_TYPE (line 032). Then, in the switch statement, we print that type as a string to stdout:

```
029     for ( i = 0; i < nArgs; i++ ) {
030             printf( "Name: '%s', type: ", args[i].name );
```

```
031
032             switch( GTK_FUNDAMENTAL_TYPE (args[i].type) ) {
033             case GTK_TYPE_CHAR :
034                     printf( "GTK_TYPE_CHAR, " );
035                     break;
036             case GTK_TYPE_UCHAR :
037                     printf( "GTK_TYPE_UCHAR, " );
038                     break;
039             case GTK_TYPE_BOOL :
040                     printf( "GTK_TYPE_BOOL, " );
041                     break;

...

080             }
```

Following the switch, on lines 081 through 101, we interpret the corresponding entry in the flags array that was returned. Remember, if NULL is sent as the second argument to gtk_object_query_args(), then no flags will be returned.

```
081             printf( "Flags: " );
082             switch( flags[i] ) {
083             case GTK_ARG_READABLE :
084                     printf( "GTK_ARG_READABLE\n" );
085                     break;
086             case GTK_ARG_WRITABLE :
087                     printf( "GTK_ARG_WRITABLE\n" );
088                     break;
089             case GTK_ARG_CONSTRUCT :
090                     printf( "GTK_ARG_CONSTRUCT\n" );
091                     break;
092             case GTK_ARG_CONSTRUCT_ONLY :
093                     printf( "GTK_ARG_CONSTRUCT_ONLY\n" );
094                     break;
095             case GTK_ARG_CHILD_ARG :
096                     printf( "GTK_ARG_CHILD_ARG\n" );
097                     break;
098             case GTK_ARG_READWRITE :
099                     printf( "GTK_ARG_READWRITE\n" );
100                     break;
101             }
```

Finally, on lines 106 through 109, the flags and args pointers are freed by a call to g_free().

```
104     /* not really needed, as we are exiting */
105
106     if ( flags )
107             g_free( flags );
108     if ( args )
109             g_free( args );
110
```

```
    return( 0 );
}
```

Getting and Setting Object Attributes

Now that we know how to obtain a list of the attributes supported by a widget class, let's discuss how to get and set the values of attributes in a widget or object instance. To retrieve attribute data from a widget, we need only make minor changes to the preceding source. Two routines can be used to read attribute data. The first is gtk_object_arg_get():

```
void
gtk_object_arg_get (GtkObject *object, GtkArg *arg, GtkArgInfo *info)
```

The first argument, object, is the widget from which object data is to be retrieved. The second argument, arg, is effectively the element in the vector returned by gtk_object_query_args() that corresponds to the attribute being queried. You can use gtk_object_query_args() to obtain this value, or you can allocate a GtkArg variable on the stack and set the name field to the attribute you want to query, for example:

```
GtkArg    myArg;
GtkWidget *myButton;

...

myArg.name = "GtkButton::label";
gtk_object_arg_get( GTK_OBJECT( myButton ), &myArg, NULL );

...
```

The final argument, info, should always be passed as NULL. In fact, there are no examples of gtk_object_arg_get() usage in the Gtk+ source code where this argument is set to anything but NULL. gtk_object_arg_get() will retrieve the value internally if you pass NULL, so perhaps this argument will be deprecated in a future version of Gtk+.

On return, myArg will contain the data that was requested. If the data could not be obtained for whatever reason (for example, the attribute does not exist), gtk_object_arg_get() will generate output to the console, for example:

```
Gtk-WARNING **: gtk_object_arg_get(): could not find argument "Yabbadabba" in
the 'GtkButton' class ancestry
```

The type field in the GtkArg struct will be set to GTK_TYPE_INVALID. This can be checked using code similar to the following:

```
if ( GTK_FUNDAMENTAL_TYPE (myArg.type) == GTK_TYPE_INVALID )

          /* Attribute could not be read for some reason */
else
          /* Attribute was read */
```

The second routine that can be used to retrieve attribute values is as follows:

```
void
gtk_object_getv (GtkObject *object, guint n_args, GtkArg *args)
```

This routine is nearly identical to gtk_object_arg_get(), except that it can be used to retrieve multiple attributes with a single function call. The argument n_args holds the number of elements in args; args is a vector of GtkArg structs.

The following code snippet illustrates how to call gtk_object_arg_get() using the return value from gtk_object_query_args(). The majority of the code is the same as in the previous listing. Here I'll just show the loop used to obtain the attribute values, one for each element in the array of GtkArg elements returned by gtk_object_query_args():

```
widget = gtk_button_new_with_label( "This is a test" );

args = gtk_object_query_args( gtk_button_get_type(), &flags, &nArgs );

if ( args == (GtkArg *) NULL ) {
        fprintf( stderr, "Unable to query widget's args\n" );
        exit( 1 );
}

for ( i = 0; i < nArgs; i++ ) {

        printf( "Name: '%s', value: ", args[i].name );

        if ( flags[i] == GTK_ARG_READABLE
                || flags[i] == GTK_ARG_READWRITE ) {

                gtk_object_arg_get( GTK_OBJECT( widget ), &args[i],
                        NULL );

                switch( GTK_FUNDAMENTAL_TYPE (args[i].type) ) {
                case GTK_TYPE_CHAR :
                        printf( "%c\n",
                                GTK_VALUE_CHAR (args[i]) );
                        break;
                case GTK_TYPE_UCHAR :
                        printf( "%c\n",
                                GTK_VALUE_UCHAR (args[i]) );
                        break;
                case GTK_TYPE_BOOL :
                        printf( "%s\n",
                                (GTK_VALUE_BOOL(args[i])==TRUE?
                                "TRUE":"FALSE"));
                        break;

...

                case GTK_TYPE_STRING :
                        printf( "%s\n",
                                GTK_VALUE_STRING (args[i]) );
                        g_free (GTK_VALUE_STRING (args[i]));
                        break;
```

```
...

095                     case GTK_TYPE_INVALID:
096                             printf( "Attribute is invalid\n" );
097                             break;
098                     case GTK_TYPE_NONE:
099                             printf( "Attribute is none\n" );
100                             break;
101                     default:
102                             break;
103                       }
104             }
105     }

...

115 }
```

On line 017, we create an instance of the GtkButton class. We need to pass an object to gtk_object_arg_get() to identify the object we are querying, and we also need, in this example, to create an instance of GtkButton so that gtk_object_query_args() can do its job.

On line 019, we call gtk_object_query_args() to obtain a list of the attributes supported by the GtkButton widget class. Then, on lines 026 through 105, we iterate through the array returned by gtk_object_query_args(). For each element, we make a call to gtk_object_arg_get(); this occurs on line 033. We then switch on the type field set by gtk_object_arg_get(), accessing this value using the GTK_FUNDAMENTAL_TYPE macro as previously described. In the switch statement, we simply use the type to determine the format string passed to printf and use the accessor macro needed to retrieve the value from the GtkArg element. Note the use of g_free(), which is needed to release storage allocated by Gtk+ for GTK_TYPE_STRING attributes, as shown on lines 074 through 078.

Gtk+ provides two routines for setting attribute values in a widget. They are:

```
void
gtk_object_set (GtkObject *object, const gchar *first_arg_name, ...)
```

and

```
void
gtk_object_setv (GtkObject *object, guint n_args, GtkArg *args)
```

Both can be used to set multiple attributes. gtk_object_setv() would be the more convenient routine to call after obtaining a GtkArg vector from gtk_object_query_args(), although this is not required, of course. In all other cases, gtk_object_set() is probably the easiest of the two to use.

gtk_object_setv() takes the very same arguments as gtk_object_getv(). The only difference is that the elements in the args vector need to contain that data to which the attribute is being set and the type. To do this, use the accessor macros used to read data from a GtkArg struct. For example, to change the label of a button, we might code the following:

```
GtkArg arg;
GtkWidget *widget;

...

arg.type = GTK_TYPE_STRING;
arg.name = "GtkButton::label";
GTK_VALUE_STRING(arg) = "Yabba Dabba Doo";
gtk_object_setv( GTK_OBJECT( widget ), 1, &arg );
```

The function gtk_object_set() accepts a variable argument list. Each attribute to be set is specified in the argument list by its name, such as GtkButton::label, followed by a variable number of arguments that specify the value of that attribute. In some cases, a single argument can be used to specify a value, for example, a button label value is a string. In some cases, the attribute being set is an aggregate, and in this case, the value arguments will correspond to the fields of a structure or the elements of a table.

The final argument to gtk_object_set() must be NULL to indicate the end of the argument list (if you forget the NULL, gtk_object_set() will read beyond the stack, leading to unpredictable behavior).

The preceding example, using gtk_object_set(), is reduced to the following:

```
GtkWidget *widget;

gtk_object_set( GTK_OBJECT( widget ), "GtkButton::label",
        "Yabba Dabba Doo", NULL );
```

Associating Client Data with an Object or Widget

Gtk+ allows applications to associate an arbitrary amount of indexed data with a widget instance. An index is nothing more than a character string used to uniquely identify the data. The data associated with an index is of type gpointer. Gtk+ maintains one list of indexed data per object or widget; there is no practical limit to the number of data items that can be attached to the list. The only restriction is that each entry on the list must have a unique index. Adding an entry using an index that corresponds to an entry already on the list will cause Gtk+ to replace that entry's data with the newly specified data.

Let's take a quick look at the functions involved, and then we'll discuss how this facility might be useful to an application.

To add an entry to an object's list, applications can use gtk_object_set_data() or gtk_object_set_data_full().

The first function, gtk_object_set_data(), takes an object, a key, and a data value as arguments:

```
void
gtk_object_set_data (GtkObject *object, const gchar *key,
        gpointer data)
```

An item on the object's data list will be added by Gtk+ as a result of making this call.

The second function is gtk_object_set_data_full():

```
void
gtk_object_set_data_full (GtkObject *object, const gchar *key,
        gpointer data, GtkDestroyNotify destroy)
```

gtk_object_set_data_full() takes the same arguments plus an additional argument named destroy, which is a pointer to a function that will be called by Gtk+ should the data indexed by key be destroyed. Destruction means that the entry indexed by key was removed from the list. The function prototype for destroy is as follows:

```
void
DestroyFunc ( gpointer data )
```

You may pass NULL as the last argument to gtk_object_set_data_full(), but then the call effectively becomes equivalent to calling gtk_object_set_data().

If an entry indexed by key already exists on the object's list prior to calling either gtk_object_set_data() or gtk_object_set_data_full(), then the gpointer stored by that entry will be replaced by data. A new entry on the list will not be created because indexes on the list must be unique.

To retrieve data from an object's list, call gtk_object_get_data():

```
gpointer
gtk_object_get_data (GtkObject *object, const gchar *key)
```

The function gtk_object_get_data() takes an object and a key. If there is no entry on the object's list indexed by key, then NULL is returned. Otherwise, the data that is stored on the list indexed by key will be returned.

To remove an entry from an object's list, call gtk_object_remove_data() or gtk_object_remove_no_notify():

```
void
gtk_object_remove_data (GtkObject *object, const gchar *key)

void
gtk_object_remove_no_notify (GtkObject *object, const gchar *key)
```

Either function will remove the entry indexed by key from the list maintained by object, if such an entry exists. If gtk_object_remove_data() was called, the destroy function registered with the entry, if any, will be invoked, and a copy of the data stored by that entry will be passed as an argument as previously discussed. If gtk_object_remove_no_notify() is used, then the destroy function will not be invoked.

Gtk+ supports the following two convenience functions:

```
void
gtk_object_set_user_data (GtkObject *object, gpointer data)

gpointer
gtk_object_get_user_data (GtkObject *object)
```

Calling one of these functions is equivalent to calling gtk_object_set_data() or gtk_object_get_data(), respectively, with a key argument that has been set to user_data.

Please be aware that some widget implementations will add a user_data entry, so setting or removing this entry may lead to incorrect behavior of the widget and your application. Calling gtk_object_get_data() or gtk_object_get_user_data() and obtaining a NULL return value cannot be taken as an indication that the list does not contain an entry indexed by user_data. It could be that the entry exists and, at the time of calling, is storing a NULL pointer as its data item. Therefore, until Gtk+ provides a routine that can be used to test for the existence of an item on a list indexed by key, I recommend playing it safe and avoid adding, setting, or removing entries keyed by user_data. Also, take reasonable precautions to ensure that keys used by your application are unique and do not collide with keys that might be in use internally by a widget implementation.

When to Use Client Data

How might one use indexed data in an application? An obvious application would be a word processor, a text editor, or for that matter, any application that allows the concurrent editing of more than one document. An image-editing tool such as The GIMP is an example of such an application.

The GIMP allows users to display and edit more than one image at a time. Each image being edited has an associated set of attributes, including width, height, image type (RGB, grayscale), the name of the file from which the image was read and to which it will be saved by default, and a flag that indicates whether or not the image is dirty and needs to be saved before the user exits The GIMP. Some of this information is reflected in the title bar of the window displaying the image data (Figure 3.6).

Figure 3.6 Title Bar of a GIMP Window

So how might The GIMP maintain information about images currently being edited? A convenient method for organizing this data would be to maintain a data structure for each image being edited. A possible candidate data structure is the following:

```
type struct _idata {
        gchar *filename;      /* file name, or NULL if untitled */
        guint width;          /* image width */
        guint height;         /* image height */
        gboolean dirty;       /* If TRUE, needs to be saved */
        gint type;            /* IMAGE_GRAY, IMAGE_RGB */
        gint fill_type;       /* FILL_BG, FILL_WHITE, FILL_CLEAR */
        GdkWindow *win;       /* Window handle for edit window */
        struct _idata *next;  /* next node in list or NULL */
} ImageData;
```

Now that we have a way to represent this data, where should we store this data structure? Whatever method we choose, we must be able to easily associate the image currently being edited or displayed by the user with the data about that image.

One possibility would be to store it in a global linked list. Whenever the user selects a window and it is brought to the front, we search the linked list for the entry with a "win" field that contains the window handle of the window that was raised; this record will contain the information about the image being edited in the window. This is a perfectly fine solution. The only problem is that the application will need to maintain code needed to support the linked list.

An alternate solution would be to use indexed data. To associate image data with a window, we simply use gtk_object_set_data() at the time the image is created or opened. For example, the routine that creates a new image and its window might perform the following:

```
...

ImageData *imageData;
GtkWidget *dialog;

imageData = (ImageData *) malloc( sizeof( ImageData ) );
imageData->filename = (gchar *) NULL;
imageData->dirty = FALSE;

 /* set defaults */

imageData-width = imageData->height = 250;
imageData->type = FILL_BG;
imageData->type = IMAGE_RGB;

/* create a window */

dialog = CreateGIMPImageDialog( imageData );
imageData->win = GTK_WIDGET(dialog)->window;

/* associate the image data with the dialog */

gtk_object_set_data( GTK_OBJECT( dialog ), "image_data",
        (gpointer) imageData );

...
```

In the preceding, CreateGIMPImageDialog() is a hypothetical routine that creates a dialog or window using the image attributes passed to it as an argument. For example, the width and height fields are used to define the size of the window.

There are two advantages in using the preceding technique. First, we didn't need to provide the linked list code; gtk_object_set_data() takes care of this for us. Second, the image data is tightly coupled with the dialog being used to display it. The result is that finding the image data that corresponds to a dialog is a straightforward task.

For example, we could associate a signal function with the dialog widget that will fire when the window becomes destroyed, as follows:

```
gtk_signal_connect (GTK_OBJECT (dialog), "destroy",
GTK_SIGNAL_FUNC(HandleDestroy), NULL);
```

HandleDestroy() can then retrieve the image_data entry from the dialog and, if the image data is "dirty", give the user the opportunity to save changes to a file:

```
void
HandleDestroy (GtkWidget *widget, gpointer data)
{
        ImageData *ptr;

        /* get the image data attached to the widget */

        ptr = gtk_object_get_data( GTK_OBJECT( dialog ), "image_data" );

        /* if we found it, and the data is dirty, give user opportunity to
           save it */

        if ( ptr != (ImageData *) NULL && ptr->dirty == TRUE )
                LetUserSaveData( ptr );

        /* free the image data */

        if ( ptr != (ImageData *) NULL )
                free( ptr );
}
```

Well, that ends my coverage of objects in this chapter. You should now have a good idea of what an object is and be aware of some of the ways that objects can be used in a Gtk+ application.

Types

You may have noticed that the code snippets and function prototypes presented in this chapter make use of nonstandard C types such as gpointer, gint, and gchar *. These types, which are defined by Glib in glib.h, are intended to aid in the portability of Gtk+, GDK, and Glib and the applications that make use of these toolkits.

You should get in the habit of using these types, particularly when declaring variables that will be passed as arguments to the Glib, GDK, or Gtk+ APIs. Using C language types such as void *, int, or char * is acceptable in other cases. Declaring a loop index variable as int as opposed to gint will not lead to any problems, unless perhaps the index variable is used as an argument to a Glib function that requires gint, for example. While perhaps unlikely, it is not guaranteed that a gint will map to an int in all implementations.

Table 3.11 lists the basic types defined by Glib for UNIX and Linux.

Table 3.11 Glib Types

C Language Type	*Glib Type*
char	gchar
signed char	gint8
unsigned char	guint8
unsigned char	guchar
short	gshort
signed short	gint16
unsigned short	guint16
unsigned short	gushort
int	gint
int	gboolean
signed int	gint32
unsigned int	guint32
unsigned int	guint
long	glong
unsigned long	gulong
float	gfloat
double	gdouble
void *	gpointer
const void *	gconstpointer

Where more than one Glib type maps to the same C type (for example, gboolean and gint both map to int in the preceding table), avoid interchanging Glib types. In other words, if a function prototype mandates the use of a gboolean, do not use a gint in its place; use a gboolean.

Summary

In this chapter, we discussed signals and signal handling. Signals are the way in which widgets communicate changes back to your application and are a required part of any meaningful Gtk+ application. You will, as a Gtk+ programmer, do much of your programming within the context of signal functions. We also covered Gtk+ events and objects and described the associated functions for each. Events are low-level when compared to signals, corresponding to events that exist at the X protocol level. Many (most) of the events we discussed are intercepted by widgets on behalf of your application and are translated into their higher level signal counterparts. Some applications, however, can make good use of events (this is especially true for applications that involve interactive graphics of some kind). We also discussed objects. Objects are fundamental to the architecture of the Gtk+ toolkit. In a practical sense, you will find yourself using the terms "object" and "widget" interchangeably. All Gtk+ widgets are descendants of GtkObject in the object/widget hierarchy. This chapter described what objects are as well as the API that exists for manipulating them. The chapter ended with a short discussion of Gtk+ data types. For the sake of portability, you should strive to use the Gtk+ types (e.g., use "guint" instead of "unsigned int"), although, as I will illustrate time and again in this book, use of the Gtk+ types is by no means a requirement.

CHAPTER

4

WIDGETS

In this chapter and the next several chapters that follow, I will describe most of the Gtk+ widget classes provided by Gtk+ 1.2. I will start in this chapter by describing the Gtk+ base widget class, GtkWidget. GtkWidget is the base widget class because most, if not all, of the Gtk+ classes you will work with as a Gtk+ programmer inherit functionality from GtkWidget. For this reason alone, GtkWidget is perhaps the most important widget class to understand completely, and it is a good place for us to start.

When describing GtkWidget and the remaining Gtk+ widgets in the chapters that follow, I will strive to provide the following information:

- An overview of the basic design of the widget, such as what it looks like and how and when it may be used in a Gtk+ application.
- Where in the widget hierarchy the widget resides. (I'll have more to say about widget hierarchies later in this chapter.)
- How instances of the widget are created and, if notable, destroyed by a Gtk+ application.
- Any modifications, features, or options supported by the widget.
- The signals supported by the widget and, in some cases, examples of their use.
- Any functions supported by the widget class (including a quick reference).

Source code will be used to illustrate concepts. However, I will try to get my points across with as little code as possible. Because of the "open source" nature of Gtk+ and the relatively large number of applications that make use of it, the Internet provides source code for numerous full-size Gtk+ application that you can download and study.

Why Widgets?

The following are the basic goals of a widget set:

- To simplify user interface development for application developers
- To promote the development of user interfaces and behavior consistent from one application to the next, simplifying application use.

Let's take a look at each of these goals independently.

Simplifying User Interface Development

There are several ways in which a toolkit can simplify user-interface development. The following sections explore some of the ways Gtk+ simplifies the development process.

API Simplification

One way to simplify development is to provide developers with a consistent programming API. In Gtk+, instances of a widget are created by calling a function provided by the widget class. The name of this function conforms to the naming convention gtk_<class>_new_<modifier>(), where <class> is the lowercase name corresponding to the widget class and <modifier> is an optional string describing additional functionality provided by the widget creation function at the time it is called. For example, to create an instance of a button widget (GtkButton), an application could call gtk_button_new(void), which will create a push button with no label, or gtk_button_new_with_label(gchar *label), which will create a push button with an application-specified label (in this case, "with_label" is the <modifier> portion of the function name). Names of public functions defined by a widget writer generally are of the form gtk_ <class>_<function>, where <class> is the lowercase name of widget class and <function> describes the functionality provided by the routine. For example, gtk_entry_set_text() sets the text displayed by an instance of the GtkEntry widget class.

Readers with Xt experience will note, with some justification, that creation of a widget instance in Xt is even simpler. While the number of functions in Gtk+ for widget creation is essentially directly proportional to the number of widget classes in the Gtk+ toolkit, only a few routines are provided for widget creation in Xt. In Xt, the widget class is identified by passing its name as an argument to the widget creation function, eliminating the need for the widget class to define a publicly callable widget creation function. It should be a simple matter to create a macro or function for Gtk+ that will accept a class identifier as an argument and use that identifier in a switch statement to call the appropriate Gtk+ widget creation function.

Widget classes are consistently named Gtk<class>, where <class>, as previously stated, describes the functionality provided by the widget class.

Finally, instances of widgets belonging to any class type can be stored as a variable of type GtkWidget *.

We'll see several examples of how Gtk+ provides API consistency throughout this book.

Abstraction

Another way in which the programming simplicity of a toolkit can be evaluated is by looking at the level of abstraction provided by the toolkit's widgets. When I refer to abstraction, it is in regard to how well the programmer is protected from the details of the underlying, native user-interface toolkit and the type of controls and user-interface "goodies" that the toolkit provides. In general, the higher the level of abstraction provided, the better.

Suppose the users of an application you are developing need to be given the capability to enter or select a calendar date, such as March 12, 2003. As a programmer using Xlib, a user interface for this feature is potentially difficult to implement. This is because Xlib provides no support for data entry of any type. An Xlib programmer would need to be very creative, designing a user interface suitable for the user to select or enter a calendar date. The level of sophistication provided by the user interface (at the lower end, a text field with perhaps a label or two; at the higher end, a more elaborate control) is perhaps linearly related to the amount of effort and time that the developer will need to spend developing it. The programmer would be forced to consider functionality (e.g, validation of user input, ensuring that a date such as "February 31" is not entered) of the control as well.

Because of the level of abstraction provided by Gtk+, the programmer using Gtk+ should have a much less difficult task implementing such a user interface. There are several ways that widgets in the Gtk+ hierarchy could be combined by a programmer to come up with a user interface capable of calendar date entry, in less time than it would take an Xlib programmer to achieve the same. However, combining existing Gtk+ widgets to create a calendar date control still requires substantial effort from the programmer. For instance, the programmer must be creative in designing the user interface of the control. Should the control be implemented as a text edit field (GtkEntry) into which the user will type a formatted date string? Or should the control function more like a real calendar, displaying a specific month chosen by the user, for example July 2003, and allowing her to click on the desired day? How should the user be allowed to specify the month and year displayed by the control? Besides the user-interface design issues, the Gtk+ programmer is still faced with identifying and implementing the functional aspects of the control, such as date validation, and providing a way for the application to retrieve the date entered/selected by the user.

Mainly because of the preceding concerns, the ideal solution for a programmer would be to use a toolkit that provides programmers with a date entry widget class. It would be unrealistic to expect the Gtk+ designers to anticipate all of the controls that might be needed by application developers now and in the future. As time goes on, needs of user interfaces change; many of you reading this book will remember the time before tab controls were introduced and used widely. To accommodate the development of new user-interface controls, Gtk+ was designed to be expandable in that new widget classes can be added to the Gtk+ widget hierarchy. Our hypothetical programmer can choose to implement her date entry control as a new widget class in the Gtk+ widget hierarchy, contributing it back to the Gtk+ development effort for inclusion in a future release of the Gtk+ toolkit. Developers should expect to see incremental additions to the Gtk+ widget hierarchy as programmers contribute new widgets to Gtk+ and subsequent releases of the toolkit are made.

Earlier in this section, I suggested that the amount of effort and time required to develop the user interface and functionality of a new control is perhaps linear with respect to the level of sophistication provided by the control that results. The degree to which this linearity holds is largely dependent on the tools used and the skill of the developer. Difficulty would generally be greater for an Xlib implementation and less for an implementation based on a combination of pre-existing Gtk+ widgets.

If the control desired by the programmer is already provided by the Gtk+ widget set, then the expected amount of effort needed to implement the control in the application user interface is constant. The use of a label, a button, a pop-up menu, or a date entry control should all require about the same amount of effort from a programmer, effort that is far less than that needed by the programmer creating the control from scratch. The reasons for this should be clear; the user interface of the control, and its functionality, have already been provided by the widget. All the programmer needs to do is instantiate the widget and interact with it at runtime using the API provided by the widget implementation.

Simplification for Users

This brings us to the second goal of a toolkit like Gtk+, which is to make life easier, not only for developers but for end users of the application. The way this is done is again through consistency. If the widget set provides a date entry widget, programmers will use that widget (assuming it is sufficient for most programmers' needs, which a good widget design will ensure) instead of implementing one of their own. This will result in a consistent user interface as well as stable and predictable behavior shared among different applications. A user who learns an application that makes use of a control instantiated from the Gtk+ widget set only needs to learn that control once because it will behave in the same manner in all other applications. This holds true for all toolkits, not just Gtk+.

Now that you have a better understanding of some of the benefits of toolkit-based programming, let's dive into the details of the first widget class we will look at in this book: GtkWidget. Since this is the first widget class described in this book, I will be overly verbose in describing how the material is organized (such descriptions in the following are *italicized*). Subsequent widget classes will be described using the same basic organization as presented here.

GtkWidget

Class Name

```
GtkWidget
```

This is the name of the class being described.

Parent Class Name

```
GtkObject
```

This is the name of the class in the Gtk+ widget hierarchy that is the parent of this widget class. Additional capabilities supported by a widget class can be discovered by reading about the parent widget class, and its parent, and so on, since a child class will inherit attributes and capabilities from its parents.

Macros

Macros are found in the widget class's include file, which in this case is named gtkwindow.h. Your application need only include gtk/gtk.h to access these macros.

Macros (Continued)

Widget type macro: `GTK_TYPE_WIDGET`

This is the type constant associated with the widget class. Casting a widget to GtkObject and passing the result to the GTK_OBJECT_TYPE macro was illustrated in Chapter 3, "Signals, Events, Objects, and Types."

Object to widget cast macro: `GTK_WIDGET(obj)`

*This macro casts a widget or an object belonging to an arbitrary class to the GtkWidget class. It is accepted practice to store the handle of a widget instance, returned by Gtk+ when the widget is created, in a variable of type GtkWidget * and then use the "object to widget cast" macro to coerce this variable to the type of class needed. We saw several examples of this in both Chapter 2, "Hello Gtk+!," and Chapter 3.*

Widget type check macro: `GTK_IS_WIDGET(obj)`

*This macro returns TRUE if the object being checked is an instance of GtkWidget; otherwise, FALSE is returned. If the variable holding the widget instance being checked is not stored in a variable of type GtkObject *, use the macro GTK_OBJECT() to coerce the variable and avoid runtime errors. For example:,*

```
GtkWidget *foo;
gboolean result;

...

result = GTK_IS_WIDGET( GTK_OBJECT( foo ) );
if ( result == TRUE ) { ... }
```

Miscellaneous Macros

Any additional macros supported by the widget class are listed as in Table 4.1.

Table 4.1 GtkWidget Miscellaneous Macros

Macro	*Description*
GTK_WIDGET_TYPE(w)	Widget type.
GTK_WIDGET_STATE(w)	Widget state (GTK_STATE_NORMAL, GTK_STATE_ACTIVE, GTK_STATE_PRELIGHT, GTK_STATE_SELECTED, GTK_STATE_INSENSITIVE).
GTK_WIDGET_SAVED_STATE(w)	Widget saved state.

Table 4.1 GtkWidget Miscellaneous Macros (Continued)

Macro	*Description*
GTK_WIDGET_FLAGS(w)	Widget flags.
GTK_WIDGET_TOPLEVEL(w)	If nonzero, it is a widget and is top-level.
GTK_WIDGET_NO_WINDOW(w)	If nonzero, it is a widget and has no window.
GTK_WIDGET_REALIZED(w)	If nonzero, it is a widget and has been realized.
GTK_WIDGET_MAPPED(w)	If nonzero, it is a widget and has been mapped.
GTK_WIDGET_VISIBLE(w)	If nonzero, it is a widget and is visible.
GTK_WIDGET_DRAWABLE(w)	If nonzero, it is a widget that is mapped and is visible.
GTK_WIDGET_SENSITIVE(w)	If nonzero, it is a widget and is sensitive.
GTK_WIDGET_PARENT_SENSITIVE(w)	If nonzero, it is a widget and its parent is sensitive.
GTK_WIDGET_IS_SENSITIVE(w)	If nonzero, it is a widget and both it and its parent are sensitive.
GTK_WIDGET_CAN_FOCUS(w)	GTK_CAN_FOCUS bit in widget flags is set.
GTK_WIDGET_HAS_FOCUS(w)	GTK_HAS_FOCUS bit in widget flags is set.
GTK_WIDGET_CAN_DEFAULT(w)	GTK_CAN_DEFAULT bit in widget flags is set.
GTK_WIDGET_HAS_DEFAULT(w)	GTK_HAS_DEFAULT bit in widget flags is set.
GTK_WIDGET_HAS_GRAB(w)	GTK_HAS_GRAB bit in widget flags is set.
GTK_WIDGET_RC_STYLE(w)	GTK_RC_STYLE bit in widget flags is set.
GTK_WIDGET_COMPOSITE_CHILD(w)	GTK_COMPOSITE_CHILD bit in widget flags is set.
GTK_WIDGET_APP_PAINTABLE(w)	GTK_APP_PAINTABLE flag in widget flags is set.
GTK_WIDGET_RECEIVES_DEFAULT(w)	GTK_RECEIVES_DEFAULT flag in widget flags is set.
GTK_WIDGET_SET_FLAGS(w,flag)	Set flag (or flags) for widget w.
GTK_WIDGET_UNSET_FLAGS(w,flag)	Clear flag (or flags) for widget w.

Signals were described in Chapter 3. Here we'll simply name the supported signals and what causes them to trigger. Table 4.2 lists the function prototypes for each of the signals.

Table 4.2 Signals

Signal Name	*Condition Causing Signal to Trigger*
show	The widget has been shown.
hide	The widget has been hidden.
map	The widget has been mapped.
unmap	The widget has been unmapped.
realize	The widget has been realized.
unrealize	The widget has been unrealized.
draw	The widget needs to be drawn.
draw_focus	The widget has focus and needs to be drawn.
draw_default	The widget has been made the default and needs to be drawn.
size_request	The widget needs to compute its requisition.
size_allocate	The widget has been allocated a size.
state_changed	The state of the widget has been changed.
parent_set	The parent of the widget has been set.
style_set	The style of the widget has been set.
add_accelerator	An accelerator was added.
remove_accelerator	An accelerator was removed.
grab_focus	The widget has grabbed the focus.
event	An X11 event has been received.
button_press_event	An X11 button press event has been received.
button_release_event	An X11 button release event has been received.
motion_notify_event	An X11 motion notify event has been received.
delete_event	An X11 window delete event has been received.
destroy_event	An X11 window destroy event has been received.
expose_event	An X11 window expose event has been received.
key_press_event	An X11 key press event has been received.
key_release_event	An X11 key release event has been received.

Table 4.2 Signals (Continued)

Signal Name	*Condition Causing Signal to Trigger*
enter_notify_event	An X11 enter notify event has been received.
leave_notify_event	An X11 leave notify event has been received.
configure_event	An X11 configure event has been received.
focus_in_event	An X11 focus in event has been received.
focus_out_event	An X11 focus out event has been received.
map_event	An X11 window map event has been received.
unmap_event	An X11 window unmap event has been received.
property_notify_event	An X11 property notify event has been received.
selection_clear_event	An X11 selection clear event has been received.
selection_request_event	An X11 selection request event has been received.
selection_notify_event	An X11 selection notify event has been received.
selection_received	The contents of a selection have been requested and received.
selection_get	A selection has been retrieved.
proximity_in_event	An XInput extension proximity in event has been received.
proximity_out_event	An XInput extension proximity out event has been received.
drag_begin	A drag has begun.
drag_motion mouse	Motion has occurred during drag and drop.
drag_leave	A drag leave event was received (e.g., the mouse left the drop site).
drag_drop	A drop has occurred.
drag_data_get	A request to the source for drag-and-drop data has been made.
drag_data_received	Data has been received by the receiving client/widget, or it has failed.
drag_data_delete	A request from the source to delete data after a drop has been made.

Table 4.2 Signals (Continued)

Signal Name	*Condition Causing Signal to Trigger*
drag_end	A drag has ended.
visibility_notify_event	An X11 visibility notify event has been received.
client_event	An X11 client event has been received.
no_expose_event	An X11 no expose event has been received.
debug_msg	A request to display a debug message has been made.

Signal Function Prototypes

This section provides the C function prototypes of the signal functions supported by the widget class. The name of the function prototype identifies the corresponding signal in the preceding table.

```
void
show(GtkWidget *widget, gpointer user_data);

void
hide(GtkWidget *widget, gpointer user_data);

void
map(GtkWidget *widget, gpointer user_data);

void
unmap(GtkWidget *widget, gpointer user_data);

void
realize(GtkWidget *widget, gpointer user_data);

void
unrealize(GtkWidget *widget, gpointer user_data);

void
draw(GtkWidget *widget, GdkRectangle *area, gpointer user_data);

void
draw_focus(GtkWidget *widget, gpointer user_data);

void
draw_default(GtkWidget *widget, gpointer user_data);

void
size_request(GtkWidget *widget, GtkRequisition *requisition, gpointer
user_data);
```

Signal Function Prototypes (Continued)

```
void
size_allocate(GtkWidget *widget, GtkAllocation *allocation, gpointer
user_data);

void
state_changed(GtkWidget *widget, GtkStateType state, gpointer
user_data);

void
parent_set(GtkWidget *widget, GtkObject *old_parent, gpointer
user_data);

void
style_set(GtkWidget *widget, GtkStyle *previous_style, gpointer
user_data);

void
add_accelerator(GtkWidget *widget, guint accel_signal_id,
GtkAccelGroup *accel_group, guint accel_key, GdkModifierType
accel_mods, GtkAccelFlags accel_flags, gpointer user_data);

void
remove_accelerator(GtkWidget *widget, GtkAccelGroup *accel_group,
guint accel_key, GdkModifierType accel_mods, gpointer user_data);

void
grab_focus(GtkWidget *widget, gpointer user_data);

gboolean
event(GtkWidget *widget, GdkEvent *event, gpointer user_data);

gboolean
button_press_event(GtkWidget *widget, GdkEventButton *event, gpointer
user_data);

gboolean
button_release_event(GtkWidget *widget, GdkEventButton *event,
gpointer user_data);

gboolean
motion_notify_event(GtkWidget *widget, GdkEventMotion *event,
gpointer user_data);
```

Signal Function Prototypes (Continued)

```
gboolean
delete_event(GtkWidget *widget, GdkEvent *event, gpointer user_data);

gboolean
destroy_event(GtkWidget *widget, GdkEvent *event, gpointer
user_data);

gboolean
expose_event(GtkWidget *widget, GdkEventExpose *event, gpointer
user_data);

gboolean
key_press_event(GtkWidget *widget, GdkEventKey *event, gpointer
user_data);

gboolean
key_release_event(GtkWidget *widget, GdkEventKey *event, gpointer
user_data);

gboolean
enter_notify_event(GtkWidget *widget, GdkEventCrossing *event,
gpointer user_data);

gboolean
leave_notify_event(GtkWidget *widget, GdkEventCrossing *event,
gpointer user_data);

gboolean
configure_event(GtkWidget *widget, GdkEventConfigure *event, gpointer
user_data);

gboolean
focus_in_event(GtkWidget *widget, GdkEventFocus *event, gpointer
user_data);

gboolean
focus_out_event(GtkWidget *widget, GdkEventFocus *event, gpointer
user_data);

gboolean
map_event(GtkWidget *widget, GdkEvent *event, gpointer user_data);

gboolean
unmap_event(GtkWidget *widget, GdkEvent *event, gpointer user_data);
```

Signal Function Prototypes (Continued)

```
gboolean
property_notify_event(GtkWidget *widget, GdkEventProperty *event,
gpointer user_data);

gboolean
selection_clear_event(GtkWidget *widget, GdkEventSelection *event,
gpointer user_data);

gboolean
selection_request_event(GtkWidget *widget, GdkEventSelection *event,
gpointer user_data);

gboolean
selection_notify_event(GtkWidget *widget, GdkEventSelection *event,
gpointer user_data);

void
selection_get(GtkWidget *widget, GtkSelectionData *data, guint info,
guint time, gpointer user_data);

void
selection_received(GtkWidget *widget, GtkSelectionData *data, guint
time, gpointer user_data);

gboolean
proximity_in_event(GtkWidget *widget, GdkEventProximity *event,
gpointer user_data);

gboolean
proximity_out_event(GtkWidget *widget, GdkEventProximity *event,
gpointer user_data);

void
drag_begin(GtkWidget *widget, GdkDragContext *drag_context, gpointer
user_data);

void
drag_end(GtkWidget *widget, GdkDragContext *drag_context, gpointer
user_data);

void
drag_data_delete(GtkWidget *widget, GdkDragContext *drag_context,
gpointer user_data);
```

Signal Function Prototypes (Continued)

```
void
drag_leave(GtkWidget *widget, GdkDragContext *drag_context, guint
time, gpointer user_data);

gboolean
drag_motion(GtkWidget *widget, GdkDragContext *drag_context, gint x,
gint y, guint time, gpointer user_data);

gboolean
drag_drop(GtkWidget *widget, GdkDragContext *drag_context, gint x,
gint y, guint time, gpointer user_data);

void
drag_data_get(GtkWidget *widget, GdkDragContext *drag_context,
GtkSelectionData *data, guint info, guint time, gpointer user_data);

void
drag_data_received(GtkWidget *widget, GdkDragContext *drag_context,
gint x, gint y, GtkSelectionData *data, guint info, guint time,
gpointer user_data);

gboolean
client_event(GtkWidget *widget, GdkEventClient *event, gpointer
user_data);

gboolean
no_expose_event(GtkWidget *widget, GdkEventNoExpose *event, gpointer
user_data);

gboolean
visibility_notify_event(GtkWidget *widget, GdkEvent *event, gpointer
user_data);

void
debug_msg(GtkWidget *widget, gchar *message, gpointer user_data);
```

Supported Arguments

See the discussion of gtk_object_setv(), gtk_object_getv(), and gtk_object_arg_get() in Chapter 3 and gtk_widget_new() and gtk_widget_newv() later in this chapter.

Prefix: `GtkWidget::`
Generally, the prefix will be of the form <class name>::.

Table 4.3 GtkWidget Arguments

Name	*Type*	*Permissions*
name	GTK_TYPE_STRING	GTK_ARG_READWRITE
parent	GTK_TYPE_CONTAINER	GTK_ARG_READWRITE
x	GTK_TYPE_INT	GTK_ARG_READWRITE
y	GTK_TYPE_INT	GTK_ARG_READWRITE
width	GTK_TYPE_INT	GTK_ARG_READWRITE
height	GTK_TYPE_INT	GTK_ARG_READWRITE
visible	GTK_TYPE_BOOL	GTK_ARG_READWRITE
sensitive	GTK_TYPE_BOOL	GTK_ARG_READWRITE
app_paintable	GTK_TYPE_BOOL	GTK_ARG_READWRITE
can_focus	GTK_TYPE_BOOL	GTK_ARG_READWRITE
has_focus	GTK_TYPE_BOOL	GTK_ARG_READWRITE
can_default	GTK_TYPE_BOOL	GTK_ARG_READWRITE
has_default	GTK_TYPE_BOOL	GTK_ARG_READWRITE
receives_default	GTK_TYPE_BOOL	GTK_ARG_READWRITE
composite_child	GTK_TYPE_BOOL	GTK_ARG_READWRITE
style	GTK_TYPE_STYLE	GTK_ARG_READWRITE
events	GTK_TYPE_GDK_EVENT_MASK	GTK_ARG_READWRITE
extension_events	GTK_TYPE_GDK_EVENT_MASK	GTK_ARG_READWRITE

Application-Level API Synopsis

In this section, the external or public functions are listed along with a brief description of the functionality that each routine provides. A later section describes each function in more detail.

Return constant GTK_TYPE_WIDGET at runtime:

```
GtkType
gtk_widget_get_type(void);
```

Create an instance of a widget of a specific type, varargs interface:

```
GtkWidget *
gtk_widget_new(GtkType type, const gchar *first_arg_name, ...);
```

Create an instance of a widget of a specific type:

```
GtkWidget *
gtk_widget_newv(GtkType type, guint nargs, GtkArg *args);
```

Increase a widget reference count by 1:

```
void
gtk_widget_ref(GtkWidget *widget);
```

Decrease a widget reference count by 1:

```
void
gtk_widget_unref(GtkWidget *widget);
```

Destroy a widget:

```
void
gtk_widget_destroy(GtkWidget *widget);
```

Set a widget pointer to NULL when the specified widget is destroyed:

```
void
gtk_widget_destroyed(GtkWidget *widget, GtkWidget **widget_pointer);
```

Get the value of a single named argument from widget:

```
void
gtk_widget_get(GtkWidget *widget, GtkArg *arg);
```

Get the values of a set of named arguments from widget:

```
void
gtk_widget_getv(GtkWidget *widget, guint nargs, GtkArg *args);
```

Set widget values, varargs interface:

```
void
gtk_widget_set(GtkWidget *widget, const gchar *first_arg_name, ...);
```

Set widget values:

```
void
gtk_widget_setv(GtkWidget *widget, guint nargs, GtkArg *args);
```

Application-Level API Synopsis (Continued)

Disassociate a widget from its parent:
```
void
gtk_widget_unparent(GtkWidget *widget);
```

Make a widget eligible for mapping. If its parent is mapped, then map it:
```
void
gtk_widget_show(GtkWidget *widget);
```

Show a widget and, if it is an unmapped top-level widget, wait for the map_event signal before returning:
```
void
gtk_widget_show_now(GtkWidget *widget);
```

Show a widget and all of its children:
```
void
gtk_widget_show_all(GtkWidget *widget);
```

Unmap a widget:
```
void
gtk_widget_hide(GtkWidget *widget);
```

If widget supports "hide all" functionality, invoke it:
```
void
gtk_widget_hide_all(GtkWidget *widget);
```

Realize a widget, if needed, and then display it:
```
void
gtk_widget_map(GtkWidget *widget);
```

Hide the window associated with the widget:
```
void
gtk_widget_unmap(GtkWidget *widget);
```

Prepare a widget and its parent, if necessary, for mapping:
```
void
gtk_widget_realize(GtkWidget *widget);
```

Unmap a widget and its children, destroying their windows:
```
void
gtk_widget_unrealize(GtkWidget *widget);
```

Add an accelerator to a widget/accelerator group:
```
void
gtk_widget_add_accelerator(GtkWidget *widget, const gchar
        *accel_signal, GtkAccelGroup *accel_group, guint accel_key,
        guint accel_mods, GtkAccelFlags accel_flags);
```

Application-Level API Synopsis (Continued)

Remove an accelerator from a widget/accelerator group:

```
void
gtk_widget_remove_accelerator(GtkWidget *widget, GtkAccelGroup
          *accel_group, guint accel_key, guint accel_mods);
```

Remove all accelerators from a widget (visible_only is unused in Gtk+ 1.2):

```
void
gtk_widget_remove_accelerators(GtkWidget *widget,
          const gchar *accel_signal, gboolean visible_only);
```

Retrieve the signal ID associated with a given accelerator:

```
guint
gtk_widget_accelerator_signal(GtkWidget *widget,
          GtkAccelGroup *accel_group, guint accel_key,
          guint accel_mods);
```

Disable the capability to add accelerators to or remove accelerators from a widget:

```
void
gtk_widget_lock_accelerators(GtkWidget *widget);
```

Re-enable the capability to add accelerators to or remove accelerators from a widget:

```
void
gtk_widget_unlock_accelerators(GtkWidget *widget);
```

Generate an event to be sent to the specified widget. Return nonzero if the widget is destroyed as a result:

```
gint
gtk_widget_event(GtkWidget *widget, GdkEvent *event);
```

If the widget supports an activate signal, generate it and return TRUE; otherwise, return FALSE:

```
gboolean
gtk_widget_activate(GtkWidget *widget);
```

Change a widget's parent to specified a widget:

```
void
gtk_widget_reparent(GtkWidget *widget, GtkWidget *new_parent);
```

Show a widget at a specific x, y location:

```
void
gtk_widget_popup(GtkWidget *widget, gint x, gint y);
```

Compute a region of intersection between a widget and a rectangle:

```
gint
gtk_widget_intersect(GtkWidget *widget, GdkRectangle *area,
         GdkRectangle *intersection);
```

Application-Level API Synopsis (Continued)

Make a widget the focus widget of its containing widget:
```
void
gtk_widget_grab_focus(GtkWidget *widget);
```

Make a widget the default widget of its containing widget:
```
void
gtk_widget_grab_default(GtkWidget *widget);
```

Set widget position:
```
void
gtk_widget_set_uposition(GtkWidget *widget, gint x, gint y);
```

Set widget size:
```
void
gtk_widget_set_usize(GtkWidget *widget, gint width, gint height);
```

Set the event solicitation mask:
```
void
gtk_widget_set_events(GtkWidget *widget, gint events);
```

Append events to the event solicitation mask:
```
void
gtk_widget_add_events(GtkWidget *widget, gint events);
```

Get the event mask associated with a widget:
```
gint
gtk_widget_get_events(GtkWidget *widget);
```

Get the top-level widget (highest ancestor in widget instance hierarchy) of widget:
```
GtkWidget *
gtk_widget_get_top-level(GtkWidget *widget);
```

Find the closest ancestor to a widget of a specific widget type:
```
GtkWidget *
gtk_widget_get_ancestor(GtkWidget *widget, GtkType widget_type);
```

Retrieve the colormap of a widget:
```
GdkColormap *
gtk_widget_get_colormap(GtkWidget *widget);
```

Retrieve the visual of a widget:
```
GdkVisual *
gtk_widget_get_visual(GtkWidget *widget);
```

Set the widget colormap (call prior to realizing widget):
```
void
gtk_widget_set_colormap(GtkWidget *widget, GdkColormap *colormap);
```

Application-Level API Synopsis (Continued)

Set the widget visual (call prior to realizing widget):

```
void
gtk_widget_set_visual(GtkWidget *widget, GdkVisual *visual);
```

Retrieve the x, y position of pointer:

```
void
gtk_widget_get_pointer(GtkWidget *widget, gint *x, gint *y);
```

Check whether a widget is an ancestor of another widget in the instance hierarchy:

```
gint
gtk_widget_is_ancestor(GtkWidget *widget, GtkWidget *ancestor);
```

Call gtk_widget_hide() and return TRUE:

```
gint
gtk_widget_hide_on_delete(GtkWidget *widget);
```

Make a widget (in)sensitive (a widget is only actually sensitive if its parent, if any, is also sensitive):

```
void
gtk_widget_set_sensitive(GtkWidget *widget, gboolean sensitive);
```

Associate a name with a widget and perform a new rc lookup if no user style for the widget is set (see text):

```
void
gtk_widget_set_name(GtkWidget *widget, const gchar *name);
```

Retrieve the name associated with a widget:

```
gchar *
gtk_widget_get_name(GtkWidget *widget);
```

Set and activate a widget's style attribute:

```
void
gtk_widget_set_style(GtkWidget *widget, GtkStyle *style);
```

Determine a widget's style from rc setting and then apply it:

```
void
gtk_widget_set_rc_style(GtkWidget *widget);
```

Make sure that either a user-defined or rc style has been applied to a widget:

```
void
gtk_widget_ensure_style(GtkWidget *widget);
```

Retrieve style data for a widget, retrieving rc style settings if needed:

```
GtkStyle *
gtk_widget_get_style(GtkWidget *widget);
```

Restore the default style of widget:

```
void
gtk_widget_restore_default_style(GtkWidget *widget);
```

Application-Level API Synopsis (Continued)

Recursively set rc style on all widgets that do not have user styles set:

```
void
gtk_widget_reset_rc_styles(GtkWidget *widget);
```

Push a style to the top of the style stack. The style will override any default styles set for the widget:

```
void
gtk_widget_push_style(GtkStyle *style);
```

Push a colormap to the top of the colormap stack. The colormap will override any default colormap set for the widget:

```
void
gtk_widget_push_colormap(GdkColormap *cmap);
```

Push a visual to the top of the visual stack. The visual will override any default visual set for the widget:

```
void
gtk_widget_push_visual(GdkVisual *visual);
```

Remove a style from a style stack:

```
void
gtk_widget_pop_style(void);
```

Remove a colormap from a colormap stack:

```
void
gtk_widget_pop_colormap(void);
```

Remove a visual from a visual stack:

```
void
gtk_widget_pop_visual(void);
```

Set the default style for a widget:

```
void
gtk_widget_set_default_style(GtkStyle *style);
```

Set the default colormap for a widget:

```
void
gtk_widget_set_default_colormap(GdkColormap *colormap);
```

Set the default visual for a widget:

```
void
gtk_widget_set_default_visual(GdkVisual *visual);
```

Retrieve the default style for a widget:

```
GtkStyle *
gtk_widget_get_default_style(void);
```

Application-Level API Synopsis (Continued)

Retrieve the default colormap for a widget:

```
GdkColormap *
gtk_widget_get_default_colormap(void);
```

Retrieve the default visual for a widget:

```
GdkVisual *
gtk_widget_get_default_visual(void);
```

Class Description

GtkWidget is the class from which all widget implementation classes in the Gtk+ widget hierarchy descend. GtkWidget provides functionality that is common to all widget classes falling below it in the Gtk+ widget class hierarchy. What makes an instance of the GtkButton widget class differ from an instance of GtkWidget is the functionality that GtkButton adds to make an instance of GtkButton look and behave as a button should. What GtkButton inherits from GtkWidget is all the code and data that make an instance of GtkButton a widget. Each and every instance of GtkButton is an instance of GtkWidget in the sense that an instance of GtkButton is able to make use of the functionality it inherits from GtkWidget.

For example, any instance of a GtkWidget can be destroyed by calling gtk_widget_destroy(). Because GtkButton is a descendant of GtkWidget, gtk_widget_destroy() can also be used to destroy an instance of GtkButton. As long as the Gtk+ class descends from GtkWidget, the GtkWidget functions and macros described here can be used for instances of the class. The relationship between a widget class and GtkWidget is also apparent by noting that most Gtk+ applications store instances of widgets, regardless of the actual widget class, in variables declared as GtkWidget *. This further substantiates the fact that all widgets can be viewed as instances of GtkWidget. This is done simply as a convenience to the programmer, mostly to eliminate the need to cast a widget instance variable to GtkWidget * when passed as an argument to functions and macros defined by GtkWidget.

Widget Creation

GtkWidget provides functions that allow you to create an instance of a widget belonging to a specific widget class. One of these functions provides a varargs interface, while the other requires that arguments be passed in as a vector. Each of these functions produces the same result; which one you use is largely a matter of personal taste.

Perhaps neither of these functions is actually used very often by application programmers. Typically, a function provided by the widget class is what most applications will call to instantiate a widget. However, using the GtkWidget interfaces allows the programmer to specify attributes of the widget instance at creation time that would normally require additional function calls using some other method. I'll return to this issue after we first take a look at the functions provided by GtkWidget.

The varargs function is gtk_widget_new():

```
GtkWidget *
gtk_widget_new(GtkType type, const gchar *first_arg_name, ...);
```

The first argument is a type that defines which widget class the instance will belong to (e.g., GtkButton). This type can be the widget type macro documented for each widget class by this book (e.g., GTK_TYPE_WINDOW), or it can be a call to the widget's type function, the name of which is formed by concatenating the string "gtk_", the class name, and "_get_type" (e.g., gtk_window_get_type() in the case of GtkWidget). It is probably better style to use the widget type macro.

The remaining arguments to gtk_widget_new() specify attributes to be assigned to the newly created widget. Each of these attributes is specified by a pair of arguments. The first of these is a string that identifies the attribute to be set. The argument that immediately follows it is the value of that attribute. The universe of attributes that can be set derives from those accepted by the widget class, by GtkWidget, or by any widget class that resides between the widget class being instantiated and GtkWidget in the class hierarchy. In the case of GtkButton, we can set values for "label", which is of type GTK_TYPE_STRING, and "relief", which is of type GTK_TYPE_RELIEF_STYLE. The arguments that can be set are defined in this book in the section "Supported Arguments" documented for each widget class. As you can see from earlier in this chapter, a large number of attributes can be set for GtkWidget, including x and y positions ("x" and "y") and the widget's width and height ("width" and "height"). The argument list is terminated by a single NULL.

For example, to create an instance of GtkButton, we might execute the following code:

```
GtkWidget *button;

...

button = gtk_widget_new( GTK_TYPE_BUTTON, "label", "Press me!",
        NULL );
```

In this example, we created a button labeled "Press me!". Here there is little advantage in using the gtk_widget_new() function to perform this task since we can make use of gtk_button_new_with_label() to perform the same thing:

```
GtkWidget *button;

...

button = gtk_button_new_with_label( "Press me!" );
```

Using gtk_button_new_with_label() is better in most cases because it is easier to read and provides a simpler interface. However, assume we want to create a button that is insensitive (e.g., the button is displayed as dimmed and does not respond to key presses). Using the GtkButton API, we would need to do the following:

```
GtkWidget *button;

...

button = gtk_button_new_with_label( "Press me!" );
gtk_widget_set_sensitive( button, FALSE );
```

Using gtk_widget_new(), this could be done using a single function call:

```
GtkWidget *button;

...

button = gtk_widget_new( GTK_TYPE_BUTTON,
         "label", "Press me!",
         "sensitive", FALSE,
         NULL );
```

There seems to be little advantage in using gtk_widget_new() in this example, but the benefit of using gtk_widget_new() increases as the number of arguments passed is increased. In the end, it is really a matter of programmer preference, but when setting more than a few attributes, it would seem to me to be easier to understand and modify a single call to gtk_widget_new() than to perform the equivalent task with a series of function calls, one for each attribute of the widget being set. The choice of using gtk_widget_new() or the functions provided by the widget class is again up to you to make.

The second function for creating a widget is gtk_widget_newv():

```
GtkWidget *
gtk_widget_newv(GtkType type, guint nargs, GtkArg *args);
```

The only difference between gtk_widget_new() and gtk_widget_newv() is in how the arguments are passed. The first argument to gtk_widget_newv() is the type of the widget to be created, specified exactly the same as for gtk_widget_new(). The second argument, nargs, is the number of arguments being passed. The final argument is a vector containing nargs arguments, each of type GtkArg. The use of GtkArg was described in Chapter 3 when gtk_object_setv() was introduced. Unless you are working with a vector of GtkArg values that was obtained through some other means (such as a call to gtk_object_getv()), I recommend that you avoid using gtk_widget_newv() and instead use gtk_widget_new(), which has a much simpler interface (this is assuming that the widget creation function exposed by the widget class is not the best alternative of all, using the guidelines previously provided).

Widget Reference Counts

A widget can have its reference count increased and decreased by one by a call to gtk_widget_ref() and get_widget_unref(), respectively:

```
void
gtk_widget_ref(GtkWidget *widget);

void
gtk_widget_unref (GtkWidget *widget);
```

When a widget is first created, it is given a reference count of one. If the reference count of a widget goes to zero, the widget will be destroyed. Destroying a widget in this manner is not recommended, however (use gtk_widget_destroy(); see the next section). You should make sure that calls to gtk_widget_ref() and gtk_widget_unref() are matched evenly.

Increasing the reference count of a widget ensures that it will persist during some operation that might otherwise lead to the destruction of the widget. Internally, Gtk+ does this in several places. One example is when Gtk+ handles a delete event in its main loop, as exhibited by the following code:

```
switch (event->type) {
        case GDK_DELETE:
                gtk_widget_ref (event_widget);
                if (!gtk_widget_event (event_widget, event) &&
                    !GTK_OBJECT_DESTROYED (event_widget))
                        gtk_widget_destroy (event_widget);
                gtk_widget_unref (event_widget);
                break;
```

In the preceding code, it is possible for the call to gtk_widget_event() to result in destruction of the widget or, if there was some failure, for the widget to still exist after the function returns and then need to be destroyed explicitly. To test whether the destruction actually occurred, the code checks both the return value from gtk_widget_event() and the widget's "object destroyed" attribute, which can only be done if the widget persists after the call to gtk_widget_destroy() was made. This is ensured by increasing the reference count of the widget by one before gtk_widget_event() is called. If the widget destruction is successful in gtk_widget_event(), the widget will still exist because the reference count is nonzero, but the call to gtk_widget_unref() will cause the widget destruction to occur. If, on the other hand, the call to gtk_widget_event() fails and the object was not destroyed, gtk_widget_destroy(), which is called in this case, will still not result in widget destruction until the call to gtk_widget_unref() is made and the reference count goes down to zero.

Destroying Widgets

To destroy a widget, applications can call gtk_widget_destroy():

```
void
gtk_widget_destroy(GtkWidget *widget);
```

The function gtk_widget_destroy() takes a single argument, a pointer to a widget. Calling this function causes the widget to be destroyed, assuming that its reference count goes to zero, as previously discussed. Otherwise, the first subsequent call to gtk_widget_unref() that reduces the widget's reference count to zero will result in the actual destruction of the widget.

A call to gtk_widget_destroy(), regardless of whether or not the widget is actually destroyed, will cause the following actions to be performed:

- Widget implementation-specific destruction code will be invoked, if any.
- Any grab that the widget may have is released.
- The reference count of the style object associated with the widget will be decreased by one. Styles will be discussed later in this chapter. If the count goes to zero, the style object will be destroyed.
- The destroy method of the parent class will be called.

GtkWidget defines a convenience routine that you can arrange to have called at the time a widget is destroyed. This routine, gtk_widget_destroyed(), has the following prototype:

```
void
gtk_widget_destroyed(GtkWidget *widget, GtkWidget **widget_pointer);
```

The first argument is the widget being destroyed; the second is a pointer to a variable in your code of type GtkWidget *. As an application programmer, you never call this routine directly. Instead, you register this function as a destroy signal handler or callback using gtk_signal_connect(). The following code, adapted from testgtk.c in the Gtk+ distribution, illustrates a typical use for this feature:

```
01  void MyCreateWindow( void ) {
02
03  static GtkWidget *mywindow = (GtkWidget *) NULL;
04
05  if (!window) {
06          mywindow = gtk_window_new (GTK_WINDOW_TOPLEVEL);
07
08          gtk_signal_connect (GTK_OBJECT (mywindow), "destroy",
09                    GTK_SIGNAL_FUNC (gtk_widget_destroyed), &mywindow);
```

On line 03, we declare a GtkWidget * variable named mywindow as a static; thus, the variable and its value will persist across calls to MyCreateWindow(). The first time MyCreateWindow() is called, mywindow will have a value of NULL, and this will cause the code in lines 06 through 09 to be invoked. On line 06, a new top-level window is created, and the handle for that window returned by Gtk+ is stored in mywindow. The next time a call is made into MyCreateWindow(), the value of mywindow will be non-NULL (assuming the window was not destroyed), so the code on lines 06 through 09 will not be invoked. The lines we are most interested in for this discussion are lines 08 and 09. Here, a call is made to gtk_signal_connect() (discussed in Chapter 3) to add gtk_widget_destroyed() to the list of functions invoked when a destroy signal is received by the widget. Signal functions are passed two arguments, as discussed in Chapter 3: The handle of the widget receiving the signal is the first argument, and the second argument passed to the signal function is the final argument passed to gtk_signal_connect(). The implementation of gtk_widget_destroyed() in Gtk+ 1.2 is simply:

```
void
gtk_widget_destroyed (GtkWidget *widget, GtkWidget **widget_pointer)
{
  /* Don't make any assumptions about the
   * value of widget!
   * Even check widget_pointer.
   */
  if (widget_pointer)
    *widget_pointer = NULL;
}
```

The effect of all this is that upon widget destruction, the static variable named mywindow will be set to NULL. The very next time MyCreateWindow() is invoked, a new window will be created because the expression !window, on line 05, will evaluate to be non-zero (TRUE).

Manipulating Widget Arguments

As we saw in the beginning of this section, GtkWidget supports many arguments. GtkWidget provides convenience routines that allow an application to set and get values of these arguments. Because these functions are largely wrappers to functions provided by GtkObject that were discussed in Chapter 3, I will not spend much time on them here other than to mention how they map to equivalent routines in GtkObject().

The first function, gtk_widget_get(), allows an application to retrieve the value of a single argument defined for a widget. The function prototype is as follows:

```
void
gtk_widget_get(GtkWidget *widget, GtkArg *arg);
```

The following code:

```
GtkWidget *widget;
GtkArg myArg;

gtk_widget_get( widget, &myArg );
```

is equivalent to:

```
GtkWidget *widget;
GtkArg myArg;

gtk_object_getv (GTK_OBJECT (widget), 1, &myArg);
```

Before calling gtk_widget_get(), you must fill in fields of the GtkArg struct that is passed. See the discussion of gtk_object_getv() in Chapter 3 for more details.

To get multiple argument values from a widget, call gtk_widget_getv(). The only difference between gtk_widget_getv() and gtk_widget_get() is a vector of GtkArg variables, and its size (cardinality, not size in bytes) is passed as arguments. Like gtk_widget_get(), gtk_widget_getv() calls gtk_object_getv(), only with a vector and count that are greater than one (typically) in size and value. The following is the prototype of gtk_widget_getv():

```
void
gtk_widget_getv(GtkWidget *widget, guint nargs, GtkArg *args);
```

This is the same prototype for gtk_object_getv(), but the first argument to gtk_object_getv() is GtkObject *, not GtkWidget *.

Widget arguments can also be set with a varargs interface with gtk_widget_set():

```
void
gtk_widget_set(GtkWidget *widget, const gchar *first_arg_name, ...);
```

The equivalent GtkObject routine is gtk_object_set(). The prototypes for these two functions are the same, except that gtk_object_set() takes a GtkObject * as its first argument, while gtk_widget_set() takes a GtkWidget *.

Finally, there is gtk_widget_setv():

```
void
gtk_widget_setv(GtkWidget *widget, guint nargs, GtkArg *args);
```

Calling gtk_widget_setv() is equivalent to calling gtk_object_setv(), except that, as you might have guessed, the first argument to gtk_object_setv() is a pointer to a GtkObject, not to a GtkWidget.

Note that for all of these functions, you should feel free to make a call to the GtkObject function if it is more convenient. Just remember that if you are dealing with a variable of type GtkWidget *, you will need to cast the widget pointer it holds to a GtkObject *, which is best done using the macro GTK_OBJECT as in the following example:

```
GtkWidget *foo;
GtkArg args;
guint size;

...

gtk_object_setv( GTK_OBJECT( foo ), size, &args[0] );
```

Realizing, Mapping, and Drawing Widgets

One area of confusion for new Gtk+ (and Xt/Motif) programmers is understanding the distinction between "realizing" a widget and "mapping" a widget. Before I introduce the next several functions, I would like to briefly clarify exactly what these two terms mean.

The good news is that, for the most part, you don't really need to know what the distinction is if you don't want to. Generally speaking, the only routines you need to be aware of to write a Gtk+ application are gtk_widget_show*() and gtk_widget_hide*(), which are discussed later in this chapter.

To realize a widget in Gtk+ effectively means to create the X window it will occupy upon being drawn. To map a window means to make it visible on the screen. GDK provides the routines that perform the actual work of creating a window and making it visible; these routines are used by Gtk+ and are themselves layered above X11, so ultimately the behavior of Gtk+ is dependent on that of X11. In X11, the creation of a window and its display are separate actions. One of the reasons for this separation is efficiency. X11 (and Gtk+) is a network-based GUI technology, which means that the application generating the user interface and the device displaying the user interface can be running on separate machines on a network, an intranet, or the Internet. Because of this separation and the inefficiencies it implies, it is in the best interest of the toolkit and application programmers to reduce the amount of traffic sent across the network between the application and the display server. One way to do this is to separate the operations of creating and destroying a window from the operations of making it visible or hidden. Granted, efficiency is not the only reason for this separation; as it turns out, other UI toolkits such as Mac Toolbox also provide this separation at the API level. But in X, the efficiency results can often be a big win. In Win32, a warning or message is usually displayed by a call to MessageBox(). MessageBox() creates and displays a modal dialog that is destroyed when dismissed by the user. In a network environment, inefficiencies in this approach may not matter in the case of a message dialog being displayed once or twice by an application, but they quickly increase their influence on the user if all dialogs in the application adopt the same approach.

Also, bear in mind that a typical message dialog has several windows and widgets associated with it. This includes the containing window or dialog, the push button that is pressed by the user to dismiss the dialog, and two label widgets: one used to display the message text and another used to display the label on the button used to dismiss the dialog.

Here is a routine I coded for my freeware application, sportslog, which I call to display a message dialog. I called it, appropriately, MessageBox():

Listing 4.1 MessageBox()

```
#include <gtk/gtk.h>

/*
 * Simple MessageBox
 */

void
MessageBox( char *message )
{
        GtkWidget *label, *button, *dialog_window;

        dialog_window = gtk_dialog_new();
        gtk_window_position (GTK_WINDOW (dialog_window),
                GTK_WIN_POS_MOUSE);

        gtk_signal_connect (GTK_OBJECT (dialog_window), "destroy",
                GTK_SIGNAL_FUNC(gtk_widget_destroyed), &dialog_window);

        gtk_window_set_title (GTK_WINDOW (dialog_window), "Message");
        gtk_container_border_width (GTK_CONTAINER (dialog_window), 0);
```

```
08        button = gtk_button_new_with_label ("OK");
09        GTK_WIDGET_SET_FLAGS (button, GTK_CAN_DEFAULT);
10        gtk_box_pack_start (
11                GTK_BOX (GTK_DIALOG (dialog_window)->action_area),
12                button, TRUE, TRUE, 0);
13        gtk_signal_connect_object (GTK_OBJECT (button), "clicked",
14                GTK_SIGNAL_FUNC (gtk_widget_destroy),
15                        GTK_OBJECT (dialog_window));

16        label = gtk_label_new (message);
17        gtk_misc_set_padding (GTK_MISC (label), 10, 10);
18        gtk_box_pack_start (GTK_BOX (GTK_DIALOG (dialog_window)->vbox),
19                label, TRUE, TRUE, 0);
20        gtk_widget_grab_default (button);
21        gtk_widget_show_all (dialog_window);
}
```

Each time I call this routine, several widgets are created. First, a dialog is created on line 01. Next, a button (and its label) are created on line 08. Finally, on line 16, a label widget is created to display the text of the message. When the user dismisses the dialog, each of these widgets is, in turn, destroyed and must be created once again. For each widget creation, we must realize the widget (create a window); this results in traffic between the X server and the application. We must also map or display each window, which is additional traffic (the call to gtk_widget_show_all(), on line 21, results in calls to map each of the widgets that are children of the dialog, including the OK button and the message label).

A more efficient alternative is the following, regardless of our being on the network or not. It assumes that we are displaying only one message window at a time, which is a fair assumption to make.

Listing 4.2 A More Efficient MessageBox()

```
#include <gtk/gtk.h>

/*
 * Simple MessageBox, more efficient
 */

void
MessageBox( char *message )
{
static GtkWidget *label, *button, *dialog_window = (GtkWidget *) NULL;

if ( dialog_window == (GtkWidget *) NULL ) {
      dialog_window = gtk_dialog_new();

      gtk_signal_connect (GTK_OBJECT (dialog_window), "destroy",
              GTK_SIGNAL_FUNC(gtk_widget_destroyed), &dialog_window);
```

```
08
09       gtk_window_set_title (GTK_WINDOW (dialog_window), "Message");
10       gtk_container_border_width (GTK_CONTAINER (dialog_window), 0);
11
12       button = gtk_button_new_with_label ("OK");
13               GTK_WIDGET_SET_FLAGS (button, GTK_CAN_DEFAULT);
14       gtk_box_pack_start (
15               GTK_BOX (GTK_DIALOG (dialog_window)->action_area),
16               button, TRUE, TRUE, 0);
17       gtk_signal_connect_object (GTK_OBJECT (button), "clicked",
18               GTK_SIGNAL_FUNC (gtk_widget_hide_all),
19               GTK_OBJECT (dialog_window));
20
21       label = gtk_label_new (message);
22       gtk_misc_set_padding (GTK_MISC (label), 10, 10);
23       gtk_box_pack_start (GTK_BOX (GTK_DIALOG (dialog_window)->vbox),
24               label, TRUE, TRUE, 0);
25 } else
26       gtk_label_set_text( label, message );
27
28 gtk_window_position (GTK_WINDOW (dialog_window), GTK_WIN_POS_MOUSE);
29 gtk_widget_grab_default (button);
30 gtk_widget_show_all (dialog_window);
}
```

The differences in this version of MessageBox() start on line 01, where the GtkWidget * variables are all declared to be static. The first reason for doing this is seen on line 03. Here, a check is made to see if the variable dialog is NULL. If it is NULL, then this is the first call to MessageBox(). (There is another possible reason that the dialog can be NULL; I will mention how a little later.) Because it is the first call, we can perform each of the following tasks that are performed by lines 04 through 24:

- Create a dialog.
- Set dialog attributes (such as name).
- Create a button with an OK label.
- Set the button attributes.
- Create a label for the message and set its value.

The dialog, button, and label widgets are stored in static variables and will be available the next time MessageBox() is called. On line 28, the window is positioned based on the current mouse position, the button is made the default widget for the dialog, and each of the widget's windows are realized and mapped by calling gtk_widget_show_all().

On lines 06 and 07, a call is made to gtk_signal_connect to associate the destroy signal for the dialog with the routine gtk_widget_destroyed() in a manner identical to that described earlier when gtk_widget_destroyed() was introduced. If for some reason the dialog (and, as a result, its children) is destroyed, the "dialog" static variable will be cleared so that the following call to our MessageBox() routine will result in a new window being created. It may be that the user decides to dismiss the MessageBox dialog by using a window manager control as opposed to clicking the OK button; this will result in destruction of the widget, which we must detect in this case and handle. Another way to handle this situation would be to register a GDK_DELETE handler for the widget and deny the user the ability to close the window in the handler. This is an acceptable way, but it reduces the flexibility of the user to dismiss the dialog in the way he or she chooses.

On lines 17 through 19, we arrange for gtk_widget_hide_all() (discussed in the next section) to be called when the OK button is clicked. The handle for the dialog widget will be passed as an argument to gtk_widget_hide_all(), which will unmap the dialog and the windows of its children widgets (the OK button and the message label). To redisplay the dialog and the children, we simply need to remap the dialog. This is discussed in the next paragraph.

Let's see what happens the second time MessageBox() is called (we assume that the dialog was not destroyed somehow, in which case "dialog" will be NULL and we revert back to the logic previously described). In this case, dialog will be non-NULL, and we skip all of the code on lines 04 through 24. As previously mentioned, to cause the dialog to redisplay, we need to remap the dialog and its children. Before we do that, however, we change the label of the button to reflect the message passed into MessageBox() with a call to gtk_label_set_text() on line 26. We then set the position of the window to reflect the current mouse position, which very likely has changed since the last time the message dialog was displayed, make the button the default widget for the dialog, and display the dialog and its children. This is all done on lines 28 through 30, exactly as was done when the message dialog was first created. However, there is one difference: In the call to gtk_widget_show_all(), Gtk+ only needs to map the widgets (instead of realizing and mapping them) because their windows were not destroyed when the user dismissed the dialog that last time it was shown.

Showing Widgets

By now you should have an understanding of the calls I am about to discuss that are related to widget realizing and mapping, so let's take a look at them in detail.

The first routine is gtk_widget_show():

```
void
gtk_widget_show(GtkWidget *widget);
```

The function gtk_widget_show() performs two operations. The first of these is to realize the widget (i.e., create its window), but only if the widget has not already been realized. The second is to map the widget (i.e., make the widget visible) and arrange for its content to be drawn.

Only the widget you specified as an argument will be realized and mapped. If that widget is a dialog, for example, and has children that are not yet realized and mapped, these child widgets will not be shown. These widgets can be displayed individually via separate calls to gtk_widget_show(), or you can call gtk_widget_show_all() as described later in this section.

A related function, gtk_widget_show_now(), will show a widget and, if it is an unmapped top-level widget, wait until a map_event signal, indicating that the window is visible, is received before returning:

```
void
gtk_widget_show_now(GtkWidget *widget);
```

As previously stated, calling gtk_widget_show() on a widget containing child widgets that are not yet shown (realized and mapped) will not cause the child widgets to be shown. The scenario is illustrated by the following code, which creates a dialog, creates a button, and then adds the button to the dialog as a child widget:

```
GtkWidget *dialog;
GtkWidget *button;

...

dialog = gtk_dialog_new();
button = gtk_button_new_with_label( "Press me!" );
gtk_box_pack_start (GTK_BOX (GTK_DIALOG (dialog)->action_area),
        button, TRUE, TRUE, 0);
gtk_widget_show( dialog );

...
```

Here, the dialog will show, but the button will not be visible because the code did not call gtk_widget_show() for the button. A way to fix this problem would be to call gtk_widget_show() for the button, and often this is exactly what is done. Another way to solve the problem would be to display the dialog widget with a call to gtk_widget_show_all():

```
void
gtk_widget_show_all(GtkWidget *widget);
```

Calling gtk_widget_show_all() will ensure that any widgets that are children of the widget being shown will be shown as well. Whether you use gtk_widget_show_all() on the parent window or gtk_widget_show() on each of the child widgets is largely a matter of convenience and personal preference on your part.

Hiding Widgets

To hide a widget, making it invisible to the user (also known as unmapping a widget), call gtk_widget_hide():

```
void
gtk_widget_hide(GtkWidget *widget);
```

The function gtk_widget_hide() takes a single argument: the widget to hide. gtk_widget_hide() does the opposite task of gtk_widget_map(). The widget's window is unmapped, but the window remains realized; it is not destroyed. You may be wondering how hiding a parent widget affects its child widgets. We now know that showing a parent widget with gtk_widget_show() does not cause the child widgets to show. But does hiding a parent widget cause the child widgets to disappear? In our previous example, where we have a push button child of a dialog, the answer is yes. If there is a parent/child relationship, then hiding the parent will cause the child widget(s) to be hidden as well.

Some widget classes implement a "hide all" function. To be precise, all widget classes have this entry point, but most widget classes do not implement this function and instead inherit from GtkWidget. In GtkWidget, the two entry points implement the same semantics because effectively gtk_widget_show() is called by the "hide all" function.

There are a few widget classes that, at the time of this writing, implement a "hide all" API. These are GtkContainer, GtkMenu, GtkMenuItem, GtkOptionMenu, and GtkWidget. The function prototype for gtk_widget_hide_all() is:

```
void
gtk_widget_hide_all(GtkWidget *widget);
```

Finally, we have gtk_widget_hide_on_delete():

```
gint
gtk_widget_hide_on_delete(GtkWidget *widget);
```

The routine gtk_widget_hide_on_delete() calls gtk_widget_hide() and returns the value TRUE.

We know that showing a widget means to realize it and then map it and that hiding a widget means to unmap it. GtkWidget allows you to perform each of these tasks independently by exposing the following functions: gtk_widget_map(), gtk_widget_unmap(), and gtk_widget_realize(). There is little difference between gtk_widget_show() and gtk_widget_map(); both will realize the window if it has not been realized yet and then map the window. However, in the case of gtk_widget_show(), the mapping only occurs if, when the widget has a parent, that parent is mapped. gtk_widget_map(), on the other hand, maps the window with no strings attached. Both gtk_widget_unmap() and gtk_widget_realize() do generally what you might expect; gtk_widget_unmap() will hide the widget, and gtk_widget_realize() will realize the widget (i.e., create the widget's window and set the state of the widget to realized). Here are the function prototypes:

```
void
gtk_widget_map(GtkWidget *widget);

void
gtk_widget_unmap(GtkWidget *widget);

void
gtk_widget_realize(GtkWidget *widget);
```

Unrealizing a widget is the opposite of realizing and mapping a widget. The widget, if visible, will be unmapped, and its window will be destroyed. If the widget is a container widget (e.g., it manages child widgets), then each of the child widgets it manages is unrealized as well. The function prototype for gtk_widget_unrealize() is what you might expect:

```
void
gtk_widget_unrealize(GtkWidget *widget);
```

Accelerators and Mnemonics

Accelerators provide a way for Gtk+ application programmers to associate menu and menu-item selection with "command-key equivalents" that will activate a menu or menu item without requiring the user to rely on a mouse or pointing device. In some cases, it may be a requirement for the user interface to be operated solely via keyboard input due to restrictions imposed by the operating environment (for example, the application is going to be run in an environment where space is very limited or the hardware is specialized and a mouse cannot be provided). More commonly, users will often demand support for accelerators because many end users find it more efficient to use shortcuts to select menu items versus using a mouse. Accelerators provide a solution for users that may be experiencing trouble with their pointing device due to device failure or, in the case of touchpad mice, erratic behavior that will occur should the users' fingers become excessively moist. Some users will not become proficient with a touchpad mouse without significant practice and may prefer to use the keyboard until proficiency has been attained.

Support for keyboard shortcuts, menus, and menu items is fairly consistent among Motif applications, although there are exceptions. Users of Motif applications have come to expect not only that File, Edit, and Help menus exist in the menu bar, but that these menus can be activated by selecting Alt+F, Alt+E, and Alt+H, respectively. Users also expect that once a menu has become active, any other menu on the menu bar can be made active by traversing the items in the menu bar using the right and left arrow keys. Once a menu is active, users also expect to be able to traverse through its items using the up and down arrow keys. Finally, once the user has highlighted a desired menu item, the expectation is that the menu item will activate once the Enter key has been pressed. This consistency is due to the Open Software Foundation (OSF) having the foresight to define a style guide for programmers.

The *OSF/Motif Style Guide* defines a base set of menus, menu items, and command-key mnemonics that should be present or used by OSF/Motif applications. However, a similar style guide does not exist for Gtk+. Because it is said that Gtk+ is Motif-like, I rely on the *OSF/Motif Style Guide* as the basis for the decisions I make regarding menus, their placement, and the mnemonics that the menus and menu items map to. I realize that my Gtk+ applications often will be sharing the desktop with OSF/Motif applications from time to time. By adopting OSF/Motif style guidelines as much as possible, I am making my application much easier to use for users that have Motif application experience. Also, I will be making it easier for my users to transition to a Motif-based application in the future.

In this book, when I use the term "mnemonic," I am referring to a command-key equivalent or shortcut. For example, the mnemonic that activates the File menu is Alt+F, and the mnemonic that activates the File menu Open menu item is Ctrl+O. This is consistent with OSF/Motif usage and puts both Motif and Gtk+ on a level playing field. When I use the term "accelerator," I am referring to the Gtk+ feature used by application developers to implement mnemonics.

In this chapter, I won't provide a comprehensive discussion of menu bars, menus, menu items, or accelerators. These subjects will be covered in far more detail in a later chapter. Here we are simply concerned with documenting the functions that GtkWidget provides that relate to accelerators and accelerator groups.

Accelerator Groups

An accelerator group is an object you associate with a widget that you want to respond to mnemonics key presses. This widget must be either an instance of GtkWindow (or one of its descendants) or an instance of GtkMenuShell (or one of its descendants).

To create an accelerator group, you must call gtk_accel_group_new(). Once the accelerator group has been created, it can be associated with a window by calling gtk_accel_group_attach(). The following code illustrates how to create an accelerator group and associate it with a window object:

```
GtkWidget *window;
GtkAccelGroup *accel_group;

window = gtk_window_new();
accel_group = gtk_accel_group_new ();
gtk_accel_group_attach (accel_group, GTK_OBJECT (window));
```

Once you have an accelerator group and it is associated with a window, you add mnemonics to one of its child widgets by calling gtk_widget_add_accelerator():

```
void
gtk_widget_add_accelerator(GtkWidget *widget,
          const gchar *accel_signal, GtkAccelGroup *accel_group,
          guint accel_key, guint accel_mods,
          GtkAccelFlags accel_flags);
```

Here, widget is the widget we had associated with the accelerator group by the call to gtk_accel_group_attach() (or one of its child widgets). The argument signal is a signal supported by the widget class that will trigger when the mnemonic is detected. The argument accel_group is the accelerator group to which the mnemonic is being added. The argument accel_key is the key that represents the mnemonic. The argument accel_mods is a bitmask of modifier keys, if any, that must be present when accel_key is pressed in order for the signal to be triggered. Finally, accel_flags is a bitmask consisting of one or more of the flags listed in Table 4.4.

Table 4.4 Accel_flags Bitmask Values

Flag	*Meaning*
GTK_ACCEL_VISIBLE	The mnemonic should be displayed by the widget, if supported by the widget.
GTK_ACCEL_SIGNAL_VISIBLE	The signal associated with the mnemonic should be displayed by the widget, if supported by the widget.
GTK_ACCEL_LOCKED	This entry cannot be removed from accelerator group, replaced, or modified.

Examples of widgets capable of displaying the mnemonic and the signal as of this writing include GtkCheckMenuItem, GtkMenuItem, and GtkRadioMenuItem. For other widgets, specifying GTK_ACCEL_VISIBLE and GTK_ACCEL_SIGNAL_VISIBLE is a no-op.

The following code associates hitting the F1 key with the "clicked" signal of a button widget. The "clicked" signal will normally trigger when the button has focus and the Return key is pressed, or when mouse button 1 is clicked. Here, we cause the button's "clicked" signal to trigger when the dialog has focus (not just the button) and the F1 key is pressed. Although typically mnemonics are associated with menus and menu items, this code illustrates that they can also be used in association with other widget types.

Listing 4.3 Accelerator Example

```
#include <gtk/gtk.h>
#include <stdio.h>
#include <gdk/gdkkeysyms.h>

static void
ClickedCallback(GtkWidget *widget, GtkWidget *dialog_window)
{
        fprintf( stderr, "In ClickedCallback\n" );
        fflush( stderr );
}

main( int argc, char *argv[] )
{
        GtkWidget *button, *dialog_window;
        GtkAccelGroup *accel_group;

        accel_group = gtk_accel_group_new();

        gtk_init( &argc, &argv );

        dialog_window = gtk_dialog_new();
        gtk_window_position (GTK_WINDOW (dialog_window), GTK_WIN_POS_MOUSE);

        button = gtk_button_new_with_label ("Press me!");

        gtk_accel_group_attach(accel_group, GTK_OBJECT(dialog_window));
        gtk_widget_add_accelerator(button, "clicked", accel_group, GDK_F1, 0,
                GTK_ACCEL_LOCKED );

        GTK_WIDGET_SET_FLAGS (button, GTK_CAN_DEFAULT);
        gtk_window_set_default( GTK_WINDOW( dialog_window ), button );
        gtk_box_pack_start (GTK_BOX (
                GTK_DIALOG (dialog_window)->action_area),
                button, TRUE, TRUE, 0);
        gtk_signal_connect (GTK_OBJECT (button), "clicked",
                GTK_SIGNAL_FUNC(ClickedCallback), button);

        gtk_widget_show_all (dialog_window);
```

```
        gtk_main();
}
```

A mnemonic can be removed from an accelerator group, assuming it is not locked, by calling gtk_widget_remove_accelerator():

```
void
gtk_widget_remove_accelerator(GtkWidget *widget,
        GtkAccelGroup *accel_group,
        guint accel_key, guint accel_mods);
```

The arguments widget, accel_group, accel_key, and accel_mods are the same arguments that were passed to gtk_widget_add_accelerator(), and they are used to identify the accelerator to be removed. If the accelerator exists and is not locked (by virtue of the GTK_ACCEL_LOCKED flag specified at creation time or because of a call made to gtk_widget_lock_accelerators(), see the following), it will be removed from the specified accelerator group.

Accelerators with the GTK_ACCEL_VISIBLE flag set that also trigger a specified signal can be removed by calling gtk_widget_remove_accelerators():

```
void
gtk_widget_remove_accelerators(GtkWidget *widget,
        const gchar *accel_signal, gboolean visible_only);
```

The arguments widget and accel_signal correspond to the same arguments that were passed to gtk_widget_add_accelerator(). The argument visible_only is unused in Gtk+ 1.2 and presumably later releases.

Given a widget, an accel_group, an accel_key, and accel_mods arguments passed to gtk_widget_add_accelerator(), an application can determine the signal associated with the mnemonic by calling gtk_widget_accelerator_signal(). The returned value, of type guint, is the same value that would be returned by passing the accel_signal argument passed to gtk_widget_add_accelerator() as an argument to gtk_signal_lookup(). For example:

```
guint    signal_id;

gtk_widget_add_accelerator(button, "clicked", accel_group, GDK_F1, 0,
        GTK_ACCEL_LOCKED);
signal_id = gtk_widget_accelerator_signal(button, accel_group,
        GDK_F1,GTK_ACCEL_LOCKED);
```

The function prototype for gtk_widget_accelerator_signal() is as follows:

```
guint
gtk_widget_accelerator_signal(GtkWidget *widget,
        GtkAccelGroup *accel_group,
        guint accel_key, guint accel_mods);
```

To disable the ability for accelerators to be added to or removed from a given widget, call gtk_widget_lock_accelerators():

```
void
gtk_widget_lock_accelerators(GtkWidget *widget);
```

Once gtk_widget_lock_accelerators() has been called, its effects can be undone by calling gtk_widget_unlock_accelerators():

```
void
gtk_widget_unlock_accelerators(GtkWidget *widget);
```

Notice that the preceding calls are no-ops if the GTK_ACCEL_LOCKED attribute was set at the time the accelerator was created. These functions are designed to give applications the ability to temporarily lock and unlock the accelerators on a widget that were not created with the GTK_ACCEL_LOCKED flag set, should that be deemed necessary.

Event-Related Functions

Events can be sent by an application to a widget by calling gtk_widget_event():

```
gint
gtk_widget_event(GtkWidget *widget, GdkEvent *event);
```

The first argument is the target widget; the second is a pointer to an event structure of type GdkEvent. The following code from GtkDrawingArea provides a usage example and illustrates, in a fairly generic way, how a call to gtk_widget_event() might be made:

```
static void
gtk_drawing_area_send_configure (GtkDrawingArea *darea)
{
  GtkWidget *widget;
  GdkEventConfigure event;

  widget = GTK_WIDGET (darea);

  event.type = GDK_CONFIGURE;
  event.window = widget->window;
  event.x = widget->allocation.x;
  event.y = widget->allocation.y;
  event.width = widget->allocation.width;
  event.height = widget->allocation.height;

  gtk_widget_event (widget, (GdkEvent*) &event);
}
```

This routine allocates a GdkEventConfigure structure on the stack, fills in its fields, and then uses gtk_widget_event() to dispatch the event to the target GtkDrawingArea widget instance that was passed to gtk_drawing_area_send_configure() as an argument. The important thing to note here is that, although gtk_widget_event() takes a GdkEvent * as its second argument, you will always be passing a pointer to a more specific GDK event structure that, as in this example, you will cast to GtkEvent *.

One place in which GtkDrawingArea makes a call to this routine is at the end of its internal realize function, which is called when the widget is realized (i.e., its window is created, as discussed earlier in this chapter). The end result of sending this event is that GtkWindow will receive and process the event in its configure event handling code, thus allowing it to handle aspects of the configure event. For example, if the window needs to be redrawn because its contents have become invalid due to the configure event (e.g., it was resized), GtkWidget will itself make a call to gtk_widget_event(), this time to send an expose event back to the widget. It is the responsibility of the expose event handler in GtkWidget to handle redrawing of the window's content by invoking the proper routine to handle the event. GtkDrawingArea doesn't handle expose events itself, which is why GtkWidget once again comes into play.

Although there are places within the Gtk+ implementation where making calls into gtk_widget_event() makes sense, does it make sense for application programs to call it? The answer probably will be "no" more often than not, but there might be special circumstances in which it might be useful.

Two routines exposed by GtkWidget can be used to solicit events of interest to the application. The first of these, gtk_widget_set_events(), was described in Chapter 3, "Signals, Events, Objects, and Types." Its function prototype is as follows:

```
void
gtk_widget_set_events(GtkWidget *widget, gint events);
```

widget is the handle of the widget for which event interest is being expressed. events is a bitmask containing the logical or of one or more of the following values: GDK_EXPOSURE_MASK, GDK_POINTER_MOTION_MASK, GDK_POINTER_MOTION_HINT_MASK, GDK_BUTTON_MOTION_MASK, GDK_BUTTON1_MOTION_MASK, GDK_BUTTON2_MOTION_MASK, GDK_BUTTON3_MOTION_MASK, GDK_BUTTON_PRESS_MASK, GDK_BUTTON_RELEASE_MASK, GDK_KEY_PRESS_MASK, GDK_KEY_RELEASE_MASK, GDK_ENTER_NOTIFY_MASK, GDK_LEAVE_NOTIFY_MASK, GDK_FOCUS_CHANGE_MASK, GDK_STRUCTURE_MASK, GDK_PROPERTY_CHANGE_MASK, GDK_VISIBILITY_NOTIFY_MASK, GDK_PROXIMITY_IN_MASK, GDK_PROXIMITY_OUT_MASK, and GDK_SUBSTRUCTURE_MASK.

A special value, GDK_ALL_EVENTS_MASK, represents the set of all masks listed here. Refer to Chapter 3 for explanations of each of these masks.

You can also append events to the list of currently solicited events for a widget by calling gtk_widget_add_events():

```
void
gtk_widget_add_events(GtkWidget *widget, gint events);
```

As before, widget is the handle of the widget for which the event mask is to be modified, and events is a bitmask that contains a logical or of the same values previously described for gtk_widget_set_events().

At any time, an application can query the events solicited for a widget by calling gtk_widget_get_events():

```
gint
```

```
gtk_wiget_get_events(GtkWidget *widget);
```

The argument widget specifies the widget being queried for its event mask. You can use gtk_widget_get_events() and get_widget_set_events() to implement a function that clears one or more events in a widgets event mask:

```
gint
ClearEvents( GtkWidget *widget, gint events )
{
        gint    mask;

        mask = gtk_widget_get_events( widget );
        mask = mask & ~events;
        gtk_widget_set_events( widget, mask );
        return( mask );
}
```

This function simply reads the current event mask for the widget, clears the bits in the mask returned, and then resets the event mask of the widget to the new value. It also returns the new mask as an added bonus.

Activating a Widget

An application can cause the "activate" signal handler of a specific widget to be executed by calling gtk_widget_activate(). We discussed the meaning of the activate signal earlier in this chapter. Here is the function prototype:

```
gboolean
gtk_widget_activate(GtkWidget *widget);
```

Reparenting a Widget

Gtk+ allows applications to reparent a widget. This functionality has limited use in an end-user Gtk+ application, but it is used in a few places in the Gtk+ widget set to implement various features. The prototype is as follows:

```
void
gtk_widget_reparent(GtkWidget *widget, GtkWidget *new_parent);
```

You must ensure that the new parent widget belongs to GtkBin or a class that inherits from GtkBin. The following wrapper function can be used to perform the task of reparenting if the new parent is of the correct type:

```
gint
WrapGtkWidgetReparent( GtkWidget *widget, GtkWidget *new_parent )
{
        g_return_val_if_fail (GTK_IS_BIN (new_parent), FALSE);

        gtk_widget_reparent( widget, new_parent );
        return( TRUE );
}
```

Showing a Widget at a Specific Location

To show a widget at a specific x and y location on the screen, you can call gtk_widget_popup():

```
void
gtk_widget_popup(GtkWidget *widget, gint x, gint y);
```

The widget will be realized and mapped as necessary, and then it will be moved to the specified x and y coordinates.

Gtk+ uses this function in the implementation of its tooltips widget. The implementation is fairly straightforward. Using functions provided by the GtkTooltips widget, the application program creates an object that contains the text of the tooltip and associates this object with a widget (e.g., a button, menu item, or entry widget). Each time an enter_notify event is detected for the object, a timeout is registered (the default timeout is 500ms). When the timeout is expired, a function is called that will pop up the tooltips window over the object, using gtk_widget_popup(), and display in that window the tooltips text associated with that object.

To hide a window that has been popped up, use gtk_widget_hide().

Computing the Intersection of a Widget and an Area

To compute a region of intersection between a widget and a rectangle, call gtk_widget_intersect():

```
gint
gtk_widget_intersect(GtkWidget *widget, GdkRectangle *area,
        GdkRectangle *intersection);
```

The intersection is computed between widget and area. The result is placed in intersection, if intersection is non-NULL. If the rectangles intersect, TRUE is returned. Otherwise, FALSE is returned.

Grabbing Focus

GtkWidget provides two convenience functions that layer above the GtkWindow routines gtk_window_set_focus() and gtk_window_set_default(). These functions are, respectively, gtk_widget_grab_focus() and gtk_widget_grab_default(). Each takes a widget as its argument. gtk_widget_grab_focus() will make widget the focus widget in its containing window, and the widget will be redrawn to indicate the change. Likewise, gtk_widget_grab_default() will make the widget the default widget in its containing window, and the widget will be redrawn to indicate the change. However, if the widget cannot be made a default widget, then gtk_widget_grab_default() will simply return without doing anything. See gtk_window_set_default() for information on how to make a widget eligible to become a default widget.

Function prototypes for gtk_widget_grab_focus() and gtk_widget_grab_default() are as follows:

```
void
gtk_widget_grab_focus(GtkWidget *widget);

void
gtk_widget_grab_default(GtkWidget *widget);
```

Specifying Widget Sensitivity

Often it is necessary to change the sensitivity of a widget based on the state of the application or the state of controls in the user interface. A sensitive widget is one that behaves normally, meaning it renders in a way that implies it is usable and will respond to events such as keyboard input or mouse presses. An insensitive widget, on the other hand, is rendered by the toolkit to imply that it is not functional.

Usually a widget indicates that it is insensitive by dimming itself and not responding to user input. Figure 4.1 shows several widgets in their sensitive and insensitive states.

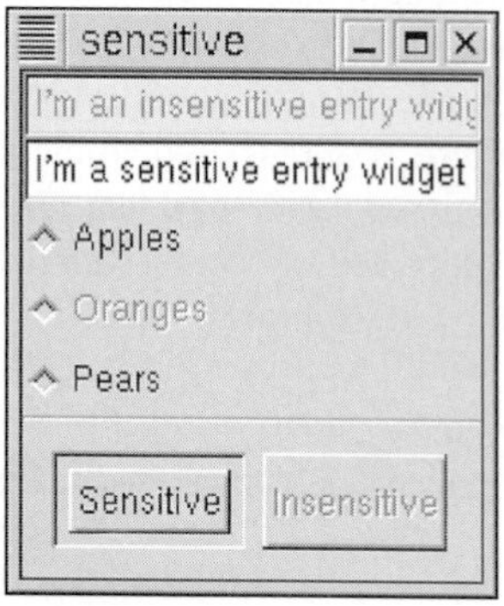

Figure 4.1 Sensitive Widgets

Mousing over an insensitive widget should result in no change in the appearance of the widget, further conveying to the user of the application that the widget is inactive. Widgets that are insensitive cannot obtain input focus, and they cannot be selected with the mouse or by Tab-key traversal.

When should you make a widget insensitive? The answer will vary based on the needs and design of the application. Sometimes it will be the state of the application that drives the sensitivity of a widget. For example, a text editor might disable the Save menu item and enable the Save As menu item for new documents, enable the Save menu item after it has been saved the first time, and regardless of whether it is a new document or not, disable the Save and the Save As menu items until the user has typed in text or has made a change that needs saving. The state of one or more widgets in the user interface may also influence the sensitivity of other widgets. For example, a printer dialog might provide two radio buttons, one labeled "Printer" and the other labeled "File," to allow the user to select a destination for the print job. Also in the dialog would be a push button that, when clicked, would display a file selection dialog, allowing the user to choose a destination file. It would make sense to enable (make sensitive) the file selection button only when the File radio button is selected and make it insensitive at all other times since selecting a file does not make sense if the user wants to print to the printer.

To make a widget sensitive or insensitive, call gtk_widget_set_sensitive():

```
void
gtk_widget_set_sensitive(GtkWidget *widget, gboolean sensitive);
```

The first argument to gtk_widget_set_sensitive() is the widget, and the second is a gboolean. If sensitive is TRUE, the widget will be made sensitive; if FALSE, it will be made insensitive.

Setting the Position and Size of a Widget

A widget's position can be set using gtk_widget_set_uposition():

```
void
gtk_widget_set_uposition(GtkWidget *widget, gint x, gint y);
```

Here, widget is the widget to be moved, and the arguments x and y specify the coordinates (with 0, 0 representing the upper-left corner) coinciding with the widget's upper-left corner after the move. The routine also accepts nonstandard x and y values that are treated specially. If either of the values for x or y is set to -2, that value will not be changed. If, for example, you want to simply change the x position of the widget to 100 and keep the same y position, you would call gtk_widget_set_position() as follows:

```
gtk_widget_set_uposition( widget, 100, -2 );
```

To set the size of a widget in terms of the width and height of its window, call gtk_widget_set_usize():

```
void
gtk_widget_set_usize(GtkWidget *widget, gint width, gint height);
```

Again, the argument widget is the handle of the widget affected. Width is the width of the window, and height is the height of the window after resizing. As with gtk_widget_set_uposition(), the value -2 has special meaning; specifying -2 for either width or height leaves that value unchanged.

Top-Level and Ancestor Widgets, and Transient Windows

Sometime, it is convenient to be aware of the top-level widget in the instance hierarchy of a particular widget. The function gtk_widget_get_toplevel() starts with the widget's parent, if any, and then checks to see what its parent is, and so forth. If the widget passed to gtk_widget_get_toplevel()

```
GtkWidget *
gtk_widget_get_toplevel(GtkWidget *widget);
```

has no parent, it is returned because it is the top-level widget. Typically a top-level widget is a dialog or window widget or some widget that inherits from the GtkWindow class.

As discussed earlier in this chapter, a transient window is a special type of window that, among other attributes, will iconify along with the top-level window of the application should the top-level window be iconified. To ensure this behavior, the client must call gtk_window_set_transient_for(), passing the window ID of the top-level window and the window ID of the window being made transient. To obtain the window ID of the top-level window, it is enough to know the widget ID of any widget contained by the top-level window. With this information, you can do the following:

```
void
SetTransientFor( GtkWindow *win, GtkWidget *widget )
{
        GtkWidget *top;

        top = gtk_widget_get_toplevel( widget );
        if ( top != (GtkWidget *) NULL ) {
                gtk_window_set_transient_for( widget->window,
                        top->window );
        }
}
```

A related function, gtk_widget_get_ancestor(), also walks up the parent list of a window, but instead of searching for the topmost widget in the instance hierarchy, it searches for the first widget belonging to a specific widget class. Here is its function prototype:

```
GtkWidget *
gtk_widget_get_ancestor(GtkWidget *widget, GtkType widget_type);
```

widget is the widget in the instance hierarchy to start the search. widget_type is the type of widget being searched. If searching for a GtkButton, you would either pass GTK_TYPE_BUTTON, which is the preferred method, or call the routine gtk_button_get_type().

If the return value is (GtkWidget *) NULL, then no such widget exists above the widget in the instance hierarchy to which the widget belongs.

Given a pair of widgets, it can be determined whether one is the ancestor of the other by calling gtk_widget_is_ancestor():

```
gint
gtk_widget_is_ancestor(GtkWidget *widget, GtkWidget *ancestor);
```

The first argument is the widget for which the query is being made, and the second is the widget that is potentially an ancestor of the first. The call returns TRUE if ancestor is an ancestor of widget; otherwise, the return value is FALSE.

Querying the Pointer Position

At any time, your application can query the x and y coordinate location of the mouse by calling gtk_widget_get_pointer():

```
void
gtk_widget_get_pointer(GtkWidget *widget, gint *x, gint *y);
```

This routine takes a pointer to a widget and two pointers to gint that will hold the x and y coordinate values upon return.

It may seem strange at first glance that this routine requires a pointer to a widget as one of its arguments. The reason for the widget argument is that the routine returns the position of the mouse relative to the window associated with the specified widget. If the widget is not yet realized, then -1 is returned in both x and y. To obtain the mouse position relative to the screen (not a widget), call gdk_window_get_pointer():

```
gint     x, y;

gdk_window_get_pointer (NULL, &x, &y, NULL);
```

Colormap and Visual Functions

Colormaps and visuals in X are a rather complex subject, but they're an important one for Gtk+ programmers to become familiar with. Because Gtk+/GDK is layered on top of X11 in the UNIX implementation (which is the focus of this book), it is best that I refer you to a book on Xlib (such as *O'Reilly Volume 1, Xlib Programming Manual*) for details on colormaps and visuals. If the program you are designing has anything to do with colors or image processing, it is really a requirement that you take the time to learn about color in X11. The reason this is important is due to the design of X11. The X server component of the X Window System was designed to accommodate a wide variety of display hardware types, ranging from 1-bit-deep terminals supporting the display of black and white only, to 8-bit displays (common years ago and still in use today) capable of displaying 256 colors at the same time, to 16-bit and 24-bit TrueColor displays that one can almost consider standard on today's desktop Linux systems. There are many variants to the preceding list; I recall back when my work focused on the X server running on hardware designs where each window displayed by the X server would be given its own private hardware colormap. Such systems are rarely, if ever, encountered, but the X server can be made to support them. As a Gtk+ programmer, I'd venture to say that the majority of display types you will encounter will be either 8-bit-deep PseudoColor or 16-bit/24-bit TrueColor. Supporting these two is perhaps a minimum, and you are advised to include each in your testing if color is important to your program. But also be aware that Gtk+ applications are, fundamentally, X applications. So, it is within the realm of possibility for your users to set their DISPLAY variables to point to a 1-bit-deep StaticGray X server and expect it to work.

Because in reality the number of users with such hardware is practically zero, it does not make much sense to support such a display. I just want you to be aware of the issue and know that X provides a solution. Here I will discuss the routines that GtkWidget provides for getting and setting colormaps and visuals. You might want to refer back to this section briefly after you've familiarized yourself with colors and visuals.

With that said, you can obtain the colormap associated with a given widget by calling gtk_widget_get_colormap():

```
GdkColormap *
gtk_widget_get_colormap(GtkWidget *widget);
```

widget, of course, is the handle of the widget you are querying. On return, a pointer to a GdkColormap structure is returned.

Several routines in GDK require a GdkColormap * as an argument. Most of these functions layer on top of X11 functions that allocate cells and colors in an X colormap. A GdkColormap is not an X colormap, but you can think of it as a client-side data structure that points to an X colormap and caches data about the colormap, notably the colors allocated in the X server colormap. As you may know, it is possible for a client other than your application to make changes to an X colormap (this is especially true regarding the default server colormap, the resource ID of which is made known to all clients during client startup). Because of this, the GDK colormap code periodically queries the colors in the X colormap pointed to by each GdkColormap allocated to ensure that values stored by the GdkColormap are correct.

More often than not, the colormap you will be passing as an argument to the GDK colormap routines will be the colormap you have obtained from a call to gtk_widget_get_colormap().In most cases, this colormap will end up being the same colormap used by all other widgets in your GUI and in fact will be the X server default shared colormap. If you are, for example, allocating colors from a colormap that you will later be using to draw in a GtkDrawingArea widget, you should ensure that the colors allocated come from the colormap being used by that drawing area widget; to do this, use gtk_widget_get_colormap().

A visual is another X data structure/concept that is best described perhaps by a book on Xlib (the same book you used to learn about colormaps will also talk about visuals, and since they are related, the information is probably in the same chapter). The short description of a visual is that it basically describes the structure of colormaps for the display device to which the client is currently connected. Usually, a given X display or server will support more than one visual type. The X11 visual classes are listed in Table 4.5.

Table 4.5 X11 Visual Classes

Visual Class	*Modifiable Colormaps?*	*Typical Depth*
PseudoColor	Yes	8-bit
GrayScale	Yes	8-bit
DirectColor	Yes	16-bit, 24-bit
StaticColor	No	Less than 8-bit (e.g., 4-bit)
StaticGray	No	1-bit
TrueColor	No	16-bit, 24-bit

For the most part, X servers and terminals developed since 1990, but prior to the widespread adoption of 16-bit and 24-bit graphics cards, are 8-bit-deep PseudoColor terminals with modifiable colormap entries. Usually the number of colors in a PseudoColor colormap of size 256 will be enough for most clients, but a common problem is running several colormap-intensive applications (e.g., The GIMP and Netscape) together on the same X server. Potentially, one of these clients will find that it cannot allocate or match the colors it needs in the default colormap because the other client(s) have allocated them already, and so the client either will give up and exit or will revert to installing a private colormap so it can get all of its colors. The problem here is one that is familiar to many users; as focus leaves a client using the default colormap and falls on the client using a private colormap, the X server swaps out the hardware colormap that displayed the default colormap colors and swaps in the hardware colormap associated with the private colormap of the other client. In doing so, the colors of all applications using the shared default colormap will go "technicolor." This is one reason it is preferable for your application to use a shared default colormap whenever possible. It is very possible that your application will be running on an 8-bit PseudoColor display; colormap flashing is not something you want to put your users through.

Most systems nowadays (since the late 1990s) come with 16-bit and 24-bit displays. Here the palette is huge, and the visual class most likely to be defaulted by the X server is TrueColor or perhaps DirectColor. There is little worry with such a visual that colors needed by an application are not already allocated (in the case of TrueColor, which is a static visual class) or cannot be allocated (in the case of DirectColor).

When would you need a visual? A visual gives your application information that can help it decide whether it makes sense to attempt what the application needs to do, and how to do it. Let's say you are writing a GIF image viewer. Let's cite a few possible scenarios: If the visual class is StaticGray and the number of map entries in the colormap is 2, then you need to either put up a dialog telling the user to buy a modern computer with a reasonable display or dither your images to bitonal before pushing the pixels into the frame buffer. If the visual class is PseudoColor and 8-bit deep, your code will need to determine whether it is feasible to use the default shared colormap or install a private colormap. If the visual is TrueColor and the number of distinct colormap entries is large, then your application only needs to worry about mapping pixel values in the image palette to colormap cells in the colormap.

Each window in an application can have its own visual class. This complicates things a bit, but in general, the situation is just like the one for colormaps in that most, if not all, widgets will reference the same visual: the X server default visual. To obtain the visual associated with a widget, call gtk_widget_get_visual():

```
GdkVisual *
gtk_widget_get_visual(GtkWidget *widget);
```

You can specify the colormap of a widget prior to it being realized (which, in most cases, means before gtk_widget_show*() is called) by calling the function gtk_widget_set_colormap():

```
void
gtk_widget_set_colormap(GtkWidget *widget, GdkColormap *colormap);
```

widget is a Gtk+ widget that has yet to be realized. colormap is a pointer to a GdkColormap struct. You can obtain the colormap with gtk_widget_get_colormap() or by creating a colormap using various means using routines provided by GDK. As you previously learned, typically a widget's colormap will be the X server default colormap shared by all widgets and other clients running on the same X server. Exceptions will be when the visual class and default X server colormap usage demand for certain applications dealing with images or a large number of colors to install a private colormap so that content is rendered accurately.

You can also specify the visual class of a widget. Setting the visual class of a widget to one that is not the same as the default visual class of the server will cause a private colormap to be created at the time the widget's window is being created. The visual class is specified by passing a pointer to a variable of type GdkVisual. The function prototype of gtk_widget_set_visual() is as follows:

```
void
gtk_widget_set_visual(GtkWidget *widget, GdkVisual *visual);
```

You can obtain a GdkVisual pointer by calling gtk_widget_get_visual(). If you have a window ID, you can also use gdk_window_get_visual() to obtain the same pointer. Several routines provided by GDK can be called to obtain a visual; these routines are summarized here.

To return the system default visual:

```
GdkVisual*
gdk_visual_get_system (void)
```

To return the best visual (e.g., the visual that has the greatest depth):

```
GdkVisual*
gdk_visual_get_best (void)
```

To return the best visual that matches the specified depth:

```
GdkVisual*
gdk_visual_get_best_with_depth (gint depth)
```

To return the best visual that matches the specified visual class:

```
GdkVisual*
gdk_visual_get_best_with_type (GdkVisualType visual_type)
```

To return the best visual that matches both the specified depth and the visual class:

```
GdkVisual*
gdk_visual_get_best_with_both (gint depth, GdkVisualType visual_type)
```

To return the GDK visual that maps to the specified X visual:

```
GdkVisual*
gdk_visual_lookup (Visual *xvisual)
```

To return the GDK visual that maps to the X visual having the specified visualid:

```
GdkVisual*
gdkx_visual_get (VisualID xvisualid)
```

Styles

A style defines the look and feel for a particular widget in a given state. As I briefly mentioned earlier in this chapter, GtkWidget defines a macro, named GTK_WIDGET_STATE, that will return one of the values listed in Table 4.6, indicating the state of a widget:

Table 4.6 Widget States

State	*Generic Meaning*
GTK_STATE_NORMAL	Sensitive widget as it appears without having the focus and not active.
GTK_STATE_ACTIVE	Sensitive widget that is active (e.g., a button that is pressed). Similar to GTK_STATE_SELECTED for some widgets.
GTK_STATE_PRELIGHT	Sensitive widget that has the focus (e.g., a button that has been moused-over).
GTK_STATE_SELECTED	Widget is selected. For example, a row in a CList widget.
GTK_STATE_INSENSITIVE	Widget that is insensitive. It cannot be made active, it cannot be selected, and it cannot be placed in a prelight state.

Note that not all widgets honor these states. Only the GtkCList, GtkCListItem, GtkCTree, GtkCTreeItem, GtkEntry, and GtkText widget classes support the idea of GTK_STATE_SELECTED, for example.

Each of the preceding states has a distinct look and feel that helps the user be aware of what a widget's state is at any given moment. Figure 4.2 illustrates, left to right, GTK_STATE_NORMAL, GTK_STATE_PRELIGHT, GTK_STATE_ACTIVE, GTK_STATE_SELECTED, and GTK_STATE_INSENSITIVE for a toggle button widget (GtkToggleButton). When a toggle button is rendered as GTK_STATE_NORMAL, a user knows (from experience) that the toggle button state cannot be changed (to GTK_STATE_ACTIVE) until the mouse is moved over it, placing the widget in GTK_STATE_PRELIGHT state. The strange appearance of GTK_STATE_SELECTED is due to the fact that a toggle button never goes into that state (my example is somewhat artificial in that sense). What the widget has done here is rendered itself in the colors associated with a selected state, appropriate for, perhaps, an item in a list (the background color is dark blue) but not a toggled button that, again, can never be "selected."

Figure 4.2 Toggle Button States

The difference in appearance from one state to another is maintained by widgets in a Gtk+ data structure named GtkWidgetStyle, which is defined in gtkstyle.h. Mostly, this information consists of colors. One such color is the background color of the widget. Because there are five distinct states that a widget can be in, five colors are recorded as the background color of a widget, one color for each widget state previously listed.

Normally, you (and your users) will control the various style attributes via a Gtk+ rc file. While not as powerful as resources in the Xt (Motif) world, the basic idea behind the Gtk+ rc file is similar. Resources in Gtk+ and Xt are not compatible with each other; for example, Gtk+ applications do not understand Motif resource files, and Motif applications are not able to read Gtk+ rc files.

Let's first take a look at rc files and the style system implemented by Gtk+. Then I will describe the relevant GtkWidget API.

Gtk+ Style System Details

As previously mentioned, a widget can be in one of five distinct states. Each of these states can be represented by a change in the widget's appearance. For each widget state, an rc file allows the attributes in Table 4.7 to be specified:

Table 4.7 Style Attributes

Attribute	*Meaning*	*Example*
fg	Foreground color	0.0, 0.0, 0.0
bg	Background color	1.0, 1.0, 1.0
bg_pixmap	Background pixmap	marble.xpm
base	Base color	1.0, 0.0, 0.0
text	Text color	0.5, 0.5, 0.5

The base attribute is used by several widget classes to specify the background color of its widgets. The GtkText class uses the text attribute to define the foreground color and base to define the background color of its widgets. In the chapters that follow, I will specify the default values for each of the preceding attributes and will mention which of the attributes is actually used by the widget class.

As you can see in the preceding table, colors can be expressed using a triplet of floating point values. The allowable range for each component in such a triplet is [0.0, 1.0]. Together, the three component values represent an RGB color; the first component indicates the amount of red in the color, the second represents the amount of green, and the third represents the amount of blue. In the preceding examples, fg is set to black, bg is set to white, base is set to red, and text is set to a medium gray. Gray values are formed by setting r, g, and b to equal values; white (1.0, 1.0, 1.0) and black (0.0, 0.0, 0.0) are grayscale values at the extreme ends of the possible range. You may, if you choose, use decimal or hexadecimal constants instead of floating-point constants. Non-floating-point values must be scaled to

65,535. For example, 1.0 is expressed as 65535 decimal or 0xffff hex; 0.5 can be expressed roughly as 32768 decimal or 0x8000 hex.

The preceding table contains only widget attributes used to show the state of a widget. A few additional attributes can be specified for a widget or widget instance in an rc file; I will discuss these widget attributes later in this section.

Attributes can be mapped to a widget class or to a specific instance of a widget created by an application. A widget class, naturally enough, corresponds to one of the Gtk+ widget classes, such as GtkButton. A name can be associated with a Gtk+ widget instance by assigning it a name after it is created, and just before it is shown, by calling gtk_widget_set_name():

```
void gtk_widget_set_name (GtkWidget *widget, gchar *name);
```

For example:

```
GtkWidget *button;

button = gtk_widget_button_new();
gtk_widget_set_name( button, "my_button" );
```

In the preceding example, "my_button" is the name assigned to this instance of the GtkButton widget class.

Both the widget class and the instance name can be used in an rc file to assign widget attributes. The following example maps the style named "global-button-style" to the GtkButton widget class.

```
widget_class "GtkButton" style "global-button-style"
```

The result of the preceding entry in an rc file is that all instances of GtkButton will render according to the style named "global-button-style." We will see how to define a style later in this section.

A specific instance of a widget can also be mapped to a style, as shown in the following example:

```
widget "my_button" style "instance-button-style"
```

In the preceding example, any widget assigned the name "my_button" will use the style named "instance-button-style."

Both the widget class name (used in widget_class) and the widget instance name can be specified using regular expressions. For example, "Gtk*Scale", when used as a widget_class name (as in the following example):

```
widget_class "Gtk*Scale" style "scale"
```

will match the GtkHScale, GtkVScale, and GtkScale widget classes. Patterns that contain '*' or '?' characters are accepted by the parser, with '*' and '?' having the standard interpretation.

One or more widgets can be identified by specifying a path consisting of widget class names and widget instance names. Components in the path are delimited by a period (.). For example:

```
widget "my window.GtkButton.GtkLabel" style "label-style"
```

Here, labels of buttons that are children of the widget named "my window" will reference the style named "label-style".

The style "instance-button-style", used earlier, might be defined in an rc file as follows:

```
style "instance-button-style"
{
  bg[NORMAL] = { 65535, 1.0, 0xffff }
}
```

Here we specify that the background color of the widget, when it is in a NORMAL state, should be rendered using white. The constants 65535, 1.0, and 0xffff all represent the same component value; use of floating-point, decimal, or hex values is largely a matter of personal preference. Only the background color of the widget in the NORMAL state will be affected by this style. The background color of the widget, in all other states (e.g., PRELIGHT) will remain unaffected by the application of this style. Other attributes (e.g., fg) are unaffected by this style definition.

Assigning attributes to a widget instance takes precedence over assigning the same attributes to a widget class. Widget class attributes, on the other hand, take precedence over default attributes defined by the widget implementation.

Within an rc file, styles can be used in the definition of other styles. For example, suppose we want to define a second GtkButton instance style that shares the same attributes as "instance-button-style" but overrides the fg and bg attributes corresponding to the button's INSENSITIVE state. To do this, we might use the following syntax:

```
style "new-instance-button-style" = "instance-button-style"
{
        fg[INSENSITIVE] = { 1.0, 0, 1.0 }
        bg[INSENSITIVE] = { 1.0, 0, 1.0 }
}
```

The style "new-instance-button-style" inherits all style information defined by the style "instance-button-style", modifying only the fg and bg attributes associated with the INSENSITIVE state.

The attribute "<parent>" is used to specify that an attribute should be set to the same value as set for the widget's parent in the widget instance hierarchy. Modifying the preceding "new-instance-button-style" style to illustrate:

```
style "new-instance-button-style" = "instance-button-style"
{
        fg[INSENSITIVE] = "<parent>"
        bg[INSENSITIVE] = { 1.0, 0, 1.0 }
}
```

Here the INSENSITIVE state foreground color of any widget using this style will be set to the INSENSITIVE state foreground color of that widget's parent in the runtime instance hierarchy.

The bg_pixmap resource specifies the name of the xpm file to be used to define the window background pixmap tile used by some of the widgets in the Gtk+ widget set. The syntax should be simple to understand at this point. Modifying, once again, the "new-instance-button-style" style:

```
style "new-instance-button-style" = "instance-button-style"
{
          fg[INSENSITIVE]  = "<parent>"
          bg[INSENSITIVE]  = { 1.0, 0, 1.0 }
          bg-pixmap[NORMAL]  = "foobar.xpm"
}
```

So that Gtk+ can find your pixmap, you must specify a path. The path consists of UNIX pathnames separated by a colon (:); each component of the path is searched until the xpm file being sought is located. To specify the xpm search path, add a pixmap_path entry to the rc file:

```
pixmap_path "/usr/include/X11R6/pixmaps:~/.sportslog"
```

Using the preceding path, xpm files are searched for starting in the standard X11R6 pixmap directory and then in the application-specific directory created by the "sportslog" application in the user's home directory.

One additional widget-style attribute that can be set by users in an rc file is the font attribute. The font name must be specified using the syntax defined by the X Logical Font Description (XLFD) format, for example:

```
-adobe-*-bold-i-normal-*-20-*-100-*-*-*-*-*
```

For more information on XLFD, see the online man page for xfontsel, a tool developed by the X Consortium and included with XFree86 that can be used to browse various XLFD settings.

The following style illustrates a font attribute specification:

```
style 'my_font_style'
{
  font = "-adobe-helvetica-medium-r-normal--*-100-*-*-*-*-*-*"
}
```

To associate an rc file with your application, you must add a call to gtk_rc_parse() to your main application, after gtk_init() has been called and before any widgets affected by style settings are created:

```
void gtk_rc_parse( char *filename );
```

The argument filename is the pathname to the rc file. It is up to you to devise a policy for the creation and location of your rc file. One suggestion would be to store it in the home or login directory of each user. Your application would create the file the first time the user runs the application, just prior to calling gtk_rc_parse():

```
char      rc_path[MAXPATH];
int       fd;

...
```

```
sprintf( rc_path, "%s/sportslog.rc", getenv( "HOME" ));

/* test to see of the file exists. if not, create one */

if ( ( fd = open( rc_path, O_RDONLY ) ) == -1 )
        MyCreateInitialRCFile( rc_path );
else
        close( fd );
gtk_rc_parse( rc_path );
```

In the preceding code, open(2) is called to test whether the file exists. Here, rc_path is simply the concatenation of the user's HOME environment variable, the name of the application (which in this case is "sportslog"), and the string ".rc". If your application supports multiple rc files, it may call gtk_rc_parse() once for each rc file supported. Styles parsed by later calls to gtk_rc_parse() will nullify the same styles defined by earlier calls.

A final style type is the user style. A user style is simply a style associated with a widget by the application via a call to gtk_widget_set_style():

```
void
gtk_widget_set_style(GtkWidget *widget, GtkStyle *style);
```

A user style takes precedence over both a default style and an rc style. Once a user style has been specified, it can be overridden by setting the widget's rc style. You can obtain a pointer to a GtkStyle struct from another widget by calling gtk_widget_get_style():

```
GtkStyle *
gtk_widget_get_style(GtkWidget *widget);
```

If necessary, rc style will be applied to the widget before the GtkStyle data is returned.

To summarize, a style is a collection of attributes that dictates how a widget is rendered when in one of five states. A default style is associated by the widget implementation. The default style can be overridden by an rc style defined by the application developer or the end user. A widget class style is a style in an rc file that pertains to any instance of the specified widget class. A widget instance style maps style information to a specific instance of a widget class. To perform this mapping, the application must assign a name to the widget instance. This is done by calling gtk_widget_set_name() after the widget is created but before it is shown:

```
void
gtk_widget_set_name(GtkWidget *widget, const gchar *name);
```

The argument widget is the widget to which the name is being assigned. If, at this point, no user style has yet been applied to the widget, Gtk+ will look up the style information that pertains to the assigned name and then apply it to the widget instance. If a user style was already applied, then only the name is associated with the widget; style information is not read. To force reading of the style information, call gtk_widget_set_rc_style():

```
void
gtk_widget_set_rc_style(GtkWidget *widget);
```

If a user style has been set for the widget, it will be overridden by this call.

You can retrieve the name associated with a widget instance by calling gtk_widget_get_name():

```
gchar *
gtk_widget_get_name(GtkWidget *widget);
```

If user and rc styles have not yet been set for a widget, the widget's rc style settings can be activated by calling gtk_widget_ensure_style():

```
void
gtk_widget_ensure_style(GtkWidget *widget);
```

Any user or rc styles applied to a widget can also be nullified and replaced with the widget's default style by calling gtk_widget_restore_default_style():

```
void
gtk_widget_restore_default_style(GtkWidget *widget);
```

Finally, an rc style can be applied to a widget, and recursively to all of its children, by calling gtk_widget_reset_rc_styles():

```
void
gtk_widget_reset_rc_styles(GtkWidget *widget);
```

Stacking Styles, Visuals, and Colormaps

You know now that several sources of style data exist. In decreasing order of precedence, these are user style, rc style, and default style. A fourth source of style data is the "style stack" maintained by GtkWidget. If the style stack is nonempty at the time a widget is being initialized, and if user style and rc style have not been applied to the widget, then the style definition at the top of the style stack will be used by the widget. Style information on the style stack is only referenced at the time the widget is created. To place a style at the top of the style stack, call gtk_widget_push_style():

```
void
gtk_widget_push_style(GtkStyle *style);
```

To pop or remove a style from the top of the style stack, call gtk_widget_pop_style():

```
void
gtk_widget_pop_style(void);
```

Colormaps and visuals also have their own stacks maintained by GtkWidget. If the colormap stack is nonempty, then the colormap used by a widget will be the colormap currently at the top of the colormap stack. Similarly, if the visual stack is nonempty, then the visual at the top of the visual stack will be used by the widget being created. To push a colormap onto the colormap stack, call gtk_widget_push_colormap():

```
void
gtk_widget_push_colormap(GdkColormap *cmap);
```

To push a visual, call gtk_widget_push_visual():

```
void
gtk_widget_push_visual(GdkVisual *visual);
```

To pop or remove the top colormap from the colormap stack, call gtk_widget_pop_colormap():

```
void
gtk_widget_pop_colormap(void);
```

Similarly, to pop or remove the top visual from the visual stack, call gtk_widget_pop_visual():

```
void
gtk_widget_pop_visual(void);
```

In either case, calling gtk_widget_pop*() against an empty stack is a no-op.

Colormaps and visuals should be pushed onto their respective stacks as a pair; it is up to your application to ensure that the tops of the colormap and visual stacks are compatible with each other. The purpose of a visual is to describe the structure of a colormap, such as how its colors are decomposed into RGB primaries or how deep its pixels are. A colormap is really nothing more than a list of colors compatible with its associated visual. To illustrate, the GDK function gdk_colormap_new(), which creates a new colormap, requires that a pointer to a GdkVisual be passed as one of its arguments. This visual is used by gdk_colormap_new() to determine how to create and initialize the colormap and is stored by gdk_colormap_new() in the private area of the GdkColormap for later use.

If you have a valid GdkColormap, you can obtain a pointer to the corresponding GdkVisual struct by using the following code:

```
GdkColormap *myColormap;
GdkVisual *myVisual;

...

myVisual = gdk_colormap_get_visual (myColormap);
```

Similarly, to get a colormap for a given visual, you can create a new colormap using gdk_colormap_new() as previously described:

```
GdkColormap *myColormap;
GdkVisual *myVisual;

...

myColormap = gdk_colormap_new (myVisual);
```

To get the server's default colormap and visual, which are compatible with each other, your application can call, respectively, gdk_colormap_get_system() and gdk_visual_get_system():

```
GdkColormap*
gdk_colormap_get_system (void)

GdkVisual*
gdk_visual_get_system (void)
```

You should not free the pointers returned by either of these functions because they are maintained internally by GDK.

The following code can be used to verify that a given visual and colormap are compatible with each other:

```
gboolean
VisualsAreEqual( GdkColormap *cmap, GdkVisual *visual )
{
        GdkVisualPrivate *a, *b;
        GdkVisual *cmapVisual;

        cmapVisual = gdk_colormap_get_visual (cmap);
        a = ((GdkVisualPrivate*) visual)->xvisual;
        b = ((GdkVisualPrivate*) cmapVisual)->xvisual;

        if ( a->visualid == b->visualid )
                return TRUE;
        else
                return FALSE;
}
```

To compare the colormap and visual on top of the GtkWidget colormap and visual stacks, you can do something like the following:

```
GdkColormap *cmap;
GdkVisual *visual;
gboolean;

cmap = gtk_widget_pop_colormap();
visual = gtk_widget_pop_visual();

if ( cmap && visual )
        ret = VisualsAreEqual( cmap, visual );
if ( cmap )
        gtk_widget_push_colormap();
if ( visual )
        gtk_widget_push_visual();
```

Style, Colormap, and Visual Defaults

GtkWidget maintains defaults for style, colormap, and visual. In the absence of any other settings (e.g., rc styles, explicit setting of colormap), these defaults are what Gtk+ associates with a new widget instance at creation time. The default values for colormap and visual are the server or system colormap and visual, respectively. As for style, the default is obtained by a call to gtk_style_new():

```
GtkStyle*
gtk_style_new (void)
```

You don't need to call this function, of course; it is done for you by gtk+. Gtk_style_new(), as of Gtk+ 1.2, sets the following default style attributes. (In Table 4.8, RGB values are in hexadecimal):

Table 4.8 Default Style Attributes

Style	*Value*
font	-adobe-helvetica-medium-r-normal--*-120-*-*-*-*-*-*, or fixed if that can't be loaded
black	0, 0, 0
white	0xffff, 0xffff, 0xffff
normal_fg	0, 0, 0
active_fg	0, 0, 0
prelight_fg	0, 0, 0
selected_fg	0xffff, 0xffff, 0xffff
insensitive_fg	0x7530, 0x7530, 0x7530
normal_bg	0xd6d6, 0xd6d6, 0xd6d6
active_bg	0xc350, 0xc350, 0xc350
prelight_bg	0xea60, 0xea60, 0xea60
selected_bg	0, 0, 0x9c40
insensitive_bg	0xd6d6, 0xd6d6, 0xd6d6

In the preceding, normal_fg corresponds to the foreground color in NORMAL state, prelight_bg corresponds to the background color in PRELIGHT state, and so on.

The text color for each state is set to the same color set for the foreground color in the same state, and the base color for each state is set to white. The only exceptions are the text and base colors corresponding to INSENSITIVE state. In both cases, the default value is insensitive_bg, shown in the preceding table.

You can override the default style for all widgets easily by obtaining a style (e.g., by calling gtk_style_new() and changing one or more of its fields) and calling gtk_widget_set_default_style():

```
void
gtk_widget_set_default_style(GtkStyle *style);
```

style is a previously allocated style. Other ways to obtain this style include calling gtk_widget_get_style() and gtk_widget_pop_style(), described earlier.

Similarly, the default colormap and default visual can be replaced with calls to gtk_widget_set_default_colormap() and gtk_widget_set_default_visual(), respectively:

```
void
gtk_widget_set_default_colormap(GdkColormap *colormap);

void
gtk_widget_set_default_visual(GdkVisual *visual);
```

Retrieving the default style, colormap, and widget is also easy to do. To get the default style, call gtk_widget_get_default_style():

```
GtkStyle *
gtk_widget_get_default_style(void);
```

To retrieve the default colormap for widget, use the following:

```
GdkColormap *
gtk_widget_get_default_colormap(void);
```

And finally, to retrieve the default visual for widget, use the following:

```
GdkVisual *
gtk_widget_get_default_visual(void);
```

Summary

We started this chapter by looking at some of the advantages of widget-based development. These advantages include abstraction and simplification for the programmer, and user interface consistency within and among applications for the end user. The remainder of this chapter described GtkWidget, a class that provides a great deal of functionality and from which most of the remaining Gtk+ widget classes inherit directly. The key point to remember is that any class in the widget hierarchy inheriting from GtkWidget (e.g., GtkButton) is in fact an instance of GtkWidget as well, so you can apply any of the functions implemented by GtkWidget to instances of these classes. If, for example, you need to set the event mask of a button widget, you would call gtk_widget_set_events(), not some function implemented by the GtkButton class. This chapter also introduced the format by which widget classes are presented in the remainder of this book.

CHAPTER

5

LABELS AND BUTTONS

In the preceding chapter, I described the GtkWidget widget class in detail. There, we learned that GtkWidget is unique among Gtk+ classes in that it provides a base class from which most of the remaining widget classes in Gtk+ inherit behavior. Although there is little doubt as to the importance of GtkWidget, an application's user interface cannot be built using GtkWidget alone. To construct a user interface, you, as a programmer, will need to utilize widget classes located elsewhere in the Gtk+ widget hierarchy.

Controls and Containers

In general, there are two fundamental widget types in Gtk+. The first type consists of widgets visible at runtime and with which users can control the behavior of the application. Push buttons, pop-up menus, text-entry fields, toggle buttons, and check buttons are some of the widget types that fall into this category. I refer to widgets of this type as control widgets because they represent the basic "controls" with which users of your application interact. The second type of widget provides application programmers with widgets that can be used to organize the layout of control widgets within the application's user interface. Widgets that belong to this category act like containers; as an application programmer, you often add control widgets and, at times, other container widgets to a container widget when constructing your user interface. A container widget is responsible for managing the widgets that have been added to it. For example, it is a container widget that ultimately must act on the resizing of a window by adjusting the geometries of its child widgets in a way best suited to the new window size.

In this chapter, we'll start our look at control widgets, covering GtkLabel as well GtkButton and related classes, as summarized in Table 5.1.

Table 5.1 Widgets Covered in This Chapter

Widget	*Description*
GtkLabel	Displays static (noneditable) text.
GtkButton	The standard push button (e.g., used to implement OK and Cancel buttons).

Table 5.1 Widgets Covered in This Chapter (Continued)

Widget	*Description*
GtkCheckButton	Allows multiple buttons within a group to be selected simultaneously ("*n* of many"). The label of each button is placed adjacent to the button.
GtkToggleButton	Similar to GtkCheckButton. The button label is placed on the button as with GtkButton, not adjacent to it.
GtkRadioButton	Similar to GtkCheckButton but multiple buttons in a group cannot be simultaneously selected ("one of many").

We'll start our discussion of the preceding widget classes with what is perhaps the most simple of the control widgets: GtkLabel. Strictly speaking, GtkLabel is not a control widget, but because it plays a part in many of the control widgets discussed (for example, the text displayed by an instance of GtkButton is actually an instance of GtkLabel), I think it is important that we start our look at Gtk+'s control widgets here.

GtkLabel

Class Name

```
GtkLabel
```

Parent Class Name

```
GtkMisc
```

Macros

Widget type macro: `GTK_TYPE_LABEL`

Object to widget cast macro: `GTK_LABEL(obj)`

Widget type check macro: `GTK_IS_LABEL(obj)`

Supported Arguments

Prefix: `GtkLabel::`

Table 5.2 GtkLabel Arguments

Name	*Type*	*Permissions*
label	GTK_TYPE_STRING	GTK_ARG_READWRITE
pattern	GTK_TYPE_STRING	GTK_ARG_READWRITE
justify	GTK_TYPE_JUSTIFICATION	GTK_ARG_READWRITE

Application-Level API Synopsis

Return GTK_TYPE_LABEL at runtime:

```
guint
gtk_label_get_type(void);
```

Create a new instance of GtkLabel with a specified string as the label value:

```
GtkWidget *
gtk_label_new(const char *str);
```

Set the text of the GtkLabel widget instance to a specified string:

```
void
gtk_label_set_text(GtkLabel *label, const char *str);
```

Set justification of the GtkLabel widget instance:

```
void
gtk_label_set_justify(GtkLabel *label, GtkJustification jtype);
```

Set the underline segment pattern for the GtkLabel instance to a specified string:

```
void
gtk_label_set_pattern(GtkLabel *label, const gchar *pattern);
```

Specify whether an instance of GtkLabel should perform word wrap:

```
void
gtk_label_set_line_wrap (GtkLabel *label, gboolean wrap);
```

Retrieve the label value string from a GtkLabel instance:

```
void
gtk_label_get(GtkLabel *label, char **str);
```

Evaluate the menu item label for an accelerator key, remove the leading underscore, and set the label's underline segment pattern (by calling gtk_label_set_pattern):

```
guint
gtk_label_parse_uline(GtkLabel *label, const gchar *string);
```

Class Description

GtkLabel is the widget class that allows for the display of static text objects in a window. This widget class is often used directly by an application and is also used by several widget classes in the GtkWidget hierarchy that are in need of displaying labels or text, including, but not limited to, the GtkButton, GtkToggleButton, GtkCheckButton, and GtkRadioButton widget classes described in this chapter. GtkLabel has limited functionality, which is appropriate for a widget class designed to do nothing more than display static text in a window. For those of you unfamiliar with the term "static text," it means text that cannot be directly manipulated by the user of the application during runtime. This is in contrast to text displayed by GtkEntry, Gtk+'s text entry widget; most of the time, users are given the ability to modify the text in a GtkEntry widget. Users can, however, indirectly affect the text displayed by a GtkLabel widget, as I will illustrate in this section. For the most part, however, once the text associated with a GtkLabel widget is set, it will usually not change during the lifetime of the window or application in which it is being displayed.

The functionality that GtkLabel provides is available through its API, which I will describe in this section. Applications can perform the following tasks: create a GtkLabel widget instance, set the text displayed by the GtkLabel widget, tell a GtkLabel widget how it should justify its text (e.g., justify right or left), and obtain the text currently being displayed by a GtkLabel widget. GtkLabel also provides routines that allow an application to identify the portions of a GtkLabel's text that should be rendered with an underscore character (_) beneath them.

Creating a Label Widget

To create a new instance of GtkLabel, call gtk_label_new():

```
GtkWidget *
gtk_label_new(const char *str);
```

The argument str is a NULL-terminated string that represents the text displayed by the label. If str is NULL, then gtk_label_new() will fail, returning NULL as its result.

Setting and Retrieving Label Text

As previously mentioned, GtkLabel is designed to be used to display static text in a window. While the user may not be able to change this text, your application can at any time. To change the text displayed by a label widget, you must call gtk_label_set_text():

```
void
gtk_label_set_text(GtkLabel *label, const char *str);
```

label is an instance of GtkLabel, as returned by a call to gtk_label_new(). str is a NULL-terminated string representing the new value of the label after the call completes. If either label or str is NULL, the routine will fail, and the text associated with the label widget will remain unchanged.

Your application can also retrieve the text currently associated with a label widget by calling gtk_label_get():

```
void
gtk_label_get(GtkLabel *label, char **str);
```

The argument label is an instance of GtkLabel, and str is a pointer to a char * variable you have declared, as in the following example:

```
GtkWidget *label;
char *str;

...

gtk_label_get( GTK_LABEL( label ), &str );
```

It is important that you do not free the memory returned through str by Gtk+.

Label Attributes

In addition to setting and getting the text of a label, applications can also specify how a label widget justifies its text when rendered and whether or not word wrap should be performed. The function gtk_label_set_justification() is used to specify the desired justification setting:

```
void
gtk_label_set_justify(GtkLabel *label, GtkJustification jtype);
```

label is an instance of GtkLabel. jtype is the desired justification value and can be set to one of the values in Table 5.3.

Table 5.3 Justification Values

Value	*Meaning*
GTK_JUSTIFY_LEFT	The origin of text on a line is at x = 0.
GTK_JUSTIFY_RIGHT	The origin of text on a line is placed as far to the right as possible.
GTK_JUSTIFY_CENTER	Text is centered on a line (default).
GTK_JUSTIFY_FILL	Wrapped text is rendered so that each line consumes the entire width of the area allocated to the label.

To specify whether text should be word wrapped or not, call gtk_label_set_line_wrap():

```
void
gtk_label_set_line_wrap (GtkLabel *label, gboolean wrap);
```

label, of course, is an instance of GtkLabel. Setting wrap to TRUE will turn on word wrap; setting wrap to FALSE will turn it off.

It is probably best to see an example usage of word wrap and justify to best appreciate how these two label attributes work together. Figures 5.1 through 5.6 are some screen shots that illustrate the settings in various combinations:

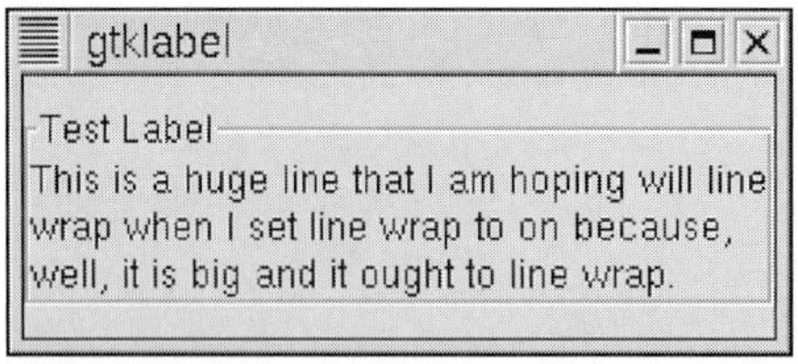

Figure 5.1 Left, Right, Center, Wrap=TRUE

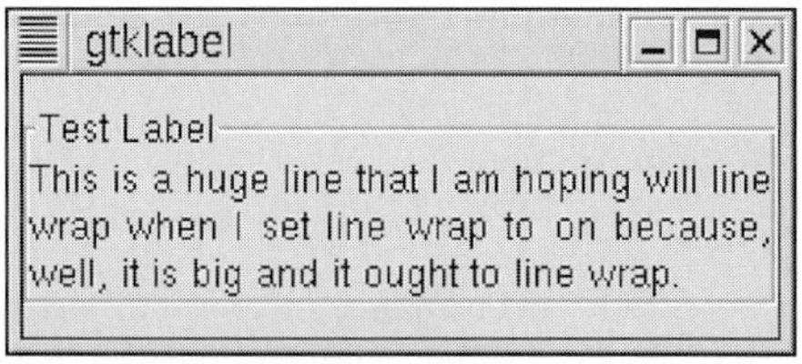

Figure 5.2 Fill, Wrap=TRUE

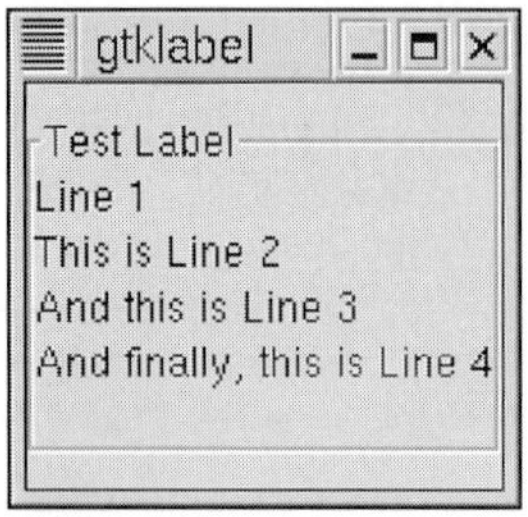

Figure 5.3 Left, Wrap=FALSE

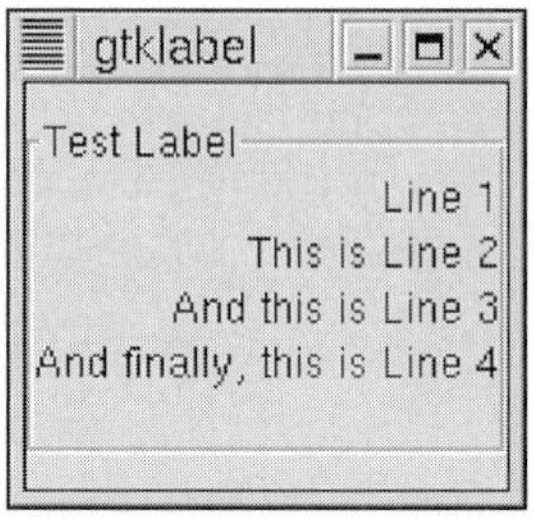

Figure 5.4 Right, Wrap=FALSE

Figure 5.5 Center, Wrap=FALSE

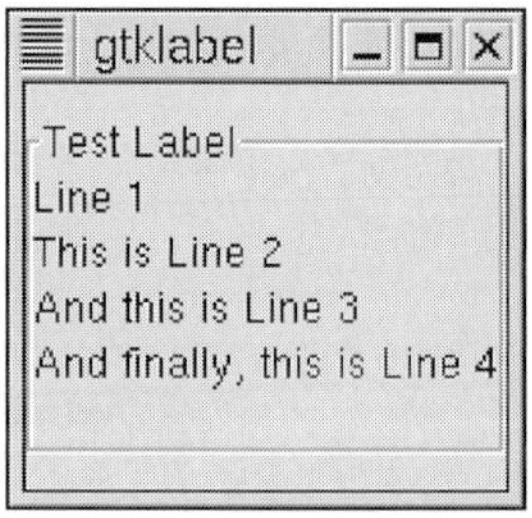

Figure 5.6 Fill, Wrap=FALSE

The source code for the application that generated the preceding screen shots shows how to call both gtk_label_set_justify() and gtk_label_set_line_wrap():

Listing 5.1 GtkLabel Attribute Sample Code

```
#include <gtk/gtk.h
#include <stdio.h

static GtkWidget *leftButton, *rightButton, *centerButton, *fillButton;
static GtkWidget *trueButton, *falseButton;

static void
QuitCallback(GtkWidget *widget, GtkWidget *dialog_window)
```

```
{
    gtk_main_quit();
    exit( 0 );
}

static void
ClickedCallback(GtkWidget *widget, GtkWidget *dialog_window)
{
    GtkWidget *window, *labelFrame, *labelTest, *vbox;

    window = gtk_window_new( GTK_WINDOW_TOPLEVEL );
    gtk_window_position (GTK_WINDOW (window), GTK_WIN_POS_MOUSE);
    gtk_widget_set_usize( window, 320, -1 );
    vbox = gtk_vbox_new (FALSE, 0);
    gtk_container_add (GTK_CONTAINER (window), vbox);

    labelFrame = gtk_frame_new ("Test Label");
    gtk_box_pack_start (GTK_BOX (vbox), labelFrame, TRUE, TRUE, 10);
        labelTest = gtk_label_new ("Line 1\n"
        "This is Line 2\n"
        "And this is Line 3\n"
        "And finally, this is Line 4\n"

    );
    gtk_container_add (GTK_CONTAINER (labelFrame), labelTest);

    if ( GTK_TOGGLE_BUTTON(leftButton)->active == TRUE ) {
        gtk_label_set_justify( GTK_LABEL(labelTest),
            GTK_JUSTIFY_LEFT );
    } else if ( GTK_TOGGLE_BUTTON(rightButton)->active == TRUE ) {
        gtk_label_set_justify( GTK_LABEL(labelTest),
            GTK_JUSTIFY_RIGHT );
    } else if ( GTK_TOGGLE_BUTTON(centerButton)->active == TRUE ) {
        gtk_label_set_justify( GTK_LABEL(labelTest),
            GTK_JUSTIFY_CENTER );
    } else if ( GTK_TOGGLE_BUTTON(fillButton)->active == TRUE ) {
        gtk_label_set_justify( GTK_LABEL(labelTest),
            GTK_JUSTIFY_FILL );
    }
    if ( GTK_TOGGLE_BUTTON(trueButton)-active == TRUE ) {
        gtk_label_set_line_wrap (GTK_LABEL(labelTest), TRUE );
        gtk_label_set_text( GTK_LABEL(labelTest),
        "This is a huge line that I am hoping will line wrap when I
set line wrap to on because, well, it is big and it ought to line wrap" );
    } else {
        gtk_label_set_line_wrap (GTK_LABEL(labelTest), FALSE );
    }
    gtk_widget_show_all( window );
}
```

The main() routine, not shown here, creates the application's main dialog. When the button in this dialog, labeled Refresh, is pressed, the routine ClickedCallback(), as shown in the preceding code, is invoked. A window is created, and within this window, a GtkFrame widget is instantiated. This GtkFrame widget has a single child that is the GtkLabel containing the text we are to display. Based on the settings made in the main dialog, text justification and line wrap attributes are applied to the GtkLabel widget. If line wrapping is disabled, a series of four text lines of differing lengths are displayed. Each of these lines is terminated by a C newline character (\n). If line wrapping is enabled, a single line of text of considerable length is displayed, illustrating the ability of the GtkLabel widget to wrap long lines of text within a region. The window is set to be 320 pixels in width to give the GtkLabel widget a fixed area, with the size of our choosing, within which to wrap its text. If line wrap is enabled, all justification settings except for GTK_JUSTIFY_FILL give the same result, as shown in Figure 5.1. If line wrap is enabled, setting GTK_JUSTIFY_FILL causes the text to fill, as shown in Figure 5.2. The justification settings GTK_JUSTIFY_LEFT, GTK_JUSTIFY_RIGHT, and GTK_JUSTIFY_CENTER are interpreted as shown in Figures 5.3, 5.4, and 5.5 only when line wrap is disabled. Specifying GTK_JUSTIFY_FILL with line wrap disabled (see Figure 5.6) gives the same result as setting GTK_JUSTIFY_LEFT with line wrap also disabled.

Placing Underscores in the Label

The final functionality provided by the GtkLabel API allows an application to specify which characters, if any, in the text of GtkLabel widget should be rendered with an underscore character (_) attribute applied to them. The function is rather simple:

```
void
gtk_label_set_pattern(GtkLabel *label, const gchar *pattern);
```

The length of the pattern must be equal to the length of the text associated with the GtkLabel instance passed as the first argument. In this pattern, an underscore (_) character indicates that the character occurring at the same position in the label's text should have an underscore applied to it. If the character in the pattern is anything else (the convention is to use a space), then the corresponding character in the label's text will render without an underscore accompanying it.

For example, given the label text "File..." and the pattern "_   ", we can expect the label to render with an underscore beneath the "F" character of the label text.

The major use of gtk_label_set_pattern() and the routine I am about to discuss, gtk_label_parse_uline(), is in GtkItemFactory, which uses it to specify the character of a menu item label that should be associated with an accelerator. An accelerator, as discussed in Chapter 4, is a key that, when pressed at the same time as an Alt or Ctrl key (depending on the context), will cause a menu to appear or a menu item to activate. These characters in a menu item or menu bar item are, by convention, rendered with an underscore.

A programmer using the GtkItemFactory to specify a menu item would specify the position of the accelerator key (in the case of a "File..." menu item, with the following string: "_File..."). GtkMenuItem passes this string, and the instance of GtkLabel associated with the menu item, to gtk_label_parse_uline():

```
guint
gtk_label_parse_uline(GtkLabel *label, const gchar *string);
```

The job of gtk_label_parse_uline() is to take the passed string, parse it for any embedded underscore characters, and construct the appropriate pattern string that will be set for the label with gtk_label_set_pattern(). The text of the label is also set to the value of string minus any embedded underscore characters. In the following example:

```
GtkWidget *label;

label = gtk_label_new( "Yabba Dabba Doo" );
gtk_label_parse_uline( label, "_File..." );
```

the text associated with label will be "File...", and the label's pattern will be set to an underscore. Note that the text and the pattern are the same length. Before drawing a character of a label's text, GtkLabel will look at the pattern and see if the character at the same position in the pattern is an underscore. If the character in the pattern is an underscore, then the corresponding letter in the text of the label will be drawn with an underscore immediately below it.

Buttons

In the next several sections, I will present Gtk+'s button classes. These button classes include GtkButton, GtkToggleButton, GtkCheckButton, and GtkRadioButton. Each is related to one other in the Gtk+ class hierarchy as depicted in Figure 5.7. I will cover the Gtk+ button classes in a top-down order starting with the GtkButton class, which is the highest class in the hierarchy and from which the remaining button classes are based, and finishing with GtkRadioButton, which is the lowest in the class hierarchy.

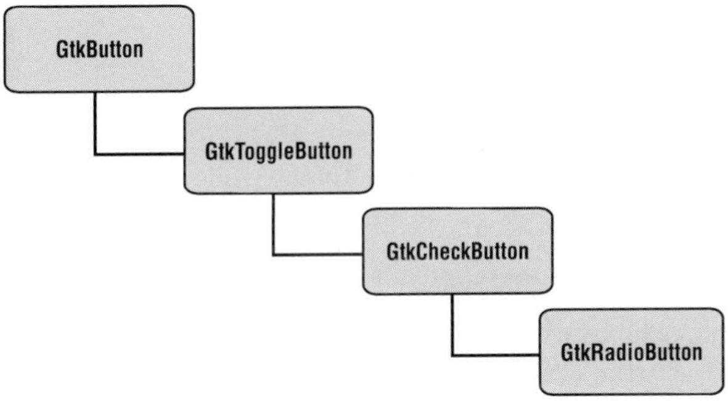

Figure 5.7 Button Widget Hierarchy

Buttons are among the most useful of the widgets provided by Gtk+. Nearly every dialog contains an instance of GtkButton or a derived class. An instance of GtkButton provides users with a way to initiate some action. In contrast, instances of GtkToggleButton, GtkCheckButton, and GtkRadioButton convey information to users and provide a way for users to make selections or choose options from the information presented, and activating an instance of one of these classes typically will not result in an action being performed.

Figures 5.8, 5.9, and 5.10 illustrate three dialogs, each containing three buttons labeled Apples, Oranges, and Pears.

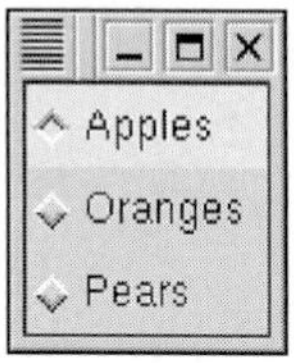

Figure 5.8 Radio Buttons

Figure 5.9 Toggle Buttons

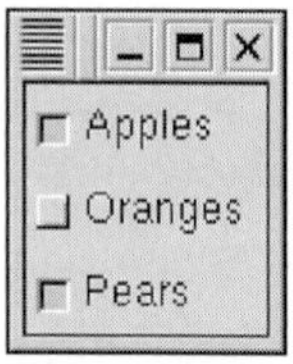

Figure 5.10 Check Buttons

The buttons in Figure 5.8 are instances of GtkRadioButton, while the buttons in Figure 5.9 and Figure 5.10 are instances of GtkToggleButton and GtkCheckButton, respectively. Radio buttons (see Figure 5.8) allow a user to make a "one of many" choice. Radio buttons, in this case the buttons labeled Apples, Oranges, and Pears, are related to each other by placing them in a "radio group." Only one radio button at a time can be selected in a radio group. Given the state of the radio group depicted in Figure 5.8, clicking on the button labeled Oranges will cause that button to become selected and will cause the button labeled Apples to become unselected. The GtkToggleButton and GtkCheckButton classes, on the other hand, allow for "many of many" selections to be made by users of your application. For example, a user could select both Apples and Pears, as shown in Figure 5.10. The GtkToggleButton and GtkCheckButton widget classes are similar in functionality; the only difference between the two classes is the appearance of the widget, as can be seen by comparing Figures 5.9 and 5.10.

GtkButton

Class Name

```
GtkButton
```

Parent Class Name

```
GtkBin
```

Macros

Widget type macro: `GTK_TYPE_BUTTON`

Object to widget cast macro: `GTK_BUTTON(obj)`

Widget type check macro: `GTK_IS_BUTTON(obj)`

Table 5.4 Signals

Signal Name	*Condition Causing Signal to Trigger*
pressed	A button widget was logically "pressed."
released	A "pressed" button widget was logically released.
clicked	The button widget was logically clicked.
enter	The mouse pointer entered the region occupied by the button.
leave	The mouse pointer left the region occupied by the button.

Signal Function Prototypes

```
void
pressed(GtkButton *button, gpointer user_data);

void
released(GtkButton *button, gpointer user_data);
```

Signal Function Prototypes (Continued)

```
void
clicked(GtkButton *button, gpointer user_data);

void
enter(GtkButton *button, gpointer user_data);

void
leave(GtkButton *button, gpointer user_data);
```

Supported Arguments

Prefix: `GtkButton::`

Table 5.5 GtkButton Arguments

Name	*Type*	*Permissions*
label	GTK_TYPE_STRING	GTK_ARG_READWRITE
relief	GTK_TYPE_RELIEF_STYLE	GTK_ARG_READWRITE

Application-Level API Synopsis

Retrieve the value GTK_TYPE_BUTTON at runtime:

```
GtkType
gtk_button_get_type(void);
```

Create an instance of GtkButton with no label string:

```
GtkWidget *
gtk_button_new(void);
```

Create an instance of GtkButton with the specified label string:

```
GtkWidget *
gtk_button_new_with_label(const gchar *label);
```

Trigger a pressed signal for the specified GtkButton instance:

```
void
gtk_button_pressed(GtkButton *button);
```

Trigger a released signal for the specified GtkButton instance:

```
void
gtk_button_released(GtkButton *button);
```

Trigger a clicked signal for the specified GtkButton instance:

```
void
gtk_button_clicked(GtkButton *button);
```

Application-Level API Synopsis (Continued)

Trigger an enter signal for the specified GtkButton instance:

```
void
gtk_button_enter(GtkButton *button);
```

Trigger a leave signal for the specified GtkButton instance:

```
void
gtk_button_leave(GtkButton *button);
```

Set the relief style for the specified GtkButton instance:

```
void
gtk_button_set_relief(GtkButton *button, GtkReliefStyle newstyle);
```

Retrieve the current relief style for the specified GtkButton instance:

```
GtkReliefStyle
gtk_button_get_relief(GtkButton *button);
```

Class Description

GtkButton is perhaps the most fundamental of the control widgets provided by the Gtk+ widget set (or by any other widget set, for that matter). The simplest and perhaps most universally used dialog imaginable is the message dialog, an example of which is shown in Figure 5.11. The only control widget needed to implement a dialog of this type is GtkButton, which, in this case, provides the push button that the user clicks to dismiss the dialog after the message has been read.

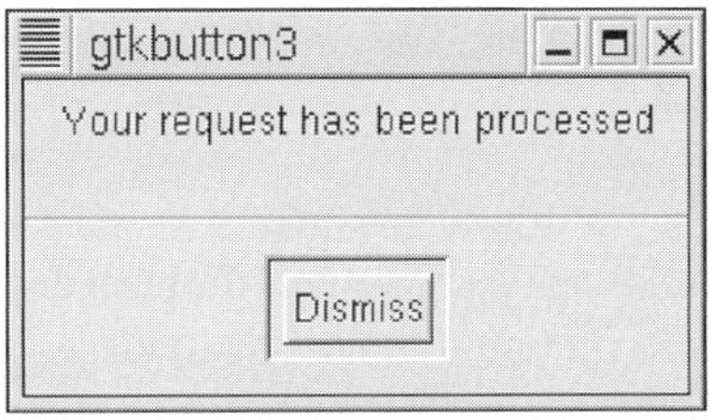

Figure 5.11 Button Widget

GtkButton is very simple, both in terms of its layout and appearance (refer to Figure 5.11) and in how it interacts with an application. With regard to appearance, a push button is little more than a rectangular area that displays a label. In the case of GtkButton, this label is an instance of GtkLabel. The parent class of GtkButton, which is GtkBin, reflects the fact that the button is a container managing an instance of GtkLabel. I will discuss the implications of this later in this chapter when I discuss the functions for creating an instance of GtkButton.

Signals

In terms of interaction, most applications are mainly interested in knowing when the button has been clicked, which is a logical term that indicates the button has been pressed and released by the user. Here again, in more detail, are the signals supported by the GtkButton widget:

- **clicked** This signal indicates that the user has physically pressed and released the mouse button within the area managed by the GtkButton instance, and as a result, the push button has been logically pressed, or clicked. The response to receiving this event should be to invoke the functionality implied by the label of the push button.
- **enter** This signal indicates that the mouse has entered the region managed by the push-button widget.
- **pressed** This signal occurs when the user has physically pressed the mouse button in the area owned by the push button. Receiving this event does not indicate that the user has logically pressed the push button; an application should not perform the action associated with the button upon receiving this event.
- **released** This signal is sent when the user has physically released the mouse button in the area owned by the push button. If this event follows a pressed event, then the push button was logically pressed, or clicked.
- **leave** This signal indicates that the mouse has left the region managed by the push-button widget.

Most applications need only handle the clicked event, and all other events generated by GtkButton for the most part can be safely ignored.

Creating a Button

Creating an instance of GtkButton is trivial. Gtk+ provides two functions for this purpose. The first of these, gtk_button_new_with_label(), is perhaps the most widely used of the two:

```
GtkWidget *
gtk_button_new_with_label(const gchar *label);
```

The argument label is a NULL-terminated C string that represents the label displayed by the push button. To create an instance of GtkButton without specifying a label, call gtk_button_new():

```
GtkWidget *
gtk_button_new(void);
```

When you create a push button by calling gtk_button_new_with_label(), GtkButton automatically creates and initializes an instance of GtkLabel, makes the label a child of the push button, and sets its text to the value you passed in as an argument. None of this is done, however, when you call gtk_button_new(). When would you ever want to create a push button that has no label? There are times when this makes sense. Perhaps the most familiar example would be to display a button that can be used to select a color. For example, instead of labeling a series of three buttons Red, Green, and Blue, a more effective (and more easily internationalized) user interface would display push buttons without a label, setting the background colors of the buttons to red, green, and blue, respectively, to convey to the user the action associated with pressing each of the buttons.

Changing the Label Text

Your application can set or change the text label of a button anytime via the label argument. Here is a short routine that illustrates the technique:

```
void
SetButtonLabel( GtkWidget *button, char *label )
{
        gtk_object_set( GTK_OBJECT( button ),
                "GtkButton::label", label, NULL );
}
```

Refer to Chapter 3, "Signals, Events, Objects, and Types," for more information on gtk_object_set().

Because the label is an instance of GtkLabel, you can make use of any of the functions provided by GtkLabel in order to modify the text. To get a handle to the GtkLabel widget managed by an instance of GtkButton, you can use the syntax illustrated by the following example, which sets the underscore pattern of the label to "_ ":

```
GtkWidget *button, *child;

...

child = GTK_BIN (button)->child;
if (child && GTK_IS_LABEL (child))
        gtk_label_set_pattern(GTK_LABEL(child), "_  " );
```

Generating Synthetic Events

GtkButton supports functions that allow applications to synthetically generate each of the signals supported by GtkButton. These functions include gtk_button_pressed(), gtk_button_released(), gtk_button_enter(), gtk_button_leave(), and gtk_button_clicked(), corresponding to GtkButtons's pressed, released, enter, leave, and clicked events, respectively. Each takes a single argument: an instance of GtkButton. Their function prototypes are as follows:

```
void
gtk_button_pressed(GtkButton *button);

void
gtk_button_released(GtkButton *button);

void
gtk_button_clicked(GtkButton *button);

void
gtk_button_enter(GtkButton *button);
```

```
void
gtk_button_leave(GtkButton *button);
```

The ability to generate synthetic events is provided mainly for use by widget writers and is not typically needed by application designers.

Relief Styles

GtkButton allows you to set the relief style of a GtkButton instance. The following relief styles are supported: GTK_RELIEF_NORMAL, GTK_RELIEF_HALF, and GTK_RELIEF_NONE. The default relief style for GtkButton is GTK_RELIEF_NORMAL. GTK_RELIEF_HALF and GTK_RELIEF_NORMAL are synonymous in Gtk 1.2 because GtkButton only distinguishes between GTK_RELIEF_NONE and other styles. Specifying GTK_RELIEF_NONE tells GtkButton not to draw a frame around a button; all that will appear when the widget does not have the focus is the text of the button. Specifying GTK_RELIEF_NORMAL or GTK_RELIEF_HALF results in a frame drawn around the button, as shown in Figures 5.12 ands 5.13.

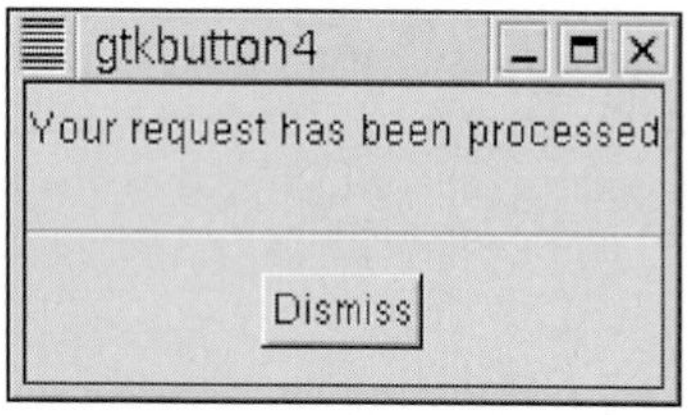

Figure 5.12 GTK_RELIEF_HALF and GTK_RELIEF_NORMAL

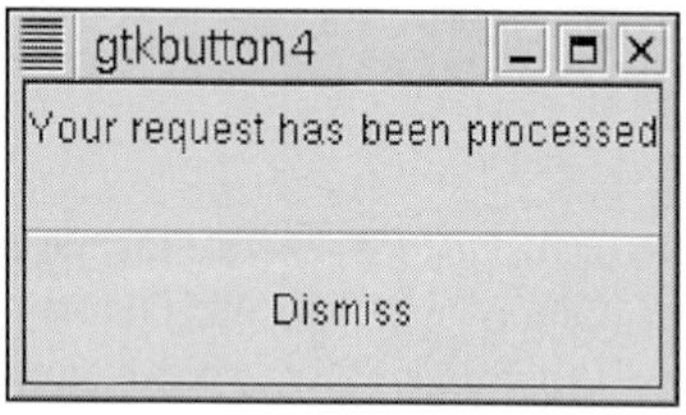

Figure 5.13 GTK_RELIEF_NONE

To set the relief style for the specified GtkButton instance, you can call gtk_button_set_relief():

```
void
gtk_button_set_relief(GtkButton *button, GtkReliefStyle newstyle);
```

To retrieve the current relief style for the specified GtkButton instance, you can call gtk_button_get_relief():

```
GtkReliefStyle
gtk_button_get_relief(GtkButton *button);
```

GtkToggleButton

Class Name

```
GtkToggleButton
```

Parent Class Name

```
GtkButton
```

Macros

Widget type macro: `GTK_TYPE_TOGGLE_BUTTON`

Object to widget cast macro: `GTK_TOGGLE_BUTTON(obj)`

Widget type check macro: `GTK_IS_TOGGLE_BUTTON(obj)`

Table 5.6 Signals

Signal Name	*Condition Causing Signal to Trigger*
toggled	The toggle-button widget changed the state (for example, from on to off).

Signal Function Prototypes

```
void toggled(GtkToggleButton *togglebutton, gpointer user_data);
```

Supported Arguments

Prefix: `GtkToggleButton::`

Table 5.7 GtkToggleButton Arguments

Name	*Type*	*Permissions*
active	GTK_TYPE_BOOL	GTK_ARG_READWRITE
draw_indicator	GTK_TYPE_BOOL	GTK_ARG_READWRITE

Application-Level API Synopsis

Retrieve the constant GTK_TYPE_TOGGLE_BUTTON at runtime:
```
GtkType
gtk_toggle_button_get_type(void);
```

Create a new instance of GtkToggleButton without a label:
```
GtkWidget *
gtk_toggle_button_new(void);
```

Create a new instance of GtkToggleButton with the specified label:
```
GtkWidget *
gtk_toggle_button_new_with_label(const gchar *label);
```

Toggle on or off the display of a toggle button indicator:
```
void
gtk_toggle_button_set_mode(GtkToggleButton *toggle_button,
         gboolean draw_indicator);
```

Set the GtkToggleButton instance as active (selected):
```
void
gtk_toggle_button_set_active(GtkToggleButton *toggle_button,
         gboolean is_active);
```

Get the active state of GtkToggleButton instance:
```
gboolean
gtk_toggle_button_get_active(GtkToggleButton *toggle_button);
```

Generate a toggled signal for the specified GtkToggleButton widget instance:
```
void
gtk_toggle_button_toggled(GtkToggleButton *toggle_button);
```

Class Description

GtkToggleButton is closely related to GtkButton (described previously), which is no surprise given that it is a child class of GtkButton. As a child class, an instance of GtkToggleButton can make use of all the facilities supported by GtkButton. This includes GtkButton's API and signals as well as its arguments.

For example, the routine SetButtonLabel(), presented earlier, can also be used to change the label text of a toggle-button widget. This is because the GtkButton:: label argument, defined by GtkButton, works for any class derived from GtkButton, including GtkToggleButton.

The main difference between GtkButton and GtkToggleButton is in how instances of these classes are used by an application. You use an instance of GtkButton to give your users a control that will perform an action when clicked, and you use an instance of GtkToggleButton to represent a state (e.g., on or off or perhaps active or inactive). A toggle button may also perform an action when it is clicked; this depends on the logic of your application.

The following screen shot of the popular Gtk+ IRC client X-Chat illustrates both types of buttons in use. Instances of GtkButton include the buttons located in the bottom-right corner of the screen, labeled Op, DeOp, Ban, and so forth. When pressed, these buttons all perform an action.

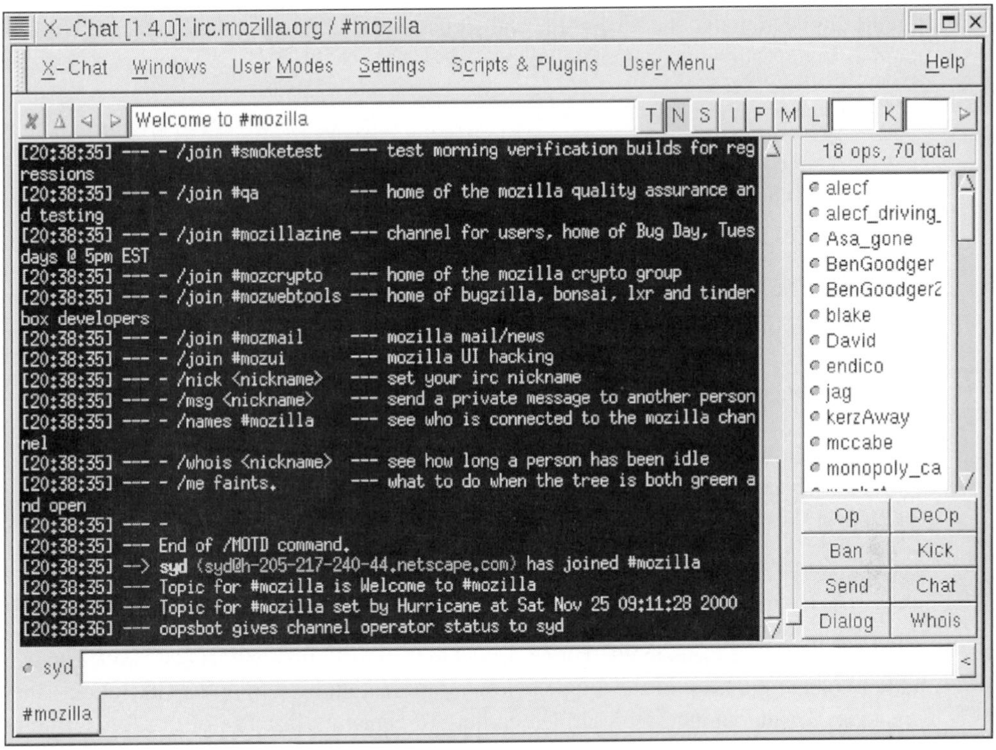

Figure 5.14 X-Chat Screen Shot

An instance of GtkButton will change its appearance as the button is clicked, and again as it is released, to indicate the activation operation as it is being performed. After the user releases the button, it reverts to its original visual state.

The buttons labeled "T," "N," "S," "I," "P," "M," and "L" near the upper-right corner of Figure 5.14 are instances of GtkToggleButton. Each of these buttons shows state information. The button that looks pressed in, labeled "N", is active or selected. The other buttons are all inactive. The default state of an instance of GtkToggleButton is inactive, which changes to active upon the first click by the user and then back to inactive upon the second click by the user, and so forth.

GtkToggleButton allows clients to change the state of the button at any time. X Chat uses this functionality in the following way. A user may click a toggle button to cause the associated action to be performed. Should the action be performed successfully, the state of the button will remain in the active state to indicate to the user that the mode represented by the button is currently active. If the action fails or it cannot be performed, the button will revert back to the inactive state. This logic is controlled by the application, and not by the toggle button widget.

Signals

When the user clicks on a toggle button, a "toggled" signal is generated by the widget to tell the application that the state of the widget has changed. The toggle signal can be registered as in the following example:

```
gtk_signal_connect (GTK_OBJECT(my_toggle_button), "toggled",
        GTK_SIGNAL_FUNC(toggle_changed), NULL);
```

The function prototype for the toggle_changed() signal function is as follows:

```
void
toggled_signal_function(GtkWidget *toggle_button, gpointer arg)
```

I'll have more to say about this function later in this chapter.

Creating Toggle Buttons

Now that we have an understanding of what GtkToggleButton instances can be used for, let's take a look at the API provided by the GtkToggleButton class.

To create an instance of GtkToggleButton without a label, your application can call gtk_toggle_button_new():

```
GtkWidget *
gtk_toggle_button_new(void);
```

This call is analogous to gtk_button_new() in the GtkButton widget class API. You can add or change the label of the toggle button after creation by setting the GtkButton::label argument for the widget, as described earlier. To create an instance of GtkToggleButton with a label, an application can call gtk_toggle_button_new_with_label():

```
GtkWidget *
gtk_toggle_button_new_with_label(const gchar *label);
```

gtk_toggle_button_new_with_label() is analogous to gtk_button_new_with_label().

Getting and Setting the State of a Toggle Button

The user generally should control the state of a toggle button. Because a toggle button looks and acts similar to a push button, users will be inclined to click on it, and this should be the catalyst for a change in the visual state of a toggle button. However, there are times when your application may want to control the state of the button. An example would be to set the initial state of a button to the active state. Another example would be to reverse the state change made by the user because of some inability to deal with the action associated with the state change, as was illustrated earlier. To change the state of a toggle button, applications can call gtk_toggle_button_set_active():

```
void
gtk_toggle_button_set_active(GtkToggleButton *toggle_button,
        gboolean is_active);
```

If is_active is TRUE, the state of the widget is changed so that the button takes on the pressed-in look associated with the active state. If is_active is FALSE, the button is set to the look associated with the inactive state. If the state changes as a result of this call, Gtk+ simulates a button click on the toggle button, meaning that any click signal functions registered for the toggle button will be invoked as a result of calling this function. Also, the toggled signal will be triggered as a result, so if a signal function has been registered by your application for the toggled signal for this widget instance, then it too will be called.

You can query the state (active or inactive) of a toggle-button widget by calling gtk_toggle_button_get_active():

```
gboolean
gtk_toggle_button_get_active(GtkToggleButton *toggle_button);
```

The argument toggle_button is an instance of GtkToggleButton (or, as we shall see later, a subclass of GtkToggleButton). If TRUE is returned, the button is active; otherwise, FALSE is returned.

There are two situations in which I can envision an application making use of the preceding call. The first is when inside of a toggled signal function. Here, you will often want to know what the current state of the widget is. Thus, the typical toggled signal function will be structured something like this:

```
void
toggled_signal_function (GtkWidget *w, gpointer arg)
{
        gboolean state;

        state = gtk_toggle_button_get_active(
                GTK_TOGGLE_BUTTON( w ) );
        if ( state == TRUE )
                // do something here
        else
                // do something else here
}
```

The other time when calling gtk_toggle_button_get_active() is important would be in the signal function associated with closing a dialog, or in a Save/Save As menu handler. Here your code will want to check the state of toggle buttons to obtain content as a part of the save operation. Let's look at a concrete example. Assume we pop up a dialog that contains three toggle buttons labeled, respectively, Apples, Oranges, and Pears. Below these toggle buttons are push buttons labeled Print and Quit. The user clicks on one or more of the toggle buttons to specify, for example, the fruits that the user eats on a regular basis. If the user clicks the Quit button, the dialog is dismissed and nothing is done. If the user clicks the Print button, the clicked signal function associated with the Print button will query the state of the toggle buttons and print the results to stdout. Here I assume that the toggle-button widgets are stored in global variables for the sake of simplicity.

```
void
print_clicked_function (GtkWidget *w, gpointer arg)
{
        gboolean apples, oranges, pears;

        apples = gtk_toggle_button_get_active(
                GTK_TOGGLE_BUTTON( apples_toggle_button_widget ) );
        oranges = gtk_toggle_button_get_active(
                GTK_TOGGLE_BUTTON( oranges_toggle_button_widget ) );
        pears = gtk_toggle_button_get_active(
                GTK_TOGGLE_BUTTON( pears_toggle_button_widget ) );

        printf( "I %s apples, %s oranges, and %s pears regularly\n",
                ( apples == TRUE ? "eat" : "do not eat" ),
                ( oranges == TRUE ? "eat" : "do not eat" ),
                ( pears == TRUE ? "eat" : "do not eat" ) );
}
```

Miscellaneous Functions

Your application can cause the toggled signal functions registered for an instance of GtkToggleButton to be invoked at any time by calling gtk_toggle_button_toggled():

```
void
gtk_toggle_button_toggled(GtkToggleButton *toggle_button);
```

The visual state of the toggle-button widget is not changed by this call.

The final function exposed by GtkToggleButton that I will describe is gtk_toggle_button_set_mode():

```
void
gtk_toggle_button_set_mode(GtkToggleButton *toggle_button,
        gboolean draw_indicator);
```

This function takes two arguments: an instance of a GtkToggleButton widget and a gboolean. This gboolean argument controls the visibility of the toggle-button widget. If set to FALSE, the toggle button is hidden from view. If TRUE, the toggle button is made visible. Effectively, passing TRUE acts as though gtk_widget_show_all() has been called on the toggle button, while passing FALSE has the opposite effect, causing the toggle button to be hidden.

GtkCheckButton

Class Name

```
GtkCheckButton
```

Parent Class Name

```
GtkToggleButton
```

Macros

Widget type macro: `GTK_TYPE_CHECK_BUTTON`

Object to widget cast macro: `GTK_CHECK_BUTTON(obj)`

Widget type check macro: `GTK_IS_CHECK_BUTTON(obj)`

Application-Level API Synopsis

Retrieve the constant GTK_TYPE_CHECK_BUTTON at runtime:

```
GtkType
gtk_check_button_get_type(void);
```

Create a new instance of GtkCheckButton without a label:

```
GtkWidget *
gtk_check_button_new(void);
```

Create a new instance of GtkCheckButton with the specified label:

```
GtkWidget *
gtk_check_button_new_with_label(const gchar *label);
```

Class Description

The next widget class in the GtkButton hierarchy is GtkCheckButton. This widget class inherits from GtkToggleButton, meaning it has full access to the functions and attributes provided by GtkToggleButton as well as those provided by GtkButton, which, as we saw earlier, is the parent of GtkToggleButton. Everything described earlier for GtkToggleButton applies to this class as well; when calling the functions or using the macros, simply pass an instance of GtkCheckButton instead of an instance of GtkToggleButton.

The only real difference between GtkCheckButton and GtkToggleButton is in how the widget is rendered (see Figure 5.10). The sensitive portion of the widget (i.e., the area that is receptive to mouse events) consists of the rectangular area that contains both the button and its label.

The API for GtkCheckButton only consists of instance-creation functions. Once again, the real functionality is provided by GtkToggleButton and its parent, GtkButton, and those classes combined define the functionality available to GtkCheckButton.

Creating a Check Button

To create a new instance of GtkCheckButton without a label, call gtk_check_button_new():

```
GtkWidget *
gtk_check_button_new(void);
```

To create a new instance of GtkCheckButton with a label, call gtk_check_button_new_with_label():

```
GtkWidget *
gtk_check_button_new_with_label(const gchar *label);
```

For details on gtk_check_button_new() and gtk_check_button_new_with_label(), refer to the information presented earlier for gtk_toggle_button_new() and gtk_toggle_button_new_with_label(), respectively.

Now let's turn our attention to GtkRadioButton, which is the remaining widget class in the GtkButton hierarchy.

GtkRadioButton

Class Name

```
GtkRadioButton
```

Parent Class Name

```
GtkCheckButton
```

Macros

Widget type macro: `GTK_TYPE_RADIO_BUTTON`

Object to widget cast macro: `GTK_RADIO_BUTTON(obj)`

Widget type check macro: `GTK_IS_RADIO_BUTTON(obj)`

Supported Arguments

Prefix: `GtkRadioButton::`

Table 5.8 GtkRadioButton Arguments

Name	*Type*	*Permissions*
group	GTK_TYPE_RADIO_BUTTON	GTK_ARG_WRITABLE

Application-Level API Synopsis

Retrieve the GTK_TYPE_RADIO_BUTTON constant at runtime:

```
GtkType
gtk_radio_button_get_type(void);
```

Create a new GtkRadioButton instance with no label and optionally add it to a button group:

```
GtkWidget *
gtk_radio_button_new(GSList *group);
```

Create a new GtkRadioButton instance with the specified label and optionally add it to a button group:

```
GtkWidget *
gtk_radio_button_new_with_label(GSList *group, const gchar *label);
```

Same as gtk_radio_button_new, but pass a widget from which the radio group to attach the new radio button will be determined:

```
GtkWidget *
gtk_radio_button_new_from_widget(GtkRadioButton *group);
```

Same as gtk_radio_button_new_with_label, but pass a widget from which the radio group to attach the new radio button will be determined:

```
GtkWidget *
gtk_radio_button_new_with_label_from_widget(GtkRadioButton *group,
        const gchar *label);
```

Retrieve the radio button group to which the specified GtkRadioButton widget instance belongs:

```
GSList *
gtk_radio_button_group(GtkRadioButton *radio_button);
```

Associate a GtkRadioButton instance with the specified radio button group:

```
void
gtk_radio_button_set_group(GtkRadioButton *radio_button, GSList *group);
```

Class Description

GtkRadioButton is far and away the most functional and specialized of the widget classes inheriting from GtkButton. An instance of GtkRadioButton differs from an instance of GtkCheckButton in appearance and in functionality. The square-shaped buttons of GtkCheckButton instances are diamond-shaped in GtkRadioButton. And, while GtkCheckButton allows for “many of many” selections, you will use a set of GtkRadioButton instances to implement “one of many” selections. Thus, you would use GtkCheckButton to implement a user interface that allows a user to, for example, respond to the question, “Which of the following are your favorite types of ice cream?” by selecting multiple answers. GtkRadioButton might be used to implement a user interface with which the user might respond to a question such as “In which month were you born?” Here, of course, only one choice is possible.

To implement “one of many” selections, GtkRadioButton requires you to group related instances of GtkRadioButton together. Doing so gives GtkRadioButton the ability to ensure that only one of the radio buttons in the group will be selected at any given moment. Whenever one of the radio buttons in the group is selected by the user (or by the application with a call to gtk_toggle_button_set_active()), GtkRadioButton will ensure that each of the other toggle buttons in the radio group is unselected.

Creating a Radio-Button Widget

Creating an instance of GtkRadioButton is slightly different than creating an instance of GtkCheckButton. The functions gtk_radio_button_new() and gtk_radio_button_new_with_label() create a radio button with and without a label, respectively:

```
GtkWidget *
gtk_radio_button_new(GSList *group);

GtkWidget *
gtk_radio_button_new_with_label(GSList *group, const gchar *label);
```

Each of these functions has an additional argument, group. When creating the first radio button in a group of related radio buttons, the group argument should be set to (GSList *) NULL. When creating subsequent radio buttons that belong to the same group, you use the widget ID of any widget that belongs to same group in order to specify the group to which the new radio button should be added. The following code and discussion should make this clear:

```
GtkWidget *apples, *oranges, *pears;

apples = gtk_radio_button_new_with_label (NULL, "Apples");

oranges = gtk_radio_button_new_with_label (
        gtk_radio_button_group (GTK_RADIO_BUTTON (apples)),
        "Oranges");

pears = gtk_radio_button_new_with_label (
        gtk_radio_button_group (GTK_RADIO_BUTTON (oranges)),
        "Pears");
```

Here, the group argument of the first button, labeled Apples, is set to NULL because we are defining the group. The group argument of the button labeled Oranges is set to the radio group to which the Apples button belongs, and the group argument of the button labeled Pears is set to the group to which the Oranges button belongs. Alternately, you could have set the Pears button radio group as follows:

```
pears = gtk_radio_button_new_with_label (
        gtk_radio_button_group (GTK_RADIO_BUTTON (apples)),
        "Pears");
```

Ultimately, any radio button in the group will work. I tend to use the first widget that was added to the group using code similar to the following:

```
GtkWidget *apples, *oranges, *pears, *group;

apples = gtk_radio_button_new_with_label (NULL, "Apples");
group = apples;

oranges = gtk_radio_button_new_with_label (
        gtk_radio_button_group (GTK_RADIO_BUTTON (group)),
        "Oranges");

pears = gtk_radio_button_new_with_label (
        gtk_radio_button_group (GTK_RADIO_BUTTON (group)),
        "Pears");
```

That is all there really is to creating a radio group. The function gtk_radio_button_group():

```
GSList *
gtk_radio_button_group(GtkRadioButton *radio_button);
```

retrieves the radio button group to which the specified GtkRadioButton instance belongs.

Two alternate functions exist for creating a radio button and adding it to a radio group. The first, gtk_radio_button_new_from_widget(), is similar to gtk_radio_button_new(), except that it takes a GtkRadioButton widget as an argument and uses that widget to determine the radio group to which the new instance of GtkRadioButton should be added. Here is the prototype:

```
GtkWidget *
gtk_radio_button_new_from_widget(GtkRadioButton *group);
```

The second of the alternate functions allows you to specify the label associated with the new instance of GtkRadioButton:

```
GtkWidget *
gtk_radio_button_new_with_label_from_widget(GtkRadioButton *group,
         const gchar *label);
```

Let's rewrite the Apples, Oranges, and Pears example using these new functions:

```
GtkWidget *apples, *oranges, *pears;

apples = gtk_radio_button_new_with_label (NULL, "Apples");

oranges = gtk_radio_button_new_with_label_from_widget( apples,
        "Oranges");

pears = gtk_radio_button_new_with_label_from_widget ( apples,
        "Pears");
```

Of the three styles, the preceding is probably the easiest to read.

The final routine we will look at here is gtk_radio_button_set_group(). This function allows you to associate a radio button with a group after the radio button has been created:

```
void
gtk_radio_button_set_group(GtkRadioButton *radio_button,
        GSList *group);
```

The first argument is an instance of GtkRadioButton returned by any of the gtk_radio_button_new*() functions mentioned earlier in this section. The argument group is a radio button group, returned by a call to gtk_radio_button_group(). One final time, let's look at our fruity example and see yet another way to create the set of radio buttons:

```
GtkWidget *apples, *oranges, *pears;

// create radio button widgets

apples = gtk_radio_button_new_with_label (NULL, "Apples");
oranges = gtk_radio_button_new_with_label (NULL, "Oranges");
pears = gtk_radio_button_new_with_label (NULL, "Pears");

// group together apples, oranges, and pears

gtk_radio_button_set_group(GTK_RADIO_BUTTON(apples),
         gtk_radio_button_group (GTK_RADIO_BUTTON (pears)));
gtk_radio_button_set_group(GTK_RADIO_BUTTON(oranges),
         gtk_radio_button_group (GTK_RADIO_BUTTON (pears)));
```

In the preceding code, I changed my tactics slightly by associating the Apples and Oranges radio buttons with the Pears radio button, as opposed to associating the Oranges and Pears radio buttons with the Apples radio button as I had done in the previous examples. It does not matter which widget in the group is passed to gtk_radio_button_group() to obtain the group ID, nor is it required that you pass the first radio-button widget of the group that was created.

However, the order in which you add radio buttons to a radio group does affect the choice of the widget that, when the widgets are shown, is toggled active. In the preceding code, the Pears radio button will be made active upon display. This is because, in the preceding code, we first add the Apples radio button to the Pears radio group. The Pears radio group does not yet exist, so a radio group is created by Gtk+ and Pears is added to the list.

Behind Pears on this list is the Apples radio button, followed eventually by the Oranges radio button. The first radio button on the list defines the radio button that will be active by default, unless your code explicitly sets the active radio button with a call to gtk_toggle_button_set_active() after the radio group is constructed.

Summary

In this chapter, we covered several widget classes. The first, GtkLabel, is used to display static text in a window or container widget. GtkButton, the next widget discussed, is used to implement push buttons such as the typical OK and Cancel buttons used in dialogs. The remaining classes discussed, GtkCheckButton, GtkToggleButton, and GtkRadioButton; all derive from GtkButton. The GtkCheckButton and GtkToggleButton controls allow users to make choices from a small group of (one or more) items. (Lists, discussed in Chapter 6, "Lists," should be used when the number of items from which the selections are to be made is large.) A set of toggle-button and check-button widgets can be combined to present the user with a way of selecting one or more items from a set of related choices (e.g., "Which of these flavors are your favorite?"). Radio buttons are similar to check-button and toggle-button widgets, except they enforce a "one of many" policy; only one item in a radio group (a set of radio buttons) can be selected at any one time.

CHAPTER

6

LISTS

This chapter continues the discussion of the Gtk+ control widgets that was started in the preceding chapter. In this chapter, I present the Gtk+ widget classes listed in Table 6.1.

Table 6.1 Widgets Covered in This Chapter

Widget	*Description*
GtkList	Single-column list
GtkCList	Multiple-column list

Figures 6.1 and 6.2 depict each of these widgets in typical use:

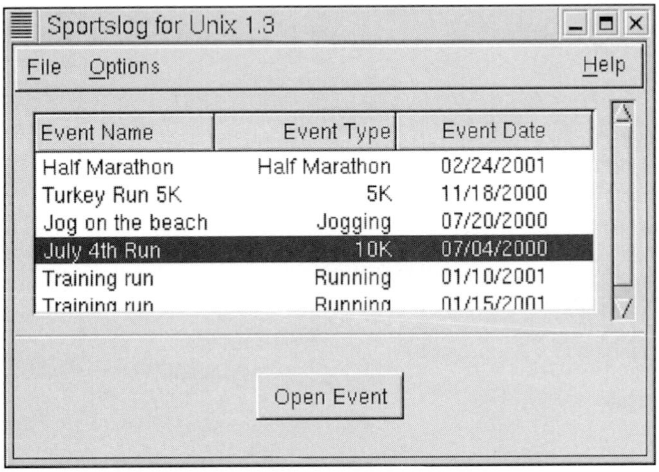

Figure 6.1 Multicolumn List Widget (GtkCList)

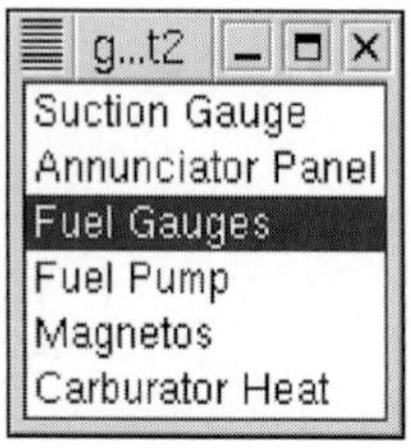

Figure 6.2 List Widget (GtkList)

Without further delay, let's begin our discussion of these widgets by taking a look at GtkList.

GtkList

Class Name

`GtkList`

Parent Class Name

`GtkContainer`

Macros

Widget type macro: `GTK_TYPE_LIST`

Object to widget cast macro: `GTK_LIST(obj)`

Widget type check macro: `GTK_IS_LIST(obj)`

Table 6.2 Signals

Signal Name	*Condition Causing Signal to Trigger*
selection_changed	The selection state of the list has been changed.
select_child	An item in the list changed the state to selected.
unselect_child	An item in the list changed the state to unselected.

Signal Function Prototypes

```
void
selection_changed(GtkList *list, gpointer user_data);

void
select_child(GtkList *list, GtkWidget *widget, gpointer user_data);

void
unselect_child(GtkList *list, GtkWidget *widget, gpointer user_data);
```

Application-Level API Synopsis

Return GTK_TYPE_LIST at runtime:

```
guint
gtk_list_get_type(void);
```

Create an instance of GtkList:

```
GtkWidget *
gtk_list_new(void);
```

Add a set of items to a list starting at the specified position:

```
void
gtk_list_insert_items(GtkList *list, GList *items, gint  position);
```

Add a set of items to the end of a list:

```
void
gtk_list_append_items(GtkList *list, GList *items);
```

Add a set of items to the start of a list:

```
void
gtk_list_prepend_items(GtkList *list, GList *items);
```

Remove a set of items from a list, releasing child widgets:

```
void
gtk_list_remove_items(GtkList *list, GList *items);
```

Remove a set of items from a list without releasing child widgets:

```
void
gtk_list_remove_items_no_unref(GtkList *list, GList *items);
```

Remove the set of list items in the specified range:

```
void
gtk_list_clear_items(GtkList *list, gint start, gint end);
```

Application-Level API Synopsis (Continued)

Select an item in a list:

```
void
gtk_list_select_item(GtkList *list, gint item);
```

Unselect an item in a list:

```
void
gtk_list_unselect_item(GtkList *list, gint item);
```

Select the item that corresponds to the specified widget:

```
void
gtk_list_select_child(GtkList *list, GtkWidget *child);
```

Unselect the item that corresponds to the specified widget:

```
void
gtk_list_unselect_child(GtkList *list, GtkWidget *child)
```

Determine the position in a list of an item that corresponds to a widget:

```
gint
gtk_list_child_position(GtkList *list, GtkWidget *child);
```

Set list selection mode:

```
void
gtk_list_set_selection_mode(GtkList *list, GtkSelectionMode  mode);
```

Select all of the items in a list:

```
void
gtk_list_select_all(GtkList *list);
```

Unselect all of the items in a list:

```
void
gtk_list_unselect_all(GtkList *list);
```

Toggle the row corresponding to the specified widget to selected or unselected:

```
void
gtk_list_toggle_row(GtkList *list, GtkWidget *item);
```

Class Description

GtkList is a simple class that supports the display of text strings in a single-column list, such as the one illustrated in Figure 6.2. Users of your program can select items in a list, and your program can arrange for a callback to be invoked as items in the list become selected or unselected. Your program can query a list at any time to determine which items have been selected. Your program can also select or unselect items programmatically if needed.

Selection Modes

There are four different selection modes, as listed in Table 6.3.

Table 6.3 GtkList Selection Modes

Mode	*Meaning*
GTK_SELECTION_SINGLE	Default mode: zero or one item is selectable at a time.
GTK_SELECTION_BROWSE	Similar to GTK_SELECTION_SINGLE, but (except when the list is initially displayed) one item is always selected.
GTK_SELECTION_MULTIPLE	More than one non-continuous selection can be made at a time.
GTK_SELECTION_EXTENDED	Continuous selections over multiple rows are possible.

These modes not only affect how many selections a user can make from the list at a time, but also how navigation from one item in the list to another is performed.

In GTK_SELECTION_SINGLE mode, a single item in the list can be selected at a time by positioning the pointer over the item in the list and pressing mouse button 1. Any previously selected item in the list will become unselected as a result. Positioning the pointer over an item in the list and pressing mouse button 2 or mouse button 3 causes the list widget to obtain focus and a solid border to be drawn around the item immediately below the pointer, as shown in Figure 6.3. I refer to an item in this mode as "preselected." Items that are neither "selected" nor "preselected" are referred to as "unselected." You can also make an item preselected by using the up arrow key or down arrow key to navigate to another item in the list from a selected item.

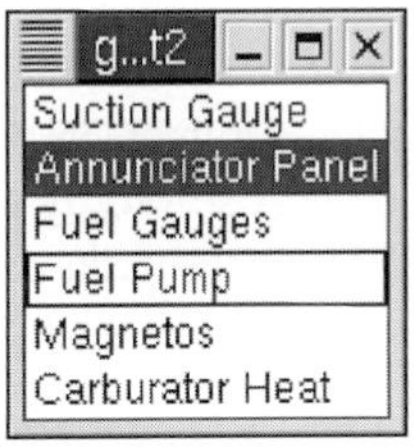

Figure 6.3 Preselected Item (Fuel Pump)

If the Enter key is pressed while an item in the list is preselected, the item becomes selected. If the up arrow key or down arrow key is pressed while an item in the list is preselected, the item immediately above or below the preselected item, respectively, will become preselected, and the item previously preselected will revert to unselected mode. The only exception to this is when the preselected item is the first or the last item in the list. If the up arrow is pressed while the first item in the list is preselected, or if the down arrow is pressed while the last item in the list is preselected, no change in the state of the list will occur.

In GTK_SELECTION_BROWSE mode, only one item in the list can be, and usually is, selected at a time. Mouse button 1 behaves as in GTK_SELECTION_SINGLE mode; clicking on an item in the list with mouse button 1 selects the item. This is also what will happen if you position the mouse over an item and click on mouse button 2 or 3. Using the up arrow key or down arrow key to traverse the list will cause the selection to follow the traversal; thus, there is no preselected state in GTK_SELECTION_BROWSE mode.

GTK_SELECTION_MULTIPLE mode is like GTK_SELECTION_SINGLE mode in terms of how it responds to arrow-key movement and mouse-button pressing. The difference is that users can select only one item in the list at a time in GTK_SELECTION_SINGLE mode, while GTK_SELECTION_MULTIPLE mode allows more than one item in the list to be selected.

The final mode, GTK_SELECTION_EXTENDED, is a bit of a variation on each of the three other modes and then some. A single click of mouse button 1 over an item will select an item and cause the previously selected item to become unselected. Moving the up arrow key or down arrow key from a selected item will cause the item above or below that item, respectively, to be selected and the previously selected item to become unselected. Positioning the pointer over an unselected item and clicking mouse button 2 or mouse button 3 will cause that item to become preselected. The previously selected item will remain selected until the up arrow key or down arrow key is moved, at which point the item that is above or below the preselected item, respectively, becomes selected. To emulate GTK_SELECTION_MULTIPLE, users must depress the Ctrl+left or Ctrl+right key while making selections to preserve previously selected items in the list.

The major difference in GTK_SELECTION_EXTENDED mode occurs when mouse button 1 is pressed while the Shift key is held down. If the list contains no selected items, then the item below the pointer becomes selected, and the fact that the Shift key is being pressed has no influence. If there is already a selected item in the list, however, then that item, the item below the pointer, and all of the items in the list between these two items will become selected.

As you can see, you have many choices when it comes to the list selection mode. Some examples should help clarify when one mode might be preferable over another. A list from which the user must select his or her country of birth would be best served by the use of GTK_SELECTION_SINGLE or GTK_SELECTION_BROWSE mode because only one item will need to be selected, and use of either of these modes will keep the user from selecting more than one item. For a list from which the user is asked to select all of the countries that he or she has visited at least once, GTK_SELECTION_MULTIPLE would be a good choice because it is an easy mode to use, and it is unlikely that the user will want to select a range of countries from the list. The ease of GTK_SELECTION_MULTIPLE is due to the ability of users to select multiple items from the list without having to press and hold down the Ctrl or Shift keys. GTK_SELECTION_EXTENDED is the most general of the supported selection modes. Its use is most appropriate in place of GTK_SELECTION_MULTIPLE when the user is likely to want to select a range of items in a list (e.g., a block of e-mail messages to be deleted in an e-mail application). Since GTK_SELECTION_EXTENDED allows the user to make single-item, multiple-item, and range selections, it is the most flexible mode of them all and probably should be used wherever the enforcement of a single selection from the list is not required. Depending on the experience of the target end users, your documentation should make the user aware of the use of the Ctrl and Shift keys whenever GTK_SELECTION_EXTENDED mode is utilized. The use of the Ctrl and Shift keys will not be obvious to more inexperienced users.

Now that you have an understanding of the various selection modes, let's take a look at the API exposed by GtkList.

Creating a List

To create a new instance of GtkList, call gtk_list_new():

```
GtkWidget *
gtk_list_new(void);
```

gtk_list_new() takes no arguments and returns a variable of type GtkWidget *. As is the case with all widget creation functions, it is generally best to save the returned value in a variable of type GtkWidget * and cast it to other types (such as GtkList *) using the provided macros (e.g., GTK_LIST) whenever necessary.

Setting the Selection Mode

Sometime after you create the list, you need to specify the list selection mode unless you plan on using the default mode of GTK_SELECTION_SINGLE. To select the mode, call gtk_list_set_selection_mode():

```
void
gtk_list_set_selection_mode(GtkList *list, GtkSelectionMode  mode);
```

list is the list returned by gtk_list_new*(). mode is one of the modes listed in the preceding table.

Adding Items to the List

Once you have a list widget, you will need to add items to it. The process is perhaps best described by looking at some example code:

```
GtkWidget *list, *list_item;
GList *item_list;

list = gtk_list_new();
item_list = NULL;
list_item = gtk_list_item_new_with_label ("Spring");
item_list = g_list_append (item_list, list_item);
list_item = gtk_list_item_new_with_label ("Summer");
item_list = g_list_append (item_list, list_item);
list_item = gtk_list_item_new_with_label ("Fall");
item_list = g_list_append (item_list, list_item);
list_item = gtk_list_item_new_with_label ("Winter");
item_list = g_list_append (item_list, list_item);
gtk_list_insert_items( GTK_LIST(list), item_list, 0 );
```

On line 04, I allocate a new instance of GtkList with a call to gtk_list_new(). Lines 05 through 14 illustrate how to add the strings "Spring", "Summer", "Fall", and "Winter" to this list. The process involves creating a vector, or list, that contains the items to be added to the list. Once the list is created, it is then passed to gtk_list_insert_items() to be added to the list:

```
void
gtk_list_insert_items(GtkList *list, GList *items, gint  position);
```

The first argument to gtk_list_insert_items() is an instance of GtkList. In the preceding code, we pass the list returned by gtk_list_new(), which is what a typical application will do. The second argument to gtk_list_insert_items() is a list of "list items." It is not possible to specify the items in a list as a set of C-language, NULL-terminated strings. Instead, you must create, for each item in the list, an instance of the Gtk+ widget class GtkListItem. A list of these "list items" (of size 1 or greater) can then be passed as the second argument to gtk_list_insert_items() in order to specify the list. The final argument to gtk_list_insert_items() is the position in the list where the first item of the items vector should be placed. To place the list of items at the start of the list, pass the value zero or use the function gtk_list_prepend_items():

```
void
gtk_list_prepend_items(GtkList *list, GList *items);
```

The arguments passed to gtk_list_prepend_items() are the same as those passed to gtk_list_insert_items(), except for position, which is not needed. Similarly, to add to the end of a list, call gtk_list_append_items():

```
void
gtk_list_append_items(GtkList *list, GList *items);
```

Let's return to the preceding sample code. To create the list of items to pass to gtk_list_insert_items(), gtk_list_prepend_items(), and gtk_list_append_items(), simply follow the recipe provided by lines 05 through 07:

```
01        GtkWidget *list_item;
02        GList *item_list;

05        item_list = NULL;
06        list_item = gtk_list_item_new_with_label ("Spring");
07        item_list = g_list_append (item_list, list_item);
```

The variable item_list is the list of items that will be passed to gtk_list_insert_items(), gtk_list_prepend_items(), or gtk_list_append_items().

First, I initialize item_list to NULL. Following that, I create an instance of GtkListItem by calling gtk_list_item_new_with_label(), passing the text of the item to be displayed in the list as an argument. Finally, on line 07, I add the instance of GtkListItem to item_list by calling g_list_append(). The first argument to g_list_append() is item_list; the second argument is the list item to add. g_list_append() will place NULL at the end of the list for you as a part of the call to mark the end. Simply repeat lines 06 and 07 for each item you want to add to the list. Once the list is constructed, you can then call gtk_list_insert_items(), gtk_list_append_items(), or gtk_list_prepend_items() to add the list of items to the GtkList instance.

Displaying Arbitrary Widget Content in a List

You are not restricted to using plain text as an item in a GtkList. Since the GtkListItem widget is a child of GtkContainer in the widget hierarchy, it is possible for you to instantiate arbitrary widgets to act as items in a list. To do this, call gtk_list_item_new() to create a new list item instead of gtk_list_item_new_with_label() (gtk_list_item_new_with_label() instantiates a GtkLabel widget and makes it a child of the GtkListItem container). Then call gtk_container_add() to place the widget within the container, as in the following example:

```
GtkWidget *list, *list_item, *pixmap;
GList *item_list;

list = gtk_list_new();
item_list = NULL;
list_item = gtk_list_item_new();
pixmap = MyCreatePixmap();
gtk_container_add( GTK_CONTAINER( list_item ), pixmap );
item_list = g_list_append (item_list, list_item);
```

The function MyCreatePixmap(), in the preceding code, creates an instance of GtkPixmap. I will discuss GtkPixmap in more detail in Chapter 8, "Separators, Arrows, Images, Pixmaps, and Entry Widgets." GDK pixmaps are discussed in the section on GtkCList, which can be found later in this chapter.

Again, anything that can be added to a container can also be added to a list item, including boxes (which are discussed in Chapter 10, "Container and Bin Classes"). You therefore have the ability, with GtkList, to create lists such as the one depicted in Figure 6.4, in which each item in the list is a horizontal box widget that itself contains a GtkPixmap and GtkLabel widget.

Figure 6.4 List Displaying Pixmaps and Labels Packed in Horizontal Boxes

The code used to construct this list is as follows:

```
GtkWidget *list, *list_item;
GList *item_list;
GtkWidget *box1, *box2, *box3, *label, *pixmap;

// create 3 boxes, each with the same pixmap, and a unique label
```

```
box1 = gtk_hbox_new (FALSE, 0);
pixmap = MyCreatePixmap();
gtk_box_pack_start (GTK_BOX (box1), pixmap, FALSE, FALSE, 0);
label = gtk_label_new(
List item 1" );
gtk_box_pack_start (GTK_BOX (box1), label, FALSE, FALSE, 0);

box2 = gtk_hbox_new (FALSE, 0);
pixmap = MyCreatePixmap();
gtk_box_pack_start (GTK_BOX (box2), pixmap, FALSE, FALSE, 0);
label = gtk_label_new( "List item 2" );
gtk_box_pack_start (GTK_BOX (box2), label, FALSE, FALSE, 0);

box3 = gtk_hbox_new (FALSE, 0);
pixmap = MyCreatePixmap();
gtk_box_pack_start (GTK_BOX (box3), pixmap, FALSE, FALSE, 0);
label = gtk_label_new( "List item 3" );
gtk_box_pack_start (GTK_BOX (box3), label, FALSE, FALSE, 0);

// create an instance of GtkList

list = gtk_list_new();

// create the GList of GtkListItems. Each GtkListItem contains
// one of the box widgets created above.

item_list = NULL;
list_item = gtk_list_item_new();
gtk_container_add( GTK_CONTAINER( list_item ), box1 );
item_list = g_list_append (item_list, list_item);
list_item = gtk_list_item_new();
gtk_container_add( GTK_CONTAINER( list_item ), box2 );
item_list = g_list_append (item_list, list_item);
list_item = gtk_list_item_new();
gtk_container_add( GTK_CONTAINER( list_item ), box3 );
item_list = g_list_append (item_list, list_item);

// Add the items to the GtkList widget

gtk_list_insert_items( GTK_LIST(list), item_list, 0 );
```

There are widgets you should avoid adding as children of GtkListItem. In the preceding code, for example, adding a GtkEntry or GtkButton widget as a child of the horizontal box will result in a button or entry widget that does not perform as expected. The problem is that GtkList will be handling the mouse and keypress events that occur within the boundary of the GtkList widget, and they will never be passed along to the button or text-entry field.

Generally speaking, widgets that do not process keyboard or mouse events as part of their normal operation are good candidates for widgets to place below GtkListItem in the widget instance hierarchy. GtkButton and GtkLabel are examples of widget classes that will work well in this situation.

Removing Items from a List

To remove a list of items from a GtkList, you call gtk_list_remove_items(). The first argument is an instance of GtkList, and the second is a list of items to remove. Note that you are not removing strings; you are removing instances of GtkListItem. Therefore, the vector you pass in must contain instances of GtkItemList that were added to the list previously with a call to gtk_list_insert_items(), gtk_list_append_items(), or gtk_list_prepend_items(). Here is the function prototype for gtk_list_remove_items():

```
void
gtk_list_remove_items(GtkList *list, GList *items);
```

By removing items with a call to gtk_list_remove_items(), you are releasing the widgets of type GtkListItem that were allocated by your application with its calls to gtk_list_item_new_with_label(). The release of GtkListItems will also happen should you destroy the GtkList widget. On return from gtk_list_remove_items(), the contents of the items vector will be set to NULL. You can, if desired, arrange to remove items from a GtkList instance without causing the GtkListItems to be released. You might want to do this should your application need to insert and/or remove items from a list more than once, to minimize the overhead involved with creating and destroying instances of GtkListItem. To remove items from a list in this manner, call gtk_list_remove_items_no_unref():

```
void
gtk_list_remove_items_no_unref(GtkList *list, GList *items);
```

Gtk+ will increment the reference count on the list items removed so that they are not released. Note, however, that the contents of the items vector will be set to NULL, so you will need to store the items in some persistent location in your application in order to reuse them. You can make a copy of a GList by calling g_list_copy():

```
GList *
g_list_copy( GList *list );
```

The argument list is the GList you want to copy. The function g_list_copy() returns a new list upon successful execution, or (GList *) NULL.

The arguments to gtk_list_remove_items_no_unref() are the same as those passed to gtk_list_remove_items().

The function gtk_list_clear_items() can be used to remove a set of items from a list in a specific range:

```
void
gtk_list_clear_items(GtkList *list, gint start, gint end);
```

The argument start is the index of the first item in the range, and end is the index of the last item in the range. If n is the number of items in the list, the allowable range for these arguments is 0 (the first item in the list) to $n - 1$ (the last item in the list). If start is greater than or equal to end, then the function will return. Setting end to a value less than zero represents the end of the list, thus

```
gtk_list_clear_items( GTK_LIST( mylist ), 3, -1 );
```

will result in the removal of all the elements in the list except for the first three (those located at indexes 0, 1, and 2).

Locating an Item in a List

We know that an item in the list is an object of type GtkListItem. Given a handle to an instance of GtkListItem, we can determine the index (in the range 0, $n - 1$) where that item is located in the list.

```
gint
gtk_list_child_position(GtkList *list, GtkWidget *child);
```

Selecting and Unselecting Items in a List

The remaining functions in the GtkList API allow applications to select and unselect items in the list. Generally, you will not want to control selections from a list programmatically because your users will want to have control over making selections. However, you might want to initialize a list by selecting an item at the time the list is created. For example, suppose you are writing a program for a car dealership that will be used by office personnel to schedule service appointments for customers. One of these dialogs might consist of a scrolled list of months. It might make sense for your program to default the selection in this list to either the current month or perhaps the first month with a free slot in the schedule that can be allocated to the customer.

To select an item in a list:

```
void
gtk_list_select_item(GtkList *list, gint item);
```

item is the index in the list (0, $n - 1$) of the item to select. After the call is made, the item specified will be selected. If the list selection mode is GTK_SELECTION_SINGLE or GTK_SELECTION_BROWSE, the previously selected item will become unselected. If the mode is GTK_SELECTION_MULTIPLE, previous selections will persist. If the mode is GTK_SELECTION_EXTENDED, the item selected and the current status of the selection dictate the result. In short, the response of selecting an item in a list with gtk_select_list_item() is similar to what would happen if the user were making the selection.

Unselecting an item, naturally, can also be performed. The call that allows this is gtk_list_unselect_item():

```
void
gtk_list_unselect_item(GtkList *list, gint item);
```

You can also select and unselect items knowing the widget ID of the GtkListItem widget of the item to be selected or unselected. To select the item that corresponds to a widget, use gtk_list_select_child():

```
void
gtk_list_select_child(GtkList *list, GtkWidget *child);
```

To unselect the item that corresponds to a specific widget, you can call gtk_list_unselect_child():

```
void
gtk_list_unselect_child(GtkList *list, GtkWidget *child);
```

Most users will find it easy to select the first item in the list and use the Shift key and mouse button 1 to select all of the items in a list while the list is in GTK_SELECTION_EXTENDED mode. However, selecting an entire list of items in this way can become bothersome, especially when the number of items in the list is large (consider selecting and removing 1,000 e-mail messages from a mailbox folder). To ease the selection and unselection of an entire list, consider adding Select All and Unselect All buttons to the user interface of your application. In the signal function for the "Select All" button, you can then call gtk_list_select_all() to select the entire list, and in the signal function for the "Unselect All" button, a call gtk_list_unselect_all() can be made to unselect the entire list.

The function prototypes for gtk_list_select_all() and gtk_list_unselect_all() are as follows:

```
void
gtk_list_select_all(GtkList *list);

void
gtk_list_unselect_all(GtkList *list);
```

The final function I will discuss can be used to toggle the state of a single item in the list, corresponding to a specific GtkItemList widget, from selected to unselected or vice versa. To toggle the state, you can call the gtk_list_toggle_row() function:

```
void
gtk_list_toggle_row(GtkList *list, GtkWidget *item);
```

Now that we have discussed GtkList in some detail, it is a good time to take a look at a similar Gtk+ class, GtkCList. Although they are similar, GtkCList and GtkList are not related to each other in the widget hierarchy. As you will see, GtkCList is more functional than GtkList. My suggestion is to try to use GtkList for simple, single-column lists. If you need multiple-column lists or are in need of the additional functionality provided by GtkCList, use GtkCList instead.

GtkCList

Class Name

```
GtkCList
```

Parent Class Name

```
GtkContainer
```

Macros

Widget type macro: `GTK_TYPE_CLIST`

Object to widget cast macro: `GTK_CLIST(obj)`

Widget type check macro: `GTK_IS_CLIST(obj)`

Table 6.4 Signals

Signal Name	*Condition Causing Signal to Trigger*
select_row	An item in the list changed the state to selected.
unselect_row	An item in the list changed the state to unselected.
row_move	A row in the list was moved to a new position with gtk_clist_row_move().
click_column	A column header button in the list was clicked.
resize_column	A column was resized by the user.
toggle_focus_row	The focus row selected state has toggled.
select_all	A select all operation was performed on the list.
unselect_all	An unselect all operation was performed on the list.
undo_selection	The list reverted to the previous selection state.

Table 6.4 Signals (Continued)

Signal Name	*Condition Causing Signal to Trigger*
start_selection	Not used as of Gtk+ 1.2.8.
end_selection	The left Shift key was released while the clist has keyboard focus.
toggle_add_mode	The add mode for the clist has toggled.
extend_selection	The current selection has been extended.
scroll_vertical	The vertical scrollbar position has changed.
scroll_horizontal	The horizontal scrollbar position has changed.
abort_column_resize	A column resize has been aborted.

Signal Function Prototypes

```
void
select_row(GtkCList *clist, gint row, gint column, GdkEventButton
*event, gpointer user_data);

void
unselect_row(GtkCList *clist, gint row, gint column, GdkEventButton
*event, gpointer user_data);

void
row_move(GtkCList *clist, gint arg1, gint arg2, gpointer user_data);

void
click_column(GtkCList *clist, gint column, gpointer user_data);

void
resize_column(GtkCList *clist, gint column, gint width, gpointer
user_data);

void
toggle_focus_row(GtkCList *clist, gpointer user_data);

void
select_all(GtkCList *clist, gpointer user_data);
```

Signal Function Prototypes (Continued)

```
void
unselect_all(GtkCList *clist, gpointer user_data);

void
undo_selection(GtkCList *clist, gpointer user_data);

void
start_selection(GtkCList *clist, gpointer user_data);

void
end_selection(GtkCList *clist, gpointer user_data);

void
toggle_add_mode(GtkCList *clist, gpointer user_data);

void
extend_selection(GtkCList *clist, GtkScrollType scroll_type, gfloat
position, gboolean auto_start_selection, gpointer user_data);

void
scroll_vertical(GtkCList *clist, GtkScrollType scroll_type, gfloat
position, gpointer user_data);

void
scroll_horizontal(GtkCList *clist, GtkScrollType scroll_type, gfloat
position, gpointer user_data);

void
abort_column_resize(GtkCList *clist, gpointer user_data);
```

Supported Arguments

Prefix: `GtkCList::`

Table 6.5 GtkCList Arguments

Name	*Type*	*Permissions*
n_columns	GTK_TYPE_UINT	GTK_ARG_READWRITE | GTK_ARG_CONSTRUCT_ ONLY
shadow_type	GTK_TYPE_SHADOW_TYPE	GTK_ARG_READWRITE
selection_mode	GTK_TYPE_SELECTION_MODE	GTK_ARG_READWRITE
row_height	GTK_TYPE_UINT	GTK_ARG_READWRITE
reorderable	GTK_TYPE_BOOL	GTK_ARG_READWRITE
titles_active	GTK_TYPE_BOOL	GTK_ARG_READWRITE
use_drag_icons	GTK_TYPE_BOOL	GTK_ARG_READWRITE

Application-Level API Synopsis

Return GTK_TYPE_CLIST at runtime:

```
guint
gtk_clist_get_type(void);
```

Create a new instance of GtkCList with the specified number of columns:

```
GtkWidget *
gtk_clist_new(gint columns);
```

Create a new instance of GtkCList with the specified number of columns and column header labels:

```
GtkWidget *
gtk_clist_new_with_titles (gint columns, gchar *titles[]);
```

Set the horizontal adjustment of the clist:

```
void
gtk_clist_set_hadjustment(GtkCList *clist, GtkAdjustment
*adjustment);
```

Application-Level API Synopsis (Continued)

Set the vertical adjustment of the clist:

```
void
gtk_clist_set_vadjustment(GtkCList *clist, GtkAdjustment
*adjustment);
```

Retrieve the horizontal adjustment of the clist:

```
GtkAdjustment *
gtk_clist_get_hadjustment(GtkCList *clist);
```

Retrieve the vertical adjustment of the clist:

```
GtkAdjustment *
gtk_clist_get_vadjustment(GtkCList *clist);
```

Set the border style of the clist:

```
void
gtk_clist_set_shadow_type(GtkCList *clist, GtkShadowType type);
```

Set the selection mode of the clist:

```
void
gtk_clist_set_selection_mode(GtkCList *clist, GtkSelectionMode
mode);
```

Enable or disable the ability of a clist to have its rows reordered:

```
void
gtk_clist_set_reorderable(GtkCList *clist, gboolean reorderable);
```

Enable or disable the use of drag icons:

```
void
gtk_clist_set_use_drag_icons(GtkCList *clist, gboolean use_icons);
```

Set clist button actions:

```
void
gtk_clist_set_button_actions(GtkCList *clist, guint button,
guint8 button_actions);
```

Freeze (disable) visual updates on the clist widget:

```
void
gtk_clist_freeze(GtkCList *clist);
```

Thaw (re-enable) visual updates on the clist widget:

```
void
gtk_clist_thaw(GtkCList *clist);
```

Show the title buttons appearing above columns in a clist:

```
void
gtk_clist_column_titles_show(GtkCList *clist);
```

Application-Level API Synopsis (Continued)

Hide the title buttons appearing above columns in a clist:
```
void
gtk_clist_column_titles_hide(GtkCList *clist);
```

Set the column title to be active (responsive to button presses, prelights, and keyboard focus):
```
void
gtk_clist_column_title_active(GtkCList *clist, gint column);
```

Set the column title to be inactive (unresponsive to button presses, prelights, and keyboard focus):
```
void
gtk_clist_column_title_passive(GtkCList *clist, gint column);
```

Set all column titles to be active (responsive to button presses, prelights, and keyboard focus):
```
void
gtk_clist_column_titles_active(GtkCList *clist);
```

Set all column titles to be inactive (unresponsive to button presses, prelights, and keyboard focus):
```
void
gtk_clist_column_titles_passive(GtkCList *clist);
```

Set the title of a column's title button to specified string:
```
void
gtk_clist_set_column_title(GtkCList *clist, gint column,
        const gchar *title);
```

Retrieve the text label of a column's title button:
```
gchar *
gtk_clist_get_column_title(GtkCList *clist, gint column);
```

Specify a widget as the "label" of a column's title button instead of using a text label:
```
void
gtk_clist_set_column_widget(GtkCList *clist, gint column,
        GtkWidget *widget);
```

Retrieve the widget parented by a column's title button:
```
GtkWidget *
gtk_clist_get_column_widget(GtkCList *clist, gint column);
```

Specify the justification setting of a column in a clist:
```
void
gtk_clist_set_column_justification(GtkCList *clist, gint column,
        GtkJustification justification);
```

Show or hide a column in the clist:
```
void
gtk_clist_set_column_visibility(GtkCList *clist, gint column,
        gboolean visible);
```

Application-Level API Synopsis (Continued)

Enable or disable column resize operations by mouse for a specific column:

```
void
gtk_clist_set_column_resizeable(GtkCList *clist, gint column,
        gboolean resizeable);
```

Specify whether a column should automatically resize itself to an optimal width based on its content:

```
void
gtk_clist_set_column_auto_resize(GtkCList *clist, gint column,
        gboolean auto_resize);
```

Make all columns in the clist automatically resize themselves to an optimal size based on their content:

```
gint
gtk_clist_columns_autosize(GtkCList *clist);
```

Retrieve the minimum size needed to display all content in the specified column, unclipped:

```
gint
gtk_clist_optimal_column_width(GtkCList *clist, gint column);
```

Explicitly set the column width of a row:

```
void
gtk_clist_set_column_width(GtkCList *clist, gint column, gint width);
```

Set the minimum width of a column:

```
void
gtk_clist_set_column_min_width(GtkCList *clist,
        gint column, gint min_width);
```

Set the maximum width of a column:

```
void
gtk_clist_set_column_max_width(GtkCList *clist, gint column,
        gint max_width);
```

Set the height of a row. The value 0 causes the height to be the same as the current font:

```
void
gtk_clist_set_row_height(GtkCList *clist, guint height);
```

Scroll the viewing area of the clist to the given column and row:

```
void
gtk_clist_moveto(GtkCList *clist, gint row, gint column,
        gfloat row_align, gfloat col_align);
```

Return visibility of a specified row in the clist:

```
GtkVisibility
gtk_clist_row_is_visible(GtkCList *clist, gint row);
```

Obtain the cell type of the specified cell in the clist:

```
GtkCellType
gtk_clist_get_cell_type(GtkCList *clist, gint row, gint column);
```

Application-Level API Synopsis (Continued)

Set the text displayed by the cell in the clist at the specified row and column:

```
void
gtk_clist_set_text(GtkCList *clist, gint row, gint column,
        const gchar *text);
```

Retrieve text displayed at the specified row and column of a clist:

```
gint
gtk_clist_get_text(GtkCList *clist, gint row, gint column,
        gchar **text);
```

Set the pixmap of the cell at the specified location in the clist:

```
void
gtk_clist_set_pixmap(GtkCList *clist, gint row, gint column,
        GdkPixmap *pixmap, GdkBitmap *mask);
```

Get the pixmap of the cell at the specified location in the clist:

```
gint
gtk_clist_get_pixmap(GtkCList *clist, gint row, gint column,
        GdkPixmap **pixmap, GdkBitmap **mask);
```

Set the pixmap and text of the cell at the specified location in the clist, replacing its current contents:

```
void
gtk_clist_set_pixtext(GtkCList *clist, gint row, gint col,
        const gchar *text, guint8 spacing, GdkPixmap *pixmap,
        GdkBitmap *mask);
```

Get the pixmap and text of the cell at the specified location in the clist:

```
gint
gtk_clist_get_pixtext(GtkCList *clist, gint row, gint column,
        gchar **text, guint8 *spacing, GdkPixmap **pixmap,
        GdkBitmap **mask);
```

Set the foreground color of a row to a previously allocated color:

```
void
gtk_clist_set_foreground(GtkCList *clist, gint row, GdkColor *color);
```

Set the background color of a row to a previously allocated color:

```
void
gtk_clist_set_background(GtkCList *clist, gint row, GdkColor *color);
```

Set the style of the cell at the specified location:

```
void
gtk_clist_set_cell_style(GtkCList *clist, gint row, gint column,
        GtkStyle *style);
```

Get the style of the cell at the specified location:

```
GtkStyle *
gtk_clist_get_cell_style(GtkCList *clist, gint row, gint column);
```

Application-Level API Synopsis (Continued)

Set the style of the specified row:

```
void
gtk_clist_set_row_style(GtkCList *clist, gint row, GtkStyle *style);
```

Get the style of the specified row:

```
GtkStyle *
gtk_clist_get_row_style(GtkCList *clist, gint row);
```

Set the horizontal and vertical shifts for drawing the contents of a cell:

```
void
gtk_clist_set_shift(GtkCList *clist, gint row, gint column,
        gint vertical, gint horizontal);
```

Set the selectable attribute of a specified row:

```
void
gtk_clist_set_selectable(GtkCList *clist, gint row, gboolean selectable);
```

Retrieve the selectable attribute of a specified row:

```
gboolean
gtk_clist_get_selectable(GtkCList *clist, gint row);
```

Prepend a row into the clist, returning the index of the row just added:

```
gint
gtk_clist_prepend(GtkCList *clist, gchar *text[]);
```

Append a row into the clist, returning the index of the row just added:

```
gint
gtk_clist_append(GtkCList *clist, gchar *text[]);
```

Insert a row at the specified index. Return the row it was actually inserted as; this may vary based on sorting attributes of the clist:

```
gint
gtk_clist_insert(GtkCList *clist, gint row, gchar *text[]);
```

Remove the specified row from the clist:

```
void
gtk_clist_remove(GtkCList *clist, gint row);
```

Associate arbitrary (client) data with a row:

```
void
gtk_clist_set_row_data(GtkCList *clist, gint row, gpointer data);
```

Associate arbitrary (client) data with a row, with destroy notification:

```
void
gtk_clist_set_row_data_full(GtkCList *clist, gint row, gpointer data,
        GtkDestroyNotify  destroy);
```

Retrieve arbitrary (client) data associated with the specified row:

```
gpointer
gtk_clist_get_row_data(GtkCList *clist, gint row);
```

Application-Level API Synopsis (Continued)

Find the row associated with the client data:

```
gint
gtk_clist_find_row_from_data(GtkCList *clist, gpointer data);
```

Select a specified row and column in the clist:

```
void
gtk_clist_select_row(GtkCList *clist, gint row, gint column);
```

Unselect the specified row and column in the clist:

```
void
gtk_clist_unselect_row(GtkCList *clist, gint row, gint column);
```

Undo the last selection made:

```
void
gtk_clist_undo_selection(GtkCList *clist);
```

Remove all items in the clist:

```
void
gtk_clist_clear(GtkCList *clist);
```

Return the row and column corresponding to the specified x and y locations:

```
gint
gtk_clist_get_selection_info(GtkCList *clist, gint x, gint y,
        gint *row, gint *column);
```

Select all rows (supported for multiple and extended selection modes only):

```
void
gtk_clist_select_all(GtkCList *clist);
```

Unselect all rows and columns (except browse mode):

```
void
gtk_clist_unselect_all(GtkCList *clist);
```

Swap the contents of the two specified rows in the clist:

```
void
gtk_clist_swap_rows(GtkCList *clist, gint row1, gint row2);
```

Move a row from one location to another:

```
void
gtk_clist_row_move(GtkCList *clist, gint source_row, gint dest_row);
```

Set a sorting compare function, replacing the default or last value set:

```
void
gtk_clist_set_compare_func(GtkCList *clist,
        GtkCListCompareFunc cmp_func);
```

Specify the column to sort by prior to a sorting operation:

```
void
gtk_clist_set_sort_column(GtkCList *clist, gint column);
```

Application-Level API Synopsis (Continued)

Specify sorting type prior to a sorting operation:
```
void
gtk_clist_set_sort_type(GtkCList *clist, GtkSortType sort_type);
```

Sort a list, using the current sorting function and type, on the previously specified column:
```
void
gtk_clist_sort(GtkCList *clist);
```

Tell GtkCList to sort automatically upon any insertions into the clist:
```
void
gtk_clist_set_auto_sort(GtkCList *clist, gboolean auto_sort);
```

Class Description

The primary use of GtkCList, like GtkList, is to display a set of text strings organized as a list from which a user can make selections. GtkList, which was previously described, allows users to select items using four different selection modes: single, browse, multiple, and extended. GtkCList supports the very same set of selection modes.

GtkCList provides additional features beyond item selection; the two features important to users are as follows:

- The ability to sort rows based on an arbitrary sort criteria
- The ability to organize data in a row as a series of sizeable columns.

Although I will cover all of the API exposed by GtkCList, I will tend to focus on the functions in the API that involve the management of columns and the sorting of data.

A Sample

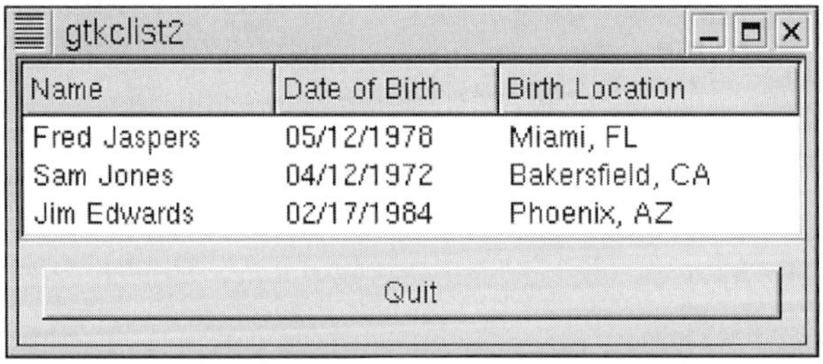

Figure 6.5 Sample GtkCList

Let's start by using the basic functions to create and display a clist like the one depicted in Figure 6.5. There are a few things to note about Figure 6.5. First, this is a three-column clist, with column one displaying the name of a person, column two displaying that person's date of birth, and column three displaying the birth location. In a clist, columns are numbered, left to right, starting with 0 and ending with $n - 1$, where n is the number of columns in the clist. Rows are numbered as in GtkList, with the topmost row assigned row number 0 and the last row assigned $m - 1$, where m is the number of rows in the table. Above the data, at the very top of the clist, is a title area that displays titles assigned to each of the columns in the clist by your program. Each of these titles is actually a button that, if your program so desires, can be made active and attached to a clicked signal function that will trigger when the title button is clicked by the user. By default, the user can change the widths of columns in the table by positioning the pointer over the boundary that separates a pair of title buttons, clicking the left mouse button and then dragging the column boundary to a new location. Your program can control various attributes of individual columns, including their minimum and maximum widths and whether or not an individual column can be resized by the user.

As with GtkList, your program can add or remove rows from a list at runtime. The only static attribute of a clist is the number of columns that each row has, and this must be specified at the time the clist is created.

Creating a Clist Widget

To create a clist, your application invokes one of the following functions: gtk_clist_new() or gtk_clist_new_with_titles(). Here are the function prototypes for these two functions:

```
GtkWidget *
gtk_clist_new(gint columns);

GtkWidget *
gtk_clist_new_with_titles (gint columns, gchar *titles[]);
```

The first routine, gtk_clist_new(), creates an instance of GtkCList that does not have a set of column title buttons. However, be aware that without column titles, GtkCList will not correctly display content that you add to the clist unless you make additional calls to explicitly set the widths of the list columns. This is because, by default, GtkCList will size the columns based on the length of the strings in the column titles, not based on the content being displayed with a cell. To cause cells (and columns) to size based on their content, call gtk_clist_set_column_auto_resize(). Calling this function will ensure that the column specified is appropriately sized for its content. I'll talk more about column sizing a bit later in this section.

The second GtkCList instance creation routine is gtk_clist_new_with_titles(). This routine takes an extra argument, a vector of char * values. Each of the C strings in the titles argument is used as a column title. Column 1's title is contained in titles[0], column 2's titles is contained in titles[1], and so forth. As previously mentioned, the default width of a column is based on the width of the column titles' text.

The following code creates an instance of GtkCList and sets the column titles to reflect the name, date of birth, and location of birth data that will be managed by the clist:

```
   GtkWidget *dialog_window, *hbox, *list;

```

```
03       static char *titles[] =
04       {
05           "Name",
06           "Date of Birth",
07           "Birth Location",
08       };
09
10       gtk_init( &argc, &argv );
11
12       dialog_window = gtk_dialog_new();
13       gtk_window_position (GTK_WINDOW (dialog_window), GTK_WIN_POS_MOUSE);
14
15       hbox = gtk_hbox_new (FALSE, 0);
16       gtk_container_add (GTK_CONTAINER (GTK_DIALOG (dialog_window)->vbox),
17               hbox);
18
19       list = gtk_clist_new_with_titles( 3, titles );
```

Notice that the titles vector is an array of size 3; each element contains a variable of type char *. This is how you should structure the titles vector passed into gtk_clist_new_with_titles(). If you want to dynamically create the title at runtime, the vector should contain pointers to the first character of dynamically created strings. Line 19 illustrates the call to gtk_clist_new_with_titles() that creates the clist. Creating a default clist couldn't be any easier. Of course, you will still need to add content to the list, and you will probably want to control other aspects of the clist as well. Such tasks can be performed using the routines that I will discuss in the next sections.

Adding and Removing Content from a Clist

To add content to an instance of GtkCList, you must first construct an array that contains pointers to NULL-terminated C strings representing the content to be displayed. Using the preceding example GtkCList instance, suppose I wanted to add a row containing the following data: name = "Rod", birthdate = "11/18/1964", and location= "Honolulu, HA". I would then declare the following array:

```
char *rowData[] = { "Rod", "11/18/1964", "Honolulu, HA" };
```

Most likely, you will not be hard-coding the clist data in your program as I have done here; the preceding is just to make it clear that the row data is an array of pointers to C strings.

Once you have the data, it is easy to add it to the clist. You may add the data to the head of the list (prepend) or to the end of the list (append), or you can add it at some specific location within the clist. To add the data to the head of the list, call gtk_clist_prepend():

```
gint
gtk_clist_prepend(GtkCList *clist, gchar *text[]);
```

The first argument is an instance of GtkCList. The second argument, text, is a vector of NULL-terminated C strings. In this vector, element 0 points to a string containing the data to display in the first column of the row being added, element 1 points to a string containing the data to display in the second column of the row being added, and so forth. The number of elements in text must be equal to the number of columns specified when the clist was created. gtk_clist_prepend() returns the index of the row where the data was inserted by the call. This may be different than row 0 if sorting is being performed on rows by the CList widget instance. The return value will always be in the range [0, $m - 1$], where m is the number of rows in the clist after the new row is added.

Your application can also insert a row at the end of a clist by calling the function gtk_clist_append():

```
gint
gtk_clist_append(GtkCList *clist, gchar *text[]);
```

The arguments passed to gtk_clist_append() are identical to those passed to gtk_clist_prepend(). gtk_clist_append() also returns a value in the range of [0, m–1]. If sorting is enabled, the row number of the inserted data will be arbitrary. If sorting is not enabled, then the value $m - 1$ will be returned.

An additional function that can be used to add a row to an instance of GtkCList is gtk_clist_insert():

```
gint
gtk_clist_insert(GtkCList *clist, gint row, gchar *text[]);
```

The arguments clist and text are the same as described for gtk_clist_prepend(). The argument row is the row that this data will occupy after insertion should sorting be disabled for the GtkCList widget. row must be in the range [0, $m - 1$], where m is the number of rows in the clist after the insertion is performed. As was the case for gtk_clist_append() and gtk_clist_prepend(), the actual row where the data is inserted is arbitrary if sorting has been enabled for the GtkCList instance. The returned value specifies the actual location of the row in the clist after sorting has been performed.

Getting and Setting Row Data

GtkCList allows applications to change the content of an existing row of data. This can be done at the column level, meaning you can change the data in a specific row and column of the clist. The function gtk_clist_set_text() is the function that provides this capability:

```
void
gtk_clist_set_text(GtkCList *clist, gint row, gint column,
        const gchar *text);
```

The arguments to gtk_clist_set_text() should be obvious. The value of row must be in the range [0, $m - 1$], where m is the number of rows in the list, while column must be in the range [0, $n - 1$], where n is the number of columns in a row. text is the NULL-terminated string that will be displayed in the specified cell, and clist is an instance of GtkCList that contains m rows of n columns.

You can retrieve the text displayed at a given row and column in a clist with a call to gtk_vlist_get_text():

```
gint
gtk_clist_get_text(GtkCList *clist, gint row, gint column,
      gchar **text);
```

clist is an instance of GtkCList, as always. row and column indicate the cell from which to retrieve text and must be in the range [0, $m - 1$] and [0, $n - 1$], respectively, as described for gtk_clist_set_text(). text is a pointer to a gchar pointer. On return, this pointer will point at a NULL-terminated string that contains the text displayed at row, column in the clist. If row or column is out of range or some other problem is encountered, then the value of text will not be changed. On success, gtk_clist_get_text() returns 1; otherwise, 0 is returned to indicate failure.

Be careful not to free or modify the memory pointed to by the value returned via the text argument to gtk_clist_get_text(). This value points to the actual string maintained by the GtkCList widget, not a copy of it.

Displaying Pixmaps

Clist cells can also display a pixmap in addition to text. GtkCList provides several routines that can be used to associate a pixmap with a cell. Each of these routines accepts a GdkPixmap, which contains the pixmap data that will be displayed, along with a GdkBitmap mask that defines the pixels within the pixmap that will be displayed in the cell.

GDK Pixmaps. Before I describe the routines, we need to go into some detail regarding the use of pixmaps in GDK. GDK provides routines that can be used to create pixmap data. GDK's pixmap routines are a thin layer of code that sits above Xlib routines that provide the same functionality. Pixmaps and bitmaps are X server resources; pixmaps contain image data with a depth that is consistent with the depth of the window into which the pixmap will be rendered, while bitmap data is always 1-bit deep. In terms of X, and GDK, pixmaps and bitmaps are the same; the only difference is in their depths (n-bit vs. 1-bit).

Pixmaps can be created using data local to your program or via X Pixmap (XPM) files stored on disk. An XPM file is an ASCII file that is best created and manipulated using a tool such as xpaint(1). XPM files are usually stored in a file with an *.xpm* extension, but this is not a requirement. Bitmap files are best manipulated using a tool such as xpaint(1) or bitmap(1). There are numerous examples of bitmap files in */usr/include/X11/bitmaps*. Both bitmap and xpaint are available on Linux and UNIX systems and, if not, can be easily obtained via ftp. For more information on these programs, consult their respective online man pages.

You can choose to read the xpm and xbm data into your program at runtime using GDK functions that I will discuss in this section, or you can incorporate the data at compile time by including the content of the XBM or XPM file(s) in your source. If you choose to provide the data at compile time, I recommend that you #include the xpm or xbm file. For example:

```
#include "MyIcon.xpm"
```

This will give you the ability to maintain the data more easily using a program like xpaint or bitmap (as opposed to editing the C source file). In the end, the amount of data involved is so minor that reading it at runtime from a file, or including it at compile time, is largely a matter of style. For more information about X pixmaps and bitmaps, refer to any good text on the X Window System.

The following is a sample bitmap file, *xlogo16*, taken from */usr/include/X11/ bitmaps*. The image stored is a 16×16, 1-bit deep image of the X Window System logo (*xlogo16*):

```
#define xlogo16_width 16
#define xlogo16_height 16
static unsigned char xlogo16_bits[] = {
   0x0f, 0x80, 0x1e, 0x80, 0x3c, 0x40, 0x78, 0x20, 0x78,
   0x10, 0xf0, 0x08, 0xe0, 0x09, 0xc0, 0x05, 0xc0, 0x02, 0x40, 0x07,
   0x20, 0x0f, 0x20, 0x1e, 0x10, 0x1e, 0x08, 0x3c, 0x04, 0x78, 0x02,
   0xf0};
```

The following is the content of an example xpm file. In the example, the width, height, number of colors, and how many ASCII characters are used to represent each pixel in the pixmap are all encoded in the first quote-delimited string of the vector openfile. You should be able to easily determine the structure of the pixmap by viewing the ASCII data (in this example, the bitmap represents a check mark):

```
/* XPM */
static char *openfile[] = {
/* width height num_colors chars_per_pixel */
"    10    9       5             1",
/* colors */
". c None",
"# c #000000",
"y c #666666",
"i c #ff1f00",
"# c #9f9f9f",
/* pixels */
"..........",
"........yy",
".......yy.",
"......yy..",
".yyy.yy...",
"..yyyy....",
"...yy.....",
"..........",
"..........",
};
```

Let's take a look at a few of the functions provided by GDK for creating GdkPixmap data, referring to the sample data previously provided.

The first function, gdk_bitmap_create_from_data(), is the only function GDK provides for creating a 1-bit-deep GdkPixmap from X bitmap data (such as *xlogo16*):

```
GdkPixmap *
gdk_bitmap_create_from_data (GdkWindow *window, const gchar *data,
gint width, gint height);
```

The first argument, window, is a handle to a GdkWindow; typically this will be the window into which the bitmap data is going to be displayed. You can obtain a window handle from an instance of GtkWidget with code similar to the following:

```
GtkWidget *myWidget;
GdkWindow *myWindow;

...

myWindow = myWidget->window;
```

The argument data is the bitmap data; width and height are self-explanatory. In the case of *xlogo16*, you would pass xlogo16_bits as the data argument, xlogo16_width as the width argument, and xlogo16_height as the height argument.

On return, you will be returned a pointer to a GdkPixmap, usable wherever 1-bit GdkPixmap data is required.

To create an *n*-bit-deep GdkPixmap from X bitmap data (e.g., *xlogo16*), call gdk_pixmap_create_from_data():

```
GdkPixmap *
gdk_pixmap_create_from_data(GdkWindow *window, const gchar *data,
        gint width, gint height, gint depth, GdkColor *fg,
        GdkColor *bg);
```

The argument window is the handle of a GdkWindow, with the same visual class, colormap, and depth as the window into which the pixmap will be displayed. Ideally, you will pass the window associated with the widget into which the GdkPixmap you are creating will eventually be displayed. If you pass –1, then the X server root window will be used. The argument data is the same as in the preceding (e.g., xlogo16_bits), as are width and height (e.g., xlogo16_width and xlogo16_height, respectively). The argument depth is the depth of the pixmap on return or, if you pass –1, is the depth of the visual associated with the window you passed as the first argument. You should ensure that the depth of the pixmap you are generating is compatible with the depth of the window into which the pixmap will later be displayed, or the X server will generate an X error event (e.g., BadMatch). The arguments fg and bg are the foreground and background pixels to be used in the resulting pixmap; any “1” cells in the input bitmap data will be converted into foreground pixels, while any “0” cells will be converted into background pixel data.

Now that you know how to deal with X bitmap data, let’s take a look at how to work with X pixmap data (e.g., XPM data such as “openfile”).

The first routine I’ll discuss is gdk_pixmap_colormap_create_from_xpm():

```
GdkPixmap*
gdk_pixmap_colormap_create_from_xpm(GdkWindow *window,
        GdkColormap *colormap, GdkBitmap **mask,
        GdkColor *transparent_color, const gchar *filename);
```

The argument window is a window handle, which in most cases should be the window into which the pixmap will ultimately be displayed or at least a window that shares the same visual class and colormap as the window into which the pixmap will be displayed. Passing

NULL will cause gdk_pixmap_colormap_create_from_xpm() to use the X server root window. The argument colormap is an instance of GdkColormap. You can obtain this colormap by calling gdk_window_get_colormap() and passing a window (of type GdkWindow *) as an argument. In most cases, you will simply want to set colormap to NULL; by doing so, gdk_pixmap_colormap_create_from_xpm() will obtain the colormap for you using the window you passed in (or using the X server root window if window was set to NULL). The argument mask is a pointer to a variable of type GdkBitmap *. On return from this function, if mask was non-NULL, mask will point to a bitmap. In this bitmap, each foreground pixel is represented by a '1' bit, and each background pixel in the image is represented by a '0' bit. This mask can be passed directly to the GdkCList functions described in the following section. The argument transparent_color can usually be set to NULL. Passing in a pointer to a GdkColor will cause gdk_pixmap_colormap_create_from_xpm() to use the specified color as the transparent color for the pixmap.

The final argument, filename, is the path (either absolute or relative) to the file that contains the X pixmap data. The function gdk_pixmap_colormap_create_from_xpm() will open and read the file for the pixmap data on behalf of the caller.

The next routine, gdk_pixmap_create_from_xpm(), is identical in functionality to gdk_pixmap_colormap_create_from_xpm(), except it does not take a colormap as an argument:

```
GdkPixmap *
gdk_pixmap_create_from_xpm(GdkWindow *window, GdkBitmap **mask,
        GdkColor *transparent_color, const gchar *filename);
```

The two remaining functions I will present here mirror the functionality of gdk_pixmap_colormap_create_from_xpm() and gdk_pixmap_create_from_xpm(), with the exception that they do not accept a path to an XPM file. Rather, both of these functions require you to pass the contents of an XPM file. These routines are used when you provide your XPM data at compile time, which again is best done by including an XPM file using a #include. If you find yourself opening the XPM file and reading it to obtain the data to pass to either of these functions, then you should be using gdk_pixmap_create_from_xpm() or gdk_pixmap_colormap_create_from_xpm(), allowing it to open and read the file for you.

Both of these routines accept a pointer to a gchar *. To create a pixmap using the example XPM data previously shown, you would simply pass openfile as the final argument. For example:

```
#include "foo.xpm" // declared the char * array "openfile"

GdkPixmap *myPixmap;
GdkWindow *myWindow;
GdkBitmap *mask;

...

myPixmap = gdk_pixmap_colormap_create_from_pixmap_d( myWindow, NULL,
        &mask, NULL, openfile );
```

The function gdk_pixmap_colormap_create_from_xpm_d() takes the same arguments as gdk_pixmap_colormap_create_from_xpm() except for the final argument, as I just mentioned.

```
GdkPixmap *
gdk_pixmap_colormap_create_from_xpm_d(GdkWindow *window, GdkColormap
*colormap, GdkBitmap **mask, GdkColor *transparent_color,
        gchar **data);
```

The functions gdk_pixmap_create_from_xpm_d() and gdk_pixmap_colormap_create_from_xpm_d() are equivalent, except gdk_pixmap_create_from_xpm_d() does not require a colormap argument.

```
GdkPixmap *
gdk_pixmap_create_from_xpm_d(GdkWindow *window, GdkBitmap **mask,
        GdkColor *transparent_color, gchar **data);
```

GtkCList Pixmap Functions. Now that I have described the routines you can use to obtain pixmap data and corresponding masks, let's continue with our discussion of GtkCList and look at the routines that make use of pixmap data.

The first function, gtk_clist_set_pixmap(), allows you to specify a pixmap to be displayed along with text in a cell of a GtkCList instance:

```
void
gtk_clist_set_pixmap(GtkCList *clist, gint row, gint column,
        GdkPixmap *pixmap, GdkBitmap *mask);
```

The argument clist is an instance of GtkCList, row and column specify the cell to which the pixmap data is to be associated, pixmap is a pointer to a GdkPixmap (returned by one of the functions previously described), and mask is a pointer to a GdkBitmap, also obtained as previously described. Since the function is void, you cannot tell if the operation was successful (except by calling gtk_clist_get_pixmap(), see the following code).

Your application can retrieve the pixmap associated with a cell at a specified location in the clist by calling gtk_clist_get_pixmap():

```
gint
gtk_clist_get_pixmap(GtkCList *clist, gint row, gint column,
        GdkPixmap **pixmap, GdkBitmap **mask);
```

The arguments to gtk_clist_get_pixmap() and gtk_clist_set_pixmap() are the same, except you must pass pointers to GdkPixmap and GdkBitmap pointers as the final two arguments, respectively. On return, gtk_clist_get_pixmap() will set pixmap and mask to values maintained by GtkCList; do not free this memory. If the function is successful (e.g., the arguments are valid), 1 is returned; otherwise, 0 is returned to indicate failure.

A function similar to gtk_clist_set_pixmap() is gtk_clist_set_pixtext(). The difference between these two functions is that gtk_clist_set_pixtext() allows you to set the text and the pixmap of the cell as opposed to just the pixmap. You also specify a spacing argument that defines how far apart the text and the pixmap are plotted from each other horizontally within the cell in pixels:

```
void
gtk_clist_set_pixtext(GtkCList *clist, gint row, gint col,
        const gchar *text, guint8 spacing, GdkPixmap *pixmap,
        GdkBitmap *mask);
```

Again, GdkCList does not pass back an indication of success or failure.

You can also retrieve the text, pixmap, and spacing between them by calling the function gtk_clist_get_pixtext():

```
gint
gtk_clist_get_pixtext(GtkCList *clist, gint row, gint column,
        gchar **text, guint8 *spacing, GdkPixmap **pixmap,
        GdkBitmap **mask);
```

The arguments clist, row, and column are identical to the same arguments as described for gtk_clist_set_pixtext(). The remaining four arguments are addresses of variables of type gchar *, guint8 *, GdkPixmap *, and GdkBitmap *. On return, these will be set to the text, spacing, pixmap, and mask associated with the cell at location [row,column] in the GtkCList, respectively. If the function fails (e.g., because of bad arguments), the value 0 will be returned. A return value of 1 indicates success.

Setting the Shadow Type

The border (or shadow) type of clist can be set with gtk_clist_set_shadow_type():

```
void
gtk_clist_set_shadow_type(GtkCList *clist, GtkShadowType type);
```

The shadow type can be one of the values shown in Figures 6.6 through 6.9. To my eyes, it is fairly difficult to discern the differences among these shadow types when using a default border width, so I have supplied pixel magnifications (obtained using xmag(1)) that show how the upper-right corner of a clist appears with each possible shadow type value.

Figure 6.6 GTK_SHADOW_IN

Figure 6.7 GTK_SHADOW_OUT

Figure 6.8 GTK_SHADOW_ETCHED_IN

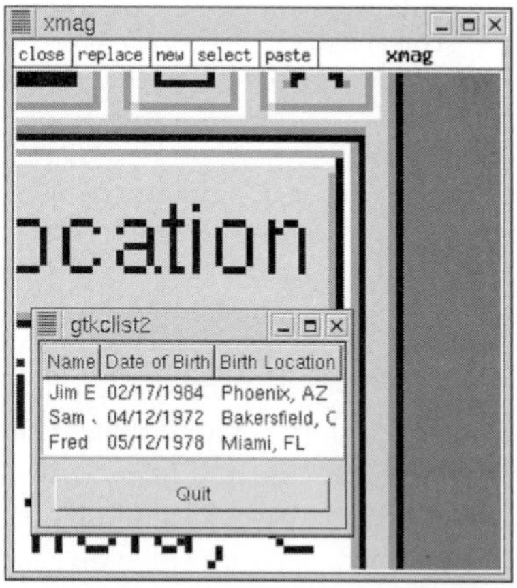

Figure 6.9 GTK_SHADOW_ETCHED_OUT

Personally, I usually go with the default shadow type defined by GtkCList.

Selection Modes

To set the selection mode of the clist, call gtk_clist_set_selection_mode():

```
void
gtk_clist_set_selection_mode(GtkCList *clist, GtkSelectionMode mode);
```

Table 6.6 is a reproduction of one that was presented for GtkList earlier in this chapter. GtkCList and GtkList selection modes are identical; for more information on selection modes and how they affect the user, refer to the "Class Description" section for GtkList presented earlier in this chapter.

Table 6.6 GtkCList Selection Modes

Selection Mode	*Meaning*
GTK_SELECTION_SINGLE	Default mode: One item is selectable at a time.
GTK_SELECTION_BROWSE	Similar to GTK_SELECTION_SINGLE.
GTK_SELECTION_MULTIPLE	More than one noncontinuous selection at a time.
GTK_SELECTION_EXTENDED	Continuous selections over multiple rows are possible.

Button Actions

GtkCList supports "button actions," which specify the actions bound to each of the buttons on the user's mouse or pointing device. X11 supports mice with up to five buttons. Most X11 programs are written with, at most, three buttons in mind (which is why three-button mouse emulation on systems with mice containing only two buttons is a good option to choose when configuring an X server).

GtkCList supports the following actions in Table 6.7. These actions apply to the rows of a clist, not the buttons in the title area.

Table 6.7 GtkCList Button Actions

Action	*Meaning*
GTK_BUTTON_IGNORED	Pressing the button does nothing.
GTK_BUTTON_SELECTS	Pressing the button selects the row.
GTK_BUTTON_DRAGS	The button can be used to drag a row from one location in the list to another.

The actions supported by a given button are expressed as the logical OR of the preceding values. By default, button 0 (in X11, buttons are numbered starting at 1, but GtkCList starts them at 0) is set to GTK_BUTTON_SELECTS | GTK_BUTTON_DRAGS. The remaining four buttons (1 through 4) are each set to GTK_BUTTON_IGNORED. I would suggest using these defaults because many other Gtk+ applications will also use the same defaults, and by changing the actions, you may confuse the users of your application who have become accustomed to a default GtkCList behavior. If you do need to change the actions, however, you can do so by calling gtk_clist_set_button_actions():

```
void
gtk_clist_set_button_actions(GtkCList *clist, guint button,
        guint8 button_actions);
```

clist is an instance of GtkCList; button is the button number (the left button is 0, the middle button is 1, and the right button is 2, unless remapped by the user). Button actions consist of GTK_BUTTON_IGNORED or any combination of the remaining values in the preceding table logically OR'd together.

Making a Clist Reorderable

To enable the ability of your users to drag a row from one place in the clist to another, you not only have to ensure that one of the buttons has a GTK_BUTTON_DRAGS action (again, by default, button 0 has this so you need do nothing), you must also explicitly enable dragging ability by calling the function gtk_clist_set_reorderable():

```
void
gtk_clist_set_reorderable(GtkCList *clist, gboolean reorderable);
```

clist is an instance of GtkCList. reorderable is a boolean value that, when set to TRUE, allows users to drag rows from one location in the clist to another. Setting reorderable to FALSE disables this ability. By default, reordering of rows by the user is disabled by GtkCList.

Freezing and Thawing a Clist

Some clist operations, such as adding items to a clist, deleting items from a clist, or setting the text or pixmap of cells in the clist, require the clist to redraw its contents. This includes not only the cells that were modified but, at times, other cells in the clist. Doing a group of these operations at a single time, such as in the following code taken from the Gtk+ distribution, can result in a large number of redraws, which is visually unappealing to the user as well as being inefficient because, ideally, a clist needs to redraw its content only once, after all of the changes to the clist have been made.

```
for (i = 0; i < 1000; i++) {
        sprintf (text[0], "CListRow %d", rand() % 10000);
        row = gtk_clist_append (clist, texts);
        gtk_clist_set_pixtext (clist, row, 3, "gtk+", 5, pixmap, mask);
}
```

A client can, when necessary, disable or "freeze" redrawing during the time that updates to a clist are made and re-enable or "thaw" redrawing when the updates have been completed.

To freeze (disable) visual updates of a clist widget, call gtk_clist_freeze():

```
void
gtk_clist_freeze(GtkCList *clist);
```

To thaw (re-enable) visual updates of a clist widget, call gtk_clist_thaw():

```
void
gtk_clist_thaw(GtkCList *clist);
```

The preceding code, using freezes and thaws, can be rewritten as follows:

```
gtk_clist_freeze( clist );
for (i = 0; i < 1000; i++) {
      sprintf (text[0], "CListRow %d", rand() % 10000);
      row = gtk_clist_append (clist, texts);
      gtk_clist_set_pixtext (clist, row, 3, "gtk+", 5, pixmap, mask);
}
gtk_clist_thaw( clist );
```

Column API

In this section, I will discuss the numerous functions supported by GtkCList that relate to columns, and the titled buttons used to label them. I will first present the routines related to column titles. Then I will discuss the routines related to the columns themselves.

Column titles are displayed as a series of push buttons above the content of a clist, as shown in Figure 6.9 and other figures in this section. There are a few things to note about the column titles. First, the width of a column title always corresponds to the width of the column it labels. Second, users can resize columns by grabbing the left or right edge of the column title button above the column, using mouse button 0, and dragging the mouse to the left or right, respectively. Finally, column title buttons can be made to respond to mouse button presses.

By default, title buttons are displayed above every instance of GtkCList, but your application can show or hide them at will. To hide the title buttons, call gtk_clist_column_titles_hide():

```
void
gtk_clist_column_titles_hide(GtkCList *clist);
```

Sensible user-interface practice would urge the avoidance of hiding and showing column titles during the execution of an application; the decision to show or hide column titles should probably be made at the time the clist is created. By default, title buttons show. If your plans involve a clist without column titles, you should make the preceding call before calling gtk_widget_show() on the GtkCList widget instance.

Showing the title buttons is done by calling gtk_clist_column_titles_show():

```
void
gtk_clist_column_titles_show(GtkCList *clist);
```

Title buttons, by default, are responsive to mouse-button presses, prelights, and keyboard focus. In many cases, you will not want this behavior regardless of the default chosen by the designers of GtkCList. To make the title buttons inactive, call gtk_clist_column_title_passive():

```
void
gtk_clist_column_title_passive(GtkCList *clist, gint column);
```

The argument column is the column to be made passive, in the range $[0, m - 1]$, where m is the number of columns in the clist. GtkCList allows you to re-enable a column title button by calling gtk_clist_column_title_active():

```
void
gtk_clist_column_title_active(GtkCList *clist, gint column);
```

The argument column is the same as previously described for gtk_clist_column_title_passive().

Your application can make all column title buttons in an instance of GtkCList active or passive. This can be done by calling gtk_clist_column_titles_active() or gtk_clist_column_titles_passive(), respectively. Both of these functions take a single argument, which is an instance of GtkCList:

```
void
gtk_clist_column_titles_active(GtkCList *clist);

void
gtk_clist_column_titles_passive(GtkCList *clist);
```

If a column title button is active, its appearance will change as the user mouses over it. This indicates that it is something that can be pressed. Should an application decide to make a column title button active, it should be designed to do something meaningful if the user clicks on the title button, something that includes visual feedback; otherwise, the user of the application will become confused into thinking that the button is inoperative or broken.

Your application can register a signal function to be called when any one of the column title buttons of a clist is clicked. Detailed information on Gtk+ signals can be found in

Chapter 3, "Signals, Events, Objects, and Types." The following code illustrates registration of a "click_column" signal function named my_click_column_func():

```
gtk_signal_connect (GTK_OBJECT (clist), "click_column",
        (GtkSignalFunc) my_click_column_func, NULL);
```

The function my_click_column_func() is defined as follows:

```
void
clist_click_column(GtkCList *clist, gint column, gpointer data)
{
        printf( "Column title button number %d was pressed",
        column + 1 );
}
```

The first argument to the signal function is the instance of GtkCList that is managing the column title button that was pressed. column is the number of the column title button pressed; the leftmost button is numbered 0, and the rightmost button is numbered $m - 1$, where again m is the number of columns in the clist. data is client data passed to all signal functions if so desired by the application. See the discussion of gtk_signal_connect() in Chapter 3 for more information on this argument.

As illustrated earlier, clist column titles are specified at the time the clist is created. Column title button text can also be set during program execution, although I do caution against making dynamic changes to column heading text. As a matter of style, I feel that column titles are best determined at the time the clist is instantiated and should generally remain fixed throughout the execution of the program.

However, you may have a special need to change or retrieve the text displayed by a column title button. To set the text displayed by a column title button, call gtk_clist_set_column_title():

```
void
gtk_clist_set_column_title(GtkCList *clist, gint column,
        const gchar *title);
```

The argument column is the number of the column that will be changed, starting on the left as always with 0. The argument title is a NULL-terminated C string that will, upon return, be the title displayed by the specified column.

You can retrieve the text displayed by a column-title button by calling gtk_clist_get_column_title():

```
gchar *
gtk_clist_get_column_title(GtkCList *clist, gint column);
```

The returned value is a NULL-terminated string maintained by the instance of GtkCList passed as the first argument. Do not free the memory associated with this string or modify it in any way; it is owned by GtkCList.

Because all GtkCList column titles are buttons and buttons (GtkButton) inherit from GtkContainer, you can choose to replace the text displayed by the column button with some other widget. An obvious replacement for a text label would be an instance of GtkPixmap. Using icons instead of text can result in a more visually appealing and intuitive user interface. Using pixmaps instead of text also makes applications easier to internationalize.

To specify a widget as the "label" of a column's title button, instead of using a text label, call gtk_clist_set_column_widget():

```
void
gtk_clist_set_column_widget(GtkCList *clist, gint column,
         GtkWidget *widget);
```

The argument clist is an instance of GtkCList, column is the column corresponding to the button widget being manipulated, and widget is an instance of GtkWidget (e.g., GtkPixmap). The following code illustrates how easy it is to set the column label of column 2 in a three-column clist to an icon:

```
GtkWidget *list, *pixmap;

static char *titles[] =
{
"Name",
"Date of Birth",
"Birth Location",
};

list = gtk_clist_new_with_titles( 3, titles );
pixmap = MyCreatePixmap();
gtk_clist_set_column_widget(GTK_CLIST(list), 1, pixmap);
```

The pixmap in the preceding code is an instance of GtkPixmap. Notice that I still set the text of the column to "Date of Birth". GtkCList takes care of disassociating this text from the column title button and using the specified widget in its place. When calling gtk_clist_new_with_titles(), make sure all of the titles in the vector are non-NULL. I could have set the second title to " ", but it really doesn't matter if the string is empty or not.

You can obtain the widget parented by a column title button by calling gtk_clist_get_column_widget(). The function accepts as arguments an instance of GtkCList and a column number and returns an instance of GtkWidget. Here is the function prototype:

```
GtkWidget *
gtk_clist_get_column_widget(GtkCList *clist, gint column);
```

The remaining column functions all set attributes on columns, as listed in Table 6.8.

Table 6.8 Functions Used to Set Column Attributes on a Clist Widget

Attribute	*Function(s)*
Column justification	gtk_clist_set_column_justification()
Column visibility	gtk_clist_set_column_visibility()
Column resize	gtk_clist_set_column_resizable()
	gtk_clist_set_column_auto_resize()
	gtk_clist_columns_autosize()

Table 6.8 Functions Used to Set Column Attributes on a Clist Widget (Continued)

Attribute	*Function(s)*
Column width	gtk_clist_optimal_column_width() gtk_clist_set_column_width() gtk_clist_set_column_min_width() gtk_clist_set_column_max_width()

The function gtk_clist_set_column_justify() allows you to specify the justification of a column in a clist:

```
void
gtk_clist_set_column_justification(GtkCList *clist, gint column,
        GtkJustification justification);
```

The argument clist is an instance of GtkCList, and column is the number of the column for which the justification style is being set. The argument justification specifies the justification style for the column and must be one of the GtkJustification enumeration values shown in Table 6.9.

Table 6.9 Column Justification Options

Option	*Meaning*
GTK_JUSTIFY_LEFT	The initial character is displayed at the first position of the cell.
GTK_JUSTIFY_RIGHT	The last character is displayed at the last position of the cell.
GTK_JUSTIFY_CENTER	Text is centered within the cell.
GTK_JUSTIFY_FILL	Identical to GTK_JUSTIFY_CENTER (the source code treats these two constants the same, which is perhaps an error).

Columns can be shown or hidden by calling gtk_clist_set_column_visibility() at runtime:

```
void
gtk_clist_set_column_visibility(GtkCList *clist, gint column,
        gboolean visible);
```

If visible is set to TRUE, the column will show; if set to FALSE, it will be hidden. Column visibility should be controllable by the user (e.g., via preference settings). For example, a "Show Date of Birth" toggle button might be used in a preferences dialog to control the display of the "Date of Birth" column in the clist example presented earlier.

As I mentioned earlier, users can resize columns by positioning the pointer over either end of the column title button, clicking mouse button 1, and dragging the button to its new size. Your application, however, can disable (or re-enable) this ability on a per-column basis by calling gtk_clist_set_column_resizeable():

```
void
gtk_clist_set_column_resizeable(GtkCList *clist, gint column,
        gboolean resizeable);
```

If the argument resizeable is set to TRUE, the column can be sized by the user (this is the default). If set to FALSE, the column size cannot be changed by the user.

The initial size of columns in a clist can be controlled by several routines provided by GtkCList. A column can be "autosized," in which case the column width is set so that the largest item displayed by the list will be visible. Otherwise, the column size is determined by the amount of space it takes to display the column title buttons.

Autosizing can be specified on a per-column basis, or once for all of the columns in a GtkCList. To specify if a column should automatically resize itself to an optimal width based on its content, call gtk_clist_set_column_auto_resize():

```
void
gtk_clist_set_column_auto_resize(GtkCList *clist, gint column,
        gboolean auto_resize);
```

The arguments clist and column should be familiar by now. If auto_resize is set to TRUE, the specified column will resize itself as data is added to or removed from the clist, to ensure that all data is viewable. If FALSE, the size of the column will be based on the width of the column's title button. You can autosize all columns in a clist with a call to gtk_clist_columns_autosize():

```
gint
gtk_clist_columns_autosize(GtkCList *clist);
```

The routine gtk_clist_optimal_column_width() returns the column size needed to display all content in the column:

```
gint
gtk_clist_optimal_column_width(GtkCList *clist, gint column);
```

This size is the same size that would be assigned to the column if the column were autosized.

Your application can explicitly set the width of a column to a specified value with a call to gtk_clist_set_column_width():

```
void
gtk_clist_set_column_width(GtkCList *clist, gint column, gint width);
```

The argument width is the desired width. If the column is not autosized, you might call gtk_clist_optimal_column_width(), which was previously described, to determine a column width that will show all content in the column without clipping.

Column sizes, including those made by GtkCList for autosized columns, can be controlled by your application by specifying maximum and minimum widths. If you specify a minimum column width, this minimum is applied before any changes are made to a column's width; if the computed or specified width is less than the minimum column size, the minimum column size is used in its place. The same holds true for maximum column sizes; a column with a maximum size will not be allowed to grow beyond that size, regardless of the content or autosize attribute of the column.

To set the minimum width of a column, call gtk_clist_set_column_min_width():

```
void
gtk_clist_set_column_min_width(GtkCList *clist, gint column,
        gint min_width);
```

To set the maximum width of a column, call gtk_clist_set_column_max_width():

```
void
gtk_clist_set_column_max_width(GtkCList *clist, gint column,
        gint max_width);
```

The arguments to the preceding functions should be self-explanatory. As always, remember that columns in a clist are numbered, left to right, starting at 0 and ending at $m - 1$, where m is the number of columns in the clist.

Row and Cell API

Now let's look at some of the functions applicable to rows of data in a clist, as well as individual cells.

Row height, by default, is set to the height of the current font. The height of a row does not include the spacing that exists between rows in the clist. You can override the computed height of a row with a call to gtk_clist_set_row_height():

```
void
gtk_clist_set_row_height(GtkCList *clist, guint height);
```

Passing a height of 0 causes the height to be the same as the current font.

Each cell in a clist has a specific type. Cell types are defined in Table 6.10.

Table 6.10 Cell Types

Cell Type	*Meaning*
GTK_CELL_EMPTY	The cell contains no data.
GTK_CELL_TEXT	The cell contains text.
GTK_CELL_PIXMAP	The cell contains pixmap data.
GTK_CELL_PIXTEXT	The cell contains both text and pixmap data.
GTK_CELL_WIDGET	This type is unimplemented in Gtk+ 1.2.

To retrieve the cell type of a cell at row = *m*, column = *n*, call gtk_clist_get_cell_type():

```
GtkCellType
gtk_clist_get_cell_type(GtkCList *clist, gint row, gint column);
```

If the cell does not exist, gtk_clist_get_cell_type() returns –1.

The foreground color and background color of a clist row can be set by calling gtk_clist_set_foreground() and gtk_clist_set_background(), respectively:

```
void
gtk_clist_set_foreground(GtkCList *clist, gint row, GdkColor *color);

void
gtk_clist_set_background(GtkCList *clist, gint row, GdkColor *color);
```

Both of these functions take a pointer to a GdkColor. The following code sets the foreground color of the fifth row of a clist to the color blue:

```
GdkColor color;
GtkWidget *clist;

...

color.red = color.green = 0; color.blue = 0xffff;
gtk_clist_set_foreground( GTK_CLIST( clist ), 4, &color );
```

It is important to ensure that the clist has been realized before setting the foreground or background colors. Refer to Chapter 4 for details on showing and realizing widgets.

Cell Styles. Styles, discussed in Chapter 4, encapsulate rendering attributes of a widget, such as font and foreground, background, and text colors. Styles are mapped to various states that a widget may be in at runtime. For example, a GtkButton, which is typically in GTK_STATE_NORMAL, will transition to GTK_STATE_PRELIGHT whenever the user positions the pointer over the button. If the user presses mouse button 1 when an instance of GtkButton is in GTK_STATE_PRELIGHT, the button will transition to GTK_STATE_ACTIVE. GtkButton maintains a style for each of these states; each state, therefore, has a unique look and feel that visually conveys to the user of the application the state the widget currently is in.

An instance of GtkCList has two styles associated with it that are applied to cells in the clist at the time they are rendered. One of these defines how the cell or row will appear normally, and the other defines how the cell or row appears when it is selected. The corresponding states are GTK_STATE_NORMAL and GTK_STATE_SELECTED, respectively. Styles can be applied to individual rows in a clist or to individual cells in a row. If your application applies a style to a cell, it overrides any style that may have been applied to the row that contains the cell, as well as the global style applied to the clist. Likewise, a style to a row overrides the clist global style but not a style that has been applied to an individual cell.

The function gtk_clist_set_cell_style() can be used to set the style of a cell at the specified location in the clist:

```
void
gtk_clist_set_cell_style(GtkCList *clist, gint row, gint column,
        GtkStyle *style);
```

The arguments clist, row, and column should be familiar to you by now. The argument style is a pointer to a GtkStyle. This can either be a style that your application has allocated or a copy of the style maintained by the GtkCList instance. You can retrieve a copy of the style using gtk_style_copy():

```
GtkStyle*
gtk_style_copy (GtkStyle *style)
```

The return value is a newly allocated style; the argument passed is the style that needs to be copied. Here is an example of its use:

```
GtkStyle *style;
GtkWidget *clist;

...

style = gtk_style_copy(GTK_WIDGET(clist)->style);
```

With a copy of the clist's current style, your application can make any changes necessary to the style while preserving default settings. In the code that follows, I will modify the cell located at row = 0, column = 3 by changing the foreground color for the GTK_STATE_ACTIVE state to red and the foreground color for the GTK_STATE_SELECTED state to green. I will also change the font used by both of these states to 16-point Helvetica.

```
GdkColor color;

// first, set up the active state color

color.red   = 0xffff;
color.green = 0;
color.blue  = 0;

style->fg[GTK_STATE_ACTIVE] = color;
```

In the preceding, I simply set up a GdkColor struct to describe the color red and assigned this color to the GTK_STATE_ACTIVE element of the style's fg member. The same is done in the following code, except the color is changed to green:

```
// next, set up the selected state colors

color.red   = 0;
color.green = 0xffff;
color.blue  = 0;

style->fg[GTK_STATE_SELECTED] = color;
```

In the following code, the font is changed to 16-point Helvetica, and the new style information is associated with a call to gtk_clist_set_cell_style():

```
// now change the font

gdk_font_unref(style->font);
style->font =
gdk_font_load("-*-helvetica-*-*-*-*-16-*-*-*-*-*-*-*");

// finally, get the new style

gtk_clist_set_cell_style(GTK_CLIST(list), 0, 3, style);
```

The function gdk_font_unref() takes an argument of type GdkFont *. It decrements the font's reference count by 1. If the reference count goes to 0, the font (or fontset) is freed. The function gdk_font_load() creates a new GdkFont, sets its reference count to 1, and returns a reference to the font (also a GdkFont *). We simply set the font field of the style to the value returned by gdk_font_load() in order to change the style's font. With the attributes of the style having been changed, a call to gtk_clist_set_cell_style() is made to associate the modified style with the cell at location 0, 3 in the clist.

A subtle point about the preceding code is that we obtained a copy of the clist's global style for use as a template for our changes. This global style was assigned to the clist at the time it was realized by GtkCList. Let's say we've made the changes to cell 0, 3, and later in the application we want to modify it once again (maybe changing the font to something else). There are two options here. One would be to once again make a copy of the clist's global style, make the same changes done before (set the foreground of the GTK_STATE_ACTIVE and GTK_STATE_SELECTED states), and then set the new font. The other option would be to grab a copy of the cell's style, which already has the desired foreground colors set, and just modify the font. To get a copy of the cell's style, you can use gtk_clist_get_cell_style() as follows:

```
GtkStyle *style;

style = gtk_clist_get_cell_style(GTK_CLIST(list), 0, 3);
style = gtk_style_copy(style);
```

At this point, you can modify the style to set the new font, as was illustrated earlier, and then call gtk_clist_set_cell_style() to affect the change. The function prototype for gtk_clist_get_cell_style() is as follows:

```
GtkStyle *
gtk_clist_get_cell_style(GtkCList *clist, gint row, gint column);
```

The arguments to gtk_clist_get_cell_style() should be self-explanatory. If any of the arguments are invalid (GtkStyle *), NULL is returned. Similarly, if the cell does not yet have a style associated with it, NULL is returned.

Functions similar to gtk_clist_set_cell_style() and gtk_clist_get_cell_style() exist for rows in a clist. The function gtk_clist_set_row_style() sets a style that will be applied to all cells in the row for which a cell style has not been set:

```
void
gtk_clist_set_row_style(GtkCList *clist, gint row, GtkStyle *style);
```

The function gtk_clist_get_row_style() is analogous to gtk_clist_get_cell_style(). The style retrieved, however, is the one applied to cells in a row that do not have a cell style applied to them. As was the case with cell styles, if no row style has yet been applied to the specified row, NULL will be returned. The following is the function prototype for gtk_clist_get_row_style():

```
GtkStyle *
gtk_clist_get_row_style(GtkCList *clist, gint row);
```

Your application may find it necessary to apply a vertical and/or horizontal offset to the upper-left corner of the pixmap or text displayed in a cell. If so, you can call gtk_clist_set_shift() to specify these offsets:

```
void
gtk_clist_set_shift(GtkCList *clist, gint row, gint column,
        gint vertical, gint horizontal);
```

The arguments clist, row, and column specify the clist and the cell to which to apply the offset. The arguments vertical and horizontal are the number of pixels, greater than or equal to 0, that should be added to the upper-left origin of the text or pixmap rendered in the cell. By default, as I discussed earlier, a cell's height is the height of the font used to render the cell content, and the width of a cell is defined by the width of the column title button of the column in which the cell is located. Adding an offset to the origin of the data displayed in a cell may result in clipping of the data; the cell will not be resized so that the data displayed is visible. Making a column autoresize does not help either; the size attribute is determined before the offset or shift is applied. The only way to ensure that the width of the column is sufficient to display content with a horizontal offset is to explicitly set the column width using one of the GtkCList functions I described earlier. However, I know of no obvious way to ensure that content with a vertical offset will not be clipped.

Your application can control the selectability of rows in a clist by calling gtk_clist_set_selectable():

```
void
gtk_clist_set_selectable(GtkCList *clist, gint row,
         gboolean selectable);
```

If selectable is set to FALSE, the row cannot be selected by the user. If set to TRUE (default), the row can be selected by the user. It is a good idea to make rows in a view-only list nonselectable; this will minimize the confusion of users who select a row and then have no operation that can be applied to the row. You can also determine at runtime whether a row is selectable by calling gtk_clist_get_selectable():

```
gboolean
gtk_clist_get_selectable(GtkCList *clist, gint row);
```

If TRUE is returned, the specified row can be selected by the user. Otherwise, FALSE is returned.

A row can easily be removed from a clist with a call to gtk_clist_remove():

```
void
gtk_clist_remove(GtkCList *clist, gint row);
```

Clist is the instance of GtkCList, and row is the row in clist to remove. Row must be in the range [0, *m*–1], with *m* equal to the number of rows in the clist. To remove all rows in a clist, use gtk_clist_clear():

```
void
gtk_clist_clear(GtkCList *clist);
```

Associating Client Data with a Row. An application can associate arbitrary, application-specific data in the form of a gpointer with a row in a clist. This data can be retrieved at any time by the application. Associating client data with a row can at times be a powerful technique, depending on the application.

Let's suppose you are using Gtk+ to develop the GUI front end of a database application. To keep it simple, the database contains a list of associates, friends, and families. Each record in the database records the contact's name, address, e-mail address, phone number, fax number, cell phone number, and up to 1,024 bytes of text that can be used to store arbitrary, unstructured data about the contact. We can ignore the details of the database in general, with the exception that we will assume the database software provides an API that can be used to retrieve a pointer to a data structure that contains the information about a contact in the database. Such a data structure might be represented in C as follows:

```
typedef struct _record {
  char *name;              // name
  char *address;           // street address
  char *email;             // e-mail address
  char *phone;             // phone number
  char *pprefix;           // phone area code
  char *fax;               // fax number
  char *fprefix;           // fax area code
  char *cell;              // cell number
  char *cprefix;           // cell area code
  char *data;              // miscellaneous data
  char dirty;              // record needs to be written to database
  char delete;             // record needs to be deleted from database
  struct _record *next;    // assume we organize this in a one-way list
} Record;
```

Upon startup, the application reads all of the records in the database, places them in an internal data structure such as a tree or a linked list of Record nodes, and then displays the data to the user using a clist. Below the clist are three buttons labeled Add, Delete, and Edit.

Clicking the Add button brings up a dialog that can be used to enter information about the contact. Once that data has been entered, it is added to the clist for display as well as to the internal data structure. The dirty field in the data structure is set to 1 to indicate that the data needs to be written to the database. Clicking on the Delete button marks the selected contact for deletion by setting the delete field in the data structure to 1. If the item has already been marked for deletion, the Delete key performs an undelete operation and changes the delete field value back to 0. Clicking on the Edit button causes the selected contact to be displayed in the same dialog used by the Add function. Changes made to contact data in this dialog are displayed in the clist but are not yet written to the database. As was the case with the Add function, the dirty field in the data structure used to store the contact is set to 1 to indicate that it needs to be written to the database.

Upon exit, if contacts were added or modified by the user (the dirty field of a record has been set to 1) or if contacts were deleted (the delete field of a record has been set to 1), then the user is asked whether the changes made to the data should be committed to the database. If the response from the user is to commit the changes, then all new contacts should be added to the database, any modified contacts should be rewritten to the database, and any deleted records should be removed from the database.

Let's focus now on how application data associated with a row in a clist can be used to implement the preceding features. Each row in the clist displays one of the nodes in our internal representation of the database, be it a linked list or a tree. Each of these nodes is a pointer to a Record (e.g., its type is Record *). As we read records from the stored database and construct the linked list maintained by the application, we also call gtk_clist_append() to add the data to the clist, to display the content of the record to the user. At this time, we also set the client data field of the record to point to the node added to the linked list. The following pseudo code illustrates the process:

```
for all records in the data base
do
        read a record from the database;
        allocate a node of type Record;
        add the node to our internal linked list;
        append a new row to the clist;
        set the client data of the row to point to the corresponding
                 node in the clist;
done
```

Notice that each row in the clist now has access to the data stored in the list. We could choose to only display a subset of the data in the clist (for example, just the name and phone number fields), but we would have immediate access to the rest of the data by dereferencing the client data stored with the row.

The practical advantages of associating each row in the clist with one node in the list become apparent as we look at how one might implement the add, modify, and delete operations that our application requires. Let's first assume that the selection mode of the clist has been set to GTK_SELECTION_SINGLE (which is the default mode). Thus, when the user hits any one of the three action buttons (add, modify, or delete), we can be sure that only one item in the list has been selected. What I am describing here can be extended, of course, to work with clists using other selection modes. The other thing I assume is that we have a select_row signal function tracking the current selection, as well as a function that we can call to retrieve the selection. For example:

```
static gint gCurrentSelection = -1;

gint
GetCurrentSelection( void )
{
        return( gCurrentSelection );
}

void
SetCurrentSelection(GtkWidget *widget, gint row, gint column,
        GdkEventButton *event, gpointer data)
{
        gCurrentSelection = row;
}
```

The data argument passed to SetCurrentSelection() by Gtk+ is not the client data that was associated with the row by the application (using the functions I am about to introduce). It is, however, the client data that was passed as the fourth argument to gtk_signal_connect(), which was called by the application to register SetCurrentSelection() as the signal handler function for the clist's select_row signal. (See Chapter 3 for more information on signals and signal functions.)

The following function, DeleteItem, is the signal function called when the Delete button located below the clist is pressed.

```
void
DeleteItem( GtkCList *widget, gpointer client_data )
{
  Record *myNode;

  // grab the client data

  if ( gCurrentSelection == -1 )
          return;                         // no selection

  myNode = (Record *) gtk_clist_get_row_data( (GTK_CLIST(clist),
          gCurrentSelection );
  if ( myNode->delete == 1 )
          myNode->delete = 0;
  else
          myNode->delete = 1;
  UpdateDeletedRowGUI( clist, gCurrentSelection, myNode->delete );
}
```

The first thing DeleteItem() does is check that a selection has been made by the user. If gCurrentSelection is –1, then there is no selection and the function returns (a more user-friendly response would be to display a message dialog that instructs the user to select an item first and try again). With the selection in hand, gtk_clist_get_row_data() is called. The function prototype for gtk_clist_get_row_data() is:

```
gpointer
gtk_clist_get_row_data(GtkCList *clist, gint row);
```

The argument clist is the clist from which to retrieve client data, and row is the row from which it is to be retrieved. The argument row, as always, is in the range [0, $m - 1$] with m equal to the number of rows currently in the clist. The return value of the function is a generic pointer of type gpointer. As you can see, I cast the return value to type Record * and assigned it to a local variable of the same type. Now that the application has retrieved the pointer from the row, it can do what it must to respond to the request to delete the item, which is to toggle the deleted state of the item. Finally, a function named UpdateDeletedRowGUI() is called to change the style associated with the deleted (or undeleted) row. In this example, I might call gtk_clist_set_row_style() to change the foreground color of the row marked as deleted to red or to revert the foreground color of a row that has been undeleted to the default color of black. An example of how to set the foreground color of a row was presented earlier when I described how styles work in GtkCList.

The basic logic for these buttons is as follows. You will need to implement a dialog that can be displayed by the clicked signal function associated with the Add and Modify buttons. The same dialog can be used for both. In the case of Modify, this dialog displays all of the data associated with the selected row, allowing it to be edited by the user. The function gtk_clist_get_row_data() can be called to retrieve the contact data corresponding to the selected row from the linked list. In the case of an Add operation, the controls of the dialog are uninitialized, and the dialog is used to obtain information about the new contact. A Cancel button in the dialog can be used to dismiss the dialog and cancel the Add or Notify operation. An OK button in the dialog can be used to accept changes made to the data. In the OK button clicked signal function, the data from the dialog is retrieved and then written to a node in the linked list. In the case of a Modify operation, this node already exists in the linked list and is already associated with a row in the clist. In the case of an Add operation, the application must create a new node of type Record, add it to the linked list, and set its fields to the data entered by the user. In addition, the application must append a new row to the clist and associate the node just added to the clist with this row. To make the association between the node in the linked list and the row in the clist, the application must call the function gtk_clist_set_row_data():

```
void
gtk_clist_set_row_data(GtkCList *clist, gint row, gpointer data);
```

The arguments to gtk_clist_set_row_data() are simple. The argument clist is the instance of GtkCList containing the row being mapped to client data. The argument row is the index of the row (in the range [0, $m - 1$]) with which the client data will be associated. The value of row in our example would be the return value of the function gtk_clist_append(), which was called to add the row to the clist. Finally, data is the client data that will be associated with the row by this function.

Yet another way to associate data with a row is gtk_clist_set_row_data_full(). This function accepts the same arguments as gtk_clist_set_row_data() plus one additional argument, as can be seen in the following function prototype:

```
void
gtk_clist_set_row_data_full(GtkCList *clist, gint row, gpointer data,
        GtkDestroyNotify destroy);
```

The argument destroy is a pointer to a function with the following prototype:

```
void
MyDestroyNotify( gpointer data )
```

The function you specify will be called when the row is deleted from the clist. GtkCList will call this function, passing the data argument that was specified as the third argument to gtk_clist_set_row_data_full(). This function comes in handy when you have client data associated with a row that is only needed by the application during the lifetime of the row. A DestroyNotify function makes it easy for you to be notified when the row has been deleted as well as to obtain the value of the client data that is no longer required and can be released.

Given a pointer, a client can determine which row (if any) has the pointer as its client data by calling gtk_clist_find_row_from_data():

```
gint
gtk_clist_find_row_from_data(GtkCList *clist, gpointer data);
```

The argument clist is an instance of GtkCList to search, and data is the client data to be searched for. The return value will be in the range $[0, m - 1]$ if some row in the clist has the specified data as its client data. Otherwise, –1 is returned to indicate that the search failed. If multiple rows in the clist have specified data as their client data, only the first row in the list found will be returned. There is no mechanism provided by GtkCList for iterating through rows that share the same client data.

Selection Functions. The next several functions involve application-initiated selections. Normally, the user is the one that controls the selection and "unselection" of rows in a clist and does so via keyboard or mouse control. However, there are times when it might be necessary for an application to select or unselect rows or cells in a clist without user involvement. First, I will describe the GtkCList functions involved with the selection and unselection of items in a clist, and then I will discuss situations when the use of these functions might be appropriate.

To select a specified row and, optionally, a column in the clist, you can call gtk_clist_select_row():

```
void
gtk_clist_select_row(GtkCList *clist, gint row, gint column);
```

The arguments clist, row, and column specify an instance of GtkClist and the location of a cell in the clist to select. If column is –1, all cells in the specified row will be selected.

To select all rows (and all columns or cells) in a clist, the function to call is gtk_clist_select_all():

```
void
gtk_clist_select_all(GtkCList *clist);
```

Selection of multiple rows is only supported for the multiple and extended list selection modes (GTK_SELECTION_MULTIPLE and GTK_SELECTION_EXTENDED).

What can be selected in a clist can also be unselected. To unselect a specified row and column in a clist, call gtk_clist_unselect_row():

```
void
gtk_clist_unselect_row(GtkCList *clist, gint row, gint column);
```

All rows in a clist can be unselected with a call to gtk_clist_unselect_all():

```
void
gtk_clist_unselect_all(GtkCList *clist);
```

Selection of multiple rows can be performed in all selection modes except for GTK_ SELECTION_BROWSE.

Selection or unselection operations performed either by the user or by your application can be undone with a call to gtk_clist_undo_selection():

```
void
gtk_clist_undo_selection(GtkCList *clist);
```

Calling this function reverts the selection state of rows and cells in a clist to their value prior to the last selection made by the user. You might provide users with an Undo Last Selection button that calls this routine from inside of its clicked signal handler.

When might it be appropriate for an application to control selections made in a clist? Let's look at an example. Assume we have been asked to write a calendar application (i.e., one similar to Gnome Calendar). We have decided in our calendar application to use a clist to display a day's agenda. Our application has the following feature requirement: The user can, at any time, invoke a search feature to locate, for example, all appointments in the month of June that contain the string "Engineering Meeting". The results of the search must be displayed by going into a "View Results" mode. Entering this mode, the calendar application displays the agenda of the first day containing a match and selects the first agenda item on that day that matches the search string entered by the user. A button labeled Next unselects the currently selected agenda item and selects the next one, switching the day of the month displayed as necessary. Similarly, a button labeled Back moves the selection to the previously matching agenda item. Hitting the button labeled Cancel takes the user out of the "View Results" mode. To implement this feature, we would use gtk_clist_select_row() to select a row in the clist upon entering "View Results" mode and as matching agenda items are highlighted as the Next and Back buttons are pressed by the user. gtk_clist_unselect_row() would be used to unselect the currently selected row before the next/previous match is highlighted.

Given an x and y coordinate relative to a clist's window, you can obtain the row and column that correspond to the coordinate by calling gtk_clist_get_selection_info():

```
gint
gtk_clist_get_selection_info(GtkCList *clist, gint x, gint y, gint
        *row, gint *column);
```

The following code (taken from Gtk+) illustrates how one can determine the following from a GDK button event:

1. That the button event occurred within the clist window
2. The row and column of the clist cell below which the button event occurred

```
GdkEventButton *event;
gint x, y, row, column;
GtkCList *clist,

if (event->window == clist->clist_window) {
        x = event->x;
        y = event->y;
        gtk_clist_get_selection_info(clist, x, y, &row, &column);
}
```

If the clist argument is not valid (clist is not an instance of GtkCList) or the x, y value does not correspond to a row in the clist, then 0 is returned. Otherwise, a return value of 1 indicates success.

Moving and Sorting Rows. GtkCList provides several routines for manipulating the position of rows in a clist. The first, gtk_clist_swap_rows(), lets you exchange the data located at two rows in the clist:

```
void
gtk_clist_swap_rows(GtkCList *clist, gint row1, gint row2);
```

Both the arguments row1 and row2 must be in the range of $[0, m - 1]$, where m is the number of rows in the clist.

I discussed earlier how the user can drag rows from one location in a clist and drop them to another with the mouse. Dragging can be performed as long as one of the buttons on the mouse has an actions mask specifying GTK_BUTTON_DRAGS (see gtk_clist_set_button_actions()) and the clist has been marked "reorderable" (see gtk_clist_set_reorderable()). An application can also control the display of drag icons during a drag operation.

Drag icons are enabled or disabled by calling gtk_clist_set_use_drag_icons():

```
void
gtk_clist_set_use_drag_icons(GtkCList *clist, gboolean use_icons);
```

The argument clist specifies the clist of interest. Setting use_icons to TRUE enables drag icons for the clist, while setting drag_icons to FALSE disables them.

Your application can move a row from one location to another with a call to gtk_clist_row_move():

```
void
gtk_clist_row_move(GtkCList *clist, gint source_row, gint dest_row);
```

The arguments source_row and dest_row specify the location of the row in the clist to be moved and the location of that row's data after the move, respectively. Both source_row and dest_row must be in the range [0, $m - 1$].

GtkCList provides sorting facilities that can be of great use to applications. By default, sorting is disabled by GtkCList; to enable it, your code must call gtk_clist_set_auto_sort():

```
void
gtk_clist_set_auto_sort(GtkCList *clist, gboolean auto_sort);
```

Setting auto_sort to TRUE enables sorting, while setting it to FALSE disables it. By default, sorting, when enabled, is performed by a clist each time a new item is added to a clist. Sorting is also performed each time gtk_clist_set_auto_sort() is called to toggle automatic sorting from disabled to enabled. Because sorting is performed each time an item is added, you may find it more efficient to disable sorting while your application is adding a large number of items to a list and then re-enable sorting as soon as the list has been constructed. For example:

```
gtk_clist_set_auto_sort( clist, FALSE );

// add items here

gtk_clist_set_auto_sort( clist, TRUE );
```

The sort order of a clist, by default, is set to GTK_SORT_ASCENDING (this can be changed by calling gtk_clist_set_sort_type(), as shown later in this chapter). By default, sorting is performed on column 0 of the clist; other columns are not a factor in the sorting results. The sort used by GtkCList (which is a merge sort) uses a compare function based on strcmp(3). The ramification of this is that data in the clist column that is being sorted is done so based on ASCII value. Although this is suitable for sorting strings of characters, it is not appropriate for use in sorting numeric data. For example, sorting the strings "1", "2", "13", and "1234" in ascending order gives you "1", "1234", "13", and "2", which is not likely to be the desired result. To get around this, you will need to create your own compare function to replace the default supplied by GtkCList. This can be done using the function gtk_clist_set_compare_func():

```
void
gtk_clist_set_compare_func(GtkCList *clist,
        GtkCListCompareFunc cmp_func);
```

The argument clist is, as usual, an instance of GtkCList, and cmp_func is a pointer to a C function used to compare list items during the sort. The prototype of this function must match the following:

```
gint
MyCompareFunc(GtkCList *clist, gconstpointer p1, gconstpointer p2)
```

Passing NULL as the second argument to gtk_clist_set_compare_func() reverts the compare function back to the GtkCList-supplied default.

It is probably worth taking a look at the default compare function supplied by Gtk+ 1.2. You should use this function as a basis for the development of your own compare functions:

Listing 6.1 Default Gtk+ 1.2 Compare Function

```
001 static gint
002 default_compare (GtkCList *clist, gconstpointer ptr1, gconstpointer ptr2)
003 {
004   char *text1 = NULL;
005   char *text2 = NULL;
006
007   GtkCListRow *row1 = (GtkCListRow *) ptr1;
008   GtkCListRow *row2 = (GtkCListRow *) ptr2;
009
010   switch (row1->cell[clist->sort_column].type)
011     {
012     case GTK_CELL_TEXT:
013       text1 = GTK_CELL_TEXT (row1->cell[clist->sort_column])->text;
014       break;
015     case GTK_CELL_PIXTEXT:
016       text1 = GTK_CELL_PIXTEXT (row1->cell[clist->sort_column])->text;
017       break;
018     default:
019       break;
020     }
021
022   switch (row2->cell[clist->sort_column].type)
023     {
024     case GTK_CELL_TEXT:
025       text2 = GTK_CELL_TEXT (row2->cell[clist->sort_column])->text;
026       break;
027     case GTK_CELL_PIXTEXT:
028       text2 = GTK_CELL_PIXTEXT (row2->cell[clist->sort_column])->text;
029       break;
030     default:
031       break;
032     }
033
034   if (!text2)
035     return (text1 != NULL);
036
037   if (!text1)
038     return -1;
039
040   return strcmp (text1, text2);
041}
```

The preceding function is rather straightforward. On lines 007 and 008, the generic pointers passed into the function are assigned to variables of type GtkCListRow. This allows us to easily access the content of the column being sorted in each of the rows. Lines 010 through 020 extract the data to be compared for row number 1, and Lines 022 through 032 do the same for row number 2. On line 010, we access the cell type for the column being sorted; the type determines how the text to be compared is obtained from a cell. Note that this check only applies to row 1 and is why there are two switch statements; it is possible that the type of data in row 1 will be different than the type of data in row 2. The cases of the switch statement on lines 012 through 017 illustrate how to extract GTK_CELL_TEXT and GTK_CELL_PIXTEXT data from a row. Lines 022 through 032 perform the same extraction but for row number 2. clist->sort_column is the column in the row on which the sorting is based. Lines 034 through 040 ensure that the extracted text is valid, and finally, on line 040, a call is made to strcmp(3), which performs the actual comparison of the strings.

There are several ways to expand upon this function. First of all, the preceding default compare function is where the limitation of GtkCList to sort only on a single column of data is introduced. Notice that we select only the text from the cell specified by clist->sort_column. We can convert this function to sort based on all of the cells in a row if needed. The following is a modified version of default_compare() that illustrates how this can be done:

Listing 6.2 Sorting Based on All Cells in a Row

```
static gint
CompareEntireRow(GtkCList *clist, gconstpointer ptr1, gconstpointer ptr2)
{
  char *text1 = NULL;
  char *text2 = NULL;
  int i, ret;

  GtkCListRow *row1 = (GtkCListRow *) ptr1;
  GtkCListRow *row2 = (GtkCListRow *) ptr2;

  for ( i = 0; i <clist->columns; i++ ) {
        switch (row1->cell[i].type)
        {
        case GTK_CELL_TEXT:
                text1 = GTK_CELL_TEXT (row1->cell[i])->text;
                break;
        case GTK_CELL_PIXTEXT:
                text1 = GTK_CELL_PIXTEXT (row1->cell[i])-text;
                break;
        default:
                break;
        }

        switch (row2->cell[i].type)
        {
        case GTK_CELL_TEXT:
                text2 = GTK_CELL_TEXT (row2->cell[i])->text;
                break;
        case GTK_CELL_PIXTEXT:
                text2 = GTK_CELL_PIXTEXT (row2->cell[i])->text;
                break;
        default:
```

```
033                 break;
034         }
035
036         if (!text2)
037                 return (text1 != NULL);
038
039         if (!text1)
040                 return -1;
041
042         ret = strcmp (text1, text2);
043         if ( ret != 0 )
044                 return( ret );
045   }
046   return( 0 );
047 }
```

The major difference in this routine is that we've added a loop, and instead of comparing a single column in each of the rows, we compare, left to right, each of the columns in the row. The number of columns in a row is specified by the columns field of the GtkCList pointer we have been passed. On lines 042 through 044, we obtain the return value from strcmp(). If this value is 0, then the column being compared contained the same value in both of the rows, and we continue at the top of the loop with the next row. If the return value is nonzero, then the rows are different and we can stop our search. If we iterate through all of the columns in the row and they all contain the same value, we will arrive at line 046, where we return a 0 to indicate that the rows contain the same data.

To make the preceding sort function the default for a clist, you need only call the following before adding content to the clist:

```
gtk_clist_set_compare_func(GTK_CLIST(clist), CompareEntireRow);
```

The remaining topic of discussion related to compare functions concerns the data being sorted. The preceding compare functions both assume that the data is ASCII. Suppose, however, your data is numeric or is based on calendar dates or some strange formatting that is incompatible with an ASCII-based compare function. The solution to the problem is to replace the call to strcmp() (as on line 042 in the preceding listing) with a call to a function that is suited to the type of data being compared. The following are examples of functions that can perform content-specific comparisons. The first function, CompareInt(), compares two strings based on the integer values they represent, not the ASCII value of the characters that make up the strings:

Listing 6.3 Comparing Integers

```
// Return -1, 0, or 1 if text1 is less than, equal to, or greater
// than text2, respectively, as an integer, not as an ASCII string.

int
CompareInt(char *text1, char *text2)
{
        int val1, val2;
```

```
            val1 = atoi( text1 );
            val2 = atoi( text2 );

            if ( val1 < val2 )
                    return( -1 );
            else if ( val1 > val2 )
                    return( 1 );
            else
                    return( 0 );
    }
```

The second function, CompareDate(), can be used to compare date strings in the format MM/DD/YYYY:

Listing 6.4 Comparing Dates

```
// Return -1, 0, or 1 if text1 is less than, equal to, or greater than text2,
// respectively, as a date, not as an ASCII string. The date must be in the
// format m{m}/d{d}/y{y}, where m, d, and y are all in range [0,9]

int
CompareDate(char *text1, char *text2)
{
        char    *m1, *m2, *d1, *d2, *y1, *y2;          // hold parts of date strs
        int     im1, im2, id1, id2, iy1, iy2;          // integer counterparts
        char    delim;                                 // strtok needs a char *

        char t1buf[NAME_MAX], t2buf[NAME_MAX];         // holds copies for strtok

         /* make copies to strings otherwise strtok will mangle them

        strncpy( t1buf, text1, NAME_MAX );
        strncpy( t2buf, text2, NAME_MAX );

        /* parse the first date */

        delim = '/';
        m1 = strtok( t1buf, &delim );
        d1 = strtok( NULL, &delim );
        y1 = strtok( NULL, &delim );

        /* parse the second date */

        m2 = strtok( t2buf, &delim );
        d2 = strtok( NULL, &delim );
        y2 = strtok( NULL, &delim );

        /* make sure that we have something for each component */

        if ( !m1 || !m2 || !d1 || !d2 || !y1 || !y2 )
                return( 0 );

         /* convert the components to integers so we can do the comparisons */

        im1 = atoi( m1 ); id1 = atoi( d1 ); iy1 = atoi( y1 );
```

```
        im2 = atoi( m2 ); id2 = atoi( d2 ); iy2 = atoi( y2 );

        /* Year has precedence over month, which has precedence over day */

        if ( iy1 < iy2 )
                return( -1 );
        else if ( iy1 > iy2 )
                return( 1 );
        else {
                // the year is the same

                if ( im1 < im2 )
                        return( -1 );
                else if ( im1 > im2 )
                        return( 1 );
                else {
                        // the year and the month are the same

                        if ( id1 < id2 )
                                return( -1 );
                        else if ( id1 > id2 )
                                return( 1 );

                        // fall through since dates are equal
                }
        }
        return( 0 );
}
```

As previously mentioned, your application can specify a sort column to be used by compare functions in computing row equality. The default column is column 0. However, you can make it any column you want by calling gtk_clist_set_sort_column():

```
void
gtk_clist_set_sort_column(GtkCList *clist, gint column);
```

The argument column is a value in the range $[0, n - 1]$, where n is the number of columns in a row. A mail user agent provides a familiar example of when an application might want to change the default sort column. A clist can be used to display the contents of a folder, where each row in the clist is a message, a sender, a date, a subject, and other information in the message being displayed as columns in a row. Mail users often want to sort e-mail messages by date or by sender and perhaps less often by other message fields that would be displayed as columns in the folder clist. To enable this feature, the mail program would register a callback on the buttons used as column titles (we discussed how this is done earlier). In the callback, the corresponding column in the clist would be made the sort column for the clist, and the clist would be sorted by making a call to gtk_clist_sort():

```
void
gtk_clist_sort(GtkCList *clist);
```

The function gtk_clist_sort() takes a single argument, an instance of GtkCList. Calling this function will cause the list to be sorted using the sort column and the compare function specified by the client with gtk_clist_set_sort_column() and gtk_clist_set_compare_func(), respectively, or defaults if the client has not specified alternates. The implementation of the signal function might look like this:

```
void
clist_click_column(GtkCList *clist, gint column, gpointer data)
{
        gtk_clist_set_sort_column( clist, column );
        gtk_clist_sort( clist );
}
```

The final GtkCList sorting function discussed here allows an application to specify the ordering of items in a clist after a sort. There are two possible choices, as listed in Table 6.11.

Table 6.11 Sorting Order Values

Sort Order	*Meaning*
GTK_SORT_ASCENDING	Row 0 has the smallest value and increases with row number.
GTK_SORT_DESCENDING	Row 0 has the largest value and decreases with row number.

Both of these values are defined by the Gtk+ enumeration type GtkSortType. To specify the order of items after a sort, call gtk_clist_set_sort_type():

```
void
gtk_clist_set_sort_type(GtkCList *clist, GtkSortType sort_type);
```

The argument clist is an instance of GtkCList. The argument sort_type specifies the ordering after a sort and must be one of the values specified in the preceding table.

Scrollbars

An instance of GtkCList displays itself within an area managed by its containing widget. The containing widget may be a box, a window, or some other widget that can be used for this purpose (see Chapter 10, "Container and Bin Classes"). The content of the clist may be (or may become, as content is changed or added at runtime) large enough that it cannot be displayed in the area provided, resulting in horizontal or vertical clipping. To get around this problem, your application must do one of the following:

- Increase the size of the containing widget. This may be the correct solution if the content of the list is relatively small and remains static.
- Provide horizontal and/or vertical scrollbars that allow users to navigate the clist to view content that might otherwise be clipped.

Although GtkCList supports the use of scrollbars, it cannot create them. To obtain scrollbars on a clist, an application can either make the clist a child of a container widget class that provides scrollbars or instantiate scrollbars and wire them to the clist directly. Details on scrollbars and adjustments can be found in Chapter 13, "Range Widgets and Adjustment Objects." In this section, I'm simply going to point out the issues involving GtkCList and discuss briefly the functions that GtkCList exposes.

Generally speaking, the decision to add scrolling to a clist will be based on how the clist is going to be used and how many items are going to be displayed in the list. I've come up with three possible cases:

1. The list is small and doesn't change (at runtime, can't add or delete an arbitrary number of rows).
2. The list can change.
3. Case 1 or case 2 with rows that contain a large number of columns or columns that contain lengthy data.

For case 1, a vertical scrollbar is not needed. The container that will hold your clist should size itself to the contents of the clist, in the absence of any code that specifically sets the size of the container widget. As long as the size of the clist (and thus the container) is not overly large, you need not worry about scrollbars. For case 2, if the potential changes to the list do not include adding items to the list that would cause resizing of the container in an undesirable way, then once again, a scrollbar is not needed. But you need to be careful. The following code illustrates this point rather nicely:

Listing 6.5 Comparing Dates

```
#include <gtk/gtk.h>

static GtkWidget *list;

static void
QuitCallback(GtkWidget *widget, GtkWidget *dialog_window)
{
     gtk_main_quit();
     exit( 0 );
}

static void
AddCallback(GtkWidget *widget, GtkWidget *dialog_window)
{
     char     *texts[5];
     int      i;

     for ( i = 0; i < 100; i++ ) {
              texts[0] = "36123-A";
              texts[1] = "Wood Chisel Set";
              texts[2] = "9.99";
              texts[3] = "1";
              texts[4] = "9.99";
              gtk_clist_append( GTK_CLIST( list ), texts );
     }
}

```

```
main( int argc, char *argv[] )
{
      GtkWidget *button, *hbox, *dialog_window;
      char *texts[5];

      static char *titles[] =
      {
          "Part #", "Description", "Unit Price", "Quantity", "Total"
      };

      gtk_init( &argc, &argv );

      dialog_window = gtk_dialog_new();
      gtk_window_position (GTK_WINDOW (dialog_window), GTK_WIN_POS_MOUSE);

      hbox = gtk_hbox_new (FALSE, 0);
      gtk_container_add (GTK_CONTAINER (GTK_DIALOG (dialog_window)->vbox),
              hbox);

      list = gtk_clist_new_with_titles( 5, titles );

      texts[0] = "36123-A"; texts[1] = "Wood Chisel Set";
      texts[2] = "9.99"; texts[3] = "1"; texts[4] = "9.99";
      gtk_clist_append( GTK_CLIST( list ), texts );

      texts[0] = "45661-A"; texts[1] = "Work Gloves";
      texts[2] = "5.99"; texts[3] = "1"; texts[4] = "5.99";
      gtk_clist_append( GTK_CLIST( list ), texts );

      texts[0] = "34991-Q"; texts[1] = "Claw Hammer";
      texts[2] = "7.99"; texts[3] = "1"; texts[4] = "7.99";
      gtk_clist_append( GTK_CLIST( list ), texts );

      texts[0] = "30125-S"; texts[1] = "Deluxe Lawn Rake";
      texts[2] = "12.99"; texts[3] = "1"; texts[4] = "12.99";
      gtk_clist_append( GTK_CLIST( list ), texts );

      gtk_box_pack_start (GTK_BOX (hbox), list, FALSE, FALSE, 0);

      button = gtk_button_new_with_label("Quit");
      gtk_box_pack_start(GTK_BOX(GTK_DIALOG(dialog_window)->action_area),
              button, TRUE, TRUE, 0);
      gtk_signal_connect(GTK_OBJECT(button), "clicked",
              GTK_SIGNAL_FUNC(QuitCallback), dialog_window);
      button = gtk_button_new_with_label ("Add");
      gtk_box_pack_start (GTK_BOX(GTK_DIALOG(dialog_window)->action_area),
             button, TRUE, TRUE, 0);
      gtk_signal_connect(GTK_OBJECT(button), "clicked",
             GTK_SIGNAL_FUNC(AddCallback), dialog_window);
      gtk_widget_show_all(dialog_window);
      gtk_main();
}
```

The main routine creates a dialog that consists of a clist placed in a GtkBox container, below which two buttons are added: one labeled Quit and the other labeled Add. The clist is initialized with four rows of data on lines 049 through 063. When executed, a top-level dialog is displayed that is sized to the clist (the size of the clist being determined by its contents) and to the Quit and Add buttons below it. The problem comes in when the Add button is hit, invoking the callback routine on lines 012 through 026. In this callback, 100 rows are added to the clist. The results are disastrous; the clist resizes itself to accommodate the new content, which in turn causes the box and its parent, the dialog, to resize as well. On my Linux system running the Enlightenment window manager, the dialog resizes such that the bottom of the dialog, and the Add and Quit buttons, is located well below the screen. Even if the sizing were to leave all portions of the window visible on the screen, it is better to add scrollbars to the clist and let them come and go as needed than to have the geometry of the dialog change as the clist contents grow and shrink. With that in mind, the approach I recommend for handling case 2 is to either size the clist or its container to a sufficiently large size to accommodate the addition of new items without causing a resize, or add a vertical scrollbar to the clist.

The most straightforward way to get scrollbars on a clist is to place the clist in a scrolled window (GtkScolledWindow) container. I will discuss this widget in detail in Chapter 11, "More Container Classes." The following code illustrates the types of changes to the preceding listing that are necessary to get scrollbars on the clist. The differences occur in the first several lines of main():

```
main( int argc, char *argv[] )
{
      GtkWidget *button, *scrolled_win, *dialog_window;
      char *texts[5];

      static char *titles[] =
      {
          "Part #",
          "Description",
          "Unit Price",
          "Quantity",
          "Total",
      };

      gtk_init( &argc, &argv );

      dialog_window = gtk_dialog_new();
      gtk_window_position (GTK_WINDOW (dialog_window), GTK_WIN_POS_MOUSE);

      scrolled_win = gtk_scrolled_window_new (NULL, NULL);

      gtk_widget_set_usize( scrolled_win, 300, 100 );

      gtk_container_set_border_width (GTK_CONTAINER (scrolled_win), 5);
```

```
025     gtk_scrolled_window_set_policy (GTK_SCROLLED_WINDOW (scrolled_win),
026             GTK_POLICY_AUTOMATIC, GTK_POLICY_AUTOMATIC);
027
028     gtk_container_add (GTK_CONTAINER (GTK_DIALOG (dialog_window)->vbox),
029             scrolled_win);
030
031     list = gtk_clist_new_with_titles( 5, titles );
032
033     ...
```

Instead of using an instance of GtkBox to contain the clist, I use an instance of GtkScrolledWindow. GtkScrolledWindow (Chapter 11) is similar to GtkBox (Chapter 10) in the sense that it knows how to contain a widget. It differs from GtkBox in that it can be made to add and remove vertical and horizontal scrollbars as required by the size of the content that scrolled window manages. The scrolled window is created on line 020. On line 022, an initial size is given to the scrolled window. This size defines a viewport through which the child window contained by the scrolled window widget is visible, one that I found to be more pleasing than the default that was computed by the scrolled window widget. Lines 025 and 026 set the scrolled window scrollbar policy. Here, GTK_POLICY_AUTOMATIC tells the scrolled window to automatically add a scrollbar as needed in both the vertical and the horizontal dimensions. If, for example, there is no vertical scrollbar, the number of rows in the clist is small enough so that each of the rows can be displayed within the area of the scrolled window, without clipping. Finally, on lines 028 and 029, the scrolled window is made a child of the dialog widgets' vertical box widget instance. With these minor changes, our clist now has all of the scrollbar capability it could possibly need.

The final case, case 3, is really a special case of Case 2 but applied to the horizontal dimension. Here I would suggest adding a horizontal scrollbar. The preceding code that I provided handles the horizontal case because I set the vertical and horizontal scrollbar preferences to GTK_POLICY_AUTOMATIC.

The following scrollbar-related functions are generally not used by application developers, but I will document them for completeness. In particular, see Chapter 13 for details about adjustments.

The first two functions can be used whenever a vertical scrollbar has been attached to a clist. The function gtk_clist_row_is_visible() can be used to determine if a given row, in the range of $[0, m - 1]$, is visible to the application user. The function prototype is as follows:

```
GtkVisibility
gtk_clist_row_is_visible(GtkCList *clist, gint row);
```

The argument clist is an instance of GtkCList, and row is the number of the row of interest. The return value is of type GtkVisibility and can be one of the following in Table 6.12.

Table 6.12 Row Visibility

Value	*Meaning*
GTK_VISIBILITY_NONE	The row is not visible.

Table 6.12 Row Visibility (Continued)

Value	*Meaning*
GTK_VISIBILITY_PARTIAL	The row is clipped (either top or bottom).
GTK_VISIBILITY_FULL	The row is completely visible vertically.

A row with a visibility of GTK_VISIBILITY_FULL does not necessarily mean that all columns in the row are visible; gtk_clist_row_is_visible() only reports visibility in the vertical dimension, and not in the horizontal dimension.

An application can cause the scrollbars to be moved so that the cell at a given row and column is visible. An application that allows searching of a clist for content might want to position the scrollbars so that the matching cell(s) are visible upon completion of the search. The function gtk_clist_moveto() provides this capability:

```
void
gtk_clist_moveto(GtkCList *clist, gint row, gint column,
        gfloat row_align, gfloat col_align);
```

The arguments clist, row, and column specify the clist of interest and the row and column to display, respectively. The arguments row and column are in the usual ranges of [0, $m - 1$] and [0, $n - 1$], where m is the number of rows in the clist and n is the number of columns in a row. Specifying a value that is less than 0 (e.g., –1) will leave the scrollbar position for that dimension unchanged. The arguments row_align and col_align define where the row and column, respectively, are displayed after the scroll. The values for these arguments are floating point and must be in the range [0, 1] inclusive. A value of 0.0 specified for row_align and col_align places the cell at the top of the clist vertically and as the leftmost cell horizontally, respectively. A value of 1.0 specified for row_align and col_align places the cell at the bottom of the clist vertically and as the rightmost cell horizontally, respectively. Setting row_align and col_align to 0.5 should place the cell in the center of the viewable portion of the clist. Other values in the range [0, 1] should do as expected, for example:

```
gtk_clist_moveto( clist, myRow, -1, 0.3, 0 );
```

This should position the row approximately one-third of the viewable area down from the top of the clist. In this case, col_align was ignored because –1 was specified as the column argument.

The final scrollbar routines I discuss here are used to specify and retrieve horizontal and vertical adjustments. Once again, I will talk more about adjustments in Chapter 13.

To set the horizontal adjustment of the clist, call gtk_clist_set_hadjustment():

```
void
gtk_clist_set_hadjustment(GtkCList *clist, GtkAdjustment *adjustment);
```

Similarly, to set the vertical adjustment of the clist, an application can call gtk_clist_set_vadjustment:

```
void
gtk_clist_set_vadjustment(GtkCList *clist, GtkAdjustment *adjustment);
```

Retrieving adjustments is also straightforward. To obtain the horizontal and vertical adjustments of a clist, call gtk_clist_get_hadjustment() and gtk_clist_get_vadjustment(), respectively:

```
GtkAdjustment *
gtk_clist_get_hadjustment(GtkCList *clist);

GtkAdjustment *
gtk_clist_get_vadjustment(GtkCList *clist);
```

Summary

In this chapter, we looked at two widgets capable of displaying data as a list. GtkList is a relatively simple widget that can be used for lists that consist of a single column of data. GtkCList is a much more complex widget (as can be evidenced by the size of its API) that can display rows consisting of one or more columns of data. Both widgets have their advantages and differences. For example, GtkList is more flexible in terms of the type of data it displays and is capable of displaying arbitrary widgets. GtkCList, on the other hand, only supports the display of text with an optional pixmap. GtkCList is capable of sorting its data, while GtkList is not. Both widgets allow an application to add content dynamically and users to select data from a list in one of several modes (e.g., single- or multiple-row selection).

CHAPTER

7

WINDOWS AND DIALOGS

In this chapter, we will take a look at the GtkWindow widget class. GtkWindow is a fairly simple class that allows clients to create and manage windows. Several widget classes in Gtk+ reside below GtkWindow in the widget class hierarchy and thus inherit functionality from GtkWindow. Perhaps the most important of these child classes is GtkDialog, which is also discussed in this chapter. The widgets covered in this chapter are summarized in Table 7.1.

Table 7.1 Widgets Covered in This Chapter

Class Name	*Description*
GtkWindow	Capable of creating a window into which content can be added. The base class for dialog classes discussed in this chapter.
GtkDialog	Implements a dialog that contains a vertical box to hold dialog content, and an action area designed to hold OK, Cancel, and related buttons.
GtkFileSelection	A file-selection dialog widget that allows users to traverse a file system, select a directory or file, and perform other file system–related functions.
GtkFontSelection	A widget (not related to GtkWindow) that can be used to select a font.
GtkFontSelectionDialog	A dialog that presents a font-selection dialog to the user and provides buttons useful in such a dialog.
GtkColorSelection	A widget (not related to GtkWindow) that can be used to select a color.
GtkColorSelectionDialog	A dialog that presents a color-selection widget to the user as well as buttons useful in such a dialog.

Although GtkFontSelection and GtkColorSelection are not related to GtkWindow, they are described in this chapter. I present them here because I feel that an understanding of their operation is crucial to the understanding of the GtkWindow-derived classes to which they correspond (GtkFontSelectionDialog and GtkColorSelectionDialog, respectively), and it makes sense to describe them all in one chapter instead of spreading them throughout the book.

Now that the agenda for the chapter has been set, let's take a look at the top of the GtkWindow widget hierarchy, which is, to no great surprise, the GtkWindow widget itself.

GtkWindow

Class Name

```
GtkWindow
```

Parent Class Name

```
GtkBin
```

Macros

Widget type macro: `GTK_TYPE_WINDOW`

Object to widget cast macro: `GTK_WINDOW(obj)`

Widget type check macro: `GTK_IS_WINDOW(obj)`

Supported Signals

Table 7.2 Signals

Signal Name	*Condition Causing Signal to Trigger*
set_focus	A widget in the window has obtained focus.

Signal Function Prototypes

```
void
set_focus(GtkWindow *window, GtkWidget *widget, gpointer user_data)
```

Supported Arguments

Prefix: **`GtkWindow::`**

Table 7.3 GtkWindow Argument

Name	*Type*	*Permissions*
type	GTK_TYPE_WINDOW_TYPE	GTK_ARG_READWRITE
title	GTK_TYPE_STRING	GTK_ARG_READWRITE
auto_shrink	GTK_TYPE_BOOL	GTK_ARG_READWRITE
allow_shrink	GTK_TYPE_BOOL	GTK_ARG_READWRITE
allow_grow	GTK_TYPE_BOOL	GTK_ARG_READWRITE
modal	GTK_TYPE_BOOL	GTK_ARG_READWRITE
window_position	GTK_TYPE_WINDOW_POSITION	GTK_ARG_READWRITE

Application-Level API Synopsis

Retrieve the window type constant GTK_TYPE_WINDOW at runtime:

```
GtkType
gtk_window_get_type(void);
```

Create a new instance of GtkWindow of the specified type, which can be GTK_WINDOW_TOPLEVEL, GTK_WINDOW_DIALOG, or GTK_WINDOW_POPUP:

```
GtkWidget *
gtk_window_new(GtkWindowType type);
```

Set the window title as displayed in the window manager decoration:

```
void
gtk_window_set_title(GtkWindow *window, const gchar *title);
```

Set the window manager class and class name:

```
void
gtk_window_set_wmclass(GtkWindow *window, const gchar *wmclass_name,
        const gchar *wmclass_class);
```

Set the window policy hints:

```
void
gtk_window_set_policy(GtkWindow *window, gint allow_shrink,
        gint allow_grow, gint auto_shrink);
```

Set the x and y positions of window:

```
void
gtk_window_set_position(GtkWindow *window, GtkWindowPosition
        position);
```

Set the focus widget of a window:

```
void
gtk_window_set_focus(GtkWindow *window, GtkWidget *focus);
```

Application-Level API Synopsis (Continued)

Activate a window's focus widget:
```
gint
gtk_window_activate_focus(GtkWindow *window);
```

Set the default widget of a window:
```
void
gtk_window_set_default(GtkWindow *window,
   GtkWidget *default_widget);
```

Activate a window's default widget:
```
gint
gtk_window_activate_default(GtkWindow *window);
```

Make a window transient:
```
void
gtk_window_set_transient_for(GtkWindow *window, GtkWindow *parent);
```

Set window manager geometry hints:
```
void
gtk_window_set_geometry_hints(GtkWindow *window, GtkWidget
*geometry_widget, GdkGeometry *geometry, GdkWindowHints geom_mask);
```

Set a window's default size:
```
void
gtk_window_set_default_size(GtkWindow *window, gint width,
   gint height);
```

Make the specified window modal:
```
void
gtk_window_set_modal(GtkWindow *window, gboolean modal);
```

Class Description

The GtkWindow class provides functionality needed by applications to create and manipulate windows.

Creating a Window Widget

Window creation in Gtk+ is performed by calling gtk_window_new(). This routine accepts a single argument that is the type of window to be created. A window in Gtk+ can be a top-level window (GTK_WINDOW_TOPLEVEL), a dialog (GTK_WINDOW_DIALOG), or a pop-up window (GTK_WINDOW_POPUP). Each of these window types will be discussed in the following section. First, the following code snippet illustrates the creation of a top-level window.

```
GtkWidget *window;

...

 window = gtk_window_new( GTK_WINDOW_TOPLEVEL );

if ( window != (GtkWidget *) NULL ) {

...
```

The function prototype for gtk_window_new() is:

```
GtkWidget *
gtk_window_new(GtkWindowType type);
```

The type can be GTK_WINDOW_TOPLEVEL, GTK_WINDOW_DIALOG, or GTK_WINDOW_POPUP, as previously described.

The preceding code illustrates two points worth mentioning. First, as I discussed earlier, the convention is for widgets, regardless of their type, to be stored in a variable of type GtkWidget *. You'll notice in the following code that I make use of the macro GTK_WINDOW to coerce this variable to a GtkWindow * as needed by some of the functions in the GtkWindow class API that require a GtkWindow * argument. Second, it is generally a good idea, especially during development, to always check the return value of the widget creation function, regardless of the Gtk+ widget class being instantiated, to ensure that the routine did not fail and that a widget was actually created. If failure occurs, the return type will be NULL; this holds true for all widget classes supported in Gtk+ 1.2. A widget creation function might fail for one of any number of reasons specific to the widget class or the widget creation function. Most widget creation functions fail if the application passes one or more incorrect arguments to the widget creation function (in this case, an invalid window type argument will lead to failure). Another cause for failure is an internal failure of some kind, such as an inability of the widget creation function to allocate needed memory.

Window Types

A top-level window (GTK_WINDOW_TOPLEVEL) is a window that has no parent window (in reality, the parent window will be the X server's root window). In other words, it exists on its own, independent of other application windows on the use's desktop. Typically, this window type will be used in the creation of an application's main window. Gtk+ top-level windows participate in window manager protocols; support for these protocols is requested by GDK on behalf of Gtk+ when the top-level window is created. The two window manager protocols supported by top-level windows include WM_DELETE_WINDOW and WM_TAKE_FOCUS. Readers who are interested in the details of these window manager protocols can refer to *The Xlib Programming Manual, Volume One,* from O'Reilly & Associates.

A dialog window (GTK_WINDOW_DIALOG) is similar to a top-level window in that it does not have a parent window (its parent is the X server root window). And, like a top-level window, a dialog also participates in the WM_DELETE_WINDOW and WM_TAKE_FOCUS window manager protocols. It differs from a top-level window in that the window is transient. In X, a dialog is almost always made transient by a call to

XSetTransientForHint(), and this is what GDK does on behalf of Gtk+ when a dialog window is created. A transient window is temporary in the sense that it is visible on the desktop for only a short amount of time (in contrast to a top-level window, like the main window of your application). By marking a window as transient, window managers may (and should) treat the window differently than they do a top-level window. Window manager decorations may be rendered differently for a dialog window. Some window managers, such as twm, will allow the user to control placement of top-level windows (by grabbing the pointer and presenting an outline of the window that the user must drag to a desired location, followed by a click of the left mouse button to position the application on the desktop). This is not done for dialog windows; they are placed on the desktop with no interaction required of the user. Finally, a transient window should (depending on the window manager) iconify along with the application's top-level window when iconified by the window manager or user.

Note that in Gtk+ 1.2, there appear to be bugs in the implementation. See my discussion of gtk_window_set_transient_for(), later in this chapter, for details.

A pop-up window (GTK_WINDOW_POPUP) is an X window that has its override_redirect and save_under attributes set at the time of creation. Otherwise, it is basically the same as a top-level window. The override_redirect attribute tells the window manager not to intercept the mapping of the window; thus, the window manager is not given the opportunity to add decorations to the window (such as a title bar, a menu, or minimize, maximize, and close buttons). Pop-up windows should be used only for very temporary windows, such as menus, or at times when it is important for a window to not be given window decorations. A save under window is handled specially by the X server when it is mapped and unmapped. When a save under window is mapped, the area beneath the save under window is saved by the X server to off-screen memory. Once the save under window is popped down and unmapped, the X server restores the contents of the window beneath the save under window automatically. Contrast this to a non-save under window; if a pop-up window was not marked as save_under, then the X server would need to send an expose event to the client, asking the client to redraw the contents that were destroyed, which is a highly inefficient operation in comparison. Windows typically created as pop-up windows include menus, option menus, about boxes, and splash screens.

Setting the Window Title

Applications should assign a title to each window they create (except for pop-up windows, which do not require a title). A window title is typically used by the window manager, which will display the window title in the title bar decoration or will use the title as a label to identify windows that have been iconified. In most cases, a title should be assigned before the window is displayed by the application. However, a title can be changed anytime after the window has been displayed. To set or change the title of a top-level or dialog window, call the function gtk_window_set_title():

```
void
gtk_window_set_title(GtkWindow *window, const gchar *title);
```

The argument window is a handle to an instance of type GtkWindow. The argument title is a C-language, null-terminated string that is the (new) title of the window to be displayed by the window manager.

Applications that allow the users to create documents—word processors, text editors, and image-manipulation programs like The GIMP—often need to change the title of windows they have created. Let's consider a text editor for a moment. A text editor will usually provide New and Save As items in its File menu. A sensible convention for naming newly created, unsaved text documents might be to assign them a name of the form Untitled-*n,* where *n* is 0 for the first newly created document, 1 for the second newly created document, and so forth. For example, if the user has already created three new text documents, the next "new" document created would be assigned the title Untitled-3. Once the user selects New, our text editor will respond by creating a new top-level window by making a call to gtk_window_new(). Then, once a title for the document is generated, gtk_window_set_title() will be called. Again, this should be done before the window manager maps the window.

Now, say the user invokes Save As and saves this document to a file named */home/bert/mydocument.* Most editors would extract the filename from the path (in this case, the result would be *mydocument*) after the Save As operation and use this string as the new window title. In Gtk+, we would make a call to gtk_window_set_title() to perform this change.

Setting the Window Position

Applications can control the x and y positions of windows on the user's desktop at the time the window is mapped by calling gtk_window_set_position() before showing the window. This routine takes two arguments: the window to be moved and a constant belonging to the enum type GtkWindowPosition that describes the desired location, as the following code snippet illustrates:

```
GtkWidget *window;

...

gtk_window_set_position( GTK_WINDOW(widget), GTK_WIN_POS_CENTER );
```

The function prototype for gtk_window_set_position() is as follows:

```
void
gtk_window_set_position(GtkWindow *window,
   GtkWindowPosition position);
```

The argument position can be set to one of the values listed in Table 7.4.

Table 7.4 Window Positions

Value	*Meaning*
GTK_WIN_POS_NONE	The window manager decides window placement. If no window manager is executing, the position of the upper-right corner of the window will likely be fixed at 0, 0.
GTK_WIN_POS_CENTER	The window is placed in the center of the user's desktop.
GTK_WIN_POS_MOUSE	The window is centered beneath the pointer location.

Setting the Class of the Window

An application can set the res_class and res_name fields of the XA_WM_CLASS property for the application by calling gtk_window_set_wmclass():

```
void
gtk_window_set_wmclass(GtkWindow *window, const gchar *wmclass_name,
        const gchar *wmclass_class);
```

The argument window is an instance of GtkWindow; usually this will be the top-level or main window of the application. The arguments wmclass_name and wmclass_class are the application name and application class, respectively. Generally speaking, wmclass_name is the value argv[0] passed to the application's main(), while wmclass_class is argv[0] with the initial letter capitalized. Thus, wmclass_name for The GIMP would be set to gimp, and wmclass_class would be set to Gimp. The value of wmclass_name can be used by the window manager to derive the title bar of the application's main window; note the potential for conflict with gtk_window_set_title(). The value of wmclass_class can be used by the window manager to look up resources for the application that might be stored in the resource database. This function should be called before the window has been realized.

Setting Policy Hints

The GtkWindow class allows the application to set window manager policy hints regarding window shrink and grow capabilities. The function gtk_window_set_policy() provides this support:

```
void
gtk_window_set_policy(GtkWindow *window, gint allow_shrink,
        gint allow_grow, gint auto_shrink);
```

If gtk_window_set_policy() is not called by your application, GtkWindow will internally set the defaults to allow_shrink = FALSE, allow_grow = TRUE, and auto_shrink = FALSE. For most applications, these are suitable defaults, and gtk_window_set_policy() need not be called.

The argument allow_shrink tells the window manager that the size of the window can be made smaller by the user, while allow_grow tells the window manager that the width and/or height of the window can be increased by the user.

Note that these are hints to the window manager and should be used to control the ability of the user to resize windows. These hints may or may not affect the application's ability to do the same, and your mileage may vary based on the window manager being used. For example, I experimented with fvwm2, and with allow_shrink and allow_grow both set to FALSE, I was unable to resize windows using the window manager, but the application was able to resize windows by calling gtk_widget_set_usize(). This may not be the case, however, with other window managers. Internally, Gtk+ (actually GDK) implements this feature with a call to XSetWMNormalHints(), setting the PMinSize and PMaxSize flags set as appropriate (see O'Reilly's *Volume One*, previously mentioned, for details). With these flags, the window manager is being told that users may not override the window manager's choice of size and that the application may override the window manager's choice of size but only if the window manager cooperates.

The auto_shrink flag controls resizing as widgets are added to or removed from the window, once the window has been realized (made visible). If set to TRUE, the window will automatically resize itself to accommodate the addition or removal of widgets. If set to FALSE, widgets added to a window may be hidden or partially obscured, or the removal of a widget may result in a less-than-optimal window layout where areas of the window previously owned by the widget that was removed go unused.

Making a Window Transient

In the preceding discussion of gtk_window_new(), I mentioned that a dialog window (GTK_WINDOW_DIALOG) is a transient window, and I explained what it means for a window to be transient. A nondialog window can be made transient by calling gtk_window_set_transient_for():

```
void
gtk_window_set_transient_for(GtkWindow *window, GtkWindow *parent);
```

The argument window is the instance of GtkWindow that should be marked transient, and parent is the instance of GtkWindow that is the window's parent. Transient windows are handled specially by the window manager. A transient window is supposed to be iconified along with its parent window when the parent is iconified. In addition, a transient window may be decorated differently by a window manager than top-level windows and, like pop-up windows, is often placed on the desktop without user intervention. To get full cooperation from the window manager, it is important to mark the window transient just prior to it being realized by a call to gtk_widget_show() or gtk_widget_show_all().

The following code snippet illustrates how to mark a dialog window transient:

```
GtkWidget *top, *dialog;

...

top = gtk_window_new( GTK_WINDOW_TOPLEVEL );

...

dialog = gtk_window_new( GTK_WINDOW_DIALOG );
gtk_window_set_transient_for( GTK_WINDOW(dialog), GTK_WINDOW(top) );

...

gtk_widget_show_all( top );
```

After reading the source code for gtk_window_new() and gdk_window_new(), one would be correct in concluding that a GTK_WINDOW_DIALOG window is a transient window, as it is made transient by GDK with a call to XSetTransientForHint(). However, the parent window passed to X by GDK is the X server's root window. Because of this, iconifying the top-level window of your application will not result in iconification of your application's dialog windows. The correct parent window for a transient window, in most cases, will be the top-level window of the application. To ensure that transient (dialog) windows behave as they should, applications should implement a strategy similar to the one previously presented, until Gtk+ has had a chance to address this issue in a future release.

Setting Geometry Hints

X allows clients to communicate hints to the window manager. These hints help the window manager perform operations, such as window resizing and placement, in a way best suited to the needs of the application. We saw an example of this earlier: gtk_window_set_policy() can be used to set window manager hints that control the ability of the user to resize application windows. In fact, these hints set by gtk_window_set_policy() belong to a larger group of hints called size hints or normal hints in the X11 world. In Gtk+, these hints are called geometry hints and can be set by calling gtk_window_set_geometry():

```
void
gtk_window_set_geometry_hints(GtkWindow *window,
        GtkWidget *geometry_widget, GdkGeometry *geometry,
        GdkWindowHints geom_mask);
```

The argument window is a GtkWindow instance for which the specified hints will apply. The window can be of any type except GTK_WINDOW_POPUP because a pop-up window does not need geometry hints. The argument geometry_widget is a widget contained by the window. Gtk+ uses this widget to help it make sizing computations; the widget itself is not communicated to the window manager, just the window. The arguments geometry and geom_mask together define the hints to be set and their values. Table 7.5 relates geom_mask values to fields in the geometry struct and briefly describes their meanings:

Table 7.5 Geometry Hints

Field	*Mask*	*Meaning*
min_width, min_height	GDK_HINT_MIN_SIZE	Program-specified minimum size
max_width, max_height	GDK_HINT_MAX_SIZE	Program-specified maximum size
base_width, base_size	GDK_HINT_BASE_SIZE	Program-specified base size
width_inc, height_inc	GDK_HINT_RESIZE_INC	Program-specified resize increments
min_aspect, max_aspect	GDK_HINT_ASPECT	Program-specified min and max aspect ratios

Invoking gtk_window_set_geometry_hints() is easy and is best done before the window is realized. The following code snippet sets the minimum and base sizes for a window that contains a drawing area widget:

```
GtkWidget          *window, *drawing;
GdkWindowHints     geo_mask;
```

```
GdkGeometry       geometry;

...

geo_mask = GDK_HINT_MIN_SIZE;

/* Minimum allowable size is 300 x 200 */

geometry.min_width = 300;
geometry.min_height = 200;

gtk_window_set_geometry_hints(GTK_WINDOW(window), drawing,
        &geometry, geo_mask );

gtk_widget_show( window );
```

Let's now take a closer look at each of the hints. GTK_HINT_MIN_SIZE defines a minimum size for the window, using the min_width and min_height fields of the GdkGeometry struct to define the minimum width and height allowable for the window, respectively. Most window managers won't allow users to resize windows to be smaller than this size. Likewise, GTK_HINT_MAX_SIZE defines the maximum width and height to which the window will be allowed to grow; these values are specified in the max_width and max_width fields, respectively.

In some cases, an application might want to do something like fix the height of a window to 200 pixels and let the width of the window be variable. One way to do this would be to set the min_height and max_height fields to 200, the min_width field to some reasonable value, and finally the max_height field to G_MAXINT. Make sure to set both the GDK_HINT_MIN_SIZE and GDK_HINT_MAX_SIZE bits in the mask passed to gtk_window_set_geometry_hints().

GDK_HINT_BASE_SIZE overrides GTK_HINT_MIN_SIZE if both are set. The base width is specified by the base_width field, and the base height is specified by the base_height field.

GTK_HINT_RESIZE_INC can be specified to define the algorithm used by the window manager in computing window sizes during a resize operation initiated by the user. For example, a word processor might desire a resize increment that corresponds to a font's width and height to ensure that characters displayed in the window are not clipped vertically or horizontally. Or an application displaying 32×32-pixel image thumbnails might request a 32-pixel resize increment to ensure that only complete thumbnails are visible in the window after a resize.

According to O'Reilly's *Volume One* (mentioned previously), the algorithm used by the window manager to compute resizes should result in a value that is a positive integer multiple of height_inc offset from base_height, and/or an integer multiple of width_inc offset from base_width. In other words:

```
width = base_width + (i * width_inc)
height = base_height + (j * height_inc)
```

GTK_HINT_ASPECT is a hint to the window manager that should result in window sizes that conform to an application-defined aspect ratio. An aspect ratio is a value that defines how the width of a window relates to its height as a ratio of width-to-height. The standard American television set, for example, has an aspect ratio of 4:3. X allows clients to specify minimum and maximum aspect ratios; the ratio of window width to height must fall somewhere between these two extremes after a window resize.

The fields min_aspect and max_aspect hold the values that define the aspect ratios used. Both of these values are of type gdouble and should be greater than 0 and less than or equal to G_MAXINT. Table 7.6 defines how the x and y components of the aspect ratio are computed:

Table 7.6 Computing the Aspect Ratio

Value	*X Component*	*Y Component*
min_aspect <= 1	G_MAXINT * min_aspect	G_MAXINT
min_aspect > 1	G_MAXINT	G_MAXINT/min_aspect
max_aspect <= 1	G_MAXINT * max_aspect	G_MAXINT
max_aspect > 1	G_MAXINT	G_MAXINT/max_aspect

Let's look at some example values just using min_aspect (both min_aspect and max_aspect computations are the same). If we set it to 1.0, the X component will be G_MAXINT, and the Y component will be G_MAXINT, resulting in an x-to-y ratio of 1:1. In this case, after resizing, the window should have equal width and height attributes. Now let's pick a value greater than 1.0, for example, 2.0. In this case, the X component will be the constant G_MAXINT, while the Y component is computed as G_MAXINT/2. The final x-to-y ratio will therefore be 2:1, meaning that after a resize, the window should have a width that is twice as large as its height. Finally, let's see what happens with min_aspect values less than 1.0 in value. Let's choose 0.5. In this case, the X component will be G_MAXINT * 0.5, and the Y component will be G_MAXINT. The x-to-y ratio then is 1:2, meaning that after a resize, we'd like the window manager to leave us with a window having a height attribute that is twice as large as its width.

The following code snippet illustrates the preceding concept and shows how to set the min_aspect and max_aspect fields. In this case, the minimum aspect is set to 1:1, and the maximum aspect is set to 2:1.

```
GtkWidget          *window, *drawing;
GdkWindowHints     geo_mask;
GdkGeometry        geometry;

...

geo_mask = GDK_HINT_ASPECT;

geometry.min_aspect = 1.0;
geometry.max_aspect = 2.0;

gtk_window_set_geometry_hints(GTK_WINDOW(window), drawing,
         &geometry, geo_mask );

gtk_widget_show( window );
```

Setting the Default Size of a Window

The default size of a window can be set with gtk_window_set_default_size():

```
void
gtk_window_set_default_size(GtkWindow *window, gint width,
         gint height);
```

This routine is fairly easy to understand. It accepts an instance of GtkWindow, a width, and a height. Disregarding the use of the GDK_HINT_BASE_SIZE and GTK_HINT_MIN_SIZE hints as previously described, not calling this routine (nor gtk_widget_set_usize(); see Chapter 4, "Widgets") will cause the size of the window to be made small enough to reasonably contain the child widgets of the window, if any. Calling this routine (and not gtk_widget_set_usize()) will cause the size of the window, when it is first displayed, to be the greater of the size needed to contain the child widgets and the size specified by its width and the height arguments. Once the window has been displayed, the window can be resized to a size smaller than the specified width and height but no smaller than the minimum needed to display the contained child widgets. Contrasting this to gtk_widget_set_usize(), the window will be displayed exactly using the size specified, regardless of the needs of the contained child widgets. Resizing is allowed as long as it is greater than or equal to the initially specified width and height. Thus, gtk_widget_set_usize() gives more control over the initial size of the window and allows resizing to any size possible as long as it is no smaller than the initial size specified. On the other hand, gtk_window_set_default_size() gives less control over the initial size of the window; the window can generally be any size desired by the client, but it must reasonably display any of its children. gtk_window_set_default_size() allows resizing of the window to any size with the condition that the minimum size must allow for the reasonable display of the window's child widgets. My recommendation is to use gtk_widget_set_usize() for specifying window sizes, mostly because it will fix the minimum window size to be no smaller than the specified size. The minimum size allowable by gtk_window_set_default_size(), although it may take into account the needs of its child widget sizes, is not always going to be the best, depending on the size and layout needs of the child widgets contained by the window.

Modal Windows

A modal window, while realized, is the only window in the application that is receptive to events, such as mouse button presses and keyboard input, generated by the user. Most windows in an application need not, and should not, be modal. Making a window modal is restrictive to a user because other parts of the application normally accessible to a user are not available during the time a modal window is in effect. However, there are times when a modal window is an appropriate tool. There may be times when an application finds itself unable to continue without certain input from the user. In such a circumstance, displaying a modal dialog to retrieve the user input is often the correct thing to do. While a modal dialog is in effect, a program need not concern itself with the activation of controls or menu items provided by other portions of the user interface. Usually, displaying a modal dialog is the application's way of saying "I cannot continue until I receive the information I am requesting." Because only the modal dialog can receive input from the user, Gtk+ is helping protect the application from receiving input that it is not prepared to deal with during the time the modal dialog is active.

Making a window modal is straightforward and can be done by calling the routine gtk_window_set_modal():

```
void
gtk_window_set_modal(GtkWindow *window, gboolean modal);
```

The first argument to gtk_window_set_modal() is an instance of GtkWindow. This is the window that is to have its modality changed. The second argument, modal, is used to make the window modal (TRUE) or nonmodal (FALSE). It is best to call gtk_window_set_modal() prior to making the window visible to ensure that only that window will receive input once it is made visible. It is possible to make a nonmodal window modal after it has been realized, but this situation is rarely encountered. Likewise, modal dialogs usually remain modal during their lifetimes; therefore, it is unlikely that an application will ever need to call gtk_window_set_modal() with the modal argument set to FALSE in order to switch a realized window from modal to nonmodal.

Gtk+ implements modality by looking at events arriving at the application from the X server. If the widget to which the event was directed (the event widget) is a child of a modal widget, then the event is passed to the event widget for processing. Otherwise, the event is passed to the modal widget (which, in most cases, will drop the event on the floor). Not all events get redirected to the modal window or its children. Those that do get redirected include the following:

- GDK_BUTTON_PRESS, GDK_2BUTTON_PRESS, GDK_3BUTTON_PRESS
- GDK_BUTTON_RELEASE
- GDK_KEY_PRESS, GDK_KEY_RELEASE
- GDK_MOTION_NOTIFY
- GDK_PROXIMITY_IN, GDK_PROXIMITY_OUT
- GDK_ENTER_NOTIFY and GDK_LEAVE_NOTIFY

All other events are sent to the original event widget.

Window Focus

Somewhat related to modality is the concept of window focus. Basically, window focus defines which menu, control, button, or to be more general, widget will receive events such as key and mouse button presses. Usually, the user interface provides visual clues to help the user become aware of what widget has obtained the current focus as focus moves from widget to widget. GtkEntry, for example, indicates input focus by changing the cursor to an I-beam cursor once an instance of GtkEntry has obtained the focus, and it reverts the cursor back to its previous value once focus is lost by the widget. The GtkButton widget class changes the color of a button from a darker shade of gray to a lighter shade of gray to indicate that the button has mouse and keyboard focus. Once the focus is lost, GtkButton restores the button to its original color as a visual clue to the user.

It is the user that typically controls which widget in a window has the focus, and this is how it should be in most cases. However, I can imagine there are times when an application might want to set the focus to a particular control or widget in a dialog. For example, assume we are developing a loan package for a bank, and one of its dialogs is an application that allows an applicant to enter his or her name, street, city, state, ZIP code, and loan amount. It may make sense for our application to set the widget focus to the name field before the dialog is first displayed because this is where most users will want to start working. See the discussion of default widgets later in this chapter.

As another example, assume that after the user has finished entering data in the previously mentioned form, he or she hits an OK or Submit button that, when pressed, causes our application to validate the data entered by the user to ensure that all fields were entered and that all of the data entered is sensible (for example, a numeric amount was entered in the ZIP code field). Should our application find an invalid field, it might want to keep the dialog up, display a modal message dialog telling the user which field is invalid, and once this message dialog is dismissed, set the window focus to the widget that corresponds to the data found to be invalid so that the user may enter it once again.

To set the focus to a particular widget in a window, an application should call gtk_window_set_focus():

```
void
gtk_window_set_focus (GtkWindow *window, GtkWidget *focus);
```

window is the instance of GtkWindow that contains the widget specified by the argument focus. focus is the instance of GtkWidget and is the widget in the specified window to which input focus will be set once the call returns.

The Focus Widget

For each window, Gtk+ maintains a focus widget, which is the widget in the window that currently has focus. Calling gtk_window_set_focus() changes the focus widget to the specified widget. As the user makes focus changes with the mouse or keyboard, the focus widget is changed by Gtk+ to record which widget currently has the focus.

A window's focus widget is activated by calling gtk_window_activate_focus():

```
gint
gtk_window_activate_focus(GtkWindow *window);
```

Some widget classes, including both GtkButton and GtkMenuItem, implement what is referred to as an "activate" signal. This signal is triggered by a call to gtk_widget_activate(). In the case of the GtkButton class, the activate signal is actually an alias for GtkButton's "clicked" signal. If the focus widget for a window is an instance of GtkButton, and if the Gtk+ application has registered a signal function to handle clicked signals for that instance (see Chapter 3, "Signals, Events, Objects, and Types"), then calling gtk_window_activate_focus() on the window will result in the execution of the clicked signal function registered by the application.

Default Widgets

Windows also maintain a default widget. A default widget is the widget in a window or dialog that is assigned the keyboard focus when no widget is defined as the focus widget. A default widget is sort of a fallback focus widget that responds to Enter and Return key presses without having the focus. The focus widget always has precedence over the default widget; if some widget has the focus, it will receive the keyboard input, not the default widget.

Most likely, you will make an instance of GtkButton the default widget. A common example is a prompt dialog, similar to the one shown in the following figure:

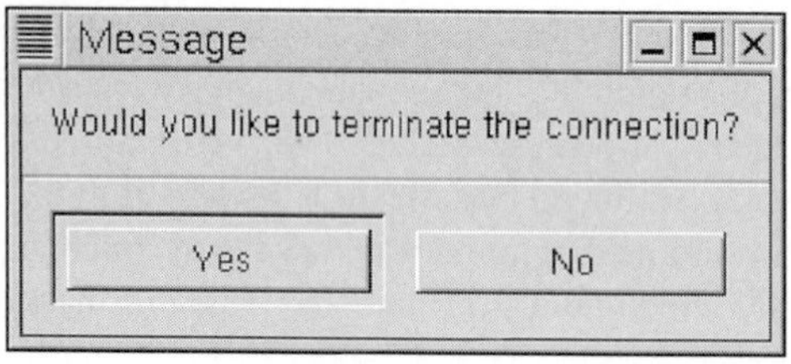

Figure 7.1 Prompt Dialog

Here, the button labeled Yes acts as the default widget. If the user hits the Enter key, the operation will be accepted. For the No button to respond to the return key in the same way, the user must tab to the No key. Doing so causes the No button to become the focus widget, and at this point, it will respond to a press of the return key press.

To make a widget the default widget, call gtk_window_set_default():

```
void
gtk_window_set_default (GtkWindow *window, GtkWidget *default_widget);
```

Prior to making the preceding call the first time for a widget, you must set a flag maintained by the widget to let Gtk+ know that the widget is allowed to be made a default widget. The call looks something like the following:

```
GTK_WIDGET_SET_FLAGS (button, GTK_CAN_DEFAULT);
```

In the preceding statement, button was declared GtkWidget *. If you do not do this (i.e., use the GTK_WIDGET_SET_FLAGS macro), Gtk+ will generate an error message at runtime, and the widget will not be made the default widget for the dialog. Here is a complete example of a routine that creates and manages a transient, modal dialog that allows a user to respond to a question with a Yes/No, OK/ Cancel type of response. The dialog created looks like the one depicted in Figure 7.1. Several parts of this example will be new to a reader at this point of the book, but perhaps it doesn't hurt to talk a little ahead of ourselves at this point. The code also illustrates the use of some of the GtkWindow class functions already discussed. Here is the code; a discussion will follow:

```
#include <gtk/gtk.h>

/*
 * Simple Yes/No OK/Cancel dialog
 */

static gboolean result;

static void
OkClickedCallback(GtkWidget *widget, GtkWidget *dialog_window)
{
   result = TRUE;
   gtk_widget_destroy( dialog_window );
```

```
   gtk_main_quit();
}

static void
CancelClickedCallback(GtkWidget *widget, GtkWidget *dialog_window)
{
   result = FALSE;
   gtk_widget_destroy( dialog_window );
   gtk_main_quit();
}

gboolean
QuestionBox( GtkWidget *parent, char *message, char *ok_label,
   char *cancel_label, gboolean okIsDefault )
{
   GtkWidget *label, *button, *dialog_window;

   dialog_window = gtk_dialog_new();
   gtk_window_position (GTK_WINDOW (dialog_window), GTK_WIN_POS_MOUSE);

   gtk_signal_connect (GTK_OBJECT (dialog_window), "destroy",
            GTK_SIGNAL_FUNC(gtk_widget_destroyed), &dialog_window);

   gtk_window_set_title (GTK_WINDOW (dialog_window), "Message");
   gtk_container_border_width (GTK_CONTAINER (dialog_window), 0);

   button = gtk_button_new_with_label (ok_label);
   GTK_WIDGET_SET_FLAGS (button, GTK_CAN_DEFAULT);
   if ( okIsDefault == TRUE )
           gtk_window_set_default( GTK_WINDOW( dialog_window ), button );
   gtk_box_pack_start (GTK_BOX (GTK_DIALOG (dialog_window)->action_area),
            button, TRUE, TRUE, 0);
   gtk_signal_connect (GTK_OBJECT (button), "clicked",
            GTK_SIGNAL_FUNC(OkClickedCallback), dialog_window);

   button = gtk_button_new_with_label (cancel_label);
   GTK_WIDGET_SET_FLAGS (button, GTK_CAN_DEFAULT);
   if ( okIsDefault == FALSE )
            gtk_window_set_default( GTK_WINDOW( dialog_window ), button
);
   gtk_box_pack_start (GTK_BOX (GTK_DIALOG (dialog_window)->action_area),
            button, TRUE, TRUE, 0);
   gtk_signal_connect (GTK_OBJECT (button), "clicked",
            GTK_SIGNAL_FUNC(CancelClickedCallback), dialog_window);

   label = gtk_label_new (message);
   gtk_misc_set_padding (GTK_MISC (label), 10, 10);
   gtk_box_pack_start (GTK_BOX (GTK_DIALOG (dialog_window)->vbox), label,
            TRUE, TRUE, 0);
   if ( parent != NULL )
            gtk_window_set_transient_for( GTK_WINDOW( dialog_window ),
                  GTK_WINDOW( parent ) );
```

```
065     gtk_window_set_modal( GTK_WINDOW( dialog_window ), TRUE );
066     gtk_widget_show_all (dialog_window);
067     gtk_main();
068     return( result );
069 }
```

The basic idea behind this routine is to display a modal dialog and wait until the user makes a choice before returning. The arguments passed to QuestionBox() include the following:

- **GtkWidget *parent** This argument is NULL if the dialog has no parent. Otherwise, it is the widget instance handle of a GtkWindow. Most likely, this will be the top-level application window, but it doesn't have to be.
- **char *message** This argument is the question being posed of the user. This should be suitable for the responses represented by ok_label, and cancel_label.
- **char *ok_label** This argument is the label for the button that causes QuestionBox to return TRUE when pressed.
- **char *cancel_label** This argument is the label for the button that causes QuestionBox to return FALSE when pressed.
- **gboolean okIsDefault** If set to TRUE, the button labeled by ok_label is made the default button of the dialog. Otherwise, the button labeled by cancel_label will be the default button of the dialog.

QuestionDialog() first creates an instance of GtkDialog; this is done on line 031. GtkDialog, as we shall see, is a child of GtkWindow, so we can make use of functions in the GtkWindow API as we do in several places of this routine. The first use of these routines is line 032, where we call the routine gtk_window_position() to cause the dialog window, when displayed, to position itself beneath the current pointer position. Other calls include line 037, which sets the title of the window to "Message," lines 063 and 064, where the dialog is made transient (if the passed parent was non-NULL), and line 066, where the window is made modal. We have already talked about each of the routines involved in this chapter. On line 040, we create an instance of GtkButton, labeling it with the ok_label that was passed by the caller. On line 041, we make the window eligible to be the default widget for the window by using the macro GTK_WIDGET_SET_FLAGS to set the GTK_CAN_DEFAULT flag. And, on lines 042 and 043, we check to see if the caller wants the button to be the default for the dialog. If so, then the gtk_window_set_default() routine is called to register the button as the default widget. Notice how here, and in the other gtk_window* calls, we use the macro GTK_WINDOW to coerce the GtkWidget * to a GtkWindow *.

While we are here, I might as well discuss a few other things related to this routine and its implementation. The GtkButton widget class implements a clicked signal; if the application registers a signal function for this signal, it will be invoked when the button is pressed. Here we register a separate signal function for each button, one that is invoked by the "OK" instance, and one that is invoked by the "Cancel" instance. Each passes as user data the instance handle for the dialog. At the bottom of the routine, after we cause the dialog and its children to display with a call to gtk_widget_show_all(), we invoke a nested gtk main loop with the call to gtk_main(). We will stay in this loop until it is exited with a call to gtk_main_exit(), which is invoked by either of the clicked signal functions that we registered. Before the signal function calls gtk_main_exit(), however, it will set a global variable that will be TRUE if OkClickedCallback() was invoked or FALSE if the other signal function, CancelClickedCallback(), was invoked. Here is the code for OkClickedCallback() again:

```
static gboolean result;

static void
OkClickedCallback(GtkWidget *widget, GtkWidget *dialog_window)
{
   result = TRUE;
   gtk_widget_destroy( dialog_window );
   gtk_main_quit();
}
```

Just as the focus widget in a window can be activated by calling the routine gtk_window_activate_focus(), the default widget can be activated by calling gtk_window_active_default():

```
gint
gtk_window_activate_default(GtkWindow *window);
```

Refer to the preceding discussion of gtk_window_activate_focus(); what was written there holds true here, except activation will be of the window's default widget, not the window's focus widget.

GtkDialog

Class Name

`GtkDialog`

Parent Class Name

`GtkWindow`

Macros

Widget type macro: `GTK_TYPE_DIALOG`

Object to widget cast macro: `GTK_DIALOG(obj)`

Widget type check macro: `GTK_IS_DIALOG(obj)`

Application-Level API Synopsis

Retrieve the constant GTK_TYPE_DIALOG at runtime:

```
GtkType
gtk_dialog_get_type (void);
```

Create a new instance of GtkDialog:

```
GtkWidget *
gtk_dialog_new(void);
```

Class Description

A dialog (in Gtk+) is a window that consists of two areas:

- A content area, which contains the basic content presented by the dialog
- An action area, which consists of buttons that, when clicked, perform an action on the content of the dialog and/or dismiss the dialog

A horizontal separator is situated between the content and action areas of a dialog, as a way to help the user distinguish between the action and content areas. See Figure 7.2.

Figure 7.2 Areas of a Dialog Widget

Dialogs can be simple (see Figure 7.3), with a small content in either the content or the action area, or they can be arbitrarily complex, as shown in Figure 7.4. Generally speaking, content in the action area typically consists of only instances of GtkButton, although Gtk-Dialog does not enforce this.

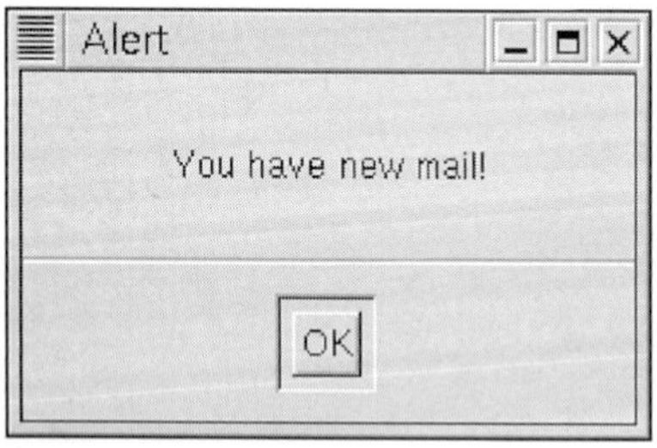

Figure 7.3 Simple Dialog Widget

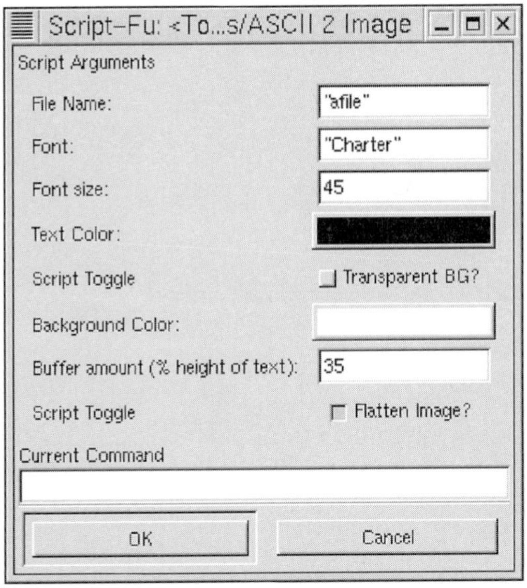

Figure 7.4 Complex Dialog Widget

The content area of a dialog widget consists of a vertical box widget (GtkVBox). The action area of a dialog widget is a horizontal box widget (GtkHBox). A vertical box is used for the content area because, typically, applications will tend to pack dialog content from top to bottom (or from bottom to top). A horizontal box widget is used for the action area because, typically, buttons in this area will be packed from left to right (or from right to left). An application can easily add a horizontal box as a child of the vertical box in the content area in order to arrange items in the content area from left to right. GtkHBox and GtkVBox widgets are described in Chapter 10, "Container and Bin Classes." You should be comfortable with both GtkHBox and GtkVBox widgets before attempting to use a dialog widget in your application.

Creating a Dialog

To create an instance of GtkDialog, call gtk_dialog_new():

```
GtkWidget *
gtk_dialog_new(void);
```

The following example code was used to create the dialog shown in Figure 7.3:

Listing 7.1 Creating a Message Dialog

```
#include <gtk/gtk.h>

main( int argc, char *argv[] )
{
   GtkWidget *dialog, *label, *button;
```

```
006
007     gtk_init( &argc, &argv );
008     dialog = gtk_dialog_new();
009
010     gtk_widget_set_usize( dialog, 214, 117 );
011     gtk_window_set_policy( GTK_WINDOW( dialog ), FALSE, FALSE, FALSE);
012
013     gtk_window_set_title( GTK_WINDOW( dialog ), "Alert" );
014
015     label = gtk_label_new("You have new mail!");
016     gtk_box_pack_start(GTK_BOX(GTK_DIALOG(dialog)->vbox),
017             label, TRUE, TRUE, 0);
018
019     button = gtk_button_new_with_label ("OK");
020     GTK_WIDGET_SET_FLAGS (button, GTK_CAN_DEFAULT);
021     gtk_box_pack_start (GTK_BOX (GTK_DIALOG (dialog)->action_area),
022             button, FALSE, FALSE, 0);
023     gtk_widget_grab_default (button);
024
025     gtk_widget_show_all( dialog );
026
027     gtk_main();
028 }
```

Dialog Sizing

The preceding source code brings to mind the issue of dialog sizing. A dialog of the type shown in Figure 7.3 looks best when it is a certain size. To determine what I felt to be an optimal size, I simply ran the program and resized the window until its size looked pleasing to me. Then I added line 010 to the program:

```
010     gtk_widget_set_usize( dialog, 214, 117 );
```

This set the initial size of the window to the result of my experiments, in this case a widget of 214 and a height of 117. On the following line, I added a call to gtk_window_set_policy():

```
011     gtk_window_set_policy( GTK_WINDOW( dialog ),
                FALSE, FALSE, FALSE);
```

The preceding change ensures that the user cannot resize the dialog, avoiding any strange (and visually unappealing) layout results that might occur if the user were given the ability to resize the dialog.

Figure 7.5 Packing Content with No Border or Padding

Obviously, 217×117 is only appropriate for the content being displayed in this example. A more generic implementation would support the display of arbitrary text in the content area. Instead of hard-coding the width and height of the dialog, you might consider alternatives such as setting the border width of the dialog and/or applying a padding value to the label when it is packed into the vertical box. Figure 7.5 illustrates a "You have new mail!" message that has been packed into a dialog sized for its content, with no border width applied to the container or padding applied to the label in the box. Figure 7.6 illustrates the result when a 5-pixel border width has been added to the dialog and the text has been packed into the action area with 20 pixels of padding. Note that the vbox padding is only applied above and below the label, not to the left or right; if we were packing a horizontal box, it would be applied to the left and right of the label, not to the top and bottom). To set a 5-pixel border for the dialog and a 20-pixel label padding for the label, lines 015 through 018 were modified as follows:

```
015      gtk_container_set_border_width (GTK_CONTAINER (dialog), 5);
016      label = gtk_label_new("You have new mail!");
017      gtk_box_pack_start(GTK_BOX(GTK_DIALOG(dialog)->vbox),
018              label, TRUE, TRUE, 20);
```

Figure 7.6 Figure 7.5 with Padding and Border Added

Also, line 010

```
010      gtk_widget_set_usize( dialog, 214, 117 );
```

was removed from the listing, enabling the dialog to size itself as necessary. See Chapter 10 for more information about gtk_container_set_border_width() and gtk_box_pack_start(). Also, see Chapter 5, "Labels and Buttons," for information on how to cause text in a label widget to wrap and fill its container (in particular, refer to the functions gtk_label_set_justify() and gtk_label_set_line_wrap()).

GtkFileSelection

Class Name

```
GtkFileSelection
```

Parent Class Name

```
GtkWindow
```

Macros

Widget type macro: `GTK_TYPE_FILE_SELECTION`

Object to widget cast macro: `GTK_FILE_SELECTION(obj)`

Widget type check macro: `GTK_IS_FILE_SELECTION(obj)`

Application-Level API Synopsis

Retrieve the constant GTK_TYPE_FILE_SELECTION at runtime:
```
GtkType
gtk_file_selection_get_type(void);
```

Create a new instance of GtkFileSelection:
```
GtkWidget *
gtk_file_selection_new(const gchar *title);
```

Set the filename (selection) field of the file-selection widget:
```
void
gtk_file_selection_set_filename(GtkFileSelection *filesel,
        const gchar *filename);
```

Retrieve the directory/file selected by the user:
```
gchar *
gtk_file_selection_get_filename(GtkFileSelection *filesel);
```

Set the initial path/file displayed by the file-selection dialog:
```
void
gtk_file_selection_complete(GtkFileSelection *filesel,
        const gchar *pattern);
```

Show the Create Dir, Delete File, and Rename File buttons:
```
void
gtk_file_selection_show_fileop_buttons(GtkFileSelection *filesel);
```

Application-Level API Synopsis (Continued)

Hide the Create Dir, Delete File, and Rename File buttons:

```
void
gtk_file_selection_hide_fileop_buttons(GtkFileSelection *filesel);
```

Class Description

Figures 7.7 and 7.8 illustrate instances of GtkFileSelection:

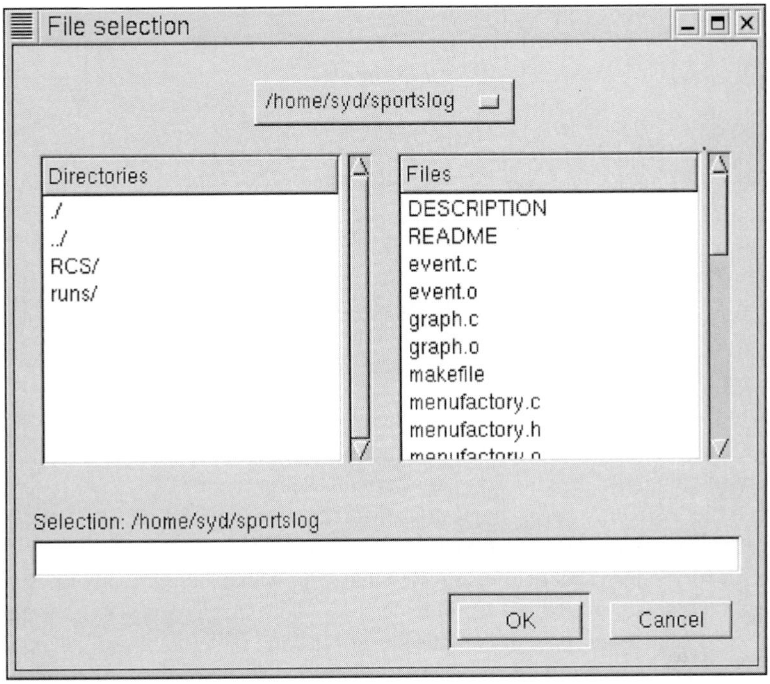

Figure 7.7 Opening a File

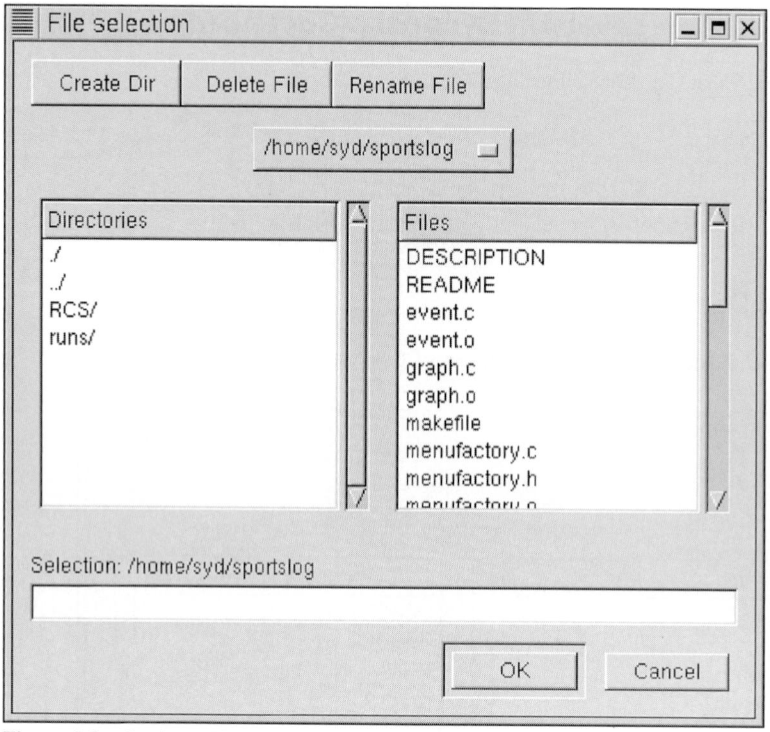

Figure 7.8 Saving a File

Figure 7.7 illustrates an instance of GtkFileSelection as it might be typically used to request a filename from a user during a file Open operation. Figure 7.8 illustrates a file-selection widget as it is typically used during a file Save As operation. These are the two most common reasons for using a file-selection widget, requesting from the user the location and name of a file to which to save content or from which to load content. Figures 7.7 and 7.8 differ only in the buttons labeled Create Dir, Delete File, and Rename File, which are seen only in Figure 7.8. In fact, these buttons are available regardless of how the file-selection widget is being used, although they make more sense at the time a user is saving a file; for example, the user might want to create a new directory into which to place the newly created file. As we shall see later, an application can show or hide these buttons as it sees fit.

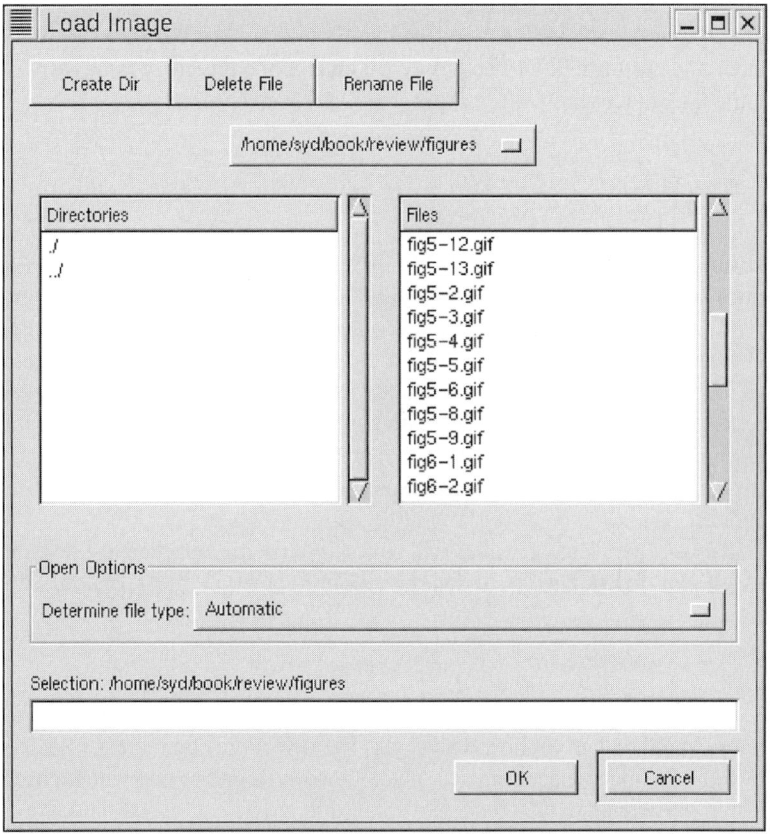

Figure 7.9 A File-Selection Widget with Custom Content

Figure 7.9 illustrates a file-selection widget used by The GIMP to open an image file. As you can see, there is extra content in the dialog that is not present in either Figure 7.7 or 7.8 (specifically, the frame labeled Open Options). I will illustrate how to add such content in the following discussion.

Creating an Instance of GtkFileSelection

Creating a file-selection widget is fairly straightforward. To do so, you call gtk_file_selection_new():

```
GtkWidget *
gtk_file_selection_new(const gchar *title);
```

The argument title will be displayed by the window manager in the title bar of the file-selection dialog when it is shown by the application. Passing the return value to gtk_widget_show() is all that is needed to cause it to be displayed as a dialog window. You do not add a file-selection widget as a child of a container widget, as you would do with a button or label.

Modifying the File-Selection Widget

By default, the current working directory will be displayed in the Directories and Files lists. The Selection text-edit field will be empty. To change the directory to be displayed before showing the file-selection dialog, call gtk_file_selection_complete():

```
void
gtk_file_selection_complete(GtkFileSelection *filesel,
        const gchar *pattern);
```

The first argument is an instance of GtkFileSelection. The second is a NULL-terminated pathname. The path can be relative or absolute. If the path names a directory, then the directory and its contents will be displayed in the Directories and Files lists, and the Selection field will remain empty. If the path names a file, then the directory portion of the path will be shown in the Directories list; the file itself will be shown in the Files list as well as being set in the Selection text-edit field. The path can contain ? and * wild-card characters. For example, */tmp/*.dat* will cause all files in the */tmp* directory that end with the characters *.dat* to be listed in the Files list. Shell-based expressions such as ~/ (user's home directory) are also supported.

You can also set the filename, which will be displayed in the Selection text field upon display of the file-selection dialog. This can be done by making a call to gtk_file_selection_set_filename():

```
void
gtk_file_selection_set_filename(GtkFileSelection *filesel,
        const gchar *filename);
```

It is not required that an application call gtk_file_selection_complete() to set the filename; these functions are independent of each other. However, a call to one will override the other if both result in a change to the filename displayed in the Selection text field. For example:

```
gtk_file_selection_set_filename(GTK_FILE_SELECTION(fileSel),
          "file.txt");

gtk_file_selection_complete(GTK_FILE_SELECTION(fileSel),
          "/tmp/fig5-14.gif" );
```

This will cause the directory contents of */tmp* to be displayed in the Directories list and *fig5-14.gif* to display in the Files list and Selection text field. If the order of the calls is changed, as follows:

```
gtk_file_selection_complete(GTK_FILE_SELECTION(fileSel),
          "/tmp/fig5-14.gif" );

gtk_file_selection_set_filename(GTK_FILE_SELECTION(fileSel),
          "file.txt");
```

then, once again, the directory contents of */tmp* will be displayed in the Directories list, the Files list will display the file contents of */tmp*, and the Selection field will display *file.txt,* as shown in the following figure:

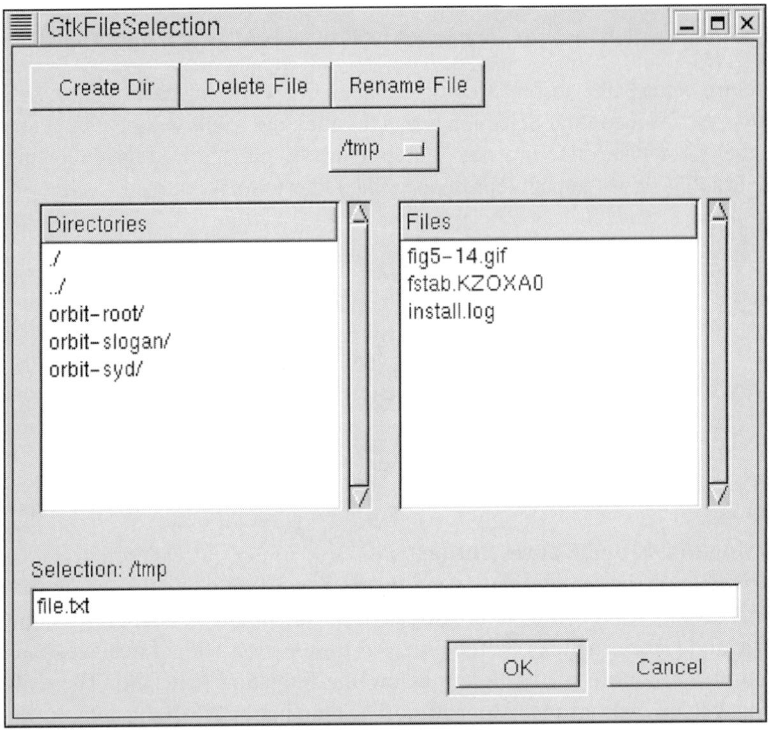

Figure 7.10 The Effect of Calling gtk_file_selection_set_filename() After gtk_file_selection_complete()

Showing and Hiding the Fileop Buttons

As previously mentioned, a file-selection dialog contains three buttons labeled Create Dir, Delete File, and Rename File. The use of these buttons is self-explanatory. You need not (in fact, cannot) attach a signal handler to these buttons; GtkFileSelection implements their functionality internally on behalf of the application. You can, however, show or hide these buttons as required. By default, they are visible. To hide them, your application must call gtk_file_selection_hide_fileop_buttons():

```
void
gtk_file_selection_hide_fileop_buttons(GtkFileSelection *filesel);
```

To show them again, you can call gtk_file_selection_show_fileop_buttons():

```
void
gtk_file_selection_show_fileop_buttons(GtkFileSelection *filesel);
```

Both functions take a file-selection widget instance as their only argument.

The final function in the GtkFileSelection API is used to extract the filename selected by the user. The function prototype for gtk_file_selection_get_filename() is:

```
gchar *
gtk_file_selection_get_filename(GtkFileSelection *filesel);
```

The return value is the absolute (complete) path of the file selected by the user. If the user did not supply a value in the Selection text field, then the result will be a directory. You can test whether the return value is a file or a directory by passing it to the following function, which returns TRUE if the path represents a file. Otherwise, it returns FALSE:

```
#include <sys/stat.h>

gboolean
IsFile( char *path )
{
        struct stat buf;

        lstat( path, &buf );
        return(S_ISREG( buf.st_mode ));
}
```

Responding to OK and Cancel Buttons

Now that we know how to get the selection and how to initialize the dialog for our needs (as well as display it), it is time to investigate how one might go about responding to clicks of the OK and Cancel buttons by the user. A file-selection widget manages three buttons, displayed at the bottom of the dialog below the Selection text field. These widgets are ok_button, cancel_button, and help_button. The help button is not, by default, visible in the dialog, so if you want to make use of it, you must show it using code like the following:

```
GtkWidget *fileSel;

...

gtk_widget_show(GTK_FILE_SELECTION(fileSel)->help_button);
```

Registering clicked signal functions for these buttons is straightforward, as illustrated by the following code snippet:

```
GtkWidget *fileSel;

...

gtk_signal_connect(GTK_OBJECT(
       GTK_FILE_SELECTION(fileSel)->ok_button),
       "clicked", (GtkSignalFunc) FileSelOk, fileSel );

// the following is only called if the help button is made visible
gtk_signal_connect(
       GTK_OBJECT(GTK_FILE_SELECTION(fileSel)->help_button),
       "clicked", (GtkSignalFunc) FileSelHelp, fileSel );
```

```
gtk_signal_connect_object(GTK_OBJECT(
       GTK_FILE_SELECTION(fileSel)->cancel_button), "clicked",
       (GtkSignalFunc) FileSelCancel, GTK_OBJECT(fileSel));
```

The GtkButton "clicked" signal is described in Chapter 5. Its handler takes two arguments: The first is the button widget instance, and the second is client data of type gpointer. Here I have arranged to pass the file-selection widget as client data. This enables the OK button signal function to retrieve the file selected by the user as follows:

```
void
FileSelOk(GtkWidget *w, gpointer arg)
{
         GtkFileSelection *fileSel = GTK_FILE_SELECTION( arg );

         // get the selection

         char *name = gtk_file_selection_get_filename(fileSel);

         // do something useful with it

         printf( "%s\n", name );

         // hide the file selection dialog

         gtk_widget_hide( GTK_WIDGET( fileSel ) );
}
```

Similarly, the Cancel button clicked signal function:

```
void
FileSelCancel(GtkWidget *w, gpointer arg)
{
          GtkFileSelection *fileSel = GTK_FILE_SELECTION( arg );
          gtk_widget_hide( GTK_WIDGET( fileSel ) );
}
```

The Help function, FileSelHelp(), is left for the reader as an exercise. Notice that the code is hiding the file-selection dialog instead of destroying it. You can either do the same or destroy the file-selection widget and create a new one each time a file-selection widget is needed. However, hiding the dialog has the nice side effect of retaining the path last traversed to by the user. As a user, I often find it annoying that after I use a file-selection dialog to traverse to some location, open a file, and process it, if I then want to save the file in the same location or perhaps open a related file, also in the same location, I am forced to traverse to that location once again because the application has forgotten to where it was that I had last traversed. You can, of course, put logic into your application to remember the file system location last traversed to by the user and restore this location (by calling gtk_file_selection_complete()) once the new file-selection widget has been created. However, I prefer to avoid this work, and instead, I create a single file-selection widget that I show and hide when needed. An additional benefit of using this technique is it reduces (to one) the number of times that a file-selection widget must be created. The following code snippet illustrates the technique for creating a file-selection widget in this manner:

```
static GtkWidget *fileSel = (GtkWidget *) NULL;

...

if ( fileSel == (GtkWidget *) NULL ) {
   fileSel = gtk_file_selection_new("File Selection");
   ...
   if ( type == OPEN )
          gtk_file_selection_hide_fileop_buttons(
              GTK_FILE_SELECTION(fileSel) );
   else
          gtk_file_selection_show_fileop_buttons(
              GTK_FILE_SELECTION(fileSel) );
}
gtk_widget_show( fileSel );
```

The static variable fileSel will initially be set to NULL and, once the file-selection widget has been created, will hold the file-selection widget created within the body of the if statement. A variable ("type" in this example) is used by the application to specify whether the dialog is being used to open a file or to save one. If type is OPEN (OPEN is an application-defined constant), then the Create Dir, Delete File, and Rename File buttons are hidden; otherwise, they are shown. The last statement shows the file-selection widget.

Adding Arbitrary Widget Content to a File-Selection Widget

The remaining topic to be discussed is adding arbitrary content to a file-selection widget, as was done in the example illustrated by Figure 7.9. The technique is rather simple. The content displayed above the Selection entry widget is contained in a vertical box widget named main_vbox, which is managed by the file-selection widget. To add content, just create it and pack it into this vertical box widget. The following code adds a checkbox widget to the file-selection dialog:

```
GtkWidget *hbox, *checkbutton;

hbox = gtk_hbox_new( FALSE, 0 );

gtk_box_pack_start( GTK_BOX(
         GTK_FILE_SELECTION(fileSel)->main_vbox ),
         hbox, FALSE, FALSE, 0 );

checkbutton = gtk_check_button_new_with_label(
         "Automatically create a log file" );
gtk_box_pack_start( GTK_BOX( hbox ), checkbutton, FALSE, FALSE, 0 );

gtk_widget_show( hbox );
gtk_widget_show( checkbutton );
```

See Chapter 10 for information on how to work with vertical and horizontal boxes. The results of the preceding code are shown in Figure 7.11:

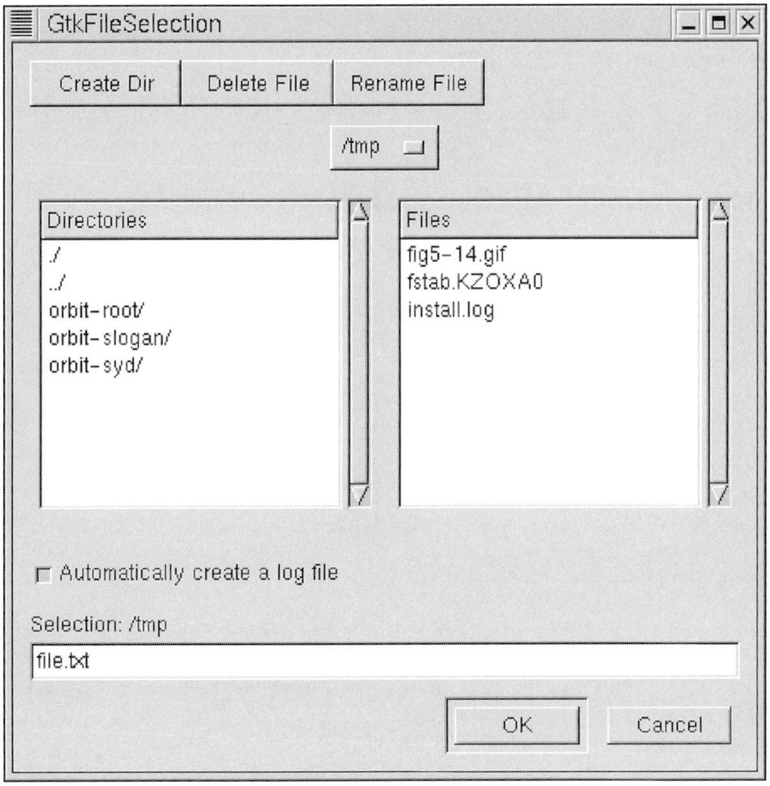

Figure 7.11 Adding Content to a File-Selection Widget

GtkFontSelection

Class Name

```
GtkFontSelection
```

Parent Class Name

```
GtkNotebook
```

Macros

Widget type macro: `GTK_TYPE_FONT_SELECTION`

Object to widget cast macro: `GTK_FONT_SELECTION(obj)`

Widget type check macro: `GTK_IS_FONT_SELECTION(obj)`

Application-Level API Synopsis

Retrieve the constant GTK_TYPE_FONT_SELECTION at runtime:
```
GtkType
gtk_font_selection_get_type(void);
```

Create a new font-selection widget:
```
GtkWidget *
gtk_font_selection_new(void);
```

Retrieve the XLFD name of the currently selected font:
```
gchar *
gtk_font_selection_get_font_name(GtkFontSelection *fontsel);
```

Open and retrieve the currently selected font:
```
GdkFont *
gtk_font_selection_get_font(GtkFontSelection *fontsel);
```

Set the XLFD font name to be displayed by the font-selection widget:
```
gboolean
gtk_font_selection_set_font_name(GtkFontSelection *fontsel,
         const gchar *fontname);
```

Set the filter applied to the font displayed by the selection widget:
```
void
gtk_font_selection_set_filter(GtkFontSelection *fontsel,
        GtkFontFilterType filter_type, GtkFontType font_type,
        gchar **foundries, gchar **weights, gchar **slants,
        gchar **setwidths, gchar **spacings, gchar **charsets);
```

Retrieve the preview text displayed by the font-selection widget:
```
gchar *
gtk_font_selection_get_preview_text(GtkFontSelection *fontsel);
```

Set the text displayed by the font-selection widget:
```
void
gtk_font_selection_set_preview_text(GtkFontSelection *fontsel,
         const gchar *text);
```

Class Description

A GtkFontSelection widget is used to retrieve a font from a user, much like an instance of Gtk-ColorSelection is used to retrieve a color from a user. Either an X Logical Font Description (XLFD) name or an open instance of a font can be obtained directly from a font-selection widget.

Font-Selection Widget User Interface

A font-selection widget consists of three panels, illustrated in Figures 7.12, 7.13, and 7.14 (the OK button in these dialogs is not part of the font-selection widget). The Font panel (Figure 7.12) is where font selection takes place. Three lists (Font, Font Style, and Size) are used to select a specific font. As can be seen in Figure 7.12, the user has selected a 9-point medium courier font. The XFLD name of the font (on my machine, given the fonts I have installed and my current font path), as returned by the font-selection widget, is: -bitstream-courier-medium-r-normal-*-*-90-*-*-m-*-iso8859-1.

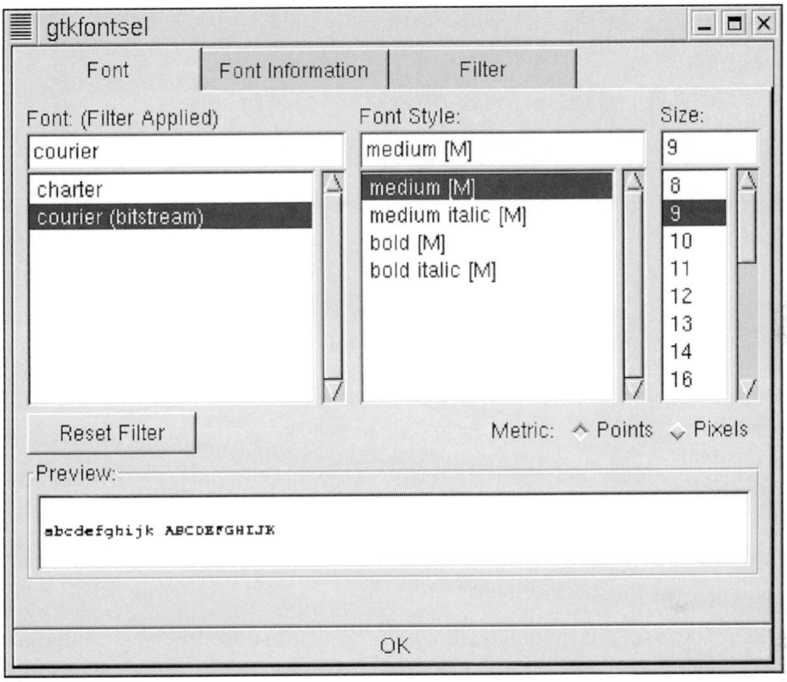

Figure 7.12 Font Panel

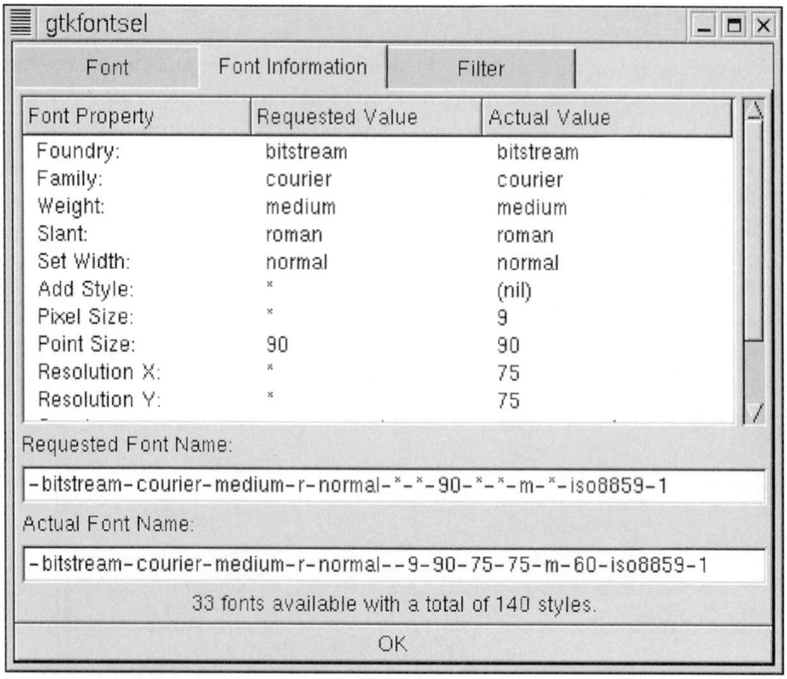

Figure 7.13 Font Information Panel

This font name can be used to obtain an open font by calling gdk_font_load() and passing the font name an argument, as illustrated in the following code snippet:

```
GdkFont *font;
char *name;

name = "-bitstream-courier-medium-r-normal-*-*-90-*-*-m-*-iso8859-1";
font = gdk_font_load( name );
if ( font != (GdkFont *) NULL ) {
        // success
        ...
```

A reference count is maintained within the GdkFont structure, initialized to 1 by gdk_font_load() when the font is loaded. An application can increment this reference count by calling gdk_font_ref():

```
gdk_font_ref( font );
```

Releasing a font is done by calling gdk_font_unref() and passing the GdkFont reference as an argument:

```
gdk_font_unref( font );
```

Only when the reference count goes to zero will the font actually be released.

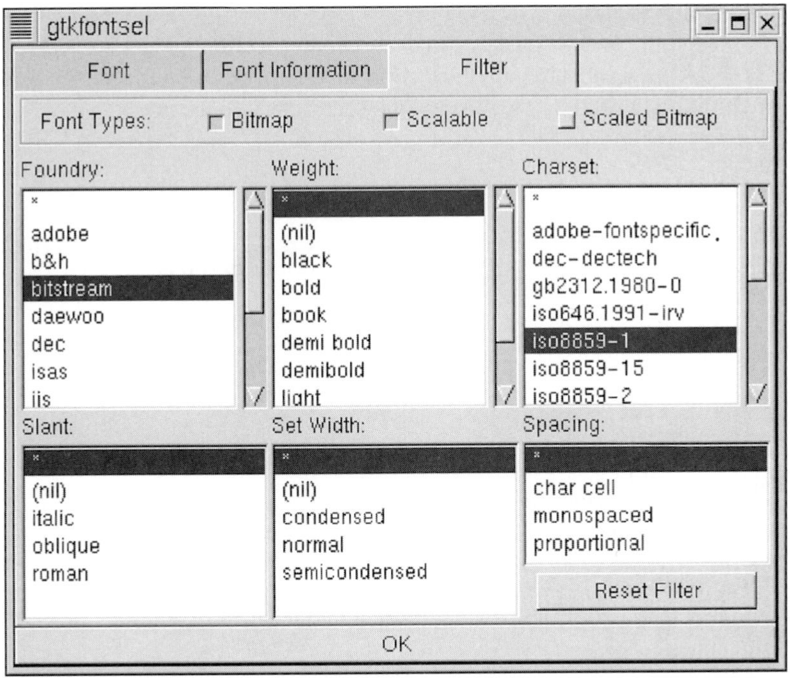

Figure 7.14 Filter Panel

Let's look at the remaining font-selection panels. The Font Information panel, shown in Figure 7.13, can be used to view the Requested Font Name (this is the font name returned by the font-selection widget when queried for an XFLD font name). The actual name of the font that, on a given machine, satisfies the requested font name is displayed as the Actual Font Name. This is the name of the font that would be opened by a call to gdk_font_load(), were it called. A multicolumn list above the font names is used to explain the meaning of the requested and actual font names in human-understandable terms.

The final panel, Filter, is shown in Figure 7.14. The Filter panel is basically used to narrow (or increase) the fonts displayed in the Font panel. As you can see in Figure 7.14, I have restricted the foundry to bitstream and the charset to iso8859-1. All other font characteristics (weight, slant, set width, and spacing) are set to *, which is the XLFD way of saying "match all." The result of this is that, in the Font panel, only bitstream iso8859-1 fonts are available for selection. If I want to further restrict the set of fonts available in the Font panel to bold fonts, I would select bold in the Weight list. The Foundry, Weight, Charset, Slant, Set Width, and Spacing list widgets each allow multiple selections (unless * is selected, as this will clear all other selections made by the user). For example, it is possible to set the filter to display only adobe and bitstream fonts by selecting "adobe" and "bitstream" in the Foundry list. A button, Reset Filter, can be used to reset the choices in the Filter panel to the default values.

Creating a Font-Selection Widget

Now that we know how the various panels in a font-selection widget are used, let's take a look at how to create and add a font-selection widget to a user interface.

To create a font-selection widget, call gtk_font_selection_new():

```
GtkWidget *
gtk_font_selection_new(void);
```

The return value is in the form of an instance of GtkWidget. You can convert this widget to a GtkFontSelection widget with the GTK_FONT_SELECTION macro:

```
GtkWidget *widget;
GtkFontSelection *fs;

widget = gtk_font_selection_new();
fs = GTK_FONT_SELECTION( fs );
```

Modifying the Font-Selection Widget

Once created, you can modify a font-selection widget by doing the following:

- Setting its filter
- Specifying the preview text displayed by the font-selection widget
- Setting the font name

I will describe how to do these optional steps in the following three sections.

Setting The Filter. In some cases, you will want to preset the choices in the Filter panel of the font-selection widget. For example, if a font-selection widget is being used to retrieve a bold font from the user, then it makes sense to initialize the filter so that only bold fonts will be selectable. Specification of the filter can also ease the process of selecting a font for the user by reducing the number of choices the user has to select from. To set the filter, you must call gtk_font_selection_filter():

```
void
gtk_font_selection_set_filter(GtkFontSelection *fontsel,
        GtkFontFilterType filter_type, GtkFontType font_type,
        gchar **foundries, gchar **weights, gchar **slants,
        gchar **setwidths, gchar **spacings, gchar **charsets);
```

The argument fontsel is an instance of GtkFontSelection. The filter_type argument can be one of the following values in Table 7.7.

Table 7.7 Filter Types

Filter Type	*Meaning*
GTK_FONT_FILTER_BASE	The user cannot modify this filter.
GTK_FONT_FILTER_USER	The user can modify, or reset, the filter.

Setting filter_type to GTK_FONT_FILTER_BASE causes a font-selection widget to restrict the changes you can make to the filter, based on the font filter attributes (foundries, weights, slants, set widths, spacings, and charsets) that you pass as arguments. These restrictions are reflected in the Filter panel, as shown in Figure 7.15:

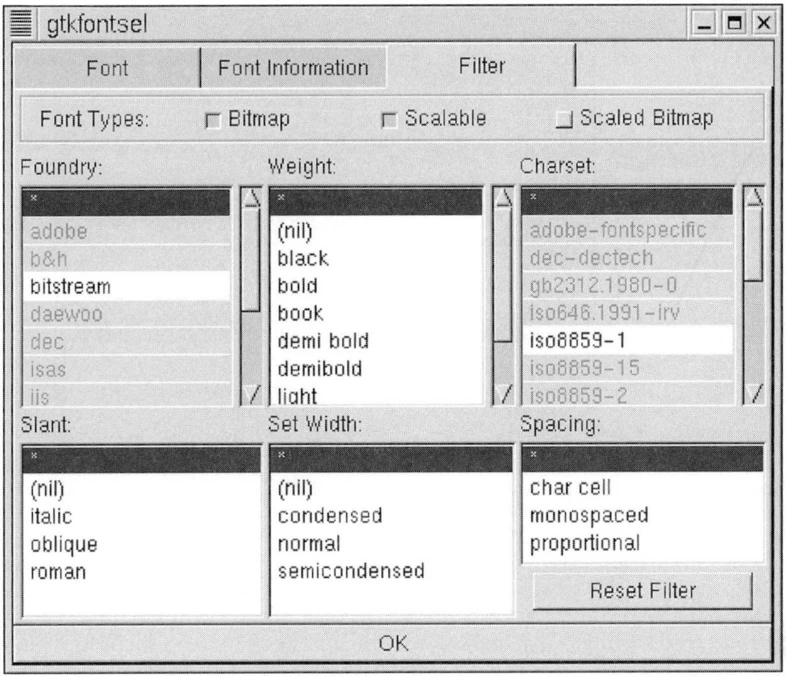

Figure 7.15 GTK_FONT_FILTER_BASE

To obtain the results in Figure 7.15, I set filter_type to GTK_FONT_FILTER_BASE and used the foundries and charsets arguments to set the foundry to bitstream and the charset to iso8859-1. All other attributes of the font were left to default values. As you can see, all choices in the Foundry and Charset lists are dimmed, and therefore unselectable, except for * and the values that I specified. Setting the filter_type to GTK_FONT_FILTER_USER would yield the same results, except all foundries and charsets would be selectable by the user, as shown in Figure 7.16:

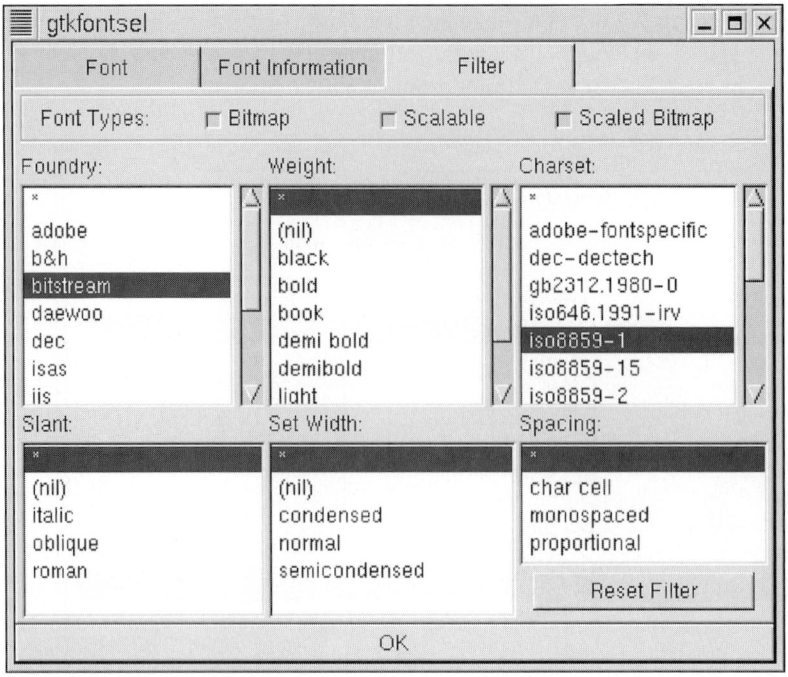

Figure 7.16 GTK_FONT_FILTER_USER

The font_type argument is a mask consisting of one or more of the values bit-wise OR'd together (see Table 7.8).

Table 7.8 Font Types

Font Type	*Meaning*
GTK_FONT_BITMAP	Show only bitmap fonts.
GTK_FONT_SCALABLE	Show only scalable fonts.
GTK_FONT_SCALABLE_BITMAP	Show only scalable bitmap fonts.
GTK_FONT_ALL	Show all fonts.

The convention specified by the XLFD (as of X11R4) is that a scalable font is a font that has an XLFD name that has no wildcards and contains the single digit "0" in the PIXEL_SIZE, POINT_SIZE, and AVERAGE_WIDTH fields. The XLFD goes on to state that scalable fields of an XLFD name are PIXEL_SIZE, POINT_SIZE, RESOLUTION_X, RESOLUTION_Y, and AVERAGE_WIDTH.

The font type (GTK_FONT_SCALABLE, GTK_FONT_BITMAP, or GTK_FONT_SCALABLE_BITMAP) is determined by the following code executed by the font-selection widget:

```
if (pixels == 0 && points == 0) {
        if (res_x == 0 && res_y == 0)
                type = GTK_FONT_SCALABLE;
        else
                type = GTK_FONT_SCALABLE_BITMAP;
}
else
        type = GTK_FONT_BITMAP;
```

In the preceding code, the variables pixels, points, res_x, and res_y refer to the PIXEL_SIZE, POINT_SIZE, RESOLUTION_X, and RESOLUTION_Y portions of an XLFD font name, respectively. The interpretation is that by setting the font_type argument of gtk_font_selection_set_filter() to GTK_FONT_SCALABLE, you are telling the font-selection widget to only display fonts that have "0" values in the PIXEL_SIZE, POINT_SIZE, RESOLUTION_X, and RESOLUTION_Y fields of the XLFD name. By setting font_type to GTK_FONT_SCALABLE_BITMAP, you are instructing the font-selection dialog to display only fonts with a 0 value in the PIXEL_SIZE and POINT_SIZE fields, and either RESOLUTION_X and RESOLUTION_Y must be nonzero. Finally, by setting font_type to GTK_FONT_BITMAP, only fonts with a nonzero PIXEL_SIZE or POINT_SIZE field in the XLFD name will be displayed.

Some of you may have noticed that the AVERAGE_WIDTH field is not being checked for in the preceding code snippet. This is based on an assumption that a font that has no pixel size and no point size cannot have a nonzero width, which may be true. However, to be literal to the XLFD spec, the font-selection widget should probably be checking for AVERAGE_WIDTH set to 0 as well before determining a font to be scalable.

The remaining arguments to gtk_font_selection_set_filter() specify font attributes used by the filter to determine the set of fonts selectable by the user. In each case, the argument is a pointer to an array of pointers to char, with the last pointer in the array set to NULL. Or, if you don't want to change the default for a particular filter, specifying NULL will cause gtk_font_selection_set_filter() to ignore that attribute. In Figure 7.15, I allow the user to select only bitstream iso8859-1 fonts. The code that implements this is as follows:

```
char *foundries[] = { "bitstream", NULL };
char *charsets[] = { "iso8859-1", NULL };

gtk_widget_show_all( window );
gtk_font_selection_set_filter(GTK_FONT_SELECTION(fontSel),
        GTK_FONT_FILTER_USER, GTK_FONT_ALL,
        foundries, NULL, NULL, NULL, NULL, charsets );
```

By setting the weights, slants, set widths, and spacings arguments to the value NULL, these attributes of the filter are unaffected by my call. Notice that I call gtk_widget_show_all() to display the window that is the parent of the font-selection widget before calling gtk_font_selection_set_filter(). It so happens that Gtk+ will generate errors and incorrectly display the window and font-selection widget if the window containing the font-selection widget is not made visible at the time gtk_font_selection_set_filter() is called (this is a bug in Gtk+ 1.2 apparently).

Let's take a look at what values can be specified for these remaining arguments passed to gtk_font_selection_set_filter(). All of these are defined by the XLFD. Here I simply summarize what the XLFD states about these attributes and refer those readers in need of more information to the XLFD for more details.

- **foundries** Entries in this vector correspond to the FOUNDRY field of the XLFD font name. Examples include "bitstream" and "adobe." Names in this field have been registered with the X Consortium.
- **weights** The weight name is a string that identifies the typographic weight of the font (e.g., its nominal "blackness"), according to the judgment of the foundry. Perhaps the most common weights are "bold" and "normal." Others include such names as "demibold," "demi bold," "light," "black," and "regular." Each entry in this vector corresponds to the WEIGHT_NAME field in the XLFD name of the font.
- **slants** A slant defines how upright characters rendered in the font will appear. Most fonts are either roman (upright) or italic. The XLFD defines the codes that can be used as entries in this vector, as summarized in Table 7.9.

Table 7.9 XLFD Slant Codes

Code	*Translation*	*Description*
"R"	"Roman"	Upright design
"I"	"Italic"	Italic design, slanted clockwise from the vertical
"O"	"Oblique"	Obliqued upright design, slanted clockwise from the vertical
"RI"	"Reverse italic"	Italic design, slanted counterclockwise from the vertical
"RO"	"Reverse oblique"	Obliqued upright design, slanted counterclockwise from the vertical
"OT"	"Other"	Other
numeric	Polymorphic	See XLFD, Section 6 for more details

The slant of a font is described by the SLANT field of the XLFD name.

- **setwidths** Entries in this vector correspond to the SETWIDTH_NAME field of the XLFD font name. Examples include "Normal," "Condensed," "Narrow," and "Wide."
- **spacings** Entries in this vector correspond to the SPACING field in the XLFD name of a font. Table 7.10 lists the possible values.

Table 7.10 XLFD Spacing Values

Value	*Translation*	*Meaning*
"P"	"Proportional"	Logical character width varies for each glyph.
"M"	"Monospaced"	Every glyph in the font has the same logical width.
"C"	"Charcell"	Glyphs in the font must fit within a "box" of constant width and height.

- **charsets** A charsets vector entry corresponds to a concatenation of the CHARSET_REGISTRY and CHARSET_ENCODING portions of an XLFD font name. There will always be a single dash (-) character in such a string to separate these two components. The CHARSET_REGISTRY portion is a name registered with the X Consortium that identifies the registration authority that owns the specified encoding. CHARSET_ENCODING is a registered name that identifies the coded character set as defined by the registration authority and, optionally, a subsetting hint. Examples of strings that can be passed include "jisx0201.1976-0," "iso8859-1," "adobe-fontspecific," and "sunolglyph-1."

Setting and Retrieving the Preview Text. Preview text is text displayed in the Preview area of the Font panel (see Figure 7.12). As the user changes the attributes of the font, the font-selection widget will redraw the text in the Preview area to give the user an indication of what the effect of the selected font is on the preview text.

To set the preview text, call gtk_font_selection_set_preview_text():

```
void
gtk_font_selection_set_preview_text(GtkFontSelection *fontsel,
        const gchar *text);
```

The fontsel argument is an instance of GtkFontSelection, and text is a NULL-terminated C string that will be displayed in the Preview area of the Font panel. A copy of the string is made by GtkFontSelection, so you are free to release or modify the memory pointed to by text in any way you see fit, once gtk_font_selection_set_preview() has returned, of course.

The default preview text is "abcdefghijk ABCDEFGHIJK." You can obtain a copy of the current preview text by calling gtk_font_selection_get_preview():

```
gchar *
gtk_font_selection_get_preview_text(GtkFontSelection *fontsel);
```

The returned value is not a copy of, but a pointer to, the NULL-terminated C string maintained by the font-selection widget. Therefore, your application must make a copy of it if it plans to modify the string in any way.

Initializing the Font Name. You can initialize the font selection by passing the XLFD font name of the font to the function gtk_font_selection_set_font_name():

```
gboolean
gtk_font_selection_set_font_name(GtkFontSelection *fontsel,
        const gchar *fontname);
```

The fontname argument is the XLFD name of the desired font. For example:

```
GtkWidget *widget;
gboolean ret;

ret = gtk_font_selection_set_font_name( GTK_FONT_SELECTION( widget ),
        "-bitstream-courier-medium-r-normal--15-140-75-75-m-90-iso8859-1" );
```

If the font name was valid, TRUE is returned; otherwise, FALSE is returned. If successful (i.e., TRUE is returned), then this call nullifies a previous call made either to this function or to gtk_font_selection_set_filter(), even if the filter you describe happens to match the font name you pass.

Retrieving the Font Selected by the User. You can query the font-selection widget for the XLFD name of the font chosen by the user, or you can request that the font-selection widget open and return a reference to the font on your behalf. To get the XLFD name of the font, call gtk_font_selection_get_font_name():

```
gchar *
gtk_font_selection_get_font_name(GtkFontSelection *fontsel);
```

If the user has not yet selected a font, then NULL is returned. To open the current selected font and obtain a handle to that font, you can call gtk_font_selection_get_font():

```
GdkFont *
gtk_font_selection_get_font(GtkFontSelection *fontsel);
```

Again, if the user has not selected a font or if some error causes the call to fail, then NULL will be returned. Otherwise, a GdkFont with a ref count of 1 will be returned.

GtkFontSelectionDialog

Class Name

```
GtkFontSelectionDialog
```

Parent Class Name

```
GtkWindow
```

Macros

Widget type macro: `GTK_TYPE_FONT_SELECTION_DIALOG`

Object to widget cast macro: `GTK_FONT_SELECTION_DIALOG(obj)`

Widget type check macro: `GTK_IS_FONT_SELECTION_DIALOG(obj)`

Application-Level API Synopsis

Retrieve the constant GTK_TYPE_FONT_SELECTION_DIALOG at runtime:

```
GtkType
gtk_font_selection_dialog_get_type(void);
```

Create a new font-selection dialog widget:

```
GtkWidget *
gtk_font_selection_dialog_new(const gchar *title);
```

Retrieve the XLFD font name of the selected font or NULL if no font has been selected. Corresponds to gtk_font_selection_get_font_name():

```
gchar *
gtk_font_selection_dialog_get_font_name(GtkFontSelectionDialog *fsd);
```

Open the font selected by the user, returning a GdkFont reference or NULL if the font could not be opened. Corresponds to gtk_font_selection_get_font():

```
GdkFont *
gtk_font_selection_dialog_get_font(GtkFontSelectionDialog *fsd);
```

Initialize the XLFD name of the selected font. Corresponds to gtk_font_selection_set_font_name():

```
gboolean
gtk_font_selection_dialog_set_font_name(GtkFontSelectionDialog *fsd,
        const gchar *fontname);
```

Application-Level API Synopsis (Continued)

Set the filter applied to fonts selectable by the user. Corresponds to gtk_font_selection_set_filter():

```
void
gtk_font_selection_dialog_set_filter(GtkFontSelectionDialog *fsd,
        GtkFontFilterType filter_type, GtkFontType font_type,
        gchar **foundries, gchar **weights, gchar **slants,
        gchar **setwidths, gchar **spacings, gchar **charsets);
```

Retrieve the preview text displayed by the font-selection dialog widget. Corresponds to gtk_font_selection_get_preview_text():

```
gchar *
gtk_font_selection_dialog_get_preview_text(GtkFontSelectionDialog *fsd);
```

Set the preview text displayed by the font-selection dialog widget. Corresponds to gtk_font_selection_set_preview_text():

```
void
gtk_font_selection_dialog_set_preview_text(GtkFontSelectionDialog *fsd,
       const gchar *text);
```

Class Description

The GtkFontSelectionDialog widget is simply an instance of GtkFontSelection that has been conveniently placed inside of a dialog, as shown in Figure 7.17:

The font-selection dialog adds three buttons, labeled OK, Cancel, and Apply. The Apply button is, by default, hidden from users, much in the same way that the Help button is hidden by the FileSelection widget.

The functions supplied by the GtkFontSelectionDialog widget API are, with only one exception (gtk_font_selection_dialog_new), wrappers of functions provided by GtkFontSelection. The only difference between the GtkFontSelection function and its counterpart in GtkFontSelectionDialog is in the name of the function and the type of its first argument. To determine the corresponding function in the GtkFontSelection API, given a function from the GtkFontSelectionDialog API in the following form:

```
<rettype>
gtk_font_selection_dialog_<x>(GtkFontSelectionDialog *fsd,
         arg1, ..., argn);
```

the corresponding GtkFontSelection function will be:

```
<rettype>
gtk_font_selection_<x>(GtkFontSelection *fontsel, arg1, ..., argn);
```

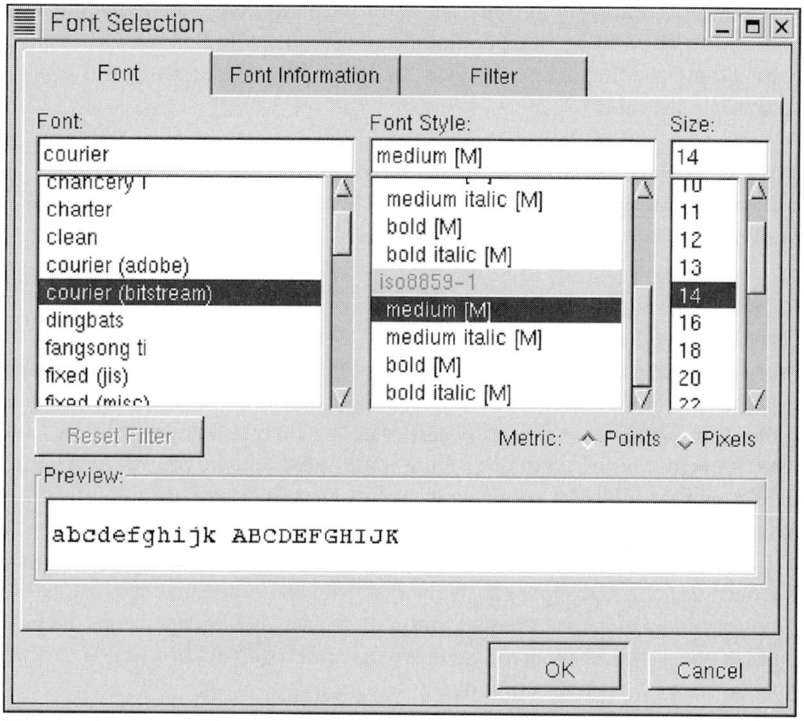

Figure 7.17 GtkFontSelectionDialog

In the preceding, <rettype> is the type of the function return value, and <x> is the portion of the function name that describes what the function actually does. For those who might still be confused, the following example should help make things clearer. In the following font-selection dialog function:

```
GtkWidget *
gtk_font_selection_dialog_set_preview_text(GtkFontSelectionDialog
        *fsd, const gchar *text);
```

<rettype> is GtkWidget *, and <x> is "set_preview_text." Thus, the function that will correspond to gtk_font_selection_dialog_set_preview_text() in the GtkFileSelection API is as follows:

```
GtkWidget *
gtk_font_selection_set_preview_text(GtkFontSelection *fontsel,
         const gchar *text);
```

Because the GtkFontSelectionDialog documentation for a given function is (again, except in only one case) identical to the documentation for the corresponding function in GtkFontSelection, I refer you to the GtkFontSelection documentation previously presented for descriptions on how the functions are called and behave. In the API reference section for GtkFontSelectionDialog, I mentioned, for each GtkFontSelectionDialog function, the name of the corresponding function in GtkFontSelection. In this section, I will cover how to create a font-selection dialog and will also show how to handle presses of the OK, Cancel, and Apply buttons.

Creating an Instance of GtkFontSelectionDialog

To create an instance of GtkFontSelectionDialog, an application must call gtk_font_selection_dialog_new():

```
GtkWidget *
gtk_font_selection_dialog_new(const gchar *title);
```

The title argument specifies the title displayed in the title bar of the dialog by the window manager.

In the section on GtkFileSelection earlier in this chapter, I described a basic strategy for creating, showing, hiding, and destroying a file-selection widget. All of what I said there applies to the font-selection dialog as well. Once you have created a font-selection dialog, you can optionally initialize it in the same manner that you would initialize a font-selection widget, as described in the earlier section on GtkFontSelection. Once the font-selection dialog has been initialized, calling gtk_widget_show() causes the dialog to display, and calling gtk_widget_hide() hides the dialog (so that it can be shown once again the next time the user places your application in a state that requires a font-selection dialog to be shown). Or you can destroy the font-selection dialog widget by calling gtk_widget_destroy(), passing the font-selection dialog widget instance as an argument. Destroying or hiding the font-selection dialog is done in the button "clicked" signal function of the ok_button and cancel_button button widget instances maintained by the font-selection dialog widget. Refer to the section "Responding to OK and Cancel Buttons" in the earlier section on GtkFileSelection for details on how to handle OK and Cancel buttons in a font-selection dialog.

The font-selection dialog widget does not have a Help button like the file-selection widget (which is perhaps a consistency issue that should be addressed because, from my point of view, a font-selection dialog is probably a widget that is going to confuse more users than a file-selection widget).

The font-selection dialog has an Apply button, which is hidden by default. To show the Apply button, you can call gtk_widget_show() as in the following code snippet:

```
GtkWidget *fsd;

fsd = gtk_font_selection_dialog_new("Select a Font");

gtk_widget_show( GTK_FILE_SELECTION_DIALOG(fsd)->apply_button );
```

Just as with the other buttons (OK and Cancel), a "clicked" signal function can and should be assigned to the Apply button. In this function, you should query the font-selection dialog widget for the currently selected XLFD font name, or the corresponding font, and apply it in the manner that is appropriate for your application. My suggestion would be to leave the dialog up, instead of hiding or destroying it in the clicked signal function, because the user might decide after applying the font that the result is not what was intended and want to select (and apply) another font.

GtkColorSelectionDialog

Class Name

```
GtkColorSelectionDialog
```

Parent Class Name

```
GtkWindow
```

Macros

Widget type macro: `GTK_TYPE_COLOR_SELECTION_DIALOG`

Object to widget cast macro: `GTK_COLOR_SELECTION_DIALOG(obj)`

Widget type check macro: `GTK_IS_COLOR_SELECTION_DIALOG(obj)`

Application-Level API Synopsis

Retrieve the constant GTK_TYPE_COLOR_SELECTION_DIALOG at runtime:

```
GtkType
gtk_color_selection_dialog_get_type(void);
```

Create a new instance of GtkColorSelectionDialog:

```
GtkWidget *
gtk_color_selection_dialog_new(void);
```

Class Description

A color-selection dialog displays a dialog like the one shown in Figure 7.18. With this dialog, a user can select a color by specifying either HSV (Hue, Saturation, Value) or RGB (Red, Green, Blue) values or by positioning the pointer over the desired color displayed by a color wheel and clicking mouse button 1.

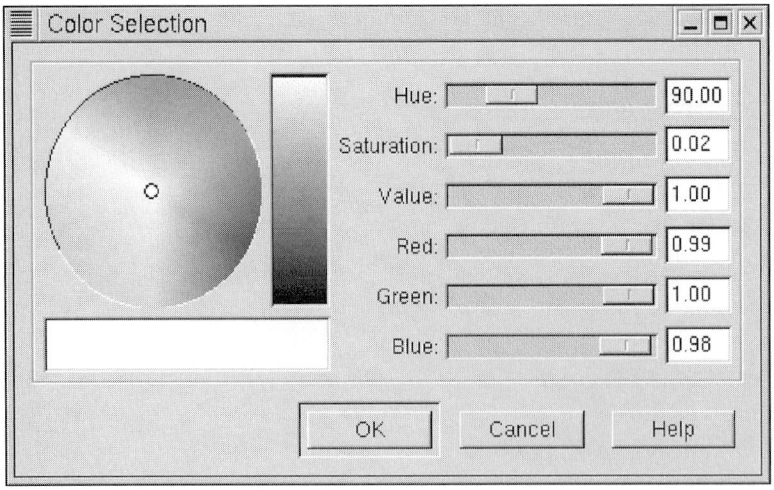

Figure 7.18 GtkColorSelectionDialog

The action area of a color-selection dialog displays three buttons labeled OK, Cancel, and Help, respectively. Clicked signal functions are not registered for these buttons by the color-selection widget; the application must assign a clicked signal function to each of these buttons (or hide the buttons that are not desired, as I will illustrate later). To use a color-selection dialog, an application must call functions provided by the GtkColorSelection widget API that is described later in this chapter. I will briefly illustrate the use of these functions in the sample code presented in this section.

Creating a Color-Selection Dialog

GtkColorSelectionDialog provides only one function, gtk_color_selection_new(), that can be used to create an instance of a color-selection dialog:

```
GtkWidget *
gtk_color_selection_dialog_new(void);
```

Like most widget creation functions in Gtk+, the return value is an instance of GtkWidget. Usually, an application will create an instance of GtkColorSelectionDialog from within the clicked handler of a button or the activate handler of a menu item. The corresponding button or menu item should be labeled in a way that indicates to the user that a color will be solicited by the application when the control is activated (e.g., “Select a color...”).

Example

The following code illustrates how to use a color-selection dialog in an application. The focus here is on application structure; details regarding the color-selection widget (GtkColorSelection), which forms the basis of the color-selection dialog widget, are provided in detail later in this chapter.

Listing 7.2 Using a Color-Selection Dialog

```
#include <gtk/gtk.h>

void
ColorSelDialogOk( GtkWidget *widget, GtkWidget *colorsel )
{
    GtkColorSelectionDialog *cseldialog =
             GTK_COLOR_SELECTION_DIALOG( colorsel );
    GtkColorSelection *csel = GTK_COLOR_SELECTION(cseldialog->colorsel);
    gdouble color[4];

    gtk_color_selection_get_color(csel, color);

    printf( "r %d g %d b %d\n", (int)( color[0] * 255 ),
             (int) (color[1] * 255), (int) (color[2] * 255 ));
    gtk_widget_destroy( colorsel );
}

void
ColorSelDialogCancel( GtkWidget *widget, GtkWidget *colorsel )
{
    gtk_widget_destroy( colorsel );
}

void
PopupColorSelection( GtkWidget *widget, gpointer ignored )
{
    GtkWidget *colorsel;

    colorsel = gtk_color_selection_dialog_new("Select a color!");

    gtk_signal_connect(GTK_OBJECT(
             GTK_COLOR_SELECTION_DIALOG(colorsel)->ok_button),
             "clicked", GTK_SIGNAL_FUNC(ColorSelDialogOk), colorsel );

    gtk_signal_connect(GTK_OBJECT(
            GTK_COLOR_SELECTION_DIALOG(colorsel)->cancel_button),
            "clicked", GTK_SIGNAL_FUNC(ColorSelDialogCancel), colorsel );

    gtk_widget_show_all(colorsel);

    gtk_widget_hide(GTK_WIDGET(
             GTK_COLOR_SELECTION_DIALOG(colorsel)->help_button));
}

main( int argc, char *argv[] )
{
    GtkWidget *button, *dialog_window;

    gtk_init( &argc, &argv );
```

```
050
051     dialog_window = gtk_dialog_new();
052     gtk_window_position(GTK_WINDOW (dialog_window), GTK_WIN_POS_MOUSE);
053
054     button = gtk_button_new_with_label ("Get Color...");
055     gtk_signal_connect(GTK_OBJECT (button), "clicked",
056             GTK_SIGNAL_FUNC(PopupColorSelection), NULL );
057     gtk_box_pack_start(GTK_BOX (GTK_DIALOG (dialog_window)->action_area),
058             button, FALSE, FALSE, 0);
059
060     gtk_widget_show_all(dialog_window);
061
062     gtk_main();
063 }
```

In the preceding code, main() creates a dialog with a single button in its action area labeled "Get Color...". Clicking on this button causes the clicked signal function PopupColorSelection() to be invoked. In this function, a new instance of GtkColorSelectionDialog is created (line 029). On line 031, I set the clicked signal function of the OK button to ColorSelDialogOk(), which I will describe later in this chapter. The action area, as I mentioned, has three buttons labeled OK, Cancel, and Help. You can reference the GtkButton widget instances corresponding to these buttons as fields of the color-selection dialog, as illustrated on lines 032 (ok_button), 036 (cancel_button), and 042 (help_button). For example, the OK button can be accessed as follows:

```
GtkWidget *colorsel, *button;

button = GTK_COLOR_SELECTION_DIALOG(colorsel)->ok_button;
```

On line 041, I hide the Help button because my sample program is incapable of providing help. Generally, applications should not hide the OK button but may decide to hide the Cancel button if selection of a color is for whatever reason mandatory.

The Cancel button signal function is set to ColorSelDialogCancel() on lines 035 through 037. The color-selection dialog widget is passed as client data; it is the job of this callback to simply destroy the color-selection dialog:

```
018  void
019  ColorSelDialogCancel( GtkWidget *widget, GtkWidget *colorsel )
020  {
021      gtk_widget_destroy( colorsel );
022  }
```

The OK button signal function, ColorSelDialogOk(), is much more interesting:

```
003  void
004  ColorSelDialogOk( GtkWidget *widget, GtkWidget *colorsel )
005  {
006      GtkColorSelectionDialog *cseldialog =
007              GTK_COLOR_SELECTION_DIALOG( colorsel );
008      GtkColorSelection *csel = GTK_COLOR_SELECTION(cseldialog->colorsel);
```

```
009     gdouble color[4];
010
011     gtk_color_selection_get_color(csel, color);
012
013     printf( "r %d g %d b %d\n", (int)( color[0] * 255 ),
014             (int) (color[1] * 255), (int) (color[2] * 255 ));
015     gtk_widget_destroy( colorsel );
016 }
```

ColorSelDialogOk(), like ColorSelDialogCancel(), receives as client data the color-selection dialog containing the button that was pressed. On line 006, I convert the client data to an instance of GtkColorSelectionDialog, and then, on the very next line, I retrieve from the color-selection dialog the instance of GtkColorSelection that it manages (line 008). It is at this point that I must use the API of GtkColorSelection. The goal here is to retrieve the color selection made by the user so that I can display it. On line 009, a gdouble array with four elements is allocated. This array is passed to gtk_color_selection_get_color() on line 011. The first three elements of this array contain, in order, the red, green, and blue components of the color that was selected. The range of these values is [0.0, 1.0]. On line 013 and 014, I scale these values to integer RGB components in the range [0, 255], and then I display them to the console. Finally, on line 015, I destroy the color-selection dialog widget by calling gtk_widget_destroy(), just as I had done in ColorSelDialogCancel(). More details on gtk_color_selection_get_color() are provided in the next section, which describes the GtkColorSelection widget API.

GtkColorSelection

Class Name

```
GtkColorSelection
```

Parent Class Name

```
GtkVBox
```

Macros

Widget type macro: `GTK_TYPE_COLOR_SELECTION`

Object to widget cast macro: `GTK_COLOR_SELECTION(obj)`

Widget type check macro: `GTK_IS_COLOR_SELECTION(obj)`

Supported Signals

Table 7.11 Signals

Signal Name	*Condition Causing Signal to Trigger*
color_changed	The user has selected a different color.

Signal Function Prototypes

```
void
color_changed(GtkColorSelection *colorselection, gpointer user_data);
```

Supported Arguments

Prefix: `GtkColorSelection::`

Table 7.12 GtkColorSelection Arguments

Name	*Type*	*Permissions*
policy	GTK_TYPE_UPDATE_TYPE	GTK_ARG_READWRITE
use_opacity	GTK_TYPE_BOOL	GTK_ARG_READWRITE

Application-Level API Synopsis

Retrieve the constant GTK_TYPE_COLOR_SELECTION at runtime:

```
GtkType
gtk_color_selection_get_type(void);
```

Create a new instance of GtkColorSelection:

```
GtkWidget *
gtk_color_selection_new(void);
```

Set the update policy of the color-selection widget to GTK_UPDATE_CONTINUOUS, GTK_UPDATE_DISCONTINUOUS, or GTK_UPDATE_DELAYED:

```
void
gtk_color_selection_set_update_policy(GtkColorSelection *colorsel,
        GtkUpdateType policy);
```

Enable or disable the use of opacity by the color-selection widget:

```
void
gtk_color_selection_set_opacity(GtkColorSelection *colorsel,
        gint use_opacity);
```

Application-Level API Synopsis (Continued)

Set the color of the color-selection widget:
```
void
gtk_color_selection_set_color(GtkColorSelection *colorsel,
        gdouble *color);
```

Get the color of the color-selection widget:
```
void
gtk_color_selection_get_color(GtkColorSelection *colorsel,
        gdouble *color);
```

Class Description

The preceding section described GtkColorSelectionDialog, a widget that displays an instance of GtkColorSelection in a dialog and provides buttons that can be used to accept the changes made by the user (OK), cancel the color-selection dialog (Cancel), or get help from the application (Help). In this section, I describe GtkColorSelection. While most applications will use GtkColorSelectionDialog to retrieve a color selection from users, GtkColorSelection is useful if you want to embed the color-selection widget in a dialog of your own design (e.g., a dialog that allows the user to choose a foreground and a background color).

Creating a Color-Selection Widget

Color-selection widgets are fairly easy to use. To create one, an application must call gtk_color_selection_new():

```
GtkWidget *
gtk_color_selection_new(void);
```

Once the widget is created, it can be added to a dialog or some other container widget.

Color-Selection Widget Attributes

There are two attributes of a color-selection widget that you can control. The first is its update policy. This basically is a preference that globally controls the update policy of the scale widgets the color-selection widget displays that can be used to change HSV, RGB, and opacity values in the widget. To change the update policy, call gtk_color_selection_set_update_policy():

```
void
gtk_color_selection_set_update_policy(GtkColorSelection *colorsel,
        GtkUpdateType policy);
```

The argument colorsel is an instance of GtkColorSel, and policy is one of the following constants: GTK_UPDATE_CONTINUOUS, GTK_UPDATE_DISCONTINUOUS, or GTK_UPDATE_DELAYED. See the description of gtk_range_set_update_policy() in

Chapter 13, "Range Widgets and Adjustment Objects," for more details on the effect these values have on the scale widgets displayed by the color-selection dialog.

The other attribute that can be changed is the use of opacity in the selection of a color. By default, opacity is disabled (but a bug in the color-selection widget results in the opacity scale still displaying in the user interface, a problem I will address later in this chapter). To enable or disable the use of opacity by the color-selection widget, call gtk_color_selection_set_opacity():

```
void
gtk_color_selection_set_opacity(GtkColorSelection *colorsel,
        gint use_opacity);
```

The argument use_opacity can be set to either FALSE (default) or TRUE. Before I describe what opacity is, let's get to the issue of how to hide the opacity scale and label in the dialog when opacity is disabled. Internally, the label for the opacity scale is stored in a field of the color-selection widget named opacity_label. The entry widget into which an opacity value may be typed is stored in a vector named entries at element 6, and the scale widget is stored in a vector named scales, also located at element 6. So after you have shown (realized and mapped) the color-selection widget, you can hide the widgets I just described to remove the opacity-related controls from the widget by executing code like the following:

```
GtkWidget *colorsel;

colorsel = gtk_color_selection_new();

gtk_widget_show( colorsel );
gtk_widget_hide( GTK_COLOR_SELECTION(colorsel)->opacity_label );
gtk_widget_hide( GTK_COLOR_SELECTION(colorsel)->scales[6] );
gtk_widget_hide( GTK_COLOR_SELECTION(colorsel)->entries[6] );
```

This sort of code is obviously highly dependent on the internal structure of GtkColorSelection and is not recommended in code that needs to be portable to more than one version of Gtk+; the correct solution would be for the color-selection widget to show and hide the opacity controls based on the opacity attribute currently set by the application.

What Is Opacity?

Opacity is a value in the range [0.0, 1.0] that describes the transparency of a color relative to its background. A fully opaque color (opacity = 1.0) will, when placed over a background, completely replace the pixel below it in the background. A fully transparent color (opacity = 0.0) will allow the background color to show through completely. A color with an opacity of 0.25 will contribute 25% of the color that is shown, while the background contributes 75%. An opaque color is computed at rendering time using a blending equation:

```
pixel = color * opacity + ( 1 - opacity ) * background
```

With an opacity of 0.25, the equation reduces to the following:

```
color * 0.25 + 0.75 * background.
```

Some image formats encode pixels as RGBA. The fourth channel (A) is referred to as an alpha channel and is usually 8 bits in depth (opacity values falling in the range [0.0, 1.0] would be scaled to the range [0, 255] in this case).

You only need to request opacity values if your application makes use of them in some way. Most applications do not need to retrieve opacity values when asking for a color.

Setting and Retrieving Colors

Some applications need to initialize the color-selection widget to reflect a color that is being changed. For example, a color-selection widget that requests the value of a new background color should be initialized to display the current background color. All applications must retrieve the color that was set by the user; otherwise, there is little purpose in displaying a color-selection dialog in the first place (granted, there might be exceptions).

To set the color and (if enabled) the opacity values displayed by a color-selection widget, you can call gtk_color_selection_set_color():

```
void
gtk_color_selection_set_color(GtkColorSelection *colorsel,
         gdouble *color);
```

The argument colorsel is an instance of GtkColorSel, and color is a vector of type gdouble that contains four elements. The first element holds the red component of the color, the second holds the green component, the third holds the blue component, and finally, the fourth holds the opacity value. All of the values must be in the range of [0.0, 1.0].

To retrieve the current color and opacity values from a color-selection widget, you can call gtk_color_selection_get_color():

```
void
gtk_color_selection_get_color(GtkColorSelection *colorsel,
         gdouble *color);
```

The arguments passed to gtk_color_selection_get_color() are the same as those previously described for gtk_color_selection_set_color().

Summary

In this chapter, we took a look at the following widgets: GtkWindow, GtkDialog, GtkFileSelection, GtkFontSelection, GtkFontSelectionDialog, GtkColorSelection, and GtkColorSelectionDialog. An instance of GtkWindow can be used to create a window into which context is placed by an application. Chapter 10 will discuss widgets that can be used to organize such content. GtkDialog is a class that makes the creation of certain types of windows easier on applications by preloading a window with a content area and an action area, both instances of GtkBox (boxes are also discussed in Chapter 10). A file-selection widget (GtkFileSelection) puts a dialog up that allows a user to traverse the file system and select a file. Controls are provided that allow users to create directories and delete files. We also illustrated how custom content can be added to a file-selection widget. GtkFontSelection-

Dialog and GtkColorSelectionDialog are similar in concept to GtkFileSelection, except these two widgets put up dialogs that allow the user to select a font and a color, respectively. Two classes not related to GtkWindow, GtkFontSelection and GtkColorSelection were described in this chapter due to their importance to the operation of GtkFontSelectionDialog and GtkColorSelectionDialog, respectively. The rest of the widgets (GtkFileSelection, GtkFontSelectionDialog, and GtkColorSelectionDialog) all derive from GtkWindow and thus can make use of the functionality described in the section on GtkWindow.

CHAPTER

8

SEPARATORS, ARROWS, IMAGES, PIXMAPS, AND ENTRY WIDGETS

This chapter concludes the presentation of Gtk+ base widget classes by taking a look at those listed in Table 8.1.

Table 8.1 Widgets Covered in This Chapter

Class Name	***Description***
GtkSeparator	Base widget class for horizontal and vertical separators (GtkHSeparator, GtkVSeparator)
GtkHSeparator	Horizontal separator widget
GtkVSeparator	Vertical separator widget
GtkArrow	Arrow widget
GtkImage	Image display widget
GtkPixmap	Widget that supports pixmap data
GtkEntry	Single-line, text-edit field widget

Separators

A separator is a horizontal (GtkHSeparator) or vertical (GtkVSeparator) line placed by an application at an arbitrary location in a window or dialog. This is not a line in the computer graphics sense of a line (i.e., a part of a drawing or graphic). Instead, separators are used by applications to create distinct areas within a dialog, and each area contains controls that are related to one another in some way. Using separators in this way will make it easier for your users to identify related controls, and this, in turn, will make your application's user interface more effective and easy to use.

One of the most common uses of a separator widget is to visually separate the control and action areas of a dialog. Figure 7-3 (see Chapter 7, "Windows and Dialogs") illustrates an instance of GtkDialog. The control area, which is the area above the horizontal separator, is where the controls specific to the dialog are placed, and this is where the user performs the primary task of the dialog. The action area, located below the horizontal separator, is where the user decides how the content of the dialog is to be applied (in this case, the dialog is simply dismissed by a press of the OK button). Most, if not all, of your application's dialogs should be organized using separate control and action areas and be separated by a horizontal separator, as shown in the illustration. GtkDialog does this for you automatically.

Horizontal and vertical separators also can be used within the control area of a dialog to group related controls, although GtkFrame provides a better solution in some cases (GtkFrame is discussed in Chapter 11, "More Container Classes").

Horizontal separators are also used in menus to create groups of related menu items. Figure 8.1 shows a typical Edit menu with horizontal separators. It is easy to see how horizontal separators are used to break the menu items up into groups of related items, making the menu much easier for a user to work with.

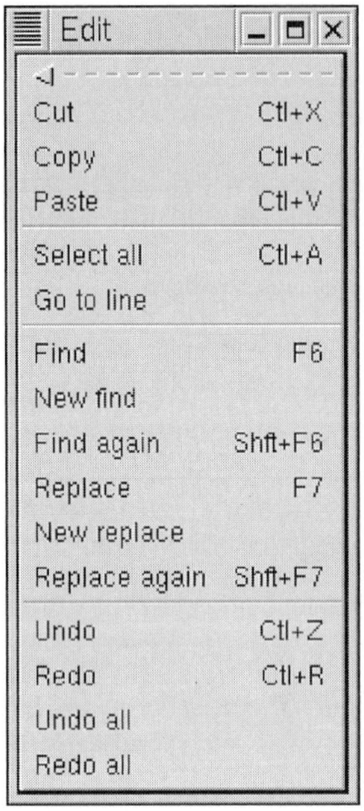

Figure 8.1 Menu Using Horizontal Separators to Group Related Items

Now that we have an idea of what separators are used for, it is time to take a detailed look at the three Gtk+ separator classes: GtkSeparator, GtkHSeparator, and GtkVSeparator.

GtkSeparator

Class Name

```
GtkSeparator
```

Parent Class Name

```
GtkWidget
```

Macros

Widget type macro: `GTK_TYPE_SEPARATOR`

Object to widget cast macro: `GTK_SEPARATOR(obj)`

Widget type check macro: `GTK_IS_SEPARATOR(obj)`

Application-Level API Synopsis

Obtain GTK_TYPE_SEPARATOR at runtime:

```
GtkType
gtk_separator_get_type(void);
```

Class Description

GtkSeparator provides the widget class from which the GtkHSeparator and GtkVSeparator classes, discussed in the following sections, inherit.

GtkHSeparator

Class Name

```
GtkHSeparator
```

Parent Class Name

```
GtkSeparator
```

Macros

Widget type macro: `GTK_TYPE_HSEPARATOR`

Object to widget cast macro: `GTK_HSEPARATOR(obj)`

Widget type check macro: `GTK_IS_HSEPARATOR(obj)`

Application-Level API Synopsis

Obtain the GTK_TYPE_HSEPARATOR constant at runtime:
```
GtkType
gtk_hseparator_get_type(void);
```

Create a new instance of GtkHSeparator:
```
GtkWidget *
gtk_hseparator_new(void);
```

Class Description

GtkHSeparator is a simple class that creates a horizontal separator (similar to the one that is often used to separate groups of related menu items in a menu or the control and action areas of a dialog). To create an instance of GtkHSeparator, call gtk_hseparator_new():

```
GtkWidget *
gtk_hseparator_new(void);
```

The horizontal separator that is returned must be added to a container widget in order to be displayed. For a horizontal separator, most likely this will be a vbox (see Chapter 10, "Container and Bin Classes"). Adding a separator to a menu will be discussed in Chapter 9, "Menus." The following code illustrates the creation of a simple message box. In Chapter 4, "Widgets," I presented a routine, MessageBox(), that creates a message box using GtkDialog. I have duplicated the code for MessageBox() here:

Listing 8.1 MessageBox

```
#include <gtk/gtk.h>

/*
 * Simple MessageBox
 */

void
MessageBox( char *message )
{
        GtkWidget *label, *button, *dialog_window;

        dialog_window = gtk_dialog_new();
        gtk_window_position (GTK_WINDOW (dialog_window),
             GTK_WIN_POS_MOUSE);

        gtk_signal_connect (GTK_OBJECT (dialog_window), "destroy",
             GTK_SIGNAL_FUNC(gtk_widget_destroyed), &dialog_window);

        gtk_window_set_title (GTK_WINDOW (dialog_window), "Message");
        gtk_container_border_width (GTK_CONTAINER (dialog_window), 0);

        button = gtk_button_new_with_label ("OK");
        GTK_WIDGET_SET_FLAGS (button, GTK_CAN_DEFAULT);
        gtk_box_pack_start (
             GTK_BOX (GTK_DIALOG (dialog_window)->action_area),
             button, TRUE, TRUE, 0);
        gtk_signal_connect_object (GTK_OBJECT (button), "clicked",
             GTK_SIGNAL_FUNC (gtk_widget_destroy),
             GTK_OBJECT (dialog_window));

        label = gtk_label_new (message);
        gtk_misc_set_padding (GTK_MISC (label), 10, 10);
        gtk_box_pack_start (GTK_BOX (GTK_DIALOG (dialog_window)->vbox),
             label, TRUE, TRUE, 0);
        gtk_widget_grab_default (button);
        gtk_widget_show_all (dialog_window);
}
```

The routine MessageBox2(), presented in Listing 8.2, performs basically the same tasks as MessageBox() (see Listing 8.1). Instead of using GtkDialog, which provides the control area, the action area, and the horizontal separator that exists between them, MessageBox2() creates its own action area, control area, and horizontal separator. The control area is a vertical box, arranging items that are added to it vertically. The action area is a horizontal box because buttons in an action area are arranged horizontally, left to right. The control area, the horizontal separator, and the action are all packed into a single vertical box widget in that order, so the control area is topmost, followed by the separator, which is then followed by the action area.

Listing 8.2 MessageBox Without Using GtkDialog

```
#include <gtk/gtk.h>

/*
 * Simple MessageBox, without using GtkDialog
 */

void
MessageBox2( char *message )
{
      GtkWidget *hbox, *vbox1, *vbox2, *separator, *label, *button,
                *dialog_window;

      dialog_window = gtk_window_new( GTK_WINDOW_TOPLEVEL );
      gtk_window_position (GTK_WINDOW (dialog_window),
              GTK_WIN_POS_MOUSE);

      gtk_signal_connect (GTK_OBJECT (dialog_window), "destroy",
              GTK_SIGNAL_FUNC(gtk_widget_destroyed), &dialog_window);

      gtk_window_set_title (GTK_WINDOW (dialog_window), "Message");
      gtk_container_border_width (GTK_CONTAINER (dialog_window), 0);

      /* create the outer vbox that holds the control area vbox, the action
         area hbox, and the separator between them */

      vbox1 = gtk_vbox_new (FALSE, 0);
      gtk_container_add (GTK_CONTAINER (dialog_window), vbox1);

      /* create the vbox that represents the control area. The message (as an
         instance of GtkLabel) will be added to this vbox. Add the control
         area vbox to the outer vbox */

      vbox2 = gtk_vbox_new (FALSE, 0);
      gtk_box_pack_start ( GTK_BOX (vbox1), vbox2, TRUE, TRUE, 0);

      /* create the separator, and add it to the outer vbox */

      separator = gtk_hseparator_new();
      gtk_box_pack_start ( GTK_BOX (vbox1), separator, TRUE, TRUE, 0);

      /* create the hbox that represents the action area. The OK button will
         be added to this hbox. Add the action area hbox to the outer vbox.
         Also, set the border width of the container so that the OK button
         and the horizontal separator have enough spacing between them to be
         visible. */
```

```
    hbox = gtk_vbox_new (FALSE, 5);
    gtk_container_set_border_width (GTK_CONTAINER (hbox), 10);

    gtk_box_pack_start ( GTK_BOX (vbox1), hbox, TRUE, TRUE, 0);

    /* now, create the message label and the OK button, and add them to the
       control and action areas, respectively. */

    button = gtk_button_new_with_label ("OK");
    GTK_WIDGET_SET_FLAGS (button, GTK_CAN_DEFAULT);
    gtk_box_pack_start ( GTK_BOX (hbox), button, TRUE, TRUE, 0);
    gtk_signal_connect_object (GTK_OBJECT (button), "clicked",
            GTK_SIGNAL_FUNC (gtk_widget_destroy),
            GTK_OBJECT (dialog_window));

    label = gtk_label_new (message);
    gtk_misc_set_padding (GTK_MISC (label), 10, 10);
    gtk_box_pack_start (GTK_BOX (vbox2), label, TRUE, TRUE, 0);
    gtk_widget_grab_default (button);
    gtk_widget_show_all (dialog_window);
}
```

Figure 8.2 illustrates the results attained by the preceding code.

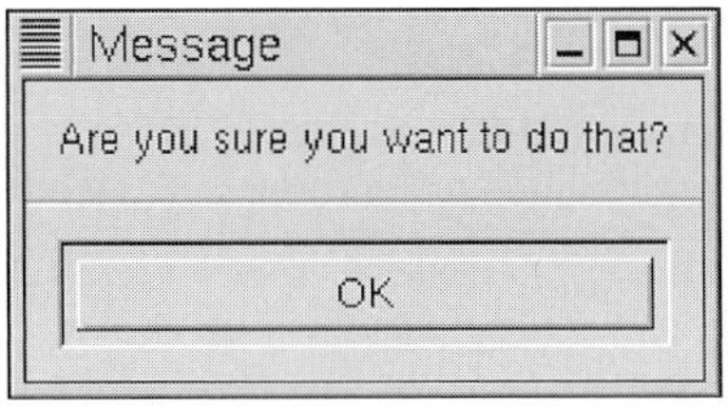

Figure 8.2 MessageBox with a Horizontal Separator

GtkVSeparator

Class Name

```
GtkVSeparator
```

Parent Class Name

```
GtkSeparator
```

Macros

Widget type macro: `GTK_TYPE_VSEPARATOR`

Object to widget cast macro: `GTK_VSEPARATOR(obj)`

Widget type check macro: `GTK_IS_VSEPARATOR(obj)`

Application-Level API Synopsis

Obtain the GTK_TYPE_VSEPARATOR constant at runtime:

```
GtkType
gtk_vseparator_get_type(void);
```

Create a new instance of GtkVSeparator:

```
GtkWidget *
gtk_vseparator_new(void);
```

Class Description

A vertical separator is very similar to a horizontal separator, except vertical separators draw themselves vertically, top to bottom, in the containing widget, as opposed to left to right, as is done by instances of GtkHSeparator.

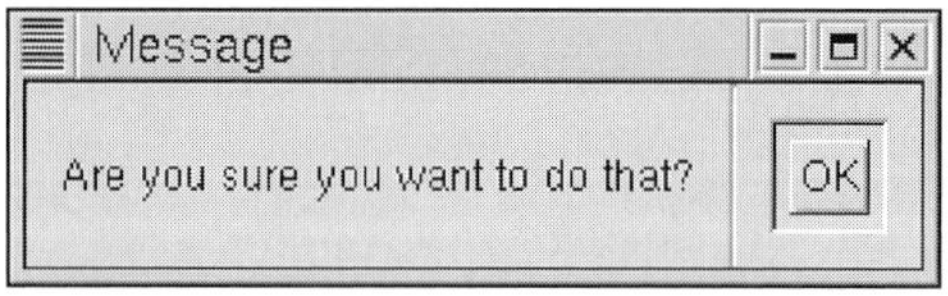

Figure 8.3 MessageBox with a Vertical Separator

My personal preference would be to use an instance of GtkFrame (see Chapter 11) to provide both vertical and horizontal separation in a control area, and my suspicion is that vertical separators, specifically, are rarely if ever used. Be that as it may, your application might find a need for a vertical separator widget. Although such an arrangement of items in a dialog is uncommon, the following code creates a message box dialog, similar to the one created by MessageBox2() but with the control and action areas arranged left to right in a horizontal box and with a vertical separator widget between the two. Figure 8.3 illustrates the result attained by this code. The routine gtk_vseparator_new() is used to create the vertical separator; its function prototype is as follows:

```
GtkWidget *
gtk_vseparator_new(void);
```

The code for MessageBox3() is presented in the following listing:

Listing 8.3 MessageBox with Vertical Separator

```
#include <gtk/gtk.h>

/*
 * Simple MessageBox, without using GtkDialog
 */

void
MessageBox3( char *message )
{
      GtkWidget *vbox1, *vbox2, *hbox, *separator, *label, *button,
                *dialog_window;

      dialog_window = gtk_window_new(GTK_WINDOW_TOPLEVEL);
      gtk_window_position (GTK_WINDOW (dialog_window), GTK_WIN_POS_MOUSE);

      gtk_signal_connect (GTK_OBJECT (dialog_window), "destroy",
              GTK_SIGNAL_FUNC(gtk_widget_destroyed), &dialog_window);

      gtk_window_set_title (GTK_WINDOW (dialog_window), "Message");
      gtk_container_border_width (GTK_CONTAINER (dialog_window), 0);

      /* create the outer hbox that holds the control area vbox, the action
         area hbox, and the separator between them */

      hbox = gtk_hbox_new (FALSE, 0);
      gtk_container_add (GTK_CONTAINER (dialog_window), hbox);

      /* create the vbox that represents the control area. The message (as an
         instance of GtkLabel) will be added to this vbox. Add the control
         area vbox to the outer hbox */

      vbox1 = gtk_vbox_new (FALSE, 0);
      gtk_box_pack_start ( GTK_BOX (hbox), vbox1, TRUE, TRUE, 0);

      /* create the separator, and add it to the outer hbox */

      separator = gtk_vseparator_new();
      gtk_box_pack_start ( GTK_BOX (hbox), separator, TRUE, TRUE, 0);

      /* create the vbox that represents the action area. The OK button will
         be added to this vbox. Add the action area vbox to the outer hbox */

      vbox2 = gtk_vbox_new (FALSE, 5);
      gtk_container_set_border_width (GTK_CONTAINER (vbox2), 10);
```

```
    gtk_box_pack_start ( GTK_BOX (hbox), vbox2, TRUE, TRUE, 0);

    /* now, create the message label and the OK button, and add them to the
       control and action areas, respectively. */

    button = gtk_button_new_with_label ("OK");
    GTK_WIDGET_SET_FLAGS (button, GTK_CAN_DEFAULT);
    gtk_box_pack_start ( GTK_BOX (vbox2), button, TRUE, TRUE, 0);
    gtk_signal_connect_object (GTK_OBJECT (button), "clicked",
            GTK_SIGNAL_FUNC (gtk_widget_destroy),
            GTK_OBJECT (dialog_window));

    label = gtk_label_new (message);
    gtk_misc_set_padding (GTK_MISC (label), 10, 10);
    gtk_box_pack_start (GTK_BOX (vbox1), label, TRUE, TRUE, 0);
    gtk_widget_grab_default (button);
    gtk_widget_show_all (dialog_window);
}
```

GtkArrow

Class Name

`GtkArrow`

Parent Class Name

`GtkMisc`

Macros

Widget type macro: `GTK_TYPE_ARROW`

Object to widget cast macro: `GTK_ARROW(obj)`

Widget type check macro: `GTK_IS_ARROW(obj)`

Supported Arguments

Prefix: `GtkArrow::`

Table 8.2 GtkArrow Arguments

Name	*Type*	*Permissions*
arrow_type	GTK_TYPE_ARROW_TYPE	GTK_ARG_READWRITE
shadow_type	GTK_TYPE_SHADOW_TYPE	GTK_ARG_READWRITE

Application-Level API Synopsis

Retrieve the GTK_TYPE_ARROW constant at runtime:

```
GtkType
gtk_arrow_get_type(void);
```

Create a new instance of GtkArrow:

```
GtkWidget *
gtk_arrow_new(GtkArrowType arrow_type, GtkShadowType shadow_type);
```

Set the arrow type and shadow type of an instance of GtkArrow:

```
void
gtk_arrow_set(GtkArrow *arrow, GtkArrowType arrow_type,
        GtkShadowType shadow_type);
```

Class Description

GtkArrow is a seldom-used widget that can be used to add an arrow decoration to a user interface. GtkArrow is similar to GtkLabel in that it does not generate any signals. If signal generation is required, the arrow must be placed in a container capable of generating a signal of the desired type, such as an instance of GtkEventBox or GtkButton. I will illustrate in the following how to incorporate an instance of GtkArrow into an instance of GtkButton.

Arrow and Shadow Types

An arrow can be one of four different types as well as one of four different shadow types. The shadow type selected has a dramatic impact on the way the arrow appears, as illustrated in Figure 8.4.

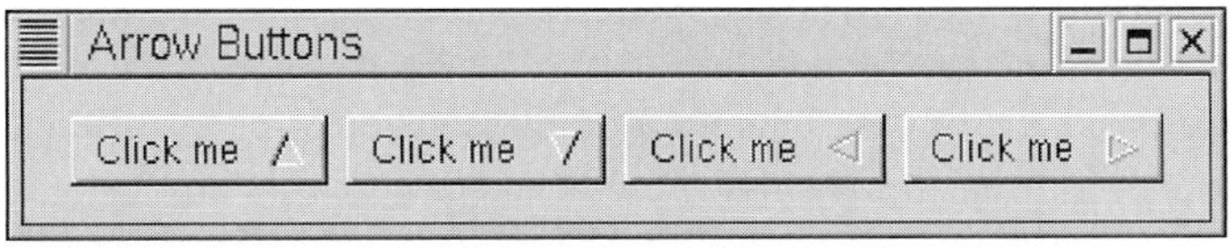

Figure 8.4 Arrow Types and Shadow Types

From left to right, the shadow types are GTK_SHADOW_IN, GTK_SHADOW_OUT, GTK_SHADOW_ETCHED_IN, and GTK_SHADOW_ETCHED_OUT. The arrow type defines the orientation of the arrow, as described in Table 8.3.

Table 8.3 Arrow Types

Type	*Orientation*
GTK_ARROW_UP	Arrow points to top of screen.
GTK_ARROW_DOWN	Arrow points to bottom of screen.
GTK_ARROW_LEFT	Arrow points to left edge of screen.
GTK_ARROW_RIGHT	Arrow points to right edge of screen.

Figure 8.4 illustrates the arrow types listed in Table 8.3 (from left to right: GTK_ARROW_UP, GTK_ARROW_DOWN, GTK_ARROW_LEFT, and GTK_ARROW_RIGHT).

The two functions provided by GtkArrow, described in the following, both allow you to specify these attributes, either at widget-creation time or sometime after widget creation.

Creating an Arrow Widget

Creating a new instance of GtkArrow is performed by calling gtk_arrow_new():

```
GtkWidget *
gtk_arrow_new(GtkArrowType arrow_type, GtkShadowType shadow_type);
```

Arrow_type is GTK_ARROW_UP, GTK_ARROW_DOWN, GTK_ARROW_LEFT, or GTK_ARROW_RIGHT, and shadow type is GTK_SHADOW_IN, GTK_SHADOW_OUT, GTK_SHADOW_ETCHED_IN, or GTK_SHADOW_ETCHED_OUT, as shown and described in the preceding figure and tables.

Setting Arrow Attributes

Once an arrow has been created, the arrow type and shadow type attributes can be changed by calling gtk_arrow_set():

```
void
gtk_arrow_set(GtkArrow *arrow, GtkArrowType arrow_type,
        GtkShadowType shadow_type);
```

arrow is an instance of GtkArrow. arrow_type and shadow_type are the same as those of the same name passed to gtk_arrow_new().

Each of the objects in Figure 8.4 is a button widget that can be clicked by a user (an instance of GtkButton). As we discussed in Chapter 5, "Labels and Buttons," GtkButton is a container widget that typically manages an instance of GtkLabel. We can create an instance of GtkButton without a label and ask it to manage some other widget. In this case, I have chosen to have it manage an instance of GtkHBox. Within the hbox, I added an instance of GtkLabel ("Click me") and, to the right of it, an instance of GtkArrow. The following code snippet illustrates the creation of the button having the GTK_ARROW_UP and GTK_SHADOW_IN attributes:

```
GtkWidget *button, *arrow, *hbox, *label;

// create a button

button = gtk_button_new();

// create an instance of GtkHBox to house the label and the arrow
// widget, and add it to the button. gtk_container_add() will fail if
// the button is already managing a child widget

hbox = gtk_hbox_new(FALSE, 0);
gtk_container_add (GTK_CONTAINER (button), hbox);

// create a label, and add it to the hbox, specifying a spacing of 5
// to keep it visually distinct from the arrow that follows

label = gtk_label_new( "Click me" );
gtk_box_pack_start (GTK_BOX (hbox), label, TRUE, TRUE, 5);

// create an arrow, and add it to the hbox

arrow = gtk_arrow_new (GTK_ARROW_UP, GTK_SHADOW_IN);
gtk_box_pack_start (GTK_BOX (hbox), arrow, TRUE, TRUE, 5);
```

Images and Pixmaps

Gtk+ 1.2 implements two classes, GtkImage and GtkPixmap, that provide wrappers above GDK's image and pixmap support, respectively. Although GDK provides most of the code necessary to support the creation and manipulation of the actual image and pixmap data, GtkImage and GtkPixmap encapsulate this functionality and allow images and pixmaps to be used in places where a GtkWidget is necessary. For example, we saw in Chapter 6, "Lists," how pixmap data can be added to a cell of an instance of GtkCList. In that chapter, I illustrated how to use GDK routines to create the actual pixmap data and then use GtkPixmap functions to create a widget that could be added to a GtkCList cell.

Information on how to use GDK to create pixmap data, as well as how GtkPixmap makes use of this data, can be found in the discussion of GtkCList in Chapter 6. In this section, I will describe the process behind creating an instance of GtkImage, including how you can use GDK routines to create and modify the image data. The APIs supported by both GtkImage and GtkPixmap will also be discussed in detail here.

GtkPixmap

Class Name

```
GtkPixmap
```

Parent Class Name

```
GtkWidget
```

Macros

Widget type macro: `GTK_TYPE_PIXMAP`

Object to widget cast macro: `GTK_PIXMAP(obj)`

Widget type check macro: `GTK_IS_PIXMAP(obj)`

Application-Level API Synopsis

Retrieve the GTK_TYPE_PIXMAP constant at runtime:
```
GtkType
gtk_pixmap_get_type(void);
```

Create a new instance of GtkPixmap, passing a previously created GDK pixmap and mask:
```
GtkWidget *
gtk_pixmap_new(GdkPixmap *pixmap, GdkBitmap *mask);
```

Set the mask and GDK pixmap associated with an instance of GtkPixmap:
```
void
gtk_pixmap_set(GtkPixmap *pixmap, GdkPixmap *val, GdkBitmap *mask);
```

Retrieve the mask and GDK pixmap associated with an instance of GtkPixmap:
```
void
gtk_pixmap_get(GtkPixmap *pixmap, GdkPixmap **val, GdkBitmap **mask);
```

Specify whether Gtk+ should maintain an insensitive version of the pixmap or bitmap corresponding to the GtkPixmap instance. If the GtkPixmap is visible at the time of the call, queue a redraw to reflect the change:
```
void
gtk_pixmap_set_build_insensitive(GtkPixmap *pixmap, guint build);
```

Class Description

In Chapter 6, I described how to use GDK routines to create pixmap data based on XPM files or XPM data embedded in your application's source code. I also illustrated how to create an instance of GtkPixmap from this data and use it to set the pixmap cell data of an instance of GtkCList. In this section, I will document the functions provided by GtkPixmap. Refer to Chapter 6 for an example of how these functions can be used.

Creating a Pixmap Widget

To create an instance of GtkPixmap, you first need to create a GdkPixmap and mask using routines supplied by GDK, passing a previously created GDK pixmap and mask. Routines such as gdk_pixmap_colormap_create_from_xpm(), described in Chapter 6, can be used to create the necessary GDK data. Given this data, you then call gtk_pixmap_new() to create the GtkPixmap wrapper class that can be used with Gtk+ functions that accept GtkPixmap widgets. The function prototype for gtk_pixmap_new() is as follows:

```
GtkWidget *
gtk_pixmap_new(GdkPixmap *pixmap, GdkBitmap *mask);
```

The first argument is a GdkPixmap. This pixmap can be prepopulated with pixmap data (e.g., using one of the functions described in Chapter 6).

Setting and Getting the Pixmap Data

You can change the pixmap and mask associated with an instance of GtkPixmap by calling gtk_pixmap_set():

```
void
gtk_pixmap_set(GtkPixmap *pixmap, GdkPixmap *val, GdkBitmap *mask);
```

The argument pixmap is an instance of GtkPixmap. The arguments val and mask are the pixmap and mask data, respectively, that were obtained using the GDK routines described in Chapter 6.

Likewise, you can retrieve the pixmap and mask data from a GtkPixmap instance by calling gtk_pixmap_get():

```
void
gtk_pixmap_get(GtkPixmap *pixmap, GdkPixmap **val, GdkBitmap **mask);
```

The argument pixmap is an instance of GtkPixmap, and on return, val will point to a GdkPixmap pointer, and mask will point to a GdkBitmap pointer. Your application will be returned pointers to the GdkPixmap and GdkBitmap being managed by the GtkPixmap widget, not copies. Therefore, be sure not to release the memory that these pointers reference.

GtkPixmap Example

The following source is a complete application that uses the preceding functions to create and swap the image data displayed by two instances of GtkButton. A click of either button will cause their images to be swapped. The code will be followed by a detailed description. The code also makes use of some of the GDK pixmap routines described in Chapter 6.

Listing 8.4 GtkPixmap Sample Application

```
#include <gtk/gtk.h>

GtkWidget *pixmap1, *pixmap2;

static void
SwitchCallback(GtkWidget *widget, GtkWidget *dialog_window)
{
      GdkPixmap *gdkPixmap1, *gdkPixmap2;
      GdkBitmap *gdkBitmap1, *gdkBitmap2;

      /* retrieve current values */

      gtk_pixmap_get(GTK_PIXMAP(pixmap1), &gdkPixmap1, &gdkBitmap1);
      gtk_pixmap_get(GTK_PIXMAP(pixmap2), &gdkPixmap2, &gdkBitmap2);

      /* and swap them */

      gtk_pixmap_set(GTK_PIXMAP(pixmap1), gdkPixmap2, gdkBitmap2);
      gtk_pixmap_set(GTK_PIXMAP(pixmap2), gdkPixmap1, gdkBitmap1);
}

static GtkWidget *
new_pixmap (char *file, GdkWindow *window, GdkColor *background)
{
      GdkPixmap *pmap;
      GdkBitmap *mask;

      pmap = gdk_pixmap_create_from_xpm(window, &mask, background, file);
      return(gtk_pixmap_new(pmap, mask));
}

main( int argc, char *argv[] )
{
      GtkWidget *button, *hbox, *dialog_window;

      gtk_init( &argc, &argv );

      dialog_window = gtk_dialog_new();
      gtk_window_position (GTK_WINDOW (dialog_window), GTK_WIN_POS_MOUSE);

      gtk_widget_show( dialog_window );

      hbox = gtk_hbox_new (FALSE, 0);
      gtk_container_add (GTK_CONTAINER (GTK_DIALOG (dialog_window)->vbox),
            hbox);

      pixmap1 = new_pixmap ("test1.xpm", dialog_window->window,
            &dialog_window->style->bg[GTK_STATE_NORMAL]);
                gtk_box_pack_start (GTK_BOX (hbox), pixmap1, TRUE, TRUE, 0);
      pixmap2 = new_pixmap ("test2.xpm", dialog_window->window,
            &dialog_window->style->bg[GTK_STATE_NORMAL]);
```

```
52         gtk_box_pack_start (GTK_BOX (hbox), pixmap2, TRUE, TRUE, 0);
53
54         button = gtk_button_new_with_label ("Switch Pixmaps");
55                 gtk_box_pack_start (GTK_BOX (
56                 GTK_DIALOG (dialog_window)->action_area), button, TRUE, TRUE, 0);
57         gtk_signal_connect (GTK_OBJECT (button), "clicked",
58                 GTK_SIGNAL_FUNC(SwitchCallback), dialog_window);
59
60         gtk_widget_show_all (dialog_window);
61         gtk_main();
62 }
```

This application creates a dialog and instantiates in its action area a button labeled Switch Pixmaps that, when clicked, invokes a routine named SwitchCallback(), discussed in the next paragraph. Two GtkPixmaps are instantiated by separate calls to new_pixmap(). The first pixmap's image will be based on the XPM data stored in *test1.xpm*, while the second pixmap's image is defined by the XPM file *test2.xpm*. The function new_pixmap() illustrates both gdk_pixmap_create_from_xpm() and gtk_pixmap_new() calls on lines 28 and 29.

When the user presses the Switch Pixmaps button, SwitchCallback() is invoked. This routine reads the pixmap and mask data from the two GtkPixmap instances, using code on lines 13 and 14. On lines 18 and 19, gtk_pixmap_set() is called to set the pixmap and mask of the first pixmap with the pixmap and mask retrieved from the second pixmap and then again to set the pixmap and mask of the second pixmap with those retrieved from the first, effectively swapping the pixmaps. Figure 8.5 illustrates the application in one of its states.

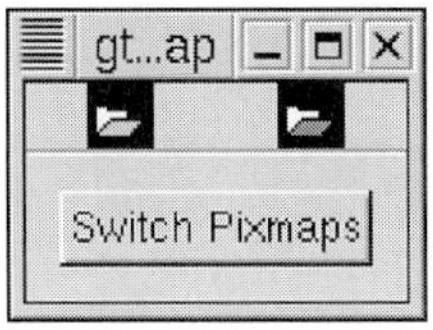

Figure 8.5 GtkPixmap Sample Application Screen Shot

Insensitive Pixmaps

A final function supported by GtkPixmap can be illustrated with a small change to the preceding listing. The function gtk_pixmap_set_build_insensitive() can be called by an application to tell GtkPixmap whether an insensitive version of a pixmap should be displayed by GtkPixmap. The function prototype is as follows:

```
void
gtk_pixmap_set_build_insensitive(GtkPixmap *pixmap, guint build);
```

The argument pixmap is an instance of GtkPixmap. The argument build is a flag that, if set to 1, causes GtkPixmap to display an insensitive version of a pixmap whenever the pixmap is made insensitive by the application with a call to gtk_widget_set_sensitive(). If build is set to 0, the pixmap will not visually change as its sensitivity is changed by the application.

The following is a modification of new_pixmap() from the preceding that illustrates how to call gtk_pixmap_set_build_sensitive():

```
static GtkWidget *
new_pixmap (char *file, GdkWindow *window, GdkColor *background)
{
   GdkPixmap *pmap;
   GdkBitmap *mask;
   GtkWidget *wpmap;

   pmap = gdk_pixmap_create_from_xpm(window, &mask, background, file);
   wpmap = gtk_pixmap_new(pmap, mask);
   gtk_pixmap_set_build_insensitive(GTK_PIXMAP(wpmap), 1);
   return( wpmap );
}
```

The preceding code illustrates how gtk_pixmap_set_build_insensitive() can be called immediately after the pixmap widget has been created.

The callback function SwitchCallback() has been modified in the following so that button presses by the user will not only swap the buttons' pixmaps, but also cause pixmap sensitivity to toggle from sensitive to insensitive. A static variable, makeSensitive, keeps track of the current sensitivity of the two pixmaps between invocations of the callback.

```
static void
SwitchCallback(GtkWidget *widget, GtkWidget *dialog_window)
{
        GdkPixmap *gdkPixmap1, *gdkPixmap2;
        GdkBitmap *gdkBitmap1, *gdkBitmap2;
        static int makeSensitive = 0;

        /* retrieve current values */

        gtk_pixmap_get(GTK_PIXMAP(pixmap1), &gdkPixmap1, &gdkBitmap1);
        gtk_pixmap_get(GTK_PIXMAP(pixmap2), &gdkPixmap2, &gdkBitmap2);

        /* and swap them */

        gtk_pixmap_set(GTK_PIXMAP(pixmap1), gdkPixmap2, gdkBitmap2);
        gtk_pixmap_set(GTK_PIXMAP(pixmap2), gdkPixmap1, gdkBitmap1);

        if ( makeSensitive == 0 ) {

                  /* make pixmaps insensitive */

                makeSensitive = 1;
                gtk_widget_set_sensitive( pixmap1, FALSE );
                gtk_widget_set_sensitive( pixmap2, FALSE );
        } else {

                  /* otherwise, make pixmaps sensitive */

                makeSensitive = 0;
                gtk_widget_set_sensitive( pixmap1, TRUE );
                gtk_widget_set_sensitive( pixmap2, TRUE );
```

```
        }
}
```

Figure 8.6 illustrates the insensitive versions of the pixmaps that were illustrated in Figure 8.5.

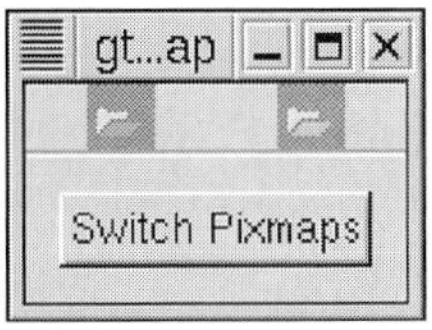

Figure 8.6 Insensitive Pixmaps

GtkImage

Class Name

```
GtkImage
```

Parent Class Name

```
GtkMisc
```

Macros

Widget type macro: `GTK_TYPE_IMAGE`

Object to widget cast macro: `GTK_IMAGE(obj)`

Widget type check macro: `GTK_IS_IMAGE(obj)`

Application-Level API Synopsis

Retrieve the constant GTK_TYPE_IMAGE at runtime:

```
GtkType
gtk_image_get_type(void);
```

Create an instance of GtkImage, supplying a clip mask and a previously created GDK image:

```
GtkWidget *
gtk_image_new(GdkImage *val, GdkBitmap *mask);
```

Set the GDK image and clip mask associated with an instance of GtkImage:

```
void
gtk_image_set(GtkImage *image, GdkImage *val, GdkBitmap *mask);
```

Application-Level API Synopsis (Continued)

Retrieve the GDK image and clip mask associated with an instance of GtkImage:

```
void
gtk_image_get(GtkImage *image, GdkImage **val, GdkBitmap **mask);
```

Class Description

The purpose of GtkImage is to provide a Gtk+ widget wrapper class for the image display and manipulation facilities and objects provided by GDK. GtkImage allows image data to be used in certain places where Gtk+ requires a widget to be present. Much of understanding GtkImage comes from being able to work with GDK image data. In this section, I will do my best to describe GDK's image support and to show how it is used with GtkImage.

Imaging in GDK

GDK's image support itself acts as a wrapper, in this case, layered above the image support provided by the core X11 protocol. As of this writing, GDK does not make use of the features provided by the X11R6 X Image Extension (XIE).

For an application to support image formats such as PNG or JPEG, it typically will need to make use of an image support library (e.g., libpng or libjpeg). Such a library is capable of converting the image data stored in an encoded form into an unencoded form that can be passed to GDK at the time the GDK image object is created. I will illustrate this later in this section, using TIFF as the image format/encoding for the example.

An image is nothing more than a rectangular grid of pixels. The grid has both a width and a height, measured in terms of pixels. Each pixel in the grid has a depth, usually specified in terms of bits but occasionally specified in terms of bytes. The pixel depth of an image defines how many colors can potentially be displayed for each pixel of the image. The pixel depth of the image alone is insufficient to determine how many colors can actually be displayed per pixel, however, because this is also a function of the window into which the image is going to be displayed.

Each window has an associated colormap. Typically, applications and windows will share a common colormap, the X server default colormap, but X allows clients to install private colormaps on windows if they so desire. Colormaps are nothing more than lookup tables. A simple example will illustrate how they work. Let's suppose you have an image, and each pixel in the image is set to the color blue. Each pixel in the image will contain the RGB triplet (R = 0, G = 0, B = 255), assuming RGB component intensities are in the range [0, 255], with 0 used to represent fully off, or no intensity, and 255 used to represent full intensity. For the X server to correctly display image data, the client must convert each pixel in the image into a value indexing a cell of the colormap associated with the window into which the image is to be displayed. The client must also ensure that a colormap cell being indexed by a pixel value in the image contains the appropriate RGB intensity. So, for this example, we need to allocate a single cell in the colormap, store the RGB triplet (0, 0, 255) in that cell, and convert all pixels in the image from the RGB triplet (0, 0, 255) to the index of that cell in order for the image to be displayed correctly.

X11 was designed to support a wide variety of display types, from simple, 1-bit-deep, monochrome displays to 24-bit-deep color displays. Images come in a wide variety of pixel depths. For example, CCITT G32D FAX image data is 1-bit deep, while JPEG supports 8-bit grayscale and 24-bit color image data. To keep things simple here, I will assume we are displaying 24-bit color image data into a 24-bit TrueColor window. In this case, the image data is already in the form of pixel values correctly indexing the colormap of the window. The set of visual classes supported by X11 is listed in Table 8.4.

Table 8.4 Visual Classes

Visual Class	*Pixel Depth*	*Image Type (Typical)*	*Modifiable Colormap?*
StaticGray	1 bit	Grayscale, bitonal	No
StaticColor	4 bits	Color	No
TrueColor	16 or 24 bits	Color	No
GrayScale	8 bits or less	Grayscale	Yes
PseudoColor	8 bits	Color	Yes
DirectColor	16 or 24 bits	Color	Yes

To effectively write image-display software for Gtk+, or X11, you must consider both the structure of pixels in the the image being displayed and the visual class and pixel depth of the display onto which the image data will be displayed, and you must write your software so that it can work with various combinations of image and visual/display types. Books that discuss color and image-display programming in X11 include *Introduction to The X Window System* (Prentice Hall), *Xlib Programming Manual, Volume 1* (O'Reilly & Associates), and *Developing Imaging Applications with XIElib* (Prentice Hall). I am going to avoid this topic here by assuming that we are displaying a 24-bit TIFF image into a 24-bit TrueColor window. In this case, there is no need to convert image pixels into colormap indexes because intensity values stored in cells of a 24-bit TrueColor colormap are equal in value to the pixel values used to index them.

An Example Using libtiff

Let's now take a look at some code that we can use to open and read our 24-bit TIFF image and get uncompressed intensity values compatible with the image we are constructing. Along the way, we will see how to create and use a GtkImage widget.

The following sample code is based on libtiff, which is included with most Linux distributions as */usr/lib/libtiff.a* (or */usr/lib/ligtiff.so*). The header file for libtiff can be found at */usr/include/tiffio.h*. Source code for libtiff can be obtained from various locations on the net, including *ftp://ftp.uu.net/graphics/tiff/*. Using a library like libtiff is a great timesaver; other image libraries that may prove useful include libjpeg *(www.ijg.org)*, libpng *(www.cdrom.com/pub/png)* and the Portable Pixmap Libraries (libppm, libpgm, and libpbm, which can be found on the Internet at various locations).

Reading a 24-bit TrueColor image with libtiff is easy. To use libtiff, include the file *<tiffio.h>* and link libtiff with your application, adding -ltiff to the build command line. The following code illustrates what is needed to open a TIFF image file and obtain information about the image data it stores. I assume here that the first argument to the application contains the name of the TIFF file to be opened and read.

```
TIFF    *tif;
uint16  bitspersample, samplesperpixel;
uint32  width, height;

tif = TIFFOpen(argv[1], "r");

if ( !tif ) {
        printf( "Unable to open tiff file %s\n", argv[1] );
        exit( 1 );
}

TIFFGetField(tif, TIFFTAG_IMAGEWIDTH, &width);
TIFFGetField(tif, TIFFTAG_IMAGELENGTH, &height);
TIFFGetField(tif, TIFFTAG_BITSPERSAMPLE, &bitspersample);
TIFFGetField(tif, TIFFTAG_SAMPLESPERPIXEL, &samplesperpixel);

if ( bitspersample != 8 || samplesperpixel != 3 ) {
        printf( "Error: image is not RGB or is not 24-bit\n" );
        exit( 1 );
}
```

We use width and height later when creating a GDK image. Both width and height can also be used to size the window into which the image data will be displayed. The variables bitspersample and samplesperpixel can be used to check whether the image data we have read is grayscale (samplesperpixel == 1) or color (samplesperpixel == 3) and whether the image is 24 bits (bitspersample == 8 && samplesperpixel == 3). The uncompressed image data can then be obtained as a single raster by calling the function TIFFReadRGBAImage():

```
uint32 *raster;

...

raster = (uint32*) malloc(width * height * sizeof (uint32));
if ( !raster ) {
        perror( "malloc" );
        exit( 1 );
}
if (!TIFFReadRGBAImage(tif, width, height, raster, 0)) {
        printf( "TIFFReadRGBAImage failed\n" );
        exit( 1 );
}
```

Before calling TIFFReadRGBAImage(), we must allocate a buffer to hold width * height pixels, each of size uint32.

Creating an Image with GDK

Now that we have the TIFF image data read in, we can allocate a GDK image with a call to gdk_image_new(), using the width and height information obtained from the TIFF image data:

```
GdkImage *
gdk_image_new(GdkImageType type, GdkVisual *visual, gint width,
          gint height);
```

The arguments width and height define the raster dimensions of the image data. The argument type can be one of the following values in Table 8.5.

Table 8.5 GdkImageType Values

Type	*Meaning*
GDK_IMAGE_SHARED	The image is stored in shared memory.
GDK_IMAGE_NORMAL	The image is not stored in shared memory.
GDK_IMAGE_FASTEST	The fastest of the preceding two techniques is used.

Your application can safely set type to GDK_IMAGE_FASTEST, as this will cause GDK to first create the image as GDK_TYPE_SHARED and, if that fails, then try to create the image a second time using GDK_IMAGE_NORMAL.

The argument visual defines the display characteristics of the window and is analogous to the Visual type of Xlib. As you can see in the following, I obtain this visual directly from the GtkWindow widget into which the image data will be displayed, with a call to the Gtk-Widget function gtk_widget_get_visual(). Here is the code that is relevant to creating a new GdkImage instance:

```
GdkImage *gimage;
GdkVisual *visual;
GtkWidget *window;

...

window = gtk_window_new( GTK_WINDOW_TOPLEVEL );
visual = gtk_widget_get_visual(window);

...

gimage = gdk_image_new( GDK_IMAGE_FASTEST, visual, width, height );
```

Setting the Image Data

The next step in creating our GDK image is to transfer the image data from the raster that was read using libtiff into our newly created GDK image. This can be done using gdk_image_put_pixel():

```
void
gdk_image_put_pixel(GdkImage *image, gint x, gint y, guint32 pixel);
```

The argument image is the GDK image that was previously created with gtk_image_new(). The values x and y specify where in the image the data is to be placed. Images in X11 are organized such that pixel (x = 0, y = 0) is located in the upper-left corner of the image, and pixel (x = width-1, y = height-1) is located in the lower-right corner of the image. In TIFF, the rows run from the bottom to the top; hence, pixel (x = 0, y = 0) is located at the bottom-left corner of the image, while pixel (x = width-1, y = height-1) is located in the upper-right corner. Because of this, we must pack image data read from row i of the raster into row height-i of the GDK image. Pixel (x, y) can be pulled from the raster as follows:

```
uint32 RGB;

RGB = raster[y * width + x];
```

Each pixel in the raster is 32 bits in length and contains the R, G, B, and A (alpha component) of the pixel (each of these is 8 bits in length). The R, G, and B components can be extracted easily from the raster with the libtiff macros TIFFGetR, TIFFGetG, and TIFFGetB, respectively. Each of these takes as a single argument a 32-bit pixel from the raster. Once extracted from the raster, the next step is to pack them into a 32-bit value that can then be placed at the corresponding pixel location of the GDK image. Each component occupies its own 8-bit segment of the 32-bit pixel. We must take into consideration the X server image byte order when constructing the GDK image pixel. If the image byte order of the server is LSBFirst, then we want to pack image pixels as RGBRGBRGB...; otherwise, the image byte order is MSBFirst, and we will want to pack image pixels as BGRBGRBGR....

We can use the GdkVisual obtained in the preceding to determine the image byte order of the X server:

```
int byteOrder;
GdkVisual *visual;

...

byteOrder = visual->byte_order;
```

Then we can compute shift values that can be used when creating the GDK image pixel values:

```
int rshift, gshift, bshift;

gshift = 8;
if ( byteOrder == LSBFirst ) {
        rshift = 16;
        bshift = 0;
} else {
        rshift = 0;
        bshift = 16;
}
```

Now all that remains is to extract pixels from the raster and pack them into the GDK image. Here is the code:

```
int i, j;
uint32 RGB, pixel, *raster;

for ( i = 0; i < height; i++ ) {
        for ( j = 0; j < width; j++ ) {
                 RGB = raster[ i *  width + j ];

                 pixel = TIFFGetR(RGB) << rshift |
                         TIFFGetG(RGB) << gshift |
                         TIFFGetB(RGB) << bshift;
                 gdk_image_put_pixel( gimage, j,
                         (height - 1) - i, pixel );
        }
}
```

In the preceding code, we simply iterate over each row in the image and over each pixel in a row. For each pixel in a row, we read the TIFF RGBA value and compute a pixel value by using the TIFFGet* macros and shifting the components as required by the image byte order. Then we call gdk_image_put_pixel() to place the pixel into the GDK image at the correct location while taking into consideration the inverted row order of TIFF vs. X11 image data.

Now that we have created a GDK image, we can use GtkImage to construct a Gtk+ widget that can be placed in a container widget of some sort so that the image data can be displayed. Before we get to that, let's quickly look at some of the other functions provided by GDK's image support API.

Reading a Pixel Value from an Image

A pixel at a given x, y location can be read from a GDK image using the function gdk_image_get_pixel():

```
guint32
gdk_image_get_pixel(GdkImage *image, gint x, gint y);
```

The pixel returned is packed using the X server image byte format. If LSBFirst, the RGB components can be obtained as follows:

```
guint8 r, g, b;
guint32 pixel;

         ...

r = pixel & 0xff0000;
g = pixel & 0xff00;
b = pixel & 0xff;
```

For MSBFirst, the code would be as follows:

```
r = pixel & 0xff;
g = pixel & 0xff00;
b = pixel & 0xff0000;
```

Destroying an Image

Once your application is done working with a GDK image, it can be destroyed by calling gdk_image_destroy():

```
void
gdk_image_destroy(GdkImage *image);
```

Retrieving Image Data from a Window

GDK image provides a function named gdk_image_get() that can be used to create a GDK image containing the contents of a window:

```
GdkImage *
gdk_image_get(GdkWindow *window, gint x, gint y, gint width,
        gint height);
```

The argument window is a GDK window. Given a GtkWidget, you can obtain the corresponding GDK window with the following code:

```
GtkWidget *myWidget;
GdkWindow *myWindow;

myWindow = myWidget->window;
```

The x, y, width, and height attributes define a rectangular region within the specified window from which the image data will be obtained. To obtain the entire contents of the window, set x and y to 0 and set width and height to the width and height of the window, respectively. Upon return, the GdkImage variable will be ready to use with GtkImage, as I will describe next.

Creating the GtkImage Widget

Now that we have constructed a GDK image, it is time to create an instance of GtkImage. Recall that GtkImage is a wrapper above the GDK image that allows an application to place image data within a Gtk container widget so that it can be displayed; the GDK image maintains all of the nitty-gritty image detail.

Given a GDK image and an optional mask, it is trivial to create a corresponding GtkImage. All you need to do is call gtk_image_new(), passing the GDK image and mask as arguments:

```
GtkWidget *
gtk_image_new(GdkImage *val, GdkBitmap *mask);
```

An instance of GtkImage is returned (as a GtkWidget *). In most cases, you can set the mask argument to NULL. However, you can use a non-NULL mask to specify a clip mask, and if so, it must be a 1-bit-deep pixmap (i.e., a GdkBitmap). If a bit in the bitmap is set to 1, then the corresponding pixel in the image will render. Pixels that are not represented by a set bit in the clip mask will not be rendered, and as a result, the window below the pixel will remain unchanged.

One way to create a clip mask is to call gdk_bitmap_create_from_data():

```
GdkPixmap *
gdk_bitmap_create_from_data(GdkWindow *window, const gchar *data,
        gint width, gint height);
```

This function was discussed in detail in Chapter 6. The returned GdkPixmap * can be cast to GdkBitmap * and be passed directly to gtk_image_new().

The following is the complete program that can be used to display a TIFF 24-bit True-Color image in a window using GtkImage:

Listing 8.5 GtkImage Sample Application

```
#include <tiffio.h>
#include <stdlib.h>

#include <gtk/gtk.h>
#include <X11/Xlib.h>

#include "mask.bmp" // clip mask, XBM image data

int main( int argc, char *argv[] )
{
        uint32   RGB, pixel, width, height, *raster;
        uint16   bitspersample, samplesperpixel;
        int      i, j, byteOrder, rshift, gshift, bshift;
        TIFF     *tif;
        GtkWidget *window, *image, *vbox;
        GdkImage *gimage;
        GdkVisual *visual;
        GdkBitmap *mask;

        /* initialize Gtk+, and create a toplevel window to display the
           image data in */

        gtk_init( &argc, &argv );

        window = gtk_window_new( GTK_WINDOW_TOPLEVEL );
        if ( !window ) {
                printf( "Unable to create a window\n" );
                exit( 1 );
        }

        /* retrieve the visual of the window, then, using the server byte
           order, compute shift values used when computing pixel values
           from data read from the TIFF image raster */

        visual = gtk_widget_get_visual(window);
        byteOrder = visual->byte_order;
        gshift = 8;
        if ( byteOrder == LSBFirst ) {
                rshift = 16;
                bshift = 0;
        } else {
                rshift = 0;
                bshift = 16;
        }
```

```
/* open and parse the TIFF image file, path is argument 1 */

tif = TIFFOpen(argv[1], "r");

if ( !tif ) {
        printf( "Unable to open tiff file %s\n", argv[1] );
        exit( 1 );
}

/* retrieve width, height, and fields that are used to determine if
   the image is color and 24-bit */

TIFFGetField(tif, TIFFTAG_IMAGEWIDTH, &width);
TIFFGetField(tif, TIFFTAG_IMAGELENGTH, &height);
TIFFGetField(tif, TIFFTAG_BITSPERSAMPLE, &bitspersample);
TIFFGetField(tif, TIFFTAG_SAMPLESPERPIXEL, &samplesperpixel);

/* make sure it is the kind of image we support */

if ( bitspersample != 8 || samplesperpixel != 3 ) {
        printf( "Error: image is not RGB or is not 24-bit\n" );
        exit( 1 );
}

/* allocate a buffer big enough to hold the uncompressed image */

raster = (uint32*)malloc(width * height * sizeof (uint32));
if ( !raster ) {
        perror( "malloc" );
        exit( 1 );
}

/* retrieve the uncompressed image data */

if (!TIFFReadRGBAImage(tif, width, height, raster, 0)) {
        printf( "TIFFReadRGBAImage failed\n" );
        exit( 1 );
}

/* set the window to the size of the image, and create a vertical
   box widget into which the GtkImage will be placed */

gtk_widget_set_usize( window, width, height );
vbox = gtk_vbox_new (FALSE, 0);
gtk_container_add(GTK_CONTAINER(window), vbox);

/* create a GDK image */

gimage = gdk_image_new( GDK_IMAGE_FASTEST, visual, width, height );
if ( !gimage ) {
        printf( "Unable to create a GDK image\n" );
        exit( 1 );
}

/* extract RGB values from TIFF raster, and store in the GDK image */

for ( i = 0; i < height; i++ ) {
```

```
		for ( j = 0; j < width; j++ ) {
			RGB = raster[ i *  width + j ];

			pixel = TIFFGetR(RGB) << rshift |
				TIFFGetG(RGB) << gshift |
				TIFFGetB(RGB) << bshift;
			gdk_image_put_pixel( gimage, j,
				(height - 1) - i, pixel );
		}
	}

	/* create a clip mask. Normally, applications will not do this except
	   for special effects, I do it here to illustrate how it is done */

	mask = (GdkBitmap *) gdk_bitmap_create_from_data (window->window,
		mask_bits, mask_width, mask_height );

	/* create the gtk image. Most applications will pass NULL as the
	   second argument if no clip mask is desired */

	image = gtk_image_new( gimage, mask );

	if ( !image ) {
		printf( "Unable to create a Gtk+ image\n" );
		exit( 1 );
	}

	/* add the GtkImage widget to the vbox, and show everything */

	gtk_box_pack_start( GTK_BOX(vbox), image, TRUE, TRUE, 0);
	gtk_widget_show_all( window );
	gtk_main();
}
```

Modifying the Image

Once you have a GtkImage widget, you can change the GdkImage and/or mask with a call to gtk_image_set():

```
void
gtk_image_set(GtkImage *image, GdkImage *val, GdkBitmap *mask);
```

The argument image is an instance of GtkImage, val is an instance of GdkImage, and mask is an instance of GdkBitmap (or, a 1-bit-deep GdkPixmap). The arguments val or mask can be set to NULL if desired. Setting val to NULL will cause the GtkImage widget's requisition to be set to width = 0, height = 0, which will likely cause the containing widget to be resized. Setting mask to NULL will remove the clip mask applied to the image so that all pixels in the image will be rendered to the display.

Retrieving the Image Data and Clip Mask

To retrieve the GDK image and clip mask associated with an instance of GtkImage, call gtk_image_get():

```
void
gtk_image_get(GtkImage *image, GdkImage **val, GdkBitmap **mask);
```

The argument image is an instance of GtkImage. The argument val is a pointer to a variable of type GdkImage *, and mask is a pointer to a variable of type GdkBitmap *. On return, GdkImage will hold a reference to the GdkImage instance maintained by the GtkImage, and mask will hold a reference to its clip mask (or NULL, if no clip mask has been specified for the GtkImage instance).

GtkEntry

Class Name

```
GtkEntry
```

Parent Class Name

```
GtkEditable
```

Macros

Widget type macro: `GTK_TYPE_ENTRY`

Object to widget cast macro: `GTK_ENTRY(obj)`

Widget type check macro: `GTK_IS_ENTRY(obj)`

Supported Arguments

Prefix: `GtkEntry::`

Table 8.6 GtkEntry Arguments

Name	*Type*	*Permissions*
max_length	GTK_TYPE_UINT	GTK_ARG_READWRITE
visibility	GTK_TYPE_BOOL	GTK_ARG_READWRITE

Application-Level API Synopsis

Obtain the constant GTK_TYPE_ENTRY at runtime:
```
GtkType
gtk_entry_get_type(void);
```

Create a new instance of GtkEntry:
```
GtkWidget *
gtk_entry_new(void);
```

Create a new instance of GtkEntry with the specified max length attribute:
```
GtkWidget *
gtk_entry_new_with_max_length(guint16 max);
```

Set the text associated with the entry field:
```
void
gtk_entry_set_text(GtkEntry *entry, const gchar *text);
```

Append the text to the current text associated with the entry field:
```
void
gtk_entry_append_text(GtkEntry *entry, const gchar *text);
```

Prefix the current text associated with the entry field with text:
```
void
gtk_entry_prepend_text(GtkEntry *entry, const gchar *text);
```

Move the caret to a specified position:
```
void
gtk_entry_set_position(GtkEntry *entry, gint position);
```

Obtain a reference to the current text:
```
gchar *
gtk_entry_get_text(GtkEntry *entry);
```

Select a range of characters from the currently displayed text:
```
void
gtk_entry_select_region(GtkEntry *entry, gint start, gint end);
```

Hide or show text in an entry field. When hidden, characters that are otherwise visible are replaced by *:
```
void
gtk_entry_set_visibility(GtkEntry *entry, gboolean visible);
```

Enable or disable the user's ability to edit text:
```
void
gtk_entry_set_editable(GtkEntry *entry, gboolean editable);
```

Specify the maximum length for text, truncating the current value if needed:
```
void
gtk_entry_set_max_length(GtkEntry *entry, guint16 max);
```

Class Description

GtkEntry is Gtk+'s text field edit widget. GtkEntry supports single-line text-edit fields. Multiple-line text-editing support in Gtk+ is provided by the GtkText widget, which I will discuss in a later chapter.

The GtkEntry widget API allows you to do the following:

- Set the value displayed in the text-edit field.
- Append text to the end or prepend text to the front of the current text.
- Retrieve the value displayed in the text-edit field.
- Set the maximum length of text in a text field.
- Select text in a text field as though it were selected by the user using a pointer.
- Make text visible or invisible. Characters in an invisible text-edit field display as a series of asterisks (*).
- Make text editable (read/write) or noneditable (read-only).
- Change the position of the I-beam caret.

I will discuss each of the preceding functions in this section.

Creating an Entry Widget

There are two ways to create an instance of GtkEntry. The first is by calling gtk_entry_new():

```
GtkWidget *
gtk_entry_new(void);
```

Like most gtk_*_new() functions, gtk_entry_new() takes no arguments. It simply creates an instance of GtkEntry. The other function for creating an instance of GtkEntry is gtk_entry_new_with_max_length():

```
GtkWidget *
gtk_entry_new_with_max_length(guint16 max);
```

The argument max is used to specify a maximum length for the text to be managed by the text-edit field. Specifying a value of 0 causes GtkEntry to use the largest length allowable, which in Gtk+ 1.2 is 2,047 characters. This is also the default maximum that will be set if you call gtk_entry_new() to create the GtkEntry widget instance.

There are many times that setting the max length of a text-edit field, either at creation time or later, will be appropriate. One example would be edit fields for numeric values such as Social Security numbers, dates, phone numbers, and so forth. By fixing the length of the text allowable in the edit field, you are making it easier for users to give your application correctly formatted values.

Setting and Getting the Value of the Text Buffer

To set the value of the text buffer, call gtk_entry_set_text():

```
void
gtk_entry_set_text(GtkEntry *entry, const gchar *text);
```

The first argument is a pointer to the GtkEntry widget, and the second, text, is a pointer to the text that should be displayed. GtkEntry will make a copy of the text that you pass, so you are free to modify the passed-in string or release its memory after the call has returned.

Two additional but perhaps seldom-used functions are gtk_entry_append_text() and gtk_entry_prepend_text(). The function gtk_entry_append_text() allows you to add text to the end of the text managed by an instance of GtkEntry:

```
void
gtk_entry_append_text(GtkEntry *entry, const gchar *text);
```

The function gtk_entry_prepend_text(), on the other hand, takes the passed-in text and adds it to the front of the text managed by the GtkEntry widget.

```
void
gtk_entry_prepend_text(GtkEntry *entry, const gchar *text);
```

To obtain the text from an instance of GtkEntry, call gtk_entry_get_text():

```
gchar *
gtk_entry_get_text(GtkEntry *entry);
```

The GtkEntry will return a pointer to a buffer that it manages, so be careful not to change the contents or free the memory returned.

Changing the Attributes of an Entry Widget

To change the maximum length of an existing text-edit field, call gtk_entry_set_max_length():

```
void
gtk_entry_set_max_length(GtkEntry *entry, guint16 max);
```

As previously mentioned, setting this value to 0 or to a value greater than 2,047 will cause Gtk+ to use the value 2,047. Changing this length argument to a value that is less than the length of the currently displayed text will cause that text to be truncated.

Another attribute you can set is the visibility of the text displayed by the GtkEntry widget. The function to call is gtk_entry_set_visibility():

```
void
gtk_entry_set_visibility(GtkEntry *entry, gboolean visible);
```

The argument entry, as always, is an instance of GtkEntry. The argument visible, a gboolean, can be either TRUE or FALSE. The default value of visible for a newly created instance of GtkEntry is TRUE. If visible is set to TRUE, all characters in the text string displayed by the GtkEntry widget will be visible. If visible is set to FALSE, GtkEntry will display each character in the string as an asterisk (*), so that the true value of the text string is hidden from the user. As the user types characters into a field that is invisible, asterisks (*) will appear in place of the characters that are typed.

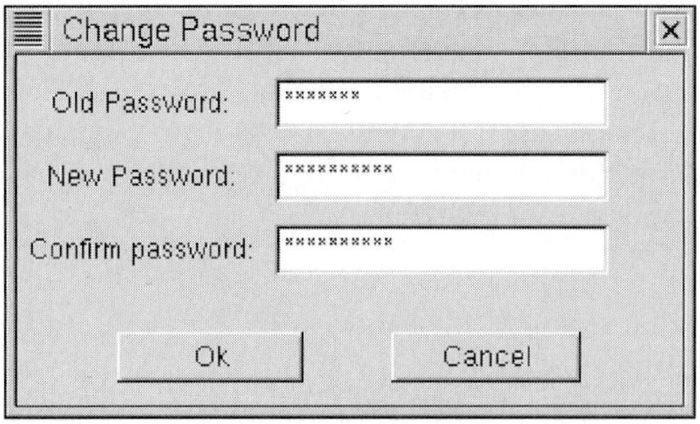

Figure 8.7 Invisible Text-Entry Field

The most common use for an invisible text-edit field is to collect a password from the user, as shown in Figure 8.7. The first field, labeled Username, has its visibility attribute set to the default TRUE value, while the field labeled Password has its visibility attribute set to FALSE.

Changing the Editable Attribute of an Edit Widget

You can cause the text displayed in a GtkEntry field to change from editable to noneditable, or from noneditable to editable, with gtk_entry_set_editable(). The default for a newly created instance of GtkEntry is TRUE. The following is the function prototype for gtk_entry_set_editable():

```
void
gtk_entry_set_editable(GtkEntry *entry, gboolean editable);
```

If editable is TRUE, the user can type into the field and make changes. If editable is FALSE, then the text is static and read-only.

One thing you might expect to happen when setting the editable attribute to FALSE would be for the GtkEntry field to become insensitive with the text rendered in a grayish color. This is not the case, however. To make a widget noneditable and insensitive, you must also call gtk_widget_set_sensitive(), as shown in the following function:

```
void
ChangeEditableAttribute( GtkEntry *w, gboolean editable )
{
        gtk_entry_set_editable( w, editable );
        gtk_widget_set_sensitive( GTK_WIDGET( w ), editable );
}
```

In some cases, users may find it confusing for an editable field that they cannot type into to be sensitive. Because of this, I recommend that you consider ensuring that the editable state and the sensitivity of the GtkEntry widget be set to the same value at all times.

Setting the Position of the Caret

The final function that allows you to set or change an attribute of a GtkEntry widget is gtk_entry_set_position():

```
void
gtk_entry_set_position(GtkEntry *entry, gint position);
```

Position is the index of the character that will appear to the right of the caret after the call is made. To set the caret to the head of the text, pass the value 0.

Simplifying Entry Widget Creation

As we saw in the preceding, the gtk_entry_new*() functions only allow you to specify the max length attribute of the text at creation time. A more general-purpose function for creating an instance of GtkEntry would also allow you to specify the text to be displayed (whether or not the field is editable), its visibility, its max length, and a selection range for the text. Here is a function that does all of this:

```
GtkWidget *
CreateGtkEntry( gchar *text, gboolean editable, gboolean visible,
        guint16 max, gint start, gint end )
{
        GtkWidget *w;

        w = gtk_entry_new_with_max_length( max );
        if ( w != (GtkWidget *) NULL ) {
                ChangeEditableAttribute( w, editable );
                gtk_entry_set_visibility( w, visible );
                if ( start < end )
                        gtk_entry_select_region( w, start, end );
                if ( text )
                        gtk_entry_set_text( w, text );
        }
        return ( w );
}
```

Here is a description of the arguments to CreateGtkEntry():

- **text** If non-NULL, the entry text will be set to the NULL-terminated string pointed to by text.
- **editable** If TRUE, the entry field is editable. If FALSE, it cannot be edited. The entry field becomes disabled if FALSE. This is due to the call to ChangeEditableAttribute().
- **visible** If TRUE, the text will be displayed normally. If FALSE, the text will display as a series of asterisks (*).
- **max** See the preceding description of gtk_entry_set_max_length().
- **start, end** If start is greater than or equal to end, these arguments are ignored. Otherwise, the text starting at index start and ending at index end will be selected.

Selecting Text

You can select a range of characters in the currently displayed text by calling gtk_entry_select_region():

```
void
gtk_entry_select_region(GtkEntry *entry, gint start, gint end);
```

The argument entry is an instance of GtkEntry. The argument start is the index of the first or leftmost character of a substring of the text currently displayed that is to be selected. The argument end is the index of the last or rightmost character to be selected. The index of the first character in an entry field is 0, while the index of the last character is the length of the text minus 1. GtkEntry does not provide a function with which you can query the current length of the text displayed. You can, however, compute the length by retrieving the text with gtk_entry_get_text() and pass the result to strlen(), or you can make use of the text_length field of the GtkEntry widget pointer. For example:

```
GtkWidget *entry;
guint16 size;

size = GTK_ENTRY( entry )->text_length;
```

I recommend that you use the gtk_entry_get_text()/strlen() approach because it is not going to break if the implementation of GtkEntry changes, and the text_length field ceases to exist. A much better solution would be for the GtkEntry widget to implement a function that could be called to obtain the current length of the text that it manages.

Summary

In this chapter, we looked at several base control classes in Gtk+. Of these, perhaps the most commonly used widget is GtkEntry. An entry widget is used to retrieve single-line text input from a user. GtkText, which is described in Chapter 14, "Text and SpinButton Widgets," can be used to retrieve multiline text. Separators, also discussed in this chapter, can be used to partition the content of a window or dialog into distinct areas. Use separators sparingly; too many can become distracting to users. Perhaps the most common use of a separator is to delimit the control and action areas in a dialog. In some cases, a frame (GtkFrame, see Chapter 11) is a more appropriate way to separate content in a window. Horizontal separators are also used in menus; see Chapter 9 for more details. This chapter also spent some time discussing GtkArrow, GtkImage, and GtkPixmap.

CHAPTER

9

MENUS

In this chapter, I will cover menus and the Gtk+ widget classes listed in Table 9.1.

Table 9.1 Widgets Covered in This Chapter

Class Name	***Description***
GtkItemFactory	A class that facilitates the creation of menus.
GtkMenu	Vertical grouping of menu items.
GtkMenuBar	Horizontal grouping of menu items.
GtkMenuItem	A selectable item in a menu or menu bar.
GtkCheckMenuItem	A menu item that can be toggled on or off; more than one check menu item can be toggled on at a time.
GtkRadioMenuItem	A menu item that can be toggled on or off; only one radio menu item in a group can be toggled on at a time.
GtkTearoffMenuItem	A menu item that facilitates tear-away menus.
GtkOptionMenu	A dialog control that consists of a button and a menu; selections from the menu change the label displayed by the button.

An additional class, GtkMenuShell, which provides a base class for both GtkMenu and GtkMenuBar, will not be covered in this chapter.

Figure 9.1 illustrates most of the Gtk+ menu system components that I discuss in this chapter. In this figure, you can see a menu bar (GtkMenuBar) that contains four menu items (GtkMenuItem) labeled File, Edit, Options, and Help. The Help menu item is activated, showing a menu (GtkMenu) that has three menu items (GtkMenuItem) labeled One, Two, and Three. The menu item labeled Two is activated, showing a pullright menu (GtkMenu) that contains five radio menu items (GtkRadioItem) labeled A, B, C, D, and E. The second of these radio menu items (labeled B) is in the selected state, meaning the user has the pointer currently positioned over the menu item but has not activated the menu item by either hitting the Enter key or releasing mouse button 1. Only one radio menu item can be selected at a time by the user (radio menu items are somewhat analogous to radio buttons, which are discussed in Chapter 5, "Labels and Buttons").

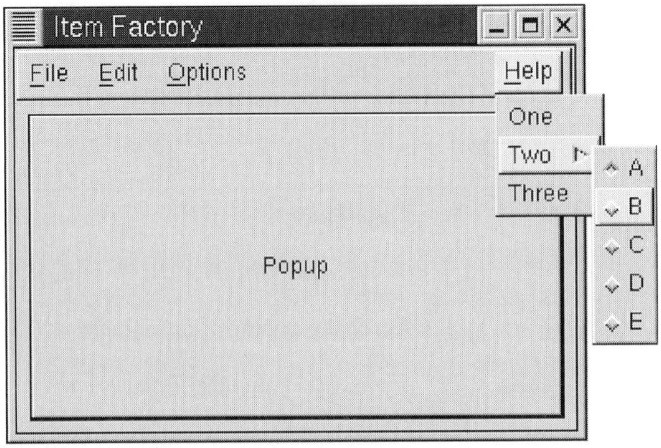

Figure 9.1 Menu System Components

Figure 9.2 illustrates the same menu bar (GtkMenuBar) shown in Figure 9.1 but with the Options menu item activated. The dashed line immediately below the Options menu item is a tearoff menu item (GtkTearOffMenuItem) that will, when activated, cause the entire Options menu to display on the user's desktop detached from the parent menu or menu bar. The Options menu's menu items are all instances of GtkCheckMenuItem. GtkCheckMenu-Item is similar to GtkRadioMenuItem except that more than one check menu item can be selected at a time by the user.

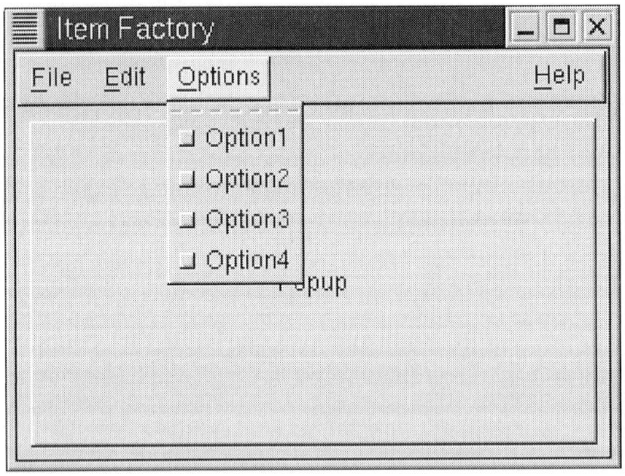

Figure 9.2 Tearoff Menus

Three classes listed in Table 9.1 that are not represented in the preceding figures are GtkMenuShell, GtkItemFactory, and GtkOptionMenu. Briefly, GtkMenuShell is a parent class for GtkMenu and GtkMenuBar. GtkMenu and GtkMenuBar are related in that they both provide a container widget for menu item children. Implementation details that would otherwise be shared by GtkMenu and GtkMenuBar are instead implemented in GtkMenuShell; GtkMenu and GtkMenuBar in turn inherit this common functionality from GtkMenuShell. GtkItemFactory is a widget class that helps simplify the creation of application menus. For many of you, GtkItemFactory is all you will need to know to add a menu to your application, and for that reason, I will present a discussion of GtkItemFactory early in this chapter.

GtkOptionMenu is the final menu widget class that I will be discussing in this chapter. GtkOptionMenu is a subclass of GtkButton. When clicked, an option menu displays a menu; selecting one of the menu items in the menu changes the value of the option menu to reflect the selected menu item. Because an option menu requires the programmer to create menu items, I cover option menus here instead of in Chapter 5 (which covers GtkButton and related classes).

GtkItemFactory

Class Name

```
GtkItemFactory
```

Parent Class Name

```
GtkObject
```

Macros

Widget type macro: `GTK_TYPE_ITEM_FACTORY`

Object to widget cast macro: `GTK_ITEM_FACTORY(obj)`

Widget type check macro: `GTK_IS_ITEM_FACTORY(obj)`

Application-Level API Synopsis

Return the constant GTK_TYPE_ITEM_FACTORY at runtime:

```
GtkType
gtk_item_factory_get_type(void);
```

Application-Level API Synopsis (Continued)

Create an instance of GtkItemFactory with an optional acceleration group:

```
GtkItemFactory *
gtk_item_factory_new(GtkType container_type, const gchar *path,
        GtkAccelGroup *accel_group);
```

Given a path (such as the path passed to gtk_item_factory_new()) and an item factory, obtain the corresponding widget (e.g., menu bar):

```
GtkWidget *
gtk_item_factory_get_widget(GtkItemFactory *ifactory,
        const gchar *path);
```

Given a widget (e.g., menu bar), find the corresponding item factory:

```
GtkItemFactory *
gtk_item_factory_from_widget(GtkWidget *widget);
```

Given a widget (e.g., menu bar) find the corresponding path:

```
gchar *
gtk_item_factory_path_from_widget(GtkWidget *widget);
```

Equivalent to gtk_item_factory_get_widget(), except retrieval is based on the numeric action that was specified at creation time:

```
GtkWidget *
gtk_item_factory_get_widget_by_action(GtkItemFactory *ifactory,
        guint action);
```

Add a new item to the factory:

```
void
gtk_item_factory_create_item(GtkItemFactory *ifactory,
GtkItemFactoryEntry *entry, gpointer callback_data,
        guint callback_type);
```

Add a set of new items to the factory:

```
void
gtk_item_factory_create_items(GtkItemFactory *ifactory,
        guint n_entries, GtkItemFactoryEntry *entries,
        gpointer callback_data);
```

Delete an item matching the specified path from the factory:

```
void
gtk_item_factory_delete_item(GtkItemFactory *ifactory,
        const gchar *path);
```

Delete an item matching the specified entry from the factory:

```
void gtk_item_factory_delete_entry(GtkItemFactory *ifactory,
        GtkItemFactoryEntry *entry);
```

Delete items matching the specified entries from the factory:

```
void
gtk_item_factory_delete_entries(GtkItemFactory *ifactory,
        guint n_entries, GtkItemFactoryEntry *entries);
```

Application-Level API Synopsis (Continued)

Display the menu defined by the factory as though the user clicked a specific mouse button at a given location and time. Factory must be for a menu (not a menu bar or an option menu):

```
void
gtk_item_factory_popup(GtkItemFactory *ifactory, guint x, guint y,
        guint mouse_button, guint32 time);
```

Same as gtk_item_factory_popup(), except specify a function to be invoked when the menu is destroyed and generic data that will be passed to the destroy function:

```
void
gtk_item_factory_popup_with_data(GtkItemFactory *ifactory,
        gpointer popup_data, GtkDestroyNotify destroy, guint x,
        guint y, guint mouse_button, guint32 time);
```

Retrieve pop-up data from an ifactory:

```
gpointer
gtk_item_factory_popup_data(GtkItemFactory *ifactory);
```

Given an ifactory's menu widget, obtain pop-up data:

```
gpointer
gtk_item_factory_popup_data_from_widget(GtkWidget *widget);
```

Specify a translation function that can be applied to menu paths as items are added to the factory:

```
void
gtk_item_factory_set_translate_func(GtkItemFactory *ifactory,
        GtkTranslateFunc func, gpointer data,
        GtkDestroyNotify notify);
```

Class Description

An item factory provides a convenient way for applications to create and manage menus, menu bars, and option menus. Using an item factory amounts to defining a data structure in your source code and making a few calls to the GtkItemFactory API. The data structure specifies the labels used for the menus and menu items and associates each menu item with a callback function that will be invoked by Gtk+ should the menu item be activated by the user.

The following is the data structure used to specify menus:

```
typedef struct _GtkItemFactoryEntry
{
        gchar *path;
        gchar *accelerator;
        GtkItemFactoryCallback callback;
        guint callback_action;
        gchar *item_type;
} GtkItemFactoryEntry;
```

The path field defines the logical position of a menu or menu item in the menu hierarchy, as well as the (untranslated) label that will be displayed by the menu or menu item in the user interface. (I have more to say about menu label translation later in this chapter.) Paths always begin with a slash (/) character and consist of one or more nodes separated by / characters. The last node in a path may have a single underscore (_) character used to define an accelerator key for the menu or menu item. If the node that contains an underscore represents a menu, the menu can be activated by the user by holding down the Alt key and pressing the key prefixed by the underscore. If the node containing the underscore is the last node in the path, then the menu item the node represents can be activated by displaying the menu and then depressing the key that is prefixed by the underscore.

The accelerator field defines the command key equivalent for the menu item. The format of this argument is a string of zero or more modifiers, followed by a string of characters used to represent a single key on the keyboard of the user. Modifiers can be any one of the following listed in Table 9.2.

Table 9.2 Modifiers

Modifier	*Key*
<alt>	Alt+_L or Alt+_R
<ctl>, <ctrl>, <control>	Control+_L or Control+_R
<shft>, <shift>	Shift+_L or Shift+_R
<mod1>, <mod2>, ..., <mod5>	X Modifier keys

Values of mod1 through mod5 are X server-dependent; to see them, you can run xmodmap:

```
$ xmodmap -pm
xmodmap:  up to 2 keys per modifier, (keycodes in parentheses):

shift       Shift_L (0x32),  Shift_R (0x3e)
lock        Caps_Lock (0x42)
control     Control_L (0x25),  Control_R (0x6d)
mod1        Alt_L (0x40),  Alt_R (0x71)
mod2        Num_Lock (0x4d)
mod3
mod4        Meta_L (0x73),  Meta_R (0x74)
mod5        Scroll_Lock (0x4e)
```

The string of characters following the modifiers defines the key to be pressed, and these strings are recognized by the Xlib function XStringToKeysym(3X11). Standard KeySym names are obtained from <X11/keysymdef.h> by removing the XK_ prefix from each name. Additional names may be supported in an implementation-dependent manner. Certain keys are not supported for use as accelerators; the GDK defines that correspond to these unsupported keys are: GDK_BackSpace, GDK_Delete, GDK_KP_Delete, GDK_Shift_L, GDK_Shift_R, GDK_Shift_Lock, GDK_Caps_Lock, GDK_ISO_Lock, GDK_Control_L, GDK_Control_R, GDK_Meta_L, GDK_Meta_R, GDK_Super_L, GDK_Super_R, GDK_

Hyper_L, GDK_Hyper_R, GDK_Mode_switch, GDK_Num_Lock, GDK_Multi_key, GDK_Scroll_Lock, GDK_Sys_Req, GDK_Up, GDK_Down, GDK_Left, GDK_Right, GDK_Tab, GDK_ISO_Left_Tab, GDK_KP_Up, GDK_KP_Down, GDK_KP_Left, GDK_KP_Right, GDK_KP_Tab, GDK_First_Virtual_Screen, GDK_Prev_Virtual_Screen, GDK_Next_Virtual_Screen, GDK_Last_Virtual_Screen, GDK_Terminate_Server, and GDK_AudibleBell_Enable.

You may notice that lock, mod2, mod4, and mod5 are not legal modifiers for the server that generated the preceding xmodmap output because GDK_Lock, GDK_Num_Lock, GDK_Meta_L, GDK_Meta_R, and GDK_Scroll_Lock are all in the list of unsupported keys. For this reason, it is probably best to not use <mod1> through <mod5> as modifiers because it is possible that the X server assigned values for these meta keys cannot be used as accelerators with Gtk+. <lock> is not a valid modifier string to begin with, so it can never be used regardless of the X server.

The field callback is a function that will be invoked once a menu item is activated. The prototype for the function depends on the callback type specified when the item is added to the item factory. Using the GtkMenuItem API discussed here, the prototype will always be as follows:

```
void
callback_fun( gpointer data, guint callback_action, GtkWidget *w );
```

An alternate API is supported for backward compatibility with GtkMenuFactory, which is not discussed in this book, and is subject to deprecation in a future release of Gtk+.

The field callback_action is an arbitrary unsigned integer value that is not interpreted by Gtk+ (however, we shall see that callback_action can be used to create categories of menus and menu items that can be acted upon as a group by some of the GtkItemFactory functions). The field widget is the widget associated with the item factory; see the following discussion of gtk_item_factory_get_widget().

The field item_type defines the type of the item in the factory, and is a string in one the following possible formats listed in Table 9.3.

Table 9.3 Factory Item Types

Type	*Meaning*
NULL, “”, “<Title>”, or “<Item>”	Simple menu item
“<CheckItem>”, “<ToggleItem>”	Check menu item
“<RadioItem>”	Radio menu item
“path”	Path of the radio item group to which the menu item being defined belongs
“<Separator>”	Menu item separator
“<Branch>”	An item to hold subitems
“<LastBranch>”	Right-justified item to hold subitems

Table 9.3 Factory Item Types (Continued)

Type	*Meaning*
“<Tearoff>”	Tearoff menu items

Creating an Item Factory

Typically, you create an array of GtkItemFactory structures and initialize the preceding fields of each element in the array to describe your menu. The following declaration defines the menu that was illustrated in Figure 9.1:

```
static GtkItemFactoryEntry menu_items[] = {
001  { "/_File",             NULL,          NULL, 0, "<Branch>" },
002  { "/File/_New",         "<control>N", handle_new, 0, NULL },
003  { "/File/_Open",        "<control>O", handle_open, 0, NULL },
004  { "/File/_Save",        "<control>S", handle_save, 0, NULL },
005  { "/File/Save _As",     NULL,          handle_save_as, 0, NULL },
006  { "/File/sep1",         NULL,          NULL, 0, "<Separator>" },
007  { "/File/Quit",         "<control>Q", gtk_main_quit, 0, NULL },
008  { "/_Edit",             NULL,          NULL, 0, "<Branch>" },
009  { "/Edit/Cu_t",         "<control>X", handle_cut, 0, NULL },
010  { "/Edit/_Copy",        "<control>C", handle_copy, 0, NULL },
011  { "/Edit/_Paste",       "<control>V", handle_paste, 0, NULL },
012  { "/_Options",          NULL,          NULL, 0, "<Branch>" },
013  { "/Options/Option1", NULL,          handle_option, 1, "<CheckItem>" },
014  { "/Options/Option2", NULL,          handle_option, 2, "<CheckItem>" },
015  { "/Options/Option3", NULL,          handle_option, 3, "<CheckItem>" },
016  { "/Options/Option4", NULL,          handle_option, 4, "<CheckItem>" },
017  { "/_Help",             NULL,          NULL, 0, "<LastBranch>" },
018  { "/Help/One",          NULL,          handle_help, 1, NULL },
019  { "/Help/Two",          NULL,          NULL, 0, "<Branch>" },
020  { "/Help/Two/A",        NULL,          handle_help, 'A', "<RadioItem>" },
021  { "/Help/Two/B",        NULL,          handle_help, 'B', "/Help/Two/A" },
022  { "/Help/Two/C",        NULL,          handle_help, 'C', "/Help/Two/A" },
023  { "/Help/Two/D",        NULL,          handle_help, 'D', "/Help/Two/A" },
024  { "/Help/Two/E",        NULL,          handle_help, 'E', "/Help/Two/A" },
025  { "/Help/Three",        NULL,          handle_help, 3, NULL },
};
```

Menus. There are five menus in the preceding array; each is denoted by an item_type field set to <Branch> (lines 001, 008, 012, and 019) or <LastBranch> (line 017). Of these entries, those with an item_type of <Branch> that contain a single / define menus in the menu bar (the object being created by the item factory in this example is a menu bar). <Branch> entries that contain more than one / character represent submenus (e.g., line 019). Using <LastBranch> causes the menu to be located to the far-right end of the menu bar. Only the last menu bar menu that is specified in the preceding array can be given an item_type of <LastBranch>.

Menu Items. Entries with an item_type field of NULL (lines 002 through 005, 007, 009 through 011, 018, and 025) are simple menu items (e.g., New, Open, Save, Cut, Copy, Paste). Each menu item can be mapped to a callback function that will be invoked by Gtk+ when the user activates the menu item. On line 002, for example, the menu item */File/_New* is mapped to the function handle_new():

```
void
handle_new( GtkWidget *w, gpointer data, guint callback_action )
```

Each simple menu item may have an accelerator, for example, <control>N is the accelerator for the */File/_New* menu item, or none (denoted by NULL). Menu items also specify a callback_action, which is an unsigned integer passed to the callback function as the third argument. For most of the menu items here, I pass 0 because the callback function makes no use of the callback_action argument. However, notice that handle_option() (lines 013 through 016) and handle_help() (lines 018, 020 through 025) both pass a callback_action argument. In handle_option(), the callback_action argument identifies which menu item was selected by the user, as in the following example:

```
void
handle_option( GtkWidget *w, gpointer data, guint callback_action )
{
        switch( callback_action ) {
                case 1: printf( "Option1 was selected\n" );
                         display_option1_help();
                         break;
                case 2: printf( "Option2 was selected\n" );
                         display_option2_help();
                         break;
                case 3: printf( "Option3 was selected\n" );
                         display_option3_help();
                         break;
                case 4: printf( "Option4 was selected\n" );
                         display_option4_help();
                         break;
        };
}
```

Simple menu items can all be defined with an item_type of "", NULL, <Title>, or <Item>.

Check Menu Items. Lines 013 through 016 all define check menu items:

```
013  { "/Options/Option1",    NULL,       handle_option, 1, "<CheckItem>" },
014  { "/Options/Option2",    NULL,       handle_option, 2, "<CheckItem>" },
015  { "/Options/Option3",    NULL,       handle_option, 3, "<CheckItem>" },
016  { "/Options/Option4",    NULL,       handle_option, 4, "<CheckItem>" },
```

A check menu item is by default unchecked; this is illustrated in Figure 9.2. Activation of a check menu item causes the check menu item's state to toggle between unchecked and checked; Figure 9.3 shows how the menu item labeled Option2 would display when selected. More than one check menu item can be selected at a single time. Determining the checked state of a check menu item will be discussed in the section later in this chapter that covers GtkCheckMenuItem.

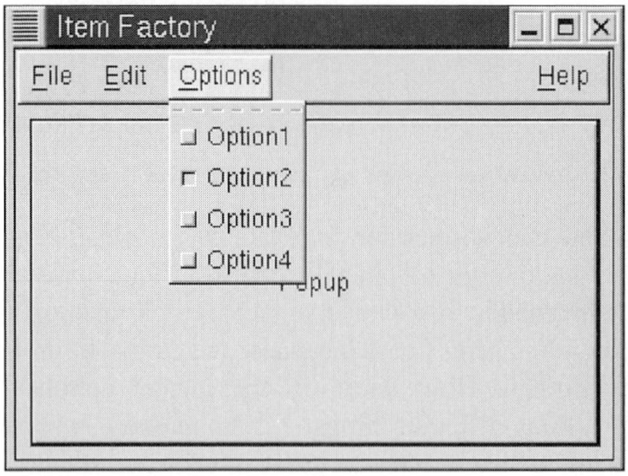

Figure 9.3 A Checked Check Menu Item

The item_type <ToggleItem> can be used in place of <CheckItem> if desired.

Radio Menu Items. Radio menu items are similar to check menu items, with the exception that only one menu item in a set of radio menu items can be selected at one time. Selecting a radio menu item causes the previously selected radio menu item to become unselected. Radio menu items are defined on lines 020 through 024:

```
020  { "/Help/Two/A",   NULL,        handle_help, 'A', "<RadioItem>" },
021  { "/Help/Two/B",   NULL,        handle_help, 'B', "/Help/Two/A" },
022  { "/Help/Two/C",   NULL,        handle_help, 'C', "/Help/Two/A" },
023  { "/Help/Two/D",   NULL,        handle_help, 'D', "/Help/Two/A" },
024  { "/Help/Two/E",   NULL,        handle_help, 'E', "/Help/Two/A" },
```

To define a radio group, create a menu item with an item_type of <RadioItem>. This menu item defines the radio menu group and its first member; specifying the path of this item in place of <RadioItem> when defining additional menu items adds them to the radio menu group. This is illustrated by the menu items defined on lines 021 through 024, each of which specifies /Help/Two/A as the item_type to add themselves to the radio group defined on line 020. I will discuss how to retrieve the state of radio items (selected vs. unselected) in the section on GtkRadioMenuItem presented later in this chapter.

Separators. Separators are defined by specifying the path of the separator and an item_type of <Separator>. The path defines the location of the separator, similar to the way in which the location of a menu item is specified. The only difference is that a Gtk+ horizontal separator widget is used as the label of the menu item, and the menu item is not selectable. The callback_action can be assigned an arbitrary value (as is the case for other menu items); the remaining fields should be set to NULL.

Tearoff Menus. Tearoff menus are, like separators, a special type of menu item. A tearoff menu should be specified as the first menu item of a menu. Like a separator, a path must be supplied. The name assigned to the tearoff menu is not used as a label; it is only used to identify the menu item. A series of dashes is displayed as the label of the menu item to indicate to the user that the menu is a tearoff menu. Generally speaking, the remaining fields should be set to NULL or zero, where applicable. The following example illustrates how one might define a File menu as a tearoff menu:

```
static GtkItemFactoryEntry file_menu_items[] =
  { "/_File",            NULL,          0,                0, "<Branch>" },
  { "/File/tearoff1",    NULL,          0,                0, "<Tearoff>" },
  { "/File/_New",        "<control>N", new_cb,            0, NULL },
  { "/File/_Open",       "<control>O", open_cb,           0, NULL },
  { "/File/_Save",       "<control>S", save_cb,           0, NULL },
  { "/File/Save _As...", NULL,          saveas_cb,        0, NULL }
}
```

The tearoff menu item is identified by the path /File/tearoff1 in the preceding example. Tearoff menus are described in more detail later in this chapter.

Creating the Application Menu Bar and Menus

Given an array of GtkItemFactoryEntry elements as previously described, it is really a simple matter to create a menu bar and the menus to which it provides access.

Creating the Item Factory. The first step is to create an instance of GtkItemFactory. This is done with a call to gtk_item_factory_new():

```
GtkItemFactory *
gtk_item_factory_new(GtkType container_type, const gchar *path,
        GtkAccelGroup *accel_group);
```

The argument container_type defines the type of menu being defined. Possible values include GTK_TYPE_MENU_BAR, GTK_TYPE_MENU, and GTK_TYPE_OPTION_MENU. Here I describe how to use GTK_TYPE_MENU_BAR; I will describe the other container types later. The argument path is a unique string that can be used to identify the item factory instance. Just about any string of printable ASCII characters will do. The argument accel_group can be set to NULL, in which case accelerators will not be supported, or it can be an instance of GtkAccelGroup, which GtkItemFactory will use when processing accelerators specified by menu item elements in your GtkItemFactoryEntry array.

The following code illustrates the creation of an an item factory named <main>, of type GTK_TYPE_MENU_BAR, that supports accelerators:

```
GtkAccelGroup *accel_group;
GtkItemFactory *item_factory;

accel_group = gtk_accel_group_new ();

item_factory = gtk_item_factory_new(GTK_TYPE_MENU_BAR, "<main>",
        accel_group );
```

Adding Menu Items to the Item Factory. The next step involved with making our menu bar is to add the items specified by the array of GtkItemFactoryEntry elements to the item factory. This can be done in one of two ways. The easiest way is to call the function gtk_item_factory_create_items():

```
void
gtk_item_factory_create_items(GtkItemFactory *ifactory,
         guint n_entries, GtkItemFactoryEntry *entries,
         gpointer callback_data);
```

The first argument, ifactory, is the item_factory returned by the call to gtk_item_factory_new(). The argument n_entries is the number of elements in the array of GtkItemFactoryEntry elements. Assuming the name of the array is menu_items, as in the preceding, pass the value sizeof(menu_items) / sizeof(GtkItemFactoryEntry). The argument entry is the address of the first element in the array of GtkItemFactoryElement elements. The argument callback_data is data passed by Gtk+ to the callback function as the first argument (and is of type gpointer, see the preceding discussion of callback function prototypes). If you have no data to pass to the callback, set this argument to NULL. Continuing the preceding example:

```
gtk_item_factory_create_items(item_factory,
         sizeof( menu_items ) / sizeof( GtkItemFactoryEntry ),
         menu_items, NULL );
```

The other way to add the items in the array would be to iterate the array and, for each item, call gtk_item_factory_create_item():

```
void
gtk_item_factory_create_item(GtkItemFactory *ifactory,
         GtkItemFactoryEntry *entry, gpointer callback_data,
         guint callback_type);
```

The argument ifactory is the item factory to add the item to, entry is a pointer to the element of type GtkItemFactoryEntry describing the item to be added, callback_data is the same as previously described for gtk_item_factory_create_items(), and callback_type should always be set to the value 1. Code that is equivalent to the preceding code which used gtk_item_factory_create_items() is:

```
int i;

for (i = 0; i < sizeof(menu_items)/sizeof(GtkItemFactoryEntry); i++)
      gtk_item_factory_create_item(item_factory,
                 &menu_items[i], NULL, 1 );
```

Retrieving the Item Factory Widget. Now that we have supplied the item factory with a description of our menu bar and the menus it contains, we need to obtain a widget that can be added to the user interface. This can be done by calling gtk_item_factory_get_widget(), passing it the item factory and the path to the menu bar:

```
GtkWidget *
gtk_item_factory_get_widget(GtkItemFactory *ifactory,
        const gchar *path);
```

To conclude our menu bar example, we would execute the following code:

```
GtkWidget *menu_bar;

menu_bar = gtk_item_factory_get_widget (item_factory, "<main>");
```

The returned widget (assuming it is not (GtkWidget *) NULL) can be added to the user interface like any other widget, for example, to a vertical box:

```
GtkWidget *vbox;

gtk_box_pack_start (GTK_BOX (vbox), menu_bar, FALSE, TRUE, 0);
```

At this point, the menu bar is a fully functioning part of our user interface.

Retrieving the Widget Corresponding to an Item in the Menu

We can obtain the widget corresponding to any element of the menu hierarchy we described to the item factory. The following code will return the GtkRadioMenuItem widget described by /Help/Two/B in the item factory:

```
myWidget = gtk_item_factory_get_widget (item_factory, "/Help/Two/B");
```

We can then use the result to interact with the radio menu item widget directly by using the functions provided by GtkRadioMenuItem and its parent classes.

Retrieving an Item Factory and Path from a Widget

We can also go the other way. Given a widget, and obtain the corresponding item factory (if any) from a widget by calling gtk_item_factory_from_widget():

```
GtkItemFactory *
gtk_item_factory_from_widget(GtkWidget *widget);
```

Given the same widget, we can also find the corresponding path:

```
gchar *
gtk_item_factory_path_from_widget(GtkWidget *widget);
```

Thus, the following code is possible:

```
GtkItemFactory *myFactory;
GtkWidget *myWidget;
gchar *path;

/* obtain the widget at path "/Help/Two/B" from item factory */

myWidget = gtk_item_factory_get_widget(item_factory, "/Help/Two/B");

/* after the following call, myFactory and item_factory should be the
```

```
   same */

myFactory = gtk_item_factory_from_widget( myWidget );

/* after the following call, path should point to the string
   "Help/Two/B" */

path = gtk_item_factory_path_from_widget( myWidget );
```

Retrieving Widgets Based on Action

Equivalent to gtk_item_factory_get_widget(), except retrieval is based on the numeric action specified at creation time, is the GtkItemFactory function gtk_item_factory_get_widget_by_action():

```
GtkWidget *
gtk_item_factory_get_widget_by_action(GtkItemFactory *ifactory,
        guint action);
```

For the preceding function to be useful, you should assign unique values to the callback_action field of the GtkItemFactoryEntry elements in your item array that describes your menus. Otherwise, gtk_item_factory_get_widget_by_action() returns the first encountered item with the specified action argument.

Deleting Items from an Item Factory

Deleting an item from the item factory can be done in one of several ways. The first of these methods deletes the item from the factory matching a path specified at factory creation time. This can be done by calling gtk_item_factory_delete_item():

```
void
gtk_item_factory_delete_item(GtkItemFactory *ifactory,
        const gchar *path);
```

The argument ifactory is, of course, the item factory. The argument path is the path of any menu or menu item. You must ensure that any underscore (_) characters that were used to define accelerators have been removed from the path argument. For example, to delete the Copy menu item defined on line 010 earlier in this chapter:

```
010  { "/Edit/_Copy",       "<control>C", handle_copy, 0, NULL },
```

You would call:

```
gtk_item_factory_delete_item( item_factory, "/Edit/Copy" );
```

The code assumes that item_factory is a handle to the item factory. If the item being deleted is a <branch> item (for example, /Edit), then each child of that branch will also be deleted. I noticed that in Gtk+ 1.2, deleting /Edit does not remove the Edit menu itself from the menu bar, which is likely a bug that may be fixed in a later version of Gtk+.

You can also delete an item matching the specified entry from the factory by calling gtk_item_factory_delete_entry():

```
void
gtk_item_factory_delete_entry(GtkItemFactory *ifactory,
```

```
GtkItemFactoryEntry *entry);
```

The argument entry is the address of the GtkItemFactoryEntry structure that was used to define the item. To delete the same entry as in the preceding example, you would call gtk_item_factory_delete_entry() as follows:

```
gtk_item_factory_delete_item( item_factory, &menu_items[9] );
```

This is because the /Edit/Copy menu item is the 10th entry in the menu_items vector. More than one entry can be deleted by passing an array of GtkItemFactoryEntry elements to gtk_item_factory_delete_entries():

```
void
gtk_item_factory_delete_entries(GtkItemFactory *ifactory,
        guint n_entries, GtkItemFactoryEntry *entries);
```

The argument n_entries is the number of elements being passed, and entries is the address of the first element in the item factory. To delete the entire menu and all of its items (using the preceding example):

```
gtk_item_factory_delete_entries(item_factory,
        sizeof( menu_items ) / sizeof( GtkItemFactoryEntry ),
        menu_items );
```

You must ensure that the n_entries elements pointed to by entries are valid and match the entries used to define the item factory in the first place.

Pop-up Menus

Given an item factory, you can display the menu defined by the factory as a pop-up menu, as though the user clicked a specific mouse button at a given location and time. For this to work, the item factory must correspond to a menu (not a menu bar or an option menu); the container_type argument passed to gtk_item_factory_new() to create the item factory must be set to GTK_TYPE_MENU for the item factory to be used as a pop-up. The function used to pop up a menu created by an item factory is gtk_item_factory_popup():

```
void
gtk_item_factory_popup(GtkItemFactory *ifactory, guint x, guint y,
        guint mouse_button, guint32 time);
```

The argument ifactory is the item factory. The remaining arguments define the nature of the button press that was used to pop up the menu. These arguments may be created by your application or come from an event. x and y specify screen-relative (not window-relative) coordinates where the menu should be placed, mouse_button is the button that was pressed, and time is the time at which the button was pressed. As I mentioned, these values can be manufactured by your application if the situation requires you to do so, but most applications will retrieve the x, y, mouse_button, and time arguments from a button_press_event event.

The following code snippet creates a File menu as a pop-up and invokes it each time the user clicks one of the mouse buttons anywhere in the application's 300×200 top-level window. The event passed to the button_press_event callback is used as a source for most of the arguments passed to gtk_item_factory_popup().

```
...

GtkItemFactory *item_factory;

gint
ButtonPressCallback( GtkWidget *widget, GdkEventButton *event,
     gpointer callback_data )
{
     gint x, y;

     gdk_window_get_origin(widget->window, &x, &y );

     gtk_item_factory_popup(item_factory, event->x + x, event->y + y,
              event->button, event->time );
}

static GtkItemFactoryEntry menu_items[] = {
 { "/_File",         NULL,          NULL, 0, "<Branch>" },
 { "/File/_New",     "<control>N", print_hello, 0, NULL },
 { "/File/_Open",    "<control>O", print_hello, 0, NULL },
 { "/File/_Save",    "<control>S", print_hello, 0, NULL },
 { "/File/Save _As", NULL,          NULL, 0, NULL },
 { "/File/sep1",     NULL,          NULL, 0, "<Separator>" },
 { "/File/Quit",     "<control>Q", gtk_main_quit, 0, NULL },
};

void get_main_menu( GtkWidget  *window )
{
     GtkAccelGroup *accel_group;
     gint nmenu_items = sizeof (menu_items) / sizeof (menu_items[0]);

     accel_group = gtk_accel_group_new ();

     item_factory = gtk_item_factory_new (GTK_TYPE_MENU, "<main>",
          accel_group);

     gtk_item_factory_create_items(item_factory, nmenu_items, menu_items, NULL);

     gtk_accel_group_attach (accel_group, GTK_OBJECT (window));
}

int main( int argc, char *argv[] )
{
     GtkWidget *window;
     GtkWidget *menu;

     gtk_init (&argc, &argv);

     window = gtk_window_new (GTK_WINDOW_TOPLEVEL);
     gtk_signal_connect (GTK_OBJECT(window), "destroy",
          GTK_SIGNAL_FUNC (gtk_main_quit), "WM destroy");
     gtk_window_set_title (GTK_WINDOW(window), "Item Factory");
     gtk_widget_set_usize (GTK_WIDGET(window), 300, 200);

     get_main_menu (window);

     gtk_widget_set_events (window, GDK_BUTTON_PRESS_MASK);
```

```
056     gtk_signal_connect (GTK_OBJECT (window), "button_press_event",
057         GTK_SIGNAL_FUNC(ButtonPressCallback), NULL);
058
059     gtk_widget_show (window);
060     gtk_main ();
061
062     return(0);
063 }
```

The item factory is defined on lines 015 through 023. Lines 025 through 038 illustrate how the item factory is created, as discussed earlier in this chapter. Note that the call to gtk_item_factory_new() sets the container type to GTK_TYPE_MENU. In main(), on lines 045 through 062, I create a simple top-level window and give it a size of 300×200. On line 053, I then call get_main_menu() to create the pop-up menu. Then the final major task of main() is to solicit button press events from the window (line 055) and register ButtonPressCallback() as the signal function to be invoked should a button press be made.

ButtonPressCallback(), on lines 003 through 013, is passed an event structure, which we use to retrieve the x, y, button, and time arguments passed to gtk_item_factory_popup(). The x and y coordinates reported are window-relative, so a call to gdk_window_get_origin() is made to retrieve the screen-relative position of the window; these offsets are added to the event coordinates to derive the screen-relative position of the mouse button press passed to gtk_item_factory_popup().

Pop-up Data. A similar function, gtk_item_factory_popup_with_data(), can be used in place of gtk_item_factory_popup(). The function gtk_item_factory_popup_with_data() requires you to specify a function to be invoked when the menu is destroyed and generic data that will be passed to the destroy function. Its function prototype is as follows:

```
void
gtk_item_factory_popup_with_data(GtkItemFactory *ifactory,
      gpointer popup_data,GtkDestroyNotify destroy,
      guint x, guint y, guint mouse_button, guint32 time);
```

The function prototype for the GtkDestroyNotifiy callback function, destroy, is as follows:

```
void
DestroyNotifyFunc( gpointer data );
```

The argument data is set by Gtk+ to the value of the popup_data argument that was passed to gtk_item_factory_popup_with_data(). The destroy (noitify) callback function is called by Gtk+ when the user selects an item from the pop-up menu or dismisses the menu by clicking outside of it (or hitting the Escape key).

You can retrieve the pop-up data associated with an item factory by making a call to gtk_item_factory_popup_data():

```
gpointer
gtk_item_factory_popup_data(GtkItemFactory *ifactory);
```

Or, given an item factory's menu widget, you can obtain the pop-up data by calling gtk_item_factory_popup_data_from_widget():

```
gpointer
gtk_item_factory_popup_data_from_widget(GtkWidget *widget);
```

Widget can be obtained from an item factory with gtk_item_factory_get_widget().

Using Pop-up Menu Data. You might wonder what purpose there would be in associating data with a pop-up menu. Pop-up menu data provides a way to set the context for a pop-up menu that can be retrieved from a menu item callback indirectly through the item factory. An example is probably the easiest way to illustrate the concept. Assume you have an application that implements an image map. An image map essentially associates portions of an image (defined as regions with an x, y offset, width, and height) with logic or data. A user mousing over, or clicking on, one portion of the image has a different context than the same operation if it were to occur over (or on) a different portion of an image. For example, a Web page might display as an image map an image of a house. Clicking on the roof might take the user to a page that discusses how roofs are built. The browser uses the x and y coordinates of the mouse press to determine in which portion of the image the button press occurred. It then performs the action associated with that portion of the image, as defined by the Web page designer.

An application might choose to implement a feature similar to Web image maps, but instead of associating an action with a button press, the application might instead pop up a menu with options for the user to select from. Referring back to the house image map example, we might display a menu with options such as Techniques, Style, Materials, Colors, and so forth, whenever the user clicks a mouse button on a particular portion of the house. What we want is for the selection of any of these menu items to be driven by the position of the menu when it was popped up. If the mouse was positioned over the image of a roof when clicked, then, for example, selecting the menu item Styles should result in the display of something related to styles of roofing. To implement such a feature, we might execute the following steps in the button press handler:

1. Correlate the button press to an object in the image, for example, a roof or a window.
2. Obtain a reference to an object that contains, or can be used to obtain, detailed information about the image object obtained in step 1.
3. Call gtk_item_factory_popup_with_data() to pop up the menu, setting the popup_data argument to the reference obtained in step 2.

Assume that we have the following data structure:

```
typedef struct _houseData {
        char *techniques;
        char *styles;
        char *materials;
        char *colors;
} HouseData;
```

And the following declaration:

```
#define WINDOW 0
#define DOOR 1
#define ROOF 2

HouseData myHouseData[] = {
        { "Cut a hole in the wall, install the window",
          "Round, Square, Clear, Opaque",
          "Saw, hammer, nails, and one window (wood, aluminum)",
          "Any color can be used" },
        { "Cut a hole in the wall, install the door",
          "Square",
         "Saw, hammer, nails, and one door (wood, steel, aluminum)",
         "Any color can be used" },
        { "Cut a hole in the ceiling, install the roof (shake, tile)",
          "Gable, flat",
          "Saw, hammer, nails, and one roof",
          "Brown, rust, gray, red" }
};
```

Element 0 of myHouseData contains data about windows, element 1 contains data about doors, and element 2 has data about roofs. The image for this example is 500 pixels wide and 400 pixels high, and there are three windows, two doors, and one roof located within the image, as defined by the following regions (the coordinates are somewhat arbitrary, and the actual values are not relevant to this discussion):

```
XRectangle roof = { 50, 50, 400, 75 };
XRectangle doors[] = { { 300, 275, 40, 100 }, { 10, 275, 40, 100 } };
XRectangle windows[] = { { 200, 140, 20, 30 }, { 140, 200, 20, 30 },
        { 380, 200, 25, 75 } };
```

An XRectangle is defined in X11/Xlib.h as follows:

```
typedef struct {
        short x, y;
        unsigned short width, height;
} XRectangle;
```

Given the preceding, we might code the button_press_event callback for the window displaying the image as follows:

```
gint
ButtonPressCallback( GtkWidget *widget, GdkEventButton *event,
     gpointer callback_data )
{
     gint i, x, y;
     gint found = 0;
     gpointer data = (gpointer) NULL;

     /* map the coordinate of the button press to an image object */

     /* check roof */

     if ( event->x >= roof.x && event->x < roof.x + roof.width &&
```

```
013                 event->y >= roof.y && event->y < roof.y + roof.height ) {
014                 data = &myHouseData[ ROOF ];
015                 found = 1;
016         }
017 
018         /* if not the roof, check for windows */
019 
020         if ( found == 0 )
021                 for ( i = 0; i < sizeof(windows) / sizeof(XRectangle); i++ )
022                         if ( event->x >= windows[i].x &&
023                                 event->x < windows[i].x + windows[i].width &&
024                                 event->y >= windows[i].y &&
025                                 event->y < windows[i].y + windows[i].height ) {
026                                         data = &myHouseData[ WINDOW ];
027                                         found = 1;
028                                 }
029 
030         /* finally, check for doors */
031 
032         if ( found == 0 )
033                 for ( i = 0; i < sizeof(doors) / sizeof(XRectangle); i++ )
034                         if ( event->x >= doors[i].x &&
035                                 event->x < doors[i].x + doors[i].width &&
036                                 event->y >= doors[i].y &&
037                                 event->y < doors[i].y + doors[i].height ) {
038                                         data = &myHouseData[ DOOR ];
039                                         found = 1;
040                                 }
041 
042         /* if user clicked in any of the image maps, then display a popup
043            menu, otherwise just return */
044 
045         if ( found == 1 ) {
046                 gdk_window_get_origin(widget->window, &x, &y );
047                 gtk_item_factory_popup_with_data(item_factory, data,
048                         NULL, event->x + x, event->y + y, event->button,
049                         event->time);
050         }
051 }
```

Basically, the preceding code checks to see if the mouse button press maps to any of the regions in the window that represent the roof or one of the doors or windows.

If a match is found, then the variable data is set to the address of the element in myHouseData that pertains to the type of object that was clicked on. On line 038, for example, data is assigned to the address of myHouseData[DOOR] because the coordinates of the mouse button press fell inside the boundaries of one of the regions specified in the array doors. The function gtk_item_factory_popup_with_data() is then called, with the popup_data argument set to *data*.

The final step is to extract the pop-up data argument from the item factory in the callback function of the pop-up menu, if and when the user selects one of the items in the pop-up menu that was displayed in the preceding. For example, the callback for the Techniques menu item would be as follows:

```
void
handle_techniques( GtkWidget *w, gpointer data,
        guint callback_action )
{
        /* assume here that item_factory is a global */

        void DisplayHelp( char *text );
        HouseData *myHouseData;

        myHouseData = (HouseData *)
                gtk_item_factory_popup_data(item_factory);

        DisplayHelp( myHouseData->techniques );
}
```

Here, we simply call gtk_item_factory_popup_data() to obtain the popup_data we assigned back in ButtonPressCallback(). The data that is retrieved is stored in a variable of type HouseData * so that we can access the techniques field, which is passed to a hypothetical function DisplayHelp(), which in turn displays the help text to the user.

Option Menus

Option menus are similar in many ways to regular or pop-up menus. However, while regular and pop-up menus are displayed dynamically, an option menu is a dialog control and is given a fixed position in the layout of the dialog. Option menus are typically used in a situation in which a user needs to select an item from a larger number of choices; for example, a dialog that lets the user select a color from a palette of 10 colors might display the color names in an option menu. The current selection of an option menu will always be displayed by the option menu, even when it is not activated. In this section, I won't go too deeply into the details of option menus, except to show how they can be created with the help of an item factory. The technique is similar to the technique used to create a menu, as described earlier in this chapter. Although gtk_item_factory_new() takes a container type argument of GTK_TYPE_OPTION_MENU, it is better to use item factory for creating the menu items displayed by the option menu and use the GtkOptionMenu API to tie the menu created to the option menu. I will now illustrate how this can be done. See the section on GtkOptionMenu later in this chapter for more details on the GtkOptionMenu API functions used in the following discussion.

The following is an array of GtkItemFactoryEntry elements that can be used to create the menu portion of an option menu:

```
static GtkItemFactoryEntry menu_items[] = {
 { "/Option1",  NULL,     handle_option, 1, NULL },
 { "/Option2",  NULL,     handle_option, 2, NULL },
 { "/Option3",  NULL,     handle_option, 3, NULL },
 { "/Option4",  NULL,     handle_option, 4, NULL },
};
```

Notice that the item_type in each of these entries is NULL. Generally, items in an option menu will be regular menu items, so you will want to specify NULL, " ", "<Title>", or "<Item>". You can, if desired, specify <separator>, <RadioItem>, or <CheckItem>, but for option menus, these choices are generally not appropriate given the way in which option menus are used. The path should consist of a slash (/) character concatenated with the menu item name. Hierarchies (e.g., /foo/bar) are not usable in option menus. The rest of the GtkItemFactoryEntry fields can be set as desired. Many applications will want to specify a callback function so that changes to the option menu can be recorded as they are made. Notice in the preceding that I register the same callback function for each menu item and use the callback_action argument to communicate to the callback function which menu item was selected by the user.

Once you have constructed a vector similar to menu_items, as shown in the preceding code, call gtk_item_factory_new() to obtain the menu. The first argument to gtk_item_factory_new() should be GTK_TYPE_MENU; the remaining arguments are as discussed earlier. Once you have the menu, you need to create an option menu and associate it with the menu created by the item factory. The following code shows how this can be done:

```
static GtkItemFactoryEntry menu_items[] = {
 { "/Option1",  NULL,      handle_option, 1, NULL },
 { "/Option2",  NULL,      handle_option, 2, NULL },
 { "/Option3",  NULL,      handle_option, 3, NULL },
 { "/Option4",  NULL,      handle_option, 4, NULL },
};

...

void
get_option_menu_menu( GtkWidget *window, GtkWidget **menu )
{
     GtkAccelGroup *accel_group;
     gint nmenu_items = sizeof (menu_items) / sizeof (menu_items[0]);

     accel_group = gtk_accel_group_new ();

     item_factory =
              gtk_item_factory_new(GTK_TYPE_MENU, "<main>", accel_group );

     gtk_item_factory_create_items(item_factory, nmenu_items, menu_items,
              NULL);

     gtk_accel_group_attach (accel_group, GTK_OBJECT (window));

     if (menu)
              /* return the actual menu created by the item factory. */
              *menu = gtk_item_factory_get_widget (item_factory, "<main>");
}

GtkWidget *window, *menu, *optionMenu;

get_option_menu_menu( window, &menu );
optionMenu = gtk_option_menu_new();
gtk_option_menu_set_menu( GTK_OPTION_MENU( optionMenu ), menu );

...
```

The function get_option_menu_menu(), called on line 031, creates the menu defined by menu_items, using GtkItemFactory. It is nearly identical to the function get_main_menu() that I presented earlier in this chapter. The second argument, on return from get_option_menu_menu(), contains the menu widget created by the item factory. On line 032, we create an option menu with a call to gtk_option_menu() and, finally, associate the menu created by the item factory with the option menu with a call to gtk_option_menu_set_menu() on line 033. Both gtk_option_menu() and get_option_menu_set_menu() are described later in this chapter. Because the menu created by the item factory is a child of the option menu after the call to gtk_option_menu_set_menu(), there is no need to call gtk_widget_show() on the menu; ensuring that the option menu widget is visible is all that is required.

Translating Menu Paths

The final item factory function I will describe allows a client to specify a translation to menu paths as they are added to a menu by the item factory:

```
void
gtk_item_factory_set_translate_func(GtkItemFactory *ifactory,
        GtkTranslateFunc func, gpointer data, GtkDestroyNotify
        notify);
```

The argument ifactory specifies the item factory, func is the translation function that your application provides, data is call data that will be passed by GtkItemFactory to the translation function (and to the notify function), and notify is a function that will be called when either the translation function previously associated with the same item factory is replaced with a new translation function (with a call to gtk_item_factory_set_translate_func()) or the item factory itself has been destroyed. In Gtk+ 1.2, for the notify function to be called, the data argument must be non-NULL.

The function prototype for a translation function is as follows:

```
gchar *
TranslateFunction(const gchar *path, gpointer func_data);
```

The path argument is the path to be translated, and func_data is the data argument that your application passed to gtk_item_factory_set_translate_func(). The entire path, including any hierarchy separators (/) and accelerator key prefixes (_) that were present when the path was defined, are also present in the passed-in path.

Although it is important to preserve each of the hierarchy separators in the path, everything else is subject to change as your translation function sees fit.

As I mentioned earlier, GtkItemFactory provides most, and for many all, of what is needed to add a menu bar and menus to your application. The rest of this chapter details most of the menu-related Gtk+ classes that GtkItemFactory makes use of. I recommend, at some point, that you take the time to read though the remainder of this chapter. Most of you, however, will find that GtkItemFactory is all you need to know to work with menus.

GtkMenuBar

Class Name

```
GtkMenuBar
```

Parent Class Name

```
GtkMenuShell
```

Macros

Widget type macro: `GTK_TYPE_MENU_BAR`

Object to widget cast macro: `GTK_MENU_BAR(obj)`

Widget type check macro: `GTK_IS_MENU_BAR(obj)`

Supported Arguments

Prefix: `GtkMenuBar::`

Table 9.4 GtkMenuBar Arguments

Name	*Type*	*Permission*
shadow	GTK_TYPE_SHADOW_TYPE	GTK_ARG_READWRITE

Application-Level API Synopsis

Retrieve the constant GTK_TYPE_MENU_BAR at runtime:

```
GtkType
gtk_menu_bar_get_type(void);
```

Create a new instance of GtkMenuBar:

```
GtkWidget *
gtk_menu_bar_new(void);
```

Insert a menu item at the end of the menu bar:

```
void
gtk_menu_bar_append(GtkMenuBar *menu_bar, GtkWidget *child);
```

Application-Level API Synopsis

Insert a menu item at the head (position 0) of a menu bar:
```
void
gtk_menu_bar_prepend(GtkMenuBar *menu_bar, GtkWidget *child);
```

Insert a menu item at an arbitrary location in a menu bar:
```
void
gtk_menu_bar_insert(GtkMenuBar *menu_bar, GtkWidget *child, gint position);
```

Set the shadow type of the menu bar:
```
void
gtk_menu_bar_set_shadow_type(GtkMenuBar *menu_bar, GtkShadowType type);
```

Class Description

A menu bar should be thought of as being a container widget designed to present and manage a set of menu items (i.e., instances of GtkMenuItem or a related class) in an application window or dialog. Most applications require only one menu bar, displayed in the application's main window. Gtk+ allows you to place a menu bar in any window or dialog, however, as needed (an example of an application that makes good use of menu bars in more than one window is the Mozilla Web browser). Your application can also have more than one menu bar in a window, but doing so is not generally considered to be a good user-interface-design decision.

Creating a Menu Bar

Using GtkMenuBar is fairly easy. The first step is to create the menu bar; this is done by calling gtk_menu_bar_new():

```
GtkWidget *
gtk_menu_bar_new(void);
```

Adding Menu Items to the Menu Bar

The next step is to add menu items to the menu bar. Menu items are displayed in a menu bar from left to right (as opposed to being displayed in a menu from top to bottom). In most cases, you add menu items to the menu bar by appending them. The first menu item appended to the menu bar will be the leftmost menu item displayed in the menu bar, and the last menu item appended to the menu bar will be displayed as the rightmost menu item.

Menu items can also be prepended to the menu bar, in which case the ordering is reversed: The first menu item that is prepended will be the rightmost menu item displayed in the menu bar. Finally, menu items can be inserted at arbitrary positions in a menu bar based on their index.

GtkMenuBar provides functions for appending (gtk_menu_bar_append()), prepending (gtk_menu_bar_prepend()), and inserting (gtk_menu_bar_insert()) menu items into a menu bar. The prototypes for gtk_menu_bar_append() and gtk_menu_bar_prepend() are identical (except for the names):

```
void
gtk_menu_bar_append(GtkMenuBar *menu_bar, GtkWidget *child);

void
gtk_menu_bar_prepend(GtkMenuBar *menu_bar, GtkWidget *child);
```

The argument menu_bar is an instance of GtkMenuBar created by a call to gtk_menu_bar_new(). The argument child is an instance of GtkWidget, an instance of GtkMenuItem (or one of its subclasses) that has been cast to GtkWidget using the GTK_WIDGET macro.

The function gtk_menu_bar_insert() allows you to place a menu item at an arbitrary location in the menu bar:

```
void
gtk_menu_bar_insert(GtkMenuBar *menu_bar, GtkWidget *child,
        gint position);
```

The function gtk_menu_bar_insert() takes an additional argument, position. Assume that the menu bar, prior to calling gtk_menu_bar_insert(), has n items. Setting position to –1, n, or any value that is greater than n has the same effect as making a call to gtk_menu_bar_append(). Setting position to 0 is equivalent to calling gtk_menu_bar_prepend(). Setting position to a value in the range $[1, n - 1]$ will cause the menu item to be inserted at the corresponding position in the menu bar.

Setting the Shadow Type

The final function discussed here, gtk_menu_bar_set_shadow_type(), allows you to set the shadow type applied to the menu bar as a whole:

```
void
gtk_menu_bar_set_shadow_type(GtkMenuBar *menu_bar,
        GtkShadowType type);
```

For a description of the possible values for type, and illustrations, see the discussion of gtk_clist_set_shadow_type() in Chapter 6.

I will present code in the next section that illustrates the use of the functions gtk_menu_bar_new() and gtk_menu_bar_append(). To present a meaningful example, I will first need to describe how GtkMenuItem works, which I will do in the following section.

GtkMenuItem

Class Name

```
GtkMenuItem
```

Parent Class Name

```
GtkItem
```

Macros

Widget type macro: `GTK_TYPE_MENU_ITEM`

Object to widget cast macro: `GTK_MENU_ITEM(obj)`

Widget type check macro: `GTK_IS_MENU_ITEM(obj)`

Supported Signals

Table 9.5 Signals

Signal Name	*Condition Causing Signal to Trigger*
activate	The menu item was activated by the user.

Signal Function Prototypes

```
void
activate(GtkMenuItem *menuitem, gpointer user_data);
```

Application-Level API Synopsis

Retrieve the constant GTK_TYPE_MENU_ITEM at runtime:

```
GtkType
gtk_menu_item_get_type(void);
```

Create a new instance of GtkMenuItem:

```
GtkWidget *
gtk_menu_item_new(void);
```

Application-Level API Synopsis (Continued)

Create a new instance of GtkMenuItem with a label:
```
GtkWidget *
gtk_menu_item_new_with_label(const gchar *label);
```

Associate a menu with a menu item:
```
void
gtk_menu_item_set_submenu(GtkMenuItem *menu_item, GtkWidget *submenu);
```

Disassociate a menu from a menu item:
```
void
gtk_menu_item_remove_submenu(GtkMenuItem *menu_item);
```

Set the placement attribute (GTK_TOP_BOTTOM or GTK_LEFT_RIGHT) of a submenu that is associated with a menu item:
```
void
gtk_menu_item_set_placement(GtkMenuItem *menu_item,
        GtkSubmenuPlacement placement);
```

Cause the specified menu item to be displayed in the selected mode (i.e., as if the user had popped up the menu containing the menu item and had traversed to the menu item without activating it):
```
void
gtk_menu_item_select(GtkMenuItem *menu_item);
```

Undo the effects from a call to gtk_menu_item_select() or from a user manually selecting a menu item:
```
void
gtk_menu_item_deselect(GtkMenuItem *menu_item);
```

Activate the specified menu item (emulates the user clicking mouse button 1 or hitting Enter when the menu item is in the selected state):
```
void
gtk_menu_item_activate(GtkMenuItem *menu_item);
```

Make the last menu item in the menu bar right-justified:
```
void
gtk_menu_item_right_justify(GtkMenuItem *menu_item);
```

Class Description

GtkMenuItem implements the visual appearance and behavior of menu items. A menu item is displayed as text in a menu bar (e.g., File, Edit, Help) or a menu (e.g., Open, Save, Quit). A menu item can be selected and activated by the user to display a menu (in the case of menu items in a menu bar, or menu items in a menu that have a submenu associated with them). Selecting and activating menu items in a menu that are not assigned a submenu causes Gtk+ to call an activate signal function that has been associated with the menu item by the application.

Creating a Menu Item

Creating a new instance of GtkMenuItem is similar to creating a new instance of GtkLabel. To create a menu item without a label, just call gtk_menu_item_new():

```
GtkWidget *
gtk_menu_item_new(void);
```

GtkMenuItem is a descendent of GtkContainer, and so a label can be associated with a menu item by calling gtk_container_add(). For example:

```
GtkWidget *label, *menu_item;

label = gtk_label_new( "File" );
gtk_container_add( GTK_CONTAINER( menu_item ), label );
```

I will illustrate the importance of separately creating menu items and their labels, as previously shown, later in this section when I illustrate how to create menu bar menu items without the use of GtkItemFactory.

If you prefer, the label displayed by a menu item can also be specified at the time the menu item is created by calling gtk_menu_item_new_with_label():

```
GtkWidget *
gtk_menu_item_new_with_label(const gchar *label);
```

The argument label is a NULL-terminated C string. Notice that gtk_menu_item_new_with_label() will not, at least in Gtk+ 1.2, parse any underscore (_) characters that you specify in the label to identify accelerator keys. For this reason, gtk_menu_item_new() is a better choice should the menu item need to have an accelerator key sequence associated with it. I present an example illustrating why this is so at the end of this section.

Submenus

A submenu can be associated with any menu item. A menu item that does not have a submenu, when activated, results in the invocation of the activate signal function assigned to the menu item, as I previously mentioned. Activating a menu item that has a submenu results in the display of the submenu. (If the menu item selected is located in the menu bar, the submenu will usually be displayed vertically. If the menu item selected is located in a menu, then the submenu will usually be displayed as a pullright menu.)

It is fairly easy to associate a submenu with a menu item or to remove a submenu from a menu item. To set the submenu of a menu item, simply make a call to gtk_menu_item_set_submenu():

```
void
gtk_menu_item_set_submenu(GtkMenuItem *menu_item, GtkWidget *submenu);
```

The argument menu_item is an instance of GtkMenuItem or one of its subclasses. The argument submenu is an instance of GtkMenu. An example call to this function will be given in the following code.

To remove a menu item's submenu, call gtk_menu_item_remove_submenu():

```
void
gtk_menu_item_remove_submenu(GtkMenuItem *menu_item);
```

A menu item's placement defines how a submenu is placed relative to the menu item that, when activated, leads to the submenu being displayed. The routine gtk_menu_item_set_placement() allows you to specify this preference:

```
void
gtk_menu_item_set_placement(GtkMenuItem *menu_item,
        GtkSubmenuPlacement placement);
```

The argument placement can be either GTK_TOP_BOTTOM or GTK_LEFT_RIGHT. By default, the placement of submenus corresponding to menu items in a menu bar is GTK_TOP_BOTTOM, and the placement of submenus corresponding to menu items in traditional menus is GTK_LEFT_RIGHT.

Right-Justifying Menu Items

Most readers have seen a menu bar that includes a menu item labeled Help and is located on the far right of the menu bar, as illustrated in Figure 9.1. The function gtk_menu_item_right_justify() is what you call in Gtk+ to position a menu in this manner:

```
void
gtk_menu_item_right_justify(GtkMenuItem *menu_item);
```

The function gtk_menu_item_right_justify() takes a single argument, the menu item to be positioned at the far right of the menu bar. It is important that the menu item be the last menu item in the menu bar; there can be no menu items to the right of the specified menu item (see gtk_menu_bar_insert() earlier). If this is not the case, the call to gtk_menu_item_right_justify() is a no-op.

Selecting and Unselecting Menu Items

The remaining calls in the GtkMenuItem API will rarely, if ever, find their way into a typical Gtk+ application.

The first, gtk_menu_item_select(), can be used to cause the specified menu item to be displayed in the selected mode. That is, gtk_menu_item_select() acts as if the user had popped up the menu containing the menu item and had traversed to the menu item without activating it (see gtk_menu_item_activate() later in this section):

```
void
gtk_menu_item_select(GtkMenuItem *menu_item);
```

The argument menu_item, of course, is an instance of GtkMenuItem that defines the menu item to be selected. To undo the effect of a selected menu item, an application can call gtk_menu_item_deselect():

```
void
gtk_menu_item_deselect(GtkMenuItem *menu_item);
```

Activating a selected menu item will cause the menu item to go to the unselected state and the activate signal function assigned to the menu item, if there is one, to be invoked. An application can activate a selected menu item with a call to gtk_menu_item_activate():

```
void
gtk_menu_item_activate(GtkMenuItem *menu_item);
```

As I mentioned earlier, I don't see the preceding functions (gtk_menu_item_select(), gtk_menu_item_deselect(), and gtk_menu_item_activate()) being used much, if at all, in an average application. These functions are used by other Gtk+ classes, however; gtk_menu_item_select() and gtk_menu_item_deslect() are used by GtkMenuShell (not covered in this book), while gtk_menu_item_activate() is used by subclasses of GtkMenuItem (e.g., GtkCheckMenuItem).

An Example

The goal of this example is to illustrate another way of implementing the GtkItemFactory example discussed earlier in this chapter. In the following, I have reproduced the declaration of the GtkItemFactoryEntry presented earlier, which was used to create the File, Edit, Options, and Help menus using GtkItemFactory:

```
static GtkItemFactoryEntry menu_items[] = {
    { "/_File",             NULL,           NULL, 0, "<Branch>" },
    { "/File/_New",         "<control>N",   handle_new, 0, NULL },
    { "/File/_Open",        "<control>O",   handle_open, 0, NULL },
    { "/File/_Save",        "<control>S",   handle_save, 0, NULL },
    { "/File/Save _As",     NULL,           handle_save_as, 0, NULL },
    { "/File/sep1",         NULL,           NULL, 0, "<Separator>" },
    { "/File/Quit",         "<control>Q",   gtk_main_quit, 0, NULL },
    { "/_Edit",             NULL,           NULL, 0, "<Branch>" },
    { "/Edit/Cu_t",         "<control>X",   handle_cut, 0, NULL },
    { "/Edit/_Copy",        "<control>C",   handle_copy, 0, NULL },
    { "/Edit/_Paste",       "<control>V",   handle_paste, 0, NULL },
    { "/_Options",          NULL,           NULL, 0, "<Branch>" },
    { "/Options/Option1",   NULL,           handle_option, 1, "<CheckItem>" },
    { "/Options/Option2",   NULL,           handle_option, 2, "<CheckItem>" },
    { "/Options/Option3",   NULL,           handle_option, 3, "<CheckItem>" },
    { "/Options/Option4",   NULL,           handle_option, 4, "<CheckItem>" },
    { "/_Help",             NULL,           NULL, 0, "<LastBranch>" },
    { "/Help/One",          NULL,           handle_help, 1, NULL },
    { "/Help/Two",          NULL,           NULL, 0, "<Branch>" },
    { "/Help/Two/A",        NULL,           handle_help, 'A', "<RadioItem>" },
    { "/Help/Two/B",        NULL,           handle_help, 'B', "/Help/Two/A" },
    { "/Help/Two/C",        NULL,           handle_help, 'C', "/Help/Two/A" },
    { "/Help/Two/D",        NULL,           handle_help, 'D', "/Help/Two/A" },
    { "/Help/Two/E",        NULL,           handle_help, 'E', "/Help/Two/A" },
    { "/Help/Three",        NULL,           handle_help, 3, NULL },
};
```

For this example, I will still make use of GtkItemFactory to create the File, Edit, Options, and Help menus, but I won't use GtkItemFactory to create the menu bar or the menu items in the menu bar. Instead, I will use the functions provided by GtkMenuBar and GtkMenuItem to create the menu bar; create the File, Edit, Options, and Help menu items; and attach to these menu items the menus created by the GtkItemFactory. If you are not familiar with GtkItem-Factory, I recommend that you return to the start of this chapter and read about it.

The following are the GtkItemFactoryEntry vectors used to create the menus that will be attached to the File, Edit, Options, and Help menus.

```
static GtkItemFactoryEntry menu_items_1[] = {
         { "/_New",      "<control>N", print_hello, 2, NULL },
         { "/_Open",     "<control>O", print_hello, 0, NULL },
         { "/_Save",     "<control>S", print_hello, 0, NULL },
         { "/Save _As", NULL,          NULL, 0, NULL },
         { "/sep1",     NULL,          NULL, 0, "<Separator>" },
         { "/Quit",     "<control>Q", gtk_main_quit, 0, NULL },
};

static GtkItemFactoryEntry menu_items_2[] = {
         { "/Cu_t",      "<control>X", print_hello, 0, NULL },
         { "/_Copy",     "<control>C", print_hello, 0, NULL },
         { "/_Paste",    "<control>V", print_hello, 0, NULL },
};

static GtkItemFactoryEntry menu_items_3[] = {
         { "/Option1",  NULL,       handle_option, 1, "<CheckItem>" },
         { "/Option2",  NULL,       handle_option, 2, "<ToggleItem>" },
         { "/Option3",  NULL,       handle_option, 3, "<CheckItem>" },
         { "/Option4",  NULL,       handle_option, 4, "<ToggleItem>" },
};

static GtkItemFactoryEntry menu_items_4[] = {
         { "/One",      NULL,             NULL, 0, NULL },
         { "/Two",      NULL,             NULL, 0, "<Branch>" },
         { "/Two/A",    NULL,             NULL, 0, "<RadioItem>" },
         { "/Two/B",    NULL,             NULL, 0, "/Two/A" },
         { "/Two/C",    NULL,             NULL, 0, "/Two/A" },
         { "/Two/D",    NULL,             NULL, 0, "/Two/A" },
         { "/Two/E",    NULL,             NULL, 0, "/Two/A" },
         { "/Three",    NULL,             NULL, 0, NULL },
}        ;
```

Essentially what I've done here is remove the <Branch> menu items associated with the File, Edit, Options, and Help menus, as well as the portion of the path associated with each of these branches from the remaining paths in the declarations. For example, I removed the following line:

```
012  { "/_Options", NULL, NULL, 0, "<Branch>" },
```

and I changed the following line:

```
013 { "/Options/Option1", NULL, handle_option, 1, "<CheckItem>" },
```

to:

```
{ "/Option1",  NULL, handle_option, 1, "<CheckItem>" },
```

The only change to line 013, as you can see, is that the /Options portion of the path, corresponding to line 012 that was removed, has been removed from the path that defines the Option1 menu item.

I placed the menu definitions in separate GtkItemFactoryEntry vectors because we are going to create separate instances of GtkItemFactory for each menu.

Creating the Menu Bar and Attaching the Accelerator Group. The first code of interest creates an instance of GtkMenuBar:

```
GtkWidget *menubar;

menubar = gtk_menu_bar_new();
```

The function gtk_menu_bar_new() was described earlier in this chapter. After adding the menu bar widget to the window, I then create an accelerator group that is used to manage the accelerators (keyboard shortcuts) for each of the menu items in the menu bar as well as each of the menu items in the menus created by GtkItemFactory:

```
GtkWidget *window;
GtkAccelGroup *accel_group;

accel_group = gtk_accel_group_new ();
gtk_accel_group_attach (accel_group, GTK_OBJECT (window));
```

We will only need one accelerator group attached to the window within which the menu bar, and the menus that it manages, are placed.

Creating the Menus. Next I call the functions that create the menus previously described, utilizing GtkItemFactory for this purpose. To make the code a little easier to read for this sample, I wrote one function for each menu (File, Edit, Options, and Help) created. The function get_file_menu(), for example, is used to create the File menu:

```
void
get_file_menu( GtkWidget **menu, GtkAccelGroup *accel_group )
{
        gint nmenu_items_1 = sizeof (menu_items_1) /
        sizeof (menu_items_1[0]);

        item_factory = gtk_item_factory_new (GTK_TYPE_MENU,
                "<main_1>", accel_group);

        gtk_item_factory_create_items(item_factory, nmenu_items_1,
                menu_items_1, NULL);

        /* Return the actual menu bar created by the item factory. */
```

```
        if (menu)
                *menu = gtk_item_factory_get_widget (item_factory,
                        "<main_1>");
}
```

This function is similar to the function get_main_menu() presented earlier in the chapter; a major difference is that we now pass an accelerator group to get_file_menu() as opposed to creating one (because all menus can share the same accelerator group, as I mentioned earlier).

The call to get_file_menu() looks like this:

```
GtkWidget *menu1;

...

get_file_menu(&menu1, accel_group);
```

The code presented so far should be no surprise if you read the description of GtkItemFactory presented earlier in the chapter. Now that we have the menus and a menu bar, let's take a look at how to add the File, Edit (and so on) menu items to the menu bar and associate the menus created with GtkItemFactory with these menu items.

Adding Menu Items. Let's start with the File menu. First we create a menu item for the File menu:

```
GtkWidget *menu_item_1;

menu_item_1 = gtk_menu_item_new();
```

Notice that I did not use gtk_menu_item_new_with_label(). To get the Alt+F accelerator to work with the menu item, you must create the menu item and its label separately. For example, the following code will not work in Gtk+ 1.2:

```
menu_item_1 = gtk_menu_item_new_with_label( "_File" );
```

This is because gtk_menu_item_new_with_label() does not process underscore (_) characters embedded in the label. To get the accelerator to work, we make use of GtkAccelLabel:

```
GtkWidget *label;

label = gtk_accel_label_new( "_File" );
```

We also make use of gtk_label_parse_uline() (described in Chapter 5):

```
guint accel_key;

accel_key = gtk_label_parse_uline (GTK_LABEL(label), "_File" );
```

The returned accelerator key (in this case, GDK_F) is associated with the menu item and the accelerator group with a call to gtk_widget_add_accelerator():

```
gtk_widget_add_accelerator (menu_item_1, "activate_item",
        accel_group, accel_key, GDK_MOD1_MASK, GTK_ACCEL_LOCKED);
```

Associating the Menu with Its Menu Item. That does it for the complicated work. Now all we need to do is add the label to the menu item (recall that a menu item is a container), add the menu item to the menu bar, and then associate the File menu we created earlier with GtkItemFactory with our menu item. The following three lines of code accomplish this:

```
gtk_container_add( GTK_CONTAINER( menu_item_1 ), label );
gtk_menu_bar_append( GTK_MENU_BAR( menubar ), menu_item_1 );
gtk_menu_item_set_submenu( GTK_MENU_ITEM( menu_item_1 ), menu1 );
```

One additional call is made to cause the Help menu item to be displayed at the far-right end of the menu bar:

```
GtkWidget *menu_item_4;          // Help menu

gtk_menu_item_right_justify( menu_item_4 );
```

Check Menu Items and Radio Menu Items

The next two classes I will cover in this chapter, GtkCheckMenuItem and GtkRadioMenu-Item, are subclasses of GtkMenuItem. Instances of either class may be used wherever an instance of GtkMenuItem is used. Each of these subclasses adds to the core functionality of GtkMenuItem. GtkCheckMenuItem allows users to toggle the menu item on or off, as does GtkRadioMenuItem. In the case of GtkCheckMenuItem, more than one check menu item can be toggled on in a menu, which is not the case for menus containing radio menu items. In menus containing radio menu items, only one radio menu item in a menu may be toggled on at any given time. Toggle indicators are displayed to the left of the menu item label for both check menu and radio menu items. Squares are used for check menu items, and diamonds are used for radio menu items. Figures 9.1 and 9.2 illustrate menus that use radio menu and check menu items, respectively.

Because the only differences between GtkCheckMenuItem and GtkRadioMenuItem are in how the toggled indicator is rendered and the number of toggled items allowed in a menu, GtkRadioMenuItem is implemented as a subclass of GtkCheckMenuItem. This means that all attributes, signals, and APIs associated with GtkMenuItem are available for use by instances of GtkCheckMenuItem, and similarly, GtkRadioMenuItem may make use of whatever functionality is available to either GtkCheckMenuItem or GtkMenuItem.

GtkCheckMenuItem

Class Name

```
GtkCheckMenuItem
```

Parent Class Name

```
GtkMenuItem
```

Macros

Widget type macro: `GTK_TYPE_CHECK_MENU_ITEM`

Object to widget cast macro: `GTK_CHECK_MENU_ITEM(obj)`

Widget type check macro: `GTK_IS_CHECK_MENU_ITEM(obj)`

Supported Signals

Table 9.6 Signals

Signal Name	*Condition Causing Signal to Trigger*
toggled	Generated whenever the menu item is activated or an application toggles the menu item.

Signal Function Prototypes

```
void toggled( GtkCheckMenuItem *checkmenuitem, gpointer user_data);
```

Application-Level API Synopsis

Obtain the constant GTK_TYPE_CHECK_MENU_ITEM at runtime:

```
GtkType
gtk_check_menu_item_get_type(void);
```

Create a new instance of GtkCheckMenuItem without a label:

```
GtkWidget *
gtk_check_menu_item_new(void);
```

Application-Level API Synopsis

Create a new instance of GtkCheckMenuItem with a label:

```
GtkWidget *
gtk_check_menu_item_new_with_label(const gchar *label);
```

Activate a check menu item (or a radio menu item):

```
void
gtk_check_menu_item_set_active(GtkCheckMenuItem *check_menu_item,
        gboolean is_active);
```

Specify whether toggles should be shown always or only during prelight:

```
void
gtk_check_menu_item_set_show_toggle(GtkCheckMenuItem *menu_item,
        gboolean always);
```

Class Description

A menu containing check menu items provides users with a way to choose one or more of the items present in the menu. A toggle indicator, rendered as a filled square to the left of the menu item label, indicates the selections that have been made by the user. Selecting a check menu item results in the invocation of a callback menu of the same type invoked for a regular menu item (GtkMenuItem). This allows an application to easily associate an action in response to the toggling of a check menu item by the user.

Because GtkCheckMenuItem inherits from GtkMenuItem, you should take the time to become familiar with GtkMenuItem (described earlier in this chapter). With the exception of the functions gtk_menu_item_get_type(), gtk_menu_item_new(), and gtk_menu_item_new_with_label(), all of the functions available to instances of GtkMenuItem can also be used by instances of GtkCheckMenuItem. For example, if you want to set the submenu of a check menu item, your application may call gtk_menu_item_set_submenu(). The function gtk_menu_item_set_submenu(), as well as the other functions provided by GtkMenuItem, take a GtkMenuItem instance as an argument; therefore, you will need to cast instances of GtkCheckMenuItem (or instances of GtkWidget, depending on how you declared the variable holding the instance of GtkCheckMenuItem) to GtkMenuItem using the GTK_MENU_ITEM macro. For example:

```
GtkWidget *myCheckMenuItem;

...

gtk_menu_item_set_submenu( GTK_MENU_ITEM( myCheckMenuItem ), menu1 );
```

Check menu items prove themselves useful in much the same context as a group of check buttons (see GtkCheckButton, Chapter 5) proves useful. Both allow a user to choose multiple options from a set of many. However, using check menu items allows the programmer to embed the choices to be provided to the user in a menu. Often, this will require far less space than would be required by an equivalent set of check buttons displayed in a dialog.

Creating Check Menu Items

Menus with check menu items are constructed just like menus containing regular menu items. You can use GtkItemFactory (described earlier in this chapter) to create menus containing check menu items by specifying "<CheckItem>" instead of "<Item>", " ", or NULL as the item type of the check menu item in the GtkItemFactoryEntry vector.

Check menu items can also be created using functions similar to those used to create instances of GtkMenuItem. The function gtk_check_menu_item_new() creates a menu item without a label:

```
GtkWidget *
gtk_check_menu_item_new(void);
```

The function gtk_check_menu_item_new_with_label(), on the other hand, creates an instance of GtkCheckMenuItem with a label:

```
GtkWidget *
gtk_check_menu_item_new_with_label(const gchar *label);
```

Analogous routines defined by GtkMenuItem are gtk_menu_item_new() and gtk_menu_item_new_with_label(), respectively. If your application must provide accelerators for one or more of its check menu items and you will not be using GtkItemFactory to define your menus, then you should read the sections on gtk_menu_item_new() and gtk_menu_item_new_with_label() that I presented earlier in this chapter (see the section on GtkMenuItem).

Using Check Menu Items

As I mentioned, check menu items are useful because they allow an application user to select more than one item from a set of menu items being displayed in a menu. Check menu items provide visual feedback to the user indicating their state, either active (a filled box to the left of the menu item label) or inactive (an unfilled box to the left of the menu item label). This state will persist during the lifetime of the GtkCheckMenuItem instance and goes away as soon as the GtkCheckMenuItem instance is destroyed. Often, an application will want to persist with the choices made by the user across subsequent invocations of the application.

To implement such a feature, an application must track all selections made by the user in the menu, record these changes somewhere, and then, in subsequent invocations of the menu, activate the check menu items corresponding to previously made selections prior to showing the menu to the user. Tracking check menu item selections can be achieved by registering a "toggled" signal function with the check menu item. If the menu item was created using GtkItemFactory, the check menu item instance can be obtained by calling gtk_item_factory_get_widget() or gtk_item_factory_get_widget_by_action() (see GtkItemFactory, described earlier in this chapter).

The toggled signal function will be passed the check menu item instance as an argument, so a single toggled signal function can be used for all check menu items in a menu. The following code illustrates how one might code a toggled signal function to track selections in a menu containing three check menu items, as well as register the signal function with each check menu item instance. The code assumes that the three check menu items have already been created and that their handles are stored in variables named checkMenuItem1, checkMenuItem2, and checkMenuItem3. To make the example simple, three gint variables are statically declared to hold the toggled state of each check menu item and are passed by reference to the signal function via the signal function callback data argument.

```
...

GtkWidget *chMenuItem1, *chMenuItem2, *chMenuItem3;
static gint item1State, item2State, item3State;

...

// register the toggled signal function with each menu item

gtk_signal_connect (GTK_OBJECT (checkMenuItem1), "toggled",
        GTK_SIGNAL_FUNC (ToggledFunction), (gpointer) &item1State);
gtk_signal_connect (GTK_OBJECT (checkMenuItem2), "toggled",
        GTK_SIGNAL_FUNC (ToggledFunction), (gpointer) &item2State);
gtk_signal_connect (GTK_OBJECT (checkMenuItem3), "toggled",
        GTK_SIGNAL_FUNC (ToggledFunction), (gpointer) &item3State);

...
```

The toggled signal function simply casts the passed-in widget to an instance of GtkCheckMenuItem (checkMenuItem) and the passed-in callback_data argument to a pointer to gint (state). It then retrieves the toggled state from the widget, storing it the variable pointed to by state:

```
void
ToggledFunction( GtkWidget *widget, gpointer callback_data )
{
        GtkCheckMenuItem *checkMenuItem = (GtkCheckMenuItem *)
        widget; gint *state = (gint *) callback_data;

        *state = checkMenuItem->active;
}
```

Setting the State of a Check Menu Item

As it turns out, GtkCheckMenuItem (as of Gtk+ 1.2) does not provide a function that can be called to check the toggled state of a check menu item. However, the active "member" of the GtkCheckMenuItem instance does indicate the toggled state of the menu item. If toggled on, the value will be 1; otherwise, it will be 0. When the application exits, it can store these values to disk so that they can be used, the next time the application is invoked, to set the initial state of the check menu items. To set the toggled (or active) state of a check menu item, an application calls gtk_menu_item_set_active():

```
void
gtk_check_menu_item_set_active(GtkCheckMenuItem *check_menu_item,
        gboolean is_active);
```

The first argument is an instance of GtkCheckMenuItem, and the second argument is a gboolean (possible values are TRUE (1) and FALSE (0)). The following code illustrates how one might set the toggled state of the three check menu items in the previous example using state that was stored to disk by the application when it last exited:

```
GtkWidget *chMenuItem1, *chMenuItem2, *chMenuItem3;
static gint item1State, item2State, item3State;

// read previously saved values from disk

ReadStateFromDisk( &item1State, &item2State, &item3State );

// set state of checked menu items based on this state

gtk_check_menu_item_set_active( GTK_CHECK_MENU_ITEM( chMenuItem1 ),
        item1State );
gtk_check_menu_item_set_active( GTK_CHECK_MENU_ITEM( chMenuItem2 ),
        item2State );
gtk_check_menu_item_set_active( GTK_CHECK_MENU_ITEM( chMenuItem3 ),
        item3State );
```

The final function defined by GtkCheckMenuItem that is discussed here specifies whether an inactive toggle indicator displayed to the left of a check menu item label will be displayed always or only when the check menu item is in prelight mode (e.g., when the mouse is positioned over the check menu item by the user). By default, check menu items that are active will always display an indicator, and inactive check menu items will not. The function gtk_check_menu_item_set_show_toggle() changes the default setting:

```
void
gtk_check_menu_item_set_show_toggle(GtkCheckMenuItem *menu_item,
        gboolean always);
```

The argument menu_item is an instance of GtkCheckMenuItem (or GtkRadioMenuItem). The argument always is a boolean that specifies, when set to TRUE (1), that the toggled (active) indicator should be displayed regardless of the active state of the check menu item. If set to FALSE (0), the indicator should only be drawn for the check menu item when the check menu item state is active or toggled on.

The next class discussed in this chapter, GtkRadioMenuItem, inherits from the Gtk CheckMenuItem class, so everything previously presented for check menu items is applicable to radio menu items, except where noted in the following.

GtkRadioMenuItem

Class Name

```
GtkRadioMenuItem
```

Parent Class Name

```
GtkCheckMenuItem
```

Macros

Widget Type Macro: `GTK_TYPE_RADIO_MENU_ITEM`

Object to Widget Cast Macro: `GTK_RADIO_MENU_ITEM(obj)`

Widget Type Check Macro: `GTK_IS_RADIO_MENU_ITEM(obj)`

Application-Level API Synopsis

Retrieve the constant GTK_TYPE_RADIO_MENU_ITEM at runtime:

```
GtkType
gtk_radio_menu_item_get_type(void);
```

Create a new radio menu item widget:

```
GtkWidget *
gtk_radio_menu_item_new(GSList *group);
```

Create a new radio item widget with a label:

```
GtkWidget *
gtk_radio_menu_item_new_with_label(GSList *group,
        const gchar *label);
```

Get the radio group associated with a radio menu item:

```
GSList *
gtk_radio_menu_item_group(GtkRadioMenuItem *radio_menu_item);
```

Set the radio group associated with a radio menu item:

```
void
gtk_radio_menu_item_set_group(GtkRadioMenuItem *radio_menu_item
        GSList *group);
```

Class Description

GtkRadioMenuItem is fundamentally the same as GtkCheckMenuItem, except for one major difference: Applications can define groups of radio menu items such that GtkRadioMenuItem will guarantee that only one radio menu item in a group can be toggled active by the user at any given time. The functions defined by GtkRadioMenuItem enable applications to create instances of GtkRadioMenuItem and manage groups of radio menu items. Additional functionality is inherited from GtkCheckMenuItem and GtkMenuItem.

Creating a Radio Menu Item

Working with GtkRadioMenuItem is easy and is best illustrated by an example. Assume we are creating a menu that allows the user to select his or her month of birth (e.g., January, February, and so on). We can create radio menu items using one of two functions. The function gtk_radio_menu_item_new() creates a radio menu item without a label:

```
GtkWidget *
gtk_radio_menu_item_new(GSList *group);
```

The function gtk_radio_menu_item_new_with_label() creates a radio menu item with the specified label:

```
GtkWidget *
gtk_radio_menu_item_new_with_label(GSList *group, const gchar *label);
```

These functions are similar to the instantiation functions provided by GtkMenuItem and GtkCheckMenuItem; refer to the descriptions of gtk_menu_item_new() and gtk_menu_item_new_with_label() earlier in this chapter for basic information on how to use these functions correctly. These functions differ from their counterparts in GtkMenuItem and GtkCheckMenuItem in that they both accept an argument of type GSList * as their first parameter. This argument can be used to specify the radio group to which the menu item belongs. If group is set to NULL, a new radio group is created for the radio menu item, which is added to the radio group as its first member. Also, the radio menu item is made active. If, however, group is non-NULL, then group defines the radio group to which the radio menu item is to be added.

Retrieving a Radio Button's Radio Group

Before we get into the example that I just mentioned, I need to describe one remaining function, gtk_radio_menu_item_group():

```
GSList *
gtk_radio_menu_item_group(GtkRadioMenuItem *radio_menu_item);
```

The function gtk_radio_menu_item_group() retrieves the radio group from the specified radio menu item, returning it to the caller.

An Example

Now I have presented enough information to create the example I promised earlier. Here is the listing:

```
typedef struct _menutype {
        unsigned char type;
        char *name;
        GtkSignalFunc func;
} MenuType;

void
event_menu_cb(GtkWidget *widget, int callback_data)
{
}

MenuType events[] = {
     { RUNNING, "Running", GTK_SIGNAL_FUNC(event_menu_cb) },
     { CYCLING, "Cycling", GTK_SIGNAL_FUNC(event_menu_cb) },
     { BLADING, "Blading", GTK_SIGNAL_FUNC(event_menu_cb) },
     { JOGGING, "Jogging", GTK_SIGNAL_FUNC(event_menu_cb) },
     { WALKING, "Walking", GTK_SIGNAL_FUNC(event_menu_cb) }
};

GtkWidget *
build_menu( MenuType *menudata, size_t size )
{
        GtkWidget *menu;
        GtkWidget *menuitem;
        GSList *group;
        int i;

        menu = gtk_menu_new ();
        group = NULL;

        for ( i = 0; i < size / sizeof( MenuType ); i++ ) {
                menuitem = gtk_radio_menu_item_new_with_label(group,
                               menudata[i].name);
                gtk_signal_connect(GTK_OBJECT (menuitem), "activate",
                               (GtkSignalFunc) menudata[i].func,
                               (gpointer) menudata[i].type);
                group = gtk_radio_menu_item_group(
                               GTK_RADIO_MENU_ITEM (menuitem));
                gtk_menu_append (GTK_MENU (menu), menuitem);
                gtk_widget_show(menuitem);
        }
        return menu;
}

main( int argc, char *argv[] )
{
        GtkWidget *menu;
```

```
048
049         build_menu( &events[0], sizeof( events ) );
050 }
```

The idea behind the example is to show how to create a menu that contains radio menu items. Each of the radio menu items in the menu will be placed in a single radio group; this ensures that only one item in the menu can be selected at a time by the user.

On lines 001 through 005, I define a type, MenuType, which contains three fields. The first of these fields, type, is an integer passed via the callback_data argument of the "activate" signal function, event_menu_cb(), which is defined on lines 007 through 010. The advantage to passing this type value (each constant is given a unique value, e.g., RUNNING is set to 1, CYCLING is set to 2) as an argument to the signal function is that it communicates to the signal function which of the radio menu items was activated. The second field of the MenuType type defines the label of the radio menu item. The third and final field is a pointer to the signal function that will be invoked when the radio menu item is made active by the user. The definition of all the radio menu items included in the menu is shown on lines 012 through 018.

The function build_menu() is responsible for creating a menu based on the MenuType vector passed to it as an argument (see line 049 for an example call). On line 028, an instance of GtkMenu is created; each radio menu item created in the loop on lines 031 through 041 will be appended to this menu (this is done on line 039 with a call to gtk_menu_append()).

Let's focus now on how the radio menu items are created and added to the radio group. On line 029, the variable "group" is set to NULL. This will be its value when gtk_radio_menu_item_new_with_label() is called on line 032 the first time through the loop. Since the first radio menu item is created with a NULL radio group, a new radio group will be created by GtkRadioMenuItem, and the Running radio menu item will be added to the group as its only member. On line 037, the code queries the group of the Running radio menu item and stores it in the "group" variable. Thus, the next time that gtk_radio_menu_item_new_with_label() is called, the "group" argument will be set to the radio to which the Running radio menu item belongs. The result is that the next radio menu item, Cycling, will be added to the same group to which the Running menu item belongs. From here on out, the call to gtk_radio_menu_item_group() is actually unnecessary because the group returned will always be the same group to which the previously created radio menu items belong. Therefore, all of the radio menu items will be placed in the same radio group, which is the desired result.

Setting the Radio Group of a Radio Menu Item

The final function supported by GtkRadioMenuItem is gtk_radio_menu_item_set_group():

```
void
gtk_radio_menu_item_set_group(GtkRadioMenuItem *radio_menu_item,
        GSList *group);
```

This function takes a radio menu item and a group (retrieved from some other radio menu item with a call to gtk_radio_menu_item_group()). The radio menu item will be removed from the group it currently belongs to and be placed in the specified group.

GtkTearoffMenuItem

Class Name

```
GtkTearoffMenuItem
```

Parent Class Name

```
GtkMenuItem
```

Macros

Widget type macro: `GTK_TYPE_TEAROFF_MENU_ITEM`

Object to widget cast macro: `GTK_TEAROFF_MENU_ITEM(obj)`

Widget type check macro: `GTK_IS_TEAROFF_MENU_ITEM(obj)`

Application-Level API Synopsis

Retrieve the constant GTK_TYPE_TEAROFF_MENU_ITEM at runtime:

```
GtkType
gtk_tearoff_menu_item_get_type(void);
```

Create a new instance of GtkTearoffMenuItem:

```
GtkWidget *
gtk_tearoff_menu_item_new(void);
```

Class Description

GtkTearoffMenuItem is a subclass of GtkMenuItem. For the most part, this means that GtkTearoffMenuItem instances can be used anywhere that an instance of GtkMenuItem is used. However, tearoff menu items are a special type of menu item in that a tearoff menu item does not have a callback function, nor does it have the ability to manage or contain a label. The Options menu shown in Figure 9.3 is a tearoff menu. Visually, a tearoff menu looks like any other menu, except a tearoff menu has a tearoff menu item, which is represented by a series of dashes seen in Figure 9.3 above the Option1 menu item.

Using a Tearoff Menu

Positioning the mouse over the tearoff menu item and pressing mouse button 1 will cause the tearoff menu to detach and display in its own top-level window, as illustrated in Figure 9.4. The tearoff menu item, as you can see, is still visible; selecting it once again will cause the tearoff menu to dismiss. The tearoff menu can also be dismissed by repeating the steps that were followed to display the tearoff menu item and detach it from the menu bar in the first place. While a tearoff menu is detached, selecting a menu item in the tearoff menu will result in the same behavior as if the menu item were selected from the menu while still attached in its original, undetached location. Users may redisplay the menu in its undetached state and select an item from it. Generally, this is not a problem. For example, making a menu item insensitive with a call to gtk_widget_set_sensitive() will cause both of the menu items, the one displayed in the detached tearoff menu and the one displayed in the attached menu, to be made insensitive.

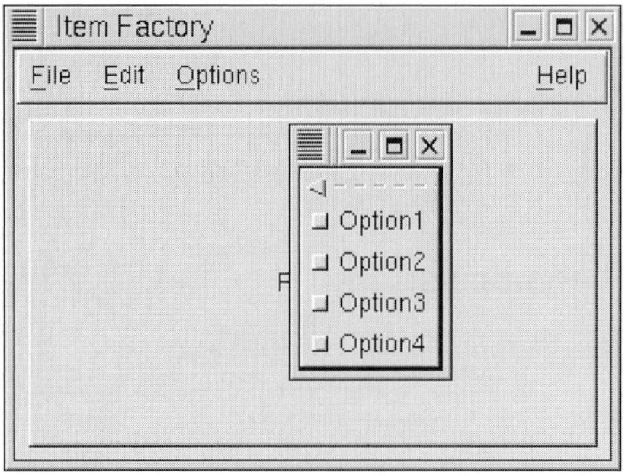

Figure 9.4 Detached Tearoff Menu

Creating a Tearoff Menu

Tearoff menu items should be made the first menu item in the menu to which they are added and should be the only tearoff menu item added to the menu. To add a tearoff menu item to a menu, create a GtkTearoffMenuItem instance by calling gtk_tearoff_menu_item_new():

```
GtkWidget *
gtk_tearoff_menu_item_new(void);
```

Once the menu item has been created, you can add the menu item to the menu with a call to gtk_menu_append() or an equivalent function, as in the following example code:

```
GtkWidget *menu, *menu_item;

menu_item = gtk_tearoff_menu_item_new();
gtk_menu_append (GTK_MENU (menu), menu_item);
gtk_widget_show (menu_item);
```

This ends my discussion of GtkMenuItem and related classes. The next class that I will discuss, GtkMenu, is similar to GtkMenuBar in that the basic purpose of a menu is to act as a container for menu items, just like a menu bar. The major difference between menu bars and menus, of course, is that a menu arranges menu items vertically, while a menu bar arranges them horizontally.

GtkMenu

Class Name

```
GtkMenu
```

Parent Class Name

```
GtkMenuShell
```

Macros

Widget type macro: `GTK_TYPE_MENU`

Object to widget cast macro: `GTK_MENU(obj)`

Widget type check macro: `GTK_IS_MENU(obj)`

Application-Level API Synopsis

Retrieve the constant GTK_TYPE_MENU at runtime:

```
GtkType
gtk_menu_get_type(void);
```

Create a new instance of GtkMenu:

```
GtkWidget *
gtk_menu_new(void);
```

Add a menu item (child) to the end of the menu:

```
void
gtk_menu_append(GtkMenu *menu, GtkWidget *child);
```

Add a menu item (child) to the start of the menu:

```
void
gtk_menu_prepend(GtkMenu *menu, GtkWidget *child);
```

Application-Level API Synopsis (Continued)

Insert a menu item (child) at an arbitrary position in the menu:

```
void
gtk_menu_insert(GtkMenu *menu, GtkWidget *child, gint position);
```

Pop up a menu, using an optional function to compute its position on the screen:

```
void
gtk_menu_popup(GtkMenu *menu, GtkWidget *parent_menu_shell,
        GtkWidget *parent_menu_item, GtkMenuPositionFunc func,
        gpointer data, guint button, guint32 activate_time);
```

Pop down a menu and remove its X server grab:

```
void
gtk_menu_popdown(GtkMenu *menu);
```

Query for the currently active menu item in a menu:

```
GtkWidget *
gtk_menu_get_active(GtkMenu *menu);
```

Set the active menu item of a menu:

```
void
gtk_menu_set_active(GtkMenu *menu, guint index);
```

Set the accelerator group of a menu:

```
void
gtk_menu_set_accel_group(GtkMenu *menu, GtkAccelGroup *accel_group);
```

Class Description

GtkMenu is similar to GtkMenuBar in that both classes are designed to manage a group of menu items. Visually, menus differ from menu bars; menus are rendered vertically, while menu bars are rendered horizontally. Also, a menu bar is usually always visible, while menus are only displayed if and when the user selects a menu item (from a menu bar or from another menu) that has a submenu attached to it.

Creating a Menu

Creating a new menu is achieved by calling gtk_menu_new():

```
GtkWidget *
gtk_menu_new(void);
```

Adding Menu Items

Menu items can be added to an instance of GtkMenu using one of three functions. The function gtk_menu_append() places the menu item at the end of the list of menu items for the menu, gtk_menu_prepend() places the menu item at the head of the list, and gtk_menu_insert() places the menu item at a specific location (specified by a position parameter in the range [0, *n*], where *n* – 1 is the number of menu items in the menu prior to making the call). Setting position to -1 is equivalent to calling gtk_menu_append(). The function prototypes for gtk_menu_append(), gtk_menu_prepend(), and gtk_menu_insert() are as follows:

```
void
gtk_menu_append(GtkMenu *menu, GtkWidget *child);

void
gtk_menu_prepend(GtkMenu *menu, GtkWidget *child);

void
gtk_menu_insert(GtkMenu *menu, GtkWidget *child, gint position);
```

Popping Up a Menu

Earlier in this chapter, the GtkItemFactory functions gtk_item_factory_popup() and gtk_item_factory_popup_with_data() were described as a way to pop up menus created by GtkItemFactory. As it turns out, both of these functions call the GtkMenu function gtk_menu_popup() to actually pop up the menu. The function prototype for gtk_menu_popup() is as follows:

```
void
gtk_menu_popup(GtkMenu *menu, GtkWidget *parent_menu_shell,
        GtkWidget *parent_menu_item, GtkMenuPositionFunc func,
        gpointer data, guint button, guint32 activate_time);
```

The argument menu is an instance of GtkMenu. The arguments parent_menu_shell and parent_menu_item are both instances of GtkWidget and can usually be set to NULL. The arguments func and data may be optionally used to specify a function to compute the position of the pop-up menu on the screen. The specified function must be of type GtkMenuPositionFunc, which means it must be a pointer to a function that has the following prototype:

```
void
MyPositionMenu (GtkMenu *menu, gint *x, gint *y, gpointer func_data)
```

The first argument is the menu to be positioned. The second and third arguments, x and y, are pointers to int that on return will hold the desired location of the menu when it is popped up. The final argument, func_data, corresponds to the data argument passed to gtk_menu_popup(). If func is set to NULL, GtkMenu will position the menu based on the location of the pointer at the time gtk_menu_popup() is called.

The final arguments to gtk_menu_popup() are mouse_button, which more often than not will be the number of the mouse button pressed by the user, and time, which will usually be the time at which the user pressed the button. As I will show below in Listing 9.1, both mouse_button and time can be obtained from the X event that triggered the posting of the pop-up menu.

An Example

Now it is time for an example. This example presented is similar to the example given for GtkItemFactory (see the section "Pop-up Menus" earlier in this chapter). Here I will use

GtkItemFactory to create the menu and illustrate how it can be popped up from a button_press_event signal function using gtk_menu_popup().

Listing 9.1 Creating and Displaying a Pop-up Menu

```
#include <gtk/gtk.h>
#include <time.h>
#include <stdio.h>

static GtkItemFactory *item_factory;

typedef struct _position
{
    int x;
    int y;
} Position;

static void
position_menu (GtkMenu *menu, gint *x, gint *y, gpointer func_data)
{
    Position *pos = func_data;

    *x = pos->x + 20;
    *y = pos->y + 20;
}

gint
ButtonPressCallback( GtkWidget *widget, GdkEventButton *event,
    gpointer callback_data )
{
    GtkWidget *menu = (GtkWidget *) callback_data;
    gint x, y;
    Position pos;

    gdk_window_get_origin(widget->window, &x, &y );

    pos.x = event->x + x;
    pos.y = event->y + y;
    gtk_menu_popup( GTK_MENU( menu ), NULL, NULL, position_menu, &pos,
            event->button, event->time );
}

static GtkItemFactoryEntry menu_items[] = {
    { "/_File",         NULL,          NULL, 0, "<Branch>" },
    { "/File/_New",     "<control>N", NULL, 0, NULL },
    { "/File/_Open",    "<control>O", NULL, 0, NULL },
    { "/File/_Save",    "<control>S", NULL, 0, NULL },
    { "/File/Save _As", NULL,          NULL, 0, NULL },
    { "/File/sep1",     NULL,          NULL, 0, "<Separator>" },
    { "/File/Quit",     "<control>Q", gtk_main_quit, 0, NULL },
};


void CreateMenu( GtkWidget *window, GtkWidget **menu )
{
    GtkAccelGroup *accel_group;
```

```
052     gint nmenu_items = sizeof (menu_items) / sizeof (menu_items[0]);
053
054     accel_group = gtk_accel_group_new ();
055
056     item_factory = gtk_item_factory_new (GTK_TYPE_MENU, "<popup_sample>",
057        accel_group);
058
059     gtk_item_factory_create_items(item_factory,nmenu_items,menu_items,NULL);
060
061     gtk_accel_group_attach (accel_group, GTK_OBJECT (window));
062
063     if (menu)
064        *menu = gtk_item_factory_get_widget (item_factory, "<popup_sample>");
065 }
066
067 int main( int argc, char *argv[] )
068 {
069     GtkWidget *window;
070     GtkWidget *menu;
071
072     gtk_init (&argc, &argv);
073
074     window = gtk_window_new (GTK_WINDOW_TOPLEVEL);
075     gtk_signal_connect (GTK_OBJECT(window), "destroy",
076        GTK_SIGNAL_FUNC (gtk_main_quit), "WM destroy");
077     gtk_window_set_title (GTK_WINDOW(window), "Popup Menu Example");
078     gtk_widget_set_usize (GTK_WIDGET(window), 300, 200);
079
080     CreateMenu (window, &menu);
081
082     gtk_widget_set_events (window, GDK_BUTTON_PRESS_MASK);
083     gtk_signal_connect (GTK_OBJECT (window), "button_press_event",
084        GTK_SIGNAL_FUNC(ButtonPressCallback), menu);
085
086     gtk_widget_show (window);
087     gtk_main ();
088
089     return(0);
090 }
```

Let's look at the code in a top-down fashion, starting with main() on line 067. On lines 074 through 078, after Gtk+ is initialized, a 300×200 window is created. On line 080, I call CreateMenu(), which is defined on lines 049 through 065. CreateMenu() creates a File menu, which will be popped up in the 300×200 window when the user presses mouse button 1 (for details on functions like CreateMenu(), refer to the discussion of GtkItemFactory earlier in this chapter). CreateMenu() also returns the widget representing the menu created. On line 082, I solicit button press events on the top-level window created earlier. Then, on line 083, I register the function ButtonPressCallback() as the signal function to handle any button_press_event signals that occur within the window (refer to Chapter 3, "Signals, Events, Objects, and Types," for information on signals and event solicitation in Gtk+). Notice that callback data passed to ButtonPressCallback() is the menu created by CreateMenu().

The function ButtonPressCallback(), shown on lines 022 through 036, is called by Gtk+ when the user positions the mouse over the window and clicks one of the mouse buttons:

```
022  gint
023  ButtonPressCallback( GtkWidget *widget, GdkEventButton *event,
024      gpointer callback_data )
025  {
026      GtkWidget *menu = (GtkWidget *) callback_data;
027      gint x, y;
028      Position pos;
029
030      gdk_window_get_origin(widget->window, &x, &y );
031
032      pos.x = event->x + x;
033      pos.y = event->y + y;
034      gtk_menu_popup( GTK_MENU( menu ), NULL, NULL, position_menu,
035              &pos, event->button, event->time );
036  }
```

The argument callback_data, as just described, is the GtkMenu that was created with the call to CreateMenu. On line 026, I assign callback_data to a variable named menu, making it easier to work with. On line 030, gdk_window_get_origin() is called to obtain the x and y positions of the window within which the button press event occurred. The window origin is needed because the coordinates of the button press event, passed via the second argument to ButtonPressCallback(), are window-relative. ButtonPressCallback() must convert these window-relative coordinates to screen-relative values when computing the coordinates that will be used by gtk_menu_popup(); this is done on lines 032 and 033. Finally, a call to gtk_menu_popup() is made. The address of the variable pos is passed as argument 5, and the address of the function position_menu() is passed as argument 4. Because arguments 4 and 5 are not NULL, this triggers GtkMenu to call position_menu(), passing the address of pos as an argument, and to use the screen-relative x and y positions that position_menu() computes as the location where the menu will be popped up on the screen. The type of the variable pos is a user-defined type, Position, defined on lines 007 through 011. position_menu() only accepts a single callback_data argument, so I invented a structure to hold the x and y coordinates, and to pass the address of a variable of type Position as the callback data, with the fields of that variable holding the x and y coordinate values needed.

The function position_menu() is defined on lines 013 through 020. This function must conform to the function prototype defined by GtkMenuPositionFunc.

```
013  static void
014  position_menu (GtkMenu *menu, gint *x,
         gint *y, gpointer func_data)
015  {
016      Position *pos = func_data;
017
018      *x = pos->x + 20;
019      *y = pos->y + 20;
020  }
```

The first argument passed by GtkMenu to position_menu() is the instance of GtkMenu to be popped up. Here I ignore this argument because it does not factor in the computation of the pop-up location. The arguments x and y are pointers that position_menu() will set to the screen-relative x and y locations, respectively, of the upper-left corner of the menu when it is popped up by GtkMenu. func_data is a generic pointer that, on line 016, I assign to a variable of type Position * so that I can access the x and y coordinates that were placed there by ButtonPressCallback(). The function position_menu(), to make things interesting, adds an offset of 20 pixels to each coordinate. This will cause the menu to display 20 pixels down and 20 pixels to the right of the pointer position at the time the mouse button was pressed by the user (see Figure 9.5).

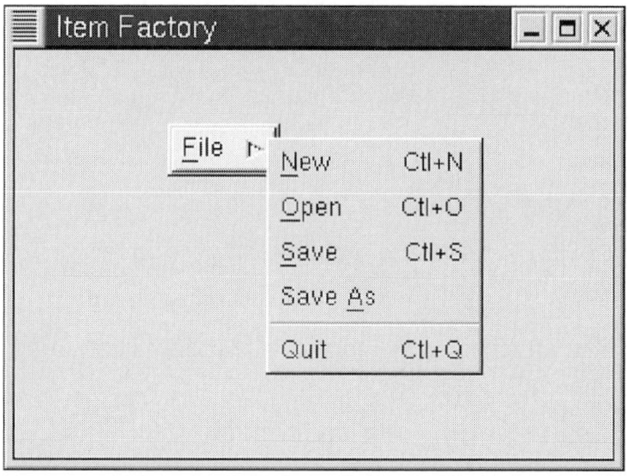

Figure 9.5 Pop-up Menu

Popping Down a Pop-up Menu

It is said that "what goes up, must come down." The same is true with a pop-up menu. Most of the time, a pop-up menu will be dismissed by the user when he or she selects and activates an item in the menu or clicks outside of the menu (or even hits the Escape key). However, if the application deems it necessary (often it is not), it can pop down the menu with a call to gtk_menu_popdown():

```
void
gtk_menu_popdown(GtkMenu *menu);
```

The only argument to gtk_menu_popdown() is an instance of GtkMenu.

Getting and Setting the Active Menu Item in a Menu

An application can query a menu for the currently active menu item, or even set the active menu item of a menu, by making calls to gtk_menu_get_active() and to gtk_menu_set_active(), respectively. The function gtk_menu_get_active() accepts a GtkMenu instance and returns an instance of GtkWidget:

```
GtkWidget *
gtk_menu_get_active(GtkMenu *menu);
```

The function gtk_menu_set_active() sets the menu item at offset index active:

```
void
gtk_menu_set_active(GtkMenu *menu, guint index);
```

Both of these functions are used in the implementation of GtkOptionMenu. It is not likely that you will need to use either of these functions in a typical application.

Accelerator Groups

Earlier in this chapter, I illustrated how to associate an accelerator group with a menu created using GtkItemFactory. An accelerator group was created with a call to gtk_accel_group_new() and was then passed as the third argument to gtk_item_factory_new():

```
GtkWidget *window;
GtkAccelGroup *accel_group;
GtkItemFactory *item_factory;

accel_group = gtk_accel_group_new ();

item_factory = gtk_item_factory_new(GTK_TYPE_MENU, "<main>",
        accel_group );
```

The accelerator group was also attached to the top-level window containing the menu with a call to gtk_accel_group_attach():

```
gtk_accel_group_attach (accel_group, GTK_OBJECT (window));
```

The routine gtk_menu_set_accel_group() can be used to set the accelerator group for a window that was not created with GtkItemFactory:

```
void
gtk_menu_set_accel_group(GtkMenu *menu, GtkAccelGroup *accel_group);
```

The argument menu is the GtkMenu instance to which the accelerator group is being assigned, and accel_group is the accelerator group (created by a call to gtk_accel_group_new()). You can even use gtk_menu_set_accel_group() to assign the accelerator group of a menu created using GtkItemFactory, although this is more difficult:

```
GtkWidget *window;
GtkAccelGroup *accel_group;
GtkItemFactory *item_factory;
GtkMenu *myMenu;

// create the accelerator group

accel_group = gtk_accel_group_new ();

// create the menu using an item factory

item_factory = gtk_item_factory_new(GTK_TYPE_MENU, "<main>",
        NULL );

// get the instance of GtkMenu created above
```

```
myMenu = (GtkMenu *) gtk_item_factory_get_widget (item_factory,
         "<main>");

// set the accelerator group using gtk_menu_set_accel_group()

gtk_menu_set_accel_group(myMenu, accel_group);

// attach the accelerator group to the window

gtk_accel_group_attach (accel_group, GTK_OBJECT (window));
```

GtkOptionMenu

Class Name

`GtkOptionMenu`

Parent Class Name

`GtkButton`

Macros

Widget type macro: `GTK_TYPE_OPTION_MENU`

Object to widget cast macro: `GTK_OPTION_MENU(obj)`

Widget type check macro: `GTK_IS_OPTION_MENU(obj)`

Application-Level API Synopsis

Retrieve the constant GTK_TYPE_OPTION_MENU at runtime:

```
GtkType
gtk_option_menu_get_type(void);
```

Create a new instance of GtkOptionMenu:

```
GtkWidget *
gtk_option_menu_new(void);
```

Retrieve the instance of GtkMenu associated with an instance of GtkOptionMenu:

```
GtkWidget *
gtk_option_menu_get_menu(GtkOptionMenu *option_menu);
```

Application-Level API Synopsis

Set the GtkMenu instance associated with an instance of GtkOptionMenu:

```
void
gtk_option_menu_set_menu(GtkOptionMenu *option_menu, GtkWidget *menu);
```

Remove the GtkMenu associated with an instance of GtkOptionMenu:

```
void
gtk_option_menu_remove_menu(GtkOptionMenu *option_menu);
```

Set the active menu item in the instance of GtkOptionMenu:

```
void
gtk_option_menu_set_history(GtkOptionMenu *option_menu, guint index);
```

Class Description

An option menu is a control that, when clicked, displays a menu. The label of an option menu displays the last menu item currently selected by the user from the menu. Figure 9.6 illustrates several instances of GtkOptionMenu. An option menu is easily identified by the small rectangle displayed to the right of the option menu's label; an instance of GtkButton is similar in appearance but does not display a rectangle next to the button label. The option menu in Figure 9.6 labeled Type of Event is one such example.

Creating an Option Menu

Creating an option menu requires that an instance of GtkOptionMenu be created, as well as an instance of GtkMenu and the instances of GtkMenuItem contained by the GtkMenu instance. To create the instance of GtkOptionMenu, make a call to gtk_option_menu_new():

```
GtkWidget *
gtk_option_menu_new( void );
```

In this chapter, we have seen that menus can be created using GtkItemFactory or directly using GtkMenuItem and GtkMenu. My recommendation is that you use GtkItemFactory to create the menu and menu items for your option menu. I will show an example of this in Listing 9.2.

Setting and Getting the Menu

Once the menu and menu items have been created, you will need to bind the menu to the option menu with a call to gtk_option_menu_set_menu():

```
void
gtk_option_menu_set_menu(GtkOptionMenu *option_menu, GtkWidget *menu);
```

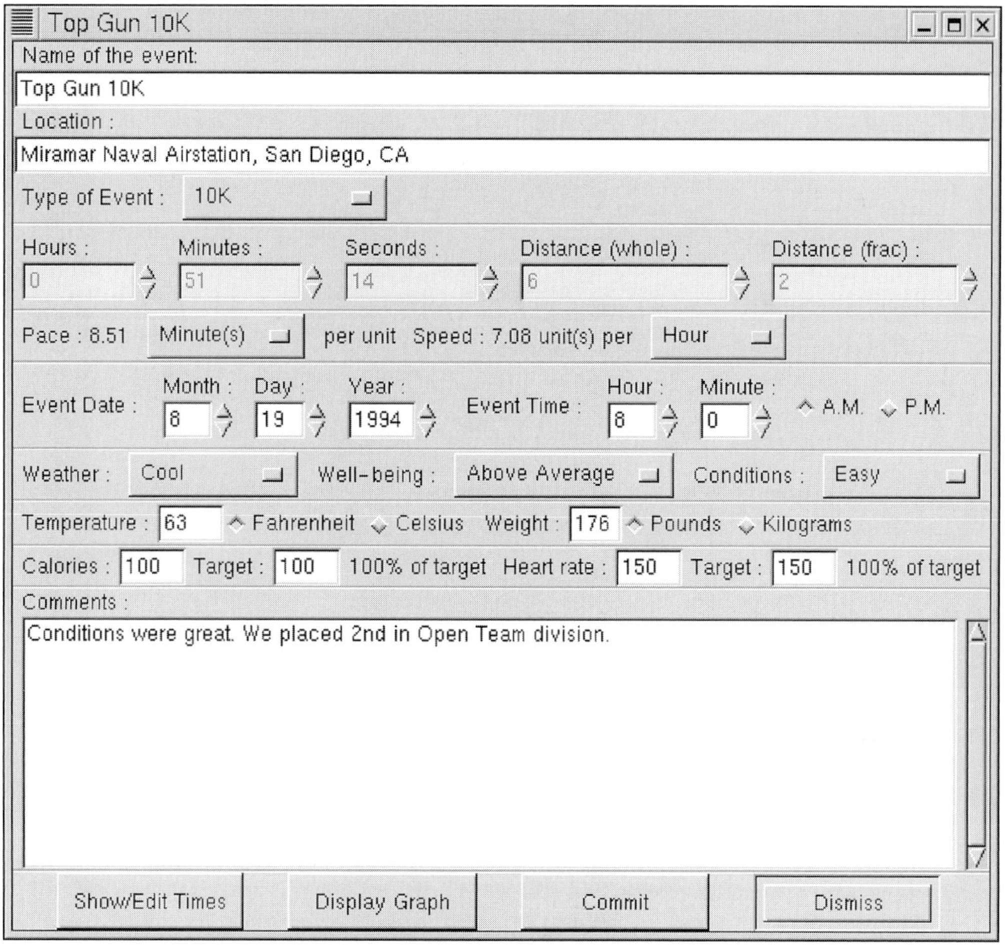

Figure 9.6 Dialog with Several Option Menu Widgets

The argument option_menu is an instance of GtkOptionMenu, and menu is an instance of GtkMenu (cast to GtkWidget *). A complementary function, gtk_option_menu_get_menu(), can be used to retrieve the menu bound to an option menu:

```
GtkWidget *
gtk_option_menu_get_menu(GtkOptionMenu *option_menu);
```

The returned instance of GtkWidget can be cast to GtkMenu.

The option menu's menu can be unbound by calling gtk_option_menu_remove_menu():

```
void
gtk_option_menu_remove_menu(GtkOptionMenu *option_menu);
```

The following function replaces the menu bound to an option menu with another menu and returns the menu that was previously bound to the option menu:

```
GtkWidget *
ReplaceOptionMenuMenu( GtkOptionMenu *optionMenu, GtkWidget *newMenu )
{
        GtkWidget *previousMenu;

        // check our arguments

        g_return_if_fail (optionMenu != NULL);
        g_return_val_if_fail (GTK_IS_OPTION_MENU (optionMenu), TRUE);
        g_return_if_fail (newMenu != NULL);
        g_return_val_if_fail (GTK_IS_MENU (newMenu), TRUE);

        // get the previously set option menu menu, if any

        previousMenu = gtk_option_menu_get_menu( optionMenu );

        // set the new option menu menu

        gtk_option_menu_set_menu( optionMenu, newMenu );

        return ( previousMenu );
}
```

The function gtk_option_menu_set_menu() makes a call to gtk_option_menu_remove_menu() before setting the new menu; because of this, it is not necessary for ReplaceOptionMenuMenu() to call gtk_option_menu_remove_menu() before calling gtk_option_menu_set_menu().

The following code illustrates how to create an option menu with four options using GtkItemFactory:

Listing 9.2 Example Option Menu

```
#include <gtk/gtk.h>

GtkItemFactory *item_factory;

static void
handle_option( gpointer data, guint callback_action, GtkWidget *w )
{
    GtkMenuItem *menuItem = (GtkMenuItem *) w;
}

static GtkItemFactoryEntry menu_items[] = {
 { "/Option1",  NULL,      handle_option, 1, NULL },
 { "/Option2",  NULL,      handle_option, 2, NULL },
 { "/Option3",  NULL,      handle_option, 3, NULL },
 { "/Option4",  NULL,      handle_option, 4, NULL },
};

```

```
018 void get_option_menu( GtkWidget **menu )
019 {
020  GtkAccelGroup *accel_group;
021  gint nmenu_items = sizeof (menu_items) / sizeof (menu_items[0]);
022
023  item_factory = gtk_item_factory_new (GTK_TYPE_MENU, "<options>", NULL );
024
025  gtk_item_factory_create_items(item_factory,nmenu_items,menu_items,NULL);
026
027  if (menu)
028    *menu = gtk_item_factory_get_widget (item_factory, "<options>");
029 }
030
031 int main( int argc, char *argv[] )
032 {
033  GtkWidget *menu;
034  GtkWidget *optionMenu;
035
036  gtk_init (&argc, &argv);
037
038  ...
039
040  get_option_menu (&menu);
041  optionMenu = gtk_option_menu_new();
042  gtk_option_menu_set_menu( GTK_OPTION_MENU( optionMenu ), menu );
043
044  ...
045
046  gtk_main ();
047
048  return(0);
049 }
```

On line 040, a call is made to get_option_menu(). This function (shown on lines 018 through 029) creates the menu that will be bound to the option menu. On line 041, an instance of GtkOptionMenu is created. The menu created on line 040 is bound to the option menu on line 042 with a call to gtk_option_menu_set_menu().

The menu is defined on lines 011 through 016. Note that the accelerator field of the GtkItemFactoryEntry struct defining each menu item is set to NULL. Typically, accelerators are not used in option menus. The function handle_option() will be invoked each time the user selects an item in the option menu. Each menu item has a unique callback_action field (1, 2, 3, or 4) that will be passed as the second argument to the callback function handle_option(). The function handle_option() can use this argument to tell which menu item in the menu was selected by the user and thereby track changes as they are made to the option menu by the user. I find it useful to store the callback_action somewhere; if the user commits the changes made to the dialog containing the option menu, the last recorded value is what I will save. For example, say the option menu contains the options Red, Green, and Blue, and the option menu is being used to edit a field named "color" in some data structure:

```
typedef struct _myData
{
        gint color;
```

```
        ...

} MyData;

static MyData myData;
```

I might define the following constants:

```
#define COLOR_RED 0x00
#define COLOR_GREEN        0x01
#define COLOR_BLUE         0x02
```

and the following static variable to hold the current selection:

```
static gint color;
```

The menu would be defined using the following:

```
static GtkItemFactoryEntry menu_items[] = {
 { "/Red",        NULL,      handle_option, COLOR_RED, NULL },
 { "/Green",      NULL,      handle_option, COLOR_GREEN, NULL },
 { "/Blue",       NULL,      handle_option, COLOR_BLUE, NULL },
};
```

The callback function would be coded as follows:

```
static void
handle_option( gpointer data, guint callback_action, GtkWidget *w )
{
         color = callback_action;
}
```

When the user commits the dialog containing the option menu, the value stored in the variable "color" would be copied into myData in the "clicked" signal function assigned to the Commit or OK button of the dialog:

```
...

myData.color = color;

...
```

Initializing the Option Menu Selection

There is one final issue regarding option menus that needs to be addressed: how to initialize the current selection of the option menu's menu. For example, if the last selection made in the preceding "color" menu was Green, we would want to initialize the option menu's menu so that Green was the current selection the next time the option menu was displayed for that data. To set the selection of an option menu's menu, call gtk_option_menu_set_history():

```
void
gtk_option_menu_set_history(GtkOptionMenu *option_menu, guint index);
```

The argument option_menu is an instance of GtkOptionMenu. The argument index is in the range [0, $n - 1$], where n is the number of menu items in the option menu's menu. Notice in the preceding how I defined the constants COLOR_RED, COLOR_GREEN, and COLOR_BLUE to be 0, 1, and 2, respectively. This makes it easy to initialize the option menu directly from the data, for example:

```
GtkOptionMenu *myOptionMenu;

...

gtk_option_menu_set_history( myOptionMenu, myData.color );
```

You may call gtk_option_menu_set_history() any time after the option menu has been created (with a call to gtk_option_menu_new()) and its menu has been attached (with a call to gtk_option_menu_set_menu()). Most applications will only set an option menu's history once before making the option menu available to the user because, generally speaking, changes made to an option menu should only be made by the user, not by the application.

Summary

Gtk+ 1.2 supports a wide variety of menu-related widgets. The easiest way to add a menu to your application is to use GtkItemFactory, the first widget class described in this chapter. To use GtkItemFactory, you simply create a data structure that defines the organization and content of your menu and that specifies callback functions to be invoked for each of the menu items in your menus. You then pass this data structure to GtkItemFactory, which will implement the menu system you have described. You can then retrieve from GtkItemFactory a widget that implements the menu and add this widget to one of your application windows.

The content of a menu is made of up menu items. For example, the Edit menu in most applications has Cut, Copy, and Paste menu items. Gtk+ supports several types of menu-item widgets. Besides the typical menu items seen in most menus (instances of GtkMenuItem), radio menu items (GtkRadioMenuItem), which allow the user to select one of many items in a menu, and check radio menu items (GtkCheckMenuItem), which allow the user to select several of many items in a menu, are both supported. Tearoff menus are menus that can be detached from their parent and displayed in a separate window. Tearoff menus persist on the desktop until they are explicitly dismissed by the user or by the application. Gtk+ allows menus to be popped up in an arbitrary window location; I illustrated the technique for popping up and popping down menus in this chapter. Finally, Gtk+ supports option menus. Option menus solve the problem of providing users with a control from which one of several items can be selected, when the list of items is too large to be displayed as a set of radio buttons and is too small to be displayed in a list widget. Option menus are also used at times when the amount of user interface real estate is restricted (i.e., when a set of radio buttons or a list simply takes up too much space).

CHAPTER

10

CONTAINER AND BIN CLASSES

This chapter, and the one that follows, will introduce the container widgets that make up the Gtk+ toolkit as of Gtk+ 1.2.

Container classes play a crucial role in Gtk+, as they do in other toolkits and widget sets for the X Window System, MacOS, and MS Windows (and countless other platforms). In the X Window System world, Xaw, Motif, and others all supply widgets that in one way or another are analogous to the Gtk+ container widgets.

So what exactly is a container widget? A container widget is simply a widget that manages other widgets. A window is a familiar example of a container. The purpose of a window is to provide an area within which user-interface objects such as buttons, text fields, radio buttons, and labels are presented to the user of an application. How this presentation is performed by a container widget helps to separate one container widget class from another. There are two attributes of a container widget that help to define it and separate it from other container widgets in the toolkit.

The first of these attributes is visibility: Is the container visible to the user or not? Windows, obviously, are visible to the user. So are button widgets, which act as a container for their labels (buttons are discussed in Chapter 5, "Labels and Buttons"). But many container widgets, as we shall see, are not visible to the user, working behind the scenes to compute the layout of the children they manage and to respond to changes in the geometry of the application windows, which in turn act as their containers.

The second attribute is the container's layout policy: How does the container place its children within the container? Some containers, such as GtkFixed in Gtk+ or Motif's BulletinBoard widget, require the programmer to precompute widget positions, specifying them at compile time or in tables read by the application at runtime. Once specified, these widget locations are, in effect, hard coded and typically will not vary once the container and its children have been instantiated and realized by the application. The majority of container widgets, in Gtk+ and in other toolkits, allow a programmer to specify abstract relationships that exist between the container and the widgets it contains, between widgets themselves within the container, or both. An example of a relationship that might exist between a container and a child widget is how the widget relates to the edges of the container. For example, are widgets, as they are added to the container, added from the left edge of the container or from the right (or perhaps from top to bottom or from bottom to top)? Or is a widget anchored to the top edge of a container (or to the left, to the right or bottom edge, or perhaps to one of the four corners), maintaining that position as the container is resized?

Container widgets often define similar relationships that exist among children of the container. One commonly encountered relationship is the amount of space that exists between widgets in the container, both vertically and horizontally. Another attribute, homogeneity, determines whether children in the container are given different sizes, each based on the needs of the widget, or are given the same size (typically the size given to a homogeneous set of children is the size needed to correctly display the largest child in the set).

Container widgets are useful because they allow programmers to easily build a user interface that not only displays its components in a consistent manner, but that responds well to changes made by a user, particularly window size. Because of container widgets, a programmer does not need to compute x, y, width, and height values for each user-interface component, spending hours trying to arrange widgets so that they center correctly or are horizontally or vertically aligned. Gone are the days when windows had to be given a fixed size that a user couldn't change, in the face of a resulting widget layout that was either difficult to recompute or, if computed at all, gave a visually unappealing or inconsistent result.

The more you become familiar with the various container widgets supplied by a toolkit, in this case Gtk+, the more likely it is that you will choose container widgets wisely and provide to your users a well-designed and visually appealing user interface that will keep its shape as the user interacts with it.

In this chapter, and the one that follows, I will present the container widget classes provided by Gtk+ 1.2 and will provide numerous examples of their use. The two container widget classes to which you should pay particular attention are GtkContainer, discussed immediately, and GtkBox and its children, GtkVBox and GtkHBox, which are described later in this chapter. A solid knowledge of these widget classes is, I believe, required if you are planning to write even the most basic Gtk+ application.

GtkContainer

Class Name

```
GtkContainer
```

Parent Class Name

```
GtkWidget
```

Macros

Widget type macro: `GTK_TYPE_CONTAINER`

Object to widget cast macro: `GTK_CONTAINER(obj)`

Macros (Continued)

Widget type check macro: `GTK_IS_CONTAINER(obj)`

Supported Signals

Table 10.1 Signals

Signal Name	*Condition Causing Signal to Trigger*
add	The child was added to the container.
remove	The child was removed from the container.
check_resize	The check resize function was called on a container.
focus	The container (or child) obtained focus.
set_focus_child	The focus child of the container was set.

Signal Function Prototypes

```
void
add(GtkContainer *container, GtkWidget *widget, gpointer user_data);

void
remove(GtkContainer *container, GtkWidget *widget, gpointer
user_data);

void
check_resize(GtkContainer *container, gpointer user_data);

GtkDirectionType
focus(GtkContainer *container, GtkDirectionType direction,
        gpointer user_data);

void
set_focus_child(GtkContainer *container, GtkWidget *widget,
        gpointer user_data);
```

Supported Arguments

Prefix: `GtkContainer::`

Table 10.2 GtkContainer Arguments

Name	*Type*	*Permissions*
border_width	GTK_TYPE_ULONG	GTK_ARG_READWRITE
resize_mode	GTK_TYPE_RESIZE_MODE	GTK_ARG_READWRITE
child	GTK_TYPE_WIDGET	GTK_ARG_WRITABLE

Application-Level API Synopsis

Return the constant GTK_TYPE_CONTAINER at runtime:

```
GtkType
gtk_container_get_type(void);
```

Set the border width of the container widget (default is 0):

```
void
gtk_container_set_border_width(GtkContainer *container, guint
        border_width);
```

Add a child widget to a container:

```
void
gtk_container_add(GtkContainer *container, GtkWidget *widget);
```

Remove a child widget from a container:

```
void
gtk_container_remove(GtkContainer *container, GtkWidget *widget);
```

Invoke a callback on each child in a container:

```
void
gtk_container_foreach(GtkContainer *container, GtkCallback callback,
        gpointer callback_data);
```

Obtain a list of each container child (one level down):

```
GList *
gtk_container_children(GtkContainer *container);
```

Set focus to the container, or to one of its children, based on a specified focus direction:

```
gint
gtk_container_focus(GtkContainer *container, GtkDirectionType
        direction);
```

Class Description

GtkContainer is a parent class to a broad category of widget classes supported by Gtk+ that are designed to manage the layout of other widgets within an area of a window. Many widget classes in Gtk+ descend from GtkContainer in the Gtk+ widget hierarchy, and most of them will be described in this chapter.

You may never actually create an instance of GtkContainer in your application; an instance of GtkContainer exists because some other class you have instantiated has inherited from it. Therefore, there is no gtk_container_new() function for you to call. However, there are a few functions in the GtkContainer API that you may find useful. In particular, gtk_container_add() will be used often in your application, as we shall see.

It is probably best to skim this section to get the general idea of what the GtkContainer class offers. Other classes described in this chapter will prove to be more useful to you as you develop your application code.

Setting the Border Widget of a Container

Let's start our look at the GtkContainer class by considering the border width of a container. The border width of a container, which defaults to 0 in Gtk+, defines how much space (in pixels) is given above and below the container, in addition to the amount of space needed by the container to lay out its children. To set the border width of a container widget, you call gtk_container_set_border_width():

```
void
gtk_container_set_border_width(GtkContainer *container,
            guint border_width);
```

Because you are unable to create an instance of GtkContainer directly from your application, you will either be working with an instance of GtkWidget or with some widget inheriting from GtkContainer (such as GtkVBox). Therefore, you must cast the first argument gtk_container_set_border_width() to a GtkContainer by using the macro GTK_CONTAINER, as in the following example:

```
GtkWidget *widget;

...

gtk_container_set_border_width( GTK_CONTAINER( widget ), 0 );
```

The same tactic is required for all of the other functions defined by the GtkContainer API because they all take as a first argument an instance of GtkContainer.

Adding and Removing Children

Child widgets can be added to most GtkContainer-derived classes with a call to gtk_container_add():

```
void
gtk_container_add(GtkContainer *container, GtkWidget *widget);
```

Similarly, a previously added child widget can be removed from a GtkContainer-derived class by calling gtk_container_remove():

```
void
gtk_container_remove(GtkContainer *container, GtkWidget *widget);
```

Adding and removing children from a container will usually result in a redraw of the container and its contents to accommodate the change in the widget's child list.

GtkContainer actually does not provide implementations of gtk_container_add() or gtk_container_remove(). These functions are supplied by classes inheriting from GtkContainer. Most of these functions are listed in Table 10.3.

Table 10.3 Add and Remove Functions

Class	*Add Function*	*Remove Function*
GtkBin	gtk_bin_add()	gtk_bin_remove()
GtkBox	gtk_box_add()	gtk_box_remove()
GtkButton	gtk_button_add()	gtk_button_remove()
GtkFixed	gtk_fixed_add()	gtk_fixed_remove()
GtkHandleBox	gtk_handle_box_add()	gtk_handle_box_remove()
GtkList	gtk_list_add()	gtk_list_remove()
GtkNotebook	gtk_notebook_add()	gtk_notebook_remove()
GtkPacker	gtk_packer_container_add()	gtk_packer_container_remove()
GtkPaned	gtk_paned_add()	gtk_paned_remove()
GtkScrolledWindow	gtk_scrolled_window_add()	gtk_scrolled_window_remove()
GtkTable	gtk_table_add()	gtk_table_remove()
GtkToolbar	gtk_toolbar_add()	gtk_toolbar_remove()
GtkTree	gtk_tree_add()	gtk_tree_remove()
GtkViewport	gtk_viewport_add()	gtk_viewport_remove()

In some cases, such as GtkBin and (most of) its child classes, the add function does little more than simply record the child widget and force a redraw. In a class that provides more functional APIs for adding child widgets, one of its add functions will be invoked, called with defaults selected by the widget implementation. In the case of GtkBox, for example, the function that will be invoked is gtk_box_pack_start_defaults() (gtk_box_pack_start_defaults() is described in this chapter in the section on GtkBox). Table 10.4 lists how gtk_container_add() is implemented in Gtk+ 1.2 by each of the classes listed in Table 10.3.

Table 10.4 Add Function Implementations

Class	*Add Function Implementations*
GtkBin	Internal
GtkBox	gtk_box_pack_start_defaults()</tr
GtkButton	Internal, gtk_bin_add()
GtkFixed	gtk_fixed_put(fixed, child, 0, 0)
GtkHandleBox	Internal, gtk_bin_add()
GtkList	Internal
GtkNotebook	gtk_notebook_insert_page_menu(notebook, child, NULL, NULL, -1)
GtkPacker	gtk_packer_add_defaults(packer, child, GTK_SIDE_TOP, GTK_ANCHOR_CENTER, 0)
GtkPaned	gtk_paned_pack1(paned, child, FALSE, TRUE)
GtkScrolledWindow	Internal
GtkTable	gtk_table_attach_defaults(table, child, 0, 1, 0, 1)
GtkToolbar	gtk_toolbar_append_widget(toolbar, child, NULL, NULL)
GtkTree	Internal

For the most part, you should try to directly call the add and remove functions provided by implementation classes, when possible. However, should the defaults be acceptable, both gtk_container_add() and gtk_container_remove() can be used instead if desired.

Iterating a Container's Children

An application can arrange to have a callback function invoked for each child widget in a container by making a call to gtk_container_foreach():

```
void
gtk_container_foreach(GtkContainer *container, GtkCallback callback,
        gpointer callback_data);
```

The argument container is an instance of GtkContainer (for example, an instance of GtkVBox), callback is a pointer to a callback function in your application, and callback_data is a pointer to application data you want to have passed to the callback function.

The callback function needs to have the following prototype:

```
void
function(GtkWidget *widget, gpointer data)
```

The argument widget is the child widget in the container, and data is the callback_data you passed to gtk_container_foreach().

The following code, taken from the testgtk.c source code supplied with Gtk+ 1.2, illustrates how this functionality might be used.

```
void
show_all_pages(GtkButton *button, GtkNotebook *notebook)
{
        gtk_container_foreach (GTK_CONTAINER (notebook),
                (GtkCallback) gtk_widget_show, NULL);
}
```

The routine is called in response to a button "clicked" event (the first argument is the button that was clicked, the second is the callback_data, an instance of GtkNotebook) to show all of the "pages" managed by a notebook widget. A similar function might be written to hide all of the pages. What happens here is that each child of the notebook will be passed to gtk_widget_show(), which will then show the widget.

Many of you will notice that gtk_widget_show() takes only one argument, but we are passing two (the widget and the callback data). Passing additional arguments is permissible in C (although it is not terribly elegant). Here, it is only required that the first argument exist and be of type GtkWidget *.

Retrieving a List of a Container's Children

The next function described here, gtk_container_children(), can be used to obtain a list of each child widget existing one level below the specified container:

```
GList *
gtk_container_children(GtkContainer *container);
```

The following implementation of the GtkButton "clicked" callback previously presented, show_all_pages(), illustrates how to retrieve and traverse the list of children returned by gtk_container_children():

```
void
show_all_pages(GtkButton *button, GtkNotebook *notebook)
{
        GList *myList;

        myList = gtk_container_children( GTK_CONTAINER( notebook ) );
        while ( myList != (GList *) NULL ) {
                gtk_show_widget( (GTK_WIDGET( myList->data ) );
                myList = myList->next;
        }
}
```

Changing Focus

The final GtkContainer function discussed here, gtk_container_focus(), is used to set the focus to a container or to one of its children:

```
gint
gtk_container_focus(GtkContainer *container,
            GtkDirectionType direction);
```

direction can be GTK_DIR_TAB_FORWARD, GTK_DIR_TAB_BACKWARD, GTK_DIR_UP, GTK_DIR_DOWN, GTK_DIR_LEFT, or GTK_DIR_RIGHT.

The focus widget will be selected by GtkContainer based on the direction specified as well as the child widget that currently has the focus. Not all directions are applicable to all containers. The basic logic employed by GtkContainer when assigning focus is as follows. First, only drawable widgets and widgets that are sensitive can attain focus. If the container is either not drawable or is currently insensitive, then gtk_container_focus() returns. If the container itself is capable of obtaining focus (GtkButton is an example of a container-derived class that can obtain focus), then focus is given to the container, and gtk_container_focus() returns. Otherwise, a list of container child widgets is retrieved, and all of the child widgets that cannot obtain the focus (i.e., widgets that are either not drawable or insensitive) are discarded from the list.

The function gtk_container_focus() then executes code, specific to the desired direction, to switch the focus to one of the child widgets obtained in the previous step.

GtkFixed

Class Name

```
GtkFixed
```

Parent Class Name

```
GtkContainer
```

Macros

Widget type macro: `GTK_TYPE_FIXED`

Object to widget cast macro: `GTK_FIXED(obj)`

Widget type check macro: `GTK_IS_FIXED(obj)`

Application-Level API Synopsis

Retrieve the constant GTK_TYPE_FIXED at runtime:

```
GtkType
gtk_fixed_get_type(void);
```

Create a new instance of GtkFixed:

```
GtkWidget *
gtk_fixed_new(void);
```

Place a child widget inside an instance of GtkFixed at location x, y:

```
void
gtk_fixed_put(GtkFixed *fixed, GtkWidget *widget, gint16 x, gint16 y);
```

Move a child widget inside an instance of GtkFixed to location x, y:

```
void
gtk_fixed_move(GtkFixed *fixed, GtkWidget *widget, gint16 x, gint16 y);
```

Class Description

Perhaps the simplest of the container classes is GtkFixed. Unlike most of the container classes, GtkFixed relies on the application to make decisions about the placement of child widgets within the real estate being managed by GtkFixed. In most other cases, the application supplies the container widget with a set of constraints (constraints are implied by the container class and often refined via the widget class API); the container widget is responsible for placing child widgets on the screen, based on the implied and specified constraints. In the case of GtkFixed, however, the application must explicitly specify the x, y coordinate of the widget within the container, and GtkFixed will happily honor the request.

You only need to use GtkFixed when the constraint system provided by the other Gtk+ container widgets does not meet the needs of your application or when you want to control the placement of child widgets explicitly. In the following section, I will provide an example that uses GtkFixed.

Creating an Instance of GtkFixed

To create an instance of GtkFixed, call gtk_fixed_new():

```
GtkWidget *
gtk_fixed_new(void);
```

The returned widget must be added to another container (for example, a window); this can be done using gtk_container_add(). You also must show the widget using gtk_widget_show() (or by calling gtk_widget_show_all() on its parent).

Adding a Child Widget

To place a child widget inside an instance of GtkFixed at location x, y, call gtk_fixed_put():

```
void
gtk_fixed_put(GtkFixed *fixed, GtkWidget *widget, gint16 x, gint16 y);
```

The argument fixed is an instance of GtkFixed, and widget is the child widget to be placed in the fixed container. The widget location is specified by the arguments x and y.

Moving a Child Widget

To reposition a child widget of an instance of GtkFixed to location x, y, an application can call gtk_fixed_move():

```
void
gtk_fixed_move(GtkFixed *fixed, GtkWidget *widget, gint16 x,
         gint16 y);
```

The arguments to gtk_fixed_move() are the same as to gtk_fixed_put().

An Example

Now it's time for an example. The example code creates a window and 10 widgets (here, I create instances of GtkLabel). A timer is created that fires 10 times a second. The timer handler (fixed_timeout()) computes a random x and y increment that is applied to the position of each widget, and uses gtk_fixed_move() to change the position of the widget. If the label widget goes off-screen in either the x or y direction, its direction of movement for that direction (x_trend and y_trend, see Listing 10.1) is changed so that the label remains within the area of the window.

A bug in GtkFixed shows up if line 069 is removed. If you run without line 069, you will notice that GtkFixed does not erase the widget at its current location before being moved. Calling gtk_widget_queue_clear() explicitly erases the widget from the window before it is moved.

Listing 10.1 GtkFixed Example

```
001 #include <gtk/gtk.h>
002 #include <stdlib.h>
003
004 /* number of GtkLabel widgets */
005
006 #define NUM_LABELS 10
007
008 /* width, height of window. used to compute if we need to change the
009    direction of movement */
010
011 #define WIN_WIDTH 300
012 #define WIN_HEIGHT 200
013
014 /* information on a label: its widget, its current position, and direction
015    of movement */
016
017 typedef struct _labels
018 {
```

```
    GtkWidget *w;
    gint x;
    gint y;
    gint x_trend;
    gint y_trend;
} Labels;

static Labels labels[NUM_LABELS];
static GtkWidget *fixed;

/* called 10 times a second to compute new positions for all of the labels,
   and adjust directions of movement if necessary */

gint
fixed_timeout (gpointer data)
{
    gint x_inc, y_inc;
    int i;

    for ( i = 0; i < NUM_LABELS; i++ ) {

            /* compute new movement in range of 0 to 10 pixels */

            x_inc = ((float) rand() / RAND_MAX) * 10;
            y_inc = ((float) rand() / RAND_MAX) * 10;

            /* add (or subtract) increment to (from)  both x and y
               positions of widget */

            labels[i].x += x_inc * labels[i].x_trend;
            labels[i].y += y_inc * labels[i].y_trend;

            /*
               if label has gone off-screen, flip the direction of
               movement for the label (only flip the component that
               went off-screen)
            */

            if ( labels[i].x > WIN_WIDTH )
                    labels[i].x_trend = -1;
            else if ( labels[i].x < 0 )
                    labels[i].x_trend = 1;
            if ( labels[i].y > WIN_HEIGHT )
                    labels[i].y_trend = -1;
            else if ( labels[i].y < 0 )
                    labels[i].y_trend = 1;

            /* clear the previous position, as GtkFixed doesn't do this
               very cleanly */

            gtk_widget_queue_clear (labels[i].w);

            /* reposition the widget */

            gtk_fixed_move( GTK_FIXED( fixed ), labels[i].w,
                    labels[i].x, labels[i].y );
    }

```

```
}

int main( int argc, char *argv[] )
{
      GtkWidget *window;
      int i, timer;

      gtk_init (&argc, &argv);

      /* create a window, sets its size and title */

      window = gtk_window_new (GTK_WINDOW_TOPLEVEL);
      gtk_signal_connect (GTK_OBJECT(window), "destroy",
              GTK_SIGNAL_FUNC (gtk_main_quit), "WM destroy");
      gtk_window_set_title (GTK_WINDOW(window), "Fixed");
      gtk_widget_set_usize (GTK_WIDGET(window), WIN_WIDTH, WIN_HEIGHT);

      /* create an instance of GtkFixed, add it to the window */

      fixed = gtk_fixed_new();
      gtk_container_add( GTK_CONTAINER( window ), fixed );
      gtk_widget_show (fixed);

      /* create the labels, placing them in the middle of the window
         using gtk_fixed_put(). Set the direction trends to random
         values */

      for ( i = 0; i < NUM_LABELS; i++ ) {
              labels[i].w = gtk_label_new ("Gtk+ Rules!");
              labels[i].x = WIN_WIDTH / 2; labels[i].y = WIN_HEIGHT / 2;
              labels[i].x_trend = (rand() > RAND_MAX / 2 ? 1 : -1 );
              labels[i].y_trend = (rand() > RAND_MAX / 2 ? 1 : -1 );
              gtk_widget_show( labels[i].w );
              gtk_fixed_put( GTK_FIXED( fixed ), labels[i].w,
                      labels[i].x, labels[i].y );
      }

      gtk_widget_show (window);

      /* register a timeout callback with Gtk+ to fire every 100ms */

      timer = gtk_timeout_add (100, fixed_timeout, NULL);
      gtk_main ();

      return(0);
}
```

GtkBox

Class Name

GtkBox

Parent Class Name

```
GtkContainer
```

Macros

Widget type macro: `GTK_TYPE_BOX`

Object to widget cast macro: `GTK_BOX(obj)`

Widget type check macro: `GTK_IS_BOX(obj)`

Supported Arguments

Prefix: `GtkBox::`

Table 10.5 GtkBox Arguments

Name	*Type*	*Permissions*
spacing	GTK_TYPE_INT	GTK_ARG_READWRITE
homogeneous	GTK_TYPE_BOOL	GTK_ARG_READWRITE
expand	GTK_TYPE_BOOL	GTK_ARG_READWRITE
fill	GTK_TYPE_BOOL	GTK_ARG_READWRITE
padding	GTK_TYPE_ULONG	GTK_ARG_READWRITE
pack_type	GTK_TYPE_PACK_TYPE	GTK_ARG_READWRITE
position	GTK_TYPE_LONG	GTK_ARG_READWRITE

Application-Level API Synopsis

Retrieve GTK_TYPE_BOX at runtime:

```
GtkType
gtk_box_get_type(void);
```

Pack a child widget into a box, left to right for a horizontal box or top to bottom for a vertical box:

```
void
gtk_box_pack_start(GtkBox *box, GtkWidget *child, gboolean expand,
        gboolean fill, guint padding);
```

Application-Level API Synopsis (Continued)

Pack a child widget into a box, right to left for a horizontal box or bottom to top for a vertical box:

```
void
gtk_box_pack_end(GtkBox *box, GtkWidget *child, gboolean expand,
        gboolean fill, guint padding);
```

Same as gtk_box_pack_start(), but use Gtk+ defaults for expand, fill, and padding:

```
void
gtk_box_pack_start_defaults(GtkBox *box, GtkWidget *widget);
```

Same as gtk_box_pack_end(), but use Gtk+ defaults for expand, fill, and padding:

```
void
gtk_box_pack_end_defaults(GtkBox *box, GtkWidget *widget);
```

Make a box homogeneous (see text):

```
void
gtk_box_set_homogeneous(GtkBox *box, gboolean homogeneous);
```

Set spacing that is added between objects in the box:

```
void
gtk_box_set_spacing(GtkBox *box, gint spacing);
```

Relocate a child of the box at a new position:

```
void
gtk_box_reorder_child(GtkBox *box, GtkWidget *child, gint position);
```

Retrieve packing settings of a child in the box:

```
void
gtk_box_query_child_packing(GtkBox *box, GtkWidget *child, gboolean
       *expand, gboolean *fill, guint *padding,
       GtkPackType *pack_type);
```

Change packing settings of a child in the box:

```
void
gtk_box_set_child_packing(GtkBox *box, GtkWidget *child, gboolean
       expand, gboolean fill, guint padding, GtkPackType pack_type);
```

Class Description

GtkBox (and its related child classes, GtkVBox and GtkHBox) is by far the most popular of the container widget classes implemented by Gtk+. This is due to the overall simplicity and flexibility that GtkBox provides; nearly any kind of layout imaginable can be achieved using the relatively small API set that GtkBox provides.

There are two types of GtkBox. Vertical boxes (implemented by GtkVBox) lay out their children vertically from top to bottom (or from bottom to top based on the packing order you specify). Horizontal boxes (implemented by GtkHBox) lay out their children horizontally from left to right (or from left to right, again, based on the packing order you specify). Using boxes involves the following steps:

Box Creation
Boxes are created using functions provided by GtkVBox and GtkHBox (both classes are described later in this chapter). Horizontal boxes can be created using the function gtk_hbox_new(), while vertical boxes are created with gtk_vbox_new().

Box Placement
A newly created box widget must be placed inside of another container widget. Typically, the first vertical or horizontal box you add will be the immediate child of a window widget or the immediate child of the vbox child of a dialog.

Box Nesting
To achieve more complicated layouts, additional instances of GtkVBox and/or GtkHBox can be created and placed as children of previously created box widgets, as the user-interface requirements dictate. Doing so forms a hierarchy of box widgets such as the one illustrated in Figure 10.8 later in this chapter. A newly instantiated box can be added within a hierarchy at any arbitrary position; however, boxes are typically added top to bottom (GtkVBox) or left to right (GtkHBox).

Widget Placement
The last step is to add the user-interface widgets that the user will see and interact with to the boxes placed in the hierarchy by the previous step. Such widgets include buttons, labels, images, and so forth. As is the case with box placement, GtkBox is flexible with regard to when and where the user-interface widgets are placed within box widgets in the box instance hierarchy.

The box nesting and widget placement steps can be, and often are, interwoven, as I will illustrate in the following section.

Packing Options
As I previously mentioned, there are two types of box. The horizontal box (GtkHBox) packs its children (other boxes or widgets) in a left to right, or right to left, manner. Vertical Boxes, on the other hand, pack children from top to bottom or from bottom to top. The direction of packing (e.g., top to bottom or bottom to top) is based on the function used by your application to add a child to the box (I'll describe the functions used in detail later).

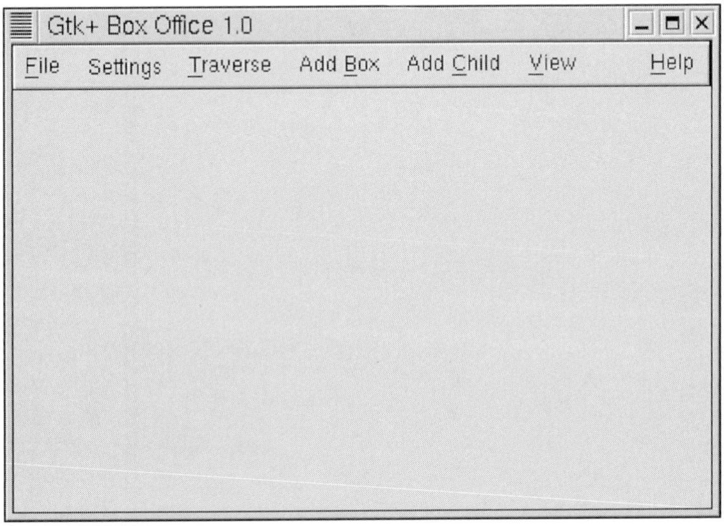

Figure 10.1 Window with a Vertical Box

The two possible packing options are "pack start" and "pack end." Figure 10.1 illustrates a window containing a single instance of GtkVBox. The box is not visible, as boxes do not draw themselves. Adding an instance of GtkButton to this box (using the default packing attributes I will discuss later) results in the layout depicted in Figure 10.2. The layout shown could have been achieved by packing the button into the vertical box with "pack end" or "pack start." Since there was no other widget yet packed into the vertical box, it did not really matter. It also does not matter whether the box containing the button, in this instance, is vertical or horizontal; the same result would have been obtained using either a vertical or horizontal box because, at this point, there is only one child that has been packed into the box.

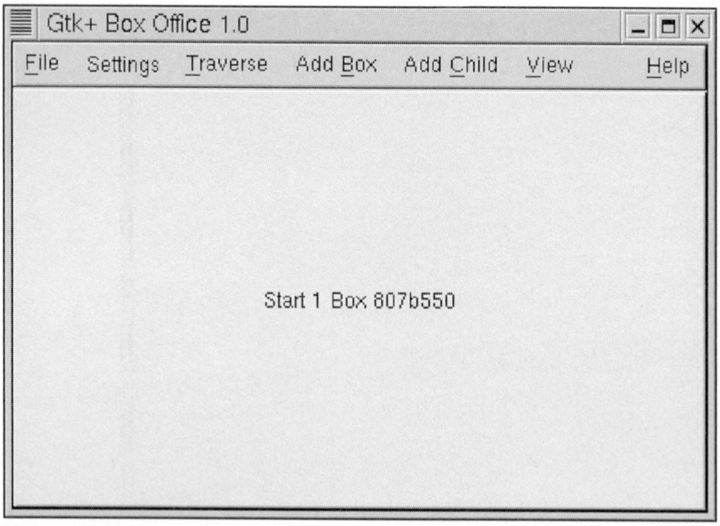

Figure 10.2 Vertical Box with a Single Button

Now let's add a second button to the vertical box. At this point, the use of a vertical or horizontal box widget as the top-level container becomes relevant. Because we are adding to a vertical box, packing with either "pack end" or "pack start" will give us the result shown in Figure 10.3 (a different result would be obtained if the first button was packed using "pack end"). The addition of a third button, however, is influenced by the packing direction selected both for the button being added and for the button added before it (button number 2). Figures 10.4 through 10.7 illustrate each of the possible results. In these figures, the order and method of packing is defined by the button label. "Start" indicates that the box was packed using "pack start," and "End" indicates a box packed using "pack end." The order of packing immediately follows 1, 2, or 3.

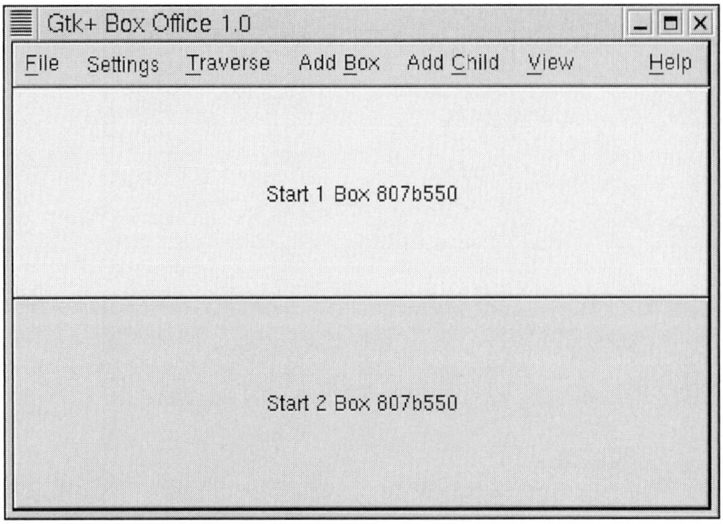

Figure 10.3 Box l and 2, Pack Start

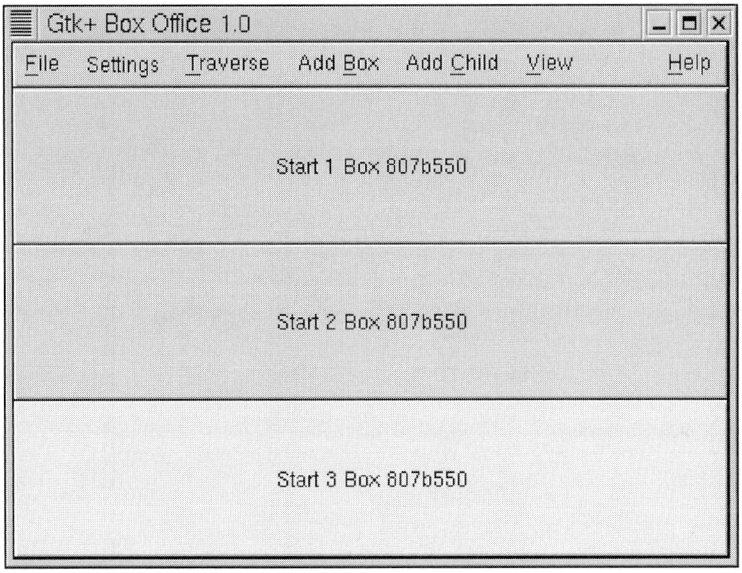

Figure 10.4 Box 1, 2, and 3, Pack Start

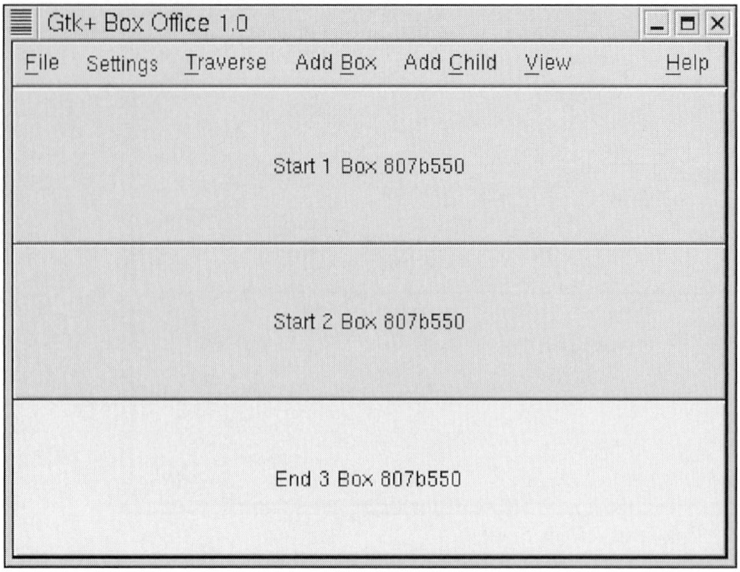

Figure 10.5 Box 1 and 2, Pack Start; Box 3 Pack End

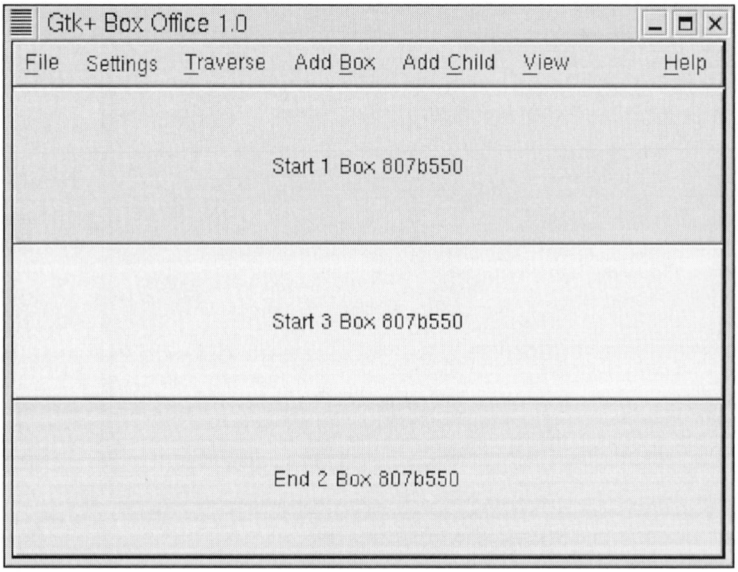

Figure 10.6 Box 1 and 3 Pack Start; Box 2 Pack End

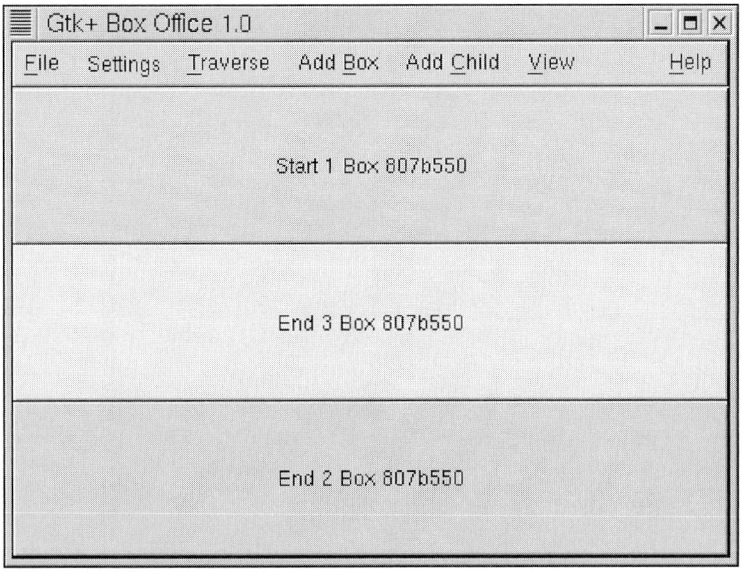

Figure 10.7 Box 1 Pack Start; Box 2 and 3 Pack End

The way to think about "pack start" and "pack end" is to imagine that a virtual, invisible widget exists at both the top and bottom sides of a vertical box (and at the left and right sides of a horizontal box). Adding a widget to this box using "pack start" binds the widget to the virtual widget attached to the top edge, while adding a widget using "pack end" binds the widget to the virtual widget attached to the bottom. Analogous situations exist for horizontal boxes, where "pack start" corresponds to the virtual widget bound to the left side of the box and "pack end" corresponds to the virtual widget bound to the right side of the box.

Once a widget has been attached to the virtual widget, that widget represents the new location to which widgets added to that end will be bound. I find it easy to think of this widget as representing the top of a stack that grows toward the other end of the box. Adding a new widget to a box results in pushing that widget onto the top of the stack that corresponds to the specified edge.

The next two examples illustrate the creation of a more complicated layout and emphasize the flexibility that GtkBox provides—allowing you to choose one of several possible ways to obtain a given layout. The layout is shown in Figure 10.8.

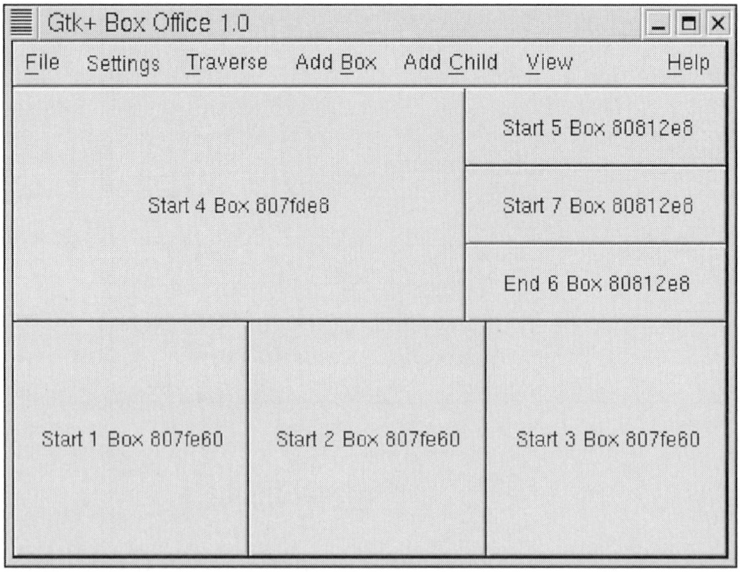

Figure 10.8 Complicated Window Layout

The first strategy adds two horizontal boxes, B and C, to a vertical box A. Both A and B, in this example, are added using "pack start." Then three button widgets, 1, 2, and 3, are added to horizontal box C using "pack start." Next, a vertical box D is added to box B using "pack end," and button widget 4 is also added to box B using "pack start." This causes the vertical box D to attach to the right-hand side of B, and button 4 to attach to the left-hand side of B. Finally, three button widgets, 5, 6, and 7, are added to the vertical box D with "pack start" to complete the layout.

The second strategy begins by adding horizontal box B using "pack start" to the vertical box A. Then button 4 is added to box B using "pack start." Next, vertical box D is added to box B using "pack start." This is followed by adding buttons 7, 6, and 5, in that order, to vertical box D using "pack end." Next, horizontal box C is added to vertical box A using "pack start," and buttons 1, 3, and 2 are added, in this order, to box C using "pack start," "pack end," and "pack start," respectively.

Take some time to convince yourself that both of the preceding strategies result in exactly the same layout.

Homogeneous, Spacing, Expand, Fill, and Padding Attributes

Now that you understand the basics of box orientation and child positioning, I can describe the attributes that can be applied to boxes. These attributes are used by your application to provide hints to a box widget, telling it how you would like the box widget to lay out its children. You should keep in mind the orientation of the box when using these attributes. For example, if the box you are packing child widgets into is a vertical box, these attributes define how child widgets will be packed vertically but not horizontally.

The attributes are described in the following sections.

Homogeneous. If homogeneous is set to TRUE, all children in a box are given the same size, based on the size required for the largest of the children to draw. If homogeneous is set to FALSE, each child widget is given only the space necessary for the child to draw itself correctly. This does not mean that the widget will actually draw itself to consume the entire size it has been given by the box. Whether this happens or not depends on the fill attribute, described below.

Spacing. This attribute defines the amount of space placed by the box between child widgets. This attribute is honored regardless of the homogeneous setting.

Expand. This attribute is only valid if homogeneous is FALSE. If homogeneous is FALSE and expand is FALSE, then widgets are packed tightly together at the end to which they have been added. If homogeneous is FALSE and expand is TRUE, then child widgets are packed so that the entire area of the box is used.

Fill. This attribute applies regardless of the homogeneous setting.

First let's consider the case when homogeneous is set to FALSE. Then, if expand is FALSE, fill is ignored. If expand is TRUE, then we have two cases—fill is FALSE or TRUE. If fill is TRUE, then widgets draw themselves to fill all of the space given to them by the expand attribute. If fill is FALSE, then a widget only draws large enough to render its content correctly.

Second, we have the case that homogeneous is TRUE. This ends up being much like the case in which homogeneous is FALSE, and it is sometimes hard to distinguish the two cases visually. Recall that homogeneous means that if your window is, say, 210 pixels wide, widgets packed into a horizontal box that consumes the entire width of the window will each be given 70 pixels of space. Fill controls whether or not the widget resizes itself to fill the entire space allocated. If fill is TRUE, the widget will resize itself; if fill is FALSE, it won't.

Padding. The final attribute is padding. Padding is somewhat independent of the preceding attributes, including homogeneous. Padding merely adds pixels around what normally would be allocated by the child widget for it to draw itself correctly. If padding is, say, 20 and the box you are packing the child widget into is horizontal, then 20 pixels will be added to the left and to the right of the widget. Or, if the box is vertical, 20 pixels will be added above and below the widget.

Packing Boxes

GtkBox supplies several functions that can be used to pack child widgets into a box. The first of these functions, gtk_box_pack_start(), can be used to pack a child widget from left to right for a horizontal box or from top to bottom for a vertical box.

```
void
gtk_box_pack_start(GtkBox *box, GtkWidget *child, gboolean expand,
        gboolean fill, guint padding);
```

The argument box is an instance of GtkVBox or GtkHBox (there are no construction functions provided by GtkBox; see GtkVBox and GtkHBox later in this chapter for the details on creating instances of vertical and horizontal boxes, respectively). If you store the instance of GtkHBox or GtkVBox in a variable of type GtkWidget *, then use the macro provided by GtkBox to cast it to an instance of GtkBox. For example:

```
GtkWidget *myWidget;

...

gtk_box_pack_start( GTK_BOX( myWidget ), .... );
```

The preceding holds true for the remaining GtkBox functions, all of which take an instance of GtkBox as their first parameter.

The second argument, child, is the child widget being packed into the box. You must also cast this widget; if not stored in a variable of type GtkWidget *, use the macro GTK_WIDGET() to perform the cast operation.

The expand, fill, and padding arguments were all described previously.

You can pack a child widget in the other direction, from right to left for a horizontal box or from bottom to top for a vertical box, with a call to gtk_box_pack_end():

```
void
gtk_box_pack_end(GtkBox *box, GtkWidget *child, gboolean expand,
        gboolean fill, guint padding);
```

The arguments for gtk_box_pack_end() are identical to those passed to gtk_box_pack_start().

In some situations, you may want to pack a child into a box using defaults provided by Gtk+ for expand, fill, and padding. If that is the case, use gtk_box_pack_start_defaults() to pack the child widget from left to right or from top to bottom, or gtk_box_pack_end_defaults() to pack the child widget from right to left or from bottom to top:

```
void
gtk_box_pack_start_defaults(GtkBox *box, GtkWidget *widget);

void
gtk_box_pack_end_defaults(GtkBox *box, GtkWidget *widget);
```

The defaults used in Gtk+ 1.2 are listed in Table 10.6.

Table 10.6 GtkBox Default Packing Attributes

Attribute	*Value*
Expand	TRUE
Fill	TRUE
Padding	0

Making a Box Homogeneous

As described earlier, packing attributes are influenced by the homogeneous attribute of the box into which the child widget is being packed. Setting homogeneous to TRUE tells a box to divide the vertical (in the case of GtkVBox) or horizontal (in the case of GtkHBox) dimension equally among each of the widgets being packed. The default homogeneous setting for a box is FALSE. You can change the homogeneous setting of a box widget at any time simply by calling gtk_box_set_homogeneous():

```
void
gtk_box_set_homogeneous(GtkBox *box, gboolean homogeneous);
```

The argument homogeneous can be either TRUE or FALSE.

Setting the Spacing

Spacing between widgets can be set by calling gtk_box_set_spacing():

```
void
gtk_box_set_spacing(GtkBox *box, gint spacing);
```

The default spacing assigned by GtkBox as of Gtk+ 1.2 is 0.

Repositioning Children

Once packed into a box, a child widget can be repositioned in one of two ways. The first method involves calling gtk_box_reorder_child(). In a box, each child is assigned a position in the range [0, $n - 1$], where n is the number of child widgets, of whatever type, currently packed into the box. Let's say we have a vertical box packed with 10 button widgets, as shown in Figures 10.9 through 10.11, all packed using gtk_box_pack_start().

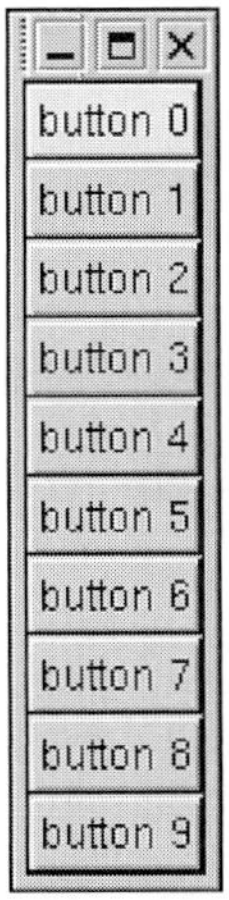

Figure 10.9 Vertical Box with 10 Buttons

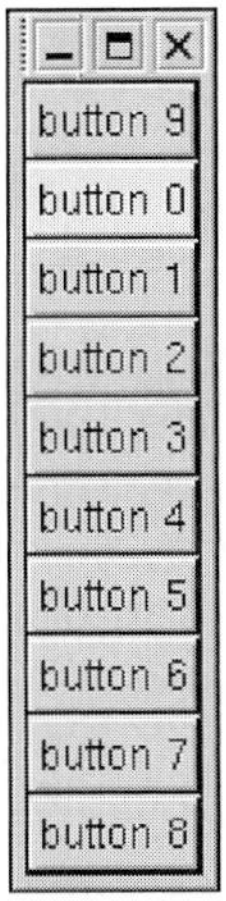

Figure 10.10 Moving Button 9 to Position 0

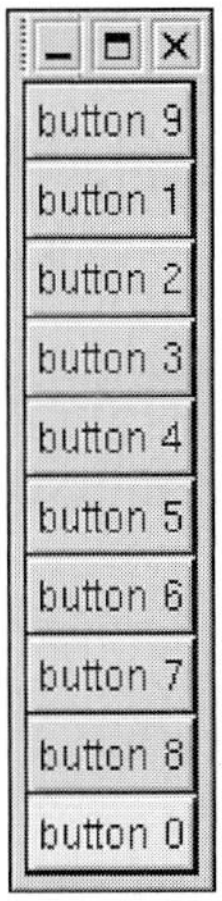

Figure 10.11 Moving Button 0 to Position 9

As you can see, I have labeled the buttons "button 0," "button 1," and so forth, to indicate the positions of each button in the box. Assume the vertical box into which the buttons have been packed is stored in the variable vbox, while the button widgets themselves are stored in a vector named button.

```
gtk_box_reorder_child( GTK_BOX( vbox ), button[ 9 ], 0 );
```

The preceding call will move the button previously at the bottom of the box to the top position (position 0), pushing the remaining buttons down one position (incrementing their positions within the box by one). See Figure 10.10.

```
gtk_box_reorder_child( GTK_BOX( vbox ), button[ 0 ], 9 );
```

Similarly, the preceding moves the button originally at the top of the box to the bottom, causing the remaining buttons to decrement their previous position attribute by one. This is illustrated in Figure 10.11.

The function prototype for gtk_box_reorder_child() should be obvious at this point:

```
void
gtk_box_reorder_child(GtkBox *box, GtkWidget *child, gint position);
```

Here, box is the vertical or horizontal box that contains the widget specified by the argument child (which is the widget that will be given a new position). position, once again, is in the range $[0, n - 1]$. It is important to understand that position values increment from top to bottom in vertical boxes when "pack start" is used and from bottom to top in vertical boxes when "pack end" is used. Likewise, position values increment from left to right in horizontal boxes when pack start is used and from right to left in horizontal boxes when pack end is used.

Setting and Getting Packing Attributes

The other way to reposition a child within a box is by changing its packing attributes using gtk_box_set_child_packing():

```
void
gtk_box_set_child_packing(GtkBox *box, GtkWidget *child,
       gboolean expand, gboolean fill, guint padding,
       GtkPackType pack_type);
```

The arguments box, child, expand, fill, and padding have all been described previously. The argument pack_type is an enum that can be set to either GTK_PACK_START or GTK_PACK_END. Changing the pack_type of a child widget moves it to the other end of the box, placing it at the next available position in the box as though it were being adding to the box using gtk_box_pack_start() or gtk_box_pack_end().

You can retrieve the packing settings of a child in the box by calling gtk_box_query_child_packing():

```
void
gtk_box_query_child_packing(GtkBox *box, GtkWidget *child,
       gboolean *expand, gboolean *fill, guint *padding,
       GtkPackType *pack_type);
```

The arguments box and child are as always: the box of interest and the child being managed by that box. The arguments expand, fill, padding, and pack_type are pointers to variables of type gboolean, gboolean, guint, and GtkPackType, respectively. On return, these variables will contain the settings that apply to the child being queried.

Now that we have a good understanding of the base class GtkBox, we can take a look at the Gtk+ classes that inherit from GtkBox, namely GtkVBox and GtkHBox. There is relatively little to say about these classes other than how to create instances of each.

GtkVBox

Class Name

```
GtkVBox
```

Parent Class Name

```
GtkBox
```

Macros

Widget type macro: `GTK_TYPE_VBOX`

Object to widget cast macro: `GTK_VBOX(obj)`

Widget type check macro: `GTK_IS_VBOX(obj)`

Application-Level API Synopsis

Retrieve the constant GTK_TYPE_VBOX at runtime:

```
GtkType
gtk_vbox_get_type(void);
```

Create a new instance of GtkVBox:

```
GtkWidget *
gtk_vbox_new(gboolean homogeneous, gint spacing);
```

Class Description

GtkVBox is a subclass of GtkBox, which was previously described. An instance of GtkVBox will pack its children from top to bottom when added to the box using the function gtk_box_pack_start() or from bottom to start when children are added to the box with gtk_box_pack_end(). To create an instance of GtkVBox, simply call gtk_vbox_new():

```
GtkWidget *
gtk_vbox_new(gboolean homogeneous, gint spacing);
```

The arguments homogeneous and spacing are described in the preceding section on GtkBox. Briefly, setting homogeneous to TRUE tells the box to give equal area to child widgets packed into the box in the vertical dimension. So, for example, if three children are packed into the box, each widget occupies one third of the vertical area available in the box. If homogeneous is FALSE, the vertical space within the box is handed out on an as-needed basis.

The argument spacing defines how many pixels are placed between children in the box, also in the vertical dimension.

All of the functions supplied by GtkBox are available for use by instances of GtkVBox. When a GtkBox argument is called for, cast it to GtkBox * using the GTK_BOX() macro.

GtkHBox

Class Name

```
GtkHBox
```

Parent Class Name

```
GtkBox
```

Macros

Widget type macro: `GTK_TYPE_HBOX`

Object to widget cast macro: `GTK_HBOX(obj)`

Widget type check macro: `GTK_IS_HBOX(obj)`

Application-Level API Synopsis

Retrieve the constant GTK_TYPE_HBOX at runtime:
```
GtkType
gtk_hbox_get_type(void);
```

Create a new instance of GtkHBox:
```
GtkWidget *
gtk_hbox_new(gboolean homogeneous, gint spacing);
```

Class Description

Similar to GtkVBox, GtkHBox is a subclass of GtkBox. Instances of GtkHBox will pack children from left to right when added to the box using the function gtk_box_pack_start() or from right to left when children are added to the box with gtk_box_pack_end(). To create an instance of GtkHBox, simply call gtk_hbox_new():

```
GtkWidget *
gtk_hbox_new(gboolean homogeneous, gint spacing);
```

The arguments homogeneous and spacing were described in the previous section on GtkBox. When homogeneous is set to TRUE, the box gives equal area to child widgets packed into the box in the horizontal dimension. So, for example, if three child widgets are packed into the box, each widget occupies one third of the horizontal area available in the box. If homogeneous is FALSE, the horizontal space within the box is allocated on an as-needed basis.

The argument spacing defines how many pixels are placed between children in the box, also in the horizontal dimension.

All of the functions supplied by GtkBox are available for use by instances of GtkHBox. When a GtkBox argument is called for by one of the GtkBox functions, cast it to GtkBox * using the GTK_BOX() macro.

GtkButtonBox

Class Name

```
GtkButtonBox
```

Parent Class Name

```
GtkBox
```

Macros

Widget type macro: `GTK_TYPE_BUTTON_BOX`

Object to widget cast macro: `GTK_BUTTON_BOX(obj)`

Widget type check macro: `GTK_IS_BUTTON_BOX(obj)`

Application-Level API Synopsis

Retrieve the constant GTK_TYPE_BUTTON_BOX at runtime:

```
GtkType
gtk_button_box_get_type (void);
```

Retrieve the default minimum width and minimum height values for child widgets:

```
void
gtk_button_box_get_child_size_default(gint *min_width,
          gint *min_height);
```

Retrieve the default button box padding:

```
void
gtk_button_box_get_child_ipadding_default(gint *ipad_x,
          gint *ipad_y);
```

Set the default minimum width and minimum height values for child widgets:

```
void
gtk_button_box_set_child_size_default(gint min_width,
          gint min_height);
```

Set the default button box padding:

```
void
gtk_button_box_set_child_ipadding_default(gint ipad_x, gint ipad_y);
```

Retrieve the interchild spacing:

```
gint
gtk_button_box_get_spacing(GtkButtonBox *widget);
```

Get the button box style (see text):

```
GtkButtonBoxStyle
gtk_button_box_get_layout(GtkButtonBox *widget);
```

Retrieve the child size:

```
void
gtk_button_box_get_child_size(GtkButtonBox *widget, gint *min_width,
         gint *min_height);
```

Application-Level API Synopsis (Continued)

Retrieve the child padding:
```
void
gtk_button_box_get_child_ipadding(GtkButtonBox *widget,
        gint *ipad_x, gint *ipad_y);
```

Set the interchild spacing:
```
void
gtk_button_box_set_spacing(GtkButtonBox *widget, gint spacing);
```

Set the button box style (see text):
```
void
gtk_button_box_set_layout(GtkButtonBox *widget,
        GtkButtonBoxStyle layout_style);
```

Set the child size:
```
void
gtk_button_box_set_child_size(GtkButtonBox *widget, gint min_width,
        gint min_height);
```

Set the child padding:
```
void
gtk_button_box_set_child_ipadding(GtkButtonBox *widget, gint ipad_x,
        gint ipad_y);
```

Class Description

Button boxes inherit from GtkBox, just as instances of GtkVBox and GtkHBox do. Therefore, functions in the API set previously described for GtkBox can be called on to operate on button boxes. However, results will not always be as I described earlier. For example, gtk_box_pack_start() and gtk_box_pack_end() can be used to add children to a button box, but these two functions will give the exact same result (which is equivalent to the result obtained by calling gtk_container_add() to add a child to the button box; the widget will be added from left to right when added to a horizontal button box or from top to bottom when added to a vertical button box).

Table 10.7 summarizes the applicability of the GtkBox API when applied to an instance of GtkButtonBox:

Table 10.7 GtkBox Functions Applied to a Button Box

Function	*Notes*
gtk_box_pack_start()	Packing direction, arguments ignored.
gtk_box_pack_end()	Packing direction, arguments ignored.

Table 10.7 GtkBox Functions Applied to a Button Box (Continued)

Function	*Notes*
gtk_box_pack_start_defaults()	Packing direction ignored.
gtk_box_pack_end_defaults()	Packing direction ignored.
gtk_box_set_homogeneous()	Not applicable, no-op.
gtk_box_set_spacing()	Not applicable, no-op.
gtk_box_reorder_child()	Fully functional.
gtk_box_query_child_packing()	Results should be ignored.
gtk_box_set_child_packing()	Results are ignored.

As you can see, only three of the GtkBox API functions—gtk_box_pack_start(), gtk_box_pack_end(), and gtk_box_reorder_child()—can be used with button boxes, and only one of those, gtk_box_reorder_child(), is fully functional if used with button boxes.

Although GtkButtonBox can be used to manage any Gtk+ widget class (including other button boxes), it was designed mainly to support the organization of instances of GtkButton. Although GtkHBox and GtkVBox certainly provide all of the capabilities necessary for managing a group of push buttons, GtkButtonBox simplifies the task considerably.

Both vertical (GtkVBox) and horizontal (GtkHBox) button boxes are supported by Gtk+. Children added to a horizontal button box are added from left to right, while children added to a vertical button box are added from top to bottom. Most applications will use a horizontal button box to organize buttons, but of course, you may decide to organize a set of buttons (or instances of any other widget class) vertically for whatever reason you find necessary.

At this point, let's take a look at the GtkButtonBox API and learn more about how button boxes can be used.

Setting and Getting the Layout Style

Every button box has a layout style attribute. This attribute defines how child widgets managed by the box are laid out. The layout styles supported by GtkButtonBox are illustrated by Figures 10.12 through 10.15.

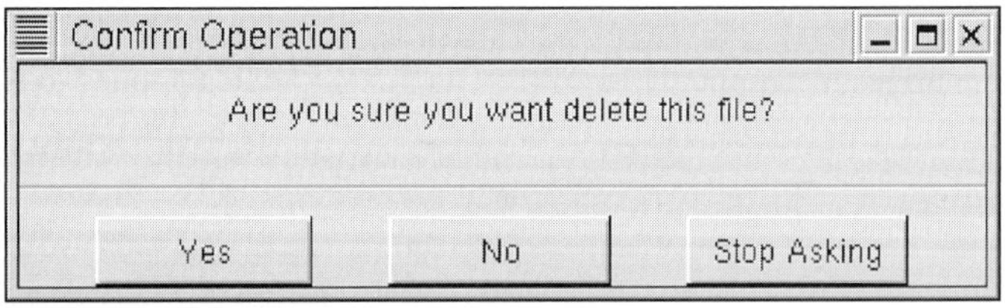

Figure 10.12 GTK_BUTTONBOX_SPREAD

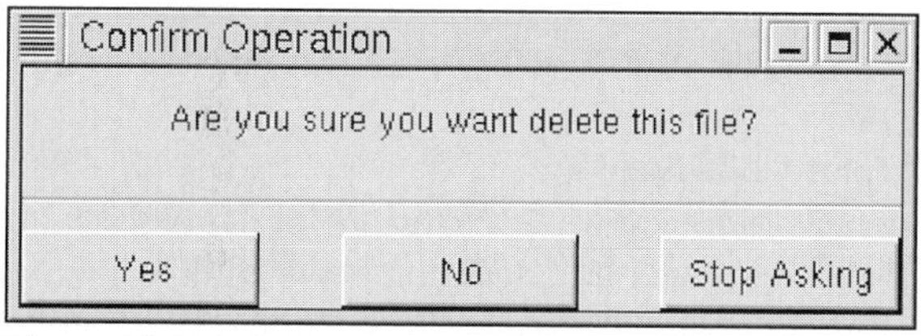

Figure 10.13 GTK_BUTTONBOX_EDGE

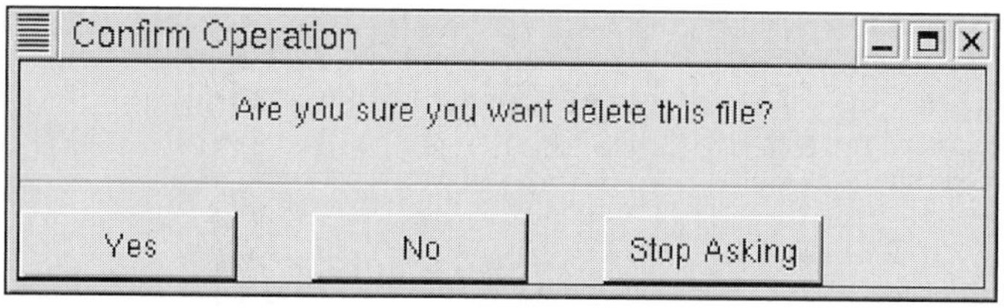

Figure 10.14 GTK_BUTTONBOX_START

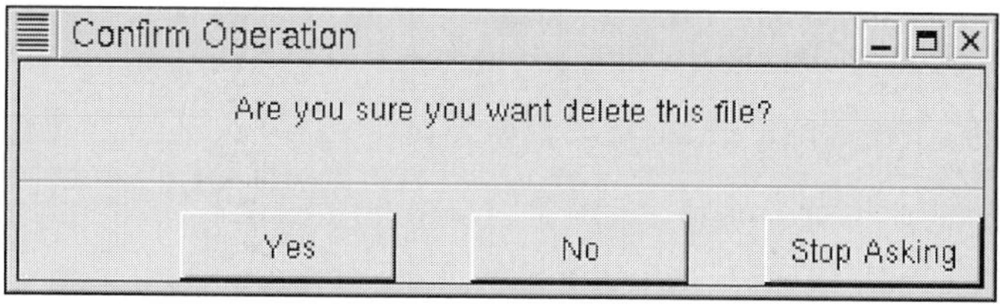

Figure 10.15 GTK_BUTTONBOX_END

The default style, GTK_BUTTONBOX_DEFAULT_STYLE, is equivalent (in Gtk+ 1.2) to specifying GTK_BUTTONBOX_EDGE.

To specify a layout style (in lieu of using the default layout style), you can call gtk_button_box_set_layout():

```
void
gtk_button_box_set_layout(GtkButtonBox *widget,
         GtkButtonBoxStyle layout_style);
```

The argument widget is an instance of GtkVButtonBox or GtkHButtonBox. The argument layout style is one of the following: GTK_BUTTONBOX_SPREAD, GTK_BUTTONBOX_EDGE, GTK_BUTTONBOX_START, GTK_BUTTONBOX_END, or GTK_BUTTONBOX_DEFAULT_STYLE.

Determining the layout style of a button box is easily done by calling gtk_button_box_get_style():

```
GtkButtonBoxStyle
gtk_button_box_get_layout(GtkButtonBox *widget);
```

One of the constants GTK_BUTTONBOX_SPREAD, GTK_BUTTONBOX_EDGE, GTK_BUTTONBOX_START, or GTK_BUTTONBOX_END is returned by this function.

Setting and Getting the Default Child Size

GtkButtonBox maintains a default minimum width and height for its children. In Gtk+ 1.2, the default minimum child width is 85, and the default minimum child height is 27.

You can set new defaults by calling gtk_button_box_set_child_size_default(), and you can determine the current default minimum width and minimum height values for child widgets with a call to gtk_button_box_get_child_size_default(). The function prototypes for these two functions are, respectively:

```
void
gtk_button_box_set_child_size_default(gint min_width,
          gint min_height);

void
gtk_button_box_get_child_size_default(gint *min_width,
          gint *min_height);
```

In addition to default child height and width values, every instance of GtkButtonBox maintains a current child height and width. When a button box is asked by its containing widget to compute its size requirement, it executes the following code, which takes into account both the current and default widths and heights:

```
// grab the default width and height values

gtk_button_box_get_child_size_default (&width_default,
          &height_default);

// if the current width has been set by the application to
// non-default value, use that, else use the default width

child_min_width = bbox-child_min_width   != GTK_BUTTONBOX_DEFAULT
        ? bbox-child_min_width : width_default;

// if the current height has been set by the application to a
// non-default value, use that, else use the default height

child_min_height = bbox-child_min_height !=GTK_BUTTONBOX_DEFAULT
        ? bbox-child_min_height : height_default;
```

Remember that the default width and height are maintained for (and shared by) all instances of GtkButtonBox created by your application. The current width and height values, however, are maintained separately for each instance of GtkButtonBox. Therefore, if you should decide to change the default width or height value, this change will affect all instances of GtkButtonBox in your application, while the current minimum width and height, if they are changed, will only affect the instance of GtkButtonBox that you specify.

Most of you will never need to change either the default or the current child size values. However, should you find a need to do so, you are likely dealing with one of the following cases:

1. You need to increase or decrease the minimum width, minimum height, or both for all button boxes in your application, which will share these values.
2. The default values are suitable for most, but not all, of the button boxes in your application.
3. Same as case 2, but the default width or height also needs to be changed.

For case 1, call gtk_button_box_set_child_size_default() once and pass it the desired defaults before adding children to the button boxes; all child widgets added to button boxes in your application will use the specified values.

For case 2, use gtk_button_box_set_child_size() to set the current child size value for the button box(es) that must use nondefault minimum width or height values.

For case 3, follow the steps outlined for case 1 and then the steps outlined for case 2.

Getting and Setting the Current Child Size Minimums

To retrieve the current child size width and height values, your application can call gtk_button_box_get_child_size():

```
void
gtk_button_box_get_child_size(GtkButtonBox *widget, gint *min_width,
       gint *min_height);
```

The argument widget is the button box being queried. On return, min_width and min_height hold the current minimum width and minimum height values, respectively. To change the current minimums, call gtk_button_box_set_child_size():

```
void
gtk_button_box_set_child_size(GtkButtonBox *widget, gint min_width,
       gint min_height);
```

The argument widget, once again, is the button box of interest. The arguments min_width and min_height are the new current minimums that will be applied to the button box.

Setting and Getting the Child Internal Padding Values

Each button box has two internal padding values that are applied to each child when computing its width and height. One of these values, ipad_x, is added to both the left- and right-hand sides of each child. The other, ipad_y, is added to both the top and bottom of each child. Just like the minimum child width and height values, GtkButtonBox maintains both default and current values for both ipad_x and ipad_y. And, as was the case for the width and height minimum values, your application can retrieve and set both the default and current values as needed. The scenarios involved are the same as described for the minimum width and height values, including the three cases previously described. Of course, the functions involved are different. To retrieve the default internal padding values, your application can call gtk_button_box_get_child_ipadding_default():

```
void
gtk_button_box_get_child_ipadding_default(gint *ipad_x, gint *ipad_y);
```

The arguments ipad_x and ipad_y, on return, will hold the internal padding defaults for the x and y dimensions, respectively. To set new default padding defaults, call gtk_button_box_set_child_ipadding_default():

```
void
gtk_button_box_set_child_ipadding_default(gint ipad_x, gint ipad_y);
```

The arguments ipad_x and ipad_y specify the new default values.

The functions for retrieving and setting the current padding values fall along the same lines as those for minimum widths and heights but require as a first argument the button box of interest. To retrieve the current padding values, call gtk_button_box_get_child_ipadding():

```
void
gtk_button_box_get_child_ipadding(GtkButtonBox *widget, gint *ipad_x,
       gint *ipad_y);
```

To change the current padding values, call gtk_button_box_set_child_ipadding():

```
void
gtk_button_box_set_child_ipadding(GtkButtonBox *widget, gint ipad_x,
       gint ipad_y);
```

The arguments for both of these functions should be self-explanatory.

Setting and Getting the Interchild Spacing

There is an additional button box attribute that we have some control over: the amount of space that exists between children in the box. Spacing is only added to the major orientation of the button box. For example, if we are working with a vertical button box, spacing will only be added between children along the y-axis, not the x-axis. As of Gtk+ 1.2, default spacing for vertical button boxes is 30 pixels, while the default spacing for horizontal button boxes is 10 pixels (we will see later that both of these values can be changed).

To obtain the interchild spacing, you can call gtk_button_box_get_spacing():

```
gint
gtk_button_box_get_spacing(GtkButtonBox *widget);
```

The argument widget is the GtkButtonBox instance of interest. To set the interchild spacing value, call gtk_button_box_set_spacing():

```
void
gtk_button_box_set_spacing(GtkButtonBox *widget, gint spacing);
```

The argument widget, again, is the button box of interest, and spacing is the new interchild spacing value.

Now that we have a good grasp of button boxes, it is time to look at how we can create instances of vertical (GtkVButtonBox) and horizontal (GtkHButtonBox) button box widgets. We will also discover how the default spacing values can be changed and queried by your application.

GtkVButtonBox

Class Name

```
GtkVButtonBox
```

Parent Class Name

```
GtkButtonBox
```

Macros

Widget type macro: `GTK_TYPE_BUTTON_BOX`

Object to widget cast macro: `GTK_VBUTTON_BOX(obj)`

Widget type check macro: `GTK_IS_VBUTTON_BOX(obj)`

Application-Level API Synopsis

Retrieve the constant GTK_TYPE_BUTTON_BOX at runtime:
```
guint
gtk_vbutton_box_get_type(void);
```

Create a new instance of GtkVButtonBox:
```
GtkWidget *
gtk_vbutton_box_new(void);
```

Get the default interchild spacing:
```
gint
gtk_vbutton_box_get_spacing_default(void);
```

Set the default interchild spacing:
```
void
gtk_vbutton_box_set_spacing_default(gint spacing);
```

Retrieve the default box layout style:
```
GtkButtonBoxStyle
gtk_vbutton_box_get_layout_default(void);
```

Set the default box layout style:
```
void
gtk_vbutton_box_set_layout_default(GtkButtonBoxStyle layout);
```

Class Description

Vertical button boxes were introduced in an earlier section (see GtkButtonBox). Less commonly used than horizontal button boxes (GtkHButtonBox, below), a vertical button box arranges its child widgets vertically based on layout style, interchild spacing, and child internal padding attributes that your application can optionally specify. If you haven't yet done so, take the time to read about GtkButtonBox (see the previous section), which is the parent class of GtkVButtonBox, to learn more about these attributes and their default values.

Creating a Vertical Button Box

Creating an instance of GtkVButtonBox is relatively easy and can be done with a call to gtk_vbutton_box_new():

```
GtkWidget *
gtk_vbutton_box_new(void);
```

The return value is an instance of GtkWidget. As is typical, this will need to be cast to GtkButtonBox if passed as the first argument to GtkButtonBox functions, using the GTK_BUTTON_BOX macro. None of the GtkVButtonBox functions accept an instance of GtkVButtonBox, so casting is not relevant when dealing with them.

Getting and Setting the Interchild Spacing

GtkVButtonBox maintains defaults for interchild spacing and layout style. It is possible for your application to query these defaults or to change them. For vertical button boxes, the default interchild spacing is 10 pixels, and the default layout style is GTK_BUTTONBOX_EDGE. To retrieve the default interchild spacing, call gtk_vbutton_box_get_spacing_default():

```
gint
gtk_vbutton_box_get_spacing_default(void);
```

gtk_vbutton_box_set_spacing_default() can be used to set the default interchild spacing:

```
void
gtk_vbutton_box_set_spacing_default(gint spacing);
```

Setting and Getting the Layout Style

To retrieve the default box layout style, make a call to gtk_vbutton_box_get_layout_default():

```
GtkButtonBoxStyle
gtk_vbutton_box_get_layout_default(void);
```

To set the default box layout style, gtk_vbutton_box_set_layout_default() can be called:

```
void
gtk_vbutton_box_set_layout_default(GtkButtonBoxStyle layout);
```

Refer to the discussion of GtkButtonBox for illustrations depicting the various layout styles as applied to vertical button boxes.

GtkHButtonBox

Class Name

```
GtkHButtonBox
```

Parent Class Name

```
GtkButtonBox
```

Macros

Widget type macro: `GTK_TYPE_BUTTON_BOX`

Object to widget cast macro: `GTK_HBUTTON_BOX(obj)`

Widget type check macro: `GTK_IS_HBUTTON_BOX(obj)`

Application-Level API Synopsis

Retrieve the constant GTK_TYPE_BUTTON_BOX at runtime:

```
guint
gtk_hbutton_box_get_type(void);
```

Create a new instance of GtkHButtonBox:

```
GtkWidget *
gtk_hbutton_box_new(void);
```

Get the default interchild spacing:

```
gint
gtk_hbutton_box_get_spacing_default(void);
```

Get the default box layout style:

```
GtkButtonBoxStyle
gtk_hbutton_box_get_layout_default(void);
```

Set the default interchild spacing:

```
void
gtk_hbutton_box_set_spacing_default(gint spacing);
```

Set the default box layout style:

```
void
gtk_hbutton_box_set_layout_default(GtkButtonBoxStyle layout);
```

Class Description

Horizontal button boxes were introduced previously (see GtkButtonBox). A horizontal button box arranges its child widgets horizontally based on layout style, interchild spacing, and child internal padding attributes that an application can optionally specify. If you haven't yet done so, take the time to read about GtkButtonBox (see the previous section), which is the parent class of GtkHButtonBox, to learn more about these attributes and their default values.

Creating a Horizontal Button Box

Creating an instance of GtkHButtonBox is relatively easy and can be done with a call to gtk_hbutton_box_new():

```
GtkWidget *
gtk_hbutton_box_new(void);
```

The return value is an instance of GtkWidget. As is typical, this will need to be cast to GtkButtonBox if passed as the first argument to GtkButtonBox functions, using the GTK_BUTTON_BOX macro. None of the GtkHButtonBox functions accept an instance of GtkHButtonBox, so casting is not relevant when dealing with them.

Getting and Setting Interchild Spacing

GtkHButtonBox maintains defaults for interchild spacing and layout style. It is possible for your application to query these defaults or to change them. For horizontal button boxes, the default interchild spacing is 30 pixels, and the default layout style is GTK_BUTTONBOX_EDGE. To retrieve the default interchild spacing, call gtk_hbutton_box_get_spacing_default():

```
gint
gtk_hbutton_box_get_spacing_default(void);
```

The function gtk_hbutton_box_set_spacing_default() can be used to set the default interchild spacing:

```
void
gtk_hbutton_box_set_spacing_default(gint spacing);
```

Getting and Setting the Default Layout Style

To retrieve the default box layout style, you can make a call to gtk_hbutton_box_get_layout_default():

```
GtkButtonBoxStyle
gtk_hbutton_box_get_layout_default(void);
```

To set the default box layout style, gtk_hbutton_box_set_layout_default() can be called:

```
void
gtk_hbutton_box_set_layout_default(GtkButtonBoxStyle layout);
```

Refer to the discussion of GtkButtonBox for illustrations depicting the various layout styles as applied to vertical button boxes.

GtkNotebook

Class Name

```
GtkNotebook
```

Parent Class Name

```
GtkContainer
```

Macros

Widget type macro: `GTK_TYPE_NOTEBOOK`

Object to widget cast macro: `GTK_NOTEBOOK(obj)`

Widget type check macro: `GTK_IS_NOTEBOOK(obj)`

Supported Signals

Table 10.8 Signals

Signal Name	*Condition Causing Signal to Trigger*
switch_page	The current page in the notebook was switched.

Signal Function Prototypes

```
void
switch_page(GtkNotebook *notebook, GtkNotebookPage *page,
      gint page_num, gpointer user_data);
```

Supported Arguments

Prefix: `GtkNotebook::`

Table 10.9 GtkNotebook Arguments

Name	*Type*	*Permissions*
page	GTK_TYPE_INT	GTK_ARG_READWRITE

Table 10.9 GtkNotebook Arguments (Continued)

Name	*Type*	*Permissions*
tab_pos	GTK_TYPE_POSITION_TYPE	GTK_ARG_READWRITE
tab_border	GTK_TYPE_UINT	GTK_ARG_WRITABLE
tab_hborder	GTK_TYPE_UINT	GTK_ARG_READWRITE
tab_vborder	GTK_TYPE_UINT	GTK_ARG_READWRITE
show_tabs	GTK_TYPE_BOOL	GTK_ARG_READWRITE
show_border	GTK_TYPE_BOOL	GTK_ARG_READWRITE
scrollable	GTK_TYPE_BOOL	GTK_ARG_READWRITE
enable_popup	GTK_TYPE_BOOL	GTK_ARG_READWRITE
tab_label	GTK_TYPE_STRING	GTK_ARG_READWRITE
menu_label	GTK_TYPE_STRING	GTK_ARG_READWRITE
position	GTK_TYPE_INT	GTK_ARG_READWRITE
tab_fill	GTK_TYPE_BOOL	GTK_ARG_READWRITE
tab_pack	GTK_TYPE_BOOL	GTK_ARG_READWRITE

Application-Level API Synopsis

Retrieve the constant GTK_TYPE_NOTEBOOK at runtime:

```
GtkType
gtk_notebook_get_type(void);
```

Create a new instance of GtkNotebook:

```
GtkWidget *
gtk_notebook_new(void);
```

Append a widget to the notebook with the specified label:

```
void
gtk_notebook_append_page(GtkNotebook *notebook, GtkWidget *child,
        GtkWidget *tab_label);
```

Append a widget to the notebook with the specified label and add a menu item to the notebook pop-up menu:

```
void
gtk_notebook_append_page_menu(GtkNotebook *notebook,
       GtkWidget *child, GtkWidget *tab_label, GtkWidget *menu_label);
```

Application-Level API Synopsis (Continued)

Prepend a widget to the notebook with the specified label:

```
void
gtk_notebook_prepend_page(GtkNotebook *notebook, GtkWidget *child,
       GtkWidget *tab_label);
```

Prepend a widget to the notebook with the specified label and add a menu item to the notebook pop-up menu:

```
void
gtk_notebook_prepend_page_menu(GtkNotebook *notebook,
      GtkWidget *child, GtkWidget *tab_label, GtkWidget *menu_label);
```

Insert a widget into the notebook with the specified label:

```
void
gtk_notebook_insert_page(GtkNotebook *notebook, GtkWidget *child,
       GtkWidget *tab_label, gint position);
```

Insert a widget into the notebook with the specified label and add a menu item to the notebook pop-up menu:

```
void
gtk_notebook_insert_page_menu(GtkNotebook *notebook,
       GtkWidget *child, GtkWidget *tab_label, GtkWidget *menu_label,
      gint position);
```

Remove a page from the notebook:

```
void
gtk_notebook_remove_page(GtkNotebook *notebook, gint page_num);
```

Retrieve the index of the currently shown page:

```
gint
gtk_notebook_get_current_page(GtkNotebook *notebook);
```

Retrieve the widget corresponding to the *n*th page of the notebook:

```
GtkWidget *
gtk_notebook_get_nth_page(GtkNotebook *notebook, gint page_num);
```

Given a widget, determine its page number in the notebook:

```
gint
gtk_notebook_page_num(GtkNotebook *notebook, GtkWidget *child);
```

Display the specified page:

```
void
gtk_notebook_set_page(GtkNotebook *notebook, gint page_num);
```

Traverse to the next page in the notebook:

```
void
gtk_notebook_next_page(GtkNotebook *notebook);
```

Traverse to the previous page in the notebook:

```
void
gtk_notebook_prev_page(GtkNotebook *notebook);
```

Application-Level API Synopsis (Continued)

Toggle the display of a border:

```
void
gtk_notebook_set_show_border(GtkNotebook *notebook,
       gboolean show_border);
```

Toggle the display of tabs:

```
void
gtk_notebook_set_show_tabs(GtkNotebook *notebook,
       gboolean show_tabs);
```

Change the location of tabs in the notebook:

```
void
gtk_notebook_set_tab_pos(GtkNotebook *notebook,
       GtkPositionType pos);
```

Enable (disable) homogeneous (same-sized) notebook tabs:

```
void
gtk_notebook_set_homogeneous_tabs(GtkNotebook *notebook,
       gboolean homogeneous);
```

Set the border width of tabs:

```
void
gtk_notebook_set_tab_border(GtkNotebook *notebook,
       guint border_width);
```

Set the horizontal border width of tabs:

```
void
gtk_notebook_set_tab_hborder(GtkNotebook *notebook,
       guint tab_hborder);
```

Set the vertical border width of tabs:

```
void
gtk_notebook_set_tab_vborder(GtkNotebook *notebook,
       guint tab_vborder);
```

Enable (disable) the ability of the notebook to scroll:

```
void
gtk_notebook_set_scrollable(GtkNotebook *notebook,
       gboolean scrollable);
```

Enable the display of the notebook pop-up menu:

```
void
gtk_notebook_popup_enable(GtkNotebook *notebook);
```

Disable the display of the notebook pop-up menu:

```
void
gtk_notebook_popup_disable(GtkNotebook *notebook);
```

Retrieve the label of the tab associated with the specified widget:

```
GtkWidget *
gtk_notebook_get_tab_label(GtkNotebook *notebook, GtkWidget *child);
```

Application-Level API Synopsis (Continued)

Set the label of the tab associated with the specified widget:

```
void
gtk_notebook_set_tab_label(GtkNotebook *notebook, GtkWidget *child,
      GtkWidget *tab_label);
```

Set the text of the label tab associated with the specified widget:

```
void
gtk_notebook_set_tab_label_text(GtkNotebook *notebook, GtkW
      idget *child, const gchar *tab_text);
```

Get the menu label associated with the specified widget:

```
GtkWidget *
gtk_notebook_get_menu_label(GtkNotebook *notebook,
      GtkWidget *child);
```

Set the menu label associated with the specified widget:

```
void
gtk_notebook_set_menu_label(GtkNotebook *notebook, GtkWidget *child,
      GtkWidget *menu_label);
```

Set the text of the menu label associated with the specified widget:

```
void
gtk_notebook_set_menu_label_text(GtkNotebook *notebook,
      GtkWidget *child, const gchar *menu_text);
```

Query the packing of a notebook tab:

```
void
gtk_notebook_query_tab_label_packing(GtkNotebook *notebook,
      GtkWidget *child,gboolean *expand, gboolean *fill,
      GtkPackType *pack_type);
```

Set the packing of a notebook tab:

```
void
gtk_notebook_set_tab_label_packing(GtkNotebook *notebook,
      GtkWidget *child, gboolean expand, gboolean fill,
      GtkPackType pack_type);
```

Change the position of a tab in the notebook:

```
void
gtk_notebook_reorder_child(GtkNotebook *notebook, GtkWidget *child,
      gint position);
```

Class Description

Notebook widgets help solve a problem that is often faced by user-interface designers: the need to present a large set of user-interface controls in a way that minimizes the amount of screen or dialog real estate used. Notebook widgets work particularly well when the user-interface controls that must be presented all fall within a somewhat general category and the category can be partitioned into a relatively small set of subcategories. The notebook widget itself can be used to represent the general category, while panels (or pages) of the notebook can be used to represent the partitioning of the general category into its constituent subcategories.

A preferences dialog provides a particularly good example of this sort of user-interface situation. Many application user interfaces contain a menu item or a button labeled Preferences or perhaps Edit Preferences. When the menu item or button is selected by the user, a dialog will typically be displayed. If the number of preference items or controls is small, they usually can be fit into a single dialog. If a partitioning of preference items exists, then horizontal separators or frames may be used to group together items that are related.

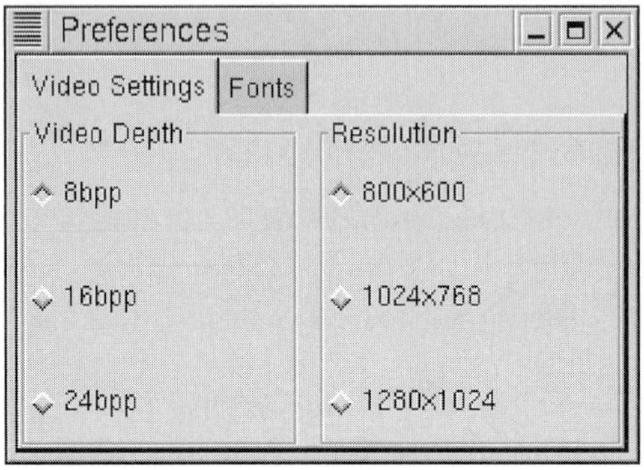

Figure 10.16 Preferences Panel

However, if the number of preference controls is large, then a notebook is an ideal choice for organizing the content. Figure 10.16 illustrates how a set of related controls might be organized in panels of a notebook widget. Notice how controls related to each other within a panel are further grouped together by surrounding them with frames.

Let's take a look at the basic components of a notebook control. All notebooks contain one or more (usually two or more) panels. A panel consists of both a tab and a content area. The tab displays a label that identifies the panel to the user (an image can also be displayed if desired). In Figure 10.16, the panel with the tab labeled Video Settings is the current panel. A panel can be made current by positioning the mouse pointer over the panel's tab and clicking mouse button 1.

GtkNotebook allows applications to create a pop-up menu that can be used at runtime to change the current panel of the notebook. The pop-up menu contains one menu item for each panel in the notebook. The labels of the menu items in the pop-up menu correspond to the labels displayed by the tabs in the notebook control. To activate the pop-up menu, the user positions the mouse pointer over any one of the panel tabs and then clicks mouse button 2. Selecting a menu item from the pop-up menu will cause the panel corresponding to the selected menu item to be made the current panel. When scrollbars are active it is possible that the tab corresponding to a panel will not be visible, making it difficult to select the panel without first scrolling the tab into view. In cases like this, the pop-up menu solution may provide an easier way for users to select the current panel. My advice is that when you enable scrolling tabs, you should also support the pop-up menu just described.

The default behavior of a notebook is to display all panel tabs, resizing them as necessary so that they are all visible to the user. If a relatively large number of tabs exists or their labels are relatively long, it may be best to enable scrolling. Figure 10.17 illustrates a notebook with scrolling disabled, and Figure 10.18 shows the same with scrolling enabled.

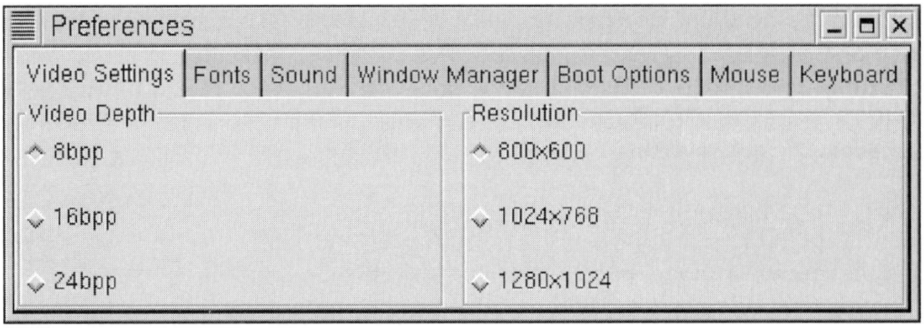

Figure 10.17 Notebook with Several Tabs

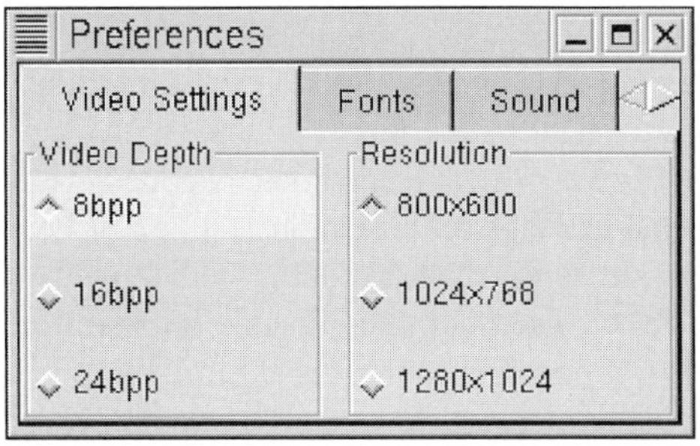

Figure 10.18 Figure 10.17 as a Scrollable Notebook

An additional notebook attribute you can specify is the placement of the tabs. GtkNotebook supports four orientations: above or below the notebook or along the left- or right-hand side of the notebook. The first two cases cause the tabs to be drawn horizontally (left to right), while the tabs in the other two cases are drawn vertically. Figure 10.19 illustrates tabs that have been placed along the bottom.

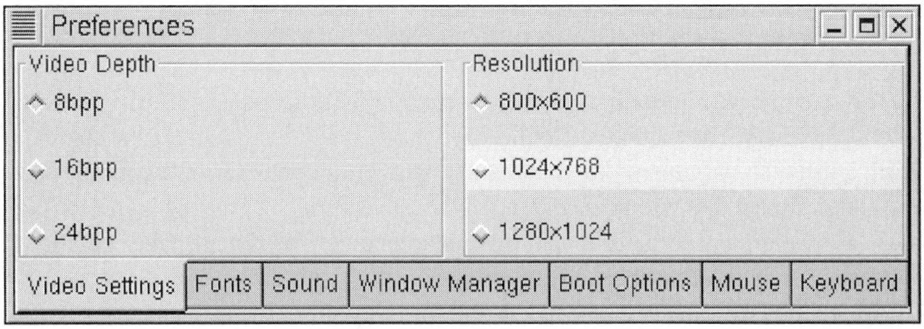

Figure 10.19 Figure 10.17 with Tabs Along the Bottom

Creating an Instance of GtkNotebook

Now that we know a bit about notebooks, let's take a look at the functions GtkNotebook provides. The function gtk_notebook_new() can be called to create a new instance of GtkNotebook:

```
GtkWidget *
gtk_notebook_new(void);
```

As usual, the return value is an instance of GtkWidget. The remainder of the GtkNotebook functions require that you pass an instance of GtkNotebook as the first argument. You can do this by casting the GtkWidget * variable to GtkNotebook using the GTK_NOTEBOOK() macro:

```
GtkWidget *notebook;

...

gtk_notebook_append_page( GTK_NOTEBOOK( notebook ), ... );
```

Creating and Adding Pages

Once you have a notebook, the next step is to create pages and add them to the notebook. A page consists of a container widget (e.g., a box) and its children. Once you have created the page, you add it to the notebook as a child. You can pretty much use any of the container widgets I describe in this chapter; this includes another notebook widget (although doing so might result in a less-than-ideal user interface/experience).

Pages can be appended to a notebook, prepended to a notebook, or added to the notebook at a specific location. In a notebook that has tabs running along the top or bottom of the notebook, the tab order is from left to right, while the tab order is from top to bottom when located on the left- or right-hand sides of the notebook. The first tab (the leftmost or top) is located at index 0, and the last tab (the rightmost or bottom) is at location $n - 1$, where n is the number of tabs or panels in the notebook.

In addition to the location of the tab or panel in the notebook, the other thing you must decide when adding a panel is whether or not the tab will be shown in the pop-up menu (when enabled). All of these choices result in six different functions that can be used to add a panel to a notebook.

To append a page to a notebook, making it the *n*th page of the notebook, your application can call gtk_notebook_append_page():

```
void
gtk_notebook_append_page(GtkNotebook *notebook, GtkWidget *child,
      GtkWidget *tab_label);
```

The argument notebook is an instance of GtkNotebook that was returned by gtk_notebook_new(). The argument child is the container widget that holds the content of the page being added. The argument tab_label is the widget (a container or a control) containing the text and/or image that will be displayed in the tab as its label. Passing NULL as tab_label will cause a default label to be provided by GtkNotebook. The default label in Gtk+ 1.2 is Page <number>, where <number>is the position of the page in the notebook, plus 1. See gtk_notebook_set_tab_label_text() for a simple way to set the text label of a notebook tab.

Prepending a page to the notebook (making it the first page) can be done with a call to gtk_notebook_prepend_page():

```
void
gtk_notebook_prepend_page(GtkNotebook *notebook, GtkWidget *child,
       GtkWidget *tab_label);
```

The arguments are the same as those passed to gtk_notebook_append_page(). To insert a page at an arbitrary position, call gtk_notebook_insert_page():

```
void
gtk_notebook_insert_page(GtkNotebook *notebook, GtkWidget *child,
       GtkWidget *tab_label, gint position);
```

The final argument, position, specifies where the page will be located after being added to the notebook. This can be in the range of [0, *n*] in a notebook that contains *n* pages prior to the insert operation being performed.

Creating and Adding Pages to a Notebook: An Example

The following code illustrates the creation of a simple three-panel notebook using the function gtk_notebook_append_page(). The child of each panel is an instance of GtkVBox that contains a single GtkLabel widget as a child. The tab label is also an instance of GtkLabel. Although it displays the same text as the label managed by the panel vbox, we must use a separate instance of GtkLabel because an instance of GtkLabel (or any widget for that matter) can only be managed by one parent.

Listing 10.2 GtkNotebook Example

```
#include <gtk/gtk.h>

int main( int argc, char *argv[] )
{
        GtkWidget *window, *vbox, *notebook, *label, *tab_label;

        gtk_init(&argc, &argv);

        // create a window

        window = gtk_window_new(GTK_WINDOW_TOPLEVEL);
        gtk_signal_connect(GTK_OBJECT(window), "destroy",
                GTK_SIGNAL_FUNC (gtk_main_quit), "WM destroy");
        gtk_window_set_title(GTK_WINDOW(window), "Notebook");
        gtk_widget_set_usize(GTK_WIDGET(window), 200, 100);

        // create a notebook and add it to the window

        notebook = gtk_notebook_new();
        gtk_container_add(GTK_CONTAINER (window), notebook);

        gtk_widget_show( notebook );
```

```

        // create the first panel, which consists of an instance of
        // GtkVBox, which in turn manages an instance of GtkLabel

        vbox = gtk_vbox_new( FALSE, 10 );

        gtk_widget_show( vbox );

        label = gtk_label_new( "Panel 1" );
        gtk_widget_show( label );
        tab_label = gtk_label_new( "Panel 1" );
        gtk_widget_show( tab_label );
        gtk_box_pack_start_defaults( GTK_BOX( vbox ), label );

        gtk_notebook_append_page( GTK_NOTEBOOK( notebook ),
                vbox, tab_label );

        // create the second panel

        vbox = gtk_vbox_new( FALSE, 10 );

        gtk_widget_show( vbox );

        label = gtk_label_new( "Panel 2" );
        gtk_widget_show( label );
        tab_label = gtk_label_new( "Panel 2" );
        gtk_widget_show( tab_label );
        gtk_box_pack_start_defaults( GTK_BOX( vbox ), label );

        gtk_notebook_append_page( GTK_NOTEBOOK( notebook ),
                vbox, tab_label );

        // create the final panel

        vbox = gtk_vbox_new( FALSE, 10 );

        gtk_widget_show( vbox );

        label = gtk_label_new( "Panel 3" );
        gtk_widget_show( label );
        tab_label = gtk_label_new( "Panel 3" );
        gtk_widget_show( tab_label );
        gtk_box_pack_start_defaults( GTK_BOX( vbox ), label );

        gtk_notebook_append_page( GTK_NOTEBOOK( notebook ),
                vbox, tab_label );

        // show the main window and call the main loop

        gtk_widget_show(window);
        gtk_main ();
```

```

        return(0);
}
```

Implementing a Pop-up menu

I mentioned earlier that GtkNotebook supports a pop-up menu that contains menu items corresponding to panels or pages in the notebook. A user can select a panel by right-clicking on the notebook, displaying the pop-up menu, and then selecting the desired panel from the pop-up menu.

GtkNotebook provides three functions that can be used to add a notebook page and, at the same time, add a menu item to the notebook pop-up menu. These functions are analogous to the preceding functions for appending, prepending, and inserting pages, but they take an additional argument, menu_label, which is a widget (typically an instance of GtkLabel, but it also can be a container) that will be displayed in the pop-up menu as a menu item that corresponds to the panel being added. To append a page and have a menu item added to the notebook pop-up menu, call gtk_notebook_append_page_menu():

```
void
gtk_notebook_append_page_menu(GtkNotebook *notebook, GtkWidget *child,
      GtkWidget *tab_label, GtkWidget *menu_label);
```

The function gtk_notebook_append_page_menu() is analogous to gtk_notebook_append_page() but results in a menu item being added to the notebook's pop-up menu. Finally, the functions gtk_notebook_prepend_page_menu() and gtk_notebook_insert_page_menu() are analogous to gtk_notebook_prepend_page() and gtk_notebook_insert_page(), respectively, but like gtk_notebook_append_page_menu() also result in a menu item being added to the notebook's pop-up menu, labeled with the label specified with the menu_label argument:

```
void
gtk_notebook_prepend_page_menu(GtkNotebook *notebook,
      GtkWidget *child, GtkWidget *tab_label, GtkWidget *menu_label);

void
gtk_notebook_insert_page_menu(GtkNotebook *notebook, GtkWidget *child,
      GtkWidget *tab_label, GtkWidget *menu_label, gint position);
```

Another way to set the menu text corresponding to a page is to make a call to gtk_notebook_set_menu_label().

The following code is similar to the example presented earlier but with the following differences:

1. It sets the page tab label to a container that manages both an image and a label.
2. It creates pop-up menu items for each page, which also consist of a container managing an image and a label.

A call is made to gtk_notebook_popup_enable() to enable the pop-up menu:

```
void
gtk_notebook_popup_enable(GtkNotebook *notebook);
```

You can also disable the pop-up menu (this is default) with a call to gtk_notebook_popup_disable():

```
void
gtk_notebook_popup_disable(GtkNotebook *notebook);
```

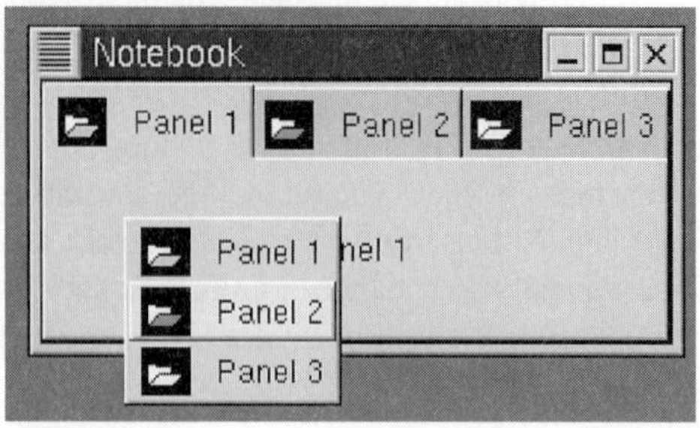

Figure 10.20 Pop-up Notebook Menu (See Listing 10.3)

Both functions take an instance of GtkNotebook as their only argument. Here is the code to implement the notebook described in this section. Figure 10.20 illustrates the result in action.

Listing 10.3 GtkNotebook Pop-up Menu Example

```
#include <gtk/gtk.h>

static GtkWidget *notebook;

// function to create a new pixmap

static GtkWidget *
new_pixmap (char *file, GdkWindow *window, GdkColor *background)
{
  GdkPixmap *pmap;
  GdkBitmap *mask;
  GtkWidget *wpmap;

  pmap = gdk_pixmap_create_from_xpm(window, &mask, background, file);
  wpmap = gtk_pixmap_new(pmap, mask);
  gtk_pixmap_set_build_insensitive(GTK_PIXMAP(wpmap), 1);
  return( wpmap );
}

// ensure the popup is disabled before exiting main loop to avoid warnings

void
CloseDown( GtkWidget *widget, gpointer unused )
{
  // disable the popup menu

  gtk_notebook_popup_disable( GTK_NOTEBOOK( notebook ) );
  gtk_main_quit();
}
```

```

int main( int argc, char *argv[] )
{
  GtkWidget *tab_label, *pixmap, *window, *hbox, *vbox,
    *hbox_menu, *label;

  gtk_init(&argc, &argv);

  // create a window

  window = gtk_window_new(GTK_WINDOW_TOPLEVEL);
  gtk_signal_connect(GTK_OBJECT(window), "destroy",
                     GTK_SIGNAL_FUNC (CloseDown), "WM destroy");
  gtk_window_set_title(GTK_WINDOW(window), "Notebook");
  gtk_widget_set_usize(GTK_WIDGET(window), 250, 100);
  gtk_widget_show(window);

  // create a notebook and add it to the window

  notebook = gtk_notebook_new();
  gtk_notebook_popup_enable( GTK_NOTEBOOK( notebook ) );
  gtk_container_add(GTK_CONTAINER (window), notebook);

  gtk_widget_show( notebook );

  // create first panel. vbox is the panel content

  vbox = gtk_vbox_new( FALSE, 10 );
  gtk_widget_show( vbox );

  // add a label to the vbox, this is what the panel displays, and
  // the user sees

  label = gtk_label_new( "Panel 1" );
  gtk_box_pack_start_defaults( GTK_BOX( vbox ), label );
  gtk_widget_show( label );

  // create the panel tab content, which will be a pixmap and label
  // managed by a horizontal box widget. First create the pixmap.

  pixmap = new_pixmap("test1.xpm", window->window,
              &window->style->bg[GTK_STATE_NORMAL]);
  gtk_widget_show( pixmap );

  // then create the label

  tab_label = gtk_label_new( "Panel 1" );
  gtk_widget_show( tab_label );

  // pack both of these into the horizontal box

  hbox = gtk_hbox_new( FALSE, 10 );
  gtk_box_pack_start_defaults( GTK_BOX( hbox ), pixmap );
  gtk_box_pack_start_defaults( GTK_BOX( hbox ), tab_label );

  // next create the menu item. This also consists of an image and
  // label packed into a horizontal box. We must create new instances
```

```
    // of each (the image, the box, and the label) since any given
    // widget can only be managed by one parent

    pixmap = new_pixmap("test1.xpm", window->window,
                  &window->style->bg[GTK_STATE_NORMAL]);
    gtk_widget_show( pixmap );

    tab_label = gtk_label_new( "Panel 1" );
    gtk_widget_show( tab_label );

    hbox_menu = gtk_hbox_new( FALSE, 10 );
    gtk_box_pack_start_defaults( GTK_BOX( hbox_menu ), pixmap );
    gtk_box_pack_start_defaults( GTK_BOX( hbox_menu ), tab_label );

    // now that we have the panel content, the tab label, and the
    // popup menu item, call gtk_notebook_append_page_menu() to
    // add all three to the notebook.

    gtk_notebook_append_page_menu( GTK_NOTEBOOK( notebook ),
      vbox, hbox, hbox_menu );

    // repeat the above steps for panels 2 and 3. First, panel 2.

    vbox = gtk_vbox_new( FALSE, 10 );

    gtk_widget_show( vbox );

    label = gtk_label_new( "Panel 2" );
    gtk_box_pack_start_defaults( GTK_BOX( vbox ), label );
    gtk_widget_show( label );

    pixmap = new_pixmap("test2.xpm", window->window,
                  &window->style->bg[GTK_STATE_NORMAL]);
    gtk_widget_show( pixmap );

    tab_label = gtk_label_new( "Panel 2" );
    gtk_widget_show( tab_label );

    hbox = gtk_hbox_new( FALSE, 10 );
    gtk_box_pack_start_defaults( GTK_BOX( hbox ), pixmap );
    gtk_box_pack_start_defaults( GTK_BOX( hbox ), tab_label );

    pixmap = new_pixmap("test2.xpm", window->window,
                  &window->style->bg[GTK_STATE_NORMAL]);
    gtk_widget_show( pixmap );

    tab_label = gtk_label_new( "Panel 2" );
    gtk_widget_show( tab_label );

    hbox_menu = gtk_hbox_new( FALSE, 10 );
    gtk_box_pack_start_defaults( GTK_BOX( hbox_menu ), pixmap );
    gtk_box_pack_start_defaults( GTK_BOX( hbox_menu ), tab_label );

    gtk_notebook_append_page_menu( GTK_NOTEBOOK( notebook ),
      vbox, hbox, hbox_menu );

    // finally, do panel 3
```

```

    vbox = gtk_vbox_new( FALSE, 10 );

    gtk_widget_show( vbox );

    label = gtk_label_new( "Panel 3" );
    gtk_box_pack_start_defaults( GTK_BOX( vbox ), label );
    gtk_widget_show( label );

    pixmap = new_pixmap("test3.xpm", window->window,
                &window->style->bg[GTK_STATE_NORMAL]);
    gtk_widget_show( pixmap );

    tab_label = gtk_label_new( "Panel 3" );
    gtk_widget_show( tab_label );

    hbox = gtk_hbox_new( FALSE, 10 );
    gtk_box_pack_start_defaults( GTK_BOX( hbox ), pixmap );
    gtk_box_pack_start_defaults( GTK_BOX( hbox ), tab_label );

    pixmap = new_pixmap("test3.xpm", window->window,
                &window->style->bg[GTK_STATE_NORMAL]);
    gtk_widget_show( pixmap );

    tab_label = gtk_label_new( "Panel 3" );
    gtk_widget_show( tab_label );

    hbox_menu = gtk_hbox_new( FALSE, 10 );
    gtk_box_pack_start_defaults( GTK_BOX( hbox_menu ), pixmap );
    gtk_box_pack_start_defaults( GTK_BOX( hbox_menu ), tab_label );

    gtk_notebook_append_page_menu( GTK_NOTEBOOK( notebook ),
      vbox, hbox, hbox_menu );

    gtk_main ();

    return(0);
  }
```

Removing a Page from a Notebook

To remove a page from the notebook, call gtk_notebook_remove_page():

```
void
gtk_notebook_remove_page(GtkNotebook *notebook, gint page_num);
```

The argument notebook is the instance of GtkNotebook from which the page will be removed, and page_num is the page, in the range [0, $n - 1$], that will be removed upon calling this function.

Reordering the Notebook Pages

Given a notebook child (page) widget instance, an application can specify a new position in the notebook for the child/page using gtk_notebook_reorder_child():

```
void
gtk_notebook_reorder_child(GtkNotebook *notebook, GtkWidget *child,
       gint position);
```

Page Functions

Several functions in the GtkNotebook API deal with pages. To get the index of the currently active page, call gtk_notebook_get_current_page():

```
gint
gtk_notebook_get_current_page(GtkNotebook *notebook);
```

The return value, not surprisingly, will be in the range [0, $n - 1$]. To get the child widget that corresponds to a given position in the notebook, you can call gtk_notebook_get_nth_page():

```
GtkWidget *
gtk_notebook_get_nth_page(GtkNotebook *notebook, gint page_num);
```

The argument page_num must be in the range of [0, $n - 1$]. If no such page is found, the value (GtkWidget *) NULL will be returned. The inverse can also be done; given a child widget, you can call gtk_notebook_page_num() to determine its position in the notebook:

```
gint
gtk_notebook_page_num(GtkNotebook *notebook, GtkWidget *child);
```

The following code snippet shows the relationship of these two functions and should, when called, cause the value 3 to be assigned to the variable position:

```
int position;
GtkWidget *notebook;

position = gtk_notebook_page_num( GTK_NOTEBOOK( notebook ),
  gtk_notebook_get_nth_page( GTK_NOTEBOOK( notebook ), 3 ) );
```

Traversing Pages

Three functions can be used to control page traversal programmatically. Although most applications will rely on the user interacting with the notebook pop-up menu or tabs to traverse from page to page, an application might want to warp the notebook to a specific page based on some other control in the user interface or even initialize the notebook so that a given page is displayed to the user upon the notebook being realized. To set, or initialize, a notebook to a specific page, call gtk_notebook_set_page():

```
void
gtk_notebook_set_page(GtkNotebook *notebook, gint page_num);
```

Once again, page_num is in the range [0, $n - 1$], where n is the number of pages currently in the notebook.

The remaining two functions allow a program to position the current page at the next or previous page relative to the currently active page. Not surprisingly, the functions that support this are named gtk_notebook_next_page() and gtk_notebook_prev_page(), respectively:

```
void
gtk_notebook_next_page(GtkNotebook *notebook);

void
gtk_notebook_prev_page(GtkNotebook *notebook);
```

Preference Functions

The remaining set of functions in the GtkNotebook API set can be used to set various attributes that control how an instance of GtkNotebook is rendered.

The first, gtk_notebook_set_show_tabs(), can be used to control the display of the user-selectable tabs that, by default, are drawn for each panel in the notebook:

```
void
gtk_notebook_set_show_tabs(GtkNotebook *notebook, gboolean show_tabs);
```

If show_tabs is set to FALSE, the tabs will not be drawn; otherwise, the default case of TRUE causes them to be drawn. Note that if your application decides to hide tabs, it must provide some user-interface control by which panel traversal can be achieved by the user. One option is to enable the notebook pop-up menu as previously described and add panels using the gtk_notebook_*_page_menu() functions. The other option would be to provide some facility by which calls to gtk_notebook_set_page(), gtk_notebook_prev_page(), and/or gtk_notebook_next_page() are made, with these functions performing the necessary page traversal.

If tabs are hidden by your application, you can also control the rendering of the page border that, by default, is drawn whenever tabs are showing:

```
void
gtk_notebook_set_show_border(GtkNotebook *notebook,
            gboolean show_border);
```

The function gtk_notebook_set_show_border() is a no-op unless gtk_notebook_set_show_tabs() has been called to turn off the display of tabs. By hiding the border, the panel area of the notebook will look more to the user like the portion of a dialog or window being managed by an instance of GtkBox because boxes do not add a border around the area they manage. The only difference will be that the notebook now provides the application with a way to easily control the display of multiple pages within the area managed by the notebook. In some applications, this can be powerful. An example of this would be a wizard dialog. A wizard leads a user through a series of panels, asking the user questions and performing tasks based on the information gathered. An example of a wizard would be an application installer.

The code to implement this wizard is as follows:

Listing 10.4 Implementing a Wizard with GtkNotebook

```
#include <gtk/gtk.h>

static int current_page = 0;
static GtkWidget *prev_button, *next_button, *finish_button;

void
SetSensitivity()
{
  if ( current_page == 2 )
    gtk_widget_set_sensitive( next_button, FALSE );
  else
    gtk_widget_set_sensitive( next_button, TRUE );
  if ( current_page > 0 )
    gtk_widget_set_sensitive( prev_button, TRUE );
  else
    gtk_widget_set_sensitive( prev_button, FALSE );
  if ( current_page == 2 )
    gtk_widget_set_sensitive( finish_button, TRUE );
  else
    gtk_widget_set_sensitive( finish_button, FALSE );
}

void
NextCallback(GtkWidget *widget, GtkNotebook *notebook)
{
  if ( current_page < 2 )
    current_page++;
  SetSensitivity();
  gtk_notebook_set_page( notebook, current_page );

}

void
PreviousCallback(GtkWidget *widget, GtkNotebook *notebook)
{
  if ( current_page > 0 )
    current_page--;
  SetSensitivity();
  gtk_notebook_set_page( notebook, current_page );
}

void
FinishCallback(GtkWidget *widget, GtkNotebook *notebook)
{
  gtk_main_quit();
}

void
CreatePanelOne( GtkWidget *notebook )
{
  GtkWidget *frame, *vbox, *radio1, *radio2, *radio3;

  frame = gtk_frame_new( "Select a Video Depth" );
  gtk_widget_show( frame );

```

```
  vbox = gtk_vbox_new( FALSE, 10 );
  gtk_widget_show( vbox );
  gtk_container_add (GTK_CONTAINER(frame), vbox );

  radio1 = gtk_radio_button_new_with_label( NULL, "8bpp" );
  gtk_box_pack_start( GTK_BOX( vbox ), radio1, TRUE, TRUE, 0 );
  gtk_widget_show( radio1 );

  radio2 = gtk_radio_button_new_with_label(
    gtk_radio_button_group( GTK_RADIO_BUTTON( radio1 )),
    "16bpp" );
  gtk_box_pack_start( GTK_BOX( vbox ), radio2, TRUE, TRUE, 0 );
  gtk_widget_show( radio2 );
  radio3 = gtk_radio_button_new_with_label(
    gtk_radio_button_group( GTK_RADIO_BUTTON( radio2 )),
    "24bpp" );
  gtk_box_pack_start( GTK_BOX( vbox ), radio3, TRUE, TRUE, 0 );
  gtk_widget_show( radio3 );

  gtk_notebook_append_page( GTK_NOTEBOOK( notebook ), frame, NULL );
}

void
CreatePanelTwo( GtkWidget *notebook )
{
  GtkWidget *frame, *vbox, *radio1, *radio2, *radio3;

  frame = gtk_frame_new( "Select a Resolution" );
  gtk_widget_show( frame );

  vbox = gtk_vbox_new( FALSE, 10 );
  gtk_widget_show( vbox );
  gtk_container_add (GTK_CONTAINER(frame), vbox );

  radio1 = gtk_radio_button_new_with_label( NULL, "800x600" );
  gtk_box_pack_start( GTK_BOX( vbox ), radio1, TRUE, TRUE, 0 );
  gtk_widget_show( radio1 );

  radio2 = gtk_radio_button_new_with_label(
    gtk_radio_button_group( GTK_RADIO_BUTTON( radio1 )),
    "1024x768" );
  gtk_box_pack_start( GTK_BOX( vbox ), radio2, TRUE, TRUE, 0 );
  gtk_widget_show( radio2 );
  radio3 = gtk_radio_button_new_with_label(
    gtk_radio_button_group( GTK_RADIO_BUTTON( radio2 )),
    "1280x1024" );
  gtk_box_pack_start( GTK_BOX( vbox ), radio3, TRUE, TRUE, 0 );
  gtk_widget_show( radio3 );

  gtk_notebook_append_page( GTK_NOTEBOOK( notebook ), frame, NULL );
}

void
CreatePanelThree( GtkWidget *notebook )
{
  GtkWidget *vbox, *label;

```

```
  vbox = gtk_vbox_new( FALSE, 10 );

  gtk_widget_show( vbox );

  label = gtk_label_new( "Use Finish to commit changes, or Quit to exit." );
  gtk_widget_show( label );
  gtk_box_pack_start_defaults( GTK_BOX( vbox ), label );

  gtk_notebook_append_page( GTK_NOTEBOOK( notebook ),
    vbox, NULL );
}

int main( int argc, char *argv[] )
{
  GtkWidget *window, *vbox, *hbox, *button, *notebook;

  gtk_init(&argc, &argv);

  // create a window

  window = gtk_window_new(GTK_WINDOW_TOPLEVEL);
  gtk_signal_connect(GTK_OBJECT(window), "destroy",
                     GTK_SIGNAL_FUNC (gtk_main_quit), "WM destroy");
  gtk_window_set_title(GTK_WINDOW(window), "Video Settings");
  gtk_widget_set_usize(GTK_WIDGET(window), 300, 200);

  // create a notebook and add it to the window

  vbox = gtk_vbox_new( FALSE, 10 );
  gtk_container_add(GTK_CONTAINER (window), vbox);

  gtk_widget_show( vbox );

  notebook = gtk_notebook_new();
  gtk_notebook_set_show_tabs( GTK_NOTEBOOK( notebook ), FALSE );
  gtk_notebook_set_show_border( GTK_NOTEBOOK( notebook ), FALSE );

  gtk_box_pack_start_defaults( GTK_BOX(vbox), notebook );

  gtk_widget_show( notebook );

  CreatePanelOne( notebook );
  CreatePanelTwo( notebook );
  CreatePanelThree( notebook );

  hbox = gtk_hbox_new( TRUE, 10 );
  gtk_box_pack_start( GTK_BOX(vbox), hbox, FALSE, FALSE, 10 );
  gtk_widget_show( hbox );

  button = gtk_button_new_with_label( "Quit" );
  gtk_box_pack_start( GTK_BOX(hbox), button, TRUE, FALSE, 0 );
  gtk_widget_show( button );
  gtk_signal_connect_object(GTK_OBJECT (button), "clicked",
            GTK_SIGNAL_FUNC(gtk_widget_destroy),
            GTK_OBJECT(window));

  prev_button = button = gtk_button_new_with_label( "Previous" );
```

```
    gtk_box_pack_start( GTK_BOX(hbox), button, TRUE, FALSE, 0 );
    gtk_widget_show( button );
    gtk_signal_connect(GTK_OBJECT (button), "clicked",
      GTK_SIGNAL_FUNC(PreviousCallback), notebook);
    gtk_widget_set_sensitive( button, FALSE );

    next_button = button = gtk_button_new_with_label( "Next" );
    gtk_box_pack_start( GTK_BOX(hbox), button, TRUE, FALSE, 0 );
    gtk_widget_show( button );
    gtk_signal_connect(GTK_OBJECT (button), "clicked",
      GTK_SIGNAL_FUNC(NextCallback), notebook);

    finish_button = button = gtk_button_new_with_label( "Finish" );
    gtk_box_pack_start( GTK_BOX(hbox), button, TRUE, FALSE, 0 );
    gtk_widget_show( button );
    gtk_signal_connect_object(GTK_OBJECT (button), "clicked",
                GTK_SIGNAL_FUNC(gtk_widget_destroy),
                GTK_OBJECT(window));
    gtk_widget_set_sensitive( button, FALSE );

    // show the main window and call the main loop

    gtk_widget_show(window);
    gtk_main ();

    return(0);
}
```

Analysis of Listing 10.4

The notebook contains three pages, as illustrated in Figures 10.21 through 10.23.

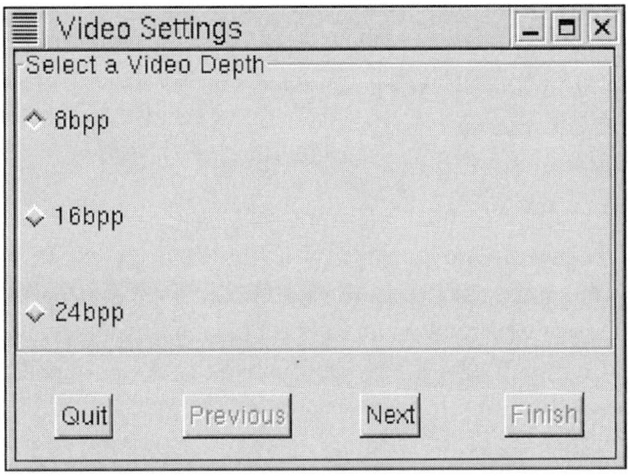

Figure 10.21 Video Settings Wizard, Page 0

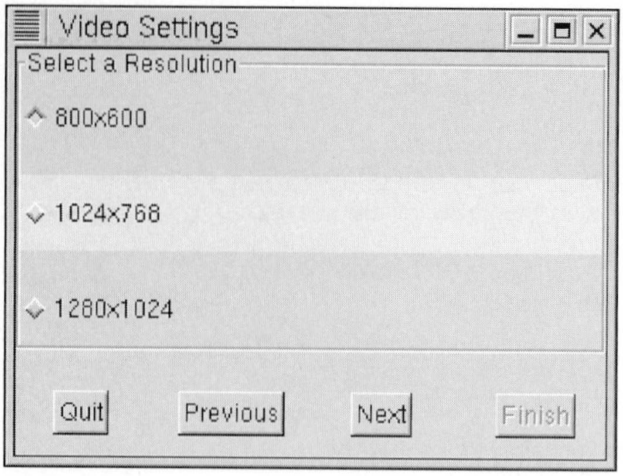

Figure 10.22 Page 1 of the Wizard

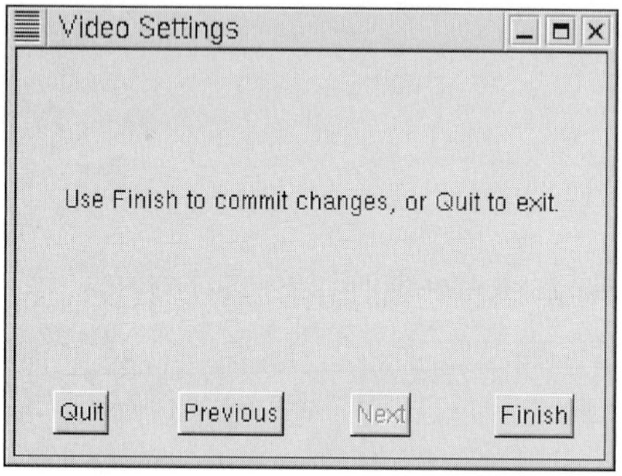

Figure 10.23 Page 2 of the Wizard

The function SetSensitivity() controls the sensitivity of the Previous, Next, and Finish push buttons, based on the current page visible in the notebook. PreviousCallback() and NextCallback() are callbacks tied to the Previous and Next buttons, respectively. Both use gtk_notebook_set_page() to change the current page as the user clicks either of these buttons and call SetSensitivity() to ensure that the Previous button is inactive when Page 0 is active (and active otherwise) and that the Next button is inactive when Page 2 is active (and active otherwise).

Functions CreatePanelOne(), CreatePanelTwo(), and CreatePanelThree() create the various notebook pages displayed by the wizard. The code in each of these has been explained in previous chapters. The function gtk_notebook_append_page() is used by each to add the panel being created to the notebook.

On line 146 of main(), the notebook itself is created. Following its creation, on lines 147 and 148, the notebook tabs and border are disabled, which gives it the main point of this example. The push buttons that lead to page traversal in the notebook are created on lines

169 through 180. Because these buttons exist, there is really no need for the display of tabs; the Next and Previous buttons provide all that is needed for the user to traverse the wizard in a sequence that the application (may) require.

If, in a wizard, random access of panels can be allowed without disrupting the flow of the wizard (in many cases, panels must be traversed serially, so random access of panels by the user is not possible), it is, in my opinion, reasonable to enable the notebook pop-up menu. Using tabs, however, seems to me to be a bad user-interface design decision in the context of wizards such as the one previously illustrated.

Setting the Orientation of the Tabs

As I mentioned earlier, an application can specify both the orientation and location of the notebook tabs. There are two vertical orientations (either on the left of the notebook or on the right) and two horizontal orientations (either above the notebook or below it). To set the orientation and placement of the tabs in a notebook, call gtk_notebook_set_tab_pos():

```
void
gtk_notebook_set_tab_pos(GtkNotebook *notebook, GtkPositionType pos);
```

The argument pos can be one of the following: GTK_POS_LEFT, GTK_POS_RIGHT, GTK_POS_TOP, or GTK_POS_BOTTOM. Depending on which value you pass, the tabs will display on the left side, right side, top, or bottom of the notebook widget, respectively. The default for a notebook widget is to display panel tabs above the panels (i.e., the default is GTK_POS_TOP).

Scrollable Tabs

A notebook, by default, will draw all of the tabs (when tabs are made visible). In a notebook that contains a large number of tabs or tabs with labels that are rather lengthy, it may not be possible for the notebook to display all of the tabs without truncating tab labels. One way to overcome this problem is to enable scrollbars on the notebook. If enabled, scrollbars are displayed should truncation of the notebook tabs be otherwise unavoidable. The notebook displays panel tabs without truncation when scrollbars are enabled and displays left and/or right scrollbars to allow traversal by the user to panels to the left, or to the right, of the currently displayed panel tabs, as necessary. To enable the display of scrollbars, call gtk_notebook_set_scrollable():

```
void
gtk_notebook_set_scrollable(GtkNotebook *notebook,
            gboolean scrollable);
```

If scrollbar is TRUE, the notebook will display scrollbars as needed.

Miscellaneous Tab Attributes

A few preference functions address tab attributes. Homogeneous tabs are tabs that have equal size, regardless of the labels they display. The size assigned to the tabs is based on the size needed to display the tab with the largest label. Tabs in a notebook widget can be made homogeneous by calling gtk_notebook_set_homogeneous_tabs() and setting homogeneous to TRUE:

```
void
gtk_notebook_set_homogeneous_tabs(GtkNotebook *notebook,
            gboolean homogeneous);
```

Setting homogeneous to FALSE has the opposite effect of causing tabs sizes to be based solely on their respective labels. By default, tabs in GtkNotebook are nonhomogeneous. Homogeneous also affects how packing works; see the section "Tab Label Packing Functions" later in this chapter for details.

A tab contains two borders. One, the horizontal border, consists of pixels to the left and right of a tab's label (or the container that bounds whatever widgets are displayed by the application in the tab). The other, the vertical border, is composed of pixels above and below the label. By default, both the horizontal and vertical borders are set to 2 pixels. Specifically, 2 pixels are added to both the left- and right-hand sides of the tab label, and 2 pixels are added above and below the tab label. Your application can change either the horizontal spacing or the vertical spacing. To change both at the same time, call gtk_notebook_set_tab_border();

```
void
gtk_notebook_set_tab_border(GtkNotebook *notebook,
            guint border_width);
```

For example, the set both the vertical and horizontal tab spacing to 5 pixels, make the following call:

```
GtkWidget *notebook;

...

gtk_notebook_set_tab_border( GTK_NOTEBOOK( notebook ), 5 );
```

To set the horizontal or the vertical notebook tab spacing individually, you call either gtk_notebook_set_tab_hborder() or gtk_notebook_set_tab_vborder(), respectively:

```
void
gtk_notebook_set_tab_hborder(GtkNotebook *notebook,
            guint tab_hborder);

void
gtk_notebook_set_tab_vborder(GtkNotebook *notebook,
            guint tab_vborder);
```

Both of the preceding take an instance of GtkNotebook as a first argument and a spacing value (greater than or equal to 0) as a second argument.

Tab Labels

The tab label widget (see the previous discussion) for a given panel can be retrieved by calling gtk_notebook_get_tab_label():

```
GtkWidget *
gtk_notebook_get_tab_label(GtkNotebook *notebook, GtkWidget *child);
```

The first argument, notebook, is the notebook of interest. The second argument, child, is the widget representing the page. You might call this function to obtain the tab label child instance so that modifications can be made to it. What modifications are possible (e.g., changing the text of the table, showing or hiding one of its children) or even appropriate is entirely dependent on the widget your application decided to use to represent the tab label.

You can also set the tab label widget for a specific panel by making a call to gtk_notebook_set_tab_label():

```
void
gtk_notebook_set_tab_label(GtkNotebook *notebook, GtkWidget *child,
       GtkWidget *tab_label);
```

The first two arguments, notebook and child, are the same as those passed to gtk_notebook_get_tab_label(). Passing NULL as the third argument causes the default tab label to be used by GtkNotebook for the panel (e.g., Page 3 for the page located at position 2 in the notebook).

As I discussed earlier, the label of a tab can be an instance of GtkLabel or perhaps an instance of GtkHBox that manages a pixmap and a label widget. If your application simply wants to use a text label, perhaps the easiest way to achieve that is to set the tab_label argument to the gtk_notebook_*_page*() function (e.g., gtk_notebook_append_page() and related functions) to NULL and call gtk_notebook_set_tab_label_text() to specify the tab label:

```
void
gtk_notebook_set_tab_label_text(GtkNotebook *notebook,
       GtkWidget *child, const gchar *tab_text);
```

The function gtk_notebook_set_tab_label_text() takes an instance of GtkNotebook (notebook), the widget that represents the panel or page of the notebook corresponding to the tab that is having its label set (child), and a simple C-language, NULL-terminated string (tab_text) that defines the label displayed by the tab after the call to gtk_notebook_set_tab_label_text() is made. This function provides a way to dynamically change the text of a page during application execution, if this is deemed necessary (and in some cases it is).

Pop-up Menu Functions

We saw that the gtk_notebook_*_page_menu() functions can be used to add a page to a notebook and give it representation in the notebook pop-up menu so that a user can pop up the menu, select the menu item corresponding to the page, and traverse the notebook to that page for viewing. The Gtk+ API exposes functions that allow you to query the child widget that corresponds to the pop-up menu item or to change the child, much like was possible for the panel tab label widget. To retrieve the menu label widget corresponding to a given panel in the notebook, call gtk_notebook_get_menu_label():

```
GtkWidget *
gtk_notebook_get_menu_label(GtkNotebook *notebook, GtkWidget *child);
```

notebook is an instance of GtkNotebook, and child is the widget that represents the page corresponding to the menu label widget being queried. The menu label widget will be returned or NULL if there is no menu label widget (e.g., your application had never specified a menu item for the page).

To set the menu item label widget corresponding to a page in the notebook, call gtk_notebook_set_menu_label():

```
void
gtk_notebook_set_menu_label(GtkNotebook *notebook, GtkWidget *child,
       GtkWidget *menu_label);
```

Here, notebook is the notebook widget, child is the page that was previously added to the notebook, and menu_label is the widget you would like to have displayed in the notebook pop-up menu for the specified page.

The simplest way to create a menu item in the notebook pop-up menu for a page is to call gtk_notebook_set_menu_label_text():

```
void
gtk_notebook_set_menu_label_text(GtkNotebook *notebook,
       GtkWidget *child, const gchar *menu_text);
```

This function takes as arguments a notebook, a child widget that defines the page that will correspond to the menu item in the pop-up menu, and a C-language, NULL-terminated string that will be displayed in the notebook pop-up menu for the page.

Tab Label Packing Functions

GtkNotebook maintains attributes that are similar to those defined for GtkBox for expand, fill, and packing order, and are used to specify how labels are packed into notebook tabs. Table 10.10 lists the attributes and their default values:

Table 10.10 Tab Label Packing Attribute Defaults

Packing Attribute	*Default Value*
expand	FALSE
fill	TRUE
pack_type	GTK_PACK_START

To query the current settings, call gtk_notebook_query_tab_label_packing():

```
void
gtk_notebook_query_tab_label_packing(GtkNotebook *notebook,
       GtkWidget *child, gboolean *expand, gboolean *fill,
       GtkPackType *pack_type);
```

The arguments notebook and child define, respectively, the GtkNotebook instance and the panel to query. The remaining arguments, expand, fill, and pack_type, are pointers to variables of type gboolean (expand and fill) and GtkPackType (pack_type). The possible returned values for expand and fill are TRUE and FALSE; pack_type can be either GTK_PACK_START or GTK_PACK_END.

The preceding attributes can be set by calling gtk_notebook_set_tab_label_packing():

```
void
gtk_notebook_set_tab_label_packing(GtkNotebook *notebook,
       GtkWidget *child, gboolean expand, gboolean fill,
       GtkPackType pack_type);
```

The argument pack_type can be set to either GTK_PACK_END or GTK_PACK_START. You can use the pack_type attribute to achieve effects similar to those achieved when packing boxes using gtk_box_pack_start() and gtk_box_pack_end(). Figure 10.24 illustrates three pages in a box. Two of these pages (those leftmost) have labels that were packed with GTK_PACK_START (the default), while the third was packed with GTK_PACK_END by calling gtk_notebook_set_tab_label_packing(), as follows:

```
gtk_notebook_set_tab_label_packing( GTK_NOTEBOOK(notebook), vbox,
        FALSE, FALSE, GTK_PACK_END );
```

Here, vbox is a vertical box that represents the content of the panel and is used to identify the panel for which the tab label packing attributes are being set. Obviously, you must call gtk_notebook_set_tab_label_packing() only after the child panel has been added to the notebook. Notice how the third panel is visually isolated from the other two as a result of the preceding call.

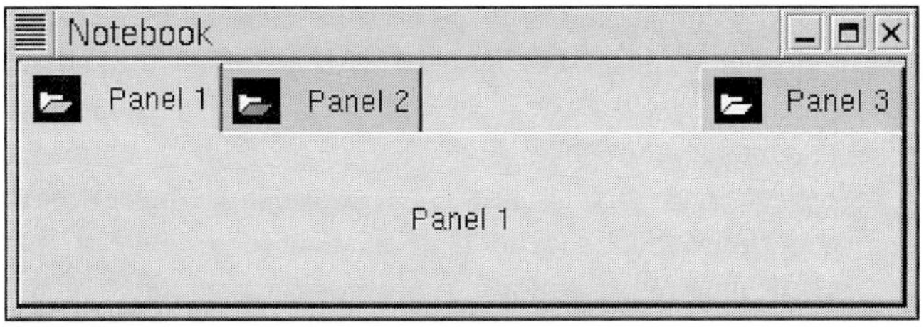

Figure 10.24 Tab Label Packing Example

You can reverse the order (visually) of all tabs in a notebook by inverting their pack_type attribute. For example, the first (leftmost) tab becomes the rightmost, while the last (rightmost) tab becomes leftmost. Note that this does not change the position attribute of the panel. The panel that was added first will continue to have a position attribute of 0, regardless of how the tabs have been packed into the tab display area or panel.

Let's look at expand and fill now. expand set to TRUE causes the tab that is specified to expand to fill the area remaining within the tab area of the notebook. fill causes the (label) widget, when possible, to completely fill the tab that manages it. If you use label widgets for tab label children or use gtk_notebook_set_tab_label() to set the tab label, then fill is a no-op. However, Figure 10.25 illustrates tab label children consisting of hbox widgets that are each managing a pixmap and label. The notebook has been set to use homogeneous tabs so that each has the same size, and expand is set to TRUE so that the entire tab area is consumed by the tabs. Pages 1 and 2 have fill set to TRUE (the default), while Page 3 has fill set to FALSE.

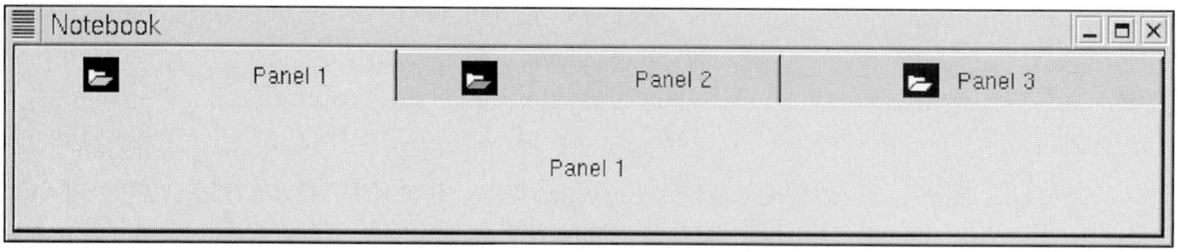

Figure 10.25 Effect of Setting Page 3 Fill Attribute to FALSE

Summary

In this chapter, I introduced container widgets. A purpose of a container widget is to organize and display, in some meaningful fashion, a set of child widgets it has been asked to manage by an application. How the container widget places its children in the area it has been allocated is based on the layout policy of the container widget and is based on constraints or hints provided by the application. Last, but not least, the resulting layout is affected by the content that the container widget has been asked to manage.

In this chapter, I discussed several container classes. The first class, GtkContainer, is a parent class to the remaining classes in the container widget hierarchy. A fixed widget (GtkFixed) lays its children out based on x and y coordinates supplied for each child by the application and is the most primitive of the container classes. A box widget (GtkBox, GtkHBox, and GtkVBox) is probably the most heavily used of the Gtk+ container widget classes. By packing boxes within boxes, arbitrarily complex layouts can be achieved; for this reason, boxes are arguably the most versatile of the container widgets supported in Gtk+ 1.2. A button box widget (GtkButtonBox) is a special case of a box widget designed to layout buttons, such as those one might find in the action area of a dialog (e.g., OK and Cancel buttons). A notebook widget (GtkNotebook) allows an application to organize related content as a series of panels or pages. A tab can (by default) be displayed above, below, to the left, or to the right of a panel to describe the panel content. Users can traverse a notebook either by clicking on a panel tab or by invoking a pop-up menu, if implemented by the application. Panel tabs can be hidden if desired, which increases the versatility of the notebook widget, provided some other mechanism for panel traversal is provided by the application. A notebook widget with hidden tabs was used in this chapter to implement a video settings wizard. In the following chapter, I will continue my discussion of the Gtk+ container widget classes.

CHAPTER

11

MORE CONTAINER CLASSES

In the preceding chapter, I introduced Gtk+ container widgets. Container widgets are widgets designed to manage a group of children. The major responsibility of a container widget is to place child widgets within the area of the window (or other container) for which the container widget is responsible. Child widget placement is based on a placement algorithm that is implemented by the container widget. Widget placement occurs when a child widget is added to the container or when geometry changes to the container have been made (for example, the user has resized the window within which the container exists).

In Chapter 10, "Container and Bin Classes," the most commonly used container widget, GtkBox, was described. Chapter 10 also described several additional container widget classes that are useful in situations for which GtkBox was not designed. This chapter continues the presentation of the Gtk+ container widget classes by describing the widget classes listed in Table 11.1.

Table 11.1 Widgets Described in This Chapter

Class Name	*Purpose*
GtkPaned	Manages a pair of child widgets; the amount of space given to each child can be adjusted by the user at runtime.
GtkVPaned	The vertical instance of GtkPaned widget.
GtkHPaned	The horizontal instance of GtkPaned widget.
GtkPacker	Implements layout policy similar to Tk's Packer widget.
GtkFrame	Places a labeled frame around its only child.
GtkAspectFrame	Same as GtkFrame but maintains a desired aspect ratio.
GtkTable	Child widgets occupy cells organized as an NxM grid.
GtkToolbar	Implements an application toolbar.

Table 11.1 Widgets Described in This Chapter (Continued)

Class Name	*Purpose*
GtkHandleBox	The child widget can be detached and displayed as a floating window and then later reattached.
GtkEventBox	Provides an X window for widgets that do not create an X window of their own.
GtkLayout	Similar to GtkFixed (Chapter 10) but implements an infinitely sized region.
GtkScrolledWindow	Provides viewport into a child widget that users can navigate using scrollbars.

GtkPaned

Class Name

```
GtkPaned
```

Parent Class Name

```
GtkContainer
```

Macros

Widget type macro: `GTK_TYPE_PANED`

Object to widget cast macro: `GTK_PANED(obj)`

Widget type check macro: `GTK_IS_PANED(obj)`

Application-Level API Synopsis

Retrieve the constant GTK_TYPE_PANED at runtime:

```
GtkType
gtk_paned_get_type(void);
```

Set the top or left pane child using packing defaults:

```
void
gtk_paned_add1(GtkPaned *paned, GtkWidget *child);
```

Application-Level API Synopsis (Continued)

Set the bottom or right pane child using packing defaults:
```
void
gtk_paned_add2(GtkPaned *paned, GtkWidget *child);
```

Set the top or left pane child:
```
void
gtk_paned_pack1(GtkPaned *paned, GtkWidget *child, gboolean resize,
       gboolean shrink);
```

Set the bottom or right pane child:
```
void
gtk_paned_pack2(GtkPaned *paned, GtkWidget *child, gboolean resize,
       gboolean shrink);
```

Set the position of the handle (control grip or sash) in pixels:
```
void
gtk_paned_set_position(GtkPaned *paned, gint position);
```

Set the height and width of the handle in pixels:
```
void
gtk_paned_set_handle_size(GtkPaned *paned, guint16 size);
```

Set the height or width of the gutter in pixels:
```
void
gtk_paned_set_gutter_size(GtkPaned *paned, guint16 size);
```

Class Description

A paned widget (an instance of GtkPaned) is designed to manage a pair of child widgets. GtkPaned places a gutter between these two widgets; the position of the gutter is modifiable by the program or, more appropriately, by a user to change the relative size given to the two child widgets that the paned widget manages. The location of the gutter is shown by a groove, which is an inset horizontal or vertical line. The size of the gutter can be changed by the application (the default is 6 pixels); the width or height of the groove remains the same (2 pixels) regardless of the size of the gutter.

The user can move the gutter by positioning the mouse pointer over a control grip located on the groove, pressing down on mouse button 1 and dragging the location of the gutter to the desired position. Each child widget, once mouse button 1 is released, will resize and redraw itself to fit the new size it has been given.

There are two types of paned widget, represented by the two GtkPaned subclasses GtkVPaned and GtkHPaned. In a vertical paned widget (GtkVPaned), the two child widgets are arranged vertically and are separated by a horizontal gutter. A horizontal paned widget (GtkHPaned) arranges its child widgets horizontally, placing a vertical gutter between them.

In most cases, you want to add container widgets as children of a paned widget, as opposed to control-like widgets such as buttons or check boxes. A paned widget is most effective when it is used to separate two work areas from each other while, at the same time, giving the user the ability to control how much of each work area dominates the total area controlled by the paned widget. You, as the developer, will need to decide whether the user should be given the ability to change the relative sizes of the two work areas or not. Figure 11.1 should help illustrate the issues involved in making this decision.

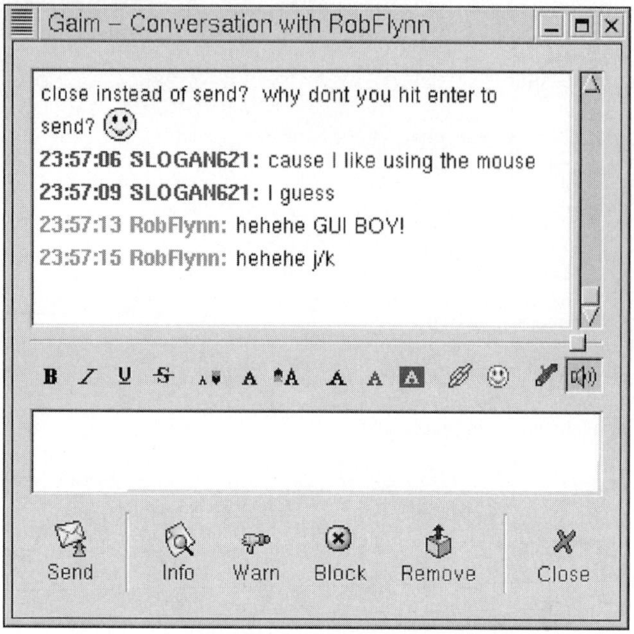

Figure 11.1 Conversation Log Window in GAIM (Default)

The conversation window of an instant-messaging or chat client, such as the Gtk+ GAIM instant-messaging client (see Figure 11.1), provides an example of when it is appropriate to use a paned widget. As can be seen, the dialog is, by default, split into two major areas: a compose area, where the sender of an instant message composes messages, and a conversation log area, where a history of the conversation can be viewed as it unfolds. Usually messages are short, hence the default shown in Figure 11.1 that gives more space to the conversation log and much less space to the compose area. For composing a long message, this default layout is not appropriate; the relative sizes of the two areas shown in Figure 11.2 increase the size of the compose window, making the task of typing in a long message easier on the user.

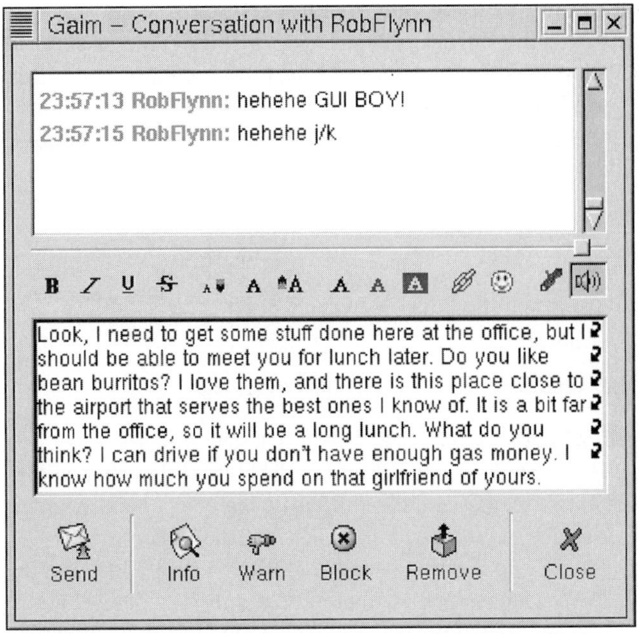

Figure 11.2 Conversation Log Window in GAIM, After Resize

A paned widget solves the problem of not knowing the optimal sizes of the compose and conversation log areas of the window at compile time by giving the user the ability to change their relative sizes at runtime.

Paned widget children can themselves be instances of GtkPaned. This can lead to very interesting and powerful user interfaces when used wisely.

Creating an Instance of GtkPaned

As with GtkBox, GtkPaned provides no functions with which an instance may be created. To create an instance of GtkPaned that's compatible with the functions provided by this class, you must use the widget creation functions provided by GtkHPaned and GtkVPaned. To create a vertical paned widget, you call the function gtk_vpaned_new():

```
GtkWidget *widget;

...

widget = gtk_vpaned_new();
```

The function gtk_vpaned_new() takes no arguments and returns an instance of GtkWidget.

Similarly, to create a horizontal paned widget, you can call gtk_hpaned_new(), which has the same prototype as gtk_vpaned_new().

Adding Children with Default Resize and Shrink Attributes

The next major step involved in using a GtkPaned widget is associating a child widget with each pane. In a vertical paned widget, the topmost pane is referred to as pane 1, and the pane below it is known as pane 2. In a horizontal paned widget, pane 1 is the leftmost pane, and pane 2 is the rightmost pane. Regardless, to specify the child widget bound to pane 1, you can call gtk_paned_add1():

```
void
gtk_paned_add1(GtkPaned *paned, GtkWidget *child);
```

Similarly, to set the pane 2 child widget, you can call gtk_paned_add2():

```
void
gtk_paned_add2(GtkPaned *paned, GtkWidget *child);
```

Both of these functions have the same argument list. The first argument, paned, is an instance of GtkPaned. The second argument, child, is the child widget that will be managed by GtkPaned. As I previously mentioned, the child is typically a container widget instance (for example, another instance of GtkPaned or an instance of GtkBox).

By using gtk_paned_add1() and/or gtk_paned_add2(), you are telling GtkPaned to pick defaults for both the resize and shrink attributes of a paned widget child. The resize attribute, a boolean, affects the size of the child widget at the time of creation relative to the size of the other child being managed by the paned widget. The shrink attribute tells GtkPaned whether the child can have its size reduced to accommodate an increase in the size of the other child, in response to a repositioning of the gutter by the user or the application.

For pane 1, the defaults assigned by GtkPaned when gtk_paned_add1() is used to add children are resize = FALSE, and shrink = TRUE. For gtk_paned_add2(), the defaults are resize = TRUE and shrink = TRUE.

Controlling the Resize and Shrink Attributes

The net result of adding children with default resize and shrink values is that pane 1 is given its needed size, and pane 2 is given the remainder of the area managed by the paned widget. Since shrink is set to TRUE for both panes, the gutter can be moved by the user to any location, causing either of the panes to shrink below the size needed to correctly display the child. In many cases, this is desired behavior—it often should be left to the user to decide whether one child pane has greater importance than the other and thus can be maximized at the cost of not fully showing the content in the other pane. However, in some cases you, as the application developer, may decide that one (or both) panes should not be resizable below the minimum size needed to display their content fully. If this is the case, you must override the defaults assigned by GtkPaned. This can be done by using the following two functions to add children to the paned widget.

The first of these functions, gtk_paned_pack1(), is used to specify child 1 of the paned widget:

```
void
gtk_paned_pack1(GtkPaned *paned, GtkWidget *child, gboolean resize,
        gboolean shrink);
```

The first two arguments to gtk_paned_pack1() are the same as those passed to gtk_paned_add1(). The argument resize, a boolean, specifies how much of the total paned widget area is initially given to child 1. If TRUE, child 1 will be given either the same amount of space given to child 2 or the remainder of the total paned widget area after child 2 is given the amount of area needed to display itself correctly. If FALSE, child 1 will be given only the area that is needed to display itself correctly, while child 2 will be given the remainder.

The argument shrink controls whether the gutter can be positioned by the user such that child 1 is given less area than is needed to correctly draw itself (TRUE) or not (FALSE).

The function gtk_paned_pack2() takes the same arguments as gtk_paned_pack1(). However, the meaning of the resize argument is influenced by the value of the resize argument passed to gtk_paned_pack1().

If the resize argument to gtk_paned_pack1() is set to FALSE, then effectively the resize argument to gtk_paned_pack2() is ignored—child 1 will always be given its needed size, and child 2 will always be given what remains. If the resize argument to gtk_paned_pack1() is set to TRUE and the resize argument to gtk_paned_pack2() is FALSE, then child 2 will be given the size needed to display its content correctly, and child 1 will be given whatever remains. If the resize arguments to both gtk_paned_pack1() and gtk_paned_pack2() are set to TRUE, then both child widgets are given equal amounts of the area managed by the paned widget. The function prototype for gtk_paned_pack2() is as follows:

```
void
gtk_paned_pack2(GtkPaned *paned, GtkWidget *child, gboolean resize,
        gboolean shrink);
```

To set the position of the gutter from your application, you must call gtk_paned_set_position():

```
void
gtk_paned_set_position(GtkPaned *paned, gint position);
```

The first argument is an instance of GtkPaned, and the second is the position of the gutter after the call has been made. Setting position to –1 (or to any negative number) will cause the gutter to revert to its original position. The position you specify will be clipped based on the shrink setting of the child widget toward which the gutter is being moved. For example, if the topmost (child 1) widget in a vertical paned widget has a minimum height of 10 pixels and you attempt to position the gutter at pixel 5, the position of the gutter will instead be set to 10, preserving the minimum size requirement of child 1. Likewise, if the minimum height of the bottom child (child 2) is 10 and the total height of the paned widget is 100 pixels, setting the position of the gutter to 95 will cause GtkPaned to position the gutter instead at location 90 so that the bottom child will be given the minimum size it requires.

Miscellaneous Functions

The preceding functions take care of the bulk of what the GtkPaned API set provides. Two additional functions supplied by GtkPaned can be used to control the size of the handle and the size of the gutter that separates the two pane children. I don't imagine that these functions will be of much use by most applications; the handle and gutter sizes that are assigned as defaults by GtkPaned should be suitable in most instances.

To set the height and the width of the separator handle or sash, you can call gtk_paned_set_handle_size():

```
void
gtk_paned_set_handle_size(GtkPaned *paned, guint16 size);
```

The size you pass defines both the width and the height of the sash, which is the square control that the user can use to reposition the separator and change the relative sizes of the paned child widgets. The sash is located a few pixels from the rightmost end of the groove in a vertical paned widget and a few pixels from the bottom of the groove in a horizontal paned widget. Again, I recommend that you not call this function and instead use the default values assigned by GtkPaned. Some readers may have noticed that the size argument is guint16. This means you cannot revert to the default handle size simply by passing a –1. The default value can be restored by calling gtk_paned_set_handle_size() with a size argument set to 10.

The gutter height can also be changed, although I recommend that applications not call this function either and simply use the default size (6 pixels) set by GtkPaned. The function prototype for gtk_paned_set_gutter_size() is as follows:

```
void
gtk_paned_set_gutter_size(GtkPaned *paned, guint16 size);
```

Changing the size of the gutter will not affect the size of the groove, which is always 2 pixels in height. In a vertical paned widget, half of the gutter will be placed above the groove, and the other half will be placed below the groove. In a horizontal paned widget, the groove separates the right and left halves of the gutter from each other.

Two following subclasses of GtkPaned—GtkVPaned and GtkHPaned—can be used to create vertical and horizontal instances of GtkPaned, respectively.

GtkVPaned

Class Name

```
GtkVPaned
```

Parent Class Name

```
GtkPaned
```

Macros

Widget type macro: `GTK_TYPE_PANED`

Object to widget cast macro: `GTK_VPANED(obj)`

Widget type check macro: `GTK_IS_VPANED(obj)`

Application-Level API Synopsis

Retrieve the constant GTK_TYPE_PANED at runtime:
```
guint
gtk_vpaned_get_type(void);
```

Create a new instance of GtkVPaned:
```
GtkWidget *
gtk_vpaned_new(void);
```

Class Description

GtkVPaned is used to create a vertical paned widget, as illustrated in Figure 11.3. The only function of interest is gtk_vpaned_new(), which is used to create a new vertical paned widget instance:

```
GtkWidget *
gtk_vpaned_new(void);
```

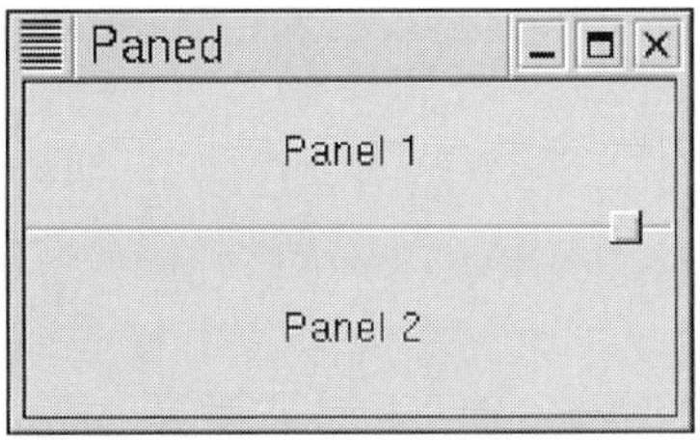

Figure 11.3 Vertical Paned Widget

The returned value can be cast to GtkPaned using the GTK_PANED macro and then passed to any of the functions defined by GtkPaned (see the preceding description of GtkPaned for more details).

GtkHPaned

Class Name

```
GtkHPaned
```

Parent Class Name

```
GtkPaned
```

Macros

Widget type macro: `GTK_TYPE_PANED`

Object to widget cast macro: `GTK_HPANED(obj)`

Widget type check macro: `GTK_IS_HPANED(obj)`

Application-Level API Synopsis

Retrieve the constant GTK_TYPE_PANED at runtime:

```
guint
gtk_hpaned_get_type(void);
```

Create a new instance of GtkHPaned:

```
GtkWidget *
gtk_hpaned_new(void);
```

Class Description

GtkHPaned is identical to GtkVPaned, except it is used to create a horizontal paned widget (as illustrated in Figure 11.4) as opposed to a vertical paned widget. Like GtkVPaned, the only function of interest in GtkHPaned is the function used to create a widget instance, which, in this case, is gtk_hpaned_new():

```
GtkWidget *
gtk_hpaned_new(void);
```

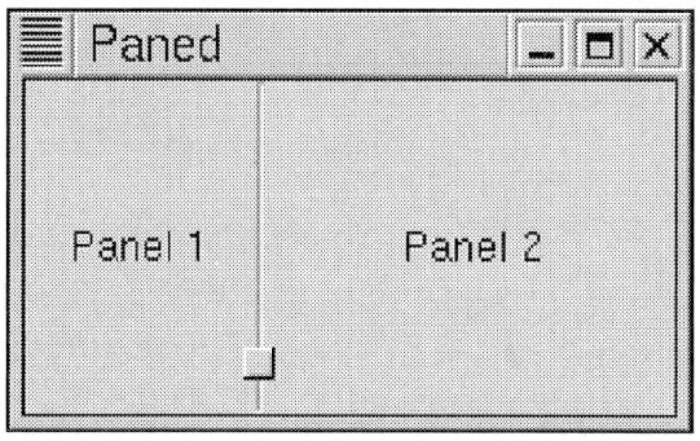

Figure 11.4 Horizontal Paned Widget

The returned value can be cast to GtkPaned with the GTK_PANED macro and then passed to any of the functions defined by GtkPaned (see GtkPaned for more details).

GtkPacker

Class Name

`GtkPacker`

Parent Class Name

`GtkContainer`

Macros

Widget type macro: `GTK_TYPE_PACKER`

Object to widget cast macro: `GTK_PACKER(obj)`

Widget type check macro: `GTK_IS_PACKER(obj)`

Supported Arguments

Prefix: `GtkPacker::`

Table 11.2 GtkPacker Arguments

Name	*Type*	*Permissions*
spacing	GTK_TYPE_UINT	GTK_ARG_READWRITE
default_border_width	GTK_TYPE_UINT	GTK_ARG_READWRITE
default_pad_x	GTK_TYPE_UINT	GTK_ARG_READWRITE
default_pad_y	GTK_TYPE_UINT	GTK_ARG_READWRITE
default_ipad_x	GTK_TYPE_UINT	GTK_ARG_READWRITE
default_ipad_y	GTK_TYPE_UINT	GTK_ARG_READWRITE
side	GTK_TYPE_SIDE_TYPE	GTK_ARG_READWRITE
anchor	GTK_TYPE_ANCHOR_TYPE	GTK_ARG_READWRITE
expand	GTK_TYPE_BOOL	GTK_ARG_READWRITE
fill_x	GTK_TYPE_BOOL	GTK_ARG_READWRITE
fill_y	GTK_TYPE_BOOL	GTK_ARG_READWRITE
use_default	GTK_TYPE_BOOL	GTK_ARG_READWRITE
border_width	GTK_TYPE_UINT	GTK_ARG_READWRITE
pad_x	GTK_TYPE_UINT	GTK_ARG_READWRITE
pad_y	GTK_TYPE_UINT	GTK_ARG_READWRITE
ipad_x	GTK_TYPE_UINT	GTK_ARG_READWRITE
ipad_y	GTK_TYPE_UINT	GTK_ARG_READWRITE
position	GTK_TYPE_LONG	GTK_ARG_READWRITE

Application-Level API Synopsis

Retrieve the constant GTK_TYPE_PACKER at runtime:

```
GtkType
gtk_packer_get_type(void);
```

Create a new instance of GtkPacker:

```
GtkWidget *
gtk_packer_new(void);
```

Application-Level API Synopsis (Continued)

Add a child widget to an instance of GtkPacker using default padding values and border width:

```
void
gtk_packer_add_defaults(GtkPacker *packer, GtkWidget *child,
        GtkSideType side, GtkAnchorType anchor,
        GtkPackerOptions options);
```

Add a child widget to an instance of GtkPacker:

```
void
gtk_packer_add(GtkPacker *packer, GtkWidget *child, GtkSideType side,
        GtkAnchorType anchor, GtkPackerOptions options,
        guint border_width, guint pad_x, guint pad_y, guint i_pad_x,
        guint i_pad_y);
```

Change the packing attributes of a GtkPacker child widget:

```
void
gtk_packer_set_child_packing(GtkPacker *packer, GtkWidget *child,
        GtkSideType side, GtkAnchorType anchor,
        GtkPackerOptions options, guint border_width, guint pad_x,
        guint pad_y, guint i_pad_x, guint i_pad_y);
```

Move a child of GtkPacker to the specified position:

```
void
gtk_packer_reorder_child(GtkPacker *packer, GtkWidget *child,
        gint position);
```

Set spacing (unused in Gtk 1.2):

```
void
gtk_packer_set_spacing(GtkPacker *packer, guint spacing);
```

Set the packer default border width:

```
void
gtk_packer_set_default_border_width(GtkPacker *packer,
        guint border);
```

Set default padding:

```
void
gtk_packer_set_default_pad(GtkPacker *packer, guint pad_x,
        guint pad_y);
```

Set default internal padding:

```
void
gtk_packer_set_default_ipad(GtkPacker *packer, guint i_pad_x,
        guint i_pad_y);
```

Class Description

GtkPacker is a container widget that implements a layout policy equivalent to the one implemented by the Tcl/Tk Packer geometry manager. Geometry managers in Tcl/Tk are, more or less, equivalent to container widgets in Gtk+.

GtkPacker is intended for programmers who are familiar with Tcl/Tk and need to write code using Gtk+ or who are porting code from Tcl/Tk to C and Gtk+. In general, programmers unfamiliar with Tcl/Tk will want to focus their attention on using GtkBox and the classes that derive from it (GtkHBox and GtkVBox). However, if you are more comfortable using the Tcl/Tk Packer, or have some Tcl/Tk user-interface code to port, GtkPacker may be what you are looking for.

In this section, I will describe each of the functions exposed by the GtkPacker API and will try to give readers familiar with Tcl/Tk a feeling for how to port Tcl/Tk packer–based user interfaces to the GtkPacker widget.

In my experience, which includes porting sample Tcl/Tk code from Brent Welch's *Practical Programming in Tcl and Tk, 3rd Edition* (Prentice Hall), Tcl/Tk packer and GtkPacker differ only in terms of the syntax used. That is, GtkPacker seems to accurately implement the semantics of a Tcl/Tk packer. I will present a few of these samples (thanks to Brent Welch for granting me permission to do this) so that you can obtain a feeling for what it takes to port Tcl/Tk packer user interfaces to GtkPacker.

A packer is much like a box widget. Like the box widget, a packer manages some area of a window or dialog. Children added to a packer are positioned based on the layout algorithm that packer implements as well as layout hints that you provide to GtkPacker when you create the packer widget and add child widgets to it.

Creating a Packer Widget

Probably the best way to get started is to look at some sample code that shows how to create a packer widget and add some child widgets to it. However, let's first take a look at a couple of functions. To create an instance of GtkPacker, call gtk_packer_new():

```
GtkWidget *
gtk_packer_new(void);
```

The return value is an instance of GtkWidget, which can be cast to an instance of GtkPacker using the macro GTK_PACKER.

In Tcl/Tk, a frame acts as the container to which child widgets are added. The Tcl/Tk Packer geometry manager decides how to place children in a frame. In Gtk+, the GtkPacker widget acts as both the container and the geometry manager. Calling gtk_packer_new() is roughly equivalent to executing a frame statement in a Tcl/Tk program.

Adding Children to a Packer

In Tcl/Tk, one or more child widgets are added to a packer by executing a pack statement. In Gtk+, child widgets are added to a packer widget by calling one of two functions:

```
void
gtk_packer_add_defaults(GtkPacker *packer, GtkWidget *child,
       GtkSideType side, GtkAnchorType anchor,
       GtkPackerOptions options);
```

The function gtk_packer_add_defaults() adds a child widget to an instance of GtkPacker using default padding values and border width. The function gtk_packer_add() performs the same function but allows the application to specify border width and padding values, overriding the defaults supplied by GtkPacker:

```
void
gtk_packer_add(GtkPacker *packer, GtkWidget *child, GtkSideType side,
       GtkAnchorType anchor, GtkPackerOptions options,
       guint border_width, guint pad_x, guint pad_y, guint i_pad_x,
       guint i_pad_y);
```

The arguments that gtk_packer_add_defaults() and gtk_packer_add() share in common are defined in Table 11.3.

Table 11.3 Arguments for gtk_packer_add_defaults() and gtk_packer_add()

Type	*Name*	*Comment*
GtkPacker *	packer	The instance of GtkPacker to which the child is being added (similar to a Tcl/Tk frame in this context).
GtkWidget *	child	The child being added to the frame or container.
GtkSideType	side	Equivalent to the -side argument to the Tcl/Tk pack command. Can be one of the following: GTK_SIDE_TOP (-side top) GTK_SIDE_BOTTOM (-side bottom) GTK_SIDE_LEFT (-side left) GTK_SIDE_RIGHT (-side right) The equivalent Tcl/Tk syntax is shown in parentheses.
GtkAnchorType	anchor	Equivalent to the -anchor argument of the Tcl/Tk pack command. Possible values include: GTK_ANCHOR_CENTER GTK_ANCHOR_NORTH (GTK_ANCHOR_N) GTK_ANCHOR_NORTH_WEST (GTK_ANCHOR_NW) GTK_ANCHOR_NORTH_EAST (GTK_ANCHOR_NE) GTK_ANCHOR_SOUTH (GTK_ANCHOR_S) GTK_ANCHOR_SOUTH_WEST (GTK_ANCHOR_SW) GTK_ANCHOR_SOUTH_EAST (GTK_ANCHOR_SE) GTK_ANCHOR_WEST (GTK_ANCHOR_W) GTK_ANCHOR_EAST (GTK_ANCHOR_E) Aliases are shown in parentheses (e.g., GTK_ANCHOR_N is an alias for GTK_ANCHOR_NORTH).

Table 11.3 Arguments for gtk_packer_add_defaults() and gtk_packer_add()

Type	*Name*	*Comment*	
GtkPackerOptions	options	A set of flags, OR'd together, that implement the following pack command arguments:	
		Flag	***Argument***
		GTK_PACK_EXPAND	-expand true
		GTK_FILL_X	-fill x
		GTK_FILL_Y	-fill y

Examples

Some examples should help illustrate the basics behind using packer widgets. These examples are derived from the book *Practical Programming in Tcl and Tk*, which was mentioned earlier. Here I will present Tcl/Tk code for the first few examples; interested readers should refer to *Practical Programming in Tcl and Tk* for the complete set of Tcl/Tk listings.

The results of the first example are illustrated in Figure 11.5. The Tcl/Tk code that implements this example is as follows:

```
. config -bg black
frame .one -width 40 -height 40 -bg white
frame .two -width 100 -height 50 -bg grey50
pack .one .two -side top
```

The preceding code basically creates two frames: one that is 40×40 in size with a white background and another that is 100×50 with a middle-gray background. The two frames are then placed in the containing window by packing them against the top edge. The result is very similar to using a vertical box (GtkVBox) and packing two widgets against the top edge using gtk_box_pack_start() (refer to Chapter 10, "Container and Bin Classes," for more information on GtkBox).

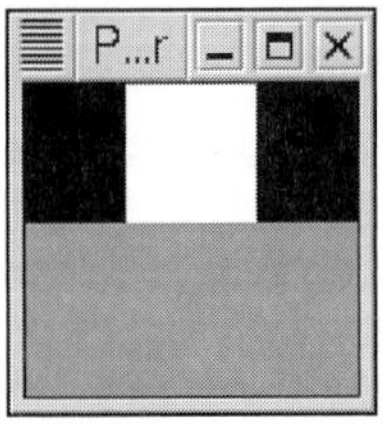

Figure 11.5 GtkPacker Example 1

A short Gtk+ program that implements the preceding Tcl/Tk code is provided in the following listing:

Listing 11.1 GtkPacker Example 1 Source

```
#include <gtk/gtk.h>

int main( int argc, char *argv[] )
{
   GtkWidget *window;
   GtkWidget *packer;
   GtkWidget *one, *two;
   GdkColor color;
   GtkStyle *style;
   GtkPackerOptions options;

   gtk_init (&argc, &argv);

   window = gtk_window_new(GTK_WINDOW_TOPLEVEL);
   gtk_signal_connect(GTK_OBJECT(window), "destroy",
           GTK_SIGNAL_FUNC(gtk_main_quit), "WM destroy");
   gtk_window_set_title(GTK_WINDOW(window), "Packer");
   style = gtk_style_new();
   color.red = 0x0;
   color.green = 0x0;
   color.blue = 0x0;
   style->bg[GTK_STATE_NORMAL] = color;
   gtk_widget_set_style( window, style );

   packer = gtk_packer_new();
   options = 0;

   one = gtk_drawing_area_new();
   gtk_widget_set_usize( one, 40, 40 );
   gtk_packer_add_defaults( GTK_PACKER( packer ), one,
           GTK_SIDE_TOP, GTK_ANCHOR_CENTER, options );
   style = gtk_style_new();
   color.red = 0xffff;
   color.green = 0xffff;
   color.blue = 0xffff;
   style->bg[GTK_STATE_NORMAL] = color;
   gtk_widget_set_style( one, style );
   gtk_widget_show( one );

   two = gtk_drawing_area_new();
   gtk_widget_set_usize( two, 100, 50 );
   gtk_packer_add_defaults( GTK_PACKER( packer ), two,
           GTK_SIDE_TOP, GTK_ANCHOR_CENTER, options );
   style = gtk_style_new();
   color.red = 0x8000;
   color.green = 0x8000;
   color.blue = 0x8000;
   style->bg[GTK_STATE_NORMAL] = color;
   gtk_widget_set_style( two, style );
   gtk_widget_show( two );
```

```
051
052       gtk_widget_show(packer);
053       gtk_container_add( GTK_CONTAINER( window ), packer );
054       gtk_widget_show(window);
055
056       gtk_main();
057
058       return(0);
059   }
```

On lines 014 through 023, a window with a black background is created, corresponding to the Tcl/Tk code

```
. config -bg black
```

On line 025, I then create an instance of GtkPacker. The packer widget is made a child of the window on line 053. The next step involves creating a pair of drawing-area widgets that will represent the two frames (one white, the other grey50) that are packed by the Tcl/Tk application into the top-level window. The first drawing area is created on line 028, and its size is set to 40×40 on the following line.

```
028       one = gtk_drawing_area_new();
029       gtk_widget_set_usize( one, 40, 40 );
```

Next I add the child widget to the packer by calling gtk_packer_add_defaults() on line 030:

```
030       gtk_packer_add_defaults( GTK_PACKER( packer ), one,
031               GTK_SIDE_TOP, GTK_ANCHOR_CENTER, options );
```

These lines are intended to be equivalent to the following Tcl/Tk line:

```
pack .one -side top
```

The side argument to gtk_packer_add_defaults() is set to GTK_SIDE_TOP, which corresponds to "-side top" in the preceding Tcl/Tk source code. The anchor argument to gtk_packer_add_defaults() is set to GTK_ANCHOR_CENTER, which will probably be the typical default value for most applications. Earlier in the program, options is set to 0. Therefore, no fill or expand options are passed to GtkPacker in this example. The code shown on lines 032 through 037 causes the background color of the drawing area to be set to white, corresponding to the "-bg white" portion of the Tcl/Tk code executed to create the 40×40 frame, which the Gtk+ code tries to emulate.

Code on lines 040 through 050 creates the second "frame," which again is in the form of a drawing-area widget in this example. The corresponding code in Tcl/Tk is as follows:

```
frame .two -width 100 -height 50 -bg grey50
pack .two -side top
```

It would be worthwhile for you, as an exercise, to take the preceding Gtk+ source code and try experiments with various side arguments (e.g., GTK_SIDE_RIGHT, GTK_SIDE_LEFT, and GTK_SIDE_BOTTOM). Try packing the first drawing area using GTK_SIDE_RIGHT and the other using GTK_SIDE_LEFT or GTK_SIDE_BOTTOM. By doing so, you will gain a good intuition for how packing works. You are free to pack an arbitrary number of child widgets to arbitrary sides of the packer widget in whatever order is needed to create the desired layout.

Nesting Packers

As is the case with boxes, a packer widget will accept another container widget (e.g., a box or a packer) as a child. By nesting packer widgets within packer widgets (or boxes within packer widgets, or packer widgets within boxes), you can achieve practically any layout desired. The following example, also derived from Brent Welch's book, illustrates two levels of nesting (see Figure 11.6 for the resulting window). First, the Tcl/Tk code is as follows:

```
001 frame .one -bg white
002 frame .two -width 100 -height 50 -bg grey50
003 foreach b {alpha beta} {
004     button .one.$b -text $b
005     pack .one.$b -side left
006 }
007 frame .one.right
008 for each b {delta epsilon} {
009     button .one.right.$b -text $b
010     pack .one.right.$b -side bottom
011 }
012 pack .one.right -side right
013 pack .one .two -side top
```

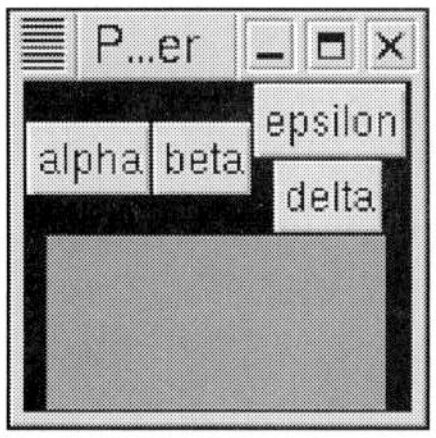

Figure 11.6 GtkPacker Example 2

Basically, the preceding code does the following. On line 001, a frame (.one) with a white background is created. The frame is packed along the top edge of the window later on line 013. One line 002, a second frame, 100 pixels wide and 50 pixels tall with a gray background, is created. It is also packed into the window on line 013, but because it follows frame .one in the packing order, it will be placed below frame .one. On lines 003 through 006, two buttons are created. Line 004 creates the button, and line 005 packs it into frame .one in a left-to-right order (-side left). Since the button labeled alpha is created first, it will be packed against the far-left edge of the frame. The second button, labeled beta, will be packed immediately to its right.

On line 007, a new frame named .one.right is created. On lines 008 through 011, two additional buttons are created and packed into this frame. As you can see on line 010, the buttons are packed against the bottom side. The button labeled delta is lower in the frame since it was packed first, while the button labeled epsilon is packed second, immediately above the delta button.

On line 012, the frame containing the delta and epsilon buttons is packed into the same frame into which the alpha and beta buttons were packed earlier, but against the right edge of that frame (using -side right) as opposed to the left edge as the buttons were on line 005. Finally, the two frames (.one and .two) are packed into the containing window on line 013. Let's look at some GtkPacker code that basically implements the Tcl/Tk code I just described:

```
026     packer = gtk_packer_new();
027     options = 0;
```

On line 026, a packer widget is instantiated. This packer corresponds to the window into which the Tcl/Tk code packs its other frames on line 013 of the Tcl/Tk code.

```
029     one = gtk_packer_new();
030     gtk_packer_add_defaults( GTK_PACKER( packer ), one,
031             GTK_SIDE_TOP, GTK_ANCHOR_CENTER, options );
032     gtk_widget_show( one );
```

On line 029, I create a packer that is analogous to frame .one in the Tcl/Tk code. On lines 030 and 031, this frame is packed into the top-level packer widget (packer); side is set to GTK_SIDE_TOP to emulate the -side top on line 013. The next several lines create buttons and pack them into the "one" packer widget, this implementing lines 003 through 006 of the Tcl/Tk code:

```
034     button = gtk_button_new_with_label( "alpha" );
035     gtk_widget_show( button );
036     gtk_packer_add_defaults( GTK_PACKER( one ), button,
037             GTK_SIDE_LEFT, GTK_ANCHOR_CENTER, options );
038
039     button = gtk_button_new_with_label( "beta" );
040     gtk_widget_show( button );
041     gtk_packer_add_defaults( GTK_PACKER( one ), button,
042             GTK_SIDE_LEFT, GTK_ANCHOR_CENTER, options );
```

The alpha and beta buttons are packed along the left side of the packer by setting the side argument to gtk_packer_add_defaults to GTK_SIDE_LEFT. The next few lines (044 through 047) create and show the packer that emulates the one.right frame in the Tcl/Tk code:

```
044     one_right = gtk_packer_new();
045     gtk_widget_show( one_right );
046     gtk_packer_add_defaults( GTK_PACKER( one ), one_right,
047             GTK_SIDE_LEFT, GTK_ANCHOR_CENTER, options );
```

As you can see, the one_right packer is packed into the one packer along the left side, adjacent to the buttons that were packed into the one packer on lines 034 through 042. Next, we create the epsilon and delta buttons and pack them into packer one_right:

```
049     button = gtk_button_new_with_label( "epsilon" );
050     gtk_widget_show( button );
```

```
051     gtk_packer_add_defaults( GTK_PACKER( one_right ), button,
052             GTK_SIDE_TOP, GTK_ANCHOR_CENTER, options );
053
054     button = gtk_button_new_with_label( "delta" );
055     gtk_widget_show( button );
056     gtk_packer_add_defaults( GTK_PACKER( one_right ), button,
057             GTK_SIDE_TOP, GTK_ANCHOR_CENTER, options );
```

Here I've decided to throw a slight monkey wrench into the process. Notice how I packed the epsilon button first and then the delta button. This is the opposite order from which the Tcl/Tk code packed its buttons into the .one.right frame. Why does this give us the same results? Careful readers will notice that the Tcl/Tk code packed the buttons using -side bottom, while in the Gtk+ code I packed them (in reverse order) by setting the gtk_packer_add_defaults() side argument to GTK_SIDE_TOP. Packing a set of buttons with side set to GTK_SIDE_TOP in the order 0, 1, 2, ..., $n - 1$ is equivalent to packing the same set of buttons with side set to GTK_SIDE_BOTTOM but packing them in the order $n - 1$, $n - 2$, $n - 3$, ..., 0. A similar argument holds true for packing widgets against GTK_SIDE_LEFT and GTK_SIDE_RIGHT.

To complete this sample, I create, on lines 059 through 069, a drawing-area widget with a medium-gray background and pack it into the top-level "packer" packer below the "one" packer widget:

```
059     two = gtk_drawing_area_new();
060     gtk_widget_set_usize( two, 100, 50 );
061     gtk_packer_add_defaults( GTK_PACKER( packer ), two,
062             GTK_SIDE_TOP, GTK_ANCHOR_CENTER, options );
063     style = gtk_style_new();
064     color.red = 0x8000;
065     color.green = 0x8000;
066     color.blue = 0x8000;
067     style-bg[GTK_STATE_NORMAL] = color;
068     gtk_widget_set_style( two, style );
069     gtk_widget_show( two );
```

Fill X and Fill Y

Let's look at some more examples. The following examples are designed to illustrate the various options that can be specified using the options argument to both gtk_packer_add() and gtk_packer_add_defaults(). So far, I have set the options argument to 0 in each of the examples presented. The first example presented here (Figure 11.7) is no different; I create a few widgets and pack them without specifying options. Examples that follow illustrate the effects that can be achieved when various options are specified by the application. The source code for the first example, which I use to illustrate the GTK_FILL_X and GTK_FILL_Y flags, is as follows:

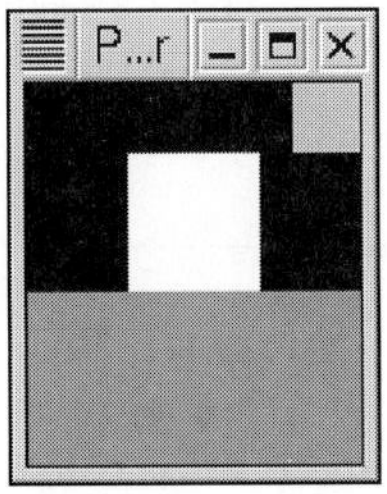

Figure 11.7 Fill X and Fill Y Example 1

Listing 11.2 Source Code for Figure 11.7

```
#include <gtk/gtk.h>

int main( int argc, char *argv[] )
{
   GtkWidget *window, *packer, *one, *two, *three;
   GdkColor color;
   GtkStyle *style;
   GtkPackerOptions options;

   gtk_init (&argc, &argv);

   window = gtk_window_new(GTK_WINDOW_TOPLEVEL);
   gtk_signal_connect(GTK_OBJECT(window), "destroy",
           GTK_SIGNAL_FUNC(gtk_main_quit), "WM destroy");
   gtk_window_set_title(GTK_WINDOW(window), "Packer");

   style = gtk_style_new();
   color.red = 0x0;
   color.green = 0x0;
   color.blue = 0x0;
   style->bg[GTK_STATE_NORMAL] = color;
   gtk_widget_set_style( window, style );

   packer = gtk_packer_new();
   options = 0;

   one = gtk_drawing_area_new();
   gtk_widget_set_usize( one, 100, 50 );
   gtk_packer_add_defaults( GTK_PACKER( packer ), one,
           GTK_SIDE_BOTTOM, GTK_ANCHOR_CENTER, options );
   style = gtk_style_new();
   color.red = 0x8000;
   color.green = 0x8000;
   color.blue = 0x8000;
   style->bg[GTK_STATE_NORMAL] = color;
   gtk_widget_set_style( one, style );
   gtk_widget_show( one );

   two = gtk_drawing_area_new();
```

```
040      gtk_widget_set_usize( two, 40, 40 );
041      gtk_packer_add_defaults( GTK_PACKER( packer ), two,
042              GTK_SIDE_BOTTOM, GTK_ANCHOR_CENTER, options );
043      style = gtk_style_new();
044      color.red = 0xffff;
045      color.green = 0xffff;
046      color.blue = 0xffff;
047      style->bg[GTK_STATE_NORMAL] = color;
048      gtk_widget_set_style( two, style );
049      gtk_widget_show( two );
050
051      three = gtk_drawing_area_new();
052      gtk_widget_set_usize( three, 20, 20 );
053      gtk_packer_add_defaults( GTK_PACKER( packer ), three,
054              GTK_SIDE_RIGHT, GTK_ANCHOR_CENTER, options );
055      style = gtk_style_new();
056      color.red = 0xbfff;
057      color.green = 0xbfff;
058      color.blue = 0xbfff;
059      style->bg[GTK_STATE_NORMAL] = color;
060      gtk_widget_set_style( three, style );
061      gtk_widget_show( three );
062
063      gtk_widget_show(packer);
064      gtk_container_add( GTK_CONTAINER( window ), packer );
065
066      gtk_widget_show(window);
067
068      gtk_main();
069
070      return(0);
071  }
```

In the preceding sample, I create a window and set its background to black (lines 012 through 022). On line 024, a packer widget is created. This packer will hold each of the three drawing-area widgets created by the remainder of the code. On lines 027 through 037, a 100×50 gray drawing area is created and packed into the bottom edge of the packer. On lines 039 through 049, a 40×40 white drawing-area widget is created and is also packed against the bottom of the packer, which causes it to be placed above the previously packed (gray) drawing area. Finally, on lines 051 through 061, a 20×20 light-gray drawing area is packed against the right side of the packer. It is placed higher than the second (white) drawing area because the second drawing-area widget effectively owns the space to its left and right (horizontally) in the packer widget. Figure 11.7 illustrates the result.

Table 11.4 presents the GTK_FILL_X and GTK_FILL_Y options I mentioned earlier.

Table 11.4 GTK_FILL_X and GTK_FILL_Y Options

Flag	*Tcl/Tk pack Argument*
GTK_FILL_X	-fill x
GTK_FILL_Y	-fill y

We can apply these options to the preceding code to see how fill works. The only change needed is on line 025:

```
025      options = GTK_FILL_X;
```

The result is illustrated in Figure 11.8:

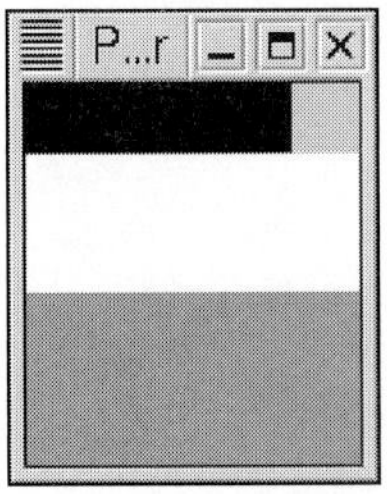

Figure 11.8 Setting GTK_FILL_X Option

What has happened here is relatively simple. Without specifying GTK_FILL_X, the drawing-area widgets will only occupy the space they need. Drawing area one is the widest of the drawing areas and thus defines the width of the area into which the other drawing areas are later added. Let's see what happens when we specify GTK_FILL_X as an option. First of all, since drawing area one is the widest of the widgets packed into the parent packer widget, it consumes the entire width of the packer. Thus, there is nothing for it to fill into. This is not the case for drawing area two, however. Drawing area two, being less wide than drawing area one, will be resized by the packer so that its width is the same as that of the "cavity" into which it is being packed. Regardless of whether or not FILL_X is specified, this cavity is, in a sense, preallocated for drawing area two, which is why drawing area three is located above drawing area two even though drawing area three was packed to the right in the parent frame.

You will notice that drawing area three does not consume the entire width of the packer; it remains 20×20 in size even though we specified GTK_FILL_X for it as well. Why is this? The reason is that when we pack a widget along the bottom, the top, the left, or the right, the widget owns that side. For example, drawing areas one and two own the bottom side of their respective areas since they were packed with GTK_SIDE_BOTTOM. Thus, they are only free to fill in the x direction. Drawing area three, on the other hand, was packed using GTK_SIDE_RIGHT. Therefore, it is free to fill in the y direction, and the GTK_FILL_X option is ignored for this widget. Thus, drawing area three retains its original size after packing. This leads us to Table 11.5.

Table 11.5 Applicable GTK_FILL_X and GTK_FILL_Y Packing Options

Options	*Applicable Packing*
GTK_FILL_X	GTK_SIDE_TOP, GTK_SIDE_BOTTOM
GTK_FILL_Y	GTK_SIDE_LEFT, GTK_SIDE_RIGHT

This table is not valid if GTK_PACK_EXPAND is specified as an option (see the following discussion).

The following figures illustrate what happens when we resize the window of the previous two sample clients. Figure 11.9 illustrates what happens with options set to 0, and Figure 11.10 illustrates with options set to GTK_FILL_X. Neither of the drawing areas one or two in Figure 11.9 resize to fill the width of the window, but they do resize in Figure 11.10.

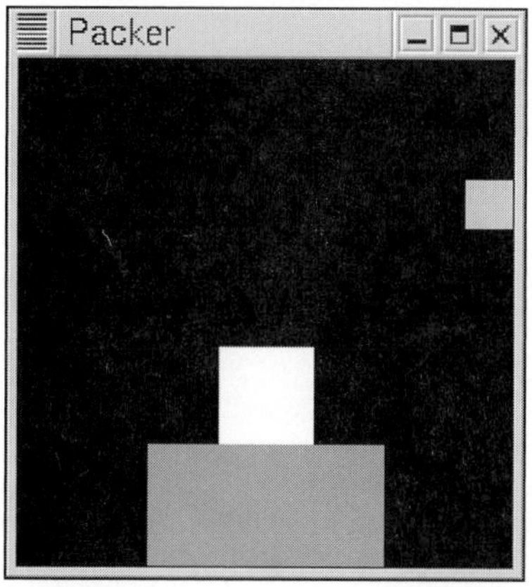

Figure 11.9 Resizing Window Depicted in Figure 11.7

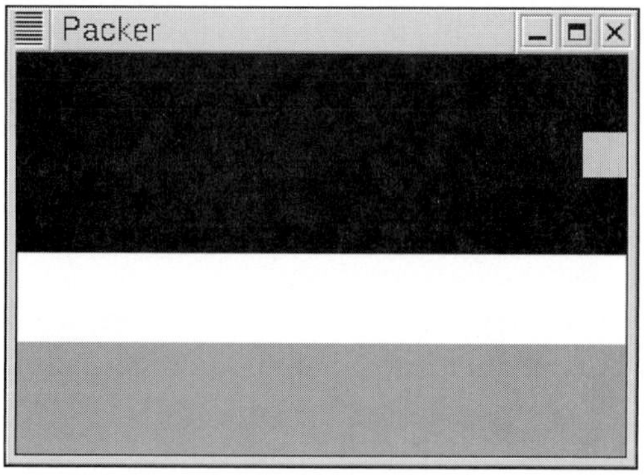

Figure 11.10 Resizing Window Depicted in Figure 11.8

By the way, OR'ing together GTK_FILL_X and GTK_FILL_Y, as in the following, is the same as specifying "-fill both" in Tcl/Tk:

```
options = GTK_FILL_X | GTK_FILL_Y;
```

Expand Option

The final options flag is GTK_PACK_EXPAND. This flag corresponds to the Tcl/Tk packer argument -expand true. It is often easy to confuse GTK_PACK_EXPAND with GTK_FILL_X and GTK_FILL_Y. After all, the previous example illustrates drawing-area widgets that have been expanded into their allocated cavities. The key to understanding the difference is to realize that the GTK_FILL_X and GTK_FILL_Y options tell the widget to fill the cavity they have been allocated, while GTK_PACK_EXPAND causes the cavity itself to be expanded.

Let's look at our original example and see how this works (refer now to Figure 11.7). By changing the options argument to GTK_PACK_EXPAND:

```
options = GTK_PACK_EXPAND;
```

we obtain the result in Figure 11.11:

Figure 11.11 Figure 11.7 Options Set to GTK_PACK_EXPAND

The cavity owned by drawing area three expanded itself horizontally to fill the remaining area of the window. The 20×20 drawing area is placed in the center of this cavity because we specified an anchor of GTK_ANCHOR_CENTER. Now let's add a GTK_FILL_X flag to the options argument:

```
options = GTK_PACK_EXPAND | GTK_FILL_X;
```

Adding GTK_FILL_X causes the 20×20 drawing area three to expand itself into the cavity created because we also specified GTK_PACK_EXPAND as an option, as shown in Figure 11.12.

Figure 11.12 Figure 11.7 Options Set to GTK_PACK_EXPAND | GTK_FILL_X

Anchoring

In all of the preceding examples, the anchor argument to gtk_packer_add() has been set to GTK_ANCHOR_CENTER, which is a good default value to use. For those of you familiar with Tcl/Tk packers, the anchor argument to gtk_packer_add() is equivalent to the -anchor argument of the pack command.

Let's return to the example shown in Figure 11.7. If we were to change the anchor argument to any other value (say, GTK_ANCHOR_NORTH) when packing drawing area three, we would still get the same result because the size of drawing area three and the cavity into which it has been packed are the same. Therefore, the anchor argument only really applies if the cavity is larger than the widget being packed into it. This is why, in Figure 11.11, drawing area three is centered within the cavity; we have caused the cavity to become larger than the drawing area, thereby adding significance to the anchor argument. If we want to force the drawing area to the right edge of the cavity in this case, we would specify an anchor argument of GTK_ANCHOR_EAST:

```
    packer = gtk_packer_new();
    options = GTK_PACK_EXPAND;

...

    three = gtk_drawing_area_new();
    gtk_widget_set_usize( three, 20, 20 );
    gtk_packer_add_defaults( GTK_PACKER( packer ), three,
            GTK_SIDE_RIGHT, GTK_ANCHOR_EAST, options );
```

GtkPacker will use whatever it can of the anchor argument that makes sense for the cavity into which the widget is being packed. If the height of the cavity is the same as the widget, then north and south components of the anchor are ignored. Likewise, if the width of the cavity equals the width of the child being packed, the east and west components are ignored. For example, the anchor GTK_ANCHOR_NORTH_EAST is equivalent to specifying GTK_ANCHOR_NORTH if the width of the cavity is the same as that of the child being packed and is equivalent to GTK_ANCHOR_EAST if the height of the cavity is the same as that of the child being packed. If the child size and the cavity size are the same, effectively the anchor argument can be set to anything, although I would recommend that you use GTK_ANCHOR_CENTER and make sure to check your application to ensure that any geometry changes to the containing window (e.g., window resizes) behave as you intend them to.

For a more detailed discussion of anchoring and additional Tcl/Tk code examples, refer to Brent Welch's book.

Border Width and Padding

You can set a border width that will be applied to all children packed into a packer widget by calling gtk_packer_set_default_border_width():

```
void
gtk_packer_set_default_border_width(GtkPacker *packer, guint border);
```

The argument packer is an instance of GtkPacker, and border is the desired border width as an unsigned integer. Figure 11.13 illustrates the effect on the layout shown in Figure 11.7 by setting a 5-pixel border around each child:

Figure 11.13 Figure 11.7 with a Default Border Width of 5 Pixels

GtkPacker recognizes two kinds of padding. Both of these paddings control how much space is allocated to widgets packed into the packer in addition to the space requested by the widget being packed. With internal padding, the size of the widget is increased by the specified value, and the widget will resize itself to accommodate that new size. With external padding, the size of the widget will not change, but GtkPacker will add extra space around the widget in much the same way that a border width is added around each widget if the border width for the packer is nonzero. The border width and external packing are two different things, however. Specifying a border width of 5 and an external padding of 5 is the visual equivalent of setting either the border width or the external padding to 10 (and setting the other value to 0). External and internal padding can be specified separately for the x and y dimensions; spacing, on the other hand, is applied both to the x and y dimensions (e.g., is added to both the width and height of the child).

Figure 11.14 illustrates the effect of setting the default external padding to 5 in the x dimension and 20 in the y dimension. The border width is set to 0 in this example. Figure 11.15 illustrates setting the internal padding to similar values. Notice, however, that the size of the widget has changed to accommodate the area it has been allocated.

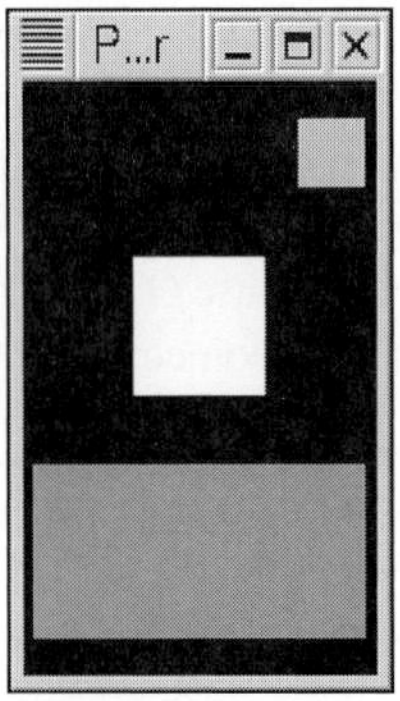

Figure 11.14 Figure 11.7 with External Padding X=5, Y=20

Figure 11.15 Figure 11.7 with Internal Padding X=5, Y=20

To set the default external padding of a packer in the x and y dimensions, call gtk_packer_set_default_pad():

```
void
gtk_packer_set_default_pad(GtkPacker *packer, guint pad_x,
        guint pad_y);
```

The arguments pad_x and pad_y specify the external padding that will be added to all children of the packer.

To set the default internal padding, call gtk_packer_set_default_ipad():

```
void
gtk_packer_set_default_ipad(GtkPacker *packer, guint i_pad_x,
        guint i_pad_y);
```

The arguments are the same as passed to gtk_packer_set_default_pad(), except the padding affected is the internal padding, not the external padding.

You can use gtk_packer_set_child_packing() to set all of the packing options for a given packer widget at one time, overriding any values that may have been specified at the time the child was originally added to the packer. The function prototype for gtk_packer_set_child_packing() is as follows:

```
void
gtk_packer_set_child_packing(GtkPacker *packer, GtkWidget *child,
        GtkSideType side, GtkAnchorType anchor,
        GtkPackerOptions options, guint border_width, guint pad_x,
        guint pad_y, guint i_pad_x, guint i_pad_y);
```

The arguments are equivalent to those passed to gtk_packer_add().

Reordering Children

The final function discussed here can be used to move a child of GtkPacker to a specified position in the packing order of the packer:

```
void
gtk_packer_reorder_child(GtkPacker *packer, GtkWidget *child,
        gint position);
```

The argument packer is the relevant instance of GtkPacker, child is the widget being moved, and position is the new position in the packing order of that child after gtk_packer_reorder_child() has returned. Position must be in the range of $[0, n - 1]$, where n is the number of children being managed by the packer. Assume we have three child widgets—a, b, and c—located at positions 0, 1, and 2. If we change the position of child a to position 1, child b will be located at position 0, and child c will remain at position 2. A move from position m to some other position $n < m$ will cause widgets at locations m through $m - 1$ to increase their position by 1. Moving a child m to some location $p > m$ will cause widgets at locations $m + 1$ through p to decrease their position value by 1.

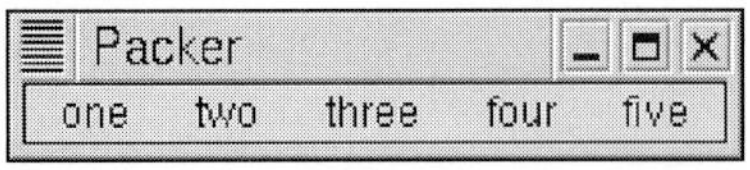

Figure 11.16 Five Buttons, Packed Left to Right

The following client positions five GtkLabel widgets in a packer. From left to right, the labels are one, two, three, four, and five, corresponding to positions 0, 1, 2, 3, and 4 in the packer (see Figure 11.16). The program arranges to fire a timer once a second. The timer callback maintains a static index variable that holds the last-assigned position of the one label widget child; the timer callback increments the value stored in this static and then calls gtk_packer_reorder_child() to move the one widget to the location specified. Notice the use of gtk_packer_set_default_pad() on line 033 and the setting of GTK_PACKER_EXPAND and GTK_FILL_X options on line 034. You might try commenting out the call to gtk_packer_set_default_pad(), set options to 0, and see what the effect is on the layout of the child widgets in the packer.

Listing 11.3 Sample Using gtk_packer_reorder_child()

```
001  #include <gtk/gtk.h>
002
003  GtkWidget *one, *two, *three, *four, *five;
004
005  gint
006  TimeoutFunc( gpointer data )
007  {
008     static int position = -1;
009     GtkPacker *packer = (GtkPacker *) data;
010
011     position++;
012     if ( position == 5 )
013             position = 0;
014     gtk_packer_reorder_child( packer, one, position );
015     return TRUE;
016  }
017
018  int main( int argc, char *argv[] )
019  {
020     GtkWidget *packer;
021     GtkWidget *window;
022     GtkPackerOptions options;
023
024     gtk_init (&argc, &argv);
025
026     window = gtk_window_new(GTK_WINDOW_TOPLEVEL);
027     gtk_signal_connect(GTK_OBJECT(window), "destroy",
028             GTK_SIGNAL_FUNC(gtk_main_quit), "WM destroy");
029     gtk_window_set_title(GTK_WINDOW(window), "Packer");
030
031     packer = gtk_packer_new();
```

```
    gtk_timeout_add( 1000, TimeoutFunc, (gpointer) packer );
    gtk_packer_set_default_pad( GTK_PACKER( packer ), 20, 0 );
    options = GTK_FILL_X | GTK_PACK_EXPAND;

    one = gtk_label_new("one");
    gtk_packer_add_defaults( GTK_PACKER( packer ), one,
            GTK_SIDE_LEFT, GTK_ANCHOR_CENTER, options );
    gtk_widget_show( one );

    two = gtk_label_new("two");
    gtk_packer_add_defaults( GTK_PACKER( packer ), two,
            GTK_SIDE_LEFT, GTK_ANCHOR_CENTER, options );
    gtk_widget_show( two );

    three = gtk_label_new("three");
    gtk_packer_add_defaults( GTK_PACKER( packer ), three,
            GTK_SIDE_LEFT, GTK_ANCHOR_CENTER, options );
    gtk_widget_show( three );

    four = gtk_label_new("four");
    gtk_packer_add_defaults( GTK_PACKER( packer ), four,
            GTK_SIDE_LEFT, GTK_ANCHOR_CENTER, options );
    gtk_widget_show( four );

    five = gtk_label_new("five");
    gtk_packer_add_defaults( GTK_PACKER( packer ), five,
            GTK_SIDE_LEFT, GTK_ANCHOR_CENTER, options );
    gtk_widget_show( five );

    gtk_widget_show(packer);
    gtk_container_add( GTK_CONTAINER( window ), packer );

    gtk_widget_show(window);
    gtk_main();
    return(0);
}
```

GtkFrame

Class Name

```
GtkFrame
```

Parent Class Name

```
GtkBin
```

Macros

Widget type macro: `GTK_TYPE_FRAME`

Object to widget cast macro: `GTK_FRAME(obj)`

Widget type check macro: `GTK_IS_FRAME(obj)`

Supported Arguments

Prefix: `GtkFrame::`

Table 11.6 GtkFrame Arguments

Name	*Type*	*Permissions*
label	GTK_TYPE_STRING	GTK_ARG_READWRITE
label_xalign	GTK_TYPE_FLOAT	GTK_ARG_READWRITE
label_yalign	GTK_TYPE_FLOAT	GTK_ARG_READWRITE
shadow	GTK_TYPE_SHADOW_TYPE	GTK_ARG_READWRITE

Application-Level API Synopsis

Retrieve the constant GTK_TYPE_FRAME at runtime:
```
GtkType
gtk_frame_get_type(void);
```

Create an instance of GtkFrame with an optional label (pass NULL if no label is desired):
```
GtkWidget *
gtk_frame_new(const gchar *label);
```

Set the label of an instance of GtkFrame to value (pass NULL if no label is desired):
```
void
gtk_frame_set_label(GtkFrame *frame, const gchar *label);
```

Set the alignment of label for an instance of GtkFrame:
```
void
gtk_frame_set_label_align(GtkFrame *frame, gfloat xalign, gfloat
yalign);
```

Set the shadow type for an instance of GtkFrame:
```
void
gtk_frame_set_shadow_type(GtkFrame *frame, GtkShadowType type);
```

Class Description

GtkFrame is a container class, like the others described in this chapter, used to manage instances of other widget classes. The parent class of GtkFrame is GtkBin, which in turn is a child class of GtkContainer. GtkFrame differs from GtkBin in that it draws a visual boundary, or a frame, around its children to indicate the area it manages. The frame can contain a label to help the user identify more readily the logical grouping to which the controls or other items in the frame belong. Like any container, an instance of GtkFrame can manage other containers, including instances of GtkFrame, GtkBox, and so forth.

Creating a Frame Widget

A frame can be created by making a call to gtk_frame_new():

```
GtkWidget *
gtk_frame_new(const gchar *label);
```

The argument label, if non-NULL, points to a NULL-terminated C string that will be used by GtkFrame to label the frame. If your application does not require the use of a label, then simply pass (gchar *) NULL.

An Example

In the following code, I create a dialog containing three instances of GtkList, each list containing the same number of items. The lists are packed, left to right, in the control area of the dialog. A #define, USE_FRAMES, will cause each of the lists to be wrapped by an instance of GtkFrame. As can be seen in Figures 11.17 and 11.18, not only do the frames provide better visual separation of the three lists, the frame labels help to identify the content of each of the lists.

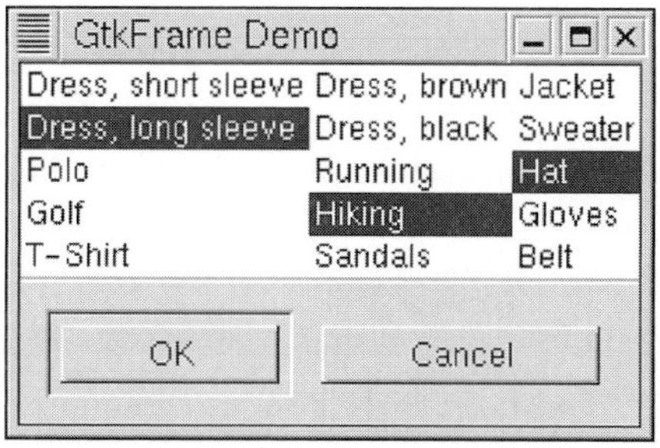

Figure 11.17 Three Lists Without Frames

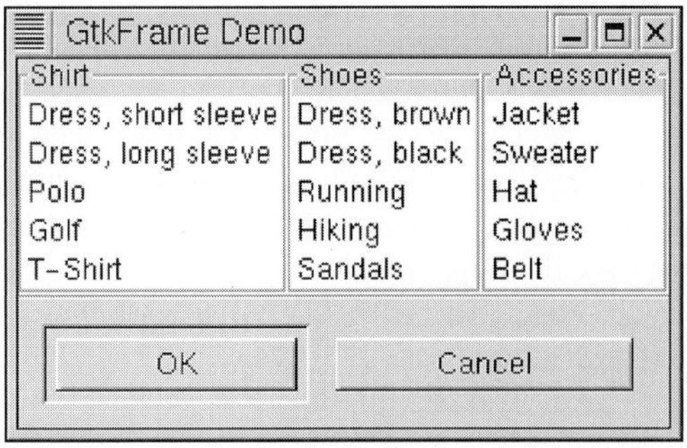

Figure 11.18 Three Lists with Frames

Listing 11.4 Partial Source Listing for Figures 11.17 and 11.18

```
#include <gtk/gtk.h>

void
GtkFrameDialog()
{
    GtkWidget *frame, *dialog_window, *hbox1, *outervbox,
        *list, *list_item;
    GList     *item_list;

    dialog_window = gtk_window_new(GTK_WINDOW_TOPLEVEL);
    gtk_window_position (GTK_WINDOW (dialog_window), GTK_WIN_POS_MOUSE);

    gtk_signal_connect (GTK_OBJECT (dialog_window), "destroy",
            GTK_SIGNAL_FUNC(gtk_widget_destroyed), &dialog_window);

    gtk_window_set_title (GTK_WINDOW (dialog_window), "GtkFrame Demo");
    gtk_container_border_width (GTK_CONTAINER (dialog_window), 0);

    outervbox = gtk_vbox_new (FALSE, 0);
    gtk_container_add (GTK_CONTAINER (dialog_window), outervbox);

    hbox1 = gtk_hbox_new (FALSE, 0);
    gtk_box_pack_start ( GTK_BOX (outervbox), hbox1, TRUE, TRUE, 0);

#if defined( USE_FRAMES )
    frame = gtk_frame_new( "Shirt" );
    gtk_box_pack_start ( GTK_BOX (hbox1), frame, TRUE, TRUE, 0);
#endif
    list = gtk_list_new();
    item_list = NULL;
    list_item = gtk_list_item_new_with_label ("Dress, short sleeve");
    item_list = g_list_append (item_list, list_item);
    list_item = gtk_list_item_new_with_label ("Dress, long sleeve");
    item_list = g_list_append (item_list, list_item);
    list_item = gtk_list_item_new_with_label ("Polo");
```

```
      item_list = g_list_append (item_list, list_item);
      list_item = gtk_list_item_new_with_label ("Golf");
      item_list = g_list_append (item_list, list_item);
      list_item = gtk_list_item_new_with_label ("T-Shirt");
      item_list = g_list_append (item_list, list_item);
      gtk_list_insert_items( GTK_LIST(list), item_list, 0 );
09 #if defined ( USE_FRAMES )
10    gtk_container_add (GTK_CONTAINER (frame), list);
11 #else
12    gtk_box_pack_start ( GTK_BOX (hbox1), list, TRUE, TRUE, 0);
13 #endif
}
```

I've only included the code needed to create the first of the three lists; the remainder of the routine follows along a similar path. On line 01, I create an instance of GtkVBox to hold the horizontal box into which the three lists (and frames) are placed, the action area, and the separator between them. Line 02 adds the vbox to the dialog. On lines 03 and 04, I create the hbox used to hold the three frames/lists and add that to the vbox previously created. All that remains for the control area is to create the three lists and pack them into the hbox (or, alternately, to create and pack the three frames). On lines 05 through 08, if the code is built with USE_FRAMES turned on, I create a frame and add that to the hbox. The call to gtk_frame_new() is passed the name of the label that will be displayed by the frame. The lines that follow this create the list and populate it with items; see Chapter 6, "Lists," for more information on GtkList. On lines 09 through 13, I add the list to the frame if USE_FRAMES is defined; otherwise, I add it to the hbox.

The preceding code should take care of illustrating most, if not all, of the cases in which a frame can be used in place of adding a control directly to a container such as a horizontal or vertical box.

Setting the Frame Label

You can change (or remove) the label of a frame with gtk_frame_set_label():

```
void
gtk_frame_set_label(GtkFrame *frame, const gchar *label);
```

The argument frame is an instance of GtkFrame, created by gtk_frame_new(). label is a NULL-terminated C string, which will, after the call, be used as the label of the frame. Passing (const gchar *) NULL as the label argument will cause the current label to be removed. Without a label, GtkFrame simply draws a solid line around the area that it manages.

Setting the Alignment of the Label

Alignment of the label can be controlled with gtk_frame_set_label_align():

```
void
gtk_frame_set_label_align(GtkFrame *frame, gfloat xalign,
        gfloat yalign);
```

By default, 0.0 and 0.5 are assigned to the xalign and yalign attributes, respectively, of a new frame when it is first created. Labels are always located on the upper horizontal edge of the frame, as shown in Figure 11.17. Alignment defines where along this edge the label is placed. The yalign value, in Gtk+ 1.2, is not used and will not be discussed further, other than to say the vertical position of the label is computed so that the topmost horizontal edge of the frame vertically bisects the label, and this computation is based on the height of the font, not the yalign value. An xalign of 0.0 places the label at the far left-end of the edge, while the value 1.0 places it at the far-right edge. The label is positioned so that all characters in the label are visible. Passing an xalign or yalign value that is outside of the range [0.0, 1.0] will cause GtkFrame to clip the value so that it falls within this range.

Setting the Shadow Type of the Frame

The final function supported by GtkFrame allows you to set the shadow type of a frame. The function, gtk_frame_set_shadow_type(), is analogous to gtk_clist_set_shadow_type(), which is described in Chapter 6.

```
void
gtk_frame_set_shadow_type(GtkFrame *frame, GtkShadowType type);
```

Most applications need not call gtk_frame_set_shadow_type() and instead can use the default type assigned by GtkFrame, GTK_SHADOW_ETCHED_IN.

GtkAspectFrame

Class Name

`GtkAspectFrame`

Parent Class Name

`GtkFrame`

Macros

Widget type macro: `GTK_TYPE_ASPECT_FRAME`

Object to widget cast macro: `GTK_ASPECT_FRAME(obj)`

Widget type check macro: `GTK_IS_ASPECT_FRAME(obj)`

Supported Arguments

Prefix: `GtkAspectFrame::`

Table 11.7 GtkAspectFrame Arguments

Name	*Type*	*Permissions*
xalign	GTK_TYPE_FLOAT	GTK_ARG_READWRITE
yalign	GTK_TYPE_FLOAT	GTK_ARG_READWRITE
ratio	GTK_TYPE_FLOAT	GTK_ARG_READWRITE
obey_child	GTK_TYPE_BOOL	GTK_ARG_READWRITE

Application-Level API Synopsis

Retrieve the constant GTK_TYPE_ASPECT_FRAME at runtime:

```
GtkType
gtk_aspect_frame_get_type(void);
```

Create a new instance of GtkAspectFrame:

```
GtkWidget *
gtk_aspect_frame_new(const gchar *label, gfloat xalign,
        gfloat yalign, gfloat ratio, gint obey_child);
```

Change attributes of an existing aspect frame:

```
void
gtk_aspect_frame_set(GtkAspectFrame *aspect_frame, gfloat xalign,
        gfloat yalign, gfloat ratio, gint obey_child);
```

Class Description

GtkAspectFrame is similar to GtkFrame, previously described, except that it allows the application to control the aspect ratio of the frame. The aspect ratio is used to compute the width of the frame based on its height. An aspect ratio of 1.0 results in a frame that has equal width and height, while a ratio set to 0.5 will cause the width of the frame to be one-half the height of the frame. The default ratio for an aspect frame widget is 1.0, and the allowable range is [0.0001, 10000.0]. A client can disable the aspect ratio setting and allow the child widget managed by the frame to determine the width and height of the frame by setting the obey_child attribute to TRUE. The default obey_child setting is TRUE.

Two additional attributes are supported by aspect frames: xalign and yalign. These attributes (which both default to 0.5), define how a frame is placed within the container that manages it whenever there is unused space, either vertically or horizontally, within the container of the frame due to the aspect ratio chosen for the frame. The following example should help clarify the use of xalign and yalign.

Assume that the aspect ratio of the frame is 0.5 and that we are placing the frame within a window that is 100 pixels tall and wide. In this case, we have a frame that is 100 pixels tall and 50 pixels wide, and we have 50 pixels of unused space to the left and/or right of the frame. The xalign attribute is used to control the location of the frame horizontally within the container and, as a result, how the unused space is distributed in the container relative to the frame. If xalign is set to 0.0, the x origin of the frame will be located at x = 0, and all 50 pixels of unused space will be situated to the right of the frame. If xalign is set to 0.5, the frame will be horizontally centered within the container, with, in this example, 25 pixels of unused parent space located to the left of the frame and 25 pixels of unused parent space to the right of the frame. This behavior is true whenever the aspect ratio is less than 1.0.

If the aspect ratio is greater than 1.0, unused space will exist either above or below the frame, and the yalign attribute is then used to determine the location of the y origin of the frame and, therefore, how the unused vertical space is distributed. If yalign is set to 0.0, the y origin of the frame will be set to 0, and unused vertical space will be located below the frame. If yalign is set to 0.5, the frame will be vertically centered in the frame, with half of the unused space occurring above and below the frame. Finally, if yalign is set to 1.0, the frame will be placed at the bottom of the container, and all unused vertical space will be located above the frame.

The valid range of values for xalign and yalign is [0.0, 1.0]. Effectively, xalign is ignored whenever ratio is 1.0 or greater, and yalign is ignored whenever ratio is 1.0 or less.

Creating an Aspect Frame Widget

To create a new instance of GtkAspectFrame, call gtk_aspect_frame_new():

```
GtkWidget *
gtk_aspect_frame_new(const gchar *label, gfloat xalign, gfloat yalign,
        gfloat ratio, gint obey_child);
```

The label argument defines the text label that will be displayed by the aspect frame. The arguments xalign, yalign, and ratio were all previously defined, as was obey_child. If obey_child is set to true, ratio is ignored, but the xalign and yalign arguments will be honored. Depending on the size requirements of the child, its aspect ratio could be not equal to 1.0, resulting in unused space above or below (or to the left or right) of the frame. The defaults for xalign, yalign, ratio, and obey_child are 0.5, 0.5, 1.0, and TRUE, respectively.

Setting the Aspect Frame Attributes

After you have created an aspect frame, you can change any of its settings by calling gtk_aspect_frame_set():

```
void
gtk_aspect_frame_set(GtkAspectFrame *aspect_frame, gfloat xalign,
        gfloat yalign, gfloat ratio, gint obey_child);
```

The arguments to gtk_aspect_frame_set() are the same as to gtk_aspect_frame_new(), except for the first argument, which in an instance of GtkAspectFrame created by an earlier call to gtk_aspect_frame_new(). You can change the label with a call to gtk_frame_set_label():

```
GtkWidget *aFrame;

...
```

```
aFrame = gtk_aspect_frame_new( "Hello", 0.5, 0.5, 1.0, TRUE);

...

gtk_frame_set_label( GTK_FRAME( aFrame ), "World" );
```

The following program illustrates the GtkAspectFrame API, showing the effects of various alignment and ratio settings. A timer is fired twice a second, and the callback invokes gtk_aspect_frame_set() to change the xalign, yalign, and ratio attributes of the frame. Changing any of these values causes GtkAspectFrame to fire an expose event that is handled by the child widget of the frame, which, in this case, is an instance of GtkDrawingArea. The drawing area widget has a signal function registered to capture the expose event, and in this signal function, it draws a number of rectangles that help to illustrate the effect of the aspect ratio change made by the timer callback. Figures 11.19 through 11.22 contain screen grabs of the client in various stages of operation.

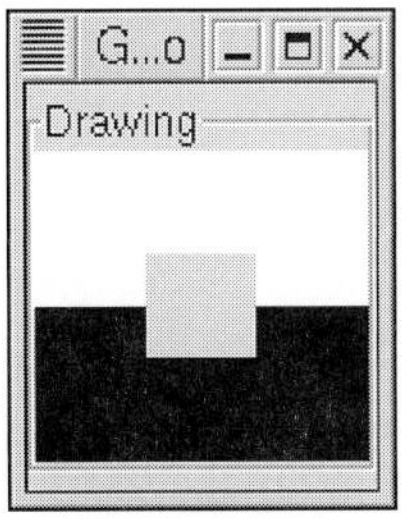

Figure 11.19

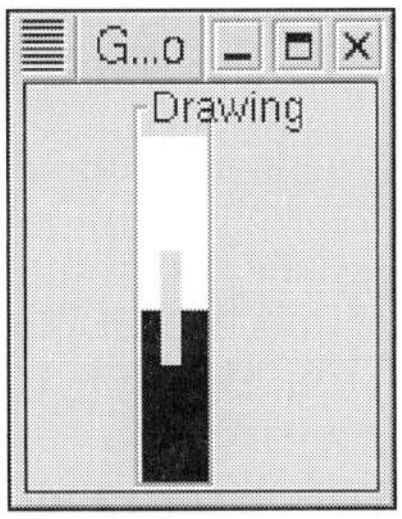

Figure 11.20

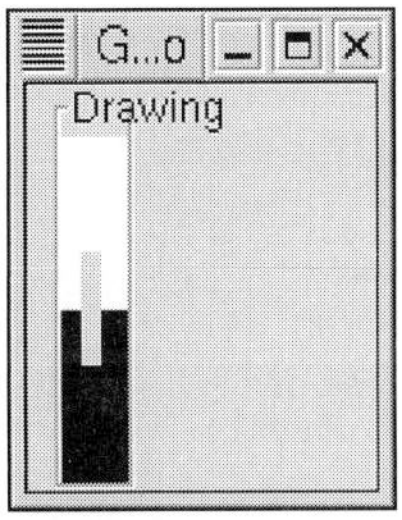

Figure 11.21

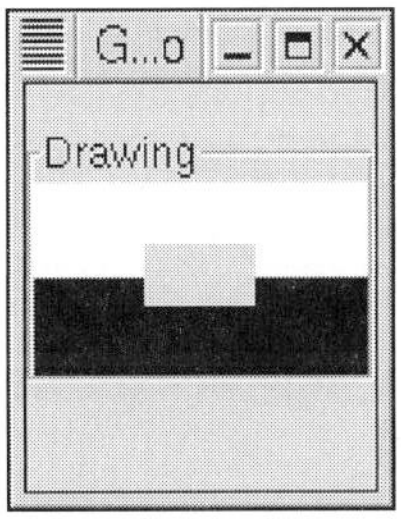

Figure 11.22

Listing 11.5 GtkAspectFrame Example

```
#include <gtk/gtk.h>

static gint
DrawingExposeFunc(GtkWidget *widget, GdkEvent *event, gpointer user_data)
{
  GtkDrawingArea *darea;
  GdkDrawable *drawable;
  GdkGC *black_gc, *gray_gc, *white_gc;
```

```
  guint max_width, max_height;

  darea = GTK_DRAWING_AREA(widget);
  drawable = widget->window;
  white_gc = widget->style->white_gc;
  gray_gc = widget->style->bg_gc[GTK_STATE_NORMAL];
  black_gc = widget->style->black_gc;
  max_width = widget->allocation.width;
  max_height = widget->allocation.height;

  gdk_draw_rectangle (drawable, white_gc,
                      TRUE,
                      0,
                      0,
                      max_width,
                      max_height / 2);

  gdk_draw_rectangle (drawable, black_gc,
                      TRUE,
                      0,
                      max_height / 2,
                      max_width,
                      max_height / 2);

  gdk_draw_rectangle (drawable, gray_gc,
                      TRUE,
                      max_width / 3,
                      max_height / 3,
                      max_width / 3,
                      max_height / 3);

  return TRUE;
}

void
MyTimeoutFunc( GtkAspectFrame *frame )
{
  static float xalign = 0.0;
  static float yalign = 0.0;
  static float ratio = 0.1;

  gtk_aspect_frame_set( frame, xalign, yalign, ratio, FALSE );
  xalign += 0.1;
  if ( xalign > 1.0 )
       xalign = 0.0;
  yalign += 0.1;
  if ( yalign > 1.0 )
       yalign = 0.0;
  ratio += 0.1;
  if ( ratio > 2.0 )
       ratio = 0.1;
}

void
GtkFrameDialog()
{
  GtkWidget *frame, *dialog_window, *drawing;
```

```

  dialog_window = gtk_window_new(GTK_WINDOW_TOPLEVEL);
  gtk_window_position (GTK_WINDOW (dialog_window), GTK_WIN_POS_MOUSE);

  gtk_signal_connect(GTK_OBJECT (dialog_window), "destroy",
        GTK_SIGNAL_FUNC(gtk_widget_destroyed), &dialog_window);

  gtk_window_set_title(GTK_WINDOW (dialog_window),"GtkAspectFrame");
  gtk_container_border_width (GTK_CONTAINER (dialog_window), 0);

  frame = gtk_aspect_frame_new( "Drawing", 0.5, 0.5, 1.0, TRUE );
  gtk_timeout_add (500, MyTimeoutFunc, frame);
  gtk_frame_set_label_align( GTK_FRAME( frame ), 0.0, 0.0 );
  gtk_container_add (GTK_CONTAINER (dialog_window), frame);

  drawing = gtk_drawing_area_new();
  gtk_drawing_area_size( GTK_DRAWING_AREA( drawing ), 100, 100 );
  gtk_signal_connect( GTK_OBJECT( drawing ), "expose_event",
        GTK_SIGNAL_FUNC( DrawingExposeFunc ), NULL);
  gtk_widget_set_events( drawing, GDK_EXPOSURE_MASK );


  gtk_container_add(GTK_CONTAINER (frame), drawing);

  gtk_widget_show_all(dialog_window);
}

main( argc, argv )
int argc;
char *argv[];
{
  gtk_init( &argc, &argv );

  GtkFrameDialog();

  gtk_main();
}
```

GtkTable

Class Name

```
GtkTable
```

Parent Class Name

```
GtkContainer
```

Macros

Widget type macro: `GTK_TYPE_TABLE`

Object to widget cast macro: `GTK_TABLE(obj)`

Widget type check macro: `GTK_IS_TABLE(obj)`

Supported Arguments

Prefix: `GtkTable::`

Table 11.8 GtkTable Arguments

Name	*Type*	*Permissions*
n_rows	GTK_TYPE_UINT	GTK_ARG_READWRITE
n_columns	GTK_TYPE_UINT	GTK_ARG_READWRITE
row_spacing	GTK_TYPE_UINT	GTK_ARG_READWRITE
column_spacing	GTK_TYPE_UINT	GTK_ARG_READWRITE
homogeneous	GTK_TYPE_BOOL	GTK_ARG_READWRITE
left_attach	GTK_TYPE_UINT	GTK_ARG_READWRITE
right_attach	GTK_TYPE_UINT	GTK_ARG_READWRITE
top_attach	GTK_TYPE_UINT	GTK_ARG_READWRITE
bottom_attach	GTK_TYPE_UINT	GTK_ARG_READWRITE
x_options	GTK_TYPE_ATTACH_OPTIONS	GTK_ARG_READWRITE
y_options	GTK_TYPE_ATTACH_OPTIONS	GTK_ARG_READWRITE
x_padding	GTK_TYPE_UINT	GTK_ARG_READWRITE
y_padding	GTK_TYPE_UINT	GTK_ARG_READWRITE

Application-Level API Synopsis

Return the constant GTK_TYPE_TABLE at runtime:

```
GtkType
gtk_table_get_type(void);
```

Create a new instance of GtkTable:

```
GtkWidget *
gtk_table_new(guint rows, guint columns, gboolean homogeneous);
```

Change the number of rows and/or columns in a table:

```
void
gtk_table_resize(GtkTable *table, guint rows, guint columns);
```

Add a cell to a table:

```
void
gtk_table_attach(GtkTable *table, GtkWidget *child,
        guint left_attach,  guint right_attach, guint top_attach,
        guint bottom_attach, GtkAttachOptions xoptions,
        GtkAttachOptions yoptions, guint xpadding,
        guint ypadding);
```

Add a cell to a table using default xoptions, yoptions, xpadding, and ypadding values:

```
void
gtk_table_attach_defaults(GtkTable *table, GtkWidget *widget,
        guint left_attach, guint right_attach, guint top_attach,
        guint bottom_attach);
```

Set the row spacing for a specific table row:

```
void
gtk_table_set_row_spacing(GtkTable *table, guint row, guint spacing);
```

Set the column spacing for a specific table column:

```
void
gtk_table_set_col_spacing(GtkTable *table, guint column, guint spacing);
```

Set the row spacing for all rows:

```
void
gtk_table_set_row_spacings(GtkTable *table, guint spacing);
```

Set the column spacing for all columns:

```
void
gtk_table_set_col_spacings(GtkTable *table, guint spacing);
```

Change the table's homogeneous setting:

```
void
gtk_table_set_homogeneous(GtkTable *table, gboolean homogeneous);
```

Class Description

A table widget manages a group of cells that are organized as an NxM matrix or grid. Cells in a table may be empty or may contain a child widget. If a cell is empty (i.e., it does not contain a child), the space that would otherwise be occupied by a child is displayed by the table widget if and only if at least one of the following is true:

- The table is homogeneous.
- Some other cell in the same row or column of the table contains a visible child widget.

For the purpose of our discussion here, each table cell is given the coordinate (*r*, *c*), where *r* is the row, and *c* is the column. Rows can range in value from 0 to $N - 1$, where N is the number of rows in the table. Columns range in value from 0 to $M - 1$, where M is the number of columns in the table.

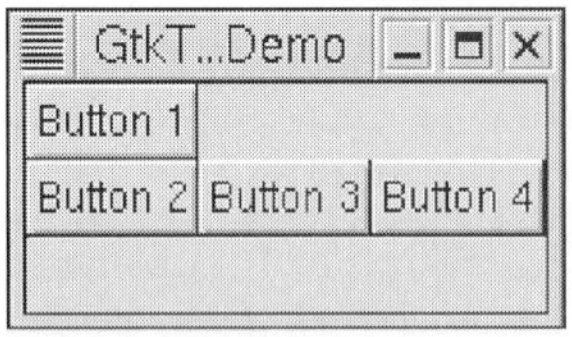

Figure 11.23 Table Widget

Figure 11.23 illustrates an instance of GtkTable containing three rows and three columns. GtkButton children have been added to the following table cells: (0, 1) (Button 1), (1, 0) (Button 2), (1, 1) (Button 3), and (1, 2) (Button 4). The homogeneous setting for the table shown in Figure 11.23 has been set to TRUE. (I will discuss how to make a table homogeneous later in this chapter.) As a result, each cell in row 3 of the table, even though it does not manage a child, has been allocated space in the user interface by the table widget. The same table, but with the homogeneous attribute set to FALSE, is illustrated in Figure 11.24. This time, no space is allocated for row 3 since it contains no cells.

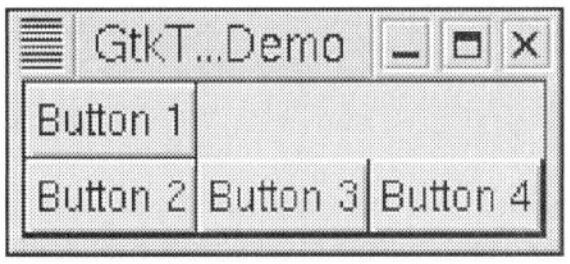

Figure 11.24 Table Widget with Homogeneous Set to FALSE

A child widget added to a table can be made to span multiple columns or rows, as illustrated in Figure 11.25. I will describe how this can be done later in this chapter.

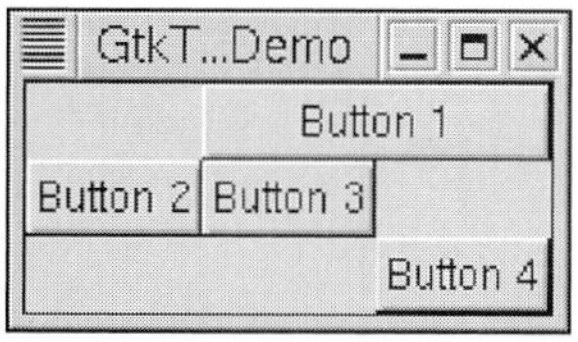

Figure 11.25 Table with Cell Spanning Multiple Columns

Cell Attributes

Each cell supports a set of attributes that can affect how a child is placed in the cell. These attributes are defined in Table 11.9.

Table 11.9 GtkTable Cell Attributes

Attribute	*Effect*
GTK_EXPAND	The table will expand to use the space available in the window or container.
GTK_SHRINK	If the table is allocated less space than requested, child widgets in the table will shrink to fit table cells. If GTK_SHRINK is not specified, cells in the table may be clipped.
GTK_FILL	Children will grow to fill available space in a cell.

The preceding attributes must be specified independently, for both the x and the y dimensions, at the time the cell is added to the table. The default value for both the x and y dimensions is GTK_EXPAND | GTK_FILL.

Each cell has two additional attributes, xpadding and ypadding, which control how much padding is placed around a child in its cell. The default padding for both the x and y dimensions is 0. Padding is added to both sides of the child. For example, specifying an xpadding of 5 will add 10 pixels to the horizontal size of the child, with 5 pixels added to both the left and right sides of the child.

Cell Coordinates and Adding Children

As previously mentioned, each cell in a table has a unique x and y coordinate. The y component ranges from 0 to $N - 1$ rows, and the x component ranging from 0 to $M - 1$ columns. Figure 11.26 illustrates the coordinate system used by a 3×3 table. Vertical and horizontal lines in bold identify edges in the table. Edges in the table are numbered in increasing order from left to right (0 to *M*) and from top to bottom (0 to *N*). The edges are important when it comes to adding a child to the table, as I will now describe.

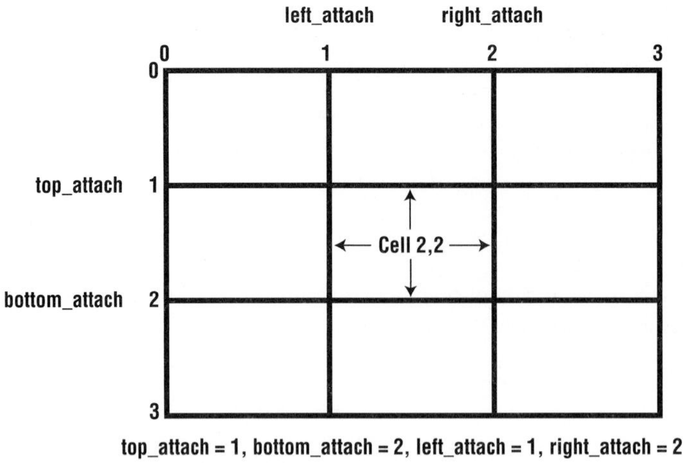

Figure 11.26 3×3 Table Widget Coordinates

To add a child to a table, you simply specify the edges that, as a group, form the boundaries of the cell into which the child is being placed. The GtkTable functions name the four boundaries of a cell left_attach, right_attach, top_attach, and bottom_attach (see Figure 11.26).

A couple of examples should make this clear. The first example adds a child to the upper-left corner of the table. The left, right, top, and bottom edges of the cell located in the upper-left corner of a table are 0, 1, 0, and 1, respectively (see Figure 11.26). Therefore, to add the child to this cell, we set left_attach to 0, right_attach to 1, top_attach to 0, and bottom_attach to 1. The left, right, top and bottom edges of the lower-right cell are 2, 3, 2, and 3, respectively (again, see Figure 11.26). To add a child there, we set left_attach to 2, right_attach to 3, top_attach to 2, and bottom_attach to 3.

GtkTable allows you to specify a bottom_edge and/or right_edge that will cause the child widget to span multiple rows and/or columns of a table. Figure 11.27 illustrates an example. Here, a button widget occupies cell (1, 0) in a 3×5 table widget (left_attach = 0, right_attach = 1, top_attach = 1, and bottom_attach = 2 were used to add the button widget). The remaining cells in row 2 are consumed by a GtkEntry widget. This was accomplished by setting left_attach = 1, right_attach = 5, top_attach = 1, and bottom_attach = 2 when adding the entry widget to the table.

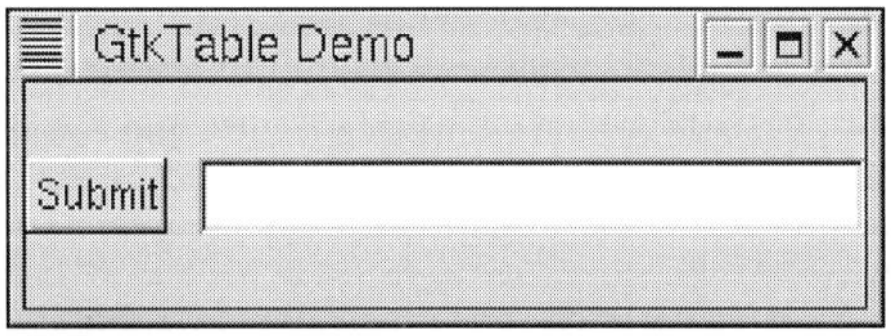

Figure 11.27 Spanning Multiple Cells

By now you should have a good idea how to use GtkTable. Let's take a look at the GtkTable API set to see how it is used.

Creating a Table Widget

Creating an instance of GtkTable is much like creating an instance of any other GtkWidget class and is done with a call to gtk_table_new():

```
GtkWidget *
gtk_table_new(guint rows, guint columns, gboolean homogeneous);
```

The rows argument specifies the number of rows that will be in the table, and columns is the number of columns in the table. The argument homogeneous, when TRUE, causes all cells to have the same size; this is the size that is needed to display the largest child in the table in terms of both width and height. If set to FALSE, the height of a row in the table is set to the height needed to display the tallest child in that row, and the width of a column is set so that it can display the widest of the child widgets located in that column.

Resizing the Table

After a table has been created, gtk_table_resize() can be called to change the number of rows and/or columns in the table:

```
void
gtk_table_resize(GtkTable *table, guint rows, guint columns);
```

The argument table is the instance of GtkTable being resized. The arguments rows and columns specify the number of rows and/or columns in the table after the resize has been performed. Passing a rows or columns value that is less than or equal to 0 will cause GtkTable to substitute the value 1 in its place (the minimum size of a table is 1×1). The function gtk_table_resize() requires you to specify both the rows and the columns—unlike some widgets APIs in Gtk+, you cannot pass a –1 as a way to tell the widget that the corresponding attribute should retain its current value. If you size a table such that it would eliminate cells in the table that are occupied by a child, GtkTable will set the size of the table so that the cells in the table will remain. Therefore, if the highest numbered row in the table that contains a child is row p, then the number of rows in the table will be set to MIN(p, rows). Likewise, if the highest number column containing a child is q, then the number of columns in the table will be set to MIN(q, columns).

Changing the Homogeneous Setting

Similarly, you can change the homogeneous setting of a table at any time with a call to gtk_table_set_homogeneous():

```
void
gtk_table_set_homogeneous(GtkTable *table, gboolean homogeneous);
```

The argument homogeneous can be set to either TRUE or FALSE.

Adding Cells to a Table

There are two ways to add a cell to a table widget. The more complicated of the two, gtk_table_attach(), allows you to specify the location of the cell that the child widget will occupy as well as the attributes I described earlier, as summarized in Table 11.10.

Table 11.10 gtk_table_attach() Option Arguments

Argument	*Meaning*
xoptions	Any combination of GTK_EXPAND, GTK_FILL, and GTK_SHRINK OR'd together
yoptions	Same as xoptions
xpadding	The amount of space, in pixels, added to the left and right of the child
ypadding	The amount of space, in pixels, added above and below the child

The function prototype for gtk_table_attach() is:

```
void
gtk_table_attach(GtkTable *table, GtkWidget *child, guint left_attach,
        guint right_attach, guint top_attach, guint bottom_attach,
        GtkAttachOptions xoptions, GtkAttachOptions yoptions,
        guint xpadding, guint ypadding);
```

The argument table is the instance of GtkTable to which the child is being added. The argument child is the widget (either another container widget or a control widget) being added. The arguments left_attach, right_attach, top_attach, and bottom_attach specify the location of the cell at which the child will be located (these arguments were described earlier in this section). The arguments xoptions, yoptions, xpadding, and ypadding were all described earlier in this section and are summarized in the preceding table.

Adding a Table Cell with Defaults

To add a cell to a table using default values for xoptions, yoptions, xpadding, and ypadding, call gtk_table_attach_defaults():

```
void
gtk_table_attach_defaults(GtkTable *table, GtkWidget *child,
        guint left_attach, guint right_attach, guint top_attach,
        guint bottom_attach);
```

The arguments table, child, left_attach, right_attach, top_attach, and bottom_attach are the same as described earlier for gtk_table_attach(). Default values for xoptions and yoptions (GTK_FILL | GTK_EXPAND), as well as xpadding and ypadding (both of these attributes default to 0), are set by gtk_table_attach_defaults().

Setting Row and Column Spacings

GtkTable allows you to set a spacing value for a specific row or column in the table. The spacing value specifies the amount of space, in pixels, that will be added between the specified row or column and the row or column, respectively, that follows it. For that reason, you cannot set spacing for the last row or column in a table; doing so will cause a warning to be generated by GtkTable. The function gtk_table_set_row_spacing() is used to set the row spacing for a specific row:

```
void
gtk_table_set_row_spacing(GtkTable *table, guint row, guint spacing);
```

The argument table is the GtkTable widget instance, row is the row being modified (in the range [0, $N-2$]), and spacing is the number of pixels that will be placed between the specified row and the row that follows it, once the change has been made. To set the column spacing, call gtk_table_set_col_spacing():

```
void
gtk_table_set_col_spacing(GtkTable *table, guint column,
        guint spacing);
```

The argument column is the column in the table that is being modified, in the range [0, $M-2$]. The argument spacing is the number of pixels that will be placed between the column and the one that follows it, after the call has been made.

The default row and column spacing is 0 pixels. Setting spacing to a value less than 0 is not caught by GtkTable, and the results are undefined.

Spacing values that will be applied to all rows or columns in a table can be set by calling gtk_table_set_row_spacings() or gtk_table_set_col_spacings(), respectively:

```
void
gtk_table_set_row_spacings(GtkTable *table, guint spacing);

void
gtk_table_set_col_spacings(GtkTable *table, guint spacing);
```

An Example: Tic-Tac-Toe Board

The following example illustrates how an instance of GtkTable might be used to implement a simple tic-tac-toe game. A vertical box widget is used in a window to hold, from top to bottom, a 3×3 table widget (the game board), an instance of GtkHSeparator, two GtkEntry widgets used to accept a board position from the user when it is time for the user to make a move, and an instance of GtkButton that, when clicked, invokes a callback that reads the row and column entered into the entry fields and places an X, if possible, in the specified location (the computer is the opponent in the game and assumes the role of player O). Below the entry fields and Move button, another horizontal separator is added. A button box is placed below this horizontal separator, to which New Game and Quit buttons are added. The code for creating the dialog is located on lines 100 through 171 in the following listing. The table widget code, in particular, is located on lines 121 and 122 and is rather simple—a call to gtk_table_new() followed by a call to gtk_box_pack_start() to add the table widget as a child of the vertical box widget.

Figure 11.28 Tic-Tac-Toe Dialog

Each cell in the table has a single child, which is a 32×32 pixel pixmap. Three pixmaps are used by the game. For empty squares on the board, a solid yellow pixmap is used. For X and O squares, a yellow pixmap superimposed with an X or O, each drawn in different color, is used (see Figure 11.28). I discussed GtkPixmap in Chapter 8, "Separators, Arrows, Images, Pixmaps, and Entry Widgets." The routine CreateXSquare() on lines 021 through 032 is used to create a GtkPixmap instance representing an X square. Similar code, not shown in the following listing, is used to create the blank and O squares.

The board itself is represented by the data structure defined on lines 010 through 013 and the array of cells declared on lines 015 through 019. The Square data type holds a type, which can be SQUARE_X, SQUARE_O, or SQUARE_BLANK, and the child widget that is currently occupied by the corresponding cell in the table. Incidentally, the cell located at row = i, column = j is indexed in the array as i * 3 + j, where row and column are both in the range [0, 2].

Cells in the tic-tac-toe playing board are initialized with SQUARE_BLANK pixmaps by calling the function InitializeBoard(), as shown on lines 051 through 069. This is done before each game is played. InitializeBoard() performs the following for each square on the playing board: First, on line 059, a SQUARE_BLANK GtkPixmap is created with a call to MakeBlankSquare(). On line 061, a check is made to see if the cell in the table already has a pixmap child widget. If it does, we call gtk_widget_destroy() to destroy the pixmap because it will be replaced by a pixmap of a different type and is no longer needed. (There are two optimizations that can be made here. First, if the cell is SQUARE_BLANK already, we do not need to do anything for that cell. Second, if the cell is not SQUARE_BLANK, we could store the pixmap in a cache to be used later when a pixmap of the same type is needed.) Next, on lines 064 and 065, we attach the new pixmap to the cell of the table with a call to gtk_table_attach_defaults(). Lines 066 and 067 record in the board array the type of the square (SQUARE_BLANK) and the pixmap widget so that it can be destroyed later in the game when an X or O piece is moved to this location on the playing board by the user or computer.

The routine TryMoveTo() uses these same principles to move an O to one of the nine board locations and is listed on lines 034 through 049.

Listing 11.6 Tic-Tac-Toe Source

```
001  #include <gtk/gtk.h>
002  #include <stdlib.h>
003
004  #define SQUARE_X 0
005  #define SQUARE_O 1
006  #define SQUARE_BLANK 2
007
008  static GtkWidget *table, *dialog, *entryrow, *entrycol;
009
010  typedef struct _square {
011     unsigned char type;
012     GtkWidget *child;
013  } Square;
014
015  static Square board[9] = {
016  { SQUARE_BLANK, NULL }, { SQUARE_BLANK, NULL }, { SQUARE_BLANK, NULL },
017  { SQUARE_BLANK, NULL }, { SQUARE_BLANK, NULL }, { SQUARE_BLANK, NULL },
018  { SQUARE_BLANK, NULL }, { SQUARE_BLANK, NULL }, { SQUARE_BLANK, NULL }
019  };
020
021  static GtkWidget *
022  MakeXSquare( GtkWidget *window )
023  {
024     GdkPixmap *pixmap;
025     GdkBitmap *mask;
026     GtkWidget *wpmap;
027
028     pixmap = gdk_pixmap_create_from_xpm( window-window, &mask,
029              &window->style->bg[GTK_STATE_NORMAL], "x.xpm" );
030     wpmap = gtk_pixmap_new(pixmap, mask);
```

```
   return( wpmap );
}

static int
TryMoveTo( int row, int col )
{
   GtkWidget *widget;
   if ( board[ row * 3 + col ].type == SQUARE_BLANK ) {
           widget = MakeOSquare( dialog );
           gtk_table_attach_defaults( GTK_TABLE( table ),
                   widget, col, col + 1, row, row + 1 );
           gtk_widget_destroy( board[ row * 3 + col ].child );
           gtk_widget_show( widget );
           board[ row * 3 + col ].type = SQUARE_O;
           board[ row * 3 + col ].child = widget;
           return( 1 );
   }
   return( 0 );
}

static void
InitializeBoard( void )
{
   GtkWidget *blank, *button;
   int i, j;

   for ( i = 0; i < 3; i ++ )
           for ( j = 0; j < 3; j++ ) {
                   blank = MakeBlankSquare( dialog );
                   gtk_widget_show( blank );
                   if ( board[ j * 3 + i ].child != NULL )
                           gtk_widget_destroy(
                                   board[ j * 3 + i ].child );
                   gtk_table_attach_defaults( GTK_TABLE( table ),
                           blank, i, i + 1, j, j + 1 );
                   board[ j * 3 + i ].type = SQUARE_BLANK;
                   board[ j * 3 + i ].child = blank;
           }
}

static void
MakeMove( gpointer ignored )
{
   char *text;
   int row, col;
   GtkWidget *widget;

   text = gtk_entry_get_text( GTK_ENTRY( entryrow ) );
   row = atoi( text );
   text = gtk_entry_get_text( GTK_ENTRY( entrycol ) );
   col = atoi( text );
```

```
    if ( row < 1 || row > 3 || col < 1 || col > 3 )
            return;
    row--; col--;
    if ( board[ row * 3 + col ].type == SQUARE_BLANK ) {
            widget = MakeXSquare( dialog );
            gtk_table_attach_defaults( GTK_TABLE( table ), widget,
                    col, col + 1, row, row + 1 );
            gtk_widget_destroy( board[ row * 3 + col ].child );
            gtk_widget_show( widget );
            board[ row * 3 + col ].type = SQUARE_X;
            board[ row * 3 + col ].child = widget;
            if ( CheckForWin() )
                    NewGame( NULL );
            else
                    MakeComputerMove();
    }
}

static GtkWidget *
GtkTTTDialog( void )
{
    GtkWidget *move, *quit, *newgame, *label, *rule, *bbox, *rlabel,
        *dialog_window, *outervbox, *hbox;

    dialog_window = gtk_window_new(GTK_WINDOW_TOPLEVEL);
    gtk_window_position( GTK_WINDOW (dialog_window), GTK_WIN_POS_MOUSE );

    gtk_signal_connect( GTK_OBJECT (dialog_window), "destroy",
        GTK_SIGNAL_FUNC(gtk_main_quit), &dialog_window );

    gtk_window_set_title( GTK_WINDOW(dialog_window), "GtkTicTacToe" );
    gtk_window_set_policy( GTK_WINDOW(dialog_window), FALSE, FALSE,
        FALSE );
    gtk_container_border_width( GTK_CONTAINER (dialog_window), 0 );

    outervbox = gtk_vbox_new( FALSE, 0 );
    gtk_box_set_spacing( GTK_BOX( outervbox ), 10 );
    gtk_container_add( GTK_CONTAINER(dialog_window), outervbox );

    table = gtk_table_new( 3, 3, TRUE );
    gtk_box_pack_start( GTK_BOX(outervbox), table, FALSE, FALSE, 0 );

    rule = gtk_hseparator_new();
    gtk_box_pack_start( GTK_BOX(outervbox), rule, FALSE, FALSE, 0 );

    hbox = gtk_hbox_new( FALSE, 0 );
    gtk_box_pack_start( GTK_BOX(outervbox), hbox, FALSE, FALSE, 0 );

    hbox = gtk_hbox_new( FALSE, 0 );
    gtk_box_set_spacing( GTK_BOX( hbox ), 10 );
    gtk_box_pack_start( GTK_BOX(outervbox), hbox, TRUE, TRUE, 0 );
```

```
    rlabel = gtk_label_new( "Row" );
    gtk_box_pack_start( GTK_BOX(hbox), rlabel, TRUE, TRUE, 0 );

    entryrow = gtk_entry_new();
    gtk_widget_set_usize( entryrow, 30, -1 );
    gtk_box_pack_start( GTK_BOX(hbox), entryrow, TRUE, TRUE, 0 );

    rlabel = gtk_label_new( "Column" );
    gtk_box_pack_start( GTK_BOX(hbox), rlabel, TRUE, TRUE, 0 );

    entrycol = gtk_entry_new();
    gtk_widget_set_usize( entrycol, 30, -1 );
    gtk_box_pack_start( GTK_BOX(hbox), entrycol, TRUE, TRUE, 0 );

    move = gtk_button_new_with_label( "Move" );
    gtk_box_pack_start( GTK_BOX(hbox), move, TRUE, TRUE, 10 );
    gtk_signal_connect(GTK_OBJECT(move), "clicked",
        GTK_SIGNAL_FUNC(MakeMove), NULL);

    rule = gtk_hseparator_new();
    gtk_box_pack_start( GTK_BOX(outervbox), rule, FALSE, FALSE, 0 );

    bbox = gtk_hbutton_box_new();
    gtk_box_pack_start( GTK_BOX(outervbox), bbox, TRUE, TRUE, 0 );

    newgame = gtk_button_new_with_label( "New Game" );
    gtk_box_pack_start( GTK_BOX(bbox), newgame, FALSE, FALSE, 10 );
    gtk_signal_connect(GTK_OBJECT(newgame), "clicked",
        GTK_SIGNAL_FUNC(NewGame), NULL);

    quit = gtk_button_new_with_label( "Quit" );
    gtk_box_pack_start( GTK_BOX(bbox), quit, FALSE, FALSE, 10 );
    gtk_signal_connect_object (GTK_OBJECT (quit), "clicked",
        GTK_SIGNAL_FUNC(gtk_widget_destroy),
        GTK_OBJECT(dialog_window));
    gtk_widget_show_all( dialog_window );
    return( dialog_window );
}

main( argc, argv )
int argc;
char *argv[];
{
    gtk_init( &argc, &argv );

    dialog = GtkTTTDialog();
    NewGame( NULL );
    gtk_main();
}
```

GtkToolbar

Class Name

```
GtkToolbar
```

Parent Class Name

```
GtkContainer
```

Macros

Widget type macro: None defined

Object to widget cast macro: `GTK_TOOLBAR(obj)`

Widget type check macro: `GTK_IS_TOOLBAR(obj)`

Supported Signals

Table 11.11 Signals

Signal Name	*Condition Causing Signal to Trigger*
orientation_changed	The orientation of the toolbar was changed.
style_changed	The style of the toolbar was changed.

Signal Function Prototypes

```
void
orientation_changed(GtkToolbar *toolbar, GtkOrientation orientation,
     gpointer user_data);

void
style_changed(GtkToolbar *toolbar, GtkToolbarStyle style,
     gpointer user_data);
```

Application-Level API Synopsis

Retrieve the GtkToolbar type at runtime:

```
guint
gtk_toolbar_get_type(void);
```

Create an instance of GtkToolbar with the specified orientation and style:

```
GtkWidget *
gtk_toolbar_new(GtkOrientation orientation, GtkToolbarStyle style);
```

Append an item to the bottom of a vertical toolbar or to the rightmost end of a horizontal toolbar (the child type of the item is GTK_TOOLBAR_CHILD_BUTTON):

```
GtkWidget *
gtk_toolbar_append_item(GtkToolbar *toolbar, const char *text,
        const char *tooltip_text, const char *tooltip_private_text,
        GtkWidget *icon, GtkSignalFunc callback, gpointer user_data);
```

Prepend an item to the top of a vertical toolbar or to the leftmost end of a horizontal toolbar (the child type of the item is GTK_TOOLBAR_CHILD_BUTTON):

```
GtkWidget *
gtk_toolbar_prepend_item(GtkToolbar *toolbar, const char *text,
        const char *tooltip_text, const char *tooltip_private_text,
        GtkWidget *icon, GtkSignalFunc callback, gpointer user_data);
```

Insert an item into the toolbar at the specified location (the child type of the item is GTK_TOOLBAR_CHILD_BUTTON):

```
GtkWidget *
gtk_toolbar_insert_item(GtkToolbar *toolbar, const char *text,
        const char *tooltip_text, const char *tooltip_private_text,
        GtkWidget *icon, GtkSignalFunc callback, gpointer user_data,
        gint position);
```

Append a space to the bottom of a vertical toolbar or to the rightmost end of a horizontal toolbar:

```
void
gtk_toolbar_append_space(GtkToolbar *toolbar);
```

Prepend a space to the top of a vertical toolbar or to the leftmost end of a horizontal toolbar:

```
void
gtk_toolbar_prepend_space(GtkToolbar *toolbar);
```

Insert a space into the toolbar at the specified location:

```
void
gtk_toolbar_insert_space(GtkToolbar *toolbar, gint position);
```

Append an element of the specified type to the toolbar:

```
GtkWidget *
gtk_toolbar_append_element(GtkToolbar *toolbar,
        GtkToolbarChildType type, GtkWidget *widget,
        const char *text,const char *tooltip_text,
        const char *tooltip_private_text,GtkWidget *icon,
        GtkSignalFunc callback, gpointer user_data);
```

Application-Level API Synopsis (Continued)

Prepend an element of the specified type to the toolbar:

```
GtkWidget *
gtk_toolbar_prepend_element(GtkToolbar *toolbar,
        GtkToolbarChildType type, GtkWidget *widget,
        const char *text, const char *tooltip_text,
        const char *tooltip_private_text,GtkWidget *icon,
        GtkSignalFunc callback, gpointer user_data);
```

Insert an element of the specified type into the toolbar:

```
GtkWidget *
gtk_toolbar_insert_element(GtkToolbar *toolbar,
        GtkToolbarChildType type, GtkWidget *widget,
        const char *text, const char *tooltip_text,
        const char *tooltip_private_text, GtkWidget *icon,
        GtkSignalFunc callback, gpointer user_data, gint position);
```

Append an item of type GTK_TOOLBAR_CHILD_WIDGET to the toolbar:

```
void
gtk_toolbar_append_widget(GtkToolbar *toolbar, GtkWidget *widget,
        const char *tooltip_text, const char *tooltip_private_text);
```

Prepend an item of type GTK_TOOLBAR_CHILD_WIDGET to the toolbar:

```
void
gtk_toolbar_prepend_widget(GtkToolbar *toolbar, GtkWidget *widget,
        const char *tooltip_text, const char *tooltip_private_text);
```

Insert an item of type GTK_TOOLBAR_CHILD_WIDGET into the toolbar:

```
void
gtk_toolbar_insert_widget(GtkToolbar *toolbar, GtkWidget *widget,
        const char *tooltip_text, const char *tooltip_private_text,
        gint position);
```

Change the orientation of the toolbar to vertical or horizontal:

```
void
gtk_toolbar_set_orientation(GtkToolbar *toolbar,
        GtkOrientation orientation);
```

Set the toolbar style:

```
void
gtk_toolbar_set_style(GtkToolbar *toolbar, GtkToolbarStyle style);
```

Set the size of spaces in the toolbar, in pixels:

```
void
gtk_toolbar_set_space_size(GtkToolbar *toolbar, gint space_size);
```

Set the space style of spaces in the toolbar:

```
void
gtk_toolbar_set_space_style(GtkToolbar *toolbar,
        GtkToolbarSpaceStyle space_style);
```

Application-Level API Synopsis (Continued)

Enable or disable tooltips for the menu bar:

```
void
gtk_toolbar_set_tooltips(GtkToolbar *toolbar, gint enable);
```

Set the button relief style:

```
void
gtk_toolbar_set_button_relief(GtkToolbar *toolbar,
        GtkReliefStyle relief);
```

Get the button relief style:

```
GtkReliefStyle
gtk_toolbar_get_button_relief(GtkToolbar *toolbar);
```

Class Description

The GtkToolbar class is designed specifically for use by applications that need to implement toolbars such as the ones shown in Figure 11.29.

A toolbar manages a set of buttons that a user can click on to activate application tasks or to bring up application dialogs. For many users, toolbars provide an easier and more intuitive way to access the features of an application than the alternatives, such as selecting an item from a menu. Because a toolbar is always visible to the user, application options presented as buttons in the toolbar can be easier to discover for users than options available as items in a menu.

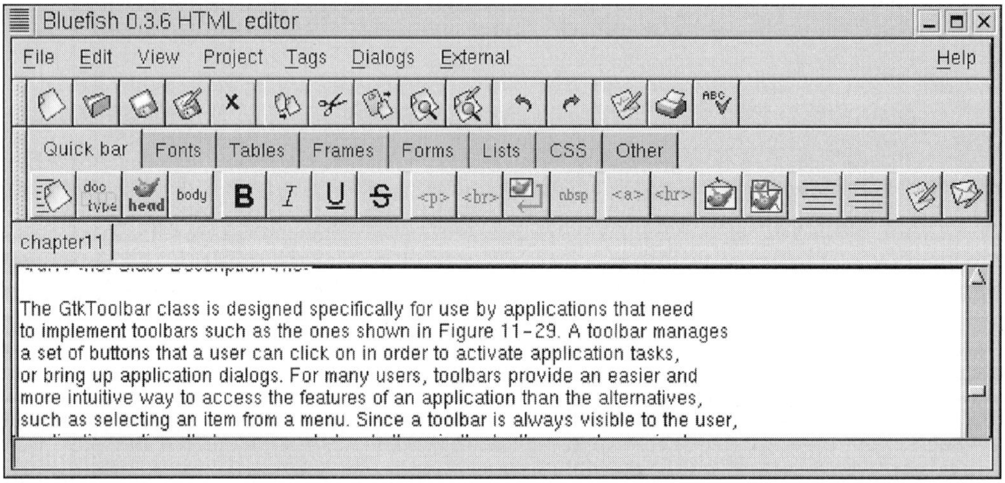

Figure 11.29 Toolbar

To add a toolbar to your application, you need to follow these steps:

1. Create an instance of GtkToolbar by calling gtk_toolbar_new(). At this point, the orientation (horizontal or vertical) and style of the toolbar are specified.
2. Add child items (typically buttons) to the toolbar.
3. (Optional) Set attributes on the toolbar that control its appearance.

Once the toolbar has been created, it can then be added as a child of some other container in the application user interface (for example, a window or vertical box widget).

A toolbar's orientation controls how the toolbar is drawn, either horizontally or vertically. A vertical toolbar can be obtained by setting the orientation to GTK_ORIENTATION_VERTICAL, and a horizontal toolbar can be obtained by setting the orientation to GTK_ORIENTATION_HORIZONTAL. The style of a toolbar controls what is displayed by the toolbar for each button. Setting the style to GTK_TOOLBAR_ICONS causes only button icons to be displayed. Setting the style to GTK_TOOLBAR_TEXT results in the display of the text label only. Setting the toolbar style to GTK_TOOLBAR_BOTH will cause both the button icon and the text label to be displayed for each button in the toolbar.

Creating a Toolbar

Now that we know a bit about toolbars, let's see how to create an instance of GtkToolbar. To create an instance of GtkToolbar, call gtk_toolbar_new():

```
GtkWidget *
gtk_toolbar_new(GtkOrientation orientation, GtkToolbarStyle style);
```

The first argument, orientation, can be set to either GTK_ORIENTATION_VERTICAL or GTK_ORIENTATION_HORIZONTAL. Possible values for style are GTK_TOOLBAR_ICONS, GTK_TOOLBAR_TEXT, and GTK_TOOLBAR_BOTH.

Adding Toolbar Children

Once you have created a toolbar, it is time to add children. At this point, you must make a decision regarding what kind of children will be added. Most Gtk+ applications will choose to add button (instances of GtkButton) children to the toolbar. If your toolbar consists of buttons, one of the following three functions can be used to add your children to the toolbar. The three functions gtk_toolbar_append(), gtk_toolbar_prepend(), and gtk_toolbar_insert() are essentially the same in terms of their function prototypes and differ only in where they place the child widget in relation to child widgets that have been previously added to the toolbar.

The first function, gtk_toolbar_append(), creates a button child and appends it to the bottom of a vertical toolbar or to the end of a horizontal toolbar:

```
GtkWidget *
gtk_toolbar_append_item(GtkToolbar *toolbar, const char *text,
        const char *tooltip_text, const char *tooltip_private_text,
        GtkWidget *icon, GtkSignalFunc callback, gpointer user_data);
```

The arguments to gtk_toolbar_append_item() are as follows:

- **toolbar** This is the instance of GtkToolbar to which the button is being added.
- **text** This is the label text that will be displayed by the button.
- **tooltip_text** This is the tooltip text shown by the button when the user mouses over it while tooltips are enabled.
- **tooltip_private_text** In most cases, you can set this to NULL. Or you can pass a string that will be used as an identifier for the tooltip in conjunction with a GtkTipsQuery widget.
- **icon** This is an instance of GtkPixmap that will be used as the icon displayed by the button. Each button must have its own GtkPixmap instance because a widget can only be managed by one parent at a time.
- **callback** This is the signal function that will be invoked when the user clicks on the toolbar button being added. The function prototype of the callback is identical to the prototype of the GtkButton "clicked" signal function.
- **user_data** This is the client data that will be passed to callback by GtkButton when the toolbar button is clicked.

An Example

The following code snippet implements the toolbar illustrated in Figure 11.30. Each toolbar is linked to a single callback that displays to stdout the text message it is passed via its second argument, data.

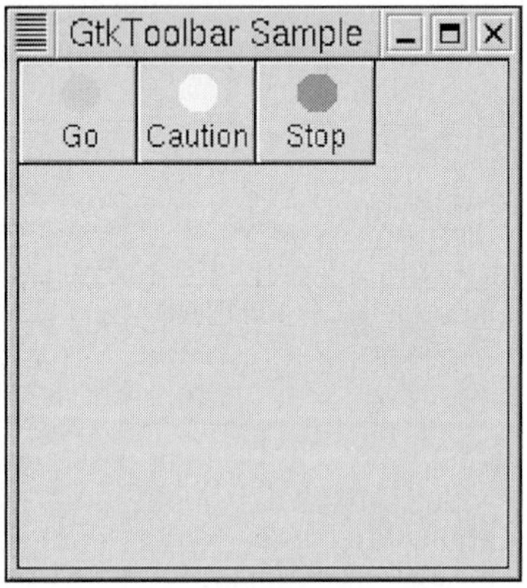

Figure 11.30 Simple Toolbar

Listing 11.7 Code Snippet that Implements Figure 11.30

```
#include <gtk/gtk.h>

static void
button_callback(GtkWidget *widget, gpointer data)
{
   printf( "%s\n" , (char *) data );
}

static GtkWidget*
make_toolbar (GtkWidget *window)
{
```

```
012     GtkWidget *toolbar;
013
014     toolbar = gtk_toolbar_new (GTK_ORIENTATION_HORIZONTAL,
015             GTK_TOOLBAR_BOTH);
016
017     gtk_toolbar_append_item (GTK_TOOLBAR (toolbar), "Go",
018             "Green Means Go", NULL, new_pixmap ("go.xpm", window->window,
019             &window->style->bg[GTK_STATE_NORMAL]),
020             (GtkSignalFunc) button_callback, "Go button was pressed" );
021     gtk_toolbar_append_item (GTK_TOOLBAR (toolbar), "Caution",
022             "Yellow Means Caution", NULL, new_pixmap ("caution.xpm",
023             window->window, &window->style->bg[GTK_STATE_NORMAL]),
024             (GtkSignalFunc) button_callback,
025             "Caution button was pressed" );
026     gtk_toolbar_append_item (GTK_TOOLBAR (toolbar), "Stop",
027             "Red Means Stop", NULL, new_pixmap ("stop.xpm",
028             window->window, &window->style->bg[GTK_STATE_NORMAL]),
029             (GtkSignalFunc) button_callback, "Stop button was pressed" );
030     return toolbar;
031 }
032
033 main( argc, argv )
034 int argc;
035 char *argv[];
036 {
037     GtkWidget *window, *toolbar, *vbox;
038
039     gtk_init( &argc, &argv );
040
041     window = gtk_window_new(GTK_WINDOW_TOPLEVEL);
042     gtk_widget_show( window );
043     gtk_window_position (GTK_WINDOW (window), GTK_WIN_POS_CENTER);
044
045     gtk_signal_connect (GTK_OBJECT (window), "destroy",
046             GTK_SIGNAL_FUNC(gtk_widget_destroy), &window);
047
048     gtk_window_set_title (GTK_WINDOW (window), "GtkToolbar Sample");
049     gtk_container_border_width (GTK_CONTAINER (window), 0);
050
051     toolbar = make_toolbar(window);
052
053     vbox = gtk_vbox_new( FALSE, 0 );
054     gtk_container_add (GTK_CONTAINER (window), vbox);
055
056     gtk_box_pack_start( GTK_BOX( vbox ), toolbar, FALSE, FALSE, 0 );
057     gtk_widget_show_all( vbox );
058
059     gtk_main();
060 }
```

Most of the interesting work happens in the function make_toolbar() on lines 009 through 031. On line 014, a horizontal toolbar that displays both the button image and the text on each toolbar button is created by calling gtk_toolbar_new(). On lines 017 through 026, calls are made to gtk_toolbar_append_item() to create each of the buttons in the toolbar:

```
017    gtk_toolbar_append_item (GTK_TOOLBAR (toolbar), "Go",
018            "Green Means Go", NULL, new_pixmap ("go.xpm", window-window,
019            &window-style-bg[GTK_STATE_NORMAL]),
020            (GtkSignalFunc) button_callback, "Go button was pressed" );
```

For example, on line 017, a button is created with the text label "Go," tooltip text set to "Green Means Go," and an image based on the xpm image contained in the file go.xpm. The function new_pixmap() is a function provided by the application and creates an instance of GtkPixmap based on the image file passed as its first argument. The remaining arguments to gtk_toolbar_append_item() specify the "clicked" signal function that will be invoked whenever the toolbar button is pressed, and its data argument, which will be printed to stdout by the signal function when it is invoked.

Care needs to be taken when creating or selecting the pixmap that will be used as the toolbar button image to ensure that the background of the image integrates correctly with the color of the toolbar button. The GIMP can be used to create an image that is appropriate for use as a toolbar button pixmap. For example, to create a 20×19 xpm file like the ones used in Figure 11.30, you might follow these steps:

1. Launch The GIMP (by typing "gimp" at the shell command-line prompt).
2. Once The GIMP loads, select New from the File menu.
3. In the dialog that displays, specify the width and height of the icon (in this example, width = 20 and height = 19), select the Transparent radio button from the Fill Type radio group, and then click OK. Resize the window that results and use the "=" key to zoom in, as this will make editing the pixmap easier.
4. Use tools provided by The GIMP to draw the image desired and then use Save As from the File menu to save the image as an XPM file.

The key step in the preceding process is specifying a fill type of Transparent when the image is first created. I have tried creating pixmap images that contain transparent fill types using xpaint(1) but have been unsuccessful.

The next two functions are identical to gtk_toolbar_append_item(), for the most part. The function gtk_toolbar_prepend_item() takes exactly the same arguments as gtk_t oolbar_append_item(). The difference is that it prepends the button to the top of a vertical toolbar or to the leftmost end of a horizontal toolbar.

```
GtkWidget *
gtk_toolbar_prepend_item(GtkToolbar *toolbar, const char *text,
        const char *tooltip_text, const char *tooltip_private_text,
        GtkWidget *icon, GtkSignalFunc callback, gpointer user_data);
```

The final function in this group, gtk_toolbar_insert_item(), can be used by an application to add a button at a specified location in the toolbar. Each button in a toolbar is assigned a position in the range [0, *n* – 1], where *n* is the total number of buttons in the toolbar. Position 0 is the leftmost button, and position *n* – 1 is the rightmost button in a horizontal toolbar. In a vertical toolbar, position 0 is the topmost button, and position *n* – 1 is the bottommost button. the function prototype for gtk_toolbar_insert_item() is the same as for gtk_toolbar_append_item() and gtk_toolbar_prepend_item(), except for an additional argument, position, which specifies the location of the button in the toolbar upon return from the function:

```
GtkWidget *
gtk_toolbar_insert_item(GtkToolbar *toolbar, const char *text,
        const char *tooltip_text, const char *tooltip_private_text,
        GtkWidget *icon, GtkSignalFunc callback, gpointer user_data,
        gint position);
```

The argument position must be in the range [0, *n*], where *n* is the number of buttons in the toolbar before the call is made. Setting position to 0 is equivalent to calling gtk_toolbar_prepend_item(), while setting position to *n* is equivalent to calling gtk_toolbar_append_item().

Button Spacings

For purely aesthetic reasons, applications can place one or more spaces within a toolbar to provide visual separation between two buttons or two sets of unrelated buttons in the toolbar. Essentially, you can think of space items in a toolbar as buttons that do not display text or pixmap data and that are insensitive to user input. The reason you might think of them as buttons is that they occupy a position in the toolbar. For example, appending a space item to a toolbar places it at position 0 and increments the position value of the remaining space items and buttons in the toolbar.

To append a space to the bottom of a vertical toolbar (or to the leftmost end of a horizontal toolbar), call gtk_toolbar_append_space():

```
void
gtk_toolbar_append_space(GtkToolbar *toolbar);
```

Similarly, to prepend a space to the top of a vertical toolbar (or to the rightmost end of a horizontal toolbar), call gtk_toolbar_prepend_space():

```
void
gtk_toolbar_prepend_space(GtkToolbar *toolbar);
```

Finally, you can insert a space into the toolbar at a specified location with a call to gtk_toolbar_insert_space():

```
void
gtk_toolbar_insert_space(GtkToolbar *toolbar, gint position);
```

Two attributes apply to space items in a toolbar. The first, the size of the space, is a value in pixels that determines how much space, vertically in a vertical toolbar and horizontally in a horizontal toolbar, is consumed by each space inserted into the toolbar. You can set this space value by calling gtk_toolbar_set_space_size():

```
void
gtk_toolbar_set_space_size(GtkToolbar *toolbar, gint space_size);
```

The argument space_size is specified in pixels.

The second attribute, space style, can be one of two values:

- **GTK_TOOLBAR_SPACE_EMPTY** The space is just that, empty space between adjacent buttons.
- **GTK_TOOLBAR_SPACE_LINE** A vertical separator (horizontal toolbars) or horizontal separator (vertical toolbars) is placed in the middle of the area occupied by each space item in the toolbar. Figure 11.31 illustrates a toolbar that contains a space between the Go and Caution buttons and that is using GTK_TOOLBAR_SPACE_LINE style spaces.

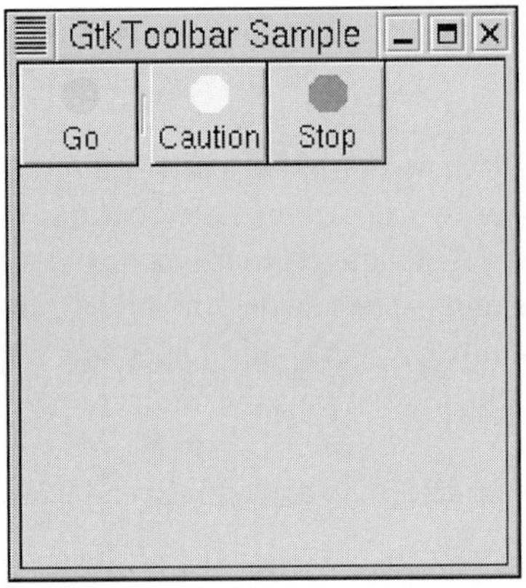

Figure 11.31 The GTK_TOOLBAR_SPACE_LINE Space Attribute

You can set the space style with a call to gtk_toolbar_set_space_style():

```
void
gtk_toolbar_set_space_style(GtkToolbar *toolbar,
        GtkToolbarSpaceStyle space_style);
```

The argument space_style can be set to either GTK_TOOLBAR_SPACE_LINE or GTK_TOOLBAR_SPACE_EMPTY. The default space value (used when gtk_toolbar_set_space_style() is not called by your application) is GTK_TOOLBAR_SPACE_EMPTY.

Adding Children of Arbitrary Type

Now that I have covered how applications can add buttons with images and text to a toolbar, I can present the more general GtkToolbar API that can be used to add widgets of arbitrary type as elements of a toolbar. If your application is among those that only adds buttons and spaces to a toolbar, you can get by using the functions already described, and the next six GtkToolbar functions that I will describe are probably not meaningful to you. One major exception will be application authors who want their toolbar buttons to behave like toggle buttons or radio buttons. If you are such an author, the following will be of interest to you.

The three functions gtk_toolbar_append_element(), gtk_toolbar_prepend_element(), and gtk_toolbar_insert_element() that I am about to describe differ from their gtk_toolbar_*_item() counterparts (which I previously described) in that they take two additional arguments: a type and a widget. The gtk_toolbar_*_item() functions previously described create and manage a button widget for you automatically; all you must do is pass a pixmap image and label for the button, and these functions take care of creating and managing the button widget that displays them.

There are five values that can be passed as the type, as defined in the enum GtkToolbarChildType:

```
typedef enum
{
        GTK_TOOLBAR_CHILD_SPACE,
        GTK_TOOLBAR_CHILD_BUTTON,
        GTK_TOOLBAR_CHILD_TOGGLEBUTTON,
        GTK_TOOLBAR_CHILD_RADIOBUTTON,
        GTK_TOOLBAR_CHILD_WIDGET
} GtkToolbarChildType;
```

Let's look at each of these values individually. When GTK_TOOLBAR_CHILD_SPACE is passed as type, a space is added to the toolbar. The widget argument to gtk_toolbar_*_element() is ignored. Other arguments ignored include the text, tooltip_text, tooltip_private_text, icon, callback, and user_data arguments. Making a call to one of the gtk_toolbar_*_space() functions will give identical results and is the recommended way to add spaces to your toolbars.

Setting type to GTK_TOOLBAR_CHILD_BUTTON gives the same results as calling the gtk_toolbar_*_item() functions. In this case, you also must pass a NULL widget argument because GtkToolbar expects to allocate it for you. The rest of the arguments are honored, however. Like GTK_TOOLBAR_CHILD_SPACE, there is little need for most Gtk+ applications to use this function, and I recommend that, for buttons, you stick with one of the gtk_toolbar_*_item() functions.

Setting type to GTK_TOOLBAR_CHILD_TOGGLEBUTTON causes GtkToolbar to instantiate and add to the toolbar an instance to GtkToggleButton. widget must be NULL or an error will occur. The remainder of the arguments are honored and act identically to those passed to the gtk_toolbar_*_item() functions. A toggle button might be used in lieu of a regular button to communicate a state that is independent of other buttons in the toolbar (that is, the selection of one button does not imply the selection, or deselection, of other buttons in the toolbar). If you need to communicate the state of a button that is not mutually exclusive of the state of other buttons in a toolbar, you can use the set of buttons in this category as radio button toggle buttons by setting the type field to GTK_TOOLBAR_CHILD_RADIOBUTTON. If widget is NULL, the radio button created and returned defines a radio button group to which other radio buttons can be added. Figure 11.32 illustrates a typical use of radio buttons in a toolbar. Here I have created a toolbar that contains the standard Play, Stop, Pause, Back, and Forward buttons that you might find in a CD-ROM player or similar application.

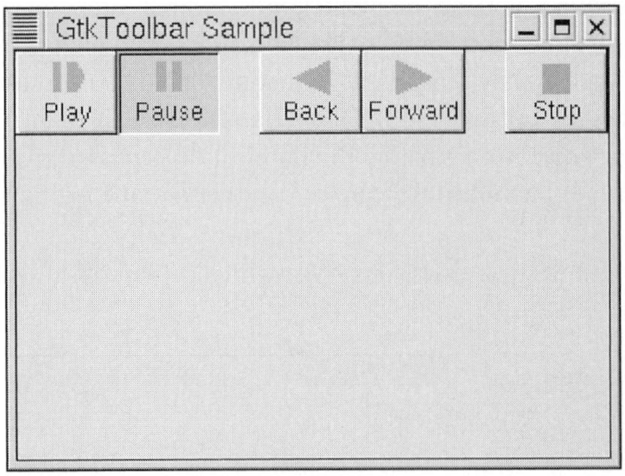

Figure 11.32 Using Radio Buttons in a Toolbar

The Back and Forward buttons are regular toolbar buttons, and therefore I used gtk_toolbar_append_item() to add both of these buttons to the toolbar. The reason for this is that these buttons do not convey state; when pressed, they simply do their job and then return to a deselected state. The remaining buttons, however, need to act like toggle buttons, on the one hand, because it is desirable for the Play button to be inset when the CD-ROM (or whatever) is being played, for example. But it is not possible for the player to simultaneously play, pause, and stop the CD-ROM; only one state can be active at any one time. For this reason, each of these buttons is a radio button and has been made to belong to the same radio group.

The relevant code (similar to code presented earlier) is as follows:

```
static GtkWidget*
CreateControlToolbar(GtkWidget *window)
{
  GtkWidget *toolbar;
  GtkWidget *radio_group;

  toolbar = gtk_toolbar_new(GTK_ORIENTATION_HORIZONTAL, GTK_TOOLBAR_BOTH);
  gtk_toolbar_set_space_size( GTK_TOOLBAR (toolbar), 20 );

  radio_group = gtk_toolbar_append_element (GTK_TOOLBAR (toolbar),
    GTK_TOOLBAR_CHILD_RADIOBUTTON, NULL, "Play",
    "Click here to play the current selection", NULL,
    new_pixmap ("play.xpm",
    window->window, &window->style->bg[GTK_STATE_NORMAL]),
    (GtkSignalFunc) button_callback, "" );
  gtk_toolbar_append_element (GTK_TOOLBAR (toolbar),
    GTK_TOOLBAR_CHILD_RADIOBUTTON, radio_group, "Pause",
    "Click here to pause the current selection", NULL,
    new_pixmap ("pause.xpm", window->window,
    &window->style->bg[GTK_STATE_NORMAL]),
    (GtkSignalFunc) button_callback, "" );
  gtk_toolbar_append_space( GTK_TOOLBAR (toolbar) );
  gtk_toolbar_append_element (GTK_TOOLBAR (toolbar),
    GTK_TOOLBAR_CHILD_BUTTON, NULL, "Back",
    "Click here to go to previous selection", NULL,
```

```
055       new_pixmap ("back.xpm", window->window,
056       &window->style->bg[GTK_STATE_NORMAL]),
057       (GtkSignalFunc) button_callback, "" );
058     gtk_toolbar_append_element (GTK_TOOLBAR (toolbar),
059       GTK_TOOLBAR_CHILD_BUTTON, NULL, "Forward",
060       "Click here to go to next selection", NULL,
061       new_pixmap ("forward.xpm", window->window,
062       &window->style->bg[GTK_STATE_NORMAL]),
063       (GtkSignalFunc) button_callback, "" );
064     gtk_toolbar_append_space( GTK_TOOLBAR (toolbar) );
065     gtk_toolbar_append_element (GTK_TOOLBAR (toolbar),
066       GTK_TOOLBAR_CHILD_RADIOBUTTON, radio_group, "Stop",
067       "Click here to stop the current selection", NULL,
068       new_pixmap ("stop.xpm", window->window,
069       &window->style->bg[GTK_STATE_NORMAL]),
070       (GtkSignalFunc) button_callback, "" );
071     return toolbar;
072   }
```

On lines 052 and 058, the Back and Forward buttons are created. Since they are basic toolbar buttons, I could have created them by calling gtk_toolbar_append_item(). On line 039, I create the Play button and, at the same time, define the radio group to which the Pause and Stop buttons are later added (on lines 045 and 066, respectively). Gtk_toolbar_append_space() is also called on lines 051 and 064 to add some visual separation to groups of related buttons. I could have used gtk_toolbar_append_element() here as well, setting type to GTK_TOOLBAR_CHILD_SPACE, but that would have made the code harder to read, (perhaps immeasurably) slower to execute, and would have gained nothing. The final type of toolbar item that can be created is GTK_TOOLBAR_CHILD_WIDGET. Here we have license to add pretty much any widget that we like in place of a button. For example, you might add a widget of your own design that displays an animated PNG graphic or a text-edit field (i.e., an instance of GtkEntry). Of course, the application will need to register its own signal functions as appropriate for the widget being added. The argument widget must be an instance of GtkWidget (or a derived class) that is not currently managed by a container widget (e.g., its parent is NULL). The arguments tooltip_text and toolkit_private_text are supported by GtkToolbar for widgets of arbitrary type. The arguments text, icon, callback, and user_data are all ignored when type is set to GTK_TOOLBAR_CHILD_WIDGET and should be set to NULL.

Now that we understand the theory and usage behind the gtk_toolbar_*_element() functions, let's look at the function prototypes. To append the element to the toolbar, call gtk_toolbar_append_element():

```
GtkWidget *
gtk_toolbar_append_element(GtkToolbar *toolbar,
        GtkToolbarChildType type, GtkWidget *widget, const char *text,
        const char *tooltip_text, const char *tooltip_private_text,
        GtkWidget *icon, GtkSignalFunc callback, gpointer user_data);
```

To prepend an element, call gtk_toolbar_prepend_element():

```
GtkWidget *
gtk_toolbar_prepend_element(GtkToolbar *toolbar,
       GtkToolbarChildType type, GtkWidget *widget, const char *text,
       const char *tooltip_text, const char *tooltip_private_text,
       GtkWidget *icon, GtkSignalFunc callback, gpointer user_data);
```

And predictably, to insert an element, call gtk_toolbar_insert_element():

```
GtkWidget *
gtk_toolbar_insert_element(GtkToolbar *toolbar,
       GtkToolbarChildType type, GtkWidget *widget, const char *text,
       const char *tooltip_text, const char *tooltip_private_text,
       GtkWidget *icon, GtkSignalFunc callback, gpointer user_data,
       gint position);
```

The arguments to each of these functions were previously described.

Convenience Functions

GtkToolbar supplies three convenience functions that can be used to add widgets to a toolbar. I call these convenience functions because they simply wrap calls to gtk_toolbar_*element() and require you to only pass a subset of arguments actually used by GtkToolbar when adding toolbar children of type GTK_TOOLBAR_CHILD_WIDGET. The arguments omitted are type (it defaults to GTK_TOOLBAR_CHILD_WIDGET), text, icon, callback, and user_data. As you might expect, three functions are supported: one to append a widget, one to prepend a widget, and one to insert a widget into the toolbar. To append an item of type GTK_TOOLBAR_ CHILD_WIDGET to the toolbar, call gtk_toolbar_ append_widget():

```
void
gtk_toolbar_append_widget(GtkToolbar *toolbar, GtkWidget *widget,
       const char *tooltip_text, const char *tooltip_private_text);
```

The arguments toolbar, widget, tooltip_text, and tooltip_private_text were all as described earlier for gtk_toolbar_append_element() when type is set to GTK_TOOLBAR_ CHILD_WIDGET.

To prepend an item of type GTK_TOOLBAR_CHILD_WIDGET to the toolbar, call gtk_toolbar_prepend_widget():

```
void
gtk_toolbar_prepend_widget(GtkToolbar *toolbar, GtkWidget *widget,
       const char *tooltip_text, const char *tooltip_private_text);
```

The arguments to gtk_toolbar_prepend_widget() are identical to those passed to gtk_toolbar_append_widget(). Finally, to insert a widget at an arbitrary location of a toolbar, call gtk_toolbar_insert_widget():

```
void
gtk_toolbar_insert_widget(GtkToolbar *toolbar, GtkWidget *widget,
       const char *tooltip_text, const char *tooltip_private_text,
       gint position);
```

The arguments toolbar, widget, tooltip_text, and tooltip_private_text are the same as described for gtk_toolbar_append_widget() and gtk_toolbar_prepend_widget(). The argument position specifies the location of the widget in the toolbar after the routine returns; it must be in the range [0, *n*], where *n* is the number of items in the toolbar after the insertion is performed.

Setting the Toolbar Orientation

The remaining GtkToolbar functions have to do with visual presentation of the toolbar and the control of tooltips.

The orientation (vertical or horizontal) is specified at the time the toolbar is created with gtk_toolbar_new(). However, GtkToolbar allows the orientation to be changed after the toolbar is created. You might find it appropriate to allow users to control the orientation of the toolbar via a preference of some sort; upon changes to the preference, a call to gtk_toolbar_set_orientation() can be made to change the orientation as desired:

```
void
gtk_toolbar_set_orientation(GtkToolbar *toolbar,
        GtkOrientation orientation);
```

orientation can be either GTK_ORIENTATION_VERTICAL for a vertical toolbar or GTK_ORIENTATION_HORIZONTAL for a horizontal toolbar.

Setting the Toolbar Style

The toolbar style, which also was initially set with gtk_toolbar_new(), can be changed at runtime with a call to gtk_toolbar_set_style():

```
void
gtk_toolbar_set_style(GtkToolbar *toolbar, GtkToolbarStyle style);
```

The style argument can be one of the following listed in Table 11.12.

Table 11.12 Toolbar Styles

Style	*Meaning*
GTK_TOOLBAR_ICONS	Show only icons
GTK_TOOLBAR_TEXT	Show only text
GTK_TOOLBAR_BOTH	Show both text and icons

Note that style is only applicable to buttons in the toolbar (e.g., the child type must be GTK_TOOLBAR_CHILD_BUTTON, GTK_TOOLBAR_CHILD_TOGGLEBUTTON, or GTK_TOOLBAR_CHILD_RADIOBUTTON). Other widgets managed by the toolbar are not affected by the style setting.

Enabling and Disabling Tooltips

To enable or disable tooltips for the menu bar, call gtk_toolbar_set_tooltips():

```
void
gtk_toolbar_set_tooltips(GtkToolbar *toolbar, gint enable);
```

If enable is TRUE, tooltips will be enabled; if it's FALSE, tooltips will be disabled. Like the orientation and style settings, the hiding and showing of tooltips can be performed at runtime.

Setting and Getting the Button Relief Attribute

The final two functions in the GtkToolbar API deal with button relief settings. You can get the current relief setting with gtk_toolbar_get_button_relief():

```
GtkReliefStyle
gtk_toolbar_get_button_relief(GtkToolbar *toolbar);
```

The possible relief styles returned are GTK_RELIEF_NORMAL, GTK_RELIEF_HALF, and GTK_RELIEF_NONE. GTK_RELIEF_NORMAL and GTK_RELIEF_HALF appear to be identical in Gtk+ 1.2 (or GTK_RELIEF_HALF is not supported). See Figure 11.32 for buttons drawn with GTK_RELIEF_NORMAL and see Figure 11.33 for the same buttons drawn with GTK_RELIEF_NONE.

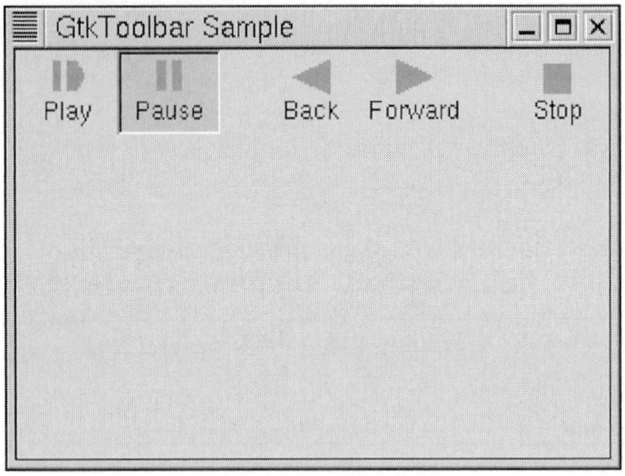

Figure 11.33 GTK_RELIEF_NONE Relief (See Also Figure 11.32)

You can change the relief style at runtime by making a call to gtk_toolbar_set_button_relief():

```
void
gtk_toolbar_set_button_relief(GtkToolbar *toolbar,
        GtkReliefStyle relief);
```

The argument relief must be GTK_RELIEF_NORMAL, GTK_RELIEF_HALF, or GTK_RELIEF_NONE. See the preceding description of gtk_toolbar_get_button_relief().

GtkHandleBox

Class Name

```
GtkHandleBox
```

Parent Class Name

```
GtkBin
```

Macros

Widget type macro: Not defined

Object to widget cast macro: `GTK_HANDLE_BOX(obj)`

Widget type check macro: `GTK_IS_HANDLE_BOX(obj)`

Supported Signals

Table 11.13 Signals

Signal Name	*Condition Causing Signal to Trigger*
child_attached	The child widget became attached to the parent.
child_detached	The child widget became detached from the parent.

Application-Level API Synopsis

Retrieve the constant GTK_TYPE_BIN at runtime:

```
guint
gtk_handle_box_get_type(void);
```

Create a new instance of GtkHandleBox:

```
GtkWidget *
gtk_handle_box_new(void);
```

Set the shadow type of the handle box (GTK_SHADOW_NONE, GTK_SHADOW_IN, GTK_SHADOW_OUT, GTK_SHADOW_ETCHED_IN, or GTK_SHADOW_ETCHED_OUT):

```
void
gtk_handle_box_set_shadow_type(GtkHandleBox *handle_box,
        GtkShadowType type);
```

Application-Level API Synopsis (Continued)

Set the position of the handle in the handle box (GTK_POS_LEFT, GTK_POS_RIGHT, GTK_POS_TOP, or GTK_POS_BOTTOM):

```
void
gtk_handle_box_set_handle_position(GtkHandleBox *handle_box,
        GtkPositionType position);
```

Set the snap edge (GTK_POS_LEFT, GTK_POS_RIGHT, GTK_POS_TOP, or GTK_POS_BOTTOM) of the handle box (see text):

```
void
gtk_handle_box_set_snap_edge(GtkHandleBox *handle_box,
        GtkPositionType edge);
```

Class Description

Figure 11.34 illustrates a handle-box widget used to contain a toolbar widget (see Figure 11.32 for the same toolbar parented in a vertical box widget). Handle boxes are container widgets that have a unique property: Application users are allowed to drag the child of the handle box to an area that is outside the area occupied by the handle-box widget; this operation is referred to as "detaching" a child. To detach a child, the user moves the mouse so that the pointer is over a grip or handle located along either the top, bottom, left (default), or right edge of the handle box. The user then presses mouse button 1 and drags the child to the desired location on the desktop. Figure 11.35 illustrates the same handle-box widget that was shown in Figure 11.34 but with its child detached. A child that has been detached will be reparented in a floating window.

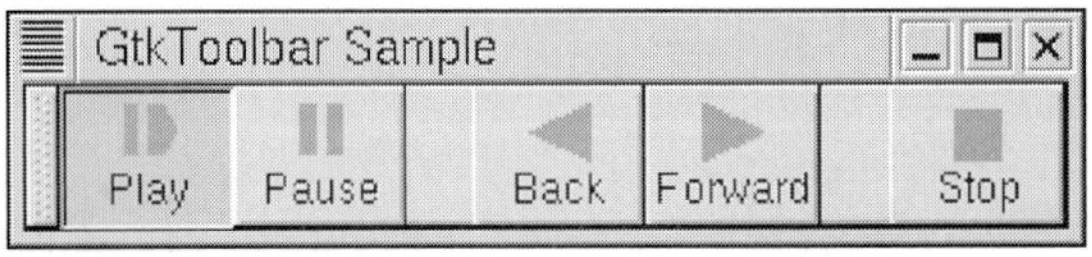

Figure 11.34 Toolbar Parented by a Handle Box

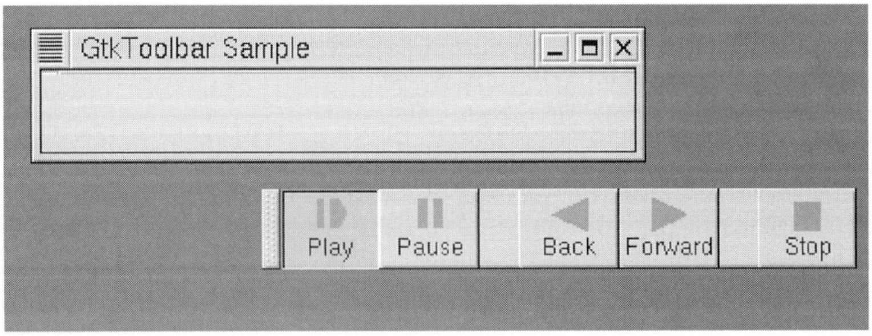

Figure 11.35 Detached Handle-Box Widget

The handle box, when a child detaches, is redrawn as a "ghost window." This ghost window provides a location to which the user can move the floating window in order to reattach the child to the handle box. Depending on the snap-edge attribute of the handle box and the container widget that manages the handle box, reattaching a floating window to its handle box parent can be a somewhat difficult task for users to become accustomed to. I'll have more to say about this issue later when I discuss the snap-edge attribute.

A child that has been detached from a handle box can be moved back (attached) to the handle box from which it was detached again by way of the grip or handle (which remains attached to the child).

Creating a Handle-Box Widget

GtkHandleBox is a relatively easy class to use. To create a new instance of GtkHandleBox, call gtk_handle_box_new():

```
GtkWidget *
gtk_handle_box_new(void);
```

The widget that is returned by gtk_handle_box_new() is a container widget. As a result, a child widget (e.g., another container such as GtkVBox or a noncontainer widget such as GtkButton) can be easily added with a call to gtk_container_add(). The following code creates a handle box and an instance of GtkToolbar and makes the toolbar a child of the handle box.

```
GtkWidget *hdlbox, *tbar;

// create a toolbar

tbar = gtk_toolbar_new(GTK_ORIENTATION_HORIZONTAL, GTK_TOOLBAR_BOTH);

// add children to the toolbar

AddSomeToolbarButtons( tbar );

// create a handle box

hdlbox = gtk_handle_box_new();

// make the toolbar a child of the handle box

gtk_container_add (GTK_CONTAINER (hdlbox), tbar);
```

At this point, you know all that you need to know to effectively use handle-box widgets in your applications.

Handle box does not implement a sophisticated child placement algorithm like other container-derived classes such as GtkBox or GtkTable. GtkHandleBox can only manage a single child. Therefore, to group a set of widgets together in a handle box, the widgets must be parented by an instance of some other container widget class such as GtkTable, GtkBox, and so forth. This container widget can then be added as the child of the handle box. The preceding toolbar example is an example of this technique. (The toolbar is the container class that is made a child of the handle box, while the toolbar buttons added by AddSomeToolbarButtons() are children managed by the instance of GtkToolbar.)

Setting the Shadow Type

Most applications will do fine using the defaults provided by GtkHandleBox and therefore can ignore the three functions I am about to discuss.

An application can change the shadow type of the handle box by making a call to gtk_handle_box_set_shadow_type():

```
void
gtk_handle_box_set_shadow_type(GtkHandleBox *handle_box,
        GtkShadowType type);
```

The type argument must be one of the following: GTK_SHADOW_NONE, GTK_SHADOW_IN, GTK_SHADOW_OUT, GTK_SHADOW_ETCHED_IN, or GTK_SHADOW_ETCHED_OUT. The default is GTK_SHADOW_OUT.

Setting the Handle Location

An application can also control where the handle is located in the handle box. To position the handle or grippy along the left, right, bottom, or top edge of a handle box, an application can call gtk_handle_box_set_handle_position():

```
void
gtk_handle_box_set_handle_position(GtkHandleBox *handle_box,
        GtkPositionType position);
```

The possible values are GTK_POS_LEFT (default), GTK_POS_RIGHT, GTK_POS_TOP, and GTK_POS_BOTTOM.

Setting the Snap Edge

The snap edge, which can be set to the same value as the handle position, is used by GtkHandleBar to detect when the user has moved a detached child back into the handle box. First, let's look at the function that can be called to change the snap edge, gtk_handle_box_set_snap_edge():

```
void
gtk_handle_box_set_snap_edge(GtkHandleBox *handle_box,
        GtkPositionType edge);
```

The arguments you pass to gtk_handle_box_set_snap_edge() are the same as those you pass to gtk_handle_box_set_shadow_type(). Setting edge to –1, however, causes GtkHandleBox to derive its own snap edge value that is based on the handle position. If the handle position is GTK_POS_LEFT or GTK_POS_RIGHT, GtkHandleBox will use a snap edge of GTK_POS_TOP. Otherwise, a snap edge of GTK_POS_LEFT will be used.

How is snap edge used, exactly? First of all, if the user detaches and then reattaches a child in a single drag (e.g., there is no button release between the point at which the detach occurred and the reattach is performed), then the snap edge does not matter, and reattachment occurs when the user moves the pointer to the same position that it occupied when the drag was initiated.

If a user drags a child window away from the handle box and releases the mouse button to place the floating (child) window on the desktop, then the snap-edge attribute of the handle box may have a more direct effect on how easy it will be for the user to reattach the child widget to the handle box. In short, the edge of the floating (detached) window that corresponds to the snap-edge attribute of the handle box must be aligned (within tolerances) to that same edge of the handle-box ghost window in order for reattachment to be performed. If the size or position of the ghost window is different than the size or position of the handle box before the child was detached, and the snap edge chosen by your application for the handle box does not take this size or position change into account, users may find reattaching the detached child to the handle box difficult or perhaps impossible.

To combat this problem, you should parent the handle box so that the snap edge you choose (or the default supplied by GtkHandleBox as previously described) does not become repositioned after a detach operation is performed.

GtkEventBox

Class Name

`GtkEventBox`

Parent Class Name

`GtkBin`

Macros

Widget type macro: `GTK_TYPE_EVENT_BOX`

Object to widget cast macro: `GTK_EVENT_BOX(obj)`

Widget type check macro: `GTK_IS_EVENT_BOX(obj)`

Application-Level API Synopsis

Retrieve the constant GTK_TYPE_EVENT_BOX at runtime:

```
GtkType
gtk_event_box_get_type(void);
```

Create a new instance of GtkEventBox:

```
GtkWidget *
gtk_event_box_new(void);
```

Class Description

Many Gtk+ widget classes do not create a separate X window for each instance they are asked by an application to instantiate. Many of these widget classes are container widget classes that create instances that are never visible to users and therefore do not need a window. Others rely on a parent in the widget instance hierarchy to provide a window into which their content is rendered.

The following is a list of some of the Gtk+ widget classes that do not create a new X window for each widget instantiated: GtkFrame, GtkAspectFrame, GtkCTree, GtkHBBox, GtkVBBox, GtkHBox, GtkVBox, GtkHSeparator, GtkVSeparator, GtkToolbar, GtkImage, GtkLabel, GtkOptionMenu, GtkPacker, GtkPixmap, and GtkTable.

Let's focus on GtkTable for the remainder of the discussion. GtkTable does not create a window for itself or its cells. The content of a table cell either is drawn into a window provided by the widget that occupies the cell or is drawn into a window created by a widget higher in the widget instance hierarchy (i.e., an ancestor of the GtkTable widget instance). In the tic-tac-toe example presented earlier in this chapter, the playing board is an instance of GtkTable. The table contains nine cells, organized as three rows of three columns each. Each cell in the table manages an instance of GtkPixmap (the pixmap represents the current occupant of the cell, either an X or an O move or an unoccupied cell). Each pixmap draws itself into the top-level window (an instance of GtkWindow) based on the layout computed for it by the GtkTable widget instance. Figure 11.36 illustrates the instance hierarchy of the tic-tac-toe board I have just described:

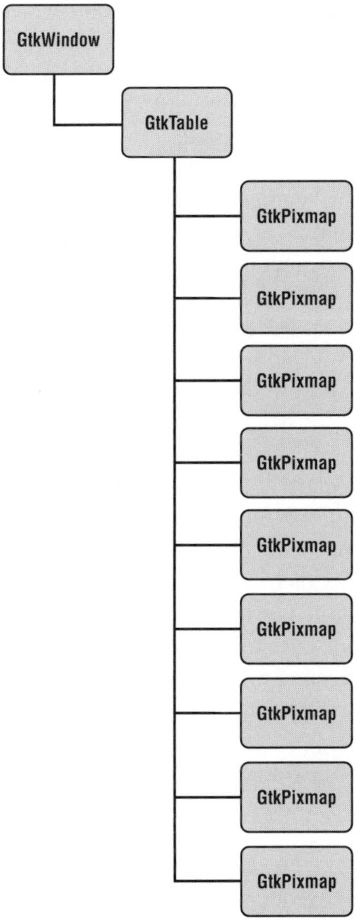

Figure 11.36 Tic-Tac-Toe Instance Hierarchy

Let's say the window created by the GtkWindow instance receives an expose event (the window was mapped, or some portion of the window became unobscured, perhaps due to the user moving a window that was higher in the window stacking order away and exposing a portion of the window). To handle this event, the GtkWindow instance will (in effect) pass this event down to each of its children (which in this case is a single instance of GtkTable). The GtkTable instance will receive the event and will handle it by calling on each of its children (instances of GtkPixmap in this case) to handle the expose event. Each instance of GtkPixmap will, in turn, handle the expose event by drawing itself in the window it is provided. Clearly, there is no need in this case for a table to create a window for itself, or for each of its children, nor is it necessary for each instance of GtkPixmap to create a window. Some widgets, on the other hand, do find it necessary to create their own windows. Once such class is GtkButton. Besides needing to draw itself (if that were its only requirement, it would not need a window), it must handle button press and key press events and respond to enter and leave events, which trigger redraws as the button transitions to and from prelight state.

If we were to place buttons, instead of pixmaps, as children of our tic-tac-toe table widget, we would gain the ability to click on them, and the buttons would respond to enter and leave notify events in the same way that any button would.

Let's say, however, that we want our pixmap widget instances to respond to one of the events to which a button widget would normally respond. How might we achieve this, given that pixmaps don't have a window and thus cannot be the target of X events? Well, there are a couple of ways we can do this. One way would be to simply replace our pixmaps with instances of GtkButton and make the pixmaps children of the buttons (see the discussion of GtkButton in Chapter 5, "Labels and Buttons"). This would work fine, but we may not want to inherit all of the overhead and extra functionality associated with using a button widget.

As another option, we might choose to associate a signal function with button press events that occur in the window created by the GtkWindow instance. The main problem with this approach is that we would need to implement code that determines which cell in the table, if any, should receive and process the button press events received by the window. This is work that is generally best left for a widget to perform, not an application. However, the solution is a reasonable one; if a mouse event were to fall inside of the area owned by one of the table cells, we would receive it, figure out which cell owned the event, and then call the function in our application that is most appropriate for handling a button press within that cell receiving the event.

Even better, we might decide to use an instance of GtkEventBox to implement our feature. GtkEventBox is designed to supply an X window to widgets that are not able to create an X window of their own. We can use the event box as a wrapper to the widget it contains; instead of creating a pixmap and adding it as the child of a cell in the table, we create a pixmap and an instance of GtkEventBox, add the pixmap as the child of the event box, and add the event box as a child of the table. The instance hierarchy of a tic-tac-toe game that applies this strategy is shown in Figure 11.37:

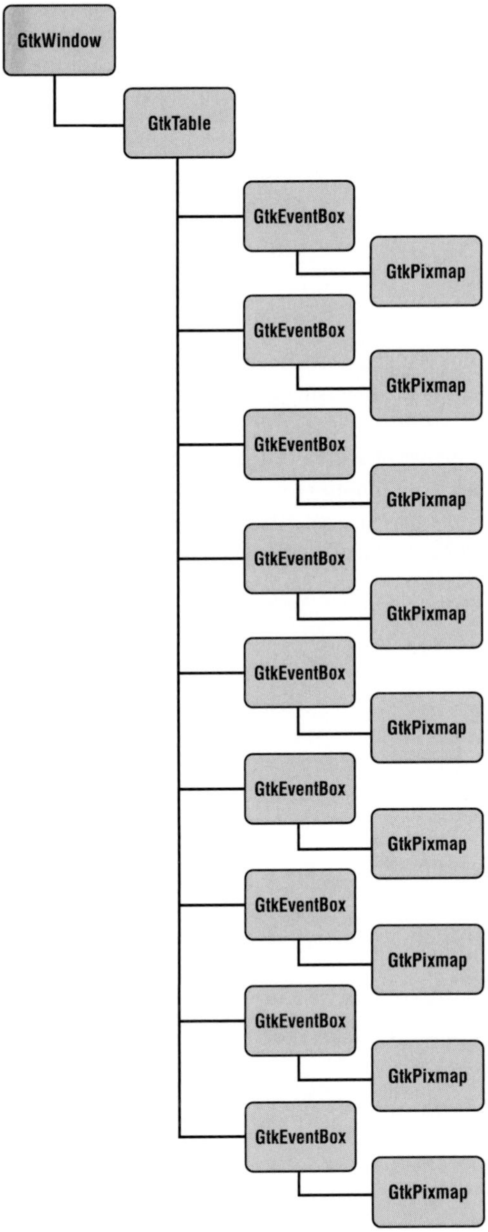

Figure 11.37 Tic-Tac-Toe Instance Hierarchy, with Event Box Widgets

If the user clicks mouse button 1 over a tic-tac-toe board cell, a button press event will be sent to the GtkEventBox widget associated with the cell over which the pointer was positioned, not to the GtkWindow instance of which the table widget instance is a child. The application can easily associate a unique button press callback function with each cell, as opposed to having to perform callback function dispatching itself based on the location of the mouse button press in the parent window. Because each cell has its own window, the application can now modify event handling on a per-cell basis if desired (it might not want to process events received by an unoccupied cell, for example).

Creating an Event Box Widget

The function gtk_event_box_new() is used to create an instance of GtkEventBox:

```
GtkWidget *
gtk_event_box_new(void);
```

The returned value, an instance of GtkWidget, is a container that creates a unique X window for its child. A child can be added to the container using gtk_container_add(), as shown in the following example.

The following code creates an instance of GtkEventBox, adds a GtkPixmap widget to the event box as its child, and solicits motion notify events on the event box. The callback function MotionNotifyCallback() will be invoked as the user moves the pointer over the pixmap drawn in the window created by the GtkEventBox instance:

```
GtkWidget *pixmap, *ebox;
GtkPixmap *pixmap;

// create the event box

ebox = gtk_event_box_new();

// solicit motion notify events on the event box, and assign
// a signal handler function

gtk_widget_set_events( ebox, GDK_POINTER_MOTION_MASK );
gtk_signal_connect( GTK_OBJECT( ebox ), "motion_notify_event",
        GTK_SIGNAL_FUNC( MotionNotifyCallback ), NULL);

// create an instance of GtkPixmap, and make it a child of the
// event box widget

pixmap = CreatePixmap();
gtk_container_add( GTK_CONTAINER(ebox), GTK_PIXMAP( widget );
```

The details of MotionNotifyCallback() are not terribly relevant; here I simply print a message to stdout:

```
gint
MotionNotifyCallback( GtkWidget *widget, GdkEvent *event,
        gpointer data )
{
        printf( "A motion notify event was received\n" );
}
```

GtkScrolledWindow

Class Name

`GtkScrolledWindow`

Parent Class Name

`GtkBin`

Macros

Widget type macro: `GTK_TYPE_SCROLLED_WINDOW`

Object to widget cast macro: `GTK_SCROLLED_WINDOW(obj)`

Widget type check macro: `GTK_IS_SCROLLED_WINDOW(obj)`

Supported Arguments

Prefix: `GtkScrolledWindow::`

Table 11.14 GtkScrolledWindow Arguments

Name	*Type*	*Permissions*
hadjustment	GTK_TYPE_ADJUSTMENT	GTK_ARG_READWRITE | GTK_ARG_CONSTRUCT
vadjustment	GTK_TYPE_ADJUSTMENT	GTK_ARG_READWRITE | GTK_ARG_CONSTRUCT
hscrollbar_policy	GTK_TYPE_POLICY_TYPE	GTK_ARG_READWRITE
vscrollbar_policy	GTK_TYPE_POLICY_TYPE	GTK_ARG_READWRITE
window_placement	GTK_TYPE_CORNER_TYPE	GTK_ARG_READWRITE

Application-Level API Synopsis

Retrieve the constant GTK_TYPE_SCROLLED_WINDOW at runtime:

```
GtkType
gtk_scrolled_window_get_type(void);
```

Create an instance of GtkScrolledWindow, optionally specifying adjustments:

```
GtkWidget *
gtk_scrolled_window_new(GtkAdjustment *hadjustment,
        GtkAdjustment *vadjustment);
```

Set or replace the horizontal adjustment of a scrolled window:

```
void
gtk_scrolled_window_set_hadjustment(GtkScrolledWindow
        *scrolled_window, GtkAdjustment *hadjustment);
```

Set or replace the vertical adjustment of a scrolled window:

```
void
gtk_scrolled_window_set_vadjustment(GtkScrolledWindow
        *scrolled_window, GtkAdjustment *vadjustment);
```

Get the horizontal adjustment of a scrolled window:

```
GtkAdjustment *
gtk_scrolled_window_get_hadjustment(GtkScrolledWindow
        *scrolled_window);
```

Get the vertical adjustment of a scrolled window:

```
GtkAdjustment *
gtk_scrolled_window_get_vadjustment(GtkScrolledWindow
        *scrolled_window);
```

Set the scrolling policies for both the horizontal and vertical scrollbars:

```
void
gtk_scrolled_window_set_policy(GtkScrolledWindow *scrolled_window,
        GtkPolicyType hscrollbar_policy,
        GtkPolicyType vscrollbar_policy);
```

Set the scrollbar placement preference for the scrolled window:

```
void
gtk_scrolled_window_set_placement(GtkScrolledWindow
        *scrolled_window, GtkCornerType window_placement);
```

Add a child widget to the scrolled window:

```
void
gtk_scrolled_window_add_with_viewport(GtkScrolledWindow
        *scrolled_window, GtkWidget *child);
```

Class Description

A scrolled window consists of a region within which content that is managed by the scrolled window is presented to the user. A pair of scrollbars that can by used by the user to navigate the content will be displayed by the scrolled window widget if the size of the content is greater than the size of the scrolled window region. A scrolled window can act as the parent of any widget, but typically it will parent a widget that displays user or application data. Here are some examples of Gtk+ widgets that might be parented by a scrolled window widget:

- A GtkCList widget that displays a record for each employee in a company
- A GtkText widget that displays the text of a document or memo
- A GtkDrawingArea widget that displays a large image
- A GtkTable widget that contains a large number of rows and/or columns

A scrolled window widget, as the preceding examples imply, addresses the problem of displaying large amounts of data within a finitely sized window or dialog (or a finitely sized portion of a window or dialog when the scrolled window shares a window or dialog with other widgets).

Using a scrolled window is fairly easy. First you create the scrolled window and make it the child of a dialog, window, or some other container widget. You then create a widget and add it as a child of the scrolled window widget.

You must decide on a scrollbar policy when creating the scrolled window. The default scrollbar policy is for GtkScrolledWindow to display scrollbars on an as-needed basis. That is, scrollbars will only be displayed when the child being managed by the scrolled window is larger in size than the area allocated to the scrolled window widget. This is the default policy, and it works well for most applications. The other scrollbar policy is to always display horizontal and vertical scrollbars, regardless of the size of the scrolled window or the child being managed.

How you add the child is determined by the type of child being added. There are two basic cases: either the child supports scrollbar adjustments or it does not. If the child does support scrollbar adjustments, you can use gtk_container_add() to add the child to the scrollbar. I will describe how to handle the other case in the section "Adding a Child to a Scrolled Window."

Creating a Scrolled Window

To create an instance of GtkScrolledWindow, call gtk_scrolled_window_new():

```
GtkWidget *
gtk_scrolled_window_new(GtkAdjustment *hadjustment,
        GtkAdjustment *vadjustment);
```

Like all gtk_*_new functions, a GtkWidget instance is returned. You can cast this to an instance of GtkScrolledWindow by using the GTK_SCROLLED_WINDOW macro. The hadjustment and vadjustment arguments specify adjustment objects that you have created or that have been obtained from some other widget that uses adjustments. In most cases, you will want to set these to NULL and use the adjustment objects created for you automatically by

GtkScrolledWindow. I will have more to say about how to use and manipulate adjustment objects later in this section.

Adding a Child to a Scrolled Window

To add a child to a scrolled window, you can do one of two things:

- Add the child using gtk_container_add() if the child widget class supports scrollbar adjustments.
- Add the child by calling gtk_scrolled_window_add_with_viewport().

You can use gtk_container_add() to add child widgets belonging to the following classes (and those that derive from them): GtkCList, GtkLayout, and GtkText. All other widget class children must be added by making a call to gtk_scrolled_window_add_with_viewport():

```
void
gtk_scrolled_window_add_with_viewport(GtkScrolledWindow
        *scrolled_window, GtkWidget *child);
```

The argument scrolled_window is an instance of GtkScrolledWindow, and child is the widget that is being made the child of the scrolled window.

Setting and Getting the Horizontal and Vertical Adjustment Objects

You can replace the horizontal or vertical adjustment objects of a scrolled window widget by calling gtk_scrolled_window_set_hadjustment() or gtk_scrolled_window_set_vadjustment(), respectively:

```
void
gtk_scrolled_window_set_hadjustment(GtkScrolledWindow
        *scrolled_window, GtkAdjustment *hadjustment);

void
gtk_scrolled_window_set_vadjustment(GtkScrolledWindow
        *scrolled_window, GtkAdjustment *vadjustment);
```

Both functions take an instance of GtkScrolledWindow as their first argument and an instance of GtkAdjustment as their second argument. Setting the adjustment argument to NULL will cause the GtkScrolledWindow object to create an adjustment object of its own, replacing the current adjustment object. As I mentioned earlier, most applications will want to let GtkScrolledWindow create adjustment objects on its own (this behavior is obtained by passing NULL as both arguments to gtk_scrolled_window_new()). However, there may be times when linking the scrolled window adjustment objects with some other widget (or widgets) can be used to achieve a more intuitive or powerful user interface.

Overriding the Default Adjustment Objects: An Example

In the following example code, I create an instance of GtkTable that contains 40 rows and 40 columns. Each table manages an instance of GtkButton. The idea is to place below the table two spin button widgets that can be used to select a specific cell in the table; one of the spin buttons specifies the row, and the other specifies the column. Each of the spin buttons creates an adjustment object. By overriding the adjustment objects of the scrolled window, changes that are made by the spin buttons will automatically cause the scrolled window to update its position. Here is the code:

Listing 11.8 Overriding the Default Adjustment Objects

```
#include <gtk/gtk.h>

#define ROWS 40
#define COLS 40

void
CreateScrolledWindow()
{
   GtkWidget *spinner, *sw, *button, *vbox, *hbox, *dlog, *table;
   GtkAdjustment *adj1, *adj2;
   int i, j;
   char buf[32];

   dlog = gtk_window_new(GTK_WINDOW_TOPLEVEL);
   gtk_window_position(GTK_WINDOW (dlog), GTK_WIN_POS_MOUSE);
   gtk_widget_set_usize( GTK_WIDGET( dlog ), 200, 200 );

   gtk_signal_connect(GTK_OBJECT (dlog), "destroy",
           GTK_SIGNAL_FUNC(gtk_widget_destroyed), &dlog);

   gtk_window_set_title(GTK_WINDOW (dlog),
           "GtkScrolledWindow Demo");
   gtk_container_border_width (GTK_CONTAINER (dlog), 0);

   vbox = gtk_vbox_new( FALSE, 0 );
   gtk_container_add (GTK_CONTAINER (dlog), vbox);

   sw = gtk_scrolled_window_new( NULL, NULL );

   gtk_box_pack_start(GTK_BOX(vbox), sw, TRUE, TRUE, 0);

   table = gtk_table_new( ROWS, COLS, TRUE );

   gtk_scrolled_window_add_with_viewport(
           GTK_SCROLLED_WINDOW( sw ), table );

   for ( i = 0; i < ROWS; i++ )
           for ( j = 0; j < COLS; j++ ) {
                   sprintf( buf, "%d, %d", i, j );
                   button = gtk_button_new_with_label( buf );
                   gtk_table_attach_defaults( GTK_TABLE( table ),
                           button, j, j + 1, i, i + 1 );
           }

   hbox = gtk_hbox_new( FALSE, 0 );
   gtk_box_pack_end(GTK_BOX(vbox), hbox, FALSE, FALSE, 0);

   adj1 = (GtkAdjustment *) gtk_adjustment_new( 0.0, 0.0,
           (gfloat) COLS - 1, 1.0, 1.0, 0.0 );
   spinner = gtk_spin_button_new(adj1, 0, 0);
```

```
051     gtk_spin_button_set_wrap(GTK_SPIN_BUTTON (spinner), TRUE);
052     gtk_box_pack_start(GTK_BOX (hbox), spinner, TRUE, TRUE, 0);
053
054     adj2 = (GtkAdjustment *) gtk_adjustment_new( 0.0, 0.0,
055             (gfloat) ROWS - 1, 1.0, 1.0, 0.0 );
056     spinner = gtk_spin_button_new (adj2, 0, 0);
057     gtk_spin_button_set_wrap(GTK_SPIN_BUTTON (spinner), TRUE);
058     gtk_box_pack_start(GTK_BOX (hbox), spinner, TRUE, TRUE, 0);
059
060     gtk_scrolled_window_set_hadjustment( GTK_SCROLLED_WINDOW( sw ), adj1 );
061     gtk_scrolled_window_set_vadjustment( GTK_SCROLLED_WINDOW( sw ), adj2 );
062
063     gtk_widget_show_all( dlog );
064 }
065
066 main( int argc, char *argv[] )
067 {
068     gtk_init( &argc, &argv );
069
070     CreateScrolledWindow();
071
072     gtk_main();
073 }
```

Unfortunately, this strategy does not actually work as we would like. Before I discuss the problem, let's take a look at the relevant portions of the code. On line 028, I create a scrolled window and pack it into a vertical box used to hold the scrolled window and the spin boxes that will later be added below the scrolled window. On lines 032 through 035, a table containing 40 rows and 40 columns is created and added to the scrolled window by making a call to gtk_scrolled_window_add_with_viewport(). On lines 037 through 043, the cells of the table are populated with instances of GtkButton. This completes the work needed to create the scrolled window and its child. CreateScrolledWindow(), on lines 045 through 058, creates a pair of spin box widgets: one for selecting a row and the other used for selecting a column in the table managed by the scrolled window. The ranges of the adjustment objects are set to 0, 39, corresponding to the number of rows and columns in the table. On lines 060 and 061, the following code sets the horizontal and vertical adjustment objects of the scrollbar to those used by the spin button widgets:

```
060   gtk_scrolled_window_set_hadjustment( GTK_SCROLLED_WINDOW( sw ), adj1 );
061   gtk_scrolled_window_set_vadjustment( GTK_SCROLLED_WINDOW( sw ), adj2 );
```

As I stated earlier, this strategy doesn't work. If you were to execute the preceding program, you would see that the adjustment ranges we specified for the spin boxes (0, 39) have been overridden by the range of pixel values that define the horizontal and vertical extent of the scrolled window child (i.e., the range of the horizontal spin box will match the range of the horizontal scrollbar, and the range of the vertical spin box will match the range of the vertical scrollbar). The problem is that the scrollbar ranges are in pixels, while the spin box ranges we tried to set are in logical units (the number of rows and columns in the table). To achieve the effect we desire, it is required that we decouple the spin box widgets from the scrolled window and allow each to have its own private adjustments. To synchronize the adjustments, we must listen to each adjustment for changes and manually set the related adjustment in the other widget as those changes occur. The code that sets an adjustment must convert from its range to the range used by the corresponding adjustment in the other widget. To implement this, the value_changed callback must have access to the corresponding adjustment in the related widget. The following routines allow an application to retrieve the scrolled window horizontal and vertical adjustments. To get the horizontal adjustment of a scrolled window, call gtk_scrolled_window_get_hadjustment():

```
GtkAdjustment *
gtk_scrolled_window_get_hadjustment(GtkScrolledWindow
        *scrolled_window);
```

The return value is an instance of GtkAdjustment. The argument scrolled_window is the scrolled window for which the horizontal adjustment is being requested.

To get the vertical adjustment, call gtk_scrolled_window_get_vadjustment():

```
GtkAdjustment *
gtk_scrolled_window_get_vadjustment(GtkScrolledWindow
        *scrolled_window);
```

The argument scrolled_window specifies the scrolled window being queried, and the return value is the vertical adjustment object of the scrolled window.

The following listing illustrates how to connect spin buttons that select rows and columns in the table with the vertical and horizontal scrollbars of the scrolled window widget:

Listing 11.9 Connecting Spin Buttons to Scrollbars

```
#include <gtk/gtk.h>

#define ROWS 40
#define COLS 40

static GtkWidget *sw, *hspinner, *vspinner;

static void
HorizontalSpinChanged (GtkWidget *widget, gpointer data)
{
   GtkAdjustment *adj;
   gint value;

   value = gtk_spin_button_get_value_as_int(GTK_SPIN_BUTTON(hspinner));
   adj = gtk_scrolled_window_get_hadjustment(GTK_SCROLLED_WINDOW(sw));
   gtk_adjustment_set_value( adj, (float) value * (int) data );
}

static void
VerticalSpinChanged (GtkWidget *widget, gpointer data)
{
   GtkAdjustment *adj;
   gint value;

   value = gtk_spin_button_get_value_as_int(GTK_SPIN_BUTTON(vspinner));
```

```
   adj = gtk_scrolled_window_get_vadjustment(GTK_SCROLLED_WINDOW(sw));
   gtk_adjustment_set_value( adj, (float) value * (int) data );
}

void
CreateScrolledWindow()
{
   GtkWidget *button, *vbox, *hbox, *dlog, *table;
   GtkAdjustment *adj1, *adj2;
   guint width, height;
   int i, j;
   char buf[32];

   dlog = gtk_window_new(GTK_WINDOW_TOPLEVEL);
   gtk_window_position(GTK_WINDOW (dlog), GTK_WIN_POS_MOUSE);
   gtk_widget_set_usize( GTK_WIDGET( dlog ), 200, 200 );

   gtk_signal_connect(GTK_OBJECT (dlog), "destroy",
           GTK_SIGNAL_FUNC(gtk_widget_destroyed), &dlog);

   gtk_window_set_title(GTK_WINDOW (dlog),
           "GtkScrolledWindow Demo");
   gtk_container_border_width(GTK_CONTAINER (dlog), 0);

   vbox = gtk_vbox_new( FALSE, 0 );
   gtk_container_add(GTK_CONTAINER (dlog), vbox);

   sw = gtk_scrolled_window_new( NULL, NULL );

   gtk_box_pack_start(GTK_BOX(vbox), sw, TRUE, TRUE, 0);

   table = gtk_table_new( ROWS, COLS, TRUE );

   gtk_scrolled_window_add_with_viewport( GTK_SCROLLED_WINDOW( sw ),
           table );

   for ( i = 0; i < ROWS; i++ )
           for ( j = 0; j < COLS; j++ ) {
                   sprintf( buf, "%d, %d", i, j );
                   button = gtk_button_new_with_label( buf );
                   gtk_table_attach_defaults( GTK_TABLE( table ),
                           button, j, j + 1, i, i + 1 );
           }

   gtk_widget_show_all(dlog);

   width = button-allocation.width;
   height = button-allocation.height;

   hbox = gtk_hbox_new( FALSE, 0 );
   gtk_box_pack_end(GTK_BOX(vbox), hbox, FALSE, FALSE, 0);
```

```
077
078       adj1 = (GtkAdjustment *) gtk_adjustment_new( 0.0, 0.0,
079               (gfloat) COLS - 1, 1.0, 1.0, 0.0 );
080       hspinner = gtk_spin_button_new(adj1, 0, 0);
081       gtk_spin_button_set_wrap(GTK_SPIN_BUTTON (hspinner), TRUE);
082       gtk_box_pack_start(GTK_BOX (hbox), hspinner, TRUE, TRUE, 0);
083       gtk_signal_connect (GTK_OBJECT (adj1), "value_changed",
084               GTK_SIGNAL_FUNC(HorizontalSpinChanged), (gpointer) width);
085
086       adj2 = (GtkAdjustment *) gtk_adjustment_new( 0.0, 0.0,
087               (gfloat) ROWS - 1, 1.0, 1.0, 0.0 );
088       vspinner = gtk_spin_button_new(adj2, 0, 0);
089       gtk_spin_button_set_wrap(GTK_SPIN_BUTTON (vspinner), TRUE);
090       gtk_box_pack_start(GTK_BOX (hbox), vspinner, TRUE, TRUE, 0);
091       gtk_signal_connect (GTK_OBJECT (adj2), "value_changed",
092               GTK_SIGNAL_FUNC(VerticalSpinChanged), (gpointer) height);
093
094       gtk_widget_show_all( hbox );
095    }
096
097    main( int argc, char *argv[] )
098    {
099       gtk_init( &argc, &argv );
100
101       CreateScrolledWindow();
102
103       gtk_main();
105    }
```

The first thing to notice is that we no longer share adjustments with the scrolled window and spin buttons. Each pair of widgets has its own pair of adjustments. A value_changed signal function is enabled for each of the spin button adjustment objects on lines 83 (for the horizontal spinner) and 91 (for the vertical spinner). The horizontal spinner signal function is passed the width of buttons managed by the table widget (the table children are homogeneous and thus each button has the same width and height), and the vertical spinner's value_changed signal function is passed the height of buttons managed by the table widget. The width and height are used to compute how far the scrollbars should be moved when the spin button values change. The vertical spin button value_changed function is on lines 019 through 028. The spin button value is queried on line 025. Next, the vertical scrollbar adjustment object is retrieved. Finally, on line 027, the vertical scrollbar adjustment object's value is changed by making a call to gtk_adjustment_set_value(). The new adjustment value is computed by multiplying the height of a button (passed as the data parameter of the signal function) and the value of the vertical spin button. The operation of the horizontal spin button value_changed callback is similar.

Setting the Scrolling Policy

As I mentioned earlier, your application can specify scrolling policies for the vertical and horizontal scrollbars of a scrolled window widget. For most applications, the default, GTK_POLICY_AUTOMATIC, will usually be the right policy choice. To set the scrolling policies for either the horizontal or the vertical scrollbars of a scrolled window widget, call gtk_scrolled_window_set_policy():

```
void
gtk_scrolled_window_set_policy(GtkScrolledWindow *scrolled_window,
        GtkPolicyType hscrollbar_policy,
        GtkPolicyType vscrollbar_policy);
```

The first argument is the scrolled window widget instance. The arguments hscrollbar_policy and vscrollbar_policy accept one of the values listed in Table 11.15.

Table 11.15 Scrolling Policies

Value	*Meaning*
GTK_POLICY_ALWAYS	Scrollbar will always show.
GTK_POLICY_AUTOMATIC	Scrollbar will only show when the child is bigger than the viewport (default).
GTK_POLICY_NEVER	Scrollbar will never show.

One bug in the API is that there is no way to retrieve the scrollbar policy. This is a problem if you want to use the preceding function to change the policy of only one of the scrollbars; somehow you must determine the policy of the other and pass it in so that it will not be changed. A minor issue, to be sure, but it would be nice if either there were separate functions for setting the vertical and horizontal scrollbar policies or either function were to accept a value such as –1 to indicate that the argument should be ignored and the current scrollbar policy be left as is.

Controlling Scrollbar Placement

The final GtkScrolledWindow function I discuss here allows you to control the placement of the scrollbars relative to the window. By default, the vertical scrollbar will be adjacent the right edge of the window, and the horizontal scrollbar will be directly below the bottom edge of the window. Your application can change this by calling gtk_scrolled_window_set_placement():

```
void
gtk_scrolled_window_set_placement(GtkScrolledWindow *scrolled_window,
        GtkCornerType window_placement);
```

There are four possible values for the window_placement. Table 11.16 specifies the resulting window placement for each value.

Table 11.16 Scrolling Policies

Value	*Vertical*	*Horizontal*
GTK_CORNER_TOP_LEFT	Right edge	Bottom edge
GTK_CORNER_BOTTOM_LEFT	Right edge	Top edge

Table 11.16 Scrolling Policies (Continued)

Value	*Vertical*	*Horizontal*
GTK_CORNER_TOP_RIGHT	Left edge	Bottom edge
GTK_CORNER_BOTTOM_RIGHT	Left edge	Top edge

The default is GTK_CORNER_TOP_LEFT. If the preceding table is confusing, remember that the window placement is always directly opposite of the corner where the vertical and horizontal scrollbars meet. For example, if the window placement is GTK_CORNER_TOP_RIGHT, the two scrollbars must meet at the bottom-left corner. Another way to think about it is as follows: Window placement defines the corner of the scrolled window where no scrollbars are located.

GtkLayout

Class Name

```
GtkLayout
```

Parent Class Name

```
GtkContainer
```

Macros

Widget type macro: `GTK_TYPE_LAYOUT`

Object to widget cast macro: `GTK_LAYOUT(obj)`

Widget type check macro: `GTK_IS_LAYOUT(obj)`

Application-Level API Synopsis

Retrieve the constant GTK_TYPE_LAYOUT at runtime:

```
GtkType
gtk_layout_get_type(void);
```

Create a new instance of GtkLayout:

```
GtkWidget *
gtk_layout_new(GtkAdjustment *hadjustment,
       GtkAdjustment *vadjustment);
```

Application-Level API Synopsis (Continued)

Add a child widget to an instance of GtkLayout at specified x, y location:
```
void
gtk_layout_put(GtkLayout *layout, GtkWidget *widget, gint x, gint y);
```

Move a child widget of an instance of GtkLayout to the specified x, y location:
```
void
gtk_layout_move(GtkLayout *layout, GtkWidget *widget, gint x,
      gint y);
```

Set the size of an instance of GtkLayout:
```
void
gtk_layout_set_size(GtkLayout *layout, guint width, guint height);
```

Retrieve the horizontal adjustment of an instance of GtkLayout:
```
GtkAdjustment *
gtk_layout_get_hadjustment(GtkLayout *layout);
```

Retrieve the vertical adjustment of an instance of GtkLayout:
```
GtkAdjustment *
gtk_layout_get_vadjustment(GtkLayout *layout);
```

Set the horizontal adjustment of an instance of GtkLayout:
```
void
gtk_layout_set_hadjustment(GtkLayout *layout,
      GtkAdjustment *adjustment);
```

Set the vertical adjustment of an instance of GtkLayout:
```
void
gtk_layout_set_vadjustment(GtkLayout *layout,
      GtkAdjustment *adjustment);
```

Class Description

GtkLayout is very similar to GtkFixed, which was described in Chapter 10. Both of these container classes implement an extremely simple layout policy that requires the application to position child widgets within the container on its own. The application positions a child by providing GtkLayout with the x, y coordinate of the child's upper-left corner. The application can move a child widget to a new location in the container as well.

There are two major differences that exist between GtkLayout and GtkFixed. The primary difference is that GtkLayout allows applications to create a container widget that appears to exceed the window size limitations imposed by the X11 protocol—width and height values in the CreateWindow protocol request are limited to 16-bit unsigned values. How GtkLayout achieves this illusion is not terribly important. Most applications will not require such large window sizes, but some applications (those that display maps or scientific data) may find a use for GtkLayout.

The second major difference that exists between GtkFixed and GtkLayout is that GtkLayout provides support for specifying adjustments, at widget creation time or after widget creation, via a function provided by the GtkLayout API. We will see in the section titled "Adjustments," how adjustment objects are used by GtkLayout.

Creating a Layout Widget

To create a new instance of GtkLayout, call gtk_layout_new():

```
GtkWidget *
gtk_layout_new(GtkAdjustment *hadjustment,
       GtkAdjustment *vadjustment);
```

The function gtk_layout_new() accepts two arguments: hadjustment and vadjustment. In most cases, you will want to set both of these arguments to NULL and let GtkLayout create adjustment objects for you.

Most applications will find it convenient to parent GtkLayout with a widget that provides scrollbars. Most likely, that widget will be GtkScrolledWindow. However, you might decide to create a separate control that allows users to navigate the content of the GtkLayout widget. I will illustrate both options later in this section. First let's take a look at the rest of the GtkLayout API.

Adding a Child Widget

You add a child widget to an instance of GtkLayout in exactly the same way that you add a child to an instance of GtkFixed (but using a function provided by GtkLayout, of course). To add a child to a layout widget, call gtk_layout_put():

```
void
gtk_layout_put(GtkLayout *layout, GtkWidget *widget, gint x, gint y);
```

The argument layout is an instance of GtkLayout, widget is some arbitrary Gtk+ widget, and x and y specify the location of the upper-left corner of the widget. The x and y values are signed int values and may exceed the unsigned 16-bit int limitation on window sizes imposed by the X11 Core Protocol.

Repositioning a Child Widget

You can move a child previously added to an instance of GtkLayout by calling gtk_layout_move():

```
void
gtk_layout_move(GtkLayout *layout, GtkWidget *widget, gint x, gint y);
```

The arguments to gtk_layout_move() are the same as to gtk_layout_put().

Setting the Size of the Layout Virtual Area

You can set the size of the virtual area managed by an instance of GtkLayout by calling gtk_layout_set_size():

```
void
gtk_layout_set_size(GtkLayout *layout, guint width, guint height);
```

The width and height arguments are unsigned int (notice that gtk_layout_move() and gtk_layout_put() accept signed int x and y parameters). This is probably a bug; there is little point in creating a layout widget that is size-limited by an unsigned int but that limits the x and y coordinates of its children to signed int values. Still, even a signed int is a pretty big number on most modern, 32-bit systems, far exceeding what most applications will ever find themselves needing to specify.

Adjustments

In this section, I will illustrate how adjustments are used with layout widgets by presenting two code examples. In the first example, I will create a layout widget and parent it with an instance of GtkScrolledWindow. In this example, the layout widget will make use of the scrollbars GtkScrolledWindow provides to control the content viewed by the user. Most applications will use GtkScrolledWindow in this way to provide scrollbars for its layout widgets.

In the second example, I will show you how to parent an instance of GtkLayout in a container that does not provide its own scrollbars. The example will provide its own controls that can be used to navigate the content managed by the layout widget. We will also take a look at the adjustment functions provided by GtkLayout.

The first example is similar to the one implemented by the testgtk program supplied with Gtk+ distributions:

Listing 11.10 Parenting a Layout Widget in a Scrollbarless Container

```
#include <gtk/gtk.h>

void
GtkLayoutDialog()
{
      GtkWidget *layout, *scrolled_window, *label, *dialog_window;
      int i, j;
      char buf[128];

      dialog_window = gtk_window_new(GTK_WINDOW_TOPLEVEL);
      gtk_window_position (GTK_WINDOW (dialog_window), GTK_WIN_POS_MOUSE);
      gtk_widget_set_usize( GTK_WIDGET( dialog_window ), 200, 200 );

      gtk_signal_connect (GTK_OBJECT (dialog_window), "destroy",
              GTK_SIGNAL_FUNC(gtk_widget_destroyed), &dialog_window);

      gtk_window_set_title (GTK_WINDOW (dialog_window), "GtkLayout Demo");
      gtk_container_border_width (GTK_CONTAINER (dialog_window), 0);

      scrolled_window = gtk_scrolled_window_new( NULL, NULL );
      gtk_container_add (GTK_CONTAINER (dialog_window), scrolled_window);
      layout = gtk_layout_new( NULL, NULL );

      gtk_layout_set_size (GTK_LAYOUT (layout), 800, 128000);

      for ( i = 0; i < 800; i+=200 )
           for ( j = 0; j < 128000; j+= 200 ) {
                sprintf( buf, "%d %ld", i, j );
                label = gtk_button_new_with_label( buf );
                gtk_layout_put( GTK_LAYOUT( layout ), label, i, j );
           }
```

```
032
033         gtk_container_add (GTK_CONTAINER (scrolled_window), layout);
034
035         gtk_widget_show_all (dialog_window);
036 }
037
038 main( argc, argv )
039 int argc;
040 char *argv[];
041 {
042      gtk_init( &argc, &argv );
043
044      GtkLayoutDialog();
045
046      gtk_main();
047 }
```

The main() routine calls GtkLayoutDialog() to create a 200×200 dialog (lines 010 through 018). On line 020, an instance of GtkScrolledWindow (discussed earlier in this chapter) is created. Notice that both the horizontal and vertical adjustments are set to NULL; this tells the scrolled window to create its own adjustments. On line 022, an instance of GtkLayout is created. As was the case with the scrolled window, I pass a NULL for both the horizontal and vertical adjustment arguments, which tells the layout widget to create adjustments as well. When the layout widget is added to the scrolled window on line 033, the layout widget adjustments will be associated with the horizontal and vertical scrollbars managed by the scrolled window widget. On line 024, a call is made to gtk_layout_set_size() to set the virtual dimensions of the layout widget. Because the scrolled window is smaller than these dimensions, both horizontal and vertical scrollbars will always be displayed by the scrolled window widget.

Finally, on lines 026 through 031, we create a number of button widgets and add them as children of the layout widget by making calls to gtk_layout_add(). There are four buttons on each row and a total of 640 rows. Each button is separated both vertically and horizontally by 200 pixels.

This is all you need to do to manage a set of widgets as children of a layout widget. GtkLayout will respond to scrollbar changes based on where the scrollbar location is and will command the correct child widgets to draw themselves.

Handling Expose Events

You can, if need be, draw content of your own into the layout area in response to an expose event, as illustrated by the next example:

Listing 11.11 Handling Expose Events

```
#include <gtk/gtk.h>

gint
HandleExposeEvent (GtkWidget *widget, GdkEventExpose *event)
{
  GtkLayout *layout;

  gint i,j;
  gint imin, imax, jmin, jmax;
```

```
010
011     layout = GTK_LAYOUT(widget);
012
013     imin = (layout->xoffset + event->area.x) / 10;
014     imax = (layout->xoffset + event->area.x + event->area.width + 9) / 10;
015
016     jmin = (layout->yoffset + event->area.y) / 10;
017     jmax = (layout->yoffset + event->area.y + event->area.height + 9) / 10;
018
019     gdk_window_clear_area (widget->window, event->area.x, event->area.y,
020             event->area.width, event->area.height);
021
022     for (i=imin; i<imax; i++)
023       for (j=jmin; j<jmax; j++)
024         if ((i+j) % 2)
025           gdk_draw_rectangle(layout->bin_window, widget->style->black_gc,
026             TRUE, 10*i - layout->xoffset, 10*j - layout-yoffset,
027             1+i%10, 1+j%10);
028     return TRUE;
029   }
030
031   void
032   GtkLayoutDialog()
033   {

...

059         gtk_widget_set_events(layout, GDK_EXPOSURE_MASK);
060         gtk_signal_connect(GTK_OBJECT (layout), "expose_event",
061             GTK_SIGNAL_FUNC (HandleExposeEvent), NULL);
062
063         gtk_layout_set_size(GTK_LAYOUT (layout), 1600, 128000);
064
065         gtk_widget_show_all(dialog_window);
066   }
067
068   main( argc, argv )
069   int argc;
070   char *argv[];
071   {
072     gtk_init( &argc, &argv );
073
074     GtkLayoutDialog();
075     gtk_main();
076   }
```

The steps followed by main() and GtkLayoutDialog() are exactly the same as in the previous example, with the exception that expose events are solicited on the layout widget on lines 059 through 061 of this last listing. It is within the expose_event signal function, HandleExposeEvent(), that drawing by the application will take place. As you can see, the event argument passed to the callback is coerced to a GdkEventExpose pointer; the area.x, area.y, area.width, and area.height fields tell you what portion of the window (e.g., the 200×200 window in our case) is in need of redrawing. If the user is scrolling the area up by 10 pixels, you might see the following values: area.x = 0, area.y = 190 (I'm conveniently ignoring the area consumed by the horizontal scrollbar), area.width = 200 (ignoring the vertical scrollbar) and area.height = 10. If the user is scrolling down by 10 pixels, the area fields will be the same except area.y will be set to 0. Your application can choose to redraw the entire window content and ignore the event data just described, but it is usually more efficient to redraw only what is in need of redrawing as opposed to redrawing the entire window contents, whenever possible.

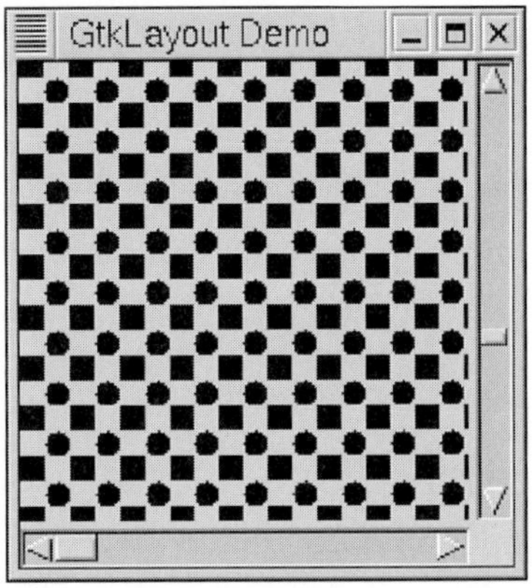

Figure 11.38 Handling Expose Events

Other data important to the expose event includes the bin_window, xoffset, and yoffset fields of the layout widget (passed as the first argument to the expose signal function, which I have cast to an instance of GtkLayout to get at these fields). The bin_window field is the window into which the content should be drawn by your expose event function. The xoffset and yoffset fields specify the current viewport into the virtual area managed by the layout widget (in this example, the area is 16000×128000). To draw your content correctly, you must map the virtual area to the area that was exposed by the user. In the following program, alternating rows of 10×10 rectangles and arcs are drawn in response to an expose event. Within each row, only every other graphic is drawn (see Figure 11.38). The user can position a scrollbar at an arbitrary location; it is up to the application to draw only those arcs and rectangles that fall in the area that was exposed. Here's the program listing that implements this:

Listing 11.12 Handling Expose Events

```
#include <gtk/gtk.h>

gint
HandleExposeEvent (GtkWidget *widget, GdkEventExpose *event)
{
  GtkLayout *layout;

  gint i,j;
  char buf[128];
  gint imin, imax, jmin, jmax;

  layout = GTK_LAYOUT (widget);

  // compute loop ranges

  imin = (layout->xoffset + event->area.x) / 10;
```

```
    imax = (layout->xoffset + event->area.x + event->area.width + 9) / 10;

    jmin = (layout->yoffset + event->area.y) / 10;
    jmax = (layout->yoffset + event->area.y + event->area.height + 9) / 10;

    // clear the area that was exposed

    gdk_window_clear_area (widget->window, event->area.x, event->area.y,
     event->area.width, event->area.height);

    for (i=imin; i<imax; i++)
      for (j=jmin; j<jmax; j++)
        if ( (i + j) % 2 == 0 ) // draw every other arc/rectangle on a line
             if ( j % 2 == 0 ) // even lines rectangles, others get arcs
                     gdk_draw_rectangle(layout->bin_window,
                             widget->style->black_gc, TRUE,
                             10*i - layout->xoffset,
                             10*j - layout->yoffset, 10, 10);
             else
                     gdk_draw_arc(layout->bin_window,
                             widget->style->black_gc, TRUE,
                             10*i - layout->xoffset,
                             10*j - layout->yoffset, 10, 10,
                             0, 360 * 64);
    return TRUE;
}

void
GtkLayoutDialog()
{
        GtkWidget    *dialog_window, *scrolledwindow, *layout;

        dialog_window = gtk_window_new(GTK_WINDOW_TOPLEVEL);
        gtk_window_position (GTK_WINDOW (dialog_window), GTK_WIN_POS_MOUSE);
        gtk_widget_set_usize (dialog_window, 200, 200);

        gtk_signal_connect (GTK_OBJECT (dialog_window), "destroy",
                GTK_SIGNAL_FUNC(gtk_widget_destroyed), &dialog_window);

        gtk_window_set_title (GTK_WINDOW (dialog_window), "GtkLayout Demo");
        gtk_container_border_width (GTK_CONTAINER (dialog_window), 0);

        scrolledwindow = gtk_scrolled_window_new (NULL, NULL);

        gtk_container_add (GTK_CONTAINER (dialog_window), scrolledwindow);

        layout = gtk_layout_new (NULL, NULL);
        gtk_container_add (GTK_CONTAINER (scrolledwindow), layout);

        // set the scrollbar step sizes to 10 pixels

        GTK_LAYOUT (layout)->hadjustment-step_increment = 10.0;
        GTK_LAYOUT (layout)->vadjustment-step_increment = 10.0;

        // solicit expose events on the layout widget

        gtk_widget_set_events (layout, GDK_EXPOSURE_MASK);
```

```
        gtk_signal_connect (GTK_OBJECT (layout), "expose_event",
            GTK_SIGNAL_FUNC (HandleExposeEvent), NULL);

        gtk_layout_set_size (GTK_LAYOUT (layout), 1600, 128000);

        gtk_widget_show_all (dialog_window);
}

main( argc, argv )
int argc;
char *argv[];
{
        gtk_init( &argc, &argv );

        GtkLayoutDialog();
        gtk_main();
}
```

Setting and Getting the Layout Adjustment Objects

All of the preceding examples used the horizontal and vertical adjustment objects created by GtkLayout. This was done because we passed NULL as arguments to gtk_layout_new(). We can retrieve the horizontal and vertical adjustment objects that were created by the layout widget by calling gtk_layout_get_hadjustment() and gtk_layout_get_vadjustment(), respectively:

```
GtkAdjustment *
gtk_layout_get_hadjustment(GtkLayout *layout);

GtkAdjustment *
gtk_layout_get_vadjustment(GtkLayout *layout);
```

Both functions take an instance of GtkLayout as their only argument and return the adjustment object being requested. You can use gtk_layout_set_hadjustment() to set or change the horizontal adjustment of a layout widget:

```
void
gtk_layout_set_hadjustment(GtkLayout *layout,
      GtkAdjustment *adjustment);
```

To set the vertical adjustment, call gtk_layout_set_vadjustment():

```
void
gtk_layout_set_vadjustment(GtkLayout *layout,
      GtkAdjustment *adjustment);
```

Both functions accept a layout widget and an adjustment object as arguments.

Layout Widgets: A Final Example

I will conclude this section by presenting the source for an example that shows how the adjustment objects of a widget can be used to control the viewport of a layout widget. In the earlier examples, the viewport into the area managed by a layout widget was controlled by a scrolled window widget to which the layout widget was added as a child. In this example, I will use a pair of spin button widgets to control what area managed by the layout widget is visible. A spin button widget creates an adjustment object that can be used as either the horizontal or vertical adjustment of a layout widget.

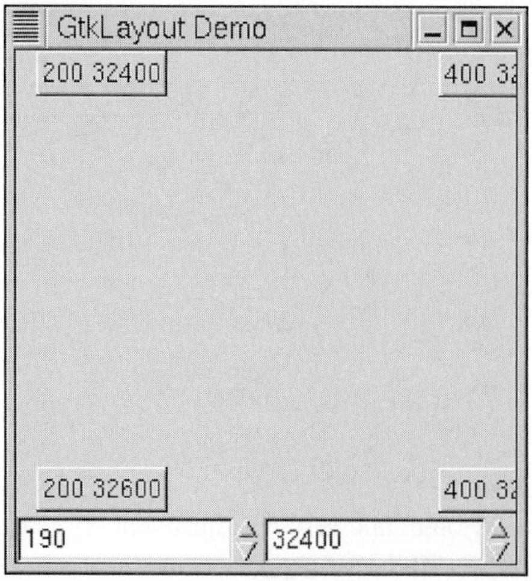

Figure 11.39 Controlling Scroll Position with Spin Buttons

Figure 11.39 illustrates the client. Together, the spin buttons specify the x and y coordinates of the origin of a view into the area being managed by the layout widget. As the value of either spin button changes, the layout widget will receive a value_changed signal from the corresponding adjustment object. The layout widget will handle this signal. The end result is that the layout widget children corresponding to the area selected by the user will draw themselves and become visible to the user.

Listing 11.13 Using Spin Buttons to Control Layout Widget Scrolling

```
#include <gtk/gtk.h>

void
GtkLayoutDialog()
{
      GtkWidget *layout, *spinner, *scrolled_window, *button, *vbox,
           *hbox, *dialog_window;
      GtkAdjustment *adj1, *adj2;
      char buf[32];
      int i, j;

      dialog_window = gtk_window_new(GTK_WINDOW_TOPLEVEL);
      gtk_window_position (GTK_WINDOW (dialog_window), GTK_WIN_POS_MOUSE);
      gtk_widget_set_usize( GTK_WIDGET( dialog_window ), 200, 200 );

      gtk_signal_connect (GTK_OBJECT (dialog_window), "destroy",
           GTK_SIGNAL_FUNC(gtk_widget_destroyed), &dialog_window);

      gtk_window_set_title (GTK_WINDOW (dialog_window), "GtkLayout Demo");
      gtk_container_border_width (GTK_CONTAINER (dialog_window), 0);

      vbox = gtk_vbox_new( FALSE, 0 );
```

```
023         gtk_container_add (GTK_CONTAINER (dialog_window), vbox);
024
025         layout = gtk_layout_new( NULL, NULL );
026
027         gtk_layout_set_size (GTK_LAYOUT (layout), 800, 128000);
028
029         for ( i = 0; i < 800; i+=200 )
030              for ( j = 0; j < 128000; j+= 200 ) {
031                      sprintf( buf, "%d %ld", i, j );
032                      button = gtk_button_new_with_label( buf );
033                      gtk_layout_put( GTK_LAYOUT( layout ), button, i, j );
034              }
035
036         gtk_box_pack_start(GTK_BOX(vbox), layout, TRUE, TRUE, 0);
037
038         hbox = gtk_hbox_new( FALSE, 0 );
039         gtk_box_pack_end(GTK_BOX(vbox), hbox, FALSE, FALSE, 0);
040
041         adj1 = (GtkAdjustment *) gtk_adjustment_new (400, 1.0, 800, 10.0,
042              100.0, 0.0);
043         spinner = gtk_spin_button_new (adj1, 0, 0);
044         gtk_spin_button_set_wrap (GTK_SPIN_BUTTON (spinner), TRUE);
045         gtk_box_pack_start (GTK_BOX (hbox), spinner, TRUE, TRUE, 0);
046
047         adj2 = (GtkAdjustment *) gtk_adjustment_new (64000, 1.0, 128000,
048              10.0, 100.0, 0.0);
049         spinner = gtk_spin_button_new (adj2, 0, 0);
050         gtk_spin_button_set_wrap (GTK_SPIN_BUTTON (spinner), TRUE);
051         gtk_box_pack_start (GTK_BOX (hbox), spinner, TRUE, TRUE, 0);
052
053         gtk_layout_set_hadjustment( GTK_LAYOUT( layout ), adj1 );
054         gtk_layout_set_vadjustment( GTK_LAYOUT( layout ), adj2 );
055
056         gtk_widget_show_all (dialog_window);
057 }
058
059 main( argc, argv )
060 int argc;
061 char *argv[];
062 {
063         gtk_init( &argc, &argv );
064
065         GtkLayoutDialog();
066
067         gtk_main();
068 }
```

In this example, the layout widget is being managed by a vertical box widget. No widgets in its containment hierarchy provide scrollbars, in contrast to the situation we saw in earlier examples in which the layout widget was being parented by a scrolled window. On lines 041 through 045, we create the adjustment object and spin button widget for the x component, and on lines 047 through 051 the same steps are performed, this time for the y component. On lines 053 and 054, the horizontal and vertical adjustments of the layout widget are set to the adjustments controlled by the spin button widgets. The net effect is that when the user changes the spin button values, the adjustment objects will fire a value_changed signal, which the layout widget will handle, causing the view of the layout widget to change as required.

Summary

In this chapter, we continued the look at container widgets that was started in Chapter 10. A paned widget (GtkPaned, GtkVPaned, and GtkHPaned) can be used to segment a dialog or window into two user-resizable areas separated vertically (GtkVPaned) or horizontally (GtkHPaned). A packer widget (GtkPacker) is a seldom-used widget that implements a layout policy very similar to the Tcl/Tk packer widget. Developers porting applications from Tcl/Tk to C/C++ and Gtk+ may find GtkPacker valuable. Developers who are not familiar with Tcl/Tk should probably stick with GtkBox, which was described in Chapter 10.

A frame widget (GtkFrame) places a labeled frame around its only child. Frames are an effective way to group related dialog content and to visually separate that content from other content in the dialog. A frame can be given a descriptive label that describes its content. Adding a label to a frame will make your dialogs easier for users to learn and use. A related widget also discussed in this chapter, GtkAspectFrame, enforces a fixed aspect ratio on the size of the frame. A table widget (GtkTable) arranges its children in a grid consisting of NxM cells.

We also examined toolbar widgets. A toolbar widget (GtkToolbar) manages a set of buttons that a user can click on to activate application tasks or to bring up application dialogs. For many users, toolbars provide an easier and more intuitive way to access the features of an application than the alternatives, such as selecting an item from a menu. Toolbars support icons, labels, and tooltips, all of which can be controlled by the application developer. A handle-box widget (GtkHandleBox) is often used to parent a toolbar widget. A handle-box widget provides a grip or handle that can be used by the application to detach the handle box from its attachment point in its container or parent and drag the handle box to the desktop.

An event box (GtkEventBox) provides an X window for widgets that do not create an X window of their own. Event boxes allow widgets without their own X window to receive and process events they would normally not receive. A layout widget (GtkLayout) is similar to GtkFixed, which was described in Chapter 10. The main difference between a layout widget and a fixed widget is that a layout widget can have an infinite size.

An important widget described in this chapter was GtkScrolledWindow. A scrolled window widget provides a viewport into a child widget that users can navigate using scrollbars. Using a scrolled window is rather simple; create the scrolled window widget, create the child it is to manage, and add the child to the scrolled window widget. GtkScrolledWindow automatically draws scrollbars based on an application-specified scrolling policy and reacts to scrollbar movement by causing the child widget to redraw its content in an appropriate manner.

CHAPTER

12

TREES

In this chapter, I introduce three widget classes: GtkTree, GtkTreeItem, and GtkCTree. The first two classes, GtkTree and GtkTreeItem, are introduced together in the first section. The reason for combining the discussion of GtkTree and GtkTreeItem is that you really can't use either of these classes without knowing something about the other. Following the general discussion of GtkTree and GtkTreeItem, I will present the API of each of these classes separately. The chapter then closes with a look at GtkCTree.

Why Use Trees?

A tree widget is similar to a list (GtkList and GtkCList)—both can be used to display a set of items that can be selected from by a user. Trees are more powerful than lists because they give the programmer the ability to organize data in ways that lists simply do not allow, and they give the end user more control over how much data is displayed at any given time. This isn't to say that you should always use trees instead of lists in your application. If you are displaying a short list of items, then trees are probably overkill. If, however, you are displaying data that can be represented as a hierarchy (e.g., a company phone book or the contents of a filesystem), or you are displaying data that can be organized as categories, or you are displaying aggregate data, then a tree will often be the best choice. The following example illustrates a situation for which the use of a tree is, I believe, preferred over the use of a list.

Say we must display the names of animals that live in the ocean, and the data we are working with contains mammals, invertebrates, and fish. An example of using a list to display such data is shown in Figure 12.1. Some of the animals listed are familiar; most readers will recognize that a Great White Shark is a fish, for example. But what is a Thornback? Is it a fish, or a mammal, or an invertebrate? It would be impractical for the application displaying this list to ask the user to select a fish because the user interface does not provide sufficient information for the user to make such a selection.

To solve this problem, we can organize our list as a tree, as shown in Figure 12.2. Here I have placed each animal into one of three categories: Mammals, Fish, and Invertebrates. When displayed as a tree, it is obvious to the user that a Thornback is a type of fish. By organizing items into categories, I have effectively reduced the number of items that the user must view to make a selection. A user can selectively show or hide categories, reducing the amount of content displayed by the control and making it easier for the user to locate a particular entry and make a selection.

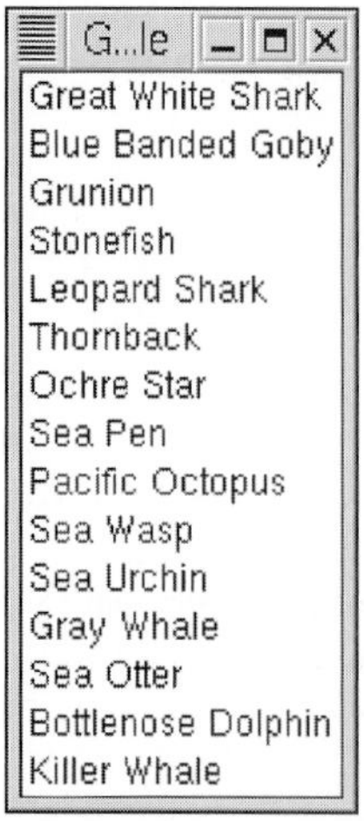

Figure 12.1 Displaying Items in a List

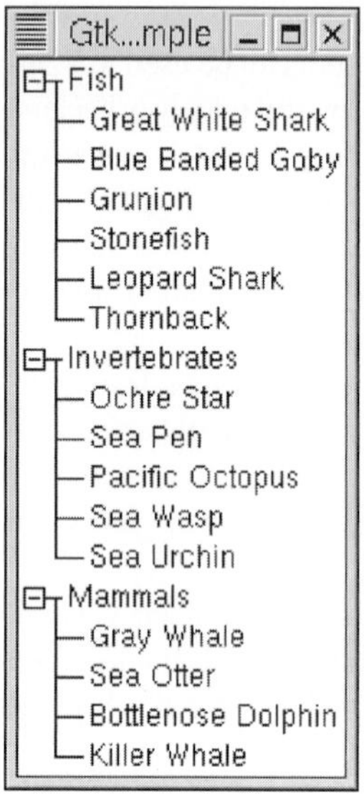

Figure 12.2 Organizing Items in a Tree

Some of you may be thinking that a multicolumn list (GtkCList) can be used to display each type of animal (see Chapter 6, "Lists"). This is correct, of course, but for the user to easily select a fish from the list, the application would need to sort the data by type (fish) or provide some way for the user to display only the fish data in the list. GtkCList is capable of sorting data by a specified column. It does not provide a way for rows to be shown or hidden by the user based on their content, although you can devise a way to do this on your own in your application, if you like.

To further illustrate how aggregate data can be displayed in a tree, consider the following code, which is used by our application to store data about ocean-dwelling animals. First some constants are defined to represent the various types of animal:

```
#define FISH_TYPE 0
#define INVERTEBRATE_TYPE 1
#define MAMMAL_TYPE 2
```

We then define a data type that can be used to hold information about each animal stored:

```
typedef struct _animal {
        unsigned char type; // e.g., FISH_TYPE
        char name[ MAXNAME ]; // e.g., "Great White Shark"
        unsigned char dangerous; // If 1, considered dangerous
        unsigned char edible; // If 1, probably tastes good
} OceanAnimal;
```

Finally, we use the preceding to define an array that contains data about the sea life we are interested in:

```
static OceanAnimal myAnimalData[] = {
        { FISH_TYPE, "Great White Shark", 1, 0 },
        { FISH_TYPE, "Blue Banded Goby", 0, 0 },
        { FISH_TYPE, "Grunion", 0, 1 },
        { FISH_TYPE, "Stonefish", 1, 0 },
        { FISH_TYPE, "Leopard Shark", 0, 0 },
        { FISH_TYPE, "Thornback", 0, 0 },
        { INVERTEBRATE_TYPE, "Ochre Star", 0, 0 },
        { INVERTEBRATE_TYPE, "Sea Pen", 0, 0 },
        { INVERTEBRATE_TYPE, "Pacific Octopus", 0, 1 },
        { INVERTEBRATE_TYPE, "Sea Wasp", 1, 0 },
        { INVERTEBRATE_TYPE, "Sea Urchin", 0, 1 },
        { MAMMAL_TYPE, "Gray Whale", 0, 0 },
        { MAMMAL_TYPE, "Sea Otter", 0, 0 },
        { MAMMAL_TYPE, "Bottlenose Dolphin", 0, 0 },
        { MAMMAL_TYPE, "Killer Whale", 1, 0 },
};
```

The preceding data structure stores a range of information about each animal (we could obviously store more data, but the preceding is sufficient for our purposes). The list displayed in Figure 12.2 does not provide enough information for a user to respond to an application request to "select a dangerous fish." The tree shown in Figure 12.3, however, facilitates such a query by organizing each fish, invertebrate, and mammal into a subcategory that conveys the needed information to the user.

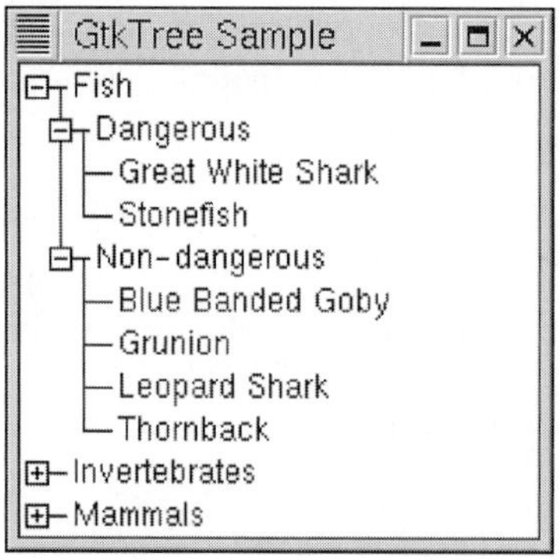

Figure 12.3 Dangerous and Non-dangerous Animals

Using GtkTree and GtkTreeItem

Now that we know why trees are useful, we can take a closer look at how to construct them.

A tree is a recursive structure that consists of nodes. The root of a tree consists of a single node. A node displays data (for example, a label or pixmap) and may act as the root node of a subtree. Figure 12.4 illustrates a tree consisting of four subtrees that are rooted at nodes 1, 4, 5, and 9. Nodes that do not act as the root of a subtree are known as leaf nodes. Nodes 2, 3, 6, 7, 8, 10, and 11 are all leaf nodes.

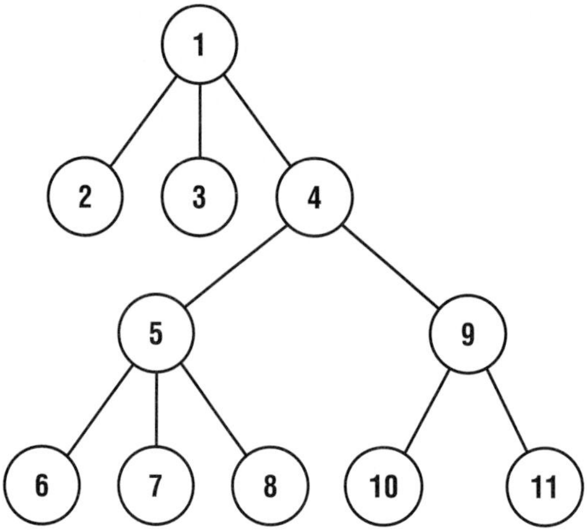

Figure 12.4 Structure

In a GtkTree instance, root nodes might be used to represent categories (e.g., Fish, Invertebrate, Mammal, Dangerous and Non-dangerous are categories). Leaf nodes, in this case, store data (Great White Shark, Thornback, and Ochre Star are all represented by leaf nodes in a tree). Figure 12.3 illustrates. Root nodes might also represent objects, with each node below these root nodes containing detailed information that describes the node immediately above it. In some cases, this information might be stored as a combination of root and leaf nodes.

For each node in a tree (except the topmost root node), your application must create an instance of GtkTreeItem. Thus, there are $n - 1$ tree items in every tree, where n is the total number of nodes in the tree.

For each subtree of a tree (including the topmost root node), your application must create an instance of GtkTree. For example, to create the tree in Figure 12.4, your application must instantiate four instances of GtkTree.

To add a subtree to a tree, you allocate an instance of GtkTree and attach it to a leaf node (an instance of GtkTreeItem) in the parent subtree. In Figure 12.4, for example, the subtree rooted at node 9 was attached to the tree by attaching it to leaf node 9 in the subtree rooted at node 5, and the subtree at node 5 was attached to the tree by attaching it to leaf node 5 in the subtree rooted at node 1.

An Example

If the previous five paragraphs did not make much sense to you, the following example should help clarify things. You might want to reread the preceding paragraphs, however, after studying the example, to ensure that the concepts introduced here are understood fully.

The following pseudocode shows how to create the tree shown in Figure 12.3. The notation used resembles (but is not) the C programming language. The functions prefixed with "gtk_" will be explained when I present the GtkTree and GtkTreeItem APIs later in this chapter. All variables are of type GtkWidget *. Because the example is lengthy, I will only show how to create the subtrees rooted at the Fish node in the root tree. The construction of the Invertebrate and Mammal subtrees follows along similar lines and is left as an exercise to the reader.

```
GtkWidget *
CreateTree()
{
        // Create the root node

        root = gtk_tree_new();

        // Add three child nodes, one for fish, one for invertebrates, and
        // one for mammals. At this point, these nodes are leaf nodes. Add
        // each of these nodes as children of the "root" node.

        node_fish = gtk_tree_item_new_with_label( "Fish" );
        gtk_tree_append(GTK_TREE(root), node_fish);

        node_inv = gtk_tree_item_new_with_label( "Invertebrates" );
        gtk_tree_append(GTK_TREE(root), node_inv);

        node_mammal = gtk_tree_item_new_with_label( "Mammals" );
        gtk_tree_append(GTK_TREE(root), node_mammal);

        // Next, create the subtrees below Fish, Invertebrates, and Mammals,
        // and attach them to the root tree.
```

```
        // Create the fish subtree

        subtree = CreateFishTree();

        // Attach the fish subtree

        gtk_tree_item_set_subtree(GTK_TREE_ITEM( node_fish ), subtree);

        // Create the invertebrate subtree

        subtree = CreateInvertebrateTree();

        // Attach the subtree

        gtk_tree_item_set_subtree(GTK_TREE_ITEM( node_inv ), subtree);

        // Create the mammal subtree

        subtree = CreateMammalTree();

        // Attach the subtree

        gtk_tree_item_set_subtree(GTK_TREE_ITEM( node_mammal ), subtree);

        // Return the tree

        return ( root );
}

GtkWidget *
CreateFishTree()
{
        // Create a subtree, to be attached by the caller to the "Fish"
        // node in the root tree

        fishtree = gtk_tree_new();

        // Create children of the subtree. One child is labeled "Dangerous",
        // the other is labeled "Non-dangerous"

        node_dangerous = gtk_tree_item_new_with_label("Dangerous");
        gtk_tree_append(GTK_TREE(fishtree), node_dangerous);

        node_nondangerous = gtk_tree_item_new_with_label("Non-dangerous");
        gtk_tree_append(GTK_TREE(fishtree), node_nondangerous);

        // Now, create the subtrees below Dangerous and Non-dangerous, and
        // attach them to the Fish tree at the appropriate nodes.

        // Create the subtree
```

```
        subtree = CreateDangerousFishTree();

        // Attach the subtree

        gtk_tree_item_set_subtree(GTK_TREE_ITEM(node_dangerous), subtree);

        // Create the subtree

        subtree = CreateNonDangerousFishTree();

        // Attach the subtree

        gtk_tree_item_set_subtree(GTK_TREE_ITEM(node_nondangerous), subtree);

        return( fishtree );
}

GtkWidget *
CreateDangerousFishTree()
{
        // Create a subtree, to be attached by the caller to the "Dangerous"
        // node in the "Fish" subtree

        dangeroustree = gtk_tree_new();

        // Create a couple of dangerous fish and add
        // them to the dangerous tree

        node = gtk_tree_item_new_with_label("Great White Shark");
        gtk_tree_append(GTK_TREE(dangeroustree), node);

        node = gtk_tree_item_new_with_label("Stonefish");
        gtk_tree_append(GTK_TREE(dangeroustree), node);

        return( dangeroustree );
}

GtkWidget *
CreateNonDangerousFishTree()
{
        // Create a subtree, to be attached by the caller to the
        // "Non-dangerous" node in the "Fish" subtree

        nondangeroustree = gtk_tree_new();

        // Create some non-dangerous fish and add
        // them to the non-dangerous tree

        node = gtk_tree_item_new_with_label("Blue Banded Goby");
        gtk_tree_append(GTK_TREE(nondangeroustree), node);
```

```
        node = gtk_tree_item_new_with_label("Grunion");
        gtk_tree_append(GTK_TREE(nondangeroustree), node);

        node = gtk_tree_item_new_with_label("Leopard Shark");
        gtk_tree_append(GTK_TREE(nondangeroustree), node);

        node = gtk_tree_item_new_with_label("Thornback");
        gtk_tree_append(GTK_TREE(nondangeroustree), node);

        return( nondangeroustree );
}
```

The following source code fully implements the tree shown in Figure 12.3. Note that the source code is less modular than the pseudocode just shown. However, the concepts are the same, and if you understand the preceding code, you should have little trouble with the following code.

Listing 12.1 Example Using GtkTree

```
#include <gtk/gtk.h>

static GtkWidget*
make_tree (GtkWidget *window)
{
   GtkWidget *root, *subtree, *node, *node1, *node2, *node3,
           *node_fish, *node_inv, *node_mammal;

   // create the root node of the tree.

   root = gtk_tree_new();
   gtk_widget_show( root );

   // create Fish, Invertebrates, and Mammals children of the root
   // node

   node_fish = node = gtk_tree_item_new_with_label("Fish");
   gtk_tree_append(GTK_TREE(root), node_fish);
   gtk_widget_show(node_fish);

   node_inv = node = gtk_tree_item_new_with_label("Invertebrates");
   gtk_tree_append(GTK_TREE(root), node_inv);
   gtk_widget_show(node_inv);

   node_mammal = node = gtk_tree_item_new_with_label("Mammals");
   gtk_tree_append(GTK_TREE(root), node_mammal);
   gtk_widget_show(node_mammal);

   // create the dangerous and non-dangerous subtrees of the Fish
   // node

   subtree = gtk_tree_new();
```

```
    gtk_widget_show( subtree );

    gtk_tree_item_set_subtree(GTK_TREE_ITEM( node_fish ), subtree);

    node1 = node = gtk_tree_item_new_with_label("Dangerous");
    gtk_tree_append(GTK_TREE(subtree), node);
    gtk_widget_show(node);

    node2 = node = gtk_tree_item_new_with_label("Non-dangerous");
    gtk_tree_append(GTK_TREE(subtree), node);
    gtk_widget_show(node);

    // create the dangerous subtree of the Fish tree

    subtree = gtk_tree_new();
    gtk_widget_show( subtree );

    gtk_tree_item_set_subtree(GTK_TREE_ITEM( node1 ), subtree);

    // Create the leaf nodes of the dangerous subtree of the Fish
    // tree

    node = gtk_tree_item_new_with_label("Great White Shark");
    gtk_tree_append(GTK_TREE(subtree), node);
    gtk_widget_show(node);

    node = gtk_tree_item_new_with_label("Stonefish");
    gtk_tree_append(GTK_TREE(subtree), node);
    gtk_widget_show(node);

    // create the non-dangerous subtree of the Fish tree

    subtree = gtk_tree_new();
    gtk_widget_show( subtree );

    gtk_tree_item_set_subtree(GTK_TREE_ITEM( node2 ), subtree);

    // Create the leaf nodes of the non-dangerous subtree of the Fish
    // tree

    node = gtk_tree_item_new_with_label("Blue Banded Goby");
    gtk_tree_append(GTK_TREE(subtree), node);
    gtk_widget_show(node);

    node = gtk_tree_item_new_with_label("Grunion");
    gtk_tree_append(GTK_TREE(subtree), node);
    gtk_widget_show(node);

    node = gtk_tree_item_new_with_label("Leopard Shark");
    gtk_tree_append(GTK_TREE(subtree), node);
    gtk_widget_show(node);
```

```

    node = gtk_tree_item_new_with_label("Thornback");
    gtk_tree_append(GTK_TREE(subtree), node);
    gtk_widget_show(node);

    // create the dangerous and non-dangerous subtrees of the
    // Invertebrates node

    subtree = gtk_tree_new();
    gtk_widget_show( subtree );

    gtk_tree_item_set_subtree(GTK_TREE_ITEM( node_inv ), subtree);

    node1 = node = gtk_tree_item_new_with_label("Dangerous");
    gtk_tree_append(GTK_TREE(subtree), node);
    gtk_widget_show(node);

    node2 = node = gtk_tree_item_new_with_label("Non-dangerous");
    gtk_tree_append(GTK_TREE(subtree), node);
    gtk_widget_show(node);

    // create the dangerous subtree of the Invertebrates tree

    subtree = gtk_tree_new();
    gtk_widget_show( subtree );

    gtk_tree_item_set_subtree(GTK_TREE_ITEM( node1 ), subtree);

    // create the leaf nodes of the dangerous Invertebrates tree

    node = gtk_tree_item_new_with_label("Sea Wasp");
    gtk_tree_append(GTK_TREE(subtree), node);
    gtk_widget_show(node);

    // create the non-dangerous subtree of the Invertebrates tree

    subtree = gtk_tree_new();
    gtk_widget_show( subtree );

    gtk_tree_item_set_subtree(GTK_TREE_ITEM( node2 ), subtree);

    // create the leaf nodes of the non-dangerous Invertebrates tree

    node = gtk_tree_item_new_with_label("Ochre Star");
    gtk_tree_append(GTK_TREE(subtree), node);
    gtk_widget_show(node);

    node = gtk_tree_item_new_with_label("Sea Pen");
    gtk_tree_append(GTK_TREE(subtree), node);
    gtk_widget_show(node);

```

```
    node = gtk_tree_item_new_with_label("Pacific Octopus");
    gtk_tree_append(GTK_TREE(subtree), node);
    gtk_widget_show(node);

    node = gtk_tree_item_new_with_label("Sea Urchin");
    gtk_tree_append(GTK_TREE(subtree), node);
    gtk_widget_show(node);

    // create the dangerous and non-dangerous subtrees of the
    // Mammals node

    subtree = gtk_tree_new();
    gtk_widget_show( subtree );

    gtk_tree_item_set_subtree(GTK_TREE_ITEM( node_mammal ), subtree);

    node1 = node = gtk_tree_item_new_with_label("Dangerous");
    gtk_tree_append(GTK_TREE(subtree), node);
    gtk_widget_show(node);

    node2 = node = gtk_tree_item_new_with_label("Non-dangerous");
    gtk_tree_append(GTK_TREE(subtree), node);
    gtk_widget_show(node);

    // create the dangerous subtree of the Mammals tree

    subtree = gtk_tree_new();
    gtk_widget_show( subtree );

    gtk_tree_item_set_subtree(GTK_TREE_ITEM( node1 ), subtree);

    // create the leaf nodes of the dangerous Mammals tree

    node = gtk_tree_item_new_with_label("Killer Whale");
    gtk_tree_append(GTK_TREE(subtree), node);
    gtk_widget_show(node);

    // create the non-dangerous subtree of the Mammals tree

    subtree = gtk_tree_new();
    gtk_widget_show( subtree );

    gtk_tree_item_set_subtree(GTK_TREE_ITEM( node2 ), subtree);

    // create the leaf nodes of the non-dangerous Mammals tree

    node = gtk_tree_item_new_with_label("Gray Whale");
    gtk_tree_append(GTK_TREE(subtree), node);
    gtk_widget_show(node);

    node = gtk_tree_item_new_with_label("Sea Otter");
```

```
   gtk_tree_append(GTK_TREE(subtree), node);
   gtk_widget_show(node);

   node = gtk_tree_item_new_with_label("Bottlenose Dolphin");
   gtk_tree_append(GTK_TREE(subtree), node);
   gtk_widget_show(node);

   return root;
}

main( argc, argv )
int argc;
char *argv[];
{
   GtkWidget *window, *tree, *vbox;

   gtk_init( &argc, &argv );

   window = gtk_window_new(GTK_WINDOW_TOPLEVEL);
   gtk_widget_show( window );
   gtk_window_position(GTK_WINDOW (window), GTK_WIN_POS_CENTER);

   gtk_signal_connect(GTK_OBJECT (window), "destroy",
          GTK_SIGNAL_FUNC(gtk_widget_destroy), &window);

   gtk_window_set_title(GTK_WINDOW (window), "GtkTree Sample");
   gtk_container_border_width(GTK_CONTAINER (window), 0);

   tree = make_tree(window);

   vbox = gtk_vbox_new( FALSE, 0 );
   gtk_container_add(GTK_CONTAINER (window), vbox);

   gtk_box_pack_start( GTK_BOX( vbox ), tree, FALSE, FALSE, 0 );
   gtk_widget_show_all( vbox );

   gtk_main();
}
```

Now that I have explained the basics of constructing trees out of GtkTree and GtkTreeItem instances, let's take a look at the GtkTree and GtkTreeItem classes in greater detail.

GtkTree

Class Name

```
GtkTree
```

Parent Class Name

```
GtkContainer
```

Macros

Widget type macro: `GTK_TYPE_TREE`

Object to widget cast macro: `GTK_TREE(obj)`

Widget type check macro: `GTK_IS_TREE(obj)`

Miscellaneous Macros:

GTK_IS_ROOT_TREE(obj)—Returns 1 if obj is the root node of the tree to which it belongs.

GTK_TREE_ROOT_TREE(obj)—Returns the root of the tree to which obj belongs, or obj if there is no root.

GTK_TREE_SELECTION(obj)—Returns the list of currently selected items in the tree rooted at obj.

Supported Signals

Table 12.1 Signals

Signal Name	*Condition Causing Signal To Trigger*
selection_changed	The selection of some tree item has been changed.
select_child	A specific (sub)tree child has been selected.
unselect_child	A specific (sub)tree child has been unselected.

Signal Function Prototypes

```
void
selection_changed(GtkTree *tree, gpointer user_data);

void
select_child(GtkTree *tree, GtkWidget *widget, gpointer user_data);

void
unselect_child(GtkTree *tree, GtkWidget *widget, gpointer user_data);
```

Application-Level API Synopsis

Return the constant GTK_TYPE_TREE at runtime:
```
GtkType
gtk_tree_get_type(void);
```

Create a new instance of GtkTree:
```
GtkWidget *
gtk_tree_new(void);
```

Append an instance of GtkTreeItem to a subtree:
```
void
gtk_tree_append(GtkTree *tree, GtkWidget *tree_item);
```

Prepend an instance of GtkTreeItem to a subtree:
```
void
gtk_tree_prepend(GtkTree *tree, GtkWidget *tree_item);
```

Insert an instance of GtkTreeItem into a subtree:
```
void
gtk_tree_insert(GtkTree *tree, GtkWidget *tree_item, gint position);
```

Remove items from a tree:
```
void
gtk_tree_remove_items(GtkTree *tree, GList *items);
```

Remove a range of items from a subtree:
```
void
gtk_tree_clear_items(GtkTree *tree, gint start, gint end);
```

Select an item in a subtree:
```
void
gtk_tree_select_item(GtkTree *tree, gint item);
```

Unselect an item in a subtree:
```
void
gtk_tree_unselect_item(GtkTree *tree, gint item);
```

Application-Level API Synopsis (Continued)

Select the item corresponding to the specified tree widget item:

```
void
gtk_tree_select_child(GtkTree *tree, GtkWidget *tree_item);
```

Unselect the item corresponding to the specified tree widget item:

```
void
gtk_tree_unselect_child(GtkTree *tree, GtkWidget *tree_item);
```

Determine the position of a child in a subtree:

```
gint
gtk_tree_child_position(GtkTree *tree, GtkWidget *child);
```

Specify the tree selection mode:

```
void
gtk_tree_set_selection_mode(GtkTree *tree, GtkSelectionMode mode);
```

Specify the tree view mode:

```
void
gtk_tree_set_view_mode(GtkTree *tree, GtkTreeViewMode mode);
```

Specify whether tree lines are viewable or not:

```
void
gtk_tree_set_view_lines(GtkTree *tree, guint flag);
```

Class Description

In the following sections I will describe how to create an instance of GtkTree, as well as how to add and remove items from a tree. Issues related to the selections of items in a tree will be explored. I will also describe the various view modes supported by GtkTree, and the GtkTree API functions that support them.

Creating an Instance of GtkTree

An instance of GtkTree is created by making a call to gtk_tree_new():

```
GtkWidget *
gtk_tree_new(void);
```

The returned tree can be used by your application as the root node of a tree, or it can added to an existing tree as a subtree by attaching it to any tree item in the tree. An overview of trees and their construction was provided at the start of this chapter; tree items are described in the section on GtkTreeItem, which immediately follows this section.

Adding Items

Once you have created an instance of GtkTree, tree items can be created and added to the tree. The section on GtkTreeItem discusses how to create tree items. Once it has been created, a tree item can be added to a tree by calling one of the following functions: gtk_tree_append(), gtk_tree_prepend(), or gtk_tree_insert().

A tree acts as a container of tree items. Each tree item that is managed by a tree has an index that determines its placement relative to other tree items in the tree. The index of tree items must be in the range [0, *n* – 1], where *n* is the number of tree items managed by the containing tree. The tree item at index *n* – 1 will appear higher in the tree (closer to the top) than the tree item at index *n*; the tree item at index 0 will be displayed at the top of the tree, while the tree item at index *n* – 1 will be displayed at the bottom of the tree.

To append a tree item to a tree, call gtk_tree_append():

```
void
gtk_tree_append(GtkTree *tree, GtkWidget *tree_item);
```

The argument tree is the instance of GtkTree to which tree_item is being added. The index of the tree item after being added is *n*, which is the number of tree items that were in the tree prior to the append operation.

To prepend (add to the top of a tree) an instance of GtkTreeItem, you can call gtk_tree_prepend():

```
void
gtk_tree_prepend(GtkTree *tree, GtkWidget *tree_item);
```

The arguments passed to gtk_tree_prepend() are the same as those passed to gtk_tree_append(). A tree item added by gtk_tree_prepend() will become the topmost child of the tree to which it was added (i.e., its index is 0). The index of each of the remaining tree items in the tree will be increased by 1 as a result of making this call.

Finally, you can insert an instance of GtkTreeItem into a subtree at a specific location with a call to gtk_tree_insert():

```
void
gtk_tree_insert(GtkTree *tree, GtkWidget *tree_item, gint position);
```

The first two arguments are the same as those passed to gtk_tree_append() and gtk_tree_prepend(). The final argument, position, unambiguously specifies the location of the tree item, relative to other tree items contained by the tree, after gtk_tree_insert() returns. Setting position to 0 emulates a call to gtk_tree_prepend(), while setting position to -1 results in gtk_tree_insert() behaving as though gtk_tree_append() were being called instead. Passing a position argument of *m*, in the range [0, *n* – 1] causes tree items previously located at positions [*m*, *n* – 1] to increase their position in the tree by one. For example, the item that was previously located at position *m* will be located at position *m* + 1 in the tree once gtk_tree_prepend() returns.

Removing Items from a Tree

Removing items from a tree can be accomplished in one of two ways, depending on the needs of the application. In situations in which your application provides a menu item or button that the user can select or click to remove items that the user has selected from the tree (by "selected," I mean the user has clicked on one or more of the tree items using the mouse, causing them to become selected), the easiest way to remove these items is to call the function gtk_tree_remove_items() from the menu item or button callback function:

```
void
gtk_tree_remove_items(GtkTree *tree, GList *items);
```

The first argument is the instance of GtkTree from which the items are to be removed. The second argument is the list of items to remove. Where does this list of items come from? Fortunately, GtkTree provides a macro, GTK_TREE_SELECTION, which can be used to obtain a list of the selected items in a tree that can be used by gtk_tree_remove_items(). The following code illustrates:

```
GtkWidget *tree, *button;

// create a tree, add its children, etc..

tree = make_tree();

// create a "Remove" button

button = gtk_button_new_with_label( "Remove" );

// set the clicked signal function of the button. Pass the GtkTree
// instance as an argument so we can pass it to GTK_TREE_SELECTION

gtk_signal_connect(GTK_OBJECT(button), "clicked",
      GTK_SIGNAL_FUNC(remove_cb), tree);
```

The preceding code creates a tree and a button labeled Remove. The "clicked" signal function of the Remove button is set to remove_cb(). The function remove_cb is rather simple:

```
001 void
002 remove_cb(GtkWidget* w, GtkTree* tree)
003 {
004     GList* selected_list;
005
006     selected_list = GTK_TREE_SELECTION(tree);
007     gtk_tree_remove_items(tree, selected_list);
008 }
```

As you can see, deleting the selected items in a tree is as simple as calling GTK_TREE_SELECTION to obtain the list of selected tree children, as shown on line 006, and then passing this list directly to gtk_tree_remove_items(), as illustrated on line 007.

You might also want to maintain a list of tree items yourself, bypassing the need to call GTK_TREE_SELECTION. This might be useful if the user, instead of being provided a Remove button as in the preceding example, is presented with a control that represents a more abstract operation such as "Remove all animals that are considered dangerous to man." To implement such a feature, your application will need to map GtkTreeItem widget instances with the application data that these tree items represent. To give a simple example:

```
// data structure that holds the animal name, an indication of its
// danger toman, and the instance of GtkTreeItem representing the
// animal in the tree

typedef struct animal {
        gchar name[MAXNAME];                // e.g., Great White Shark
        gboolean isDangerous;               // in this case, TRUE
        GtkWidget *treeItem;                // holds the related tree item
} Animal;

...

// declare a table of animals

Animal myAnimals[] = {
{ "Great White Shark", TRUE, 0 },
{ "Grunion", FALSE, 0 },

...

};
        // create tree items for each animal, storing the resulting
        // widget in the treeItem field

        for ( i = 0; i < sizeof( myAnimals ) / sizeof( Animal ); i++ )
                myAnimals[i].treeItem =
                        gtk_tree_item_new_with_label
                                ( myAnimals[i].name );
```

The following routine can be used to iterate through the Animals data structure, creating a GList vector of animals, based on their danger to man, that can be passed to gtk_tree_remove_items() for removal from the tree:

```
GList *
GetAnimalsOfType( gboolean isDangerous )
{
   GList *list = NULL;
   int i;

   for ( i = 0; i < sizeof( myAnimals ) / sizeof( Animal ); i++ )
           if ( myAnimals[i].isDangerous == isDangerous )
                 list = g_list_prepend( list, myAnimals[i].treeItem );
```

```
    return( list );
}
```

A code snippet from the caller of this function might look like the following:

```
GList *list;
GtkWidget *tree;

// here we attempt to delete all the dangerous animals

list = GetAnimalsOfType( TRUE );
if ( list != NULL )
        gtk_tree_remove_items(GTK_TREE( tree ), list);
```

Be careful not to attempt to remove widgets that have already been removed from the tree; doing so will likely lead to a core dump or undefined behavior.

Removing Items Based on Position

You can also remove items from a (sub)tree based on their position. The function gtk_tree_clear_items() makes this possible:

```
void
gtk_tree_clear_items(GtkTree *tree, gint start, gint end);
```

tree is an instance of GtkTree, start is the position of the first element to be removed, and end is the position of the last element to be removed. start must be less than or equal to end, and both must be within the range of $[0, n - 1]$, where n is the number of tree items in the (sub)tree prior to making the call. To delete only one item, set start and end to the position of the element you want to delete. For example, to delete the third item in a subtree, you can execute the following code:

```
GtkWidget *tree;

...

gtk_tree_clear_items( GTK_TREE( tree ), 2, 2 );
```

Selecting Items

The user can select tree items from a tree by positioning the pointer over the item to be selected and clicking mouse button 1. Users can select either leaf tree items (such as Great White Shark) or tree items that represent the root of a subtree (e.g., Mammals). By default, only one item can be in the selected state at a time. Applications can, and often do, change this behavior by making a call to gtk_tree_set_selection_mode():

```
void
gtk_tree_set_selection_mode(GtkTree *tree, GtkSelectionMode mode);
```

tree is the instance of GtkTree that will be affected by the call, and mode is the selection mode that will be in effect when gtk_tree_set_selection_mode() returns. Possible mode values are listed in Table 12.2.

Table 12.2 GtkTree Selection Modes

Value	*Meaning*
GTK_SELECTION_SINGLE	One item selectable at a time (default mode)
GTK_SELECTION_BROWSE	Similar to GTK_SELECTION_SINGLE
GTK_SELECTION_MULTIPLE	More than one noncontinuous selection at a time
GTK_SELECTION_EXTENDED	Continuous selections over multiple rows possible

For more information on these modes, see gtk_list_set_selection_mode(), which is described in detail in Chapter 6.

An application can select an item in a subtree without user interaction. When might this be useful? Consider the implementation of a Select All menu item in the Edit menu. Selecting this menu item should cause all items in the tree to be selected. Or, perhaps, it might cause all items in a selected subtree to also become selected, depending on the semantics you desire. Regardless of the exact semantics adopted, clearly an operation like Select All, which is not supported by GtkTree directly, must be implemented by the application. By making a call to gtk_tree_select_item() for each item in a (sub)tree, you can implement the semantics of a Select All operation. Here is the function prototype for gtk_tree_select_item():

```
void
gtk_tree_select_item(GtkTree *tree, gint item);
```

The argument tree is an instance of GtkTree and can be either a root tree or a subtree. The argument item is the position of the tree item to be selected, in the range $[0, n - 1]$. There is no clear way to determine the number of tree items in a subtree; at least, there is no GtkTree function for doing this. To obtain the upper bound of a loop that implements a Select All operation, you might need to call the following code, which obtains the number of tree items managed by a tree by looking at the size of the list used to hold the tree items:

```
GtkWidget *tree;
gint nchildren;          // number of tree items in the tree

nchildren = g_list_length(GTK_TREE(tree)->children);

// now we can select all of the children in the subtree

for ( i = 0; i < nchildren; i++ )
       gtk_tree_select_item(GTK_TREE(tree), i );
```

Perhaps GtkTree will provide a better solution in a future release, one that better hides the implementation of GtkTree.

If you have an instance of GtkTreeItem handy, you can easily determine its position in a (sub)tree by calling gtk_tree_child_position():

```
gint
gtk_tree_child_position(GtkTree *tree, GtkWidget *child);
```

One additional point I should mention regarding gtk_tree_select_item()is that it enforces the semantics defined by the selection mode of the subtree. In other words, if the user can only select one item in the list at a time using the mouse, then your application can only select one item as well.

Unselecting an item in a subtree is largely analogous to selecting an item and can be performed by calling gtk_tree_unselect_item():

```
void
gtk_tree_unselect_item(GtkTree *tree, gint item);
```

You can select or unselect any tree item in a tree by naming the GtkTreeItem instance that implements the tree item to be (un)selected. Recall the gtk_tree_remove_items() example, previously shown, which implemented the operation “Delete all dangerous animals from the tree.” We can make use of the function that we wrote, GetAnimalsOfType(), to retrieve a list of tree item widgets based on their danger to humans, as we did before. The resulting list can then be traversed to implement the operation “Select all dangerous animals in the tree,” as shown in the following listing:

```
GList *list;
GtkWidget *tree;

// here we attempt to delete all the dangerous animals

list = GetAnimalsOfType( TRUE );
while ( list != NULL ) {
        gtk_tree_select_child(GTK_TREE( tree ),
                GTK_WIDGET(list->data));
        list = list->next;
}
```

The function gtk_tree_select_child(), which I will describe now, was used in the preceding code to perform the actual selection of tree children:

```
void
gtk_tree_select_child(GtkTree *tree, GtkWidget *tree_item);
```

Unselecting a tree item is analogous and can be performed by making a call to gtk_tree_unselect_child():

```
void
gtk_tree_unselect_child(GtkTree *tree, GtkWidget *tree_item);
```

The arguments to gtk_tree_select_child() and gtk_tree_unselect_child() are the same: tree is the (sub)tree that contains the tree item to (un)select, and tree item is the instance of GtkTreeItem that was created and added to the tree at some prior point in time.

View Modes

The view mode of a tree dictates how tree items in the tree display themselves. There are two possible modes, both of which are listed in Table 12.3.

Table 12.3 GtkTree View Modes

View Mode	*Meaning*
GTK_TREE_VIEW_LINE	Horizontal and vertical lines are drawn to make tree item relationships easier to see (default).
GTK_TREE_VIEW_ITEM	Just the tree items are drawn.

You can specify the tree view mode by passing one of the values in the preceding table to gtk_tree_set_view_mode():

```
void
gtk_tree_set_view_mode(GtkTree *tree, GtkTreeViewMode mode);
```

tree is the (sub)tree to which the mode will be applied. It appears that this function is a no-op in Gtk 1.2.

GtkTree supports one additional function that appears to be unnecessary when compared to gtk_tree_set_view_mode(), which was just described, if it were not for the fact that gtk_tree_set_view_mode() appears to be a no-op. You can call gtk_tree_set_view_lines() to control the display of lines:

```
void
gtk_tree_set_view_lines(GtkTree *tree, guint flag);
```

The default for view lines is TRUE, so there is really no need to call it if, as in most applications, you find the display of lines acceptable. Figures 12.5 and 12.6 illustrate the differences.

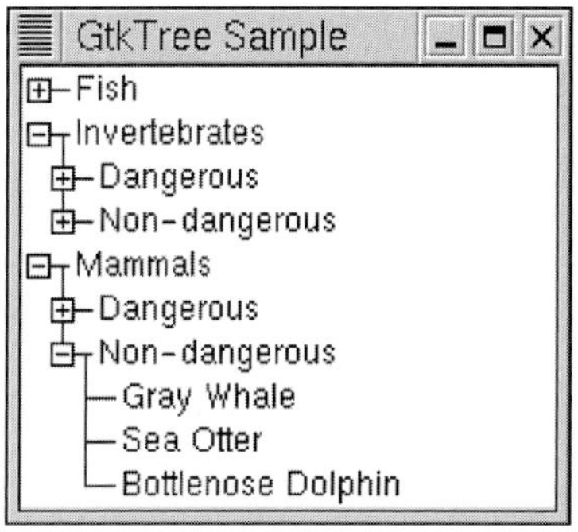

Figure 12.5 Viewing Lines

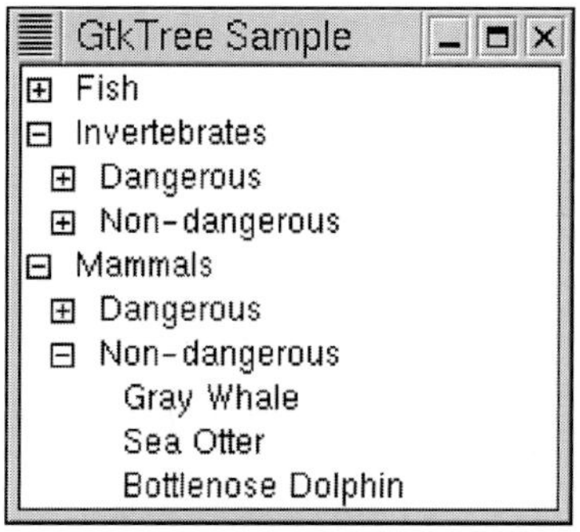

Figure 12.6 Hiding Lines

GtkTreeItem

Class Name

`GtkTreeItem`

Parent Class Name

`GtkItem`

Macros

Widget type macro: `GTK_TYPE_TREE_ITEM`

Object to widget cast macro: `GTK_TREE_ITEM(obj)`

Widget type check macro: `GTK_IS_TREE_ITEM(obj)`

Supported Signals

Table 12.4 Signals

Signal Name	*Condition Causing Signal to Trigger*
expand	A tree item has been expanded.
collapse	A tree item has been collapsed.

Signal Function Prototypes

```
void
expand(GtkTreeItem *treeitem, gpointer user_data);

void
collapse(GtkTreeItem *treeitem, gpointer user_data);
```

Application-Level API Synopsis

Retrieve the constant GTK_TYPE_TREE_ITEM at runtime:

```
GtkType
gtk_tree_item_get_type(void);
```

Create a new tree item:

```
GtkWidget *
gtk_tree_item_new(void);
```

Create a new tree item with a label:

```
GtkWidget *
gtk_tree_item_new_with_label(gchar *label);
```

Associate a subtree (an instance of GtkTree) with a tree item in its parent:

```
void
gtk_tree_item_set_subtree(GtkTreeItem *tree_item, GtkWidget *subtree);
```

Detach the subtree that has been previously attached to the specified tree item:

```
void
gtk_tree_item_remove_subtree(GtkTreeItem *tree_item);
```

Select a tree item:

```
void
gtk_tree_item_select(GtkTreeItem *tree_item);
```

Unselect a tree item:

```
void
gtk_tree_item_deselect(GtkTreeItem *tree_item);
```

Expand a tree item, showing the first level of the subtree that exists below it:

```
void
gtk_tree_item_expand(GtkTreeItem *tree_item);
```

Collapse a tree item, hiding the entire subtree that exists below it:

```
void
gtk_tree_item_collapse(GtkTreeItem *tree_item);
```

Class Description

GtkTreeItem, as I discussed at the start of this chapter, is tightly coupled to the GtkTree class. This is because GtkTree is a container class that was specifically designed to manage GtkTreeItem instances. If you attempt to add a child to a tree that is not an instance of GtkTreeItem (using the gtk_tree_append() function, for example), GtkTree will display an error, and the operation will not be performed.

Like trees, tree items are also containers. Unlike trees, however, tree items are flexible in terms of the types of children they will manage. All of the examples presented so far in this chapter have created tree items that manage instances of GtkLabel. However, you can (within reason) create tree items that manage a variety of widget types, including other layout widgets such as GtkBox, GtkPixmap, and so forth. In this section, I will show how you can add GtkPixmap and GtkBox children to a tree.

Creating a Tree Item Widget

Tree items are as easily created as instances of any other Gtk+ widget class. To create a new tree item with a label (probably the most common type of tree item is one that simply displays text), you can call gtk_tree_item_new_with_label():

```
GtkWidget *
gtk_tree_item_new_with_label(gchar *label);
```

The argument label is a C-language, NULL-terminated ASCII string. The following code creates a tree item that displays the text “Echinodermata”:

```
GtkWidget *widget;

widget = gtk_tree_item_new( "Echinodermata" );
```

Tree items can be created without text labels by calling gtk_tree_item_new():

```
GtkWidget *
gtk_tree_item_new(void);
```

A tree item created without a label is essentially a container in need of a child widget. Knowing that most applications will want to instantiate GtkLabel widgets for this purpose, GtkTreeItem provides gtk_tree_item_new_with_label() as a convenience routine. For some applications, labels are not enough. This is particularly true when items in the tree have a visual and textual representation.

Displaying colors from a fixed palette in a subtree provides a good example of this. Suppose your tree is designed to display all the red colors present in the X11 rgb.txt file. Figure 12.7 illustrates how this data might be displayed in a tree that uses standard label-based tree items.

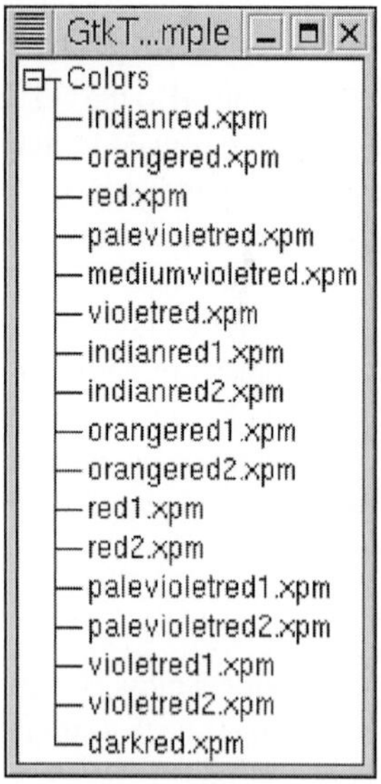

Figure 12.7 Displaying Color Names in a Tree

It should be obvious that these names do not sufficiently convey to the user the visual distinction that exists between OrangeRed and OrangeRed2. We might solve this problem by providing a button below the tree, labeled Display Color, that opens up a color selection dialog and displays the color currently selected in the tree by the user based on its RGB value. However, this solution is a tedious one for the user; a better solution would involve displaying the color as a part of the tree item itself.

Our first attempt will illustrate the basics of how a tree item can be made to manage a widget other than an instance of GtkLabel. In this example, instead of displaying a text label, we choose to display a 16×16 image as a child of the tree item, to better convey the color than a name might. To do this, we create a tree item with a call to gtk_tree_item_new(), create a pixmap widget that contains the image we want to display, and then make the pixmap widget a child of the tree item. The following code illustrates:

Listing 12.2 First Attempt at Display Colors in a Tree

```
#include <gtk/gtk.h>

// data structure to hold information about our colors

typedef struct _colorent {
   unsigned char red;       // red component of rgb value
   unsigned char green;     // green component of rgb value
   unsigned char blue;      // blue component of rgb value
   char *label;             // label to display for tree item
   char *filename;          // filename that stores the image
} colorent;

// table describing the colors we will be displaying
```

```

colorent colortable[] = {
{ 205,  92,  92, "indian red", "indianred.xpm"},
{ 255,  69,   0, "orange red", "orangered.xpm"},
{ 255,   0,   0, "red", "red.xpm"},
{ 219, 112, 147, "pale violet red", "palevioletred.xpm"},
{ 199,  21, 133, "medium violet red", "mediumvioletred.xpm"},
{ 208,  32, 144, "violet red", "violetred.xpm"},
{ 255, 106, 106, "IndianRed1", "indianred1.xpm"},
{ 238,  99,  99, "IndianRed2", "indianred2.xpm"},
{ 255,  69,   0, "OrangeRed1", "orangered1.xpm"},
{ 238,  64,   0, "OrangeRed2", "orangered2.xpm"},
{ 255,   0,   0, "red1", "red1.xpm"},
{ 238,   0,   0, "red2", "red2.xpm"},
{ 255, 130, 171, "PaleVioletRed1", "palevioletred1.xpm"},
{ 238, 121, 159, "PaleVioletRed2", "palevioletred2.xpm"},
{ 255,  62, 150, "VioletRed1", "violetred1.xpm"},
{ 238,  58, 140, "VioletRed2", "violetred2.xpm"},
{ 139,   0,   0, "dark red", "darkred.xpm"},
};

static GtkWidget*
new_pixmap (char *filename, GdkWindow *window, GdkColor *background)
{
   GtkWidget *wpixmap;
   GdkPixmap *pixmap;
   GdkBitmap *mask;

   pixmap = gdk_pixmap_create_from_xpm(window, &mask, background,
           filename);
   wpixmap = gtk_pixmap_new (pixmap, mask);

   return wpixmap;
}

static GtkWidget *
make_tree(GtkWidget *window)
{
   GtkWidget *root, *image, *subtree, *node, *node_colors;
   int i;

   // create the root node of the tree.

   root = gtk_tree_new();
   gtk_widget_show( root );

   node_colors = node = gtk_tree_item_new_with_label("Colors");
   gtk_tree_append(GTK_TREE(root), node_colors);
   gtk_widget_show(node_colors);

   subtree = gtk_tree_new();
   gtk_widget_show( subtree );

   gtk_tree_item_set_subtree(GTK_TREE_ITEM( node_colors ), subtree);

   for ( i = 0; i < sizeof( colortable ) / sizeof( colorent ); i++ ) {
           node = gtk_tree_item_new();
```

```
071             image = new_pixmap(colortable[i].filename,
072                     window->window, &window->style->bg[GTK_STATE_NORMAL]);
073             gtk_container_add(GTK_CONTAINER(node), image);
074             gtk_tree_append(GTK_TREE(subtree), node);
075             gtk_widget_show_all(node);
076         }
077
078         return root;
079     }
```

On lines 005 through 011, I define a type that can be used to hold information about the items stored in the tree. Of importance for this example is the filename field. This field is passed as an argument to new_pixmap(), defined on lines 035 through 047, which creates an instance of GtkPixmap based on its contents. The tree items are created and added to the tree on lines 069 through 076. For each entry in the color table defined on lines 015 through 033, we create a new tree item (line 070), create a new pixmap widget (line 071), and add the pixmap widget to the tree item as its child with a call to gtk_container_add() (line 073). The result is displayed in Figure 12.8.

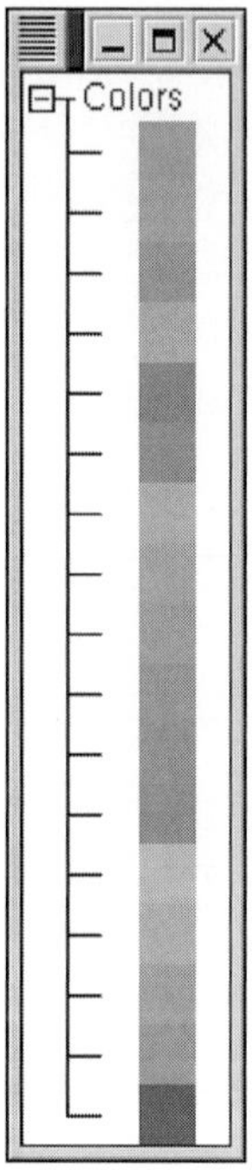

Figure 12.8 Displaying Colors in a Tree

One thing that is rather unappealing about the tree in Figure 12.8 is that the pixmap image is not well aligned with the tree structure. It would be nice if the image were closer to the tree structure and made the tree easier for users to interact with. To control the placement of the tree item child, we might choose to instantiate a container widget, add the pixmap as a child of the container widget, and then add the container widget as a child of the tree item. A horizontal box (GtkHBox) widget is able to solve our problem. The loop on lines 069 through 076 can be recoded as follows:

```
    for ( i = 0; i < sizeof( colortable ) / sizeof( colorent ); i++ ) {
            node = gtk_tree_item_new();
            image = new_pixmap(colortable[i].filename,
                 window->window, &window->style->bg[GTK_STATE_NORMAL]);
001         hbox = gtk_hbox_new( FALSE, 0 );
002         gtk_container_add(GTK_CONTAINER(node), hbox);
003         gtk_box_pack_start( GTK_BOX( hbox ), image, FALSE, FALSE, 0 );
            gtk_tree_append(GTK_TREE(subtree), node);
            gtk_widget_show_all(node);
    }
```

On line 001, we create an instance of GtkHBox. On line 002, the horizontal box is made the child of the tree item, not the pixmap. On line 003, the pixmap is made a child of the hbox, which aligns it to the far left edge of the area managed by the box. The result is in Figure 12.9.

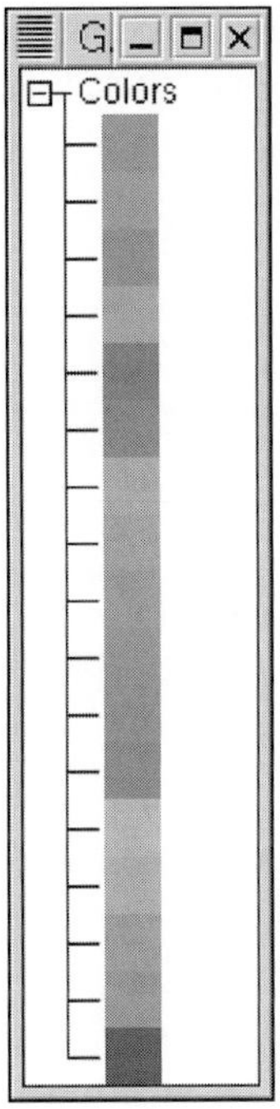

Figure 12.9 Displaying Colors in a Tree Using a GtkHBox Widget

One final change and we will be finished with our example. After looking at Figure 12.9, you might agree with me in thinking that the best solution of all would be to show both a label and a pixmap for each color displayed in the tree. It turns out that it is easy to modify the code we have developed so far in order to do this. Since the child of the tree item is a horizontal box, it is trivial to add additional children to the horizontal box instance. Here, we decide to add an instance of GtkLabel:

```
for ( i = 0; i < sizeof( colortable ) / sizeof( colorent ); i++ ) {
        node = gtk_tree_item_new();
        image = new_pixmap(colortable[i].filename,
              window->window, &window->style->bg[GTK_STATE_NORMAL]);
001     label = gtk_label_new( colortable[i].label );
        hbox = gtk_hbox_new( FALSE, 0 );
002     gtk_box_set_spacing( GTK_BOX( hbox ), 10 );
        gtk_container_add(GTK_CONTAINER(node), hbox);
        gtk_box_pack_start( GTK_BOX( hbox ), image, FALSE, FALSE, 0 );
003     gtk_box_pack_start( GTK_BOX( hbox ), label, FALSE, FALSE, 0 );
        gtk_tree_append(GTK_TREE(subtree), node);
        gtk_widget_show_all(node);
}
```

I will just discuss those lines that were added. On line 001, an instance of GtkLabel was created. The label text is supplied by the label field of the colortable data structure. On line 002, I set the box spacing to 10 pixels so that the pixmap and label are given sufficient horizontal separation. On line 003, I simply added the label widget as a child of the horizontal box, immediately following the pixmap. The result is shown in Figure 12.10.

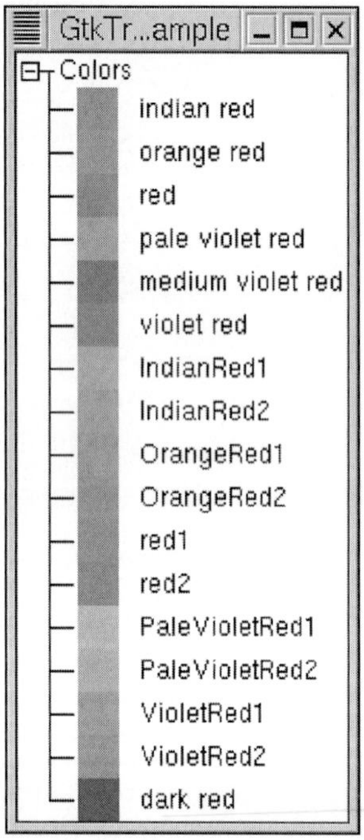

Figure 12.10 Displaying Colors and Color Names in a Tree

Subtrees

Tree items can do two things. First, they are capable of displaying content, typically a label. This has been illustrated several times in this chapter. Second, they can act as anchor points for subtrees. A tree item that just displays a label or other widget can be selected by the user. A tree item that anchors a subtree can be selected as well, or it can be opened to reveal the first level of content in the subtree that it anchors. Generally speaking, the name you give the tree item to which a subtree is attached should provide the user with a good indication of the content that will be found in the subtree once the subtree is opened.

Subtrees are trees. You create them by calling gtk_tree_new() and populate them by creating tree items that you attach to the tree by calling one of the GtkTree functions: gtk_tree_append(), gtk_tree_prepend(), or gtk_tree_insert(). You attach a subtree onto a parent tree by calling gtk_tree_item_set_subtree():

```
void
gtk_tree_item_set_subtree(GtkTreeItem *tree_item, GtkWidget *subtree);
```

The argument subtree is an instance of GtkTree, the contents of which are arbitrary. (It can contain subtrees, for example; the structure of the tree is not relevant.) The argument tree_item is the tree item in the parent tree that will act as the anchor for the subtree being added.

A tree item can only act as an anchor for one subtree. It is an error to call gtk_tree_item_set_subtree(), passing a tree_item that anchors a subtree prior to the call.

You can detach a subtree from a tree item with gtk_tree_item_remove_subtree(). This makes the subtree eligible for being attached to some other tree item as well as making the tree item eligible for anchoring some other subtree. The function prototype for gtk_tree_item_remove_subtree() is as follows:

```
void
gtk_tree_item_remove_subtree(GtkTreeItem *tree_item);
```

The argument tree_item is the tree item that anchors the subtree to be removed. If the tree item does not currently anchor a subtree, the call is a no-op.

Tree Operations

The remaining functions in the GtkTreeItem API allow an application to perform the following tasks:

- Select and deselect tree items
- Expand and collapse a subtree anchored by a specific tree item

Selecting and Deselecting Tree Items. To select a tree item, call gtk_tree_item_select():

```
void
gtk_tree_item_select(GtkTreeItem *tree_item);
```

The argument tree_item is the tree item to be selected. To deselect (or unselect) a tree item, call gtk_tree_item_deselect():

```
void
gtk_tree_item_deselect(GtkTreeItem *tree_item);
```

In this case, the argument tree_item is the tree item that will be unselected once the call returns. The advantage to using gtk_tree_item_select() or gtk_tree_item_deselect() is that using either of these does not require you to know the tree within which the tree item is located or its position relative to other tree items managed by its parent tree. This is in contrast to gtk_tree_select_item(), gtk_tree_unselect_item(), gtk_tree_select_child(), and gtk_tree_unselect_child(), which require more information to perform the same task. (Yes, I agree with you that the use of "deselect" by GtkTreeItem and "unselect" by GtkTree is confusing.)

Expanding and Collapsing Tree Items. Your application can also expand and collapse a subtree (if any) anchored by a tree item by calling gtk_tree_item_expand() and gtk_tree_item_collapse(), respectively:

```
void
gtk_tree_item_expand(GtkTreeItem *tree_item);

void
gtk_tree_item_collapse(GtkTreeItem *tree_item);
```

Only the first level below the tree item is exposed by gtk_tree_item_expand(). Collapsing a tree item will cause all subtrees that descend from the tree anchored by tree_item to collapse as well.

The following code shows how to write a recursive function that expands all of the subtrees that descend from a given tree.

```
001 void
002 ShowAll( GtkTree *tree )
003 {
004     GList *list;
005     GtkTree *subtree;
006
007     list = tree->children;
008     while ( list ) {
009             subtree = (GtkTree *) GTK_TREE_ITEM(list->data)->subtree;
010             if ( subtree ) {
011                     gtk_tree_item_expand(
012                             GTK_TREE_ITEM( subtree->tree_owner ) );
013                     ShowAll( subtree );
014             }
015             list = list->next;
016     }
017 }
```

Essentially, this function grabs the list of children (tree items) managed by the tree (line 007) and, for each child, checks to see if it anchors a subtree (line 010). If so, the tree item that anchors that subtree is expanded (line 011), and then ShowAll() is called recursively to expand the contents of the subtree that was just expanded. You can pass a subtree at any level to start the ball rolling; to expand the entire tree, pass the tree root.

A function like ShowAll() is rather dangerous to write because it presumes that the internal structure of GtkTree and GtkTreeItem remains the same in releases that follow the one for which the code was developed. Should you find yourself developing general-purpose code such as the preceding, which might be useful to other developers, it might be a good time to contact the Gtk+ owners (or, more specifically, the author of the widget for which the code you are developing pertains) and explore with him or her the possibility of contributing your code to the Gtk+ effort. This will allow others to benefit from your changes and will help ensure that implementation-specific changes are being dealt with by Gtk+ as future versions are developed.

GtkCTree

Class Name

```
GtkCTree
```

Parent Class Name

```
GtkCList
```

Macros

Widget type macro: `GTK_TYPE_CTREE`

Object to widget cast macro: `GTK_CTREE(obj)`

Widget type check macro: `GTK_IS_CTREE(obj)`

Supported Signals

Table 12.5 Signals

Signal Name	*Condition Causing Signal to Trigger*
tree_select_row	The row was selected by the user.
tree_unselect_row	The row was unselected by the user.
tree_expand	The subtree was expanded to show children.
tree_collapse	The subtree was collapsed to hide children.

Table 12.5 Signals (Continued)

Signal Name	*Condition Causing Signal to Trigger*
tree_move	The subtree was moved to some other location.
change_focus_row_expansion	Keyboard expansion/collapse of the selected tree has occurred (see text).

Signal Function Prototypes

```
void
tree_select_row(GtkCTree *ctree, GList *node, gint column,
     gpointer user_data);

void
tree_unselect_row(GtkCTree *ctree, GList *node, gint column,
     gpointer user_data);

void
tree_expand(GtkCTree *ctree, GList *node, gpointer user_data);

void
tree_collapse(GtkCTree *ctree, GList *node, gpointer user_data);

void
tree_move(GtkCTree *ctree, GList *node, GList *new_parent,
     GList *new_sibling, gpointer user_data);

void
change_focus_row_expansion(GtkCTree *ctree,
      GtkCTreeExpansionType expansion, gpointer user_data);
```

Supported Arguments

Prefix: `GtkCTree::`

Table 12.6 GtkCTree Arguments

Name	*Type*	*Permissions*
n_columns	GTK_TYPE_UINT	GTK_ARG_READWRITE | GTK_ARG_CONSTRUCT_ ONLY
tree_column	GTK_TYPE_UINT	GTK_ARG_READWRITE | GTK_ARG_CONSTRUCT_ ONLY

Table 12.6 GtkCTree Arguments (Continued)

Name	*Type*	*Permissions*
indent	GTK_TYPE_UINT	GTK_ARG_READWRITE
spacing	GTK_TYPE_UINT	GTK_ARG_READWRITE
show_stub	GTK_TYPE_BOOL	GTK_ARG_READWRITE
line_style	GTK_TYPE_CTREE_LINE_STYLE	GTK_ARG_READWRITE
expander_style	GTK_TYPE_CTREE_EXPANDER_STYLE	GTK_ARG_READWRITE

Application-Level API Synopsis

Return the constant GTK_TYPE_CTREE at runtime:

```
GtkType
gtk_ctree_get_type(void);
```

Create an instance of GtkCTree with the specified number of columns and titles:

```
GtkWidget *
gtk_ctree_new_with_titles(gint columns, gint tree_column,
        gchar *titles[]);
```

Create an instance of GtkCTree with the specified number of columns. This is equivalent to calling gtk_ctree_new_with_titles() with a NULL titles argument:

```
GtkWidget *
gtk_ctree_new(gint columns, gint tree_column);
```

Create a new node and add it to the tree:

```
GtkCTreeNode *
gtk_ctree_insert_node(GtkCTree *ctree, GtkCTreeNode *parent,
        GtkCTreeNode *sibling, gchar *text[], guint8 spacing,
        GdkPixmap *pixmap_closed, GdkBitmap *mask_closed,
        GdkPixmap *pixmap_opened, GdkBitmap *mask_opened,
        gboolean is_leaf, gboolean expanded);
```

Remove a node from the tree:

```
void
gtk_ctree_remove_node(GtkCTree *ctree, GtkCTreeNode *node);
```

Walk the tree, calling func(ctree, node, data) for each node in the tree. The traversal order is post-order:

```
void
gtk_ctree_post_recursive(GtkCTree *ctree, GtkCTreeNode *node,
        GtkCTreeFunc func, gpointer data);
```

Application-Level API Synopsis (Continued)

Walk the tree, calling func(ctree, node, data) for each node in the tree. The traversal order is post-order, and only includes nodes to the specified depth:

```
void
gtk_ctree_post_recursive_to_depth(GtkCTree *ctree,
        GtkCTreeNode *node, gint depth, GtkCTreeFunc func,
        gpointer data);
```

Walk the tree, calling func(ctree, node, data) for each node in the tree. The traversal order is pre-order:

```
void
gtk_ctree_pre_recursive(GtkCTree *ctree, GtkCTreeNode *node,
        GtkCTreeFunc func, gpointer data);
```

Walk the tree, calling func(ctree, node, data) for each node in the tree. The traversal order is pre-order and only includes nodes to the specified depth:

```
void
gtk_ctree_pre_recursive_to_depth(GtkCTree *ctree,
        GtkCTreeNode *node, gint depth, GtkCTreeFunc func,
        gpointer data);
```

Return TRUE if the node is viewable:

```
gboolean
gtk_ctree_is_viewable(GtkCTree *ctree, GtkCTreeNode *node);
```

Return TRUE if the specified child is a sibling or child of the specified node in the tree:

```
gboolean
gtk_ctree_find(GtkCTree *ctree, GtkCTreeNode *node,
        GtkCTreeNode *child);
```

Return TRUE if the specified node is a parent of the specified child:

```
gboolean
gtk_ctree_is_ancestor(GtkCTree *ctree, GtkCTreeNode *node,
        GtkCTreeNode *child);
```

Find the first child or sibling of the specified node by row data:

```
GtkCTreeNode *
gtk_ctree_find_by_row_data(GtkCTree *ctree, GtkCTreeNode *node,
        gpointer data);
```

Find all children or siblings of the specified node by row data:

```
GList *
gtk_ctree_find_all_by_row_data(GtkCTree *ctree, GtkCTreeNode *node,
        gpointer data);
```

Find the first child or sibling of the specified node by row data, using a custom comparison function:

```
GtkCTreeNode *
gtk_ctree_find_by_row_data_custom(GtkCTree *ctree,
        GtkCTreeNode *node, gpointer data, GCompareFunc func);
```

Application-Level API Synopsis (Continued)

Find all children or siblings of the specified node by row data, using a custom compare function:

```
GList *
gtk_ctree_find_all_by_row_data_custom(GtkCTree *ctree,
        GtkCTreeNode *node, gpointer data, GCompareFunc func);
```

Return TRUE if the specified x, y coordinate corresponds to an expander box in the tree:

```
gboolean
gtk_ctree_is_hot_spot(GtkCTree *ctree, gint x, gint y);
```

Reposition the specified node in the tree so that it has the specified parent and sibling:

```
void
gtk_ctree_move(GtkCTree *ctree, GtkCTreeNode *node,
        GtkCTreeNode *new_parent, GtkCTreeNode *new_sibling);
```

Expand the specified node, displaying its immediate children:

```
void
gtk_ctree_expand(GtkCTree *ctree, GtkCTreeNode *node);
```

Recursively expand the specified node, displaying all nodes that descend from it:

```
void
gtk_ctree_expand_recursive(GtkCTree *ctree, GtkCTreeNode *node);
```

Recursively expand the specified node to the specified depth:

```
void
gtk_ctree_expand_to_depth(GtkCTree *ctree, GtkCTreeNode *node,
        gint depth);
```

Collapse the specified node, hiding its immediate children:

```
void
gtk_ctree_collapse(GtkCTree *ctree, GtkCTreeNode *node);
```

Recursively collapse the specified node and all nodes that descend from it:

```
void
gtk_ctree_collapse_recursive(GtkCTree *ctree, GtkCTreeNode *node);
```

Recursively collapse the specified node to the specified depth:

```
void
gtk_ctree_collapse_to_depth(GtkCTree *ctree, GtkCTreeNode *node,
        gint depth);
```

If the node is expanded, collapse it; otherwise, expand it:

```
void
gtk_ctree_toggle_expansion(GtkCTree *ctree, GtkCTreeNode *node);
```

Recursively expand or collapse the node, depending on its previous state:

```
void
gtk_ctree_toggle_expansion_recursive(GtkCTree *ctree,
        GtkCTreeNode *node);
```

Application-Level API Synopsis (Continued)

Select the row corresponding to the specified node:

```
void
gtk_ctree_select(GtkCTree *ctree, GtkCTreeNode *node);
```

Recursively select the row corresponding to the specified node and all of its children:

```
void
gtk_ctree_select_recursive(GtkCTree *ctree, GtkCTreeNode *node);
```

Unselect the row corresponding to the specified node:

```
void
gtk_ctree_unselect(GtkCTree *ctree, GtkCTreeNode *node);
```

Recursively unselect the row corresponding to the specified node and all of its children:

```
void
gtk_ctree_unselect_recursive(GtkCTree *ctree, GtkCTreeNode *node);
```

Set the text for the specified node and column:

```
void
gtk_ctree_node_set_text(GtkCTree *ctree, GtkCTreeNode *node,
        gint column, const gchar *text);
```

Set the pixmap for the specified node and column:

```
void
gtk_ctree_node_set_pixmap(GtkCTree *ctree, GtkCTreeNode *node,
        gint column, GdkPixmap *pixmap, GdkBitmap *mask);
```

Set the text and pixmap for the specified node and column:

```
void
gtk_ctree_node_set_pixtext(GtkCTree *ctree, GtkCTreeNode *node,
        gint column, const gchar *text, guint8 spacing,
        GdkPixmap *pixmap, GdkBitmap *mask);
```

Change the attributes of the specified node:

```
void
gtk_ctree_set_node_info(GtkCTree *ctree, GtkCTreeNode *node,
        const gchar *text, guint8 spacing, GdkPixmap *pixmap_closed,
        GdkBitmap *mask_closed, GdkPixmap *pixmap_opened,
        GdkBitmap *mask_opened, gboolean is_leaf, gboolean expanded);
```

Offset the display of data corresponding to the specified column in the specified node by the specified number of pixels:

```
void
gtk_ctree_node_set_shift(GtkCTree *ctree, GtkCTreeNode *node,
        gint column, gint vertical, gint horizontal);
```

Make the specified node in the tree selectable or not:

```
void
gtk_ctree_node_set_selectable(GtkCTree *ctree, GtkCTreeNode *node,
        gboolean selectable);
```

Application-Level API Synopsis (Continued)

Determine whether the specified node can be selected or not:

```
gboolean
gtk_ctree_node_get_selectable(GtkCTree *ctree, GtkCTreeNode *node);
```

Determine the type of data stored by a node in the specified column:

```
GtkCellType
gtk_ctree_node_get_cell_type(GtkCTree *ctree, GtkCTreeNode *node,
        gint column);
```

Retrieve the text from the specified node, if any:

```
gint
gtk_ctree_node_get_text(GtkCTree *ctree, GtkCTreeNode *node,
        gint column, gchar **text);
```

Retrieve the pixmap from the specified node, if any:

```
gint
gtk_ctree_node_get_pixmap(GtkCTree *ctree, GtkCTreeNode *node,
        gint column, GdkPixmap **pixmap, GdkBitmap **mask);
```

Retrieve the pixmap and the text from the specified node, if any:

```
gint
gtk_ctree_node_get_pixtext(GtkCTree *ctree, GtkCTreeNode *node,
        gint column, gchar **text, guint8 *spacing,
        GdkPixmap **pixmap, GdkBitmap **mask);
```

Retrieve attributes and data from the specified node:

```
gint
gtk_ctree_get_node_info(GtkCTree *ctree, GtkCTreeNode *node,
        gchar **text, guint8 *spacing, GdkPixmap **pixmap_closed,
        GdkBitmap **mask_closed, GdkPixmap **pixmap_opened,
        GdkBitmap **mask_opened, gboolean *is_leaf,
        gboolean *expanded);
```

Set style data for the specified node:

```
void
gtk_ctree_node_set_row_style(GtkCTree *ctree, GtkCTreeNode *node,
        GtkStyle *style);
```

Retrieve style data from the specified node:

```
GtkStyle *
gtk_ctree_node_get_row_style(GtkCTree *ctree, GtkCTreeNode *node);
```

Set style data for the specified column:

```
void
gtk_ctree_node_set_cell_style(GtkCTree *ctree, GtkCTreeNode *node,
        gint column, GtkStyle *style);
```

Application-Level API Synopsis (Continued)

Get style data for the specified column:
```
GtkStyle *
gtk_ctree_node_get_cell_style(GtkCTree *ctree, GtkCTreeNode *node,
        gint column);
```

Set the foreground color of the specified node:
```
void
gtk_ctree_node_set_foreground(GtkCTree *ctree, GtkCTreeNode *node,
        GdkColor *color);
```

Set the background color of the specified node:
```
void
gtk_ctree_node_set_background(GtkCTree *ctree, GtkCTreeNode *node,
        GdkColor *color);
```

Set the data attribute of the specified row:
```
void
gtk_ctree_node_set_row_data(GtkCTree *ctree, GtkCTreeNode *node,
        gpointer data);
```

Set the data attribute and destroy function of the specified row:
```
void
gtk_ctree_node_set_row_data_full(GtkCTree *ctree,
       GtkCTreeNode *node, gpointer data, GtkDestroyNotify destroy);
```

Get the data attribute of the specified row:
```
gpointer
gtk_ctree_node_get_row_data(GtkCTree *ctree, GtkCTreeNode *node);
```

Scroll the tree so that the specified node and column are visible:
```
void
gtk_ctree_node_moveto(GtkCTree *ctree, GtkCTreeNode *node,
        gint column, gfloat row_align, gfloat col_align);
```

Return the visibility of the specified node. Options are GTK_VISIBILITY_NONE, GTK_VISIBILITY_PARTIAL, or GTK_VISIBILITY_FULL:
```
GtkVisibility
gtk_ctree_node_is_visible(GtkCTree *ctree, GtkCTreeNode *node);
```

Specify the indentation of tree lines, in pixels (default is 20 pixels):
```
void
gtk_ctree_set_indent(GtkCTree *ctree, gint indent);
```

Specify the spacing of nodes in the tree, in pixels:
```
void
gtk_ctree_set_spacing(GtkCTree *ctree, gint spacing);
```

Turn on or off the display of the tree line stub (see text):
```
void
gtk_ctree_set_show_stub(GtkCTree *ctree, gboolean show_stub);
```

Application-Level API Synopsis (Continued)

Set the tree line style (see text):

```
void
gtk_ctree_set_line_style(GtkCTree *ctree, GtkCTreeLineStyle
line_style);
```

Specify the expander style. Options are GTK_CTREE_EXPANDER_NONE, GTK_CTREE_EXPANDER_SQUARE, GTK_CTREE_EXPANDER_TRIANGLE, or GTK_CTREE_EXPANDER_CIRCULAR:

```
void
gtk_ctree_set_expander_style(GtkCTree *ctree,
        GtkCTreeExpanderStyle expander_style);
```

Specify a compare procedure for drag and drop (see text):

```
void
gtk_ctree_set_drag_compare_func(GtkCTree *ctree,
        GtkCTreeCompareDragFunc cmp_func);
```

Sort the tree starting at the specified node (or the focus row if node is set to NULL):

```
void
gtk_ctree_sort_node(GtkCTree *ctree, GtkCTreeNode *node);
```

Sort all nodes recursively from the specified node (or the entire tree if node is set to NULL):

```
void
gtk_ctree_sort_recursive(GtkCTree *ctree, GtkCTreeNode *node);
```

Class Description

GtkCTree is similar to GtkTree, previously described, in very much the same way that GtkCList is similar to GtkList. GtkList, as you may recall, displays single-column lists of arbitrary widget data, while GtkCList displays multicolumn lists of text and provides support for sorting. Such is the case with GtkTree and GtkCTree. GtkTree allows your application to display single-column trees that contain arbitrary widget data, while GtkCTree supports the display of multicolumn trees of text data and, like GtkCList, supports sorting.

The similarity of GtkCTree and GtkCList is no accident; GtkCList is the parent class of GtkCTree. Because of this, you can make use of the GtkCList API when working with an instance of GtkCTree. GtkCList functions that take an instance of GtkCList can be used by coercing the GtkCTree instance into an instance of GtkCList with the GTK_CLIST macro. For example:

```
GtkWidget *ctree;
gint size, column;

...
```

```
column = 0;
size = gtk_clist_optimal_column_width(GTK_CLIST(ctree), column);
```

The preceding code returns the size needed to display the data in column 0 of a GtkCTree instance without that data being clipped.

In some cases, GtkCTree provides functions that are similar to ones provided by GtkCList. I recommend, in such cases, that you use the versions provided by GtkCTree. I will discuss how some of the GtkCList functions can be used with instances of GtkCTree. Refer to the discussion of GtkCList in Chapter 6 for additional details on the GtkCList API.

GtkCTree, like GtkCList, defines a large number of functions, which can make GtkCTree rather overwhelming for first-time users. To soften the blow, I will approach GtkCTree initially by way of example, developing three small applications that illustrate the bulk of what you will need to know to make use of GtkCTree in your own applications. A fourth application will show how to add sorting capabilities to sample application three. Once I finish presenting the sample applications, I will describe the remainder of the GtkCTree API for those of you who are interested. However, for most of you, the sample applications presented here will provide most of what you need to know to work with GtkCTree.

A First Example

Sample application one illustrates a technique that can be used to create the same tree that I developed earlier in this chapter with GtkTree (see Figure 12.3 and the accompanying source-code listing). As it turns out, I believe it is actually easier to create this tree with GtkCTree than to create it with GtkTree. The code for sample application one is as follows:

Listing 12.3 First GtkCTree Example (See Figure 12.3)

```
#include <gtk/gtk.h>

static GtkWidget *
make_tree ( void )
{
   GtkWidget *root;
   GtkCTreeNode *parent, *node;
   gchar *text[1];

   // create the root node of the tree.

   root = gtk_ctree_new( 1, 0 );

   // Fish

   text[0] = "Fish";
   parent = gtk_ctree_insert_node(GTK_CTREE(root),
           NULL, NULL, text, 5, NULL, NULL, NULL, NULL,
           FALSE, TRUE);

   text[0] = "Dangerous";
   node = gtk_ctree_insert_node(GTK_CTREE(root),
           parent, NULL, text,
```

```
                5, NULL, NULL, NULL, NULL, FALSE, TRUE);

    text[0] = "Great White Shark";
    gtk_ctree_insert_node(GTK_CTREE(root),
                node, NULL, text,
                5, NULL, NULL, NULL, NULL, TRUE, TRUE);

    text[0] = "Stonefish";
    gtk_ctree_insert_node(GTK_CTREE(root),
                node,  NULL, text,
                5, NULL, NULL, NULL, NULL, TRUE, TRUE);

    text[0] = "Non-Dangerous";
    node = gtk_ctree_insert_node(GTK_CTREE(root),
                parent,  NULL, text,
                5, NULL, NULL, NULL, NULL, FALSE, TRUE);

    text[0] = "Blue Banded Goby";
    gtk_ctree_insert_node(GTK_CTREE(root),
                node, NULL, text,
                5, NULL, NULL, NULL, NULL, TRUE, TRUE);

    text[0] = "Grunion";
    gtk_ctree_insert_node(GTK_CTREE(root),
                node,  NULL, text,
                5, NULL, NULL, NULL, NULL, TRUE, TRUE);

    text[0] = "Leopard Shark";
    gtk_ctree_insert_node(GTK_CTREE(root),
                node, NULL, text,
                5, NULL, NULL, NULL, NULL, TRUE, TRUE);

    text[0] = "Thornback";
    gtk_ctree_insert_node(GTK_CTREE(root),
                node, NULL, text,
                5, NULL, NULL, NULL, NULL, TRUE, TRUE);

    // Invertebrates

    text[0] = "Invertebrates";
    parent = gtk_ctree_insert_node(GTK_CTREE(root),
                NULL, NULL, text,
                5, NULL, NULL, NULL, NULL, FALSE, TRUE);

    text[0] = "Dangerous";
    node = gtk_ctree_insert_node(GTK_CTREE(root),
                parent, NULL, text,
                5, NULL, NULL, NULL, NULL, FALSE, TRUE);

    text[0] = "Sea Wasp";
    gtk_ctree_insert_node(GTK_CTREE(root),
```

```
                node, NULL, text,
                5, NULL, NULL, NULL, NULL, TRUE, TRUE);

        text[0] = "Non-Dangerous";
        node = gtk_ctree_insert_node(GTK_CTREE(root),
                parent, NULL, text,
                5, NULL, NULL, NULL, NULL, FALSE, TRUE);

        text[0] = "Ochre Star";
        gtk_ctree_insert_node(GTK_CTREE(root),
                node, NULL, text,
                5, NULL, NULL, NULL, NULL, TRUE, TRUE);

        text[0] = "Sea Pen";
        gtk_ctree_insert_node(GTK_CTREE(root),
                node, NULL, text,
                5, NULL, NULL, NULL, NULL, TRUE, TRUE);

        text[0] = "Pacific Octopus";
        gtk_ctree_insert_node(GTK_CTREE(root),
                node, NULL, text,
                5, NULL, NULL, NULL, NULL, TRUE, TRUE);

        text[0] = "Sea Urchin";
        gtk_ctree_insert_node(GTK_CTREE(root),
                node, NULL, text,
                5, NULL, NULL, NULL, NULL, TRUE, TRUE);

        // Mammals

        text[0] = "Mammals";
        parent = gtk_ctree_insert_node(GTK_CTREE(root),
                NULL, NULL, text,
                5, NULL, NULL, NULL, NULL, FALSE, TRUE);

        text[0] = "Dangerous";
        node = gtk_ctree_insert_node(GTK_CTREE(root),
                parent, NULL, text,
                5, NULL, NULL, NULL, NULL, FALSE, TRUE);

        text[0] = "Killer Whale";
        gtk_ctree_insert_node(GTK_CTREE(root),
                node, NULL, text,
                5, NULL, NULL, NULL, NULL, TRUE, TRUE);

        text[0] = "Non-Dangerous";
        node = gtk_ctree_insert_node(GTK_CTREE(root),
                parent, NULL, text,
                5, NULL, NULL, NULL, NULL, FALSE, TRUE);

        text[0] = "Gray Whale";
```

```
    gtk_ctree_insert_node(GTK_CTREE(root),
            node, NULL, text,
            5, NULL, NULL, NULL, NULL, TRUE, TRUE);

    text[0] = "Sea Otter";
    gtk_ctree_insert_node(GTK_CTREE(root),
            node, NULL, text,
            5, NULL, NULL, NULL, NULL, TRUE, TRUE);

    text[0] = "Bottlenose Dolphin";
    gtk_ctree_insert_node(GTK_CTREE(root),
            node, NULL, text,
            5, NULL, NULL, NULL, NULL, TRUE, TRUE);

    return root;
}

main( argc, argv )
int argc;
char *argv[];
{
    GtkWidget *window, *tree;

    gtk_init( &argc, &argv );

    window = gtk_window_new(GTK_WINDOW_TOPLEVEL);
    gtk_widget_set_usize( window, 200, -1 );

    gtk_signal_connect(GTK_OBJECT (window), "destroy",
     GTK_SIGNAL_FUNC(gtk_widget_destroy), &window);

    gtk_window_set_title(GTK_WINDOW (window), "GtkTree Sample");
    gtk_container_border_width(GTK_CONTAINER (window), 0);

    tree = make_tree();

    gtk_container_add(GTK_CONTAINER(window), tree);
    gtk_window_position(GTK_WINDOW (window), GTK_WIN_POS_CENTER);

    gtk_widget_show_all( window );

    gtk_main();
}
```

Creating a GtkCTree Instance

Only two GtkCTree functions are needed in the preceding listing to implement the tree. The first of these functions, predictably, is the one used by applications to create an instance of GtkCTree: gtk_ctree_new(). The prototype for gtk_ctree_new() is:

```
GtkWidget *
gtk_ctree_new(gint columns, gint tree_column);
```

The first argument, columns, specifies how many columns are to be defined for each row in the tree. The second argument, tree_column, specifies which column the tree controls will be displayed in. tree_column can be any integer in the range [0, columns-1], but in most cases, you will want to set tree_column to 0. On line 012 in the preceding listing, I create a single-column tree by setting columns to 1 and tree_column to 0.

Inserting Nodes

Once the tree has been created, all that remains to do is add the nodes that contain the data to be displayed. To add nodes to the tree, the preceding code makes calls to gtk_tree_insert_node():

```
GtkCTreeNode *
gtk_ctree_insert_node(GtkCTree *ctree, GtkCTreeNode *parent,
        GtkCTreeNode *sibling, gchar *text[], guint8 spacing,
        GdkPixmap *pixmap_closed, GdkBitmap *mask_closed,
        GdkPixmap *pixmap_opened, GdkBitmap *mask_opened,
        gboolean is_leaf, gboolean expanded);
```

The first argument, ctree, is the instance of GtkCTree to which the node will be added, and it is created by calling gtk_ctree_new() or one of the other GtkCTree instance creation functions that I will describe later. parent is the parent node of the node being added. The nodes labeled Fish, Invertebrates, Mammals, Dangerous, and Non-dangerous are all parent nodes to other nodes in the tree. For example, Fish is the parent node of the two nodes labeled Dangerous and Non-dangerous that descend from it. Likewise, Dangerous is the parent node of the node labeled Great White Shark, and Non-dangerous is the parent node of the node labeled Blue Banded Goby. Nodes at the top of the hierarchy (Fish, Invertebrates, and Mammals) do not have parent nodes, so when they are created, the parent argument to gtk_ctree_insert_node() is set to NULL. All other nodes will have a non-NULL parent node, which is the return value of the gtk_ctree_insert_node() call that was used to add that parent node to the tree.

The third argument, sibling, relates the node being added to some node in the tree sharing the same parent. This argument can usually be set to NULL. If it is set to NULL, then nodes will be displayed in the order in which they were added to the tree. If sibling is non-NULL, the node being added will be placed immediately above the node specified by the sibling argument. GtkCTree supports drag and drop (when enabled by a call to gtk_clist_set_reorderable()), but drag and drop will not function if you do not specify sibling values for nodes added to the tree.

The argument text defines the content of the row being added to the tree. As I mentioned earlier, GtkCTree is only capable of displaying text data; if you need to display other types of data (e.g., images) in a tree and your data can be displayed in a single column, then you should use GtkTree instead.

The argument text is an array of pointers to char, so each element in the text array is set to the address of a character string defined on the stack, on the heap, or as a string literal. GtkCTree will make a copy of each string passed to it in the text vector. In this example, I use string literals:

```
008     gchar *text[1];

        ...
```

```
016     text[0] = "Fish";
017     parent = gtk_ctree_insert_node(GTK_CTREE(root),
018             NULL, NULL, text, 5, NULL, NULL, NULL, NULL,
019             FALSE, TRUE);
```

The number of elements in text is the same as the columns argument passed to gtk_ctree_new(). In this case, I only have one column in each row of the tree, so I use the declaration shown on line 008 to declare the array. Line 016 assigned the first element of the array, corresponding to column 1 in the row, to point to the string Fish, which is the data being added.

The next argument, spacing, specifies the number of pixels that will be placed between the pixmap data I am about to describe and the beginning of the column data contained in the text argument I previously described.

The next four arguments define image data that will be displayed to the left of the text row data, separated by the number of pixels specified by the spacing argument. The first two arguments, pixmap_closed and mask_closed, define an image displayed by the node when it is unexpanded or closed, while the second two, pixmap_opened and mask_opened, define an image shown when the node is expanded or opened. If the node has no children (i.e., it is a leaf node), then pixmap_opened and mask_opened are ignored. See the discussion of pixmaps and bitmap masks in Chapter 6 for information on how to create GdkPixmap and GdkBitmap data that is compatible with GtkCTree.

The argument is_leaf should be set to TRUE if the node is not the parent node of some other node in the tree (e.g., if the node is a leaf node). If set to FALSE, the node is expected to have children and will be drawn with a control that allows users to expand or close the subtree it parents. The final argument, expanded, is ignored if the node is a leaf node (i.e., if is_leaf is set to TRUE). If is_leaf is FALSE, then setting expanded to TRUE will cause the node to initially draw expanded, showing its immediate children. Setting expanded to FALSE will hide the immediate children of the node (and any nodes below the children, regardless of their expanded state).

Analyzing the Sample Code

Now that we have discussed gtk_ctree_insert_node(), let's return to the sample code and look at how it is used in detail, focusing on adding the Fish node and its children.

```
001 #include <gtk/gtk.h>
002
003 static GtkWidget *
004 make_tree ( void )
005 {
006    GtkWidget *root;
007    GtkCTreeNode *parent, *node;
008    gchar *text[1];
009
010    // create the root node of the tree.
011
012    root = gtk_ctree_new( 1, 0 );
```

On line 012, a new single-column instance of GtkCTree is created.

```
013
014      // Fish
015
016      text[0] = "Fish";
017      parent = gtk_ctree_insert_node(GTK_CTREE(root),
018              NULL, NULL, text, 5, NULL, NULL, NULL, NULL,
019              FALSE, TRUE);
```

On lines 016 through 019, a root node containing the data "Fish" is created. It is a root node of the tree because it has no parent (parent is set to NULL). It will be the parent of some other node, so is_leaf is set to FALSE. I save the node in the variable parent so that it can be referred to below:

```
020
021      text[0] = "Dangerous";
022      node = gtk_ctree_insert_node(GTK_CTREE(root),
023              parent, NULL, text,
024              5, NULL, NULL, NULL, NULL, FALSE, TRUE);
```

On lines 021 through 024, a child of the Fish node containing the data "Dangerous" is added to the tree. Its parent node is the Fish node; this association is made by passing parent as the parent argument to gtk_ctree_insert_node(). Like the Fish node, this node will act as the parent of other nodes in the tree, so is_leaf is also set to FALSE.

Next we add the children of the Dangerous node. On lines 026 through 029, I add a node labeled Great White Shark as a child of the Dangerous node created earlier:

```
025
026      text[0] = "Great White Shark";
027      gtk_ctree_insert_node(GTK_CTREE(root),
028              node, NULL, text,
029              5, NULL, NULL, NULL, NULL, TRUE, TRUE);
```

The variable "node" contains a reference to the Dangerous node and is passed as the parent argument to gtk_ctree_insert_node(). Is_leaf is set to TRUE this time because Great White Shark is a leaf node. Similar code is executed on lines 031 through 034 to add Stonefish as a child of the Dangerous node.

```
030
031      text[0] = "Stonefish";
032      gtk_ctree_insert_node(GTK_CTREE(root),
033              node,  NULL, text,
034              5, NULL, NULL, NULL, NULL, TRUE, TRUE);
```

The next step, on lines 036 through 039, adds Non-Dangerous as a child of the Fish node. The code is the same as that executed to add the Dangerous node, except for the data passed in, which is set to Non-Dangerous on line 036.

```
035
```

```
        text[0] = "Non-Dangerous";
        node = gtk_ctree_insert_node(GTK_CTREE(root),
                parent,  NULL, text,
                5, NULL, NULL, NULL, NULL, FALSE, TRUE);
```

The rest of the code should be fairly obvious at this point. You might try, as an exercise, to compile the preceding code and then add Barracuda as a child of the Dangerous node and Sea Bass as a child of the Non-Dangerous node to make sure you understand the preceding.

A Second Example

Let's continue with a look at the second sample client. This client is a variation on the preceding client, but it adds a second column of data to each row that describes the habitat of the animal. In addition, titles are added to each column, just like the column titles supported by the GtkCList class. The source code changes needed to support these new features are minimal. First, the size of the text array increases to 2 to hold column 2's data, and a second array, titles, is declared to hold the title data that will be passed to GtkCTree:

```
        gchar *text[2];
        gchar *titles[2];
```

To create the tree, the call to gtk_ctree_new() is replaced with a call to a new function, gtk_ctree_new_with_titles():

```
GtkWidget *
gtk_ctree_new_with_titles(gint columns, gint tree_column,
        gchar *titles[]);
```

The first two arguments are the same as those passed to gtk_ctree_new(). The third argument, titles, holds pointers to strings that are used by GtkCTree to label the columns as illustrated in Figure 12.11. These strings are copied by GtkCTree, so you are free to release any memory you may have allocated to hold them after the call to gtk_ctree_new_with_titles() returns. Here is the code used to create a tree with two columns labeled Animal and Habitat:

```
        // create the root node of the tree.
        titles[0] = "Animal";
        titles[1] = "Habitat";
        root = gtk_ctree_new_with_titles( 2, 0, titles );
```

The only remaining change needed to create our tree is to specify the data to be displayed in column 2 for each node in the tree. This is simply a matter of assigning the string to the second element of the text vector, for example:

```
        text[0] = "Dangerous";
        text[1] = "";
        node = gtk_ctree_insert_node(GTK_CTREE(root),
                parent, NULL, text,
                5, NULL, NULL, NULL, NULL, FALSE, TRUE);
```

```
032     text[0] = "Great White Shark";
033     text[1] = "Open ocean";
034     gtk_ctree_insert_node(GTK_CTREE(root),
035             node, NULL, text,
036             5, NULL, NULL, NULL, NULL, TRUE, TRUE);
```

On line 027, I set the second text element to " " because there is no data to be displayed in the Habitat column for categories such as Fish or Dangerous. On line 033, I set the Habitat data to "Open ocean." See Figure 12.11 for the results.

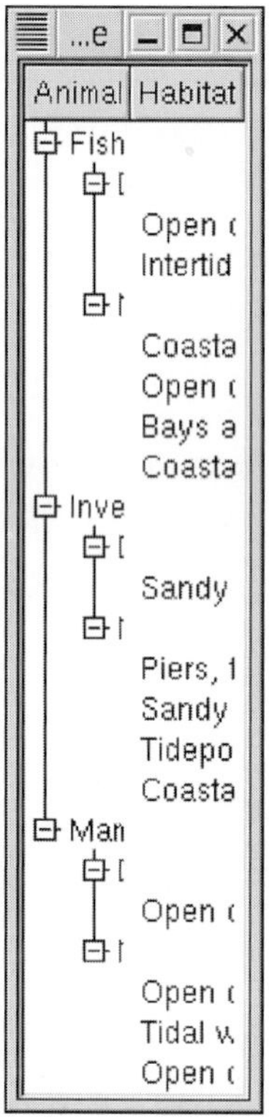

Figure 12.11 Multicolumn Tree

As you can tell by looking at Figure 12.11, there is a problem; as you can see, all of the columns are sized based on the width of the text in the column headings, not on the width of the data being displayed. In most cases, you will want at least one of the columns (usually column 0) to display with a width that makes all of its data viewable; trees sized like the one shown in Figure 12.11 are, at best, a nuisance to users.

To control the size of the columns, we must turn to the GtkCList API, which provides the functions we need. Several functions supplied by GtkCList can be used to modify the appearance of GtkCTree column headings or to make them sensitive (or insensitive) to button presses by users. The function I will use here to control the width of columns is gtk_clist_set_column_auto_resize(), which tells the tree to size each column automatically based on its content. Here are the code changes needed:

```
titles[0] = "Animal";
titles[1] = "Habitat";
root = gtk_ctree_new_with_titles( 2, 0, titles );

for ( i = 0; i < 2; i++ )
        gtk_clist_set_column_auto_resize(GTK_CLIST(root), i, TRUE );
```

This has the side effect of making the columns nonresizable; see Chapter 6 for more details. The result is shown in Figure 12.12.

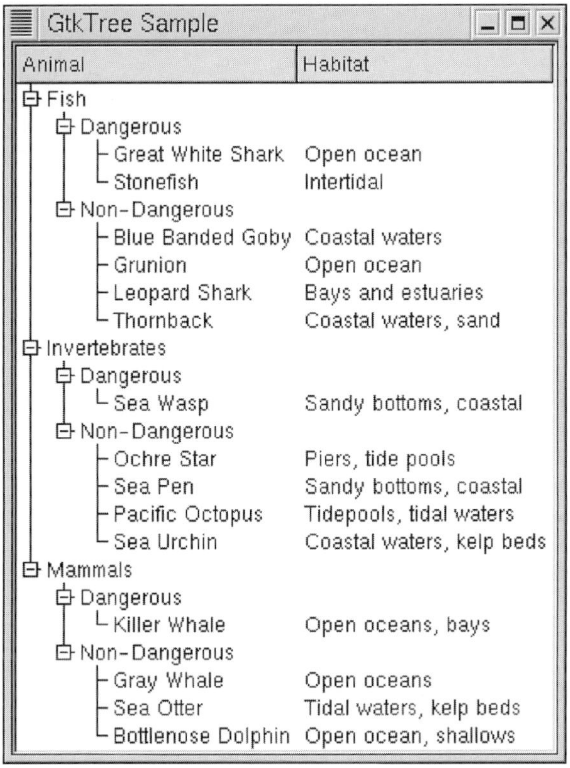

Figure 12.12 Multicolumn Tree, Columns Correctly Sized

Displaying the Contents of a Directory

As a final example of GtkCTree, I will create an application that displays the contents of a user-selected directory. Each row displays five pieces of data: the name of the item, its type (file, directory, fifo, and so on), the user and group IDs of its owner, and its size in bytes. Each directory in the tree is represented by a parent node; children of a directory node represent contents of that directory (if a directory cannot be read by the application because of permissions issues, the directory node will have no children).

The routine that does the bulk of the work is recursive; the recursion comes into play when a directory is read and processed within the inner loop of the routine. The source code for the routine PopulateTreeRecursive() is as follows:

Listing 12.4 Displaying the Contents of a Directory

```
#include <gtk/gtk.h>
#include <sys/stat.h>
#include <sys/types.h>
#include <sys/param.h>
#include <dirent.h>
#include <unistd.h>
#include <stdio.h>

static GtkWidget *
PopulateTreeRecursive( char *path, GtkCTree *tree, GtkCTreeNode *parent )
{
   GtkCTreeNode *newparent = NULL;
   struct stat buf;
   DIR *dp;
   int i;
   gchar *titles[ 5 ];
   struct dirent *dir;
   gboolean isleaf;
   char pathbuf[ MAXPATHLEN ];      // full path
   char buf1[ MAXPATHLEN ];         // file/dir name
   char buf2[ 32 ];                 // file type
   char buf3[ 32 ];                 // user
   char buf4[ 32 ];                 // group
   char buf5[ 32 ];                 // size in bytes

   gchar *text[ 5 ] = { buf1, buf2, buf3, buf4, buf5 };

   if ( tree == NULL ) {
           titles[0] = "Name"; titles[1] = "Type";
           titles[2] = "User"; titles[3] = "Group";
           titles[4] = "Size";
           tree = (GtkCTree *)
                   gtk_ctree_new_with_titles( 5, 0, titles );
           for ( i = 0; i < 5; i++ )
                   gtk_clist_set_column_auto_resize(
                           GTK_CLIST(tree), i, TRUE );
   }

   dp = opendir( path );
   if ( dp == (DIR *) NULL )
           return;
   while ( ( dir = readdir( dp ) ) !=  (struct dirent *) NULL ) {
           strcpy( buf1, dir->d_name );

           snprintf( pathbuf, MAXPATHLEN - 1, "%s/%s",
                   path, dir->d_name );

           if(lstat(pathbuf, &buf) < 0)
                   continue;

```

```
051         isleaf = TRUE;
052         if (S_ISLNK(buf.st_mode))
053             sprintf( buf2, "Symlink" );
054         else if (S_ISREG(buf.st_mode))
055             sprintf( buf2, "Regular" );
056         else if (S_ISDIR(buf.st_mode)) {
057             isleaf = FALSE;
058             sprintf( buf2, "Directory" );
059         }
060         else if (S_ISCHR(buf.st_mode))
061             sprintf( buf2, "Char Device" );
062         else if (S_ISBLK(buf.st_mode))
063             sprintf( buf2, "Block Device" );
064         else if (S_ISFIFO(buf.st_mode))
065             sprintf( buf2, "Fifo" );
066         else if (S_ISSOCK(buf.st_mode))
067             sprintf( buf2, "Socket" );
068         sprintf( buf3, "%d", buf.st_uid );
069         sprintf( buf4, "%d", buf.st_gid );
070         sprintf( buf5, "%lu", buf.st_size );
071 
072         newparent = gtk_ctree_insert_node(GTK_CTREE(tree), parent,
073             NULL, text, 5, NULL, NULL, NULL, NULL, isleaf,
074             TRUE);
075         if(lstat(pathbuf, &buf) >= 0 && S_ISDIR(buf.st_mode) &&
076             !S_ISLNK(buf.st_mode)) {
077             if (!strcmp(dir->d_name, ".") ||
078                 !strcmp(dir->d_name, ".."))
079                 continue;
080             snprintf( pathbuf, MAXPATHLEN - 1, "%s/%s",
081                 path, dir->d_name );
082             PopulateTreeRecursive( pathbuf, tree, newparent);
083         }
084     }
085     closedir( dp );
086     return( GTK_WIDGET(tree) );
087 }
```

The first call to PopulateTreeRecursive() might look like the following:

```
GtkWidget *tree;

tree = PopulateTreeRecursive( "/home/syd/src", NULL, NULL );
gtk_widget_show( tree );
```

The preceding call creates an instance of GtkCTree that recursively displays the contents of the directory */home/syd/src*.

The first time PopulateTreeRecursive() is called, the arguments tree and parent are both set to NULL, and the argument path is set to the absolute (full) path of the directory that the user wishes to recursively display. Because tree is NULL, code on lines 029 through 036 is executed to create and initialize an instance of GtkCTree. This code will only be executed once; all other calls to PopulateTreeRecursive() are made with the tree argument set to the tree created on these lines during the first call to PopulateTreeRecursive().

The next task of PopulateTreeRecursive() is to open for reading the directory that was passed in as the path argument (lines 039 through 041) and to iterate through its contents. If the directory cannot be opened due to permissions issues, we simply return. The bulk of the work happens on lines 042 through 084 inside a while loop that iterates the contents of the directory. Five character arrays (buf1, buf2, ..., buf5) are used to hold the data that makes up the row that will be added to the tree for each item in the directory. On line 048, a call to lstat(2) gives information about the directory item read during an iteration of the while loop. I use lstat(2) because it does not follow symlinks, avoiding the possibility of our code entering an infinite loop. The code on lines 051 through 070 places the information read by lstat(2) into the appropriate buffers and, on line 072, calls gtk_ctree_insert_node() to add the node to the tree. Notice how is_leaf is set to FALSE if the item read is a directory; this is because we will add children to that node when PopulateTreeRecursive() is recursively called to add its contents to the tree.

As each node is added to the tree, a check is made to see if the item added is a directory (and not a symlink). If it is a directory, then we recursively call PopulateTreeRecursive(), passing as arguments the full path of the directory to be processed (path), the tree created on lines 032 and 033 by the first call to PopulateTreeRecursive() (tree), and the node that was added to the tree that represents the directory item that will be processed (parent). A tree that is added by a recursive call to PopulateTreeRecursive() will display the contents of the directory specified by the path argument and will be placed in the tree below the node specified by the parent argument.

As an exercise, try adding pixmap data to each node, choosing an image that is appropriate for the type of item the node represents. For example, use a folder icon to represent a directory, a file icon to represent a file, and so forth.

Removing Nodes from a Tree

Nodes can be removed from a tree by calling gtk_ctree_remove_node():

```
void
gtk_ctree_remove_node(GtkCTree *ctree, GtkCTreeNode *node);
```

The argument ctree is the instance of GtkCTree to which the node belongs, and node is the node to be removed from the tree. If the node is a parent to other nodes in the tree, the children of the node will also be removed.

Setting the Indentation

In this section and the ones that follow, I will discuss some of the functions specific to GtkCTree that you might find useful. The first of these functions, gtk_ctree_set_indent(), controls how many pixels to the right of the parent's data a child's data is drawn. The default is to indent children 20 pixels. The function prototype for gtk_ctree_set_indent() is as follows:

```
void
gtk_ctree_set_indent(GtkCTree *ctree, gint indent);
```

The argument indent is an integer value that should be greater than or equal to 0. A value less than 0 will result in a runtime assertion and will cause the indent value to revert to its default of 20 pixels.

Setting the Spacing

The amount of spacing separating lines in the ctree control from the data displayed for the node can be controlled with gtk_ctree_set_spacing():

```
void
gtk_ctree_set_spacing(GtkCTree *ctree, gint spacing);
```

Spacing is an integer value 0 or greater (negative values result in an assert).

Setting the Line Style of a CTree

The line style of the ctree can be set by calling gtk_ctree_set_line_style():

```
void
gtk_ctree_set_line_style(GtkCTree *ctree,
        GtkCTreeLineStyle line_style);
```

The line_style argument can be one of the values provided in Table 12.7.

Table 12.7 GtkCTreeLineStyle

Line Style	*Result*
GTK_CTREE_LINES_NONE	No tree lines are drawn.
GTK_CTREE_LINES_SOLID	Tree lines are solid (default).
GTK_CTREE_LINES_DOTTED	Tree lines are drawn using a series of dots.
GTK_CTREE_LINES_TABBED	See Figure 12.13.

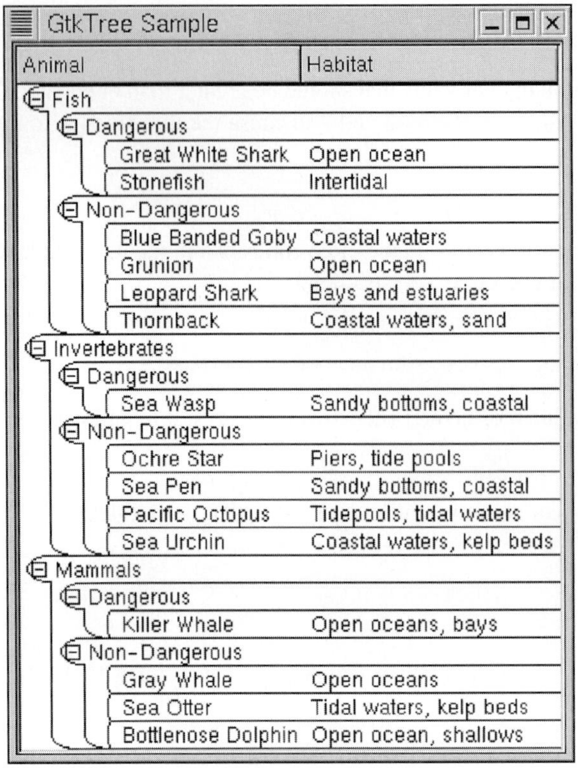

Figure 12.13 GTK_CTREE_LINES_TABBED

Setting the Expander Style

An expander is a graphic to the left of a parent node that can be clicked on by the user to expand or collapse the node, showing or hiding, respectively, the children of that node. An expander also provides visual feedback that lets users know the state of the node, either expanded or collapsed. You can change the expander style by calling gtk_ctree_set_expander_style():

```
void
gtk_ctree_set_expander_style(GtkCTree *ctree,
        GtkCTreeExpanderStyle expander_style);
```

The argument expander_style can be one of the following graphics listed in Table 12.8.

Table 12.8 GtkCTreeExpanderStyle

Expander Style	*Result*
GTK_CTREE_EXPANDER_NONE	No expander is drawn.
GTK_CTREE_EXPANDER_SQUARE	The default expander (see preceding figures).

Table 12.8 GtkCTreeExpanderStyle (Continued)

Expander Style	***Result***
GTK_CTREE_EXPANDER_TRIANGLE	See Figure 12.14.
GTK_CTREE_EXPANDER_CIRCULAR	See Figure 12.15.

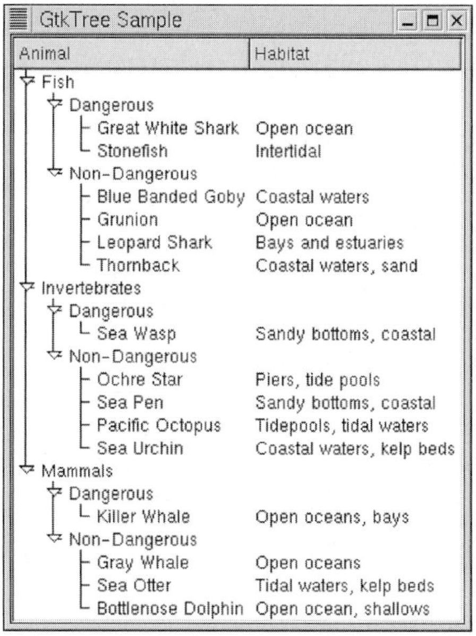

Figure 12.14 GTK_CTREE_EXPANDER_TRIANGLE

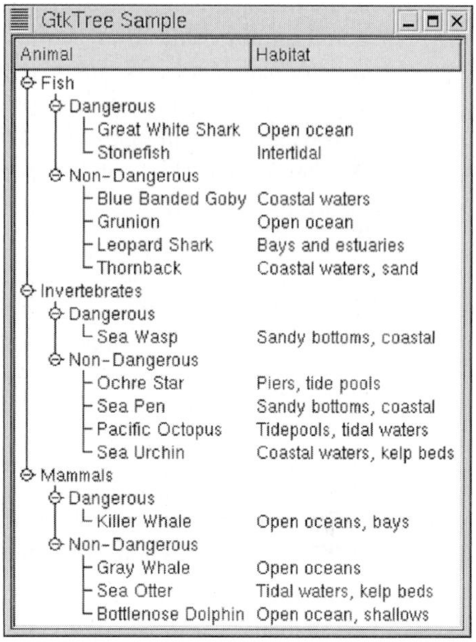

Figure 12.15 GTK_CTREE_EXPANDER_CIRCULAR

Note that users can still expand or collapse nodes if GTK_CTREE_EXPANDER_NONE is specified. This can be done by double-clicking on the node to be expanded or collapsed.

Sorting Functions

The following functions pertain to tree sorting. The first function discussed here lets you specify a comparison function that will be used in place of the default comparison function invoked during a drag-and-drop operation (should drag and drop be enabled; refer to the discussion of the sibling argument to gtk_clist_insert_node(), presented earlier). The function gtk_ctree_set_drag_compare_func() takes two arguments: an instance of GtkCTree and a pointer to a function.

```
void
gtk_ctree_set_drag_compare_func(GtkCTree *ctree,
        GtkCTreeCompareDragFunc cmp_func);
```

The function prototype of comp_func is defined by GtkCTreeCompareDragFunc:

```
typedef gboolean (*GtkCTreeCompareDragFunc) (GtkCTree *ctree,
        GtkCTreeNode *source_node, GtkCTreeNode *new_parent,
        GtkCTreeNode *new_sibling);
```

Your drag compare function should use the passed arguments to determine whether the drag-and-drop operation should be allowed or denied. The argument source_node will specify the node being moved, new_parent specifies the new parent node of source_node should the operation be allowed, and new_sibling specifies the new sibling of source_node should the drag-and-drop operation be allowed. If you want to deny the operation, your drag compare function should return FALSE. Returning TRUE will cause the drag-and-drop operation to be performed.

You can cause an instance of GtkCTree to automatically sort all data by setting the GtkCList autosort attribute of the ctree. This is done by calling gtk_clist_set_auto_sort(). Additional GtkCList sorting functions applicable to instances of GtkCTree are detailed in Chapter 6.

If you chose to disable GtkCList-style autosorting, you can still provide sort capabilities for your users by calling two functions defined by GtkCTree. The first function, gtk_ctree_sort_node(), sorts the immediate children of a specific node in the tree. Its function prototype is as follows:

```
void
gtk_ctree_sort_node(GtkCTree *ctree, GtkCTreeNode *node);
```

The sort order is defined by the last call made to gtk_clist_set_sort_type(), or GTK_SORT_ASCENDING if no such call was made. The compare function that was set by the last call to gtk_clist_set_compare_func() will be used in lieu of the default compare function (default_compare(), defined in gtkclist.c).

To extend the sort recursively to all children below a given node, you may call gtk_ctree_sort_recursive():

```
void
gtk_ctree_sort_recursive(GtkCTree *ctree, GtkCTreeNode *node);
```

The preceding remarks that were made for gtk_ctree_sort_node() apply equally to gtk_ctree_sort_recursive().

Recursive Functions

In this section, I describe GtkCTree functions that are recursive in nature. These functions allow you to invoke callback functions in your application for each node in the tree, find nodes based on data that your application has attached to a node or to a set of nodes, as well as query the ctree widget for certain attributes of the nodes that it manages.

The first four functions described allow you to walk the tree, starting at a node you specify. For each node in the tree, GtkCTree will invoke a callback function that you provide. The callback function you provide must conform to the following function prototype:

```
typedef void (*GtkCTreeFunc) (GtkCTree *ctree, GtkCTreeNode *node,
        gpointer data);
```

In the preceding function prototype, node specifies the node being visited, and data is client data that your application optionally arranges to have passed to the callback function.

The first function, gtk_ctree_post_recursive(), performs a post-order traversal of the tree starting at the specified node:

```
void
gtk_ctree_post_recursive(GtkCTree *ctree, GtkCTreeNode *node,
        GtkCTreeFunc func, gpointer data);
```

The argument ctree is the instance of GtkCTree to be traversed, node is the starting node for the traversal, func is the function that will be called for each node traversed, and data is the client data that will be passed to func via its data argument.

The function gtk_ctree_post_recursive_to_depth() is identical to gtk_ctree_post_ recursive(), except for the depth argument that restricts the traversal to the specified depth:

```
void
gtk_ctree_post_recursive_to_depth(GtkCTree *ctree, GtkCTreeNode *node,
        gint depth, GtkCTreeFunc func, gpointer data);
```

If depth is -1, the entire tree is traversed. If depth is 0, only the first (root) node is visited. Specifying a depth value of 1 will visit the root node and its immediate children, and so forth.

The final two recursive traversal functions, gtk_ctree_pre_recursive():

```
void
gtk_ctree_pre_recursive(GtkCTree *ctree, GtkCTreeNode *node,
        GtkCTreeFunc func, gpointer data);
```

and gtk_ctree_pre_recursive_to_depth():

```
void
gtk_ctree_pre_recursive_to_depth(GtkCTree *ctree, GtkCTreeNode *node,
        gint depth, GtkCTreeFunc func, gpointer data);
```

mirror gtk_ctree_post_recursive() and gtk_ctree_post_recursive_to_depth() in terms of functionality. The only difference is that the later two functions traverse the tree in pre-order, not post-order (see a book on data structures for more information on post- and pre-order traversal of trees).

Passing Client Data to a Traversal Function. I should probably give you a hint as to why it might be useful to pass client data to a recursive traversal function. There are no fixed rules that dictate when or when not to pass data to a traversal function. It is completely up to you as the developer to make use of the traversal functions in whatever way makes sense to your application. As an example to get you thinking about how you might use this feature in your application, I developed sample code that traverses a tree of address book data and that changes each phone number with a 123 area code to one with an 456 area code. I use the traversal callback function to inspect each node in the tree and to convert only those that match. To make the example simple, the area code is stored in a column of its own, apart from the rest of the phone number.

The partial source code for the example is presented in the following listing:

Listing 12.5 Searching for Data in a CTree

```
#include <gtk/gtk.h>

typedef struct _area {
   char *in;                  // old area code
   char *out;                 // new area code
} Area;

void
CallbackFunc (GtkCTree *ctree, GtkCTreeNode *node, gpointer data)
{
   Area *area = (Area *) data;
   char *text;

   gtk_ctree_node_get_text(ctree, node, 1, &text);
   if ( !strcmp( text, area->in ) )
           gtk_ctree_node_set_text(ctree, node, 1, area->out);
}

void
ChangeAreaCode(GtkWidget *widget, gpointer data)
{
   GtkCTree *tree = (GtkCTree *) data;

   Area area;

   area.in = "123"; area.out = "456";

   gtk_clist_freeze(GTK_CLIST(tree));
   gtk_ctree_post_recursive( tree, NULL, CallbackFunc, &area );
   gtk_clist_thaw(GTK_CLIST(tree));
}

static GtkWidget *
MakeAddressBookTree( void )
{
   GtkWidget *root;
   GtkCTreeNode *parent, *node;
   gchar *text[3], *titles[3];
   int i;

   // create the root node of the tree.

   titles[0] = "Name"; titles[1] = "Area"; titles[2] = "Phone";
   root = gtk_ctree_new_with_titles( 3, 0, titles );

```

```
    for ( i = 0; i < 3; i++ )
            gtk_clist_set_column_auto_resize(GTK_CLIST(root), i, TRUE);

    // Friends

    text[0] = "Friends"; text[1] = ""; text[2] = "";
    parent = gtk_ctree_insert_node(GTK_CTREE(root),
            NULL, NULL, text, 5, NULL, NULL, NULL, NULL, FALSE, TRUE);

    text[0] = "Sammy"; text[1] = "123"; text[2] = "456-7890";
    node = gtk_ctree_insert_node(GTK_CTREE(root), parent, NULL, text,
            5, NULL, NULL, NULL, NULL, FALSE, TRUE);

    text[0] = "Jamie"; text[1] = "098"; text[2] = "765-4321";
    node = gtk_ctree_insert_node(GTK_CTREE(root), parent, node, text,
            5, NULL, NULL, NULL, NULL, FALSE, TRUE);

    text[0] = "Bob"; text[1] = "019"; text[2] = "283-7465";
    node = gtk_ctree_insert_node(GTK_CTREE(root), parent, node, text,
            5, NULL, NULL, NULL, NULL, FALSE, TRUE);

    // Family

    text[0] = "Family"; text[1] = ""; text[2] = "";
    parent = gtk_ctree_insert_node(GTK_CTREE(root), NULL, NULL, text,
            5, NULL, NULL, NULL, NULL, FALSE, TRUE);

    text[0] = "Fred"; text[1] = "111"; text[2] = "222-3333";
    node = gtk_ctree_insert_node(GTK_CTREE(root), parent, NULL, text,
            5, NULL, NULL, NULL, NULL, FALSE, TRUE);

    text[0] = "Joe"; text[1] = "444"; text[2] = "555-6666";
    node = gtk_ctree_insert_node(GTK_CTREE(root), parent, node, text,
            5, NULL, NULL, NULL, NULL, FALSE, TRUE);

    text[0] = "Paul"; text[1] = "777"; text[2] = "888-9999";
    node = gtk_ctree_insert_node(GTK_CTREE(root), parent, node, text,
            5, NULL, NULL, NULL, NULL, FALSE, TRUE);

    return root;
}
```

The main application creates a window and a vertical box widget and then calls Make AddressBookTree() to create an instance of GtkCTree. Each node in the tree that holds data consists of three fields: name, area code, and phone number. The following code illustrates how a record is added to the tree.

```
    text[0] = "Sammy"; text[1] = "123"; text[2] = "456-7890";
    node = gtk_ctree_insert_node(GTK_CTREE(root), parent, NULL, text,
            5, NULL, NULL, NULL, NULL, FALSE, TRUE);
```

The tree created by MakeAddressBookTree() is added to the vertical box widget by the main program, as is the "Replace 123 with 456" button. A clicked signal function, ChangeAreaCode(), is registered with the button widget.

On line 026, a variable of type Area is initialized to hold the area code to be searched for during the traversal (in) as well as the replacement area code (out). On line 029, gtk_ctree_post_recursive() is called to traverse the tree. The call to gtk_ctree_post_ recursive() is surrounded by calls to gtk_clist_freeze() and gtk_clist_thaw() to force GtkCList to defer redrawing of the tree until the traversal is complete.

The traversal callback function, CallbackFunc(), is passed a reference to the tree being traversed (tree), the node being visited (node), and the Area data structure that holds the search parameters (data). A GtkCTree function, gtk_ctree_node_get_text(), is called to extract the data stored in column 2 (i.e., the area code). On line 015, I compare the value read from the node to the search area code passed to the callback function. If a match is found, I replace the value read with the new area code with a call to gtk_ctree_node_set_text() (line 016).

```
015      if ( !strcmp( text, area->in ) )
016              gtk_ctree_node_set_text(ctree, node, 1, area->out);
```

I will describe gtk_ctree_node_get_text() and gtk_ctree_node_set_text() in more detail later in this section.

Querying Tree and Node Attributes

The next few functions can be used to query certain attributes of a GtkCTree instance and the nodes that it contains. The first function, gtk_ctree_is_viewable(), can be used to determine whether a node in the tree is viewable:

```
gboolean
gtk_ctree_is_viewable(GtkCTree *ctree, GtkCTreeNode *node);
```

The argument ctree is an instance of GtkCTree. The argument node is an instance of GtkCTreeNode and specifies the node of interest. If each ancestor of the node is expanded, then TRUE is returned; otherwise, FALSE is returned.

The following function will return TRUE if the specified child is a sibling or child of the the specified node in the tree:

```
gboolean
gtk_ctree_find(GtkCTree *ctree, GtkCTreeNode *node,
       GtkCTreeNode *child);
```

Likewise, gtk_ctree_is_ancestor() will return TRUE if the specified node is an ancestor of the specified child:

```
gboolean
gtk_ctree_is_ancestor(GtkCTree *ctree, GtkCTreeNode *node,
       GtkCTreeNode *child);
```

Attaching and Retrieving Client Data

Before we take a look at the next set of search functions, I need to describe how you can attach client data to a node in the tree. To do so, you can call one of two functions, gtk_ctree_node_set_row_data():

```
void
gtk_ctree_node_set_row_data(GtkCTree *ctree, GtkCTreeNode *node,
        gpointer data);
```

or gtk_ctree_node_set_row_data_full():

```
void
gtk_ctree_node_set_row_data_full(GtkCTree *ctree, GtkCTreeNode *node,
        gpointer data, GtkDestroyNotify destroy);
```

Both of these functions share the first three arguments. The argument ctree is an instance of GtkCTree, node is an instance of GtkCTreeNode representing a node in ctree, and data is arbitrary data that your client wishes to attach to the node. An additional argument, destroy, is accepted by gtk_ctree_node_set_row_data_full(). Calling gtk_ctree_node_set_row_data() is equivalent to calling gtk_ctree_node_set_row_data_full() and setting destroy to NULL. Destroy, if non-NULL, must be a pointer to a function that adheres to the following function prototype:

```
typedef void (*GtkDestroyNotify) (gpointer data);
```

GtkCTree will call the function you register via the destroy function when the row or node to which the data is attached is destroyed. The data you register with either of the preceding two functions will be passed the destroy function as its only argument.

A typical use of client data is to attach, directly to a node, a pointer to a data structure or memory location that holds the data being displayed by the node. This makes the data accessible to you whenever you need it, for example, from within the context of one of the recursive traversal functions described earlier. To retrieve client data from a specific node, you can call gtk_ctree_node_get_row_data():

```
gpointer
gtk_ctree_node_get_row_data(GtkCTree *ctree, GtkCTreeNode *node);
```

The return value is the gpointer added by gtk_ctree_node_set_row_data_full() or gtk_ctree_node_set_row_data().

Searching for Nodes Based on Client Data

GtkCTree will return to you a list of all nodes in the tree (starting at a node you specify) that have a data attribute that matches a certain value. To obtain this list, call gtk_ctree_find_all_by_row_data():

```
GList *
gtk_ctree_find_all_by_row_data(GtkCTree *ctree, GtkCTreeNode *node,
        gpointer data);
```

The argument ctree is the tree to search, node is the starting node (NULL causes the entire tree to be searched), and the argument data is the data to search for.

The following code is a modification of the sample program previously presented:

Listing 12.6 Searching Based on Client Data

```
#include <gtk/gtk.h>

void
ChangeAreaCode(GtkWidget *widget, gpointer data)
{
   GList *list;
   GtkCTree *tree = (GtkCTree *) data;
   GtkCTreeNode *node;

   list = gtk_ctree_find_all_by_row_data( tree, NULL, (gpointer) 123 );

   gtk_clist_freeze(GTK_CLIST(tree));
   while ( list ) {
         node = (GtkCTreeNode *) list->data;
         gtk_ctree_node_set_text( tree, node, 1, "456" );
         gtk_ctree_node_set_row_data( tree, node, (gpointer) 456 );
         list = list->next;
   }
   gtk_clist_thaw(GTK_CLIST(tree));
}

static GtkWidget *
MakeAddressBookTree ( void )
{
   GtkWidget *root;
   GtkCTreeNode *parent, *node;
   gchar *text[3], *titles[3];
   int i;

   // create the root node of the tree.

   titles[0] = "Name"; titles[1] = "Area"; titles[2] = "Phone";
   root = gtk_ctree_new_with_titles( 3, 0, titles );

   for ( i = 0; i < 3; i++ )
         gtk_clist_set_column_auto_resize(GTK_CLIST(root), i, TRUE);

   // Friends

   text[0] = "Friends"; text[1] = ""; text[2] = "";
   parent = gtk_ctree_insert_node(GTK_CTREE(root),
         NULL, NULL, text, 5, NULL, NULL, NULL, NULL, FALSE, TRUE);

   text[0] = "Sammy"; text[1] = "123"; text[2] = "456-7890";
   node = gtk_ctree_insert_node(GTK_CTREE(root), parent, NULL, text,
```

```
046                 5, NULL, NULL, NULL, NULL, FALSE, TRUE);
047         gtk_ctree_node_set_row_data(GTK_CTREE(root), node, (gpointer) 123);
048
049         text[0] = "Jamie"; text[1] = "098"; text[2] = "765-4321";
050         node = gtk_ctree_insert_node(GTK_CTREE(root), parent, node, text,
051                 5, NULL, NULL, NULL, NULL, FALSE, TRUE);
052         gtk_ctree_node_set_row_data(GTK_CTREE(root), node, (gpointer) 098);
053
054         text[0] = "Bob"; text[1] = "019"; text[2] = "283-7465";
055         node = gtk_ctree_insert_node(GTK_CTREE(root), parent, node, text,
056                 5, NULL, NULL, NULL, NULL, FALSE, TRUE);
057         gtk_ctree_node_set_row_data(GTK_CTREE(root), node, (gpointer) 019);
058
059         // Family
060
061         text[0] = "Family"; text[1] = ""; text[2] = "";
062         parent = gtk_ctree_insert_node(GTK_CTREE(root), NULL, NULL, text,
063                 5, NULL, NULL, NULL, NULL, FALSE, TRUE);
064
065         text[0] = "Fred"; text[1] = "111"; text[2] = "222-3333";
066         node = gtk_ctree_insert_node(GTK_CTREE(root), parent, NULL, text,
067                 5, NULL, NULL, NULL, NULL, FALSE, TRUE);
068         gtk_ctree_node_set_row_data(GTK_CTREE(root), node, (gpointer) 111);
069
070         text[0] = "Joe"; text[1] = "444"; text[2] = "555-6666";
071         node = gtk_ctree_insert_node(GTK_CTREE(root), parent, node, text,
072                 5, NULL, NULL, NULL, NULL, FALSE, TRUE);
073         gtk_ctree_node_set_row_data(GTK_CTREE(root), node, (gpointer) 444);
074
075         text[0] = "Paul"; text[1] = "777"; text[2] = "888-9999";
076         node = gtk_ctree_insert_node(GTK_CTREE(root), parent, node, text,
077                 5, NULL, NULL, NULL, NULL, FALSE, TRUE);
078         gtk_ctree_node_set_row_data(GTK_CTREE(root), node, (gpointer) 777);
079
080         return root;
081     }
```

For each node I add to the tree, except the Friends and Family nodes, I attach, as client data, an integer representation of the area code displayed by that node. An example of this is on line 047, where I set the client data to 123, corresponding to the "123" text displayed by column 2 of the row. In the clicked signal function, I call gtk_ctree_find_all_by_row_data() to obtain a list of each node in the tree that has a data attribute matching the area code (123) I am trying to locate. Searching by integer value on the data attribute of nodes is much quicker than extracting the column 2 text from each node in the tree and doing a string comparison. If a match is found, I change the text of column 2 to "456" and change the data attribute of the node to 456 so that the next time a search for 123 is made, the node that is modified will not be returned as a match. The search-and-replace functionality is implemented in the clicked signal function ChangeAreaCode() (lines 003 through 020 in the preceding listing).

Performing Custom Searches

If equality is not your thing, you can perform searches on the data attribute using a comparison function of your own design. This can be done by creating a function with the following prototype:

```
typedef gint (*GCompareFunc) (gconstpointer a, gconstpointer b);
```

Then you can pass it to gtk_ctree_find_all_row_data_custom():

```
GList *
gtk_ctree_find_all_by_row_data_custom(GtkCTree *ctree,
        GtkCTreeNode *node,gpointer data, GCompareFunc func);
```

The first three arguments are the same as the first three arguments passed to gtk_ctree_find_all_by_row_data(). The final argument is a pointer to the comparison function previously defined. The comparison function will be called for each node in the tree below (and including) the specified node. If the comparison function returns TRUE, the matching node will be added to the GList returned by gtk_ctree_find_all_by_row_data_custom() when all nodes in the tree have been processed.

GtkCTree implements two slight variations of gtk_ctree_find_all_by_row_data() and gtk_ctree_find_all_by_row_data_custom(). These variations return the first node in the tree that matches the search criteria, instead of a list of all nodes that match. The first of these functions, gtk_ctree_find_by_row_data():

```
GtkCTreeNode *
gtk_ctree_find_by_row_data(GtkCTree *ctree, GtkCTreeNode *node,
        gpointer data);
```

is equivalent to gtk_ctree_find_all_by_row() data, but all searching is halted once the first node is found. The return value is the first node found, or NULL if no such node exists. If you want to use your own comparison function to perform the search, you must use gtk_ctree_find_by_row_data_custom():

```
GtkCTreeNode *
gtk_ctree_find_by_row_data_custom(GtkCTree *ctree, GtkCTreeNode *node,
        gpointer data, GCompareFunc func);
```

The arguments to gtk_ctree_find_by_row_data_custom() are the same as those passed to gtk_ctree_find_all_by_row_data_custom(). The first matching node will be returned, or NULL if no such node exists.

Moving, Expanding, Collapsing, and Selecting Rows

The following set of functions supports the moving, expanding, collapsing, and selecting of nodes (or rows) in an instance of GtkCTree.

Moving a Node. A node can be moved to a new location in the tree programmatically by calling gtk_ctree_move():

```
void
gtk_ctree_move(GtkCTree *ctree, GtkCTreeNode *node,
        GtkCTreeNode *new_parent, GtkCTreeNode *new_sibling);
```

The argument node is the node to be moved, and new_parent and new_sibling identify the new location of the node in ctree. All children of the node prior to the move will remain children of the node after the move has been completed.

Expanding a Node. Several GtkCTree functions allow you to collapse and expand nodes in the tree. To expand a node and display its immediate children, call gtk_ctree_expand():

```
void
gtk_ctree_expand(GtkCTree *ctree, GtkCTreeNode *node);
```

To recursively expand the specified node and display all nodes that descend from it, call gtk_ctree_expand_recursive():

```
void
gtk_ctree_expand_recursive(GtkCTree *ctree, GtkCTreeNode *node);
```

Finally, to recursively expand a node to a specific depth, you can call gtk_ctree_expand_to_depth():

```
void
gtk_ctree_expand_to_depth(GtkCTree *ctree, GtkCTreeNode *node,
        gint depth);
```

The argument depth is an integer in the range [1, *n*], where *n* is the depth of the tree. By the way, there is no easy way to determine the depth of a tree; GtkCTree does not provide a function or macro that can be used to query this information. If you specify a depth of 0, the entire tree starting at the specified node will be expanded.

Collapsing a Node. What can be expanded can also be collapsed (the GtkCTree version of the well-known saying "What goes up, must come down"). To collapse a node, hiding its immediate children, call gtk_ctree_collapse():

```
void
gtk_ctree_collapse(GtkCTree *ctree, GtkCTreeNode *node);
```

As usual, ctree is the tree containing the node to be collapsed. Collapsing a node does not affect the collapsed or expanded state of the children nodes or any of the nodes below these children. If you were to expand the node just collapsed, the tree would appear as it did before the node was collapsed. If you would like to recursively collapse all children of a node, you must call gtk_ctree_collapse_recursive():

```
void
gtk_ctree_collapse_recursive(GtkCTree *ctree, GtkCTreeNode *node);
```

Calling this function will collapse the node, all of its children, and so on. If you were to expand a node after it was recursively collapsed, it would not appear the same as it did before collapsing (except if the children of the node were already recursively collapsed or if all of the children of the node are leaf nodes and have no children of their own). All child nodes of a tree that was recursively collapsed need to be expanded by the user or the program in order to be viewed once again.

Of course, you can recursively collapse a node to the specified depth, just as you can recursively expand a node to a specified depth. To do so, call gtk_ctree_collapse_to_depth():

```
void
gtk_ctree_collapse_to_depth(GtkCTree *ctree, GtkCTreeNode *node,
        gint depth);
```

The argument depth is an integer in the range [1, *n*], where *n* is the depth of the tree. If depth is set to 0, the entire tree, starting at the specified node, will be collapsed. Setting node to NULL causes gtk_ctree_collapse_to_depth() to work from the root node of the tree.

Retrieving the State of a Node. The expanded/collapsed state of a node in a tree can be inverted by calling gtk_ctree_toggle_expansion():

```
void
gtk_ctree_toggle_expansion(GtkCTree *ctree, GtkCTreeNode *node);
```

The argument ctree is the tree containing the node to toggle; node is the node to toggle. If node is set to NULL, the root node is toggled.

Recursively Expanding and Collapsing Nodes. To recursively expand or collapse a node, depending on its previous state, call gtk_ctree_toggle_expansion_recursive():

```
void
gtk_ctree_toggle_expansion_recursive(GtkCTree *ctree,
        GtkCTreeNode *node);
```

The arguments to gtk_ctree_toggle_expansion_recursive() are the same as those passed to gtk_ctree_toggle_expansion().

Using the Keyboard to Collapse and Expand a Tree. GtkCTree allows users to collapse and expand a selected row via the keyboard. The supported keyboard bindings are shown in Table 12.9.

Table 12.9 Supported Keyboard Bindings

Binding	*Action*	*Description*
'+', GDK_SHIFT_MASK	GTK_CTREE_EXPANSION_ EXPAND	If collapsed, row is expanded
GDK_KP_Add	GTK_CTREE_EXPANSION_ EXPAND	If collapsed, row is expanded
GDK_KP_Add, GDK_CONTROL_MASK	GTK_CTREE_EXPANSION_ EXPAND_RECURSIVE	If collapsed, row is recursively expanded
'-'	GTK_CTREE_EXPANSION_ COLLAPSE	If expanded, row is collapsed

Table 12.9 Supported Keyboard Bindings (Continued)

Binding	*Action*	*Description*
GDK_KP_Subtract	GTK_CTREE_EXPANSION_ COLLAPSE	If expanded, row is collapsed
GDK_KP_Subtract, GDK_CONTROL_MASK	GTK_CTREE_EXPANSION_ COLLAPSE_RECURSIVE	If expanded, row is recursively collapsed
'='	GTK_CTREE_EXPANSION_ TOGGLE	Collapsed, expanded state is toggled
GDK_KP_Multiply	GTK_CTREE_EXPANSION_ TOGGLE	Collapsed, expanded state is toggled
GDK_KP_Multiply, GDK_CONTROL_MASK	GTK_CTREE_EXPANSION_ TOGGLE_RECURSIVE	Collapsed, expanded state is recursively toggled

In the preceding table, GDK_SHIFT_MASK means that one of the Shift keys is held down while the other key in the binding is being depressed, and GDK_CONTROL_MASK, similarly, means that the Control key is being held down while the other key is depressed. A key that is prefixed with GDK_KP_ denotes a keypad key. For example, GDK_KP_Add is the + key on the keyboard keypad, not the - key located in the top row of the keyboard adjacent to the = and 0 keys.

Your application need do nothing for these bindings to take effect. The values in the Action column of Table 12.9 list constants passed via the expansion argument to the change_focus_row_expansion signal function that your application can optionally register with the ctree widget. This signal is dispatched whenever the user collapses or expands a row using the keyboard bindings listed in Table 12.9. See Table 12.5 for a description of this signal and the section immediately following Table 12.5, "Signal Function Prototypes," for the function prototype of the corresponding signal function.

Selecting and Unselecting Nodes

Finally, let's look at how to programmatically select nodes in a tree. The functions are similar to those described for expanding and collapsing nodes in a tree; both recursive and nonrecursive functions are provided. To nonrecursively select a row or node in the tree, call gtk_ctree_select():

```
void
gtk_ctree_select(GtkCTree *ctree, GtkCTreeNode *node);
```

As you may have guessed, ctree is the GtkCTree containing the node to select, and node is the node that will be selected once gtk_ctree_select() returns. node must be non-NULL; otherwise, gtk_ctree_select() will fail.

To recursively select a node, call gtk_ctree_select_recursive():

```
void
gtk_ctree_select_recursive(GtkCTree *ctree, GtkCTreeNode *node);
```

The arguments are the same as those passed to gtk_ctree_select().

You can unselect a node by calling gtk_ctree_unselect():

```
void
gtk_ctree_unselect(GtkCTree *ctree, GtkCTreeNode *node);
```

You can recursively unselect a node, and all of its children, by making a call to gtk_ctree_unselect_recursive():

```
void
gtk_ctree_unselect_recursive(GtkCTree *ctree, GtkCTreeNode *node);
```

Miscellaneous Functions

The final set of GtkCTree functions that I will describe represents a grab bag of functionality. The majority of these functions come in pairs; one function in the pair is used to retrieve a particular piece of information about a node or about the tree, while the other function is used to set that same piece of information.

Checking Whether a Coordinate Is in the Expander Box. The first function, gtk_ctree_is_hot_spot(), will return TRUE if the x and y coordinates it is passed define a location within any expander box that is currently visible in the tree. The function prototype is as follows:

```
gboolean
gtk_ctree_is_hot_spot(GtkCTree *ctree, gint x, gint y);
```

Both x and y are window-relative coordinate values (such as the values that would be reported by a motion notify event).

Setting and Getting the Text Displayed in a Column. A pair of functions allow you to retrieve and set the text value displayed by a column in a tree row. To retrieve the text value of a specific column, call gtk_ctree_node_get_text():

```
gint
gtk_ctree_node_get_text(GtkCTree *ctree, GtkCTreeNode *node,
        gint column, gchar **text);
```

The arguments ctree, node, and column define the data to be retrieved. The argument column must be in the range 1 to *n*, where *n* is the number of columns in a row. Both ctree and node must be non-NULL. The argument text is a pointer to a variable of type gchar *. The following code retrieves the text from column 3 of a node and prints it to stdout:

```
gint retval;
gchar *text;
GtkCTree *tree;
GtkCTreeNode *node;

...
```

```
retval = gtk_ctree_node_get_text( tree, node, 3, &text );
if ( retval == 1 )
        printf( "Retrieved text is %s\n", text );
```

The function gtk_ctree_node_get_text() returns 1 on success and 0 on failure. A pointer to the column text data is returned, not a copy. Therefore, you should take care not to free or modify the text string returned by this function.

To set the column text of a node, you can call gtk_ctree_node_set_text():

```
void
gtk_ctree_node_set_text(GtkCTree *ctree, GtkCTreeNode *node,
        gint column, const gchar *text);
```

The first three arguments are used identically to the first three arguments passed to gtk_ctree_node_get_text(). The final argument, text, is a char * that contains the text to be displayed by the node in the specified column. GtkCTree makes a copy of the text string you pass, so you are free to delete or modify the text string you passed without affecting the data displayed in the tree.

Setting and Getting Pixmap Data. A similar pair of functions exists for getting and setting whatever pixmap data might be associated with a node in a ctree. To get the pixmap from a specified node, if the pixmap exists, call gtk_ctree_node_get_pixmap():

```
gint
gtk_ctree_node_get_pixmap(GtkCTree *ctree, GtkCTreeNode *node,
        gint column, GdkPixmap **pixmap, GdkBitmap **mask);
```

The arguments ctree, node, and column are as previously described for gtk_ctree_node_get_text(). The argument pixmap is a pointer to a GdkPixmap *, and mask is a pointer to a GdkBitmap *. Note that the actual pixmap and mask data used by the tree is returned, not a copy. Therefore, do not free the memory pointed to be either of these values and be careful when modifying the image data because modifications will affect the ctree from which the data was retrieved.

To set the pixmap and mask data for the specified node and column, you can call gtk_ctree_node_set_pixmap():

```
void
gtk_ctree_node_set_pixmap(GtkCTree *ctree, GtkCTreeNode *node,
        gint column, GdkPixmap *pixmap, GdkBitmap *mask);
```

Keep in mind that GtkCTree will not make a copy of either the pixmap or the mask, but it will reference count both, and GDK will hold on to the pixmap and the bitmap until the reference count goes to 0. Also, realize that the pixmap and mask data set here is temporary in the sense that GtkCTree continues to maintain the open and closed pixmap and mask data specified when the node was added to the tree. Once the user (or your application) changes the expand or collapse state of the node, the pixmap and mask data displayed in response to the call to gtk_ctree_node_set_pixmap() will be discarded, and the pixmap and mask displayed will revert to those set when the node was created (or by a call to gtk_ctree_set_node_info(), which I will describe in the next section).

The next two functions combine the functionality of the preceding text and pixmap getter and setter functions. To retrieve both the pixmap and text data from a node in a tree, call gtk_ctree_node_get_pixtext():

```
gint
gtk_ctree_node_get_pixtext(GtkCTree *ctree, GtkCTreeNode *node,
        gint column,gchar **text, guint8 *spacing, GdkPixmap **pixmap,
        GdkBitmap **mask);
```

The arguments to gtk_ctree_node_get_pixtext() are provided in Table 12.10.

Table 12.10 gtk_ctree_node_get_pixtext() Arguments

Argument	***Type***	***Value***
ctree	GtkCTree *	On input, the ctree containing the node to query
node	GtkCTreeNode *	On input, the node containing the data
column	gint	On input, the column from which data is to be retrieved
text	gchar **	On return, points to the text displayed by the node in the specified column
spacing	guint8 *	On return, the number of pixels that separate the image and text data
pixmap	GdkPixmap **	On return, a pointer to the pixmap data displayed by the node
mask	GdkBitmap **	On return, a pointer to the bitmap mask associated with pixmap

To set the text and pixmap for the specified node and column, you can call the related function gtk_ctree_mode_set_pixtext():

```
void
gtk_ctree_node_set_pixtext(GtkCTree *ctree, GtkCTreeNode *node,
        gint column, const gchar *text, guint8 spacing,
        GdkPixmap *pixmap, GdkBitmap *mask);
```

The arguments to gtk_ctree_node_set_pixtext() are provided in Table 12.11.

Table 12.11 gtk_ctree_node_set_pixtext() Arguments

Argument	***Type***	***Value***
ctree	GtkCTree *	On input, the ctree containing the node to change

Table 12.11 gtk_ctree_node_set_pixtext() Arguments (Continued)

Argument	*Type*	*Value*
node	GtkCTreeNode *	On input, the node to modify
column	gint	On input, the column in the node that will be modified
text	gchar *	On input, points to the text that will be displayed in the specified column
spacing	guint8	On input, the number of pixels that separate the image and text data
pixmap	GdkPixmap *	On input, a pointer to the pixmap data that will displayed by the node
mask	GdkBitmap *	On input, a pointer to the bitmap mask associated with pixmap

Retrieving and Modifying Node Attributes. The next two functions allow you to retrieve and modify most of the attributes you specified when adding a node to the tree. The first function, gtk_ctree_set_node_info(), can be called to modify the attributes of a node:

```
void
gtk_ctree_set_node_info(GtkCTree *ctree, GtkCTreeNode *node,
        const gchar *text, guint8 spacing, GdkPixmap *pixmap_closed,
        GdkBitmap *mask_closed, GdkPixmap *pixmap_opened,
        GdkBitmap *mask_opened, gboolean is_leaf, gboolean expanded);
```

The arguments ctree and node identify the node to be queried. The remainder of the arguments should be familiar to you by now (if not, refer to the description of gtk_ctree_insert_node() earlier in this section). The changes made here override those made at the time the node was created or by previous calls to gtk_ctree_set_node_info().

To retrieve attributes from a node, you can call gtk_ctree_get_node_info():

```
gint
gtk_ctree_get_node_info(GtkCTree *ctree, GtkCTreeNode *node,
        gchar **text, guint8 *spacing, GdkPixmap **pixmap_closed,
        GdkBitmap **mask_closed, GdkPixmap **pixmap_opened,
        GdkBitmap **mask_opened, gboolean *is_leaf,
        gboolean *expanded);
```

As is the case with gtk_ctree_set_node_info(), ctree and node identify a node in the tree that, in this case, will be queried for attributes. The remaining arguments are the addresses of variables of their respective types and will contain the desired attribute values once gtk_ctree_get_node_info() returns.

Setting a Column Offset. To offset the display of the data corresponding to the specified column in the specified node by the specified number of pixels, call gtk_ctree_node_set_shift():

```
void
gtk_ctree_node_set_shift(GtkCTree *ctree, GtkCTreeNode *node,
        gint column, gint vertical, gint horizontal);
```

The default value for both vertical and horizontal is 0. There is no function that can be used to query the shift value of a node/column in the tree.

Getting and Setting the Selectable Attribute of a Node. Your application can control the selectability of rows in the tree by calling gtk_ctree_node_set_selectable():

```
void
gtk_ctree_node_set_selectable(GtkCTree *ctree, GtkCTreeNode *node,
        gboolean selectable);
```

The selectability of a node can be queried by gtk_ctree_node_get_selectable():

```
gboolean
gtk_ctree_node_get_selectable(GtkCTree *ctree, GtkCTreeNode *node);
```

If the node can be selected by the user or programmatically by the application, TRUE will be returned.

Determining the Type of a Cell. Applications can determine the type of data stored by a column of a specific node in the tree by calling gtk_ctree_node_get_cell_type():

```
GtkCellType
gtk_ctree_node_get_cell_type(GtkCTree *ctree, GtkCTreeNode *node,
        gint column);
```

The arguments ctree, node, and column specify the column to query. Return values are provided in Table 12.12.

Table 12.12 GtkCellType

Value	*Meaning*
GTK_CELL_EMPTY	The column does not hold any data.
GTK_CELL_TEXT	The column contains text.
GTK_CELL_PIXMAP	The column contains a pixmap and mask.
GTK_CELL_PIXTEXT	The column is both GTK_CELL_TEXT and GTK_CELL_PIXMAP.
GTK_CELL_WIDGET	The column contains a widget (unimplemented in Gtk+ 1.2).

Setting and Getting Style Objects. The next few functions allow you to query or change the Gtk+ style objects of nodes in a tree or specific columns within a row. There are two pairs of setter and getter functions. One pair is used to set and get the style object of a row or node in a tree, while the other pair is used to set and get the style object of a specific column in a specific row. Let's first take a look at the row-oriented functions. To get a row (or node) style object, you can call gtk_ctree_node_get_row_style():

```
GtkStyle *
gtk_ctree_node_get_row_style(GtkCTree *ctree, GtkCTreeNode *node);
```

The arguments ctree and node identify the tree and row, respectively. The return value is a Gtk+ style object or NULL if none has been set.

The function gtk_ctree_node_set_row_style():

```
void
gtk_ctree_node_set_row_style(GtkCTree *ctree, GtkCTreeNode *node,
        GtkStyle *style);
```

can be used to replace the style object associated with a row (if there is one) with a style object of your choosing. The arguments ctree and node, once again, identify the tree and the node to which to attach the style. The argument style is the style object that will be attached to the specified node.

The following code snippet reads a style object from a node in the tree, makes a copy of it if it exists (or creates a new one if it does not), and then changes the font to one similar to the default Gtk+ font, except bold and italicized. It then calls gtk_ctree_node_set_row_style() to attach the new style object to the row from which the original style object was obtained.

```
GtkStyle *style, *new_style;
GdkFont *font;

...

// add a node to the tree

text[0] = "Ralph"; text[1] = "888"; text[2] = "666-444";
node = gtk_ctree_insert_node(GTK_CTREE(root), parent, NULL, text,
       5, NULL, NULL, NULL, NULL, FALSE, TRUE);

// read the style object -- this will be NULL here, but the following
// code illustrates how to deal with NULL and non-NULL return values

style = gtk_ctree_node_get_row_style( GTK_CTREE(root), node );
if ( style )
       new_style = gtk_style_copy( style );    // copy the one read
else
       new_style = gtk_style_new();            // create a new one

// load the Gtk+ default font, but bold and italicized

font = gdk_font_load(
```

```
        "-adobe-helvetica-bold-o-normal--*-120-*-*-*-*-iso8859-1");

// change the font if the above load was successful

if (font) {
        gdk_font_unref(new_style->font);
        new_style->font = font;
        gdk_font_ref(new_style->font);
}

// attach the style object to the node created above

gtk_ctree_node_set_row_style( GTK_CTREE(root), node, new_style );
```

Whatever can be done for an entire row can also be done for individual columns in a row. To retrieve the style object attached to a cell (if any), you can call gtk_ctree_node_get_cell_style():

```
GtkStyle *
gtk_ctree_node_get_cell_style(GtkCTree *ctree, GtkCTreeNode *node,
        gint column);
```

As is usual, ctree and node identify the tree and the row. The argument column, in the range of [1, *n*], with *n* equal to the number of columns in the tree, identifies the column from which the style object is to be read.

Setting the style object of a column is almost as easy as reading it and can be done by calling gtk_ctree_node_set_cell_style():

```
void
gtk_ctree_node_set_cell_style(GtkCTree *ctree, GtkCTreeNode *node,
        gint column, GtkStyle *style);
```

Setting Foreground and Background Colors. Two style-related functions can be used to set the foreground and background colors used to render the contents of columns in a row. To set the foreground color, call gtk_ctree_node_set_foreground():

```
void
gtk_ctree_node_set_foreground(GtkCTree *ctree, GtkCTreeNode *node,
        GdkColor *color);
```

To set the background color, call gtk_ctree_node_set_background():

```
void
gtk_ctree_node_set_background(GtkCTree *ctree, GtkCTreeNode *node,
        GdkColor *color);
```

Both of these functions accept a ctree and a node argument, which identify the node to be modified. Both functions also take as a third argument a pointer to a GdkColor object, which your application has obtained and initialized. If you pass NULL as the color argument, the effect of the previous call to gtk_ctree_node_set_foreground() (or gtk_ctree_ node_set_background(), as the case may be) will be negated because GtkCTree will revert to its default foreground (or background) color from that point on.

Determining Whether a Node Is Visible. You can call gtk_ctree_node_is_visible() to determine whether a node is visible or not:

```
GtkVisibility
gtk_ctree_node_is_visible(GtkCTree *ctree, GtkCTreeNode *node);
```

Potential return values include GTK_VISIBILITY_NONE (the row is not visible), GTK_VISIBILITY_PARTIAL (part of the row is visible), or GTK_VISIBILITY_FULL (all of the row is visible).

Scrolling a CTree to Make a Specific Node Visible. The final function described in this chapter will, when called, cause a ctree instance to scroll so that the specified column in the specified node is visible. The function gtk_ctree_node_moveto() takes five arguments:

```
void
gtk_ctree_node_moveto(GtkCTree *ctree, GtkCTreeNode *node,
        gint column, gfloat row_align, gfloat col_align);
```

The argument ctree identifies the GtkCTree instance, and node specifies the node or row. The argument column, in the range [1, *n*], where *n* is the number of columns in the tree, specifies the column to scroll into view. The arguments row_align and col_align, both of type gfloat, described how to place the data being put into view (see the description of gtk_clist_moveto() in Chapter 6).

Summary

A tree widget is similar to a list (GtkList and GtkCList) in that both can be used to display a set of items that can be selected from by a user. Trees are more powerful than lists because they give the programmer the ability to organize data in ways that lists simply do not allow, and they give the end user more control over how much data is displayed at any given time. In this chapter, we discussed the following tree-related widgets: GtkTree, GtkTreeItem, and GtkCTree. GtkTree and GtkTreeItem are used together to display trees that contain a (theoretically) infinite number of subtrees, with each node in the tree displaying a label or, if the application prefers, managing a widget of arbitrary type. (Typically, this widget will be a box widget that, in turn, manages arbitrary content such as a pixmap and label widget; see Figure 12.10.) GtkCTree is a much more involved widget (as suggested by its rather large API) that allows for the display of tree nodes consisting of multiple columns. A ctree widget displays resizable column headings for each column in the tree and supports keyboard bindings that allow the user to collapse and expand rows via keyboard input. However, unlike a tree item being displayed in a GtkTree widget, a ctree node can only display text-based data. Therefore, if your application must display image or other arbitrary data in a tree, using GtkTree and GtkTreeItem is currently the only option available.

CHAPTER

13

RANGE WIDGETS AND ADJUSTMENT OBJECTS

In this chapter, I will describe the Gtk+ range widgets listed in Table 13.1.

Table 13.1 Widgets Described in This Chapter

Class Name	*Description*
GtkRange	Parent class of the range widget classes discussed in this chapter
GtkScale	Scale widget parent class
GtkHScale	Horizontal scale widget
GtkVScale	Vertical scale widget
GtkScrollbar	Scrollbar widget parent class
GtkHScrollbar	Horizontal scrollbar widget
GtkVScrollbar	Vertical scrollbar widget
GtkAdjustment	Adjustment objects

As an application developer, you will only ever instantiate widgets belonging to the following widget classes: GtkHScale, GtkVScale, GtkHScrollbar, or GtkVScrollbar. The other widget classes (GtkRange, GtkScale, and GtkScrollbar) are base classes that contain functionality you might find useful when working with GtkHScale, GtkVScale, GtkHScrollbar, or GtkVScrollbar, but you will never actually create instances of these classes in your applications.

This chapter includes a discussion of Gtk+ adjustment objects (GtkAdjustment). Adjustment objects are the basis upon which the widget classes we look at in this chapter implement their functionality. Several Gtk+ widget classes, including GtkScrolledWindow, GtkCList, GtkLayout, and GtkProgress, create instances of range widgets (scales and scrollbars) or adjustment objects, and some of these classes allow you to specify an adjustment object at widget-creation time to override the adjustment object that the widget would normally create for itself.

Scale Widgets

Scale widgets give users a convenient way to select a value that falls within a predefined range. Figure 13.1 illustrates the two types of scale widget that Gtk+ supports: horizontal and vertical. The horizontal or vertical area of a scale widget represents the full range of values that can be selected by the user. Within this area, a movable "thumb" indicates the current value of the scale widget and can be positioned, using the keyboard or the mouse, to change the scale widget's value. Applications can arrange to be notified whenever the scale widget has changed its value. This strategy works especially well if the application needs to respond in real-time to values as they are selected by the user. An application can also query the value of a scale widget at a time that is most convenient to the application, for example, when the user has hit the OK button in the dialog displaying the scale widget to indicate that the value he or she has selected should be read and saved.

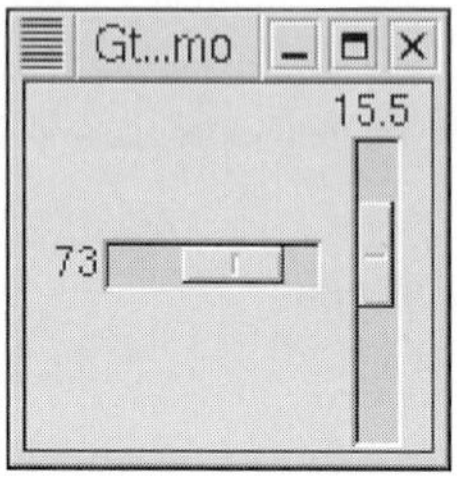

Figure 13.1 Horizontal and Vertical Scale Widgets

Scale widgets display a label, adjacent to the scale control, that indicates the current value of the scale widget. The default behavior of a scale widget is to show this label, but GtkScale allows you to hide the label if desired. You can also specify the location of the label relative to the scale control.

My presentation of GtkScale is organized as follows. First I will describe the two classes derived from GtkScale: GtkHScale and GtkVScale. These classes are the ones your application will instantiate directly, and they are both rather simple to describe. Once I have described both of these classes, I will then describe their parent class, GtkScale, in detail. I will then tie it all together with a sample application that illustrates how to respond to changes in a scale's value as they are made by a user and how to extract the value of a scale widget at a discrete point in time (e.g., when the user has dismissed a dialog containing a scale widget control).

GtkHScale

Class Name

```
GtkHScale
```

Parent Class Name

```
GtkScale
```

Macros

Widget type macro: `GTK_TYPE_HSCALE`

Object to widget cast macro: `GTK_HSCALE(obj)`

Widget type check macro: `GTK_IS_HSCALE(obj)`

Supported Arguments

Prefix: `GtkHScale::`

Table 13.2 GtkHScale Arguments

Name	*Type*	*Permissions*
adjustment	GTK_TYPE_ADJUSTMENT	GTK_ARG_READWRITE | GTK_ARG_CONSTRUCT

Application-Level API Synopsis

Return the constant GTK_TYPE_HSCALE at runtime:

```
GtkType
gtk_hscale_get_type(void)
```

Create a new instance of GtkHScale:

```
GtkWidget *
gtk_hscale_new(GtkAdjustment *adjustment)
```

Class Description

GtkHScale is a very simple class. For most applications, the only function of interest is the one used to create an instance of GtkHScale, gtk_hscale_new():

```
GtkWidget *
gtk_hscale_new(GtkAdjustment *adjustment)
```

The argument adjustment specifies an application-defined adjustment object. You must create an adjustment object of your own, or supply one created by some other widget, in order for the horizontal scale widget to work properly. I describe adjustment objects later in this chapter (see GtkAdjustment).

The following code snippet creates a horizontal scrollbar that allows the user to select values in the range of 0.0 to 99.0:

```
GtkAdjustment *adjustment;
GtkWidget *scale;

adjustment = gtk_adjustment_new(0.0, 0.0, 100.0, 0.1, 1.0, 1.0);

scale = gtk_hscale_new (GTK_ADJUSTMENT (adjustment));
```

GtkVScale

Class Name

```
GtkVScale
```

Parent Class Name

```
GtkScale
```

Macros

Widget type macro: `GTK_TYPE_VSCALE`

Object to widget cast macro: `GTK_VSCALE(obj)`

Widget type check macro: `GTK_IS_VSCALE(obj)`

Supported Arguments

Prefix: `GtkVScale::`

Table 13.3 GtkVScale Arguments

Name	*Type*	*Permissions*
adjustment	GTK_TYPE_ADJUSTMENT	GTK_ARG_READWRITE | GTK_ARG_CONSTRUCT

Application-Level API Synopsis

Return the constant GTK_TYPE_VSCALE at runtime:

```
GtkType
gtk_vscale_get_type(void)
```

Create a new instance of GtkVScale:

```
GtkWidget *
gtk_vscale_new(GtkAdjustment *adjustment)
```

Class Description

GtkVScale is nearly identical to GtkHScale, previously described, except that the widget created by GtkVScale is drawn vertically as opposed to horizontally, which is the case with GtkHScale. To create a new instance of GtkVScale, you can call gtk_hscale_new():

```
GtkWidget *
gtk_hscale_new(GtkAdjustment *adjustment)
```

As was the case with GtkHScale, adjustment is an application-defined adjustment object. For details and example code, see the preceding description of GtkHScale.

GtkScale

Class Name

`GtkScale`

Parent Class Name

```
GtkRange
```

Macros

Widget type macro: `GTK_TYPE_SCALE`

Object to widget cast macro: `GTK_SCALE(obj)`

Widget type check macro: `GTK_IS_SCALE(obj)`

Supported Arguments

Prefix: `GtkScale::`

Table 13.4 GtkScale Arguments

Name	*Type*	*Permissions*
digits	GTK_TYPE_INT	GTK_ARG_READWRITE
draw_value	GTK_TYPE_BOOL	GTK_ARG_READWRITE
value_pos	GTK_TYPE_POSITION_TYPE	GTK_ARG_READWRITE

Application-Level API Synopsis

Return the constant GTK_TYPE_SCALE at runtime:
```
GtkType
gtk_scale_get_type(void)
```

Set the number of significant digits displayed by a scale widget:
```
void
gtk_scale_set_digits(GtkScale *scale, gint digits)
```

Show or hide the scale value:
```
void
gtk_scale_set_draw_value(GtkScale *scale, gboolean draw_value)
```

Set the scale position type, controlling the location of the scale value:
```
void
gtk_scale_set_value_pos(GtkScale *scale, GtkPositionType pos)
```

Application-Level API Synopsis (Continued)

Get the width, in pixels, of the scale value text:
```
gint
gtk_scale_get_value_width(GtkScale *scale)
```

Cause the scale value to be (re)drawn:
```
void
gtk_scale_draw_value(GtkScale *scale)
```

Class Description

GtkScale is the parent class of GtkHScale and GtkVScale. As such, it provides interfaces that may be of interest to programmers who instantiate instances of either GtkHScale or GtkVScale.

Setting the Number of Significant Digits

The first function described here is gtk_scale_set_digits():

```
void
gtk_scale_set_digits(GtkScale *scale, gint digits)
```

This function allows the application to control the number of significant digits displayed by the scale widget label (when visible). Normally, the number of significant digits displayed is 1 (scale widget values are stored as floating point, as is the case for all widgets based on adjustment objects). Setting digits to 0 will cause the value to display as an integer.

Showing and Hiding the Scale Value

By default, a scale widget will display its value as a label. You can show or hide this label by calling gtk_scale_set_draw_value():

```
void
gtk_scale_set_draw_value(GtkScale *scale, gboolean draw_value)
```

The argument scale is an instance of GtkScale (GtkHScale or GtkVScale), and the argument draw_value is a boolean that controls the display of the scale widget label. If draw_value is set to TRUE, the label will be drawn; if set to FALSE, the label will be hidden from users.

Setting the Value Label Position

By default, both horizontal and vertical scale widgets will display their label above the scale widget control. You can change the default position by calling gtk_scale_set_value_pos():

```
void
gtk_scale_set_value_pos(GtkScale *scale, GtkPositionType pos)
```

The argument pos can be one of the following values listed in Table13.5.

Table 13.5 GtkPositionType Values

Value	*Meaning*
GTK_POS_LEFT	The value is displayed to the left of the control.
GTK_POS_RIGHT	The value is displayed to the right of the control.
GTK_POS_TOP	The value is displayed above the control (default).
GTK_POS_BOTTOM	The value is displayed below the control.

Miscellaneous Scale Widget Functions

Two perhaps-seldom-used functions allow you to get the width of the scale value text (gtk_scale_get_value_width()) and cause the scale to redraw its value (gtk_scale_draw_value()). The function prototypes for these two functions are as follows:

```
gint
gtk_scale_get_value_width(GtkScale *scale)

void
gtk_scale_draw_value(GtkScale *scale)
```

Each of these functions accepts an instance of GtkScale as its only argument. The function gtk_scale_get_value_width() returns the width, in pixels, of the text being (or that would be) displayed by the scale widget.

An Example

Now it is time for a sample program. The sample program creates an instance of GtkHScale, placing the scale value to the left of the slider. An instance of GtkVScale is also created and is displayed next to the horizontal scale. Its label is drawn in the default location. Both of the scales can be set, by the user and independently of each other, to a value in the range of [0, 100]. The number of significant digits displayed by the horizontal scale widget label is set to 0. The vertical scale widget displays the default value of 1 significant digit.

Each scale widget displays its current value whenever a change to the scale's thumb position is made by the user. This is done by printing the value of the scale widget to stderr from within a value_changed signal function that is registered by the application for each adjustment object created. This illustrates how an application can monitor changes made to a scale's value as they are made. An OK button (GtkButton) is also displayed below the scale widgets. Pressing this button causes a clicked signal function to be invoked; the clicked signal function queries each of the adjustment objects for its current value and displays the values retrieved to stderr as well. This illustrates how an application can retrieve the value of a scale at a discrete point in time. I will describe the use of adjustment objects in more detail later in this chapter (feel free to skip ahead and read about adjustment objects before looking at the source code I am about to present). The example presented here is simple, but it does illustrate most of what you will need to know to make use of scale widgets in your applications.

Listing 13.1 Widget Example

```
#include <gtk/gtk.h>
#include <stdio.h>

// a data type that makes it possible to pass both adjustment objects as
// client data to the HandleOkButton() signal function

typedef struct _adjustments {
    GtkAdjustment *adj1;
    GtkAdjustment *adj2;
} Adjustments;

// called when the user presses the Ok button

static void
HandleOkButton(GtkWidget *w, gpointer data)
{
    Adjustments *adjs = (Adjustments *) data;

    fprintf( stderr, "Hscale value is %d vscale value is %.1f\n",
             (int) adjs->adj1->value, adjs->adj2->value );
}

// called when the user changes the value of the first scale widget

static void
Adjustment1Changed(GtkAdjustment *w, gpointer data)
{
    fprintf( stderr, "Adjustment 1 is %d\n", (int) w->value );
}

// called when the user changes the value of the second scale widget

static void
Adjustment2Changed(GtkAdjustment *w, gpointer data)
{
    fprintf( stderr, "Adjustment 2 is %.1f\n", w->value );
}

main( argc, argv )
int argc;
```

```
char *argv[];
{
    GtkWidget *hscale, *vscale, *vbox, *hbox, *window, *button;
    GtkObject *adj1, *adj2;
    Adjustments adjustments;

    gtk_init( &argc, &argv );

    window = gtk_window_new(GTK_WINDOW_TOPLEVEL);
    gtk_window_position(GTK_WINDOW(window), GTK_WIN_POS_MOUSE);

    gtk_signal_connect(GTK_OBJECT(window), "destroy",
             GTK_SIGNAL_FUNC(gtk_widget_destroyed), &window);

    gtk_window_set_title(GTK_WINDOW (window), "GtkScale Demo");

    vbox = gtk_vbox_new( FALSE, 0 );
    gtk_container_add( GTK_CONTAINER( window ), vbox );

    hbox = gtk_hbox_new( FALSE, 0 );
    gtk_box_pack_start( GTK_BOX( vbox ), hbox, TRUE, TRUE, 0 );

    // create an adjustment object for the first scale widget

    adj1 = gtk_adjustment_new(0.0, 0.0, 100.0, 1.0, 5.0, 0.0);
    gtk_signal_connect(GTK_OBJECT(adj1), "value_changed",
             GTK_SIGNAL_FUNC(Adjustment1Changed), NULL);

    // create a horizontal scale widget. Display the value to the
    // left of the scale, and display scale value as an integer

    hscale = gtk_hscale_new( GTK_ADJUSTMENT(adj1) );
    gtk_scale_set_value_pos( GTK_SCALE(hscale), GTK_POS_LEFT );
    gtk_scale_set_digits( GTK_SCALE(hscale), 0 );

    gtk_box_pack_start( GTK_BOX( hbox ), hscale, TRUE, TRUE, 0 );

    // create an adjustment object for the second scale widget

    adj2 = gtk_adjustment_new(0.0, 0.0, 100.0, 1.0, 5.0, 0.0);
    gtk_signal_connect(GTK_OBJECT(adj2), "value_changed",
             GTK_SIGNAL_FUNC(Adjustment2Changed), NULL);

    // create a vertical scale widget using widget-supplied defaults

    vscale = gtk_vscale_new( GTK_ADJUSTMENT(adj2) );

    gtk_box_pack_start( GTK_BOX( hbox ), vscale, TRUE, TRUE, 0 );

```

```
090     adjustments.adj1 = GTK_ADJUSTMENT(adj1);
091     adjustments.adj2 = GTK_ADJUSTMENT(adj2);
092
093     button = gtk_button_new_with_label( "Ok" );
094     gtk_signal_connect(GTK_OBJECT(button), "clicked",
095             (GtkSignalFunc) HandleOkButton, &adjustments);
096
097     gtk_box_pack_end( GTK_BOX( vbox ), button, FALSE, FALSE, 0 );
098
099     gtk_widget_show_all( GTK_WIDGET( window ) );
100
101     gtk_main();
102 }
```

Perhaps the most important thing to notice about the preceding code is the use of adjustment objects. It should be clear that it is the adjustment object that is used to specify the range that the scale widget represents; this should be clear from lines 065 and 080, which create the adjustment objects and set their ranges, and by lines 072 and 086, which associate the adjustment objects with the scaled widgets that make use of them. It should also be clear that it is the adjustment object that maintains the value of the scale widget as this value is changed by the user. This is demonstrated by the value_changed signal function, which reads the adjustment object for its current value to determine the value currently being displayed by the scale widget, and by the OK button's clicked signal function, which essentially does the same thing. As an exercise, change line 086 to read as follows:

```
086     vscale = gtk_vscale_new( GTK_ADJUSTMENT(adj1) );
```

That is, change the "adj2" to "adj1" and then re-execute the program. What are the results of this change? Be sure to read the section on adjustment objects, presented later in this chapter, for details on how adjustment objects can be shared in this manner among multiple widgets.

The relationship of scale widgets to adjustment objects is the same for all of the widgets derived from GtkRange. (Currently, the only other widget class that is derived from GtkRange is GtkScrollbar.)

Scrollbars

The Gtk+ classes (GtkHScrollbar, GtkVScrollbar, and GtkScrollbar) that I will discuss in this section make up the set of Gtk+ scrollbar classes derived from GtkRange. Scrollbars are used by widget writers for the most part and not by application writers. Application writers should usually get by using a widget such as GtkScrolledWindow to parent content that needs to be scrolled. This may also be true if you are designing a widget that supports scrolling. GtkText makes use of GtkScrolledWindow, not its own scrollbars, to implement its scrolling capability. As it turns out, the only Gtk+ classes that instantiate their own scrollbars (as of Gtk 1.2.7) are GtkMain and GtkScrolledWindow.

In several ways, scrollbars as similar to scale widgets (which are described in the preceding section). Both can be used to control the value of a GtkAdjustment object, and both can be manipulated by a user to select a value within a range. However, you should always use GtkHScale or GtkVScale to create a control of this type; if there are scrollbars present in your user interface, they should be ones created by a GtkScrolledWindow or by some other widget class, not directly by your application. The reason for this is that users expect that scale widgets will be used to select a value in a range, whereas scrollbars are expected to control a view into a larger virtual set of data being managed by the application (a document or an image), and this sort of job is best handled by a container widget such as the scrolled window widget. The next few pages document the GtkScrollbar classes in detail.

GtkHScrollbar

Class Name

```
GtkHScrollbar
```

Parent Class Name

```
GtkScrollbar
```

Macros

Widget type macro: `GTK_TYPE_HSCROLLBAR`

Object to widget cast macro: `GTK_HSCROLLBAR(obj)`

Widget type check macro: `GTK_IS_HSCROLLBAR(obj)`

Application-Level API Synopsis

Return the constant GTK_TYPE_HSCROLLBAR at runtime:

```
GtkType
gtk_hscrollbar_get_type(void)
```

Create a new instance of GtkHScrollbar with an optional adjustment object:

```
GtkWidget *
gtk_hscrollbar_new(GtkAdjustment *adjustment)
```

Class Description

GtkHScrollbar is a simple class providing one function, gtk_hscrollbar_new(), that can be used to create a horizontal scrollbar:

```
GtkWidget *
gtk_hscrollbar_new(GtkAdjustment *adjustment)
```

The only argument to gtk_hscrollbar_new() is a GtkAdjustment object. This can be any adjustment object, either one created specifically for this instance of GtkHScrollbar or some other adjustment object that is in use by some other widget instance. Although you can pass NULL as a parameter, this will render the scrollbar useless; an adjustment object will be created for you, but the adjustment object's attributes will not be ones needed by your application. You can retrieve the adjustment object created on your behalf with a call to gtk_range_get_adjustment() (described later in this chapter) and set adjustment values using the GtkAdjustment API (also described later in this chapter). You also can call gtk_range_set_adjustment() to set the scrollbar adjustment object, but in the end, it is easier to simply pass a non-NULL adjustment object to gtk_hscrollbar_new() than to use any other possible method.

GtkVScrollbar

Class Name

```
GtkVScrollbar
```

Parent Class Name

```
GtkScrollbar
```

Macros

Widget type macro: `GTK_TYPE_VSCROLLBAR`

Object to widget cast macro: `GTK_VSCROLLBAR(obj)`

Widget type check macro: `GTK_IS_VSCROLLBAR(obj)`

Application-Level API Synopsis

Return the constant GTK_TYPE_VSCROLLBAR at runtime:
```
GtkType
gtk_vscrollbar_get_type(void)
```

Create a new instance of GtkVScrollbar with an optional adjustment object:
```
GtkWidget *
gtk_vscrollbar_new(GtkAdjustment *adjustment)
```

Class Description

GtkVScrollbar is similar to GtkHScrollbar, except it is used to create vertical scrollbars, not horizontal scrollbars. Like GtkHScrollbar, there is only one function of interest used to create an instance of GtkVScrollbar:

```
GtkWidget *
gtk_vscrollbar_new(GtkAdjustment *adjustment)
```

Like gtk_hscrollbar_new(), gtk_vscrollbar_new() accepts only a single argument, which is an adjustment object provided by your application. Refer to the preceding text that described gtk_hscrollbar_new() for more details regarding the adjustment argument to gtk_v scrollbar_new().

GtkScrollbar

Class Name

```
GtkScrollbar
```

Parent Class Name

```
GtkRange
```

Macros

Widget type macro: `GTK_TYPE_SCROLLBAR`

Object to widget cast macro: `GTK_SCROLLBAR(obj)`

Widget type check macro: `GTK_IS_SCROLLBAR(obj)`

Application-Level API Synopsis

Return the constant GTK_TYPE_SCROLLBAR at runtime:
```
GtkType
gtk_scrollbar_get_type(void)
```

Class Description

GtkScrollbar is simply the parent class of GtkHScrollbar and GtkVScrollbar. As such, it provides little implementation. The only function that is exposed is gtk_scrollbar_get_type(), which simply returns the constant GTK_TYPE_SCROLLBAR at runtime.

Adjustment Objects

Adjustment objects are perhaps one of the more innovative features of Gtk+. In a nutshell, an adjustment object is used to separate the widget that displays values in a range (e.g., scrollbars and scales) from the object that defines the range and maintains its current value. Therefore, instead of storing the minimum, maximum, and current values of a range within a scrollbar or scale widget instance, the data is stored in an adjustment object. The widget (e.g., the scale or scrollbar) then holds a reference to the adjustment object. If the user moves the scale widget thumb or clicks on a scrollbar arrow, the scale or scrollbar widget, as the case may be, changes the current value stored in the adjustment object to reflect the change made in the UI by the user. Likewise, if the application changes the current value of the adjustment object programmatically (see gtk_adjustment_change_value() later in this chapter), the scale widget or scrollbar widget responds by redrawing itself to reflect the newly set value of the adjustment object. Changes made to attributes of an adjustment object, other than the current value, can have similar effects on the user interface.

There are some advantages to this architecture. First, a widget does not have to invent a way to represent and manage ranges of values. It can rely on the adjustment object to implement the details; it simply needs to know how to talk to the adjustment object using the API that is provided. Second, the application writer needs only to learn about adjustment objects as opposed to learning about an API that is specific to an individual widget class. The callback used to retrieve the value from a horizontal scale widget (refer to HandleOkButton()) will work, without any modification, with any widget that uses adjustment objects. That is, the same code can be used to retrieve the value from a horizontal or vertical scale widget or from a horizontal or vertical scrollbar.

Finally, adjustment objects can be shared among widgets. For example, you might share an adjustment object among an instance of a horizontal scale widget and a vertical scrollbar widget instance. As the user changes the scale widget, the vertical scrollbar will also change, and vice-versa. Sharing an adjustment object among 2 or more widget instances is simple. All you need to do is create (or obtain) an adjustment object, and pass it to the widget creation routines of the widgets that you want to share it.

Implementation of Adjustment Objects. Let's now look at the internal structure of adjustment objects. The following is the implementation from Gtk+ 1.2.7:

```
typedef struct _GtkAdjustment GtkAdjustment;

...

struct _GtkAdjustment

  GtkData data;

  gfloat lower;
  gfloat upper;
  gfloat value;
  gfloat step_increment;
  gfloat page_increment;
  gfloat page_size;
};
```

The most important fields are summarized in Table 13.6.

Table 13.6 Important GtkAdjustment Object Fields

Field	*Value*
lower	The minimum possible value represented by the adjustment
upper	The maximum possible value represented by the adjustment, with page size affecting the user-settable upper bound

Table 13.6 Important GtkAdjustment Object Fields (Continued)

Field	*Value*
value	The current value represented by the adjustment, in the range [lower, upper - page_size]
step_increment	The smallest amount of change that can be applied to "value" by a user interface control
page_increment	The largest amount of change that can be applied to "value" by a user interface control
page_size	Interpreted in a widget-specific manner.

You use lower and upper when creating the adjustment object to define the range of allowable values to which the adjustment object can be set, and you use value to set an initial value for the control, to change its value at runtime, or to obtain its value. The fields step_increment and page_increment are basically used in the same way by both scrollbars and scale widgets. In scale widgets, step_increment specifies the smallest incremental change (negative or positive) that can be made to the value of the scale widget by the user. Such a change can be made by moving the scale widget thumb by positioning the pointer over the thumb, clicking and holding down mouse button 1, and dragging the thumb to the new position. For scrollbars, step_increment corresponds to the change in value, again either positive or negative, that occurs whenever the user clicks mouse button 1 on one of the arrows found at either end of the scrollbar. The field page_increment is used by scale widgets to position the thumb after the user clicks mouse button 1 within the trough. This is also the way that scrollbars make use of page_increment (both scale and scrollbar widgets rely on the parent class, GtkRange, for this functionality).

The field page_size is ignored by GtkScale and its derived widgets, so setting it to zero is a good idea. For scrollbars, page_size is used to size the thumb in such a way that it conveys to the user the amount of data currently being displayed by the widget controlled by the scrollbar, relative to the total size of the data that can be viewed by the user (by manipulating the position of the scrollbar thumb). The relative amount of space occupied in the trough by the scrollbar thumb can be computed by the following equation:

```
1 / ((upper - lower) / page_size)
```

For example, with the following values:

```
upper: 100
lower: 0
page_size: 1
```

the amount of space occupied by the thumb will be 1/100 (i.e., one percent of the trough size, with the scrollable area displaying one percent of the total content available for viewing). If we were to set the page size to 50, we would cause the thumb size to be much larger, covering 50 percent of the trough. In this case, the user would expect that positioning the adjustment at 0 (moving the scrollbar to the top) would expose the top 50 percent of the viewable content, while positioning the adjustment at 50 (i.e., moving the scrollbar to the bottom) would expose the bottom 50 percent of the content. page_size affects the range of values that the adjustment object can take on; in the preceding example (page size is equal to 1), the maximum value that can be set by the user is 99, while in the case of a page size that is equal to 50, the maximum value that can be set by the user is 50.

So far, I haven't mentioned the unit size of page_size, step_increment, or any of the other fields of an adjustment object. Some of you have assumed that we are working with pixels (e.g., the value of an adjustment can be set to 50 pixels). In some cases this is true, but the reality is that adjustment objects are unit-size neutral. It is up to the application to determine the unit size that the adjustment object is working with, and as far as adjustment objects are concerned, the unit size is completely arbitrary. For example, suppose we are writing a fitness program that prompts the user for his or her weight with a scale widget. In this case, the unit size of the adjustment used by the scale widget is going to be either pounds or kilograms, not pixels.

GtkAdjustment

Class Name

```
GtkAdjustment
```

Parent Class Name

```
GtkData
```

Macros

Widget type macro: `GTK_TYPE_ADJUSTMENT`

Object to widget cast macro: `GTK_ADJUSTMENT(obj)`

Widget type check macro: `GTK_IS_ADJUSTMENT(obj)`

Supported Signals

Table 13.7 Signals

Signal Name	*Condition Causing Signal to Trigger*
changed	An internal attribute of the adjustment object (e.g., page_size) has been changed.
value_changed	The user (or the application) has changed the value of the adjustment object.

Signal Function Prototypes

```
void
changed(GtkAdjustment *adjustment, gpointer user_data);

void
value_changed(GtkAdjustment *adjustment, gpointer user_data);
```

Application-Level API Synopsis

Return the constant GTK_TYPE_ADJUSTMENT at runtime:

```
GtkType
gtk_adjustment_get_type(void)
```

Create a new instance of GtkAdjustment:

```
GtkObject *
gtk_adjustment_new(gfloat value, gfloat lower, gfloat upper,
         gfloat step_increment, gfloat page_increment,
         gfloat page_size)
```

Notify an adjustment that one of its attributes has been changed, generating a changed signal:

```
void
gtk_adjustment_changed(GtkAdjustment *adjustment)
```

Notify an adjustment that its value has changed, generating a value_changed signal:

```
void
gtk_adjustment_value_changed(GtkAdjustment *adjustment)
```

Set the value of an adjustment:

```
void
gtk_adjustment_set_value(GtkAdjustment *adjustment, gfloat value)
```

Class Description

Adjustment objects were introduced earlier in this chapter. If you haven't done so already, read the preceding section entitled "Adjustment Objects." Here I will briefly describe the GtkAdjustment object API, and then I will present two sample applications that should illustrate the issues involved with the setting and use of GtkAdjustment object attributes such as page_size, value, and so on.

Creating an Adjustment Object

To create an instance of GtkAdjustment, call gtk_adjustment_new():

```
GtkObject *
gtk_adjustment_new(gfloat value, gfloat lower, gfloat upper,
         gfloat step_increment, gfloat page_increment,
         gfloat page_size)
```

The return value is a GtkObject (adjustments are objects, not widgets). You can use the GTK_ADJUSTMENT macro to coerce an object to an adjustment when needed, as I will illustrate in the following sample code. Each of the arguments to gtk_adjustment_new() corresponds to fields defined by the GtkAdjustment types documented in Table 13.6.

Changing Adjustment Object Attributes

You can set any of these fields after object creation by coercing the GtkObject returned by gtk_adjustment_new() and accessing the fields of the GtkAdjustment type directly. For example:

```
GtkObject *adj;

GTK_ADJUSTMENT( adj )->lower = 10.0;
GTK_ADJUSTMENT( adj )->upper = 30.0;
GTK_ADJUSTMENT( adj )->step_increment = 1.0;
GTK_ADJUSTMENT( adj )->page_increment = 5.0;
GTK_ADJUSTMENT( adj )->page_size = 1.0;
GTK_ADJUSTMENT( adj )->value = 25.0;
```

If you change the value of the value field in this manner, you must make a call to gtk_value_adjustment_changed() to ensure that the change to the value field will be reflected in the user interface (i.e., so that all widgets using the adjustment object will be given an opportunity to redraw themselves). The function prototype for gtk_value_adjustment_changed() is as follows:

```
void
gtk_adjustment_value_changed(GtkAdjustment *adjustment)
```

The argument adjustment is the adjustment object that has had its value changed. You can get around the need for calling gtk_adjustment_value_changed() by calling gtk_adjustment_set_value(), which sets the value of the adjustment and, if the value has changed, calls gtk_adjustment_value_changed() for you automatically. The function prototype for gtk_adjustment_set_value() is, quite predictably:

```
void
gtk_adjustment_set_value(GtkAdjustment *adjustment, gfloat value)
```

Changing any of the other fields (lower, upper, step_increment, page_increment, and page_size) requires you to notify the adjustment so that it can, in turn, make sure that all widgets using the adjustment object are given an opportunity to handle the change as necessary (e.g., to redraw themselves). To do this, call gtk_adjustment_changed():

```
void
gtk_adjustment_changed(GtkAdjustment *adjustment)
```

The function gtk_adjustment_changed() takes an adjustment object as an argument.

Working with Adjustment Objects

As I discussed earlier in this section, the unit size of an adjustment object is arbitrary. For example, an adjustment object can just as easily represent pounds or kilograms as it can represent pixels; the interpretation of units is up to the application. The following two sample applications illustrate how applications that manage their own scrollbars might deal with this issue.

In the first example, I illustrate how to display image data in a window that has a size smaller than the image. Vertical and horizontal scrollbars are used to navigate the image data. In this case, the unit of scrolling is 1 pixel, as reflected by the page_size attribute of the adjustment objects that is set to 1 by the program.

The program creates a window that is 100×75 pixels in size. This window is made nonresizeable. A vertical box widget is packed with a horizontal box and a horizontal scrollbar. The horizontal box is packed (from left to right) with a drawing-area widget, which will be used to display the image data, as well as a vertical scrollbar.

An instance of GdkPixmap is created to hold the image data by making a call to gdk_pixmap_create_from_xpm(). Because a pixmap is an X drawable resource, it has a size just like an X window does, and this size can be queried for by the application with a call to gdk_window_get_geometry(). Once we know this size, the application can give the sizes of the other user-interface components (the width of the vertical scrollbar, the height of the horizontal scrollbar, and the size of the window) and set correct values for both the horizontal and the vertical scrollbar adjustment objects. For the vertical scrollbar adjustment object, the following values are set with the following code:

```
GTK_ADJUSTMENT( adj1 )->lower = 0.0;
GTK_ADJUSTMENT( adj1 )->upper = (float) height - 1.0;
GTK_ADJUSTMENT( adj1 )->step_increment = 1.0;
GTK_ADJUSTMENT( adj1 )->page_increment = 25.0;
GTK_ADJUSTMENT( adj1 )->page_size = 1.0;
GTK_ADJUSTMENT( adj1 )->value = 0.0;
```

Here, the page_size is set to 1 pixel, and we are allowing the user to scroll to any position in the range of [0, *height* - 1], where *height* is the height of the image minus the height of the window (less the height of the horizontal scrollbar). If the user clicks on the vertical scrollbar arrows, the image will be scrolled 1 pixel (step_increment is set to 1). Clicking within the trough will result in a vertical scroll of 25 pixels (page_increment = 25). Setting the fields of the horizontal scrollbar adjustment object follows along similar lines. See the function SetAdjustments() in the following listing.

Movement of either the vertical or horizontal scrollbar results in a call to the value_changed signal function AdjustmentChanged(). In this callback, a call to gdk_draw_pixmap() is made. gdk_draw_pixmap() performs an XCopyArea of the appropriate region in the source pixmap to the window that was created for the GtkDrawingArea widget. The function prototype for gtk_draw_pixmap() is as follows:

```
void
gdk_draw_pixmap(
        GdkDrawable *drawable, // target drawable
        GdkGC *gc, // X graphics context
        GdkDrawable *src, // src drawable (the pixmap)
        gint xsrc, // x origin of data in source pixmap
        gint ysrc, // y origin of data in source pixmap
        gint xdest, // x destination of data in target drawable
        gint ydest, // y destination of data in target drawable
        gint width, // width of area to be copied
        gint height); // height of area to be copied
```

The signal function, AdjustmentChanged():

```
static void
AdjustmentChanged(GtkAdjustment *w, gpointer data)
{
        GtkWidget *drawing = (GtkWidget *) data;
        int x = GTK_ADJUSTMENT(adj2)->value;
        int y = GTK_ADJUSTMENT(adj1)->value;

        gdk_draw_pixmap(drawing->window, gc, pmap, x, y, 0, 0,
                100, 75);
}
```

retrieves the value attributes of both the vertical and horizontal scrollbar adjustment objects and uses these values to define the origin of the area to be copied from the off-screen pixmap to the destination window. As you can see, xsrc and ysrc are set to x (the horizontal scrollbar adjustment object value) and y (the vertical scrollbar adjustment object value), respectively. The destination origin is always set to 0, 0 because we want the region being viewed to be completely viewable in the drawing-area window. width and height are set to 100 and 75, respectively. In reality, we need to copy less than this because 100×75 is the size of the window, and it does not account for the width and height of the vertical and horizontal scrollbars, each of which takes some of the viewable size of the window away, leaving that much less for the drawing area widget, which is the target of the copy. If we needed to be more precise, we would query the size of the drawing-area widget window and use the result to determine the size of the area to be copied. However, we can let clipping deal with the overrun; 100×75 is close enough and does not add significantly to the amount of time it takes to copy the pixmap data.

Here is the complete source code for the sample I just described:

Listing 13.2 GtkAdjustment Example 1

```
#include <gtk/gtk.h>
#include <stdlib.h>

static GdkPixmap *pmap;
static GdkGC *gc;
GtkObject *adj1, *adj2;

void
SetAdjustments( GtkObject *adj1, GtkObject *adj2, int width, int height )
{
    GTK_ADJUSTMENT( adj1 )->lower = 0.0;
    GTK_ADJUSTMENT( adj1 )->upper = (float) height - 1.0;
    GTK_ADJUSTMENT( adj1 )->step_increment = 1.0;
    GTK_ADJUSTMENT( adj1 )->page_increment = 25.0;
    GTK_ADJUSTMENT( adj1 )->page_size = 1.0;
    GTK_ADJUSTMENT( adj1 )->value = 0.0;

    GTK_ADJUSTMENT( adj2 )->lower = 0.0;
    GTK_ADJUSTMENT( adj2 )->upper = (float) width - 1.0;
    GTK_ADJUSTMENT( adj2 )->step_increment = 1.0;
    GTK_ADJUSTMENT( adj2 )->page_increment = 25.0;
    GTK_ADJUSTMENT( adj2 )->page_size = 1.0;
    GTK_ADJUSTMENT( adj2 )->value = 0.0;
}

static void
AdjustmentChanged(GtkAdjustment *w, gpointer data)
{
    GtkWidget *drawing = (GtkWidget *) data;
    int x = GTK_ADJUSTMENT(adj2)->value;
    int y = GTK_ADJUSTMENT(adj1)->value;

    gdk_draw_pixmap(drawing->window, gc, pmap, x, y, 0, 0, 100, 75);
}

main( argc, argv )
int argc;
char *argv[];
{
    GtkWidget *window, *hsb, *vsb, *vbox, *hbox, *drawing;
    int width, height, x, y, depth;
    int hsbwidth, hsbheight, vsbwidth, vsbheight;
    GdkBitmap *mask;
```

```

        gtk_init( &argc, &argv );

        window = gtk_window_new(GTK_WINDOW_TOPLEVEL);
        gtk_window_position(GTK_WINDOW(window), GTK_WIN_POS_MOUSE);
        gtk_widget_set_usize(window, 100, 75);
        gtk_window_set_policy(GTK_WINDOW( window ), FALSE, FALSE, TRUE);
        gtk_widget_show( window );

        gtk_signal_connect(GTK_OBJECT(window), "destroy",
                GTK_SIGNAL_FUNC(gtk_widget_destroyed), &window);

        gtk_window_set_title(GTK_WINDOW (window), "GtkAdjustment Demo");

        vbox = gtk_vbox_new( FALSE, 0 );
        gtk_container_add( GTK_CONTAINER( window ), vbox );

        hbox = gtk_hbox_new( FALSE, 0 );
        gtk_box_pack_start( GTK_BOX( vbox ), hbox, TRUE, TRUE, 0 );

        drawing = gtk_drawing_area_new();

        adj1 = gtk_adjustment_new(0.0, 0.0, 0.0, 1.0, 5.0, 0.0);
        gtk_signal_connect(GTK_OBJECT(adj1), "value_changed",
                GTK_SIGNAL_FUNC(AdjustmentChanged), drawing);

        vsb = gtk_vscrollbar_new( GTK_ADJUSTMENT(adj1) );

        gtk_box_pack_end( GTK_BOX( hbox ), vsb, FALSE, TRUE, 0 );

        adj2 = gtk_adjustment_new(0.0, 0.0, 0.0, 1.0, 5.0, 0.0);
        gtk_signal_connect(GTK_OBJECT(adj2), "value_changed",
                GTK_SIGNAL_FUNC(AdjustmentChanged), drawing);

        hsb = gtk_hscrollbar_new( GTK_ADJUSTMENT(adj2) );

        gtk_box_pack_end( GTK_BOX( vbox ), hsb, FALSE, TRUE, 0 );

        gtk_box_pack_start( GTK_BOX( hbox ), drawing, TRUE, TRUE, 0 );

        gtk_widget_show_all( GTK_WIDGET( window ) );

        pmap = gdk_pixmap_create_from_xpm(drawing->window, &mask,
                (GdkColor *) NULL, "stang.xpm");

        gc = gdk_gc_new( drawing->window );

        gdk_window_get_geometry((GdkWindow *) hsb->window, &x, &y, &hsbwidth,
                &hsbheight, &depth);

        gdk_window_get_geometry((GdkWindow *) vsb->window, &x, &y, &vsbwidth,
                &vsbheight, &depth);

        gdk_window_get_geometry((GdkWindow *) pmap, &x, &y, &width, &height,
                &depth);
```

```
    SetAdjustments( adj1, adj2, (width - 100) + vsbwidth,
            (height - 75) + hsbheight );

    gtk_main();
}
```

The next sample is very similar to the preceding. Instead of loading an image, the second sample program creates an off-screen pixmap that is 512×512 pixels in size. The program tiles this pixmap with 32 rows of 16×16 rectangles (a total of 32 rectangles are drawn for each row). The color of each rectangle is randomly computed at the time the rectangle is drawn. The page_size attribute is set to 16, lower is set to 0 (as before), upper is set to the width of the window less page_size, step_increment is 16 pixels, and page_increment is set to 32 pixels. The end result is that the user will see each click of the scrollbar buttons moving the display by one row or column (depending on which scrollbar is being clicked), while clicks in the trough result in moving the display by two rows or columns. In this case, we have set our adjustment so that the user can only scroll rows or columns. Other types of data (text, cells in a spreadsheet, and so forth) should usually be scrolled at no less than the size of the data being displayed. If you are managing a table that contains cells of a certain height, the unit of scrolling should be based on the height of the cell (or the width in the case of a horizontal scrollbar). If you are displaying a body of text, the vertical scrollbar should be oriented toward a scroll unit based on the average height of a character, in pixels, in the font being used to display the text (or, perhaps, the height of the tallest character in the font). Similarly, you would initialize a horizontal scrollbar adjustment object in this scenario so that the unit of scrolling is based on the average width of characters in the font being used to display the text.

Here, I just show the function used to create the pixmap (for those of you who are interested in the details) and the changes made to the function SetAdjustments():

Listing 13.3 GtkAdjustment Example 2

```
#define RAND( x ) ((int) (((float) random() / (RAND_MAX - 1)) * x))

void
BuildPixmap( GdkWindow * window )
{
    int i, j;
    GdkColor color;

    pmap = gdk_pixmap_new( window, 512, 512, -1 );
    for ( i = 0; i < 32; i++ )
            for ( j = 0; j < 32; j++ ) {
                    color.red = RAND( 65535 );
                    color.green = RAND( 65535 );
                    color.blue = RAND( 65535 );
                    gdk_color_alloc(gdk_colormap_get_system (), &color);
                    gdk_gc_set_foreground( gc, &color );
                    gdk_draw_rectangle((GdkDrawable *) pmap, gc,
                            TRUE, i * 16, j * 16, 16, 16 );
            }
```

```
}

void
SetAdjustments( GtkObject *adj1, GtkObject *adj2, int width, int height )
{
    GTK_ADJUSTMENT( adj1 )->lower = 0.0;
    GTK_ADJUSTMENT( adj1 )->upper = (float) height - 16.0;
    GTK_ADJUSTMENT( adj1 )->step_increment = 16.0;
    GTK_ADJUSTMENT( adj1 )->page_increment = 32.0;
    GTK_ADJUSTMENT( adj1 )->page_size = 16.0;
    GTK_ADJUSTMENT( adj1 )->value = 0.0;

    GTK_ADJUSTMENT( adj2 )->lower = 0.0;
    GTK_ADJUSTMENT( adj2 )->upper = (float) width - 16.0;
    GTK_ADJUSTMENT( adj2 )->step_increment = 16.0;
    GTK_ADJUSTMENT( adj2 )->page_increment = 32.0;
    GTK_ADJUSTMENT( adj2 )->page_size = 16.0;
    GTK_ADJUSTMENT( adj2 )->value = 0.0;
}
```

The only other changes that must be made to the first example are to the window width and height arguments that are passed to the various routines that require them (100 and 75 are both changed to 512 to reflect the new window dimensions).

GtkRange

Class Name

`GtkRange`

Parent Class Name

`GtkWidget`

Macros

Widget type macro: `GTK_TYPE_RANGE`

Object to widget cast macro: `GTK_RANGE(obj)`

Widget type check macro: `GTK_IS_RANGE(obj)`

Supported Arguments

Prefix: `GtkRange::`

Table 13.8 GtkRange Argument

Name	*Type*	*Permission*
update_policy	GTK_TYPE_UPDATE_TYPE	GTK_ARG_READWRITE

Application-Level API Synopsis

Return the constant GTK_TYPE_RANGE at runtime:

```
GtkType
gtk_range_get_type(void)
```

Retrieve the adjustment object associated with a range widget:

```
GtkAdjustment *
gtk_range_get_adjustment(GtkRange *range)
```

Set the range widget update policy:

```
void
gtk_range_set_update_policy(GtkRange *range, GtkUpdateType policy)
```

Set the range adjustment object:

```
void
gtk_range_set_adjustment(GtkRange *range,
        GtkAdjustment *adjustment);
```

Class Description

GtkRange, as I stated at the start of this chapter, is the parent class of both GtkScrollbar and GtkScale. The first function provided by GtkRange can be used to retrieve the adjustment object of a GtkRange-derived widget. The prototype for gtk_range_get_adjustment() is:

```
GtkAdjustment *
gtk_range_get_adjustment(GtkRange *range)
```

The argument range is the range widget from which to retrieve the GtkAdjustment object. To coerce a GtkRange-derived widget to an instance of GtkRange, use the GTK_RANGE macro. For example:

```
GtkWidget *scrollbar;
GtkAdjustment *adj;

...

scrollbar = gtk_hscrollbar_new( adj );

...

adj = gtk_range_get_adjustment( GTK_RANGE( scrollbar ) );
```

Setting the Update Policy of a Range Widget

Scrollbars, scale widgets, and other GtkRange objects abide by an update policy that can be set by your application using gtk_range_set_update_policy():

```
void
gtk_range_set_update_policy(GtkRange *range, GtkUpdateType policy)
```

The argument range is an instance of GtkRange (more precisely, an instance of a child class, e.g., GtkHScrollbar). The argument policy can be one of the following values listed in Table 13.9.

Table 13.9 GtkUpdateType Values

Value	*Meaning*
GTK_UPDATE_CONTINUOUS	The value_changed signal is emitted continuously as the user moves the slider or scrollbar.
GTK_UPDATE_DISCONTINUOUS	The value_changed signal is emitted only once, when the slider has stopped moving and the mouse button has been released.
GTK_UPDATE_DELAYED	The value_changed signal is emitted after a short delay if the user has stopped moving the slider but still has the mouse button depressed.

The default update policy is GTK_UPDATE_CONTINUOUS.

Setting the Range Widget Adjustment Object

Finally, you can set the adjustment object of a range widget with a call to gtk_range_set_adjustment():

```
void
gtk_range_set_adjustment(GtkRange *range, GtkAdjustment *adjustment);
```

The argument range is an instance of a GtkRange-derived class in practice. The adjustment argument is an application-created adjustment object or an adjustment object retrieved from another range widget using gtk_range_get_adjustment().

Summary

This chapter described the Gtk+ range widgets (GtkRange, GtkScale, GtkVScale, GtkHScale, GtkScrollbar, GtkVScrollbar, and GtkHScrollbar) as well as adjustment objects (GtkAdjustment). A scale widget (GtkScale, GtkHScale, and GtkVScale) is a control that allows users to view and select floating-point and integer values falling within a fixed range. Scrollbar widgets (GtkScrollbar, GtkVScrollbar, and GtkHScrollbar) are generally not instantiated by applications and are primarily used by widget writers. If your application displays content that is greater in size than the container within which it is placed, you should parent it with a GtkScrolledWindow widget and allow GtkScrolledWindow to provide scrollbars when needed (see Chapter 11, "More Container Classes," for a description of GtkScrolledWindow). A range widget (GtkRange) is a parent class that abstracts the behavior of scrollbars and scale widgets. GtkRange provides functions that allow you to retrieve and set the adjustment object of a range widget, as well as specify an update policy that controls how the range widget will respond to changes made to the range control by the user (e.g., movement of a scrollbar thumb).

An adjustment object stores the current state of a range widget (i.e., the range of values that it supports) and its current value. A single adjustment object can be shared among several range widgets. If this is done, a change made to the value of one widget will immediately be reflected by the others. Most widgets classes that support scrollbars allow the application to specify an adjustment object at the time the widget is created. You can either specify an adjustment object from another widget so that the two (or more) widgets share the same adjustment object, or you can specify NULL to cause the widget to create its own adjustment object. See the sections "Creating a Scrolled Window" and "Overriding the Default Adjustment Objects: An Example" in Chapter 11 for an example.

CHAPTER

14

TEXT AND SPINBUTTON WIDGETS

In this chapter, I will describe the two widgets listed in Table 14.1.

Table 14.1 Widgets Described in This Chapter

Class Name	*Description*
GtkText	Text edit/display widget
GtkSpinButton	Spin button entry widget

A text widget is used to display multiline text. You can control attributes such as word wrap and the ability of users to edit the text that is displayed. A spin button widget is an editable control that supports the input of numeric data. A user can edit the value of a spin control by typing in an edit field or by clicking on a pair of arrow widgets displayed next to the edit field. These arrows can be used to increment or decrement the value with a specific range defined by the spin button control. At the end of this chapter, I will use a spin button widget to develop a simple image viewer/slide show application.

GtkText

Class Name

```
GtkText
```

Parent Class Name

```
GtkEditable
```

Macros

Widget type macro: `GTK_TYPE_TEXT`

Object to widget cast macro: `GTK_TEXT(obj)`

Widget type check macro: `GTK_IS_TEXT(obj)`

Supported Arguments

Prefix: `GtkText::`

Table 14.2 GtkText Arguments

Name	*Type*	*Permissions*
hadjustment	GTK_TYPE_ADJUSTMENT	GTK_ARG_READWRITE | GTK_ARG_CONSTRUCT
vadjustment	GTK_TYPE_ADJUSTMENT	GTK_ARG_READWRITE | GTK_ARG_CONSTRUCT
line_wrap	GTK_TYPE_BOOL	GTK_ARG_READWRITE
word_wrap	GTK_TYPE_BOOL	GTK_ARG_READWRITE

Application-Level API Synopsis

Retrieve the constant GTK_TYPE_TEXT at runtime:
```
GtkType
gtk_text_get_type(void);
```

Create a new instance of GtkText, optionally specifying the vertical and/or horizontal adjustment objects:
```
GtkWidget *
gtk_text_new(GtkAdjustment *hadj, GtkAdjustment *vadj);
```

Toggle the editable attribute of a text widget:
```
void
gtk_text_set_editable(GtkText *text, gboolean editable);
```

Toggle the word-wrap attribute of a text widget:
```
void
gtk_text_set_word_wrap(GtkText *text, gint word_wrap);
```

Toggle the line-wrap attribute of a text widget:
```
void
gtk_text_set_line_wrap(GtkText *text, gint line_wrap);
```

Application-Level API Synopsis (Continued)

Set the horizontal and/or vertical adjustment objects of a text widget:
```
void
gtk_text_set_adjustments(GtkText *text, GtkAdjustment *hadj,
        GtkAdjustment *vadj);
```

Set the text insertion/deletion point:
```
void
gtk_text_set_point(GtkText *text, guint index);
```

Query the text insertion/deletion point:
```
guint
gtk_text_get_point(GtkText *text);
```

Get the length of the text currently being managed by the text widget:
```
guint
gtk_text_get_length(GtkText *text);
```

Freeze the text widget (called prior to modifying text):
```
void
gtk_text_freeze(GtkText *text);
```

Thaw the text widget (undo a previous call to gtk_text_freeze()):
```
void
gtk_text_thaw(GtkText *text);
```

Insert text relative to the insertion/deletion point:
```
void
gtk_text_insert(GtkText *text, GdkFont *font, GdkColor *fore,
        GdkColor *back, const char *chars, gint length);
```

Delete n characters ahead of the insertion/deletion point:
```
gint
gtk_text_backward_delete(GtkText *text, guint nchars);
```

Delete n characters beyond the insertion/deletion point:
```
gint
gtk_text_forward_delete(GtkText *text, guint nchars);
```

Class Description

Like GtkLabel (see Chapter 5, "Labels and Buttons"), GtkText is primarily designed to display text. There are, however, significant differences between the GtkLabel and GtkText widget classes. Specifically, you use instances of GtkLabel to display small amounts of text in a dialog or in warning, error, and message dialogs. GtkText, in contrast, is designed to display significantly larger bodies of text (such as the contents of a file or the text output from a compiler).

GtkText allows applications to control the following aspects of the text it manages:

- Its style (e.g., font, background color, and so on)
- Whether or not the text can be edited by the user
- Whether or not line or word wrapping (or both) is enabled

The last two items are global, meaning they apply to the entire text widget and to all of the text it manages. The text style can be applied to portions of the text managed by the text widget, however, at the time the text is added.

Scrolling Text

In some cases, the amount of text being managed by a GtkText widget is small enough to be completely visible in the window created by the GtkText widget. More often than not, however, an instance of GtkText will be asked to manage a body of text that is larger than can be displayed within the GtkText widget's window. When the text is larger than the window that must display it, some mechanism by which users can scroll to text that is not visible must be provided. There are two solutions to this problem, and which method you choose is largely a matter of preference. The first solution is provided by GtkText intrinsically: GtkText is designed to interpret the up, down, left, and right arrow keys as well as the Page Up and Page Down keys of your keyboard. The up and down arrow keys scroll the display, respectively, up and down one line. The left and right arrow keys, as you might expect, cause a line of text to scroll left and right by one character, respectively. Finally, the Page Up and Page Down keys cause vertical scrolling of text by a predefined number of lines. The Home and End keys cause the cursor (not the insertion/deletion point) to be moved to the beginning and end of a line of text, respectively. These keys do not cause the text widget to display the first and last lines of the text being managed, as some users might otherwise expect.

The other way to deal with a GtkText widget contained by a window too small to display all of the text that the widget is managing is to make the GtkText widget the child of a scrolled window widget (GtkScrolledWindow). This is probably the better solution of the two; GtkText will modify the adjustment objects created by the scrolled window so that the text will scroll correctly based on font size. Also, scrollbars are more intuitive to users as a way to navigate the content than are keys on the keyboard.

Creating a Text Widget

To create an instance of GtkText, call gtk_text_new():

```
GtkWidget *
gtk_text_new(GtkAdjustment *hadj, GtkAdjustment *vadj);
```

The function gtk_text_new() takes two arguments: hadj is an optional horizontal adjustment object, and vadj is an optional vertical object. If you provide your own scrollbars or other control based on adjustment objects to control the display of the text managed by the text widget, then you would pass the associated adjustment object(s) to gtk_text_new(). If you want to use GtkText intrinsic scrolling (e.g., the arrow keys previously described) or you are placing the text widget inside of a scrolled window, then you should specify NULL for both hadj and vadj.

Changing the Adjustment Objects

Generally, you specify the adjustment objects at the time the text widget is created. You can also set them after the text widget has been created with a call to gtk_text_set_adjustments():

```
void
gtk_text_set_adjustments(GtkText *text, GtkAdjustment *hadj,
        GtkAdjustment *vadj);
```

The guidelines for setting hadj and vadj are the same as those previously described for gtk_text_new(). Typically, applications will never need to call gtk_text_set_adjustments().

Making a Text Widget Editable or Read-Only

Once you have created the text widget, you can (optionally) change some of its default attributes and behavior. For example, to toggle the editable attribute of a text widget, you can call gtk_text_set_editable():

```
void
gtk_text_set_editable(GtkText *text, gboolean editable);
```

The argument text is the text widget on which you want to set the editable attribute, and editable is a boolean used to control the ability of users to change the text being displayed. If editable is set to FALSE, the user cannot set the insert/delete point, nor can the user type anything into the text widget window. The application is, however, free to call functions in the GtkText API to set the insertion/deletion point, insert text, and delete text as needed. By default, a text widget is not editable, so if you want the user to be able to edit content displayed in a text widget, you must make a call to gtk_text_set_editable() with the editable argument set to TRUE.

Word Wrap

You can also toggle the word-wrap and line-wrap attributes of a text widget. By default, word wrapping is disabled, and line wrapping is enabled. If line wrapping is enabled, the text widget will automatically wrap lines of text on character boundaries, without regard to the content of the line. Thus, a line-wrapped document may contain words that are broken onto separate lines. If this is a problem, you can enable word wrapping. With word wrapping enabled, lines that are in need of wrapping will be wrapped on whitespace boundaries only. This is a somewhat simple word-wrapping algorithm; there is always the potential for GtkText to implement more sophisticated word-wrapping algorithms (such as breaking words on hyphen or syllable boundaries) in a future release. In Gtk 1.2, however, whitespace is the delimiter used to distinguish words from one another.

To toggle the word-wrap attribute of a text widget (default is FALSE), you can call gtk_text_set_word_wrap():

```
void
gtk_text_set_word_wrap(GtkText *text, gint word_wrap);
```

The argument text is an instance of GtkText, and word_wrap is an integer. To enable word wrapping, set word_wrap to TRUE; otherwise, set it to FALSE.

Similarly, to enable or disable the line-wrap attribute (default is TRUE), you can call gtk_text_set_line_wrap():

```
void
gtk_text_set_line_wrap(GtkText *text, gint line_wrap);
```

The argument text is an instance of GtkText, as usual, and line_wrap, an integer, should be set to TRUE to enable line wrapping or FALSE to disable it.

Text Widget Buffer Manipulation

GtkText provides several functions that allow applications to add to or delete from the text being managed by a text widget. This text is nothing more than a string of characters, structured much like a C-language string (e.g., a variable of type char *). The first character in the string is located at offset 0, and the last character is located at offset $n - 1$, where the number of characters in the string is equal to n. In the remainder of this section, I will refer to this text as the "buffer."

The Insertion Point. Before adding characters to or deleting characters from the buffer, you must first identify where in the buffer the insertion or deletion will be performed. This location is called the "point" and is an index in the range of $[0, n]$, where n is the current number of characters in the buffer. When a text widget is first created, its point is set to 0. As text is added to the buffer, the point is incremented by the number of characters added. Because of this, you can get away with not setting the point before each insertion, as long as you are only appending text to the buffer. The same holds true for deleting text from the buffer in the backward direction: As text is removed from the end of the buffer, the point is decremented by the number of characters removed so that it points at the current end of the buffer. I will discuss inserting and deleting text from the buffer in more detail in the section titled "Inserting and Deleting Text."

Setting and Getting the Insertion Point. If you want to insert or delete text from some point other than the end of the buffer, or if you want to reset the point to the end of the buffer, you must call the function get_text_set_point() to specify the point before performing the insertion or deletion. The function prototype for gtk_text_set_point() is as follows:

```
void
gtk_text_set_point(GtkText *text, guint index);
```

The argument text is an instance of GtkText, and index specifies the point in the range of $[0, n]$, where n in the number of characters currently in the buffer.

Getting the Length of the Text Buffer. Getting the length of the buffer is done by calling gtk_text_get_length():

```
guint
gtk_text_get_length(GtkText *text);
```

Therefore, you can set the point to the end of the buffer with code similar to the following:

```
GtkWidget *txt;

...

gtk_text_set_point(GTK_TEXT(txt),
        gtk_text_get_length(GTK_TEXT(txt)));
```

If you want to set the point to the head of the buffer, set the index to 0, as in the following example:

```
gtk_text_set_point( GTK_TEXT( txt ), 0 );
```

The current point can be read from a text widget with gtk_text_get_point():

```
guint
gtk_text_get_point(GtkText *text);
```

The return value will be in the range [0, *n*], where *n* is the length of the text widget buffer.

Inserting and Deleting Text. GtkText provides several functions that allow applications to insert or delete text from a text widget buffer. Text can be inserted and deleted by the application regardless of the editable attribute of the text widget; editable only allows or restricts users from making changes to the text via the keyboard.

To insert text into a (possibly empty) buffer, call gtk_text_insert():

```
void
gtk_text_insert(GtkText *text, GdkFont *font, GdkColor *fore,
        GdkColor *back, const char *chars, gint length);
```

The argument text is an instance of GtkText; chars is the C-language, NULL-terminated string that contains the characters to be inserted; and length is the size of the string to be inserted. The text will be inserted at the current point; see the preceding discussion for details. The arguments font, fore, and back are all optional style information that can be assigned to the text being inserted. The easiest way to insert text is to specify text, chars, and length and set fore, back, and font to NULL, which tells the text widget to use default values for these attributes.

The following example creates a text widget and sets its buffer to the string

Today was a very hot day in Texas", illustrating perhaps the simplest case of using an instance of GtkText:

```
GtkText *text;
static char *str = "Today was a very hot day in Texas";

text = gtk_text_new( NULL, NULL );
gtk_text_insert(GTK_TEXT(text), NULL, NULL, NULL, str, strlen(str));
```

The following code example illustrates how one might insert the same text into the buffer that was inserted in the preceding example, but it uses a font and colors for both the foreground and background that are specified by the application:

```
GtkText *text;
GdkFont *font;
GdkColor col1, col2;
static char *str = "Today was a very hot day in Texas";

text = gtk_text_new( NULL, NULL );

col1.red   = 0;
col1.green = 56000;
col1.blue  = 0;
gdk_color_alloc(gtk_widget_get_colormap(text), &col1);

col2.red   = 32000;
col2.green = 0;
col2.blue  = 56000;
gdk_color_alloc(gtk_widget_get_colormap(text), &col2);

font = gdk_font_load(
         "-*-helvetica-bold-r-normal-*-20-*-*-*-*-*-*");

gtk_text_insert(GTK_TEXT(text), font, col1, col2, str, strlen(str));
```

You are not required to set all three attributes (font, background color, and foreground color). For example, you are free to set only the foreground color and use defaults for the font and the background color. This can easily be done by setting both font and back arguments to NULL.

Deleting Text. Text can also be deleted from the buffer relative to the current point. Unless you know that the point is set to the end of the buffer and you are deleting characters from the end of the buffer, you will likely need to set the point prior to deleting any characters by calling gtk_text_set_point().

GtkText provides two functions that can be used to delete text from the buffer. The first function, gtk_text_backward_delete(), deletes a specified number of characters preceding the current insertion point. The function prototype for gtk_text_backward_delete() is as follows:

```
gint
gtk_text_backward_delete(GtkText *text, guint nchars);
```

The argument text is an instance of GtkText, and nchars is the number of characters to be deleted. To delete the last 10 characters in the buffer, set the point to the end of the buffer and call gtk_text_backward_delete(), as follows:

```
GtkWidget *txt;

...

gtk_text_set_point(GTK_TEXT(txt),
         gtk_text_get_length(GTK_TEXT(txt)));
gtk_text_backward_delete( GTK_TEXT( txt ), 10 );
```

If less than nchars characters are in the buffer ahead of the point, the call will fail, the buffer will remain unchanged, and FALSE will be returned to the caller. Otherwise, the specified number of characters will be deleted, and TRUE will be returned to indicate success. After successful deletion, the point will be moved back nchars characters after the call, except when the new point location would be greater than the size of the buffer, in which case the point will be positioned at the end of the buffer.

You can also delete characters that occur after the insertion point by calling gtk_text_forward_delete():

```
gint
gtk_text_forward_delete(GtkText *text, guint nchars);
```

The arguments passed to gtk_text_forward_delete() are the same as those passed to gtk_text_backward_delete(). gtk_text_forward_delete() deletes nchars characters after the insertion point. If there are less than nchars characters in the buffer after the insertion point, the operation will fail and FALSE will be returned. Otherwise, nchars characters will be deleted, and TRUE will be returned to indicate success. The location of the point is unchanged by a call to this function.

Freezing and Thawing the Text Widget. By inserting or deleting large amounts of text or by making a relatively large number of successive insertions or deletions, you increase the chances that the user will be subjected to flicker or other visual artifacts that are possible as GtkText changes the content in the buffer. To avoid this, I recommend always surrounding calls to gtk_text_insert(), gtk_text_forward_delete() and gtk_text_backward_delete() with calls to gtk_text_freeze() and gtk_text_thaw(). The function gtk_text_freeze():

```
void
gtk_text_freeze(GtkText *text);
```

will block any visual updates to the text widget UI until the following call to gtk_text_thaw() is made. The function gtk_text_thaw(), therefore, negates the effects of the previous call to gtk_text_freeze(). Its prototype is as follows:

```
void
gtk_text_thaw(GtkText *text);
```

GtkText will automatically freeze and thaw calls that cause greater than 1,024 characters to be inserted or deleted from the buffer. The following code shows how to use gtk_text_freeze() and gtk_text_thaw():

```
GtkText *text;
char *str;

...

gtk_text_freeze( GTK_TEXT(text) );
gtk_text_insert(GTK_TEXT(text), NULL, NULL, NULL, str, strlen(str));
gtk_text_thaw( GTK_TEXT(text) );
```

Retrieving Text

GtkText (like GtkEntry) inherits from GtkEditable, which is not discussed in this book. However, you must use a function in GtkEditable to obtain the content of the text widget after it has been edited by the user. To retrieve the text, you must call gtk_editable_get_chars():

```
gchar *
gtk_editable_get_chars(GtkEditable *editable, gint start_pos,
          gint end_pos);
```

The argument editable is an instance of GtkEditable or a derived class, such as GtkText. (The other class that derives from GtkEditable is GtkEntry, but it provides a function that allows an application to retrieve the contents of the entry field.) The characters that will be retrieved are defined by the arguments start_pos and end_pos. Valid ranges for start_pos and end_pos are [0, text_size – 1], where text_size is the value returned by a call to gtk_text_get_length(), as described earlier in this section. You should ensure that start_pos is less than end_pos in value. The return value is a pointer to a null-terminated gchar buffer. Your application is free to manipulate the contents of this buffer as it sees fit; it is a copy of the text, not the actual text as managed by GtkText. To release the memory pointed to by the returned buffer once it is no longer needed, your application can simply pass it to g_free().

The following code illustrates how to retrieve the contents of a text widget. In this example, I am retrieving the content from a GtkButton “clicked” signal function (assume, for this example, that this button is labeled “Check Spelling” and that the task of the clicked signal function is to retrieve the content from the text widget and pass it to a spelling checker).

```
static void
SpellCheckCB(GtkWidget *widget, GtkWidget *text)
{
        char *buf;

        // grab the entire buffer: start_pos is 0, and end_pos is the
        // number of characters in the buffer, minus 1.

        buf = gtk_editable_get_chars( GTK_EDITABLE(text), 0,
                gtk_text_get_length( GTK_TEXT( text ) ) - 1 ) );
        check_spelling( buf );
}

...

main( int argc, char *argv[] )
{
        GtkWidget *button, *text;

        ...

        text = gtk_text_new( NULL, NULL );

        ...

        button = gtk_button_new_with_label( "Check Spelling" );
```

```
        gtk_signal_connect(GTK_OBJECT(button), "clicked",
                GTK_SIGNAL_FUNC(SpellCheckCB), text);

        ...

        gtk_main();
}
```

GtkSpinButton

Class Name

`GtkSpinButton`

Parent Class Name

`GtkEntry`

Macros

Widget type macro: `GTK_TYPE_SPIN_BUTTON`

Object to widget cast macro: `GTK_SPIN_BUTTON(obj)`

Widget type check macro: `GTK_IS_SPIN_BUTTON(obj)`

Supported Arguments

Prefix: `GtkSpinButton::`

Table 14.3 GtkSpinButton Arguments

Name	*Type*	*Permissions*
adjustment	GTK_TYPE_ADJUSTMENT	GTK_ARG_READWRITE
climb_rate	GTK_TYPE_FLOAT	GTK_ARG_READWRITE
digits	GTK_TYPE_UINT	GTK_ARG_READWRITE
snap_to_ticks	GTK_TYPE_BOOL	GTK_ARG_READWRITE
numeric	GTK_TYPE_BOOL	GTK_ARG_READWRITE

Table 14.3 GtkSpinButton Arguments (Continued)

Name	*Type*	*Permissions*
wrap	GTK_TYPE_BOOL	GTK_ARG_READWRITE
update_policy	GTK_TYPE_SPIN_BUTTON_UPDATE_POLICY	GTK_ARG_READWRITE
shadow_type	GTK_TYPE_SHADOW_TYPE	GTK_ARG_READWRITE
value	GTK_TYPE_FLOAT	GTK_ARG_READWRITE

Application-Level API Synopsis

Retrieve the constant GTK_TYPE_SPIN_BUTTON at runtime:

```
GtkType
gtk_spin_button_get_type(void);
```

Create a new instance of GtkSpinButton:

```
GtkWidget *
gtk_spin_button_new(GtkAdjustment *adjustment, gfloat climb_rate,
        guint digits);
```

Set the adjustment object and other attributes of a spin button:

```
void
gtk_spin_button_configure(GtkSpinButton *spin_button,
        GtkAdjustment *adjustment, gfloat climb_rate, guint digits);
```

Set the adjustment object of a spin button:

```
void
gtk_spin_button_set_adjustment(GtkSpinButton *spin_button,
        GtkAdjustment *adjustment);
```

Retrieve the adjustment object of a spin button:

```
GtkAdjustment *
gtk_spin_button_get_adjustment(GtkSpinButton *spin_button);
```

Set the number of significant digits displayed by the spin button:

```
void
gtk_spin_button_set_digits(GtkSpinButton *spin_button,
        guint digits);
```

Get the current value of the spin button as a float:

```
gfloat
gtk_spin_button_get_value_as_float(GtkSpinButton *spin_button);
```

Get the current value of the spin button as an integer:

```
gint
gtk_spin_button_get_value_as_int(GtkSpinButton *spin_button);
```

Application-Level API Synopsis (Continued)

Set the current value of the spin button:

```
void
gtk_spin_button_set_value(GtkSpinButton *spin_button, gfloat value);
```

Set the update policy of the spin button (GTK_UPDATE_ALWAYS or GTK_UPDATE_IF_VALID; see text):

```
void
gtk_spin_button_set_update_policy(GtkSpinButton *spin_button,
        GtkSpinButtonUpdatePolicy policy);
```

Set or clear the numeric mode of a spin button widget (the default is FALSE):

```
void
gtk_spin_button_set_numeric(GtkSpinButton *spin_button,
        gboolean numeric);
```

Spin the spin button by the specified increment and direction (see the text for a definition of GtkSpinType):

```
void
gtk_spin_button_spin(GtkSpinButton *spin_button,
        GtkSpinType direction, gfloat increment);
```

Set the wrap attribute of a spin button:

```
void
gtk_spin_button_set_wrap(GtkSpinButton *spin_button, gboolean wrap);
```

Set the shadow type (GTK_SHADOW_NONE, GTK_SHADOW_IN, GTK_SHADOW_OUT, GTK_SHADOW_ETCHED_IN, or GTK_SHADOW_ETCHED_OUT) of the spin button:

```
void
gtk_spin_button_set_shadow_type(GtkSpinButton *spin_button,
        GtkShadowType shadow_type);
```

Set the snap-to-ticks attribute of a spin button:

```
void
gtk_spin_button_set_snap_to_ticks(GtkSpinButton *spin_button,
        gboolean snap_to_ticks);
```

Update the display of a spin button:

```
void
gtk_spin_button_update(GtkSpinButton *spin_button);
```

Class Description

A spin button is an entry widget specifically designed to support the entry of numeric values falling within a predefined integer or floating-point range. A spin button accepts both positive and negative integer and floating-point values of arbitrary precision. Figure 14.1 illustrates a dialog with several spin button widgets (see the fields labeled Hours, Minutes, Seconds, and Distance). As can be seen in Figure 14.1, a spin button consists of two areas. The first area is similar to an instance of GtkEntry and provides an area used by the widget to display the current value of the spin button, as well as a location for the user to type a new value into the control directly. The second area, located immediately to the right of the entry field, consists of a pair of arrow buttons. Clicking the top arrow button increments the value in the entry field, while clicking the bottom arrow button decrements the value.

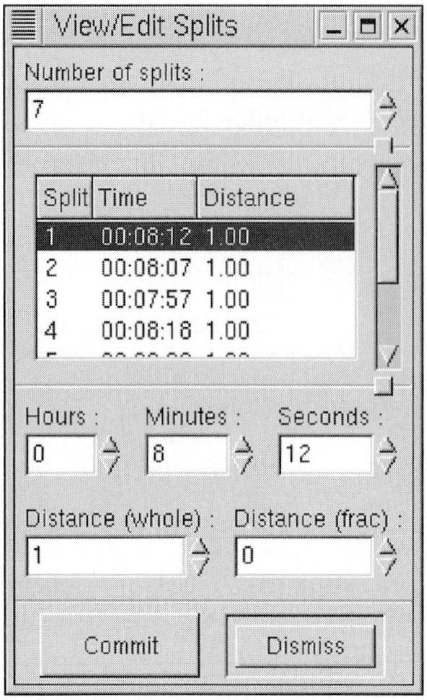

Figure 14.1 Spin Button Widgets in a Dialog

The range of values accepted by an instance of GtkSpinButton is specified by the application using a Gtk+ adjustment object (see Chapter 13, "Range Widgets and Adjustment Objects"). An adjustment object with lower set to 1, upper set to 12, and step_increment set to 1 would be appropriate for specifying the range of a spin button that accepts the month portion of a date from a user, for example.

Keyboard and Mouse Events

Spin buttons are sensitive to mouse button and key press events; GtkSpinButton specifically listens for the keypress events listed in Table 14.4.

Table 14.4 GtkSpinButton Key press Events

Key	*Action*
Up	The value is incremented by timer_step (minimum is step_increment).
Down	The value is decremented by timer_step (minimum is step_increment).
Page Up	The value is incremented by page_increment.
Page Down	The value is decremented by page_increment.

The timer_step attribute of a spin button widget will be described later in this chapter when I describe the climb_rate argument to gtk_spin_button_new(). Table 14.5 describes how mouse button press and release events affect the value of a spin button widget:

Table 14.5 GtkSpinButton Mouse Button Events

Button Event	*Action*
Button 1 press	Same as Up and Down key
Button 2 press	Same as Page Up and Page Down keys
Button 3 release, up arrow	Adjustment value is assigned the adjustment upper field
Button 3 release, down arrow	Adjustment value is assigned the adjustment lower field

For example, if the lower field of the spin button adjustment object is set to 30 and the user releases button 3 over the down arrow, then the value of the spin button (and of the adjustment object) will be set to 30 (the value of the adjustment object lower field).

Creating a Spin Button Widget

To create an instance of GtkSpinButton, call gtk_spin_button_new():

```
GtkWidget *
gtk_spin_button_new(GtkAdjustment *adjustment, gfloat climb_rate,
        guint digits);
```

The function gtk_spin_button_new () accepts three arguments. The first argument, adjustment, is a GtkAdjustment object. This can be an adjustment object that you create, an adjustment object retrieved from some other widget (e.g., from a scale or scrollbar widget), or it can be NULL. If set to NULL, an adjustment object will be created for you, and in this case, all of the adjustment object fields will be initialized to 0.0.

The second argument, climb_rate, is used to control the rate of change of the spin button value as the user causes one of the events listed in Tables 14.4 and 14.5 (except for mouse button 3 release events) to occur.

Understanding the Climb Rate

To understand how climb_rate is used, I will describe what happens when a user depresses and holds mouse button 1 over one of the spin button arrows. First, the spin button value is moved in the appropriate direction; the amount of movement is defined by the adjustment object step_increment value, and the direction (positive or negative) is determined by which arrow (up or down) was pressed. Next, the spin button widget registers a timeout that will fire after approximately 200 ms. The spin button widget saves the value of step_increment in an internal field named timer_step; this field (timer_step) will be used by the timeout function to determine how much to change the spin button value, as I will describe next.

The timeout function, when it is first invoked, resets the timer to fire every 20 ms thereafter, thus increasing the rate at which the spin button value is updated. Next, the spin button value is incremented (or decremented) by the value saved in timer_step. The timer_step value is left unchanged the first five times the timer function is called (approximately 300 ms after the user first depressed the mouse button over the arrow). Each invocation thereafter, however, the timer_step value will be incremented by the climb_rate value. The effect is an increase over time to the amount of change made to the spin button value as the user continues to press mouse button 1; the longer the mouse button is depressed, the larger the change made to the spin button value each time the timer function is invoked.

The third argument to gtk_spin_button_new(), digits, defines how many digits to the right of the decimal point are displayed by the spin button value. Accepted values for this argument are in the range [0, 5].

Configuring the Spin Button Widget

When you create a new spin button with gtk_spin_button_new(), it will make a call to gtk_spin_button_configure() to configure the spin button widget with the adjustment, climb_rate, and digits arguments it was passed. Your application can also call gtk_spin_button_configure() to change the attributes of a spin button. The function prototype is as follows:

```
void
gtk_spin_button_configure(GtkSpinButton *spin_button,
        GtkAdjustment *adjustment, gfloat climb_rate, guint digits);
```

The first argument, spin_button, is the instance of GtkSpinButton to be configured. The adjustment, climb_rate, and digits arguments are as were previously described for gtk_spin_button_new().

Setting and Getting the Adjustment Object

The next two functions allow applications to set or get the adjustment object of a spin button widget individually. To set the adjustment object, call gtk_spin_button_set_adjustment():

```
void
gtk_spin_button_set_adjustment(GtkSpinButton *spin_button,
        GtkAdjustment  *adjustment);
```

The argument spin_button is the spin button widget, and adjustment is an adjustment object. To retrieve the adjustment object, call gtk_spin_button_get_adjustment():

```
GtkAdjustment *
gtk_spin_button_get_adjustment(GtkSpinButton *spin_button);
```

The return value is a GtkAdjustment object. You will find it necessary to get the adjustment object if, when you created the spin button, you specified NULL for the adjustment argument to gtk_spin_button_new(), and you want to set the attributes of the adjustment object created on your behalf to their correct values, using the API provided by GtkAdjustment (as described in Chapter 13).

Setting the Number of Significant Digits Displayed by a Spin Button

You can also set (but not get) the number of significant digits displayed by the spin button by calling gtk_spin_button_set_digits():

```
void
gtk_spin_button_set_digits(GtkSpinButton *spin_button, guint digits);
```

The argument digits must be in the range of [0, 5]. GtkSpinButton provides no API for retrieving the digits attribute of a spin button, nor does it provide function that can be used to set or get the climb_rate attribute (climb_rate can be set with gtk_spin_button_configure(), as previously described).

Setting and Getting the Value of a Spin Button

Getter and setter functions for the spin button value are provided by GtkSpinButton. You can retrieve the current spin button value as either a float or an integer. Internally, a spin button value is always stored as a float, so only a floating-point setter is provided. To retrieve the current value of a spin button widget as a float, call gtk_spin_button_get_value_as_float():

```
gfloat
gtk_spin_button_get_value_as_float(GtkSpinButton *spin_button);
```

Or, to retrieve it as an integer, call gtk_spin_button_get_value_as_int():

```
gint
gtk_spin_button_get_value_as_int(GtkSpinButton *spin_button);
```

The implementation of gtk_spin_button_get_value_as_int() rounds the current value down or up using the following code:

```
val = spin_button->adjustment->value;
if (val - floor (val) < ceil (val) - val)
        return floor (val);
else
        return ceil (val);
```

Thus, if the current value is 3.7, gtk_spin_button_get_value_as_int() would return 4.0, whereas a current value of 3.4 would result in a return value of 3.0.

To set the current value of the spin button, call gtk_spin_button_set_value():

```
void
gtk_spin_button_set_value(GtkSpinButton *spin_button, gfloat value);
```

The argument spin_button is, of course, an instance of GtkSpinButton. Value is a floating-point number in the range allowable by the spin button adjustment object.

Changing the Spin Button Update Policy

Each spin button widget instance has an update policy as described Table 14.6.

Table 14.6 Spin Button Update Policy

Update Policy	*Meaning*
GTK_UPDATE_ALWAYS	Values out of range will be clipped (default).
GTK_UPDATE_IF_VALID	Values out of range will be ignored.

For example, assume an adjustment object implementing a range of [0, 5], the current value of the spin button is 3, and the update policy is set to GTK_UPDATE_ALWAYS. Setting the spin button value (perhaps with a call to gtk_spin_button_set_value()) to 7 would result in a spin button value of 5. Setting it to -2 would result in it being clipped to its lower bound of 0. If the update policy were GTK_UPDATE_IF_VALID, the result of both changes would be 3 (e.g., the changes would be discarded since they are out of range).

To change the update policy, call gtk_spin_button_set_update_policy():

```
void
gtk_spin_button_set_update_policy(GtkSpinButton *spin_button,
        GtkSpinButtonUpdatePolicy policy);
```

As always, spin_button is the instance of GtkSpinButton of interest. policy is one of the values listed in Table 14.6.

Using Numeric Mode

GtkSpinButton supports a numeric mode that, when enabled, causes the entry field of the spin button to reject input that is not numeric. This includes all characters except the digits 0 through 9, the sign characters + and -, and the decimal point character (the actual characters involved may be different based on locale). By default, numeric mode is disabled, but it can be enabled (or disabled again) by calling gtk_spin_button_set_numeric():

```
void
gtk_spin_button_set_numeric(GtkSpinButton *spin_button,
        gboolean numeric);
```

The argument numeric, if set to FALSE, disables numeric mode (again, this is the default). Setting numeric to TRUE enables numeric mode.

Setting the Value of a Spin Button

Applications can programmatically emulate the manipulation of the spin button control by a user (e.g., emulate the pressing of the up arrow to change the spin button's value). Some applications may want to initialize the value of a spin button control with gtk_spin_button_set_value() when the spin button is first displayed, but changes to the spin button value at runtime (other than setting initial values) should normally be made by the user, not by the application. Changes to a spin button can be made indirectly by sharing the adjustment object of a spin button with the adjustment object of some other widget in such a way that changing the value of the widget will automatically result in a corresponding change to the spin button value.

So, when does it make sense for a program to emulate the increment or decrement of a spin button by the user? One illustrative example comes to mind. Consider an image viewer application that allows the user to select an image for viewing by its number. A spin button might be used to increment through the images one at a time or to select a specific image for viewing. One feature of such an application might be a "slide show" mode that automatically increments the current image by one at some predefined interval, allowing the user to view all of the images in sequence without the need to click the up (or down) arrow of the spin button control. To implement this feature, the application might register a Gtk+ timer to fire at the desired interval and then increment (or decrement) the spin button value from within the timer callback function. I will present such an application at the end of this section. In the meantime, let's take a look at how to increment or decrement the spin button value from an application.

The function you must call to increment or decrement a spin button is called gtk_spin_button_spin():

```
void
gtk_spin_button_spin(GtkSpinButton *spin_button,
        GtkSpinType direction, gfloat increment);
```

The argument spin_button is an instance of GtkSpinButton. The remaining arguments, direction and increment, are defined in Table 14.7.

Table 14.7 GtkSpinType Values

Value	*Emulation*
GTK_SPIN_STEP_FORWARD	Button 1 press over up arrow
GTK_SPIN_STEP_BACKWARD	Button 1 press over down arrow
GTK_SPIN_PAGE_FORWARD	Button 2 press over up arrow
GTK_SPIN_PAGE_BACKWARD	Button 2 press over down arrow
GTK_SPIN_HOME	Button 3 release over up arrow
GTK_SPIN_END	Button 3 release over down arrow
GTK_SPIN_USER_DEFINED	Change current value by increment

As I described earlier, button 1 presses cause the value of the spin button to change by the adjustment object step_increment, button 2 presses cause the value to change by the adjustment object page_increment, and button 3 releases over the up or down arrow cause the spin button value to be set to the adjustment object upper and lower values, respectively.

As you can see, the increment argument is ignored unless the direction argument is set to GTK_SPIN_USER_DEFINED. A nonzero increment in this case will cause the spin button value to be incremented or decremented by the specified value. An increment occurs if the value is greater than zero, and a decrement occurs if the value is less than zero.

Controlling the Wrapping of Values

What happens to a spin button that is being incremented beyond the upper value of its adjustment object or that is being decremented beyond the lower value of the adjustment object? By default, a spin button will clip its value to the upper and lower values of the adjustment object, thereby rendering an increment of a spin button already set to upper, or the decrement of a spin button already set to lower, useless. This default can be changed so that the value of the adjustment object (and, thus, the value of the spin button) will wrap in these cases. That is, incrementing a spin button above the upper value will result in the value being set to lower, and decrementing a spin button below the lower value will cause the value to be set to upper. To enable this functionality, you must call gtk_spin_button_set_wrap():

```
void
gtk_spin_button_set_wrap(GtkSpinButton *spin_button, gboolean wrap);
```

Setting wrap to TRUE enables the wrapping behavior previously described; setting it to FALSE returns the spin button to the default action of clipping values to the upper and lower values of the spin button adjustment object.

Setting the Shadow Type

Applications can change the shadow type of a spin button, which affects how the arrows adjacent to the entry field are rendered. To set the shadow type call gtk_spin_button_set_shadow_type():

```
void
gtk_spin_button_set_shadow_type(GtkSpinButton *spin_button,
        GtkShadowType shadow_type);
```

The argument spin_button, as usual, is an instance of GtkSpinButton, and shadow type is one of the following constants: GTK_SHADOW_NONE, GTK_SHADOW_IN, GTK_SHADOW_OUT, GTK_SHADOW_ETCHED_IN, or GTK_SHADOW_ETCHED_OUT.

The Snap-to-Ticks Attribute

The final spin button attribute discussed here is snap-to-ticks. Setting this attribute to TRUE (the default is FALSE) causes the spin button to snap any values entered into the entry field of the spin button to a value that is consistent to the step_increment of the adjustment object associated with the spin button widget. For example, if snap-to-ticks is enabled and the step_increment of the adjustment object is set to 0.5, then any values entered into the spin button entry field will be modified to be divisible by 0.5.

What the spin button widget does when snap-to-ticks is enabled and the user enters a value is as follows: The value is extracted from the entry field, and if the value is closer to the next largest value evenly divisible by the step_increment than it is to the next smallest value also evenly divisible by the step_increment, it is set to that next largest value. Otherwise, it is set to the next lowest value evenly divisible by the step_increment.

An example might be useful. Say the step_increment is 0.5, and the user enters the value 43.3. In this case, the next highest candidate value is 43.5, and the next lowest candidate value is 43.0. Since 43.3 is closer to 43.5 than it is to 43.0, the spin button value will be changed to 43.5.

To enable or disable the snap-to-ticks attribute of a spin button, you can call gtk_spin_button_snap_to_ticks():

```
void
gtk_spin_button_set_snap_to_ticks(GtkSpinButton *spin_button,
        gboolean snap_to_ticks);
```

If snap_to_ticks is set to TRUE, values entered into the entry field will snap to the adjustment object step_increment value. If set to FALSE, values entered by the user will be accepted as entered.

Causing the Spin Button to Redraw

The final function exposed by the GtkSpinButton API is gtk_spin_button_update():

```
void
gtk_spin_button_update(GtkSpinButton *spin_button);
```

This function, when called, will cause the spin button widget to redraw itself. Applications normally need not call this function.

An Example

Now it is time for the sample code I promised earlier. The sample program is in the form of a simple image viewer. There is a lot to learn from the application due to the way I have designed it. The application is designed to display a fixed set of XPM images (in this case, the number of images is fixed to 3; an obvious enhancement would be to modify the program to show all of the images in a user-specified directory). Next and Previous buttons are provided that allow the user to navigate among the images as one would expect. A spin button is provided that allows the user to do a similar form of navigation using the up and down arrows that the spin button provides. The user, of course, can type an image number into the spin button entry field and hit the Enter key to cause the specified image to be displayed. Finally, a button labeled Slide Show is provided that, when pressed, causes the program to cycle through the images in forward order, changing from one image to another every 5 seconds. The Slide Show button label is changed to Cancel Slide Show, and the Next and Previous buttons are disabled as soon as the user begins the slide show. Clicking the Cancel Slide Show button re-enables the Next and Previous buttons, causes the slide show to stop, and reverts the slide show button to its original label. Figure 14.2 illustrates the application at runtime.

Figure 14.2 Spin Button Widgets in a Dialog

As it turns out, the spin button, together with its adjustment object, forms the basis of the controls and logic that I just described. To illustrate how, let's take a look at the program source code (a discussion of the source will immediately follow):

Listing 14.1 Button Slide Show Example

```
#include <gtk/gtk.h>

static int which = 1, timeout = 0;
static GtkWidget *spinner, *visible, *pixmap1, *pixmap2, *pixmap3;
static GtkWidget *button1, *button2, *button3, *label;
static GtkAdjustment *adj;

static void
NextCallback(GtkWidget *widget, gpointer dummy)
{
    which++;
    if ( which == 4 )
            which = 1;
    gtk_adjustment_set_value( adj, (float) which );
}
```

```
static void
PrevCallback(GtkWidget *widget, gpointer dummy)
{
    which--;
    if ( which == 0 )
            which = 3;
    gtk_adjustment_set_value( adj, (float) which );
}

static void
SpinnerCallback( GtkAdjustment *adj, gpointer dummy)
{
    GdkPixmap *gdkPixmap;
    GdkBitmap *gdkBitmap;
    GtkWidget *current;

    which = (int) adj->value;
    if ( which == 1 )
            current = pixmap1;
    else if ( which == 2 )
            current = pixmap2;
    else
            current = pixmap3;

    gtk_pixmap_get(GTK_PIXMAP( current ), &gdkPixmap, &gdkBitmap);
    gtk_pixmap_set(GTK_PIXMAP( visible ), gdkPixmap, gdkBitmap);
}

int
SlidesTimerCallback(gpointer dummy)
{
    gtk_spin_button_spin( GTK_SPIN_BUTTON( spinner ),
            GTK_SPIN_STEP_FORWARD, 0 );
    return 1;
}

static void
SlidesCallback(GtkWidget *widget, gpointer dummy)
{
    static void CancelCallback(GtkWidget *widget, gpointer dummy);

    if ( GTK_WIDGET_SENSITIVE( button1 ) == FALSE ) {
            CancelCallback( widget, dummy );
            return;
    }

    gtk_spin_button_set_value(GTK_SPIN_BUTTON(spinner), 1.0);
    timeout = gtk_timeout_add(5000, SlidesTimerCallback, NULL);
    gtk_widget_set_sensitive( button1, FALSE );
    gtk_widget_set_sensitive( button2, FALSE );
    gtk_label_set_text( GTK_LABEL( label ), "Cancel Slide Show" );
}

static void
CancelCallback(GtkWidget *widget, gpointer dummy)
{
```

```
    if ( timeout ) {
            gtk_timeout_remove(timeout);
            timeout = 0;
    }
    gtk_widget_set_sensitive( button1, TRUE );
    gtk_widget_set_sensitive( button2, TRUE );
    gtk_label_set_text( GTK_LABEL( label ), "Slide Show" );
}

static GtkWidget *
new_pixmap (char *file, GdkWindow *window, GdkColor *background)
{
    GdkPixmap *pmap;
    GdkBitmap *mask;
    GtkWidget *wpmap;

    pmap = gdk_pixmap_create_from_xpm(window, &mask, background, file);
    wpmap = gtk_pixmap_new(pmap, mask);
    return( wpmap );
}

main( int argc, char *argv[] )
{
    GtkWidget *dialog_window;

    gtk_init( &argc, &argv );

    dialog_window = gtk_dialog_new();
    gtk_window_position (GTK_WINDOW (dialog_window), GTK_WIN_POS_MOUSE);

    gtk_widget_show( dialog_window );

    visible = new_pixmap ("pic1.xpm", dialog_window->window,
            &dialog_window->style->bg[GTK_STATE_NORMAL]);
    gtk_box_pack_start (GTK_BOX (GTK_DIALOG (dialog_window)->vbox),
            visible, TRUE, TRUE, 0);

    pixmap1 = new_pixmap ("pic1.xpm", dialog_window->window,
            &dialog_window->style->bg[GTK_STATE_NORMAL]);
    pixmap2 = new_pixmap ("pic2.xpm", dialog_window->window,
            &dialog_window->style->bg[GTK_STATE_NORMAL]);
    pixmap3 = new_pixmap ("pic3.xpm", dialog_window->window,
            &dialog_window->style->bg[GTK_STATE_NORMAL]);

    button1 = gtk_button_new_with_label ("Next");
    gtk_box_pack_start (GTK_BOX (GTK_DIALOG (dialog_window)->action_area),
            button1, TRUE, TRUE, 0);
    gtk_signal_connect (GTK_OBJECT (button1), "clicked",
            GTK_SIGNAL_FUNC(NextCallback), dialog_window);

    button2 = gtk_button_new_with_label ("Prev");
    gtk_box_pack_start (GTK_BOX (GTK_DIALOG (dialog_window)->action_area),
            button2, TRUE, TRUE, 0);
    gtk_signal_connect (GTK_OBJECT (button2), "clicked",
            GTK_SIGNAL_FUNC(PrevCallback), dialog_window);

    adj = gtk_adjustment_new( 1.0, 1.0, 3.0, 1.0, 1.0, 1.0 );
```

```
130     gtk_signal_connect(GTK_OBJECT(adj), "value_changed",
131             GTK_SIGNAL_FUNC (SpinnerCallback), NULL);
132
133     spinner = gtk_spin_button_new( GTK_ADJUSTMENT(adj), 0.0, 0.0 );
134     gtk_spin_button_set_wrap(GTK_SPIN_BUTTON(spinner), TRUE);
135     gtk_box_pack_start (GTK_BOX (GTK_DIALOG (dialog_window)->action_area),
136             spinner, TRUE, TRUE, 0);
137
138     button3 = gtk_button_new();
139     label = gtk_label_new( "Slide Show" );
140     gtk_container_add( GTK_CONTAINER( button3 ), label );
141
142     gtk_box_pack_start (GTK_BOX (GTK_DIALOG (dialog_window)->action_area),
143             button3, TRUE, TRUE, 0);
144     gtk_signal_connect (GTK_OBJECT (button3), "clicked",
145             GTK_SIGNAL_FUNC(SlidesCallback), NULL);
146
147     gtk_widget_show_all (dialog_window);
148     gtk_main();
149 }
```

Analysis

The main program, as is typically the case, creates the application main window (in this case an instance of GtkDialog), completes the UI, and then registers callbacks on the user-interface controls before calling into gtk_main().

Our UI consists of an instance of GtkPixmap (see Chapter 8, "Separators, Arrows, Images, Pixmaps, and Entry Widgets"), which is managed by the vertical box of the dialog widget, and a series of controls placed inside of a horizontal box. The horizontal box is made an instance child of the dialog widget's control area (see Chapter 7, "Windows and Dialogs," for information on GtkDialog).

Handling Images. Let's take a quick look at how the images are dealt with before we continue our discussion of the spin button control. For this example, I chose to hard-code the images displayed and support only XPM image data (after all, this is an example for GtkSpinButton, not images). On lines 105 through 115, I create four instances of GtkImage. The first instance, created on line 105, is the most important of the four because it is the only instance I create that is used as a part of the user interface. The remaining images, created on lines 110 through 115, are used to hold image data that will be displayed as the user traverses the set of image data using the Next and Previous buttons or the spin button control.

```
105     visible = new_pixmap ("pic1.xpm", dialog_window->window,
106             &dialog_window->style->bg[GTK_STATE_NORMAL]);
107     gtk_box_pack_start (GTK_BOX (GTK_DIALOG (dialog_window)->vbox),
108             visible, TRUE, TRUE, 0);
109
110     pixmap1 = new_pixmap ("pic1.xpm", dialog_window->window,
111             &dialog_window->style->bg[GTK_STATE_NORMAL]);
112     pixmap2 = new_pixmap ("pic2.xpm", dialog_window->window,
113             &dialog_window->style->bg[GTK_STATE_NORMAL]);
```

```
114     pixmap3 = new_pixmap ("pic3.xpm", dialog_window->window,
115             &dialog_window->style->bg[GTK_STATE_NORMAL]);
```

Creating the Spin Button Controls. The spin button control and the adjustment object are created on lines 129 through 136:

```
129     adj = gtk_adjustment_new( 1.0, 1.0, 3.0, 1.0, 1.0, 1.0 );
130     gtk_signal_connect(GTK_OBJECT(adj), "value_changed",
131             GTK_SIGNAL_FUNC (SpinnerCallback), NULL);
132
133     spinner = gtk_spin_button_new( GTK_ADJUSTMENT(adj), 0.0, 0.0 );
134     gtk_spin_button_set_wrap(GTK_SPIN_BUTTON(spinner), TRUE);
135     gtk_box_pack_start (GTK_BOX (GTK_DIALOG (dialog_window)->action_area),
136             spinner, TRUE, TRUE, 0);
```

The value of the adjustment object is initialized to 1 (this is consistent with the initial image displayed by the "visible" pixmap, namely pic1.xpm). The range of values to which the spin button can be set is set to [1, 3]. The spin button widget (spinner) is created on line 133. On line 134, I set the wrap attribute of the spin button to TRUE; this allows the spin button to operate correctly in slide show mode and simplifies the use of the Next and Previous buttons. For example, hitting the Next button while displaying image 3 will cause image 1 to be displayed, and hitting the Previous button when displaying image 1 causes image 3 to be displayed.

Implementing the value_changed Signal Function. The value_changed signal function SpinnerCallback(), assigned on line 130, is the means by which changes made by the user are communicated to the application. This includes, as we shall see, not only changes to the spin button widget but also to the Next and Previous buttons. The slide show feature is also based in part on this signal. Let's look at the spin button first. If the value of the spin button is changed by the user, the spin button widget will change the adjustment value and then fire the value_changed signal, leading to a call to the SpinnerCallback() function:

```
026 static void
027 SpinnerCallback( GtkAdjustment *adj, gpointer dummy)
028 {
029     GdkPixmap *gdkPixmap;
030     GdkBitmap *gdkBitmap;
031     GtkWidget *current;
032
033     which = (int) adj->value;
034     if ( which == 1 )
035             current = pixmap1;
036     else if ( which == 2 )
037             current = pixmap2;
038     else
039             current = pixmap3;
040
041     gtk_pixmap_get(GTK_PIXMAP( current ), &gdkPixmap, &gdkBitmap);
042     gtk_pixmap_set(GTK_PIXMAP( visible ), gdkPixmap, gdkBitmap);
043 }
```

In the callback, on line 033, the adjustment value is retrieved; it will be a value in the range [1, 3] and logically reflects the image that the user has selected for viewing. On lines 034 through 039, the value is used to select an instance of GtkPixmap from which image data will be retrieved. For example, if the adjustment value is 1, then pixmap1 has been selected. On line 041, the image data is read from the selected image. Then, on line 042, the visible image data is modified to display that image.

Implementing the Next and Previous Buttons. All that remains is a description of how the Previous and Next buttons and the slide show feature work. The Previous and Next buttons are wired to PrevCallback() and NextCallback() clicked signal functions, respectively:

```
static void
NextCallback(GtkWidget *widget, gpointer dummy)
{
   which++;
   if ( which == 4 )
           which = 1;
   gtk_adjustment_set_value( adj, (float) which );
}

static void
PrevCallback(GtkWidget *widget, gpointer dummy)
{
   which--;
   if ( which == 0 )
           which = 3;
   gtk_adjustment_set_value( adj, (float) which );
}
```

These functions simply compute a new value for the currently displayed image (as stored in the global "which" variable) and then change the adjustment value by calling gtk_adjustment_set_value(). Changing the adjustment value results in SpinnerCallback() being invoked, which handles the chore of updating the image that is displayed.

Implementing the Slide Show. The slide show feature is actually pretty simple to implement and relies again on adjustment objects. The slide show button is instantiated on line 138. Instead of letting GtkButton create its own label, I create my own and add it to the button as a child on lines 139 and 140. This allows me to change the label, when the user clicks the Slide Show button, to Cancel Slide Show, and then back again when the user clicks the button to cancel. On line 144, I set the "clicked" signal function to SlidesCallback().

```
138    button3 = gtk_button_new();
139    label = gtk_label_new( "Slide Show" );
140    gtk_container_add( GTK_CONTAINER( button3 ), label );
141
142    gtk_box_pack_start (GTK_BOX (GTK_DIALOG (dialog_window)->action_area),
143            button3, TRUE, TRUE, 0);
144    gtk_signal_connect (GTK_OBJECT (button3), "clicked",
145            GTK_SIGNAL_FUNC(SlidesCallback), NULL);
```

Here is the source code for SlidesCallback():

```
053 static void
054 SlidesCallback(GtkWidget *widget, gpointer dummy)
055 {
056     static void CancelCallback(GtkWidget *widget, gpointer dummy);
057
058     if ( GTK_WIDGET_SENSITIVE( button1 ) == FALSE ) {
059             CancelCallback( widget, dummy );
060             return;
061     }
062
063     gtk_spin_button_set_value(GTK_SPIN_BUTTON(spinner), 1.0);
064     timeout = gtk_timeout_add(5000, SlidesTimerCallback, NULL);
065     gtk_widget_set_sensitive( button1, FALSE );
066     gtk_widget_set_sensitive( button2, FALSE );
067     gtk_label_set_text( GTK_LABEL( label ), "Cancel Slide Show" );
068 }
```

Let's begin our look at SlidesCallback() with the code on line 063. Here the spin button value is set to 1; this causes the first image in the set to be displayed immediately. Next, on line 065, a Gtk+ timeout function is added. The timeout will fire every 5 seconds (5000 ms), invoking the function SlidesTimerCallback(), which is responsible for displaying the next image in the slide show. On lines 065 through 067, the user interface is adjusted; the Previous and Next buttons are disabled, and the Slide Show button label is changed to Cancel Slide Show. Let's now go back and look at lines 058 through 061. When the user presses the Cancel Slide Show button, the same callback function that was registered for the Slide Show button, SlidesCallback(), will be invoked (this makes sense because they are the same button, just the label was changed). This time, button1 (the Previous button) will be insensitive, so we make a call to CancelCallback() and return. CancelCallback() simply stops the timeout function, re-enables the Next and Previous buttons, and changes the label of button3 back to Slide Show.

```
070 static void
071 CancelCallback(GtkWidget *widget, gpointer dummy)
072 {
073     if ( timeout ) {
074             gtk_timeout_remove(timeout);
075             timeout = 0;
076     }
077     gtk_widget_set_sensitive( button1, TRUE );
078     gtk_widget_set_sensitive( button2, TRUE );
079     gtk_label_set_text( GTK_LABEL( label ), "Slide Show" );
080 }
```

The last function, SlidesTimerCallback(), is called when the timeout expires (again, every 5 seconds in this example):

```
045 int
046 SlidesTimerCallback(gpointer dummy)
047 {
```

```
    gtk_spin_button_spin( GTK_SPIN_BUTTON( spinner ),
            GTK_SPIN_STEP_FORWARD, 0 );
    return 1;
}
```

SlidesTimerCallback() simply calls gtk_spin_button_spin() to advance the spin button value by 1. The function gtk_spin_button_spin() will advance the value of the adjustment object by 1, which will result in SpinnerCallback() being called as if the Next button had been pressed by the user. Note that we could have called gtk_spin_button_spin() from both NextCallback() and PrevCallback() to change the spin button adjustment object as follows:

```
static void
NextCallback(GtkWidget *widget, gpointer dummy)
{
        gtk_spin_button_spin( GTK_SPIN_BUTTON( spinner ),
                GTK_SPIN_STEP_FORWARD, 0 );
}

static void
PrevCallback(GtkWidget *widget, gpointer dummy)
{
        gtk_spin_button_spin( GTK_SPIN_BUTTON( spinner ),
                GTK_SPIN_STEP_BACKWARD, 0 );
}
```

Either technique is fine. Although deciding which to use is largely a matter of programmer preference, calling gtk_spin_button_spin() does result in code that is more readable.

Summary

A text widget (GtkText) is used to display multiline text. Functions in the GtkText API allow the application to set the text displayed, retrieve it after editing by the user, insert and delete text, control word wrap, and allow or disallow edits to the data being displayed. If your application needs to display single-line text edit fields, you should use GtkEntry instead (see Chapter 8). If your application needs to display text data in a message dialog, you should use GtkLabel (Chapter 5), not GtkText for this purpose (see Figure 7-1 in Chapter 7). A spin button widget is an editable control that supports the input of numeric data. A user can edit the value of a spin control by typing in an edit field or can use arrows displayed by the spin button control to increment or decrement the value within a specific range. If your application requires the user to enter numeric data, a spin button widget is your best choice. A scale widget (GtkScale) provides a second alternative but may be more difficult for users to interact with.

CHAPTER

15

MISCELLANEOUS WIDGETS

This chapter completes my coverage of the Gtk+ widget classes. In this chapter, the set of widget classes described includes those that are less commonly used in Gtk+ applications or that do not fit easily into one of the other chapters of this book and are too simple to deserve a chapter of their own. The widgets I will document in this chapter are listed in Table 15.1.

Table 15.1 Widgets Described in This Chapter

Class Name	*Description*
GtkRuler	Base ruler class
GtkHRuler	Horizontal ruler (derived from GtkRuler)
GtkVRuler	Vertical ruler (derived from GtkRuler)
GtkPreview	Displays RGB and grayscale data
GtkProgress	Base class for widgets that display progress
GtkProgressBar	Progress bar widget (derived from GtkProgress)
GtkTooltips	Tooltips collection widget
GtkTipsQuery	Displays additional tooltips data in a window
GtkCombo	Combo box widget
GtkStatusbar	Stack-based status bar widget
GtkAccelLabel	Label that supports display of accelerator text
GtkDrawingArea	Widget that supports drawing of graphics and images
GtkCalendar	Calendar display widget

GtkRuler

Class Name

```
GtkRuler
```

Parent Class Name

```
GtkWidget
```

Macros

Widget type macro: `GTK_TYPE_RULER`

Object to widget cast macro: `GTK_RULER(obj)`

Widget type check macro: `GTK_IS_RULER(obj)`

Supported Arguments

Prefix: `GtkRuler::`

Table 15.2 GtkRuler Arguments

Name	*Type*	*Permissions*
lower	GTK_TYPE_FLOAT	GTK_ARG_READWRITE
upper	GTK_TYPE_FLOAT	GTK_ARG_READWRITE
position	GTK_TYPE_FLOAT	GTK_ARG_WRITABLE
max_size	GTK_TYPE_FLOAT	GTK_ARG_WRITABLE

Application-Level API Synopsis

Return the constant GTK_TYPE_RULER at runtime:

```
GtkType
gtk_ruler_get_type(void);
```

Set the "metric type" attribute of a rule to either GTK_PIXELS, GTK_INCHES or GTK_CENTIMETERS:

```
void
gtk_ruler_set_metric(GtkRuler *ruler, GtkMetricType metric);
```

Application-Level API Synopsis (Continued)

Set the range of values represented by the ruler (see text):

```
void
gtk_ruler_set_range(GtkRuler *ruler, gfloat lower, gfloat upper,
        gfloat position, gfloat max_size);
```

Class Description

GtkRuler is a parent class for the GtkHRuler and GtkVRuler classes, both of which I will describe in this chapter. Like many parent classes of this type, you do not create instances of GtkRuler directly in your applications. Instead, you create instances of GtkHRuler and/or GtkVRuler, depending on your needs. Instances of GtkHRuler and GtkVRuler can be passed to GtkRuler functions by casting them to GtkRuler using the GTK_RULER macro, as follows:

```
GtkWidget *hruler;

hruler = gtk_hruler_new();

gtk_ruler_set_metric( GTK_RULER( hruler ), GTK_PIXELS );
```

Setting the Ruler Metric

Two functions provided by GtkRuler are useful to applications. The first lets you specify the "metric type" attribute of the horizontal or vertical ruler. The function prototype for gtk_ruler_set_metric() is as follows:

```
void
gtk_ruler_set_metric(GtkRuler *ruler, GtkMetricType metric);
```

The argument metric can be one of the values listed in Table 15.3.

Table 15.3 GtkMetricType Values

Metric	*Pixels Per Unit*
GTK_PIXELS	1
GTK_INCHES	72 pixels per inch
GTK_CENTIMETERS	28.35 pixels per centimeter

The choice of metric affects how many ticks are displayed by the ruler widget and how the ticks are labeled. For example, when metric is set to GTK_INCHES, each inch will be displayed with major ticks and a numerical label, while a minor tick and no label will be used to identify 1/4-, 1/2-, and 3/4-inch values that fall in between.

The metric attribute is influenced by the size of the ruler, the range of values associated with the ruler, the physical resolution of the screen, and the data being displayed inside the area that the ruler measures. To illustrate this, let's start with the simple case of displaying a 300×300 image in a 300×300 window on a screen that has a 72×72-dots-per-inch resolution. Here, if we were to display a horizontal ruler with the default metric of GTK_PIXELS, its ticks would naturally range from 0 to 300 in value, would consume a total of 300 pixels on screen, and would be spaced at 72 dots per inch, meaning that pixel 71 of the image would be shown exactly 1 inch from the edge of the window if we were to measure it with a measuring tape (ignoring any spacing or bordering applied to the widget managing the ruler and the content area). If the metric were changed to GTK_INCHES, the same relationship would hold, and if you were to place a measuring tape or ruler, scaled in inches, against the screen, the scale of the measuring tape and that of the ruler widget would correspond to each other exactly. The same one-to-one correspondence between screen and physical realities will hold if you were to change the metric argument of the ruler to GTK_CENTIMETERS.

On a 100-dpi screen, GtkRuler correctly labels our 300×300 image data when the metric attribute is set to GTK_PIXELS. However, by setting the metric attribute to GTK_INCHES or GTK_CENTIMETERS, the labels of the ruler now (incorrectly) give us information for a 72-dpi device, which is inconsistent with the display and, therefore, does not correspond to the real-world physical measurement.

To summarize:

- Real-world devices are not always 72 dpi (or 28.35 pixels per centimeter).
- Only the ruler metric GTK_PIXELS will accurately reflect reality regardless of the screen resolution.

For these reasons, your only safe bet is to use the default GTK_PIXELS as the metric attribute for a ruler. It is not easy for many workstations to report accurately the true screen resolution of the display; this is especially true for Linux-based systems that may run with arbitrary displays of varying sizes. Even if the system could report its screen resolution accurately, GtkRuler does not allow the 72 dpi value to be changed, so there is no hope that an application can tell a ruler widget how to accurately convert pixels to inches or centimeters.

Setting the Range of a Ruler

The following function, gtk_ruler_set_range(), must be called for each ruler widget to define the full extent of values represented by the ruler:

```
void
gtk_ruler_set_range(GtkRuler *ruler, gfloat lower, gfloat upper,
        gfloat position, gfloat max_size);
```

The argument ruler is an instance of GtkHRuler or GtkVRuler, lower is the lowest value represented by the ruler, upper is the highest value, and position is the initial location of the ruler thumb. The argument max_size controls how the ruler labels and tick marks are drawn by the vertical and horizontal ruler widgets. The use of this argument is not entirely clear to me; hopefully, the following will make some sense. The file *gtkruler.c* defines the following array used internally by GtkRuler:

```
static const GtkRulerMetric ruler_metrics[] =
{
        {"Pixels", "Pi", 1.0,
        { 1, 2, 5, 10, 25, 50, 100, 250, 500, 1000 },
        { 1, 5, 10, 50, 100 }},
        {"Inches", "In", 72.0,
        { 1, 2, 4, 8, 16, 32, 64, 128, 256, 512 },
        { 1, 2, 4, 8, 16 }},
        {"Centimeters", "Cn", 28.35,
        { 1, 2, 5, 10, 25, 50, 100, 250, 500, 1000 },
        { 1, 5, 10, 50, 100 }},
};
```

Let's focus on the first entry, which is used whenever the metric attribute is set to GTK_PIXELS, because it is what most applications use, and it is the easiest to understand. The fourth field of the "Pixels" entry is an array of integers:

```
{ 1, 2, 5, 10, 25, 50, 100, 250, 500, 1000 }
```

Each of these values represents a label increment. Let's assume that the range of the ruler is [0, 300]. The entry 5 would mean labels are drawn by the ruler in increments of 5. That is, the 0, 5, 10, ..., 300 ticks would all be labeled by the ruler widget for the range [0, 300]. If the label only ranges in value from [0, 10], the only increments that make sense are 1, 2, and 5. The width or height of the ruler, and the width or height of the font used to draw the labels, affect what increments can be drawn by the ruler: The wider or taller the font and the less wide (tall) the ruler translates into fewer ticks that can be labeled, thus favoring the label increments that are larger.

So exactly what part does the max_size argument play in all of this? The best way to understand the effect it has is to look at the source code. (Both of the ruler widgets, GtkHRuler and GtkVRuler, implement similar code in their methods that draw the ruler ticks, e.g., gtk_hruler_draw_ticks().) First, the width of the ruler widget is obtained on line 001. Following this, two variables, lower and upper, are computed (lines 002 and 003):

```
001 width = widget->allocation.height;
002 upper = ruler->upper / ruler->metric->pixels_per_unit;
003 lower = ruler->lower / ruler->metric->pixels_per_unit;
```

For this example, the variable width is 282, ruler->upper = 300, ruler->lower = 0, and ruler->metric->pixels_per_unit is 1 (since the metric is GTK_PIXELS). As a result, upper is assigned 300, and lower is assigned 0. With these values, the variable increment is given the value 4.06320275e-34 on line 004:

```
004 increment = (gfloat) width / (upper - lower);
```

For the following code, let ruler->max_size = 1 and font->ascent = 11.

```
005 scale = ceil (ruler->max_size / ruler->metric->pixels_per_unit);
006 sprintf (unit_str, "%d", scale);
007 digit_height = font->ascent; /* assume descent == 0 ? */
```

Then we have scale = 1 and digit_height = 11. On line 008, text_height is assigned the value 12:

```
008 text_height = strlen (unit_str) * digit_height + 1;
```

Then we go into a loop, looking at values in the metric ruler_scale field until it, times the increment, is greater than twice the text_height (24 in this case):

```
009 for (scale = 0; scale < MAXIMUM_SCALES; scale++)
010      if (ruler->metric->ruler_scale[scale] * fabs(increment) >
                             2 * text_height)
011           break;
```

The loop terminates with scale = 5, meaning the label increment is 50. Let's try again with a max_size of 128. In this case, increment is 2.01992702, and the loop on lines 009 through 011 terminates with scale set to 6, which indexes the value 100 in the metric_ruler scale field. Accordingly, only ticks 0, 100, and 200 are drawn this time.

Let's increase the size of the ruler by widening the window and see how that affects the drawing of labels. Here the ruler size is 706 pixels, and with a ruler->max_size set to 1, the loop stops with scale = 4, meaning the label increment is 25. Thus, labels are drawn at the following locations: 0, 25, 50, 75, ..., 300. If we change the max_size attribute to 128, ticks are labeled at intervals of 50.

My advice is to either set max_size to 0 or experiment with various values to see how they affect the labeling of rulers in your application, and then use the value that gives you the most pleasing results.

Tracking Mouse Movement

You (and users of your application) will notice that when the pointer is placed within the ruler widget, it will respond to mouse movement by tracking the pointer. As the pointer is tracked, the ruler widget will redraw the thumb so that it corresponds to the current pointer position. By default, rulers do not respond to any movement that occurs outside of the ruler widget. However, such behavior is often desirable. For an example of this behavior, display an image in The GIMP and move the mouse around inside the window displaying the image. The rulers will track the mouse movement within the image window to indicate approximately over which pixel the mouse is located as it is moved. To achieve this effect, use code similar to the following:

```
GtkWidget *ruler, *window;

window = gtk_window_new(GTK_WINDOW_TOPLEVEL);
ruler = gtk_hruler_new();

gtk_signal_connect_object( GTK_OBJECT(window),
          "motion_notify_event",
          GTK_SIGNAL_FUNC(GTK_WIDGET_CLASS(
          GTK_OBJECT(ruler)->klass)->motion_notify_event),
          GTK_OBJECT (ruler));
```

In the preceding code, window is the top-level window containing the ruler widget. Here we ensured that motion_notify_event signals that are generated as movement within the containing window occurs are also dispatched to the ruler widget for processing. The ruler widget will handle the event as though it had occurred within its own window and will update the ruler thumb to indicate the pointer position as it is tracked.

Sample Code

The following is the typical sample code presented for GtkRuler. In this case, a 300×300 window is created. An instance of GtkTable containing two rows and two columns is added to the window. A horizontal scrollbar is instantiated and inserted in the top row of the table. A vertical scrollbar is instantiated and inserted in the leftmost column of the table. The remaining cells of the table are intended to hold the content that the rulers represent; this might be either a pixmap or an image widget, for example.

Listing 15.1 GtkRuler Example

```
#include <gtk/gtk.h>

main( int argc, char *argv[] )
{
   GtkWidget *dialog_window, *table;
   GtkWidget *vruler, *hruler;

   gtk_init( &argc, &argv );

   dialog_window = gtk_window_new( GTK_WINDOW_TOPLEVEL );
   gtk_window_position(GTK_WINDOW(dialog_window), GTK_WIN_POS_MOUSE);

   gtk_widget_set_usize(dialog_window, 300, 300);

   table = gtk_table_new(2, 2, FALSE);
   gtk_container_add(GTK_CONTAINER (dialog_window), table );

   hruler = gtk_hruler_new();
   gtk_ruler_set_range(GTK_RULER (hruler), 0, 300, 0, 1);
   gtk_table_attach(GTK_TABLE (table), hruler, 1, 2, 0, 1,
           GTK_EXPAND | GTK_FILL, GTK_FILL, 0, 0);

   vruler = gtk_vruler_new();
   gtk_ruler_set_range(GTK_RULER(vruler), 0, 300, 0, 1);
   gtk_table_attach(GTK_TABLE(table), vruler, 0, 1, 1, 2,
           GTK_FILL, GTK_EXPAND | GTK_FILL, 0, 0);

   gtk_widget_show_all(dialog_window);
   gtk_main();
}
```

GtkHRuler

Class Name

```
GtkHRuler
```

Parent Class Name

```
GtkRuler
```

Macros

Widget type macro: `GTK_TYPE_RULER`

Object to widget cast macro: `GTK_HRULER(obj)`

Widget type check macro: `GTK_IS_HRULER(obj)`

Application-Level API Synopsis

Retrieve the constant GTK_TYPE_RULER at runtime:

```
guint
gtk_hruler_get_type(void);
```

Create an instance of GtkHRuler:

```
GtkWidget *
gtk_hruler_new(void);
```

Class Description

GtkHRuler is a derived class of GtkRuler, which was previously described. GtkHRuler is used to create a horizontal ruler. (GtkVRuler, the other class derived from GtkRuler, creates a vertical instance of GtkRuler.) The only function of interest in this class is gtk_hruler_new():

```
GtkWidget *
gtk_hruler_new(void);
```

See the preceding discussion of GtkRuler for a sample program that makes use of GtkHRuler and calls gtk_hruler_new().

GtkPreview

Class Name

```
GtkPreview
```

Parent Class Name

```
GtkWidget
```

Macros

Widget type macro: `GTK_TYPE_PREVIEW`

Object to widget cast macro: `GTK_PREVIEW(obj)`

Widget type check macro: `GTK_IS_PREVIEW(obj)`

Supported Arguments

Prefix: `GtkPreview::`

Table 15.4 GtkPreview Arguments

Name	*Type*	*Permission*
expand	GTK_TYPE_BOOL	GTK_ARG_READWRITE

Application-Level API Synopsis

Return the constant GTK_TYPE_PREVIEW at runtime:

```
GtkType
gtk_preview_get_type(void);
```

Create a new instance of GtkPreview, of the specified type:

```
GtkWidget *
gtk_preview_new(GtkPreviewType type);
```

Set the width and height of an instance of GtkPreview:

```
void
gtk_preview_size(GtkPreview *preview, gint width, gint height);
```

Application-Level API Synopsis (Continued)

Copy data from a preview widget to the specified window:

```
void
gtk_preview_put(GtkPreview *preview, GdkWindow *window, GdkGC *gc,
        gint srcx, gint srcy, gint destx, gint desty, gint width,
        gint height);
```

Place a row of data in the preview widget:

```
void
gtk_preview_draw_row(GtkPreview *preview, guchar *data, gint x,
        gint y, gint w);
```

Specify whether a preview widget should expand to fit its allocation:

```
void
gtk_preview_set_expand(GtkPreview *preview, gboolean expand);
```

Set gamma correction on the preview widget:

```
void
gtk_preview_set_gamma(double gamma);
```

Set the dither mode of the preview widget:

```
void
gtk_preview_set_dither(GtkPreview *preview, GdkRgbDither dither);
```

Retrieve global information about preview widgets:

```
GtkPreviewInfo *
gtk_preview_get_info(void);
```

Class Description

GtkPreview is perhaps the quickest method for displaying arbitrary image data, either RGB or grayscale, without the need to concern yourself with the conversion of the image data into a format that is compatible with the window in which it is being displayed (e.g., its colormap, depth, visual class). It is not in the scope of this book to discuss the problem of displaying image data in an X window; see my book on the X Image Extension (XIE) (*Developing Imaging Applications With XIElib*, Prentice Hall, 1998) or any good book on Xlib to learn the issues involved. To briefly introduce the problem here, X requires that the image data you display in a window be compatible with that window. The depth of the image must be the same as that of the window in which it is being displayed (dithering is one technique that can be used to reduce the pixel size of an image to correspond to that of the window for which it is targeted). Also, RGB or grayscale data must be converted by the application into pixel values that index a colormap maintained by the server and associated with the target window.

GtkPreview basically converts an RGB or grayscale image into pixel values. The pixels in the result preserve the image content and are acceptable for display by the X server in a given window.

The following example illustrates the basics involved with using a GtkPreview widget to display a TIFF color image in a window. After I provide an overview of the program and its structure, I will explain in detail the GtkPreview API that it uses.

Listing 15.2 Using GtkPreview to Display a TIFF Color Image

```
#include <tiffio.h>
#include <stdlib.h>

#include <gtk/gtk.h>
#include <X11/Xlib.h>

static uint32 *raster;
static int width, height;
static GtkWidget *preview;

void
SizeAllocation( GtkWidget *widget, GtkAllocation  *allocation)
{
    guint i, j, k, RGB;
    guchar *buf;

    buf = (guchar *) malloc(width * 3);
    if ( !buf )
            return;

    for ( i = 0; i < height; i++ ) {
            for ( j = 0, k = 0; j < width; j++ ) {
                    RGB = raster[((height - 1) - i) * width + j];
                    buf[k+0] = TIFFGetR(RGB);
                    buf[k+1] = TIFFGetG(RGB);
                    buf[k+2] = TIFFGetB(RGB);
                    k += 3;
            }
            gtk_preview_draw_row(GTK_PREVIEW(preview), buf, 0, i, width);
    }
    if ( buf )
            free( buf );
}

int main( int argc, char *argv[] )
{
    uint32 RGB, pixel;
    uint16 bitspersample, samplesperpixel;
    GtkWidget *window, *vbox;
    TIFF *tif;

    gtk_init( &argc, &argv );

    window = gtk_window_new( GTK_WINDOW_TOPLEVEL );

    tif = TIFFOpen(argv[1], "r");
```

```
047
048         if ( !tif ) {
049                 printf( "Unable to open tiff file %s\n", argv[1] );
050                 exit( 1 );
051         }
052
053         TIFFGetField(tif, TIFFTAG_IMAGEWIDTH, &width);
054         TIFFGetField(tif, TIFFTAG_IMAGELENGTH, &height);
055         TIFFGetField(tif, TIFFTAG_BITSPERSAMPLE, &bitspersample);
056         TIFFGetField(tif, TIFFTAG_SAMPLESPERPIXEL, &samplesperpixel);
057
058         if ( samplesperpixel != 3 ) {
059                 printf( "Error: image is not RGB.\n" );
060                 exit( 1 );
061         }
062
063         raster = (uint32*)malloc(width * height * sizeof (uint32));
064
065         if ( !raster ) {
066                 perror( "malloc" );
067                 exit( 1 );
068         }
069
070         if (!TIFFReadRGBAImage(tif, width, height, raster, 0)) {
071                 printf( "TIFFReadRGBAImage() failed\n" );
072                 exit( 1 );
073         }
074
075         gtk_widget_set_usize( window, width, height );
076         vbox = gtk_vbox_new(FALSE, 0);
077         gtk_container_add(GTK_CONTAINER(window), vbox);
078
079         preview = gtk_preview_new(GTK_PREVIEW_COLOR);
080         gtk_preview_size(GTK_PREVIEW (preview), width, height);
081         gtk_preview_set_expand(GTK_PREVIEW (preview), TRUE);
082
083         gtk_signal_connect(GTK_OBJECT (preview), "size_allocate",
084                 GTK_SIGNAL_FUNC (SizeAllocation), NULL);
085
086         gtk_box_pack_start( GTK_BOX(vbox), preview, TRUE, TRUE, 0);
087
088         gtk_widget_show_all( window );
089
090         gtk_main();
091 }
```

The sample program is split into two functions, the obligatory main() and a routine called SizeAllocation(). The purpose of main() in this example is to create a window into which the image will be displayed, to read and parse the TIFF image data from the user-specified file, and to create an instance of GtkPreview into which the image data will be displayed.

Lines 046 through 073 are dedicated to reading the TIFF image data into a buffer that can be used by GtkPreview. This body of code (which would be better expressed as a function) can be replaced with code that can handle other image types such as GIF, JPG, and so forth.

The point of this code (or any image code you would execute in its place) is to get the image data and its width and height.

```
046     tif = TIFFOpen(argv[1], "r");
047
048     if ( !tif ) {
049             printf( "Unable to open tiff file %s\n", argv[1] );
050             exit( 1 );
051     }
052
053     TIFFGetField(tif, TIFFTAG_IMAGEWIDTH, &width);
054     TIFFGetField(tif, TIFFTAG_IMAGELENGTH, &height);
055     TIFFGetField(tif, TIFFTAG_BITSPERSAMPLE, &bitspersample);
056     TIFFGetField(tif, TIFFTAG_SAMPLESPERPIXEL, &samplesperpixel);
057
058     if ( samplesperpixel != 3 ) {
059             printf( "Error: image is not RGB.\n" );
060             exit( 1 );
061     }
062
063     raster = (uint32*)malloc(width * height * sizeof (uint32));
064
065     if ( !raster ) {
066             perror( "malloc" );
067             exit( 1 );
068     }
069
070     if (!TIFFReadRGBAImage(tif, width, height, raster, 0)) {
071             printf( "TIFFReadRGBAImage() failed\n" );
072             exit( 1 );
073     }
```

Here, the width and height of the image are stored in global variables of the same names, and the image data is stored in a uint32 * variable named raster. Notice on line 058 that I check to see if libtiff reported a samples-per-pixel attribute of 3. If so, this is sufficient to indicate that the data I am dealing with is RGB. If the image isn't RGB, then I exit the program because I only support RGB data in this example. The other possible value is 1; this would indicate that the data is grayscale. For simplicity sake, I have chosen to ignore grayscale image data as well for this example. For more information on libtiff, the library used to read and parse the TIFF file, you can execute the following command:

```
$ man libtiff
```

Creating a Preview Widget

The code that is tasked with creating and configuring the preview widget is on lines 079 through 084. On line 079, gtk_preview_new() is called to create an instance of GtkPreview:

```
079     preview = gtk_preview_new(GTK_PREVIEW_COLOR);
```

The function prototype for gtk_preview_new() is as follows:

```
GtkWidget *
gtk_preview_new(GtkPreviewType type);
```

The argument type can be one of the following values: GTK_PREVIEW_COLOR, used when the image is triple-band RGB color, or GTK_PREVIEW_GRAYSCALE, used when the image data is single-band grayscale. Here, I use GTK_PREVIEW_COLOR because I am only supporting RGB color data in this example.

Setting the Image Size

On the following line, I tell the preview widget the size of the image it is going to be displaying:

```
gtk_preview_size(GTK_PREVIEW (preview), width, height);
```

The function prototype for gtk_preview_size() is as follows:

```
void
gtk_preview_size(GtkPreview *preview, gint width, gint height);
```

The first argument is an instance of GtkPreview. The remaining two arguments are the width and height that the preview widget would like to be allocated in response to a size request from a containing widget.

Setting the Expand Attribute

The next two functions, gtk_review_set_expand() and the corresponding call to gtk_signal_connect(), need some explanation:

```
gtk_preview_set_expand(GTK_PREVIEW (preview), TRUE);

gtk_signal_connect(GTK_OBJECT (preview), "size_allocate",
        GTK_SIGNAL_FUNC (SizeAllocation), NULL);
```

The function gtk_preview_set_expand() takes a boolean argument, expand:

```
void
gtk_preview_set_expand(GtkPreview *preview, gboolean expand);
```

The intent of the default value of FALSE is to tell the preview widget to make sure its size is never made larger than the size specified by gtk_preview_set_size() or, if gtk_preview_set_size() has not been called, no larger than the initial size requisition of the preview widget. In practice, the preview widget will accept whatever allocation it has been given. In its internal size_allocation function, if expand has been set to TRUE, the upper-left corner of the preview widget's window will be aligned with the x and y coordinates of its allocation, and its width and height will correspond to the width and height of its allocation. If expand is set to FALSE, the width and height of the preview widget will be the smaller of the allocation width and height, or the preview widget's requisition width and height. (Again, the requisition width and height is either the original width and height of the preview widget or the width and height of the preview widget assigned by a call to gtk_preview_size().) Also, if expand is FALSE and the allocation width and/or height is greater than the size given, the preview widget window will be centered within the area described by the allocation.

I am not particularly fond of this aspect of GtkPreview (the centering of the preview widget window in its allocation). For this reason, I advocate setting the expand attribute to TRUE, as I do on line 081. The size_allocation signal function that I registered on line 083 is invoked by Gtk+ when the widget is initially created and anytime the widget is resized. The code for SizeAllocation() is duplicated in the following:

```
011  void
012  SizeAllocation( GtkWidget *widget, GtkAllocation  *allocation)
013  {
014     guint i, j, k, RGB;
015     guchar *buf;
016
017     buf = (guchar *) malloc(width * 3);
018     if ( !buf )
019             return;
020
021     for ( i = 0; i < height; i++ ) {
022             for ( j = 0, k = 0; j < width; j++ ) {
023                     RGB = raster[((height - 1) - i) * width + j];
024                     buf[k+0] = TIFFGetR(RGB);
025                     buf[k+1] = TIFFGetG(RGB);
026                     buf[k+2] = TIFFGetB(RGB);
027                     k += 3;
028             }
029             gtk_preview_draw_row(GTK_PREVIEW(preview), buf, 0, i, width);
030     }
031     if ( buf )
032             free( buf );
033  }
```

On line 017, I allocate a buffer big enough to hold a row of image data. For each row in the image (line 021) and for each pixel in a row (line 022), I extract the RGB components of the pixel and pack them into the row buffer (lines 023 through 027).

Setting the Image Data

Continuing with the example, once a row has been constructed, I then call, on line 029, gtk_preview_draw_row() to add the row data to the preview widget so that it can be drawn to the window. The function prototype for gtk_preview_draw_row() is as follows:

```
void
gtk_preview_draw_row(GtkPreview *preview, guchar *data, gint x,
        gint y, gint w);
```

The argument preview is an instance of GtkPreview, and data is the row of data (because I am dealing with RGB data, each pixel is 3 bytes wide; when dealing with grayscale image data, each pixel is 1 byte in width). The argument x indicates an offset within the row, in the range

[0, width – 1], while y indicates the row number and is in the range [0, height – 1]. The argument w is the width of the data in pixels (not bytes) and must be in the range of [0, width – x]. (Practically speaking, w is never set to 0, however, because it makes no sense to write a zero-length row of data to a preview widget.)

As you can see, I am writing complete rows of data by setting x to 0, y to the row number, and w to the width in pixels of the image I am rendering. Also, I am ignoring the allocation entirely, and I am always drawing the image at its original width and height (e.g., the requisition of the preview widget).

If I wanted to scale the image data to fit the allocation, I would do the following: First, I would make a call to gtk_preview_size() to change the size of the preview widget to match the allocation. Next, I would scale the image data by whatever means are available to the new preview widget size and then draw the image data using gtk_preview_draw_row() as before. Adding the following code to the top of SizeAllocation() illustrates the basic technique I have just described:

```
uint32 *newraster;

if ( allocation->width != widget->requisition.width ||
        allocation->height != widget->requisition.height &&
        preview->expand == TRUE )
{
        width = allocation->width;
        height = allocation->height;

        gtk_preview_size( preview, width, height );
        newraster = scale( raster, width, height );
} else
        newraster = raster;

 ...

                        RGB = newraster[((height - 1) - i) * width + j];
```

Here, raster holds the original, unscaled data, and scale() is a function (not discussed in detail here) that scales the image in the raster from its original dimensions of oldwidth, oldheight to the new dimensions specified by the allocation object.

Drawing the Image Data

Calling gtk_preview_draw_row() is not sufficient for the actual rendering to the preview widget window to take place. An expose event is needed to cause this to happen. This can be done by calling gtk_widget_queue_draw(), passing the preview widget as an argument.

The function gtk_preview_put() transfers the image data you have previously placed in the preview image with a call to gtk_preview_draw_row(); it is called by the GtkPreview widget expose signal function. You can call this function at any time to render the image data to an arbitrary window. The function prototype for gtk_preview_put() is as follows:

```
void
gtk_preview_put(GtkPreview *preview, GdkWindow *window, GdkGC *gc,
        gint srcx, gint srcy, gint destx, gint desty, gint width,
        gint height);
```

The argument preview is an instance of GtkPreview that has data to be displayed, and window is the GdkWindow that will receive that data. The argument gc is a GdkGC that is compatible with window. The arguments srcx and srcy identify the location of the pixel corresponding to the upper-left corner of the image data that is to be displayed, while destx and desty define the upper-left corner of the area within the target window to which the data will be rendered. Finally, the arguments width and height define the size of the image data, in pixels, that will be copied to the window. Let's look at how the GtkPreview expose signal function calls gtk_preview_put():

```
static gint
gtk_preview_expose(GtkWidget *widget, GdkEventExpose *event)
{
  GtkPreview *preview;
  gint width, height;

  preview = GTK_PREVIEW (widget);

  gdk_window_get_size (widget->window, &width, &height);

  gtk_preview_put (GTK_PREVIEW (widget),
        widget->window, widget->style->black_gc,
        event->area.x - (width - preview->buffer_width)/2,
        event->area.y - (height - preview->buffer_height)/2,
        event->area.x, event->area.y,
        event->area.width, event->area.height);

  return FALSE;
}
```

Here, the expose function is copying only those pixels from the image data that correspond to the area exposed. The source x and y coordinates and the destination x and y coordinates are a function of the expose event origin (event->area.x, event->area.y), and the size of the image copied is defined by the size of the area exposed (event->area.width, event->area.height).

Miscellaneous GtkPreview Functions. The next two functions allow you to control the gamma correction of the image data and to choose a dithering technique to be applied to the image data if dithering is required prior to display.

Setting the Dither Preference. The function gtk_preview_set_dither():

```
void
gtk_preview_set_dither(GtkPreview *preview, GdkRgbDither dither);
```

allows an application to tell GDK when to dither (or not dither) images of a higher fidelity than the display supports. The argument dither can be one of the values specified in Table 15.5.

Table 15.5 GdkRgbDither Values

Dither Mode	*Meaning*
GDK_RGB_DITHER_NONE	The image will not be dithered.
GDK_RGB_DITHER_NORMAL	Perform dithering in 8-bit or lesser visuals.
GDK_RGB_DITHER_MAX	Perform dithering in 16-bit or lesser visuals.

Note that if GDK_RGB_DITHER_NONE is selected, the image data will be levels-adjusted so that it is compatible with the visual class and depth of the window to which it is rendered. This may introduce a posterization effect if the levels reduction is dramatic (i.e., 24-bit RGB data displayed in an 8-bit PseudoColor window).

My recommendation is to always call this function and pass GDK_RGB_DITHER_MAX as the argument. This will ensure that the image data you display will show at its best, regardless of the display or X server to which your application is connected.

Setting the Gamma. You can set the gamma used by all GtkPreview widgets by calling the function gtk_preview_set_gamma():

```
void
gtk_preview_set_gamma(double gamma);
```

The argument gamma can be any value in the range [0.0, 1.0]. Often, 0.8 is a good choice because many monitors are adjusted for a gamma of 0.8, but the default value of 1.0 yields acceptable results as well. A gamma of 0.0 renders the image black by driving the brightness of the image to an absolute minimum. At the other end of the range, 1.0 sets the brightness of the image to the highest possible value.

Retrieving Global Information About Preview Widgets. The final GtkPreview function, gtk_preview_get_info():

```
GtkPreviewInfo *
gtk_preview_get_info(void);
```

retrieves global information about preview widgets. The function takes no arguments and returns a pointer to a GtkPreviewInfo structure, which is defined as follows:

```
struct _GtkPreviewInfo
{
  GdkVisual *visual;
  GdkColormap *cmap;
  guchar *lookup;
  gdouble gamma;
};
```

The field visual is obtained by GtkPreview by calling gdk_rgb_get_visual(), and cmap is obtained via a call to gdk_rgb_get_cmap(). These functions return the visual and colormap, respectively, chosen by GDK when it was initialized at startup. The field lookup is a 256-element lookup table created by GtkPreview that is used internally by GtkPreview when applying gamma values (other than 1.0) to the image data as it is drawn. The field gamma holds the preview widget gamma value, either 1.0 (the default) or the value set by a call to gtk_preview_set_gamma().

GtkProgress

Class Name

`GtkProgress`

Parent Class Name

`GtkWidget`

Macros

Widget type macro: `GTK_TYPE_PROGRESS`

Object to widget cast macro: `GTK_PROGRESS(obj)`

Widget type check macro: `GTK_IS_PROGRESS(obj)`

Supported Arguments

Prefix: `GtkProgress::`

Table 15.6 Arguments

Name	*Type*	*Permissions*
activity_mode	GTK_TYPE_BOOL	GTK_ARG_READWRITE
show_text	GTK_TYPE_BOOL	GTK_ARG_READWRITE
text_xalign	GTK_TYPE_FLOAT	GTK_ARG_READWRITE
text_yalign	GTK_TYPE_FLOAT	GTK_ARG_READWRITE

Application-Level API Synopsis

Retrieve the constant GTK_TYPE_PROGRESS at runtime:

```
GtkType
gtk_progress_get_type(void);
```

Enable or disable the display of the progress widget text:

```
void
gtk_progress_set_show_text(GtkProgress *progress, gint show_text);
```

Set the horizontal and vertical alignment of the progress widget text:

```
void
gtk_progress_set_text_alignment(GtkProgress *progress,
        gfloat x_align, gfloat y_align);
```

Set the progress widget format string (see text):

```
void
gtk_progress_set_format_string(GtkProgress *progress,
        const gchar *format);
```

Set the progress widget adjustment object (see text):

```
void
gtk_progress_set_adjustment(GtkProgress *progress,
        GtkAdjustment *adjustment);
```

Initialize the range and value attributes of the progress widget:

```
void
gtk_progress_configure(GtkProgress *progress, gfloat value,
        gfloat min, gfloat max);
```

Set the progress widget percentage:

```
void
gtk_progress_set_percentage(GtkProgress *progress,
        gfloat percentage);
```

Set the progress widget value:

```
void
gtk_progress_set_value(GtkProgress *progress, gfloat value);
```

Retrieve the progress widget value:

```
gfloat
gtk_progress_get_value(GtkProgress *progress);
```

Set the progress widget activity mode (TRUE or FALSE, see text):

```
void
gtk_progress_set_activity_mode(GtkProgress *progress,
        guint activity_mode);
```

Retrieve the current text associated with the progress widget:

```
gchar *
gtk_progress_get_current_text(GtkProgress *progress);
```

Application-Level API Synopsis (Continued)

Get the text that would be displayed by the progress widget, given a value:

```
gchar *
gtk_progress_get_text_from_value(GtkProgress *progress,
        gfloat value);
```

Get the current percentage displayed by the progress widget:

```
gfloat
gtk_progress_get_current_percentage(GtkProgress *progress);
```

Given a value, determine what percentage it represents:

```
gfloat
gtk_progress_get_percentage_from_value(GtkProgress *progress,
        gfloat value);
```

Class Description

GtkProgress is a base or parent class that is not directly instantiated by an application. In Gtk 1.2, GtkProgress acts as the parent class of GtkProgressBar (GtkProgressBar is described in the next section). Mainly, GtkProgress allows an application to control the aspects of widgets (in Table 15.7) that derive from it.

Table 15.7 GtkProgress Attributes

Attribute	*Explanation*
initial state	Controls the range and adjustment attributes of a progress widget.
text	Toggles the display of text, formats its display, and retrieves its current value.
value and percentage	Gets or sets the current value or percentage of the progress widget.
activity mode	Controls how the progress widget displays its current state (either discretely or continuously).

The next several sections describe each of these attributes and the functions that control them in detail. The discussion is biased towards GtkProgressBar usage; how these attributes are interpreted by other classes that derive from GtkProgress will vary to some degree.

Initialization

Because GtkProgress is a base class, no widget creation functions are provided. And because the only class inheriting from GtkProgress in Gtk 1.2 is GtkProgressBar, you create an instance of GtkProgressBar indirectly by calling gtk_progress_bar_new(), which is described later in this chapter. Regardless of the widget inheriting from GtkProgress, once you have created an instance of a widget that inherits from GtkProgress, you may call any of the functions I describe in this section and in the following sections.

When you instantiate a derived class of GtkProgress, you either provide it an adjustment object (see gtk_progress_bar_new_with_adjustment()) or allow it to create its own adjustment (as is the case with gtk_progress_bar_new()). Regardless of how the original adjustment object is created, you can replace the adjustment object with a new one by calling gtk_progress_set_adjustment():

```
void
gtk_progress_set_adjustment(GtkProgress *progress,
          GtkAdjustment *adjustment);
```

The argument progress is an instance of a GtkProgress-derived class that has been coerced to an instance of GtkProgress. The argument adjustment is an adjustment object (see Chapter 13, "Range Widgets and Adjustment Objects," for details on creating and using adjustment objects). In general, let the adjustment object be created for you if the adjustment object is not to be shared with one or more additional Gtk+ widgets that make use of adjustment objects, or if the GtkProgress-derived widget is the first widget of a set of widgets that will share a common adjustment object. The remaining widgets in the set, in this case, should not be creating their own adjustment objects; instead, they should be provided, at the time of their creation, the adjustment object that was created by the progress-derived widget.

The following code sections:

```
GtkWidget *w;
GtkAdjustment *adj;

w = gtk_progress_bar_new();
adj = gtk_adjustment_new(0, 1, 300, 0, 0, 0);
gtk_progress_set_adjustment( (GTK_PROGRESS( w ), adj );
```

and

```
GtkWidget *w;
GtkAdjustment *adj;

adj = gtk_adjustment_new(0, 1, 300, 0, 0, 0);
w = gtk_progress_bar_new_with_adjustment( adj );
```

generate the same result.

The second and final function in this category, gtk_progress_configure():

```
void
gtk_progress_configure(GtkProgress *progress, gfloat value,
        gfloat min, gfloat max);
```

is used to set the lower, upper, and value attributes of a GtkProgress-derived widget. The argument progress is an instance of a GtkProgress-derived widget, and value, min, and max correspond to that widget's value, lower, and upper adjustment object attributes, respectively, which will become effective once the function returns.

Text

GtkProgress widgets maintain a text string that can be used by the derived widget class to display a label that conveys the following information to the user: percentage complete, current value, minimum (lower) value, and maximum (upper) value.

The application can determine not only whether the string should be displayed (if supported by the GtkProgress-derived class), but the format of the text that is displayed. The format of the text is defined by a format string that is similar to the format string used in the printf(3) family of functions. Let's discuss the format string in detail first. A format string consists of any arbitrary text you care to include, as well as directives that are parsed for and replaced by GtkProgress when it is asked by the subclass instance to construct a string for display. A directive is a substring of the format string that matches the following regular expression: %{0-2}[%pPvVlLuU]. That is, a % character, followed by an optional 0, 1, or 2, followed by one of the following characters: p, P, v, V, l, L, u, or U. Table 15.8 lists the meanings assigned to this last set of characters.

Table 15.8 Format String Directives

Character	*Meaning*
%	Literal %
p or P	Current percentage
v or V	Current value
l or L	Low value in the range
u or U	Upper value in the range

The optional 0, 1, or 2 indicates the number of significant digits to display after a value.

Some examples will help make this clear. The format string "Hello World" will result in a text value of "Hello World" because no directives are included in the format string. The format string "The value is %v in the range [%l, %u]", given a lower bound of 0, an upper bound of 100, and a current value of 75, results in the text value "The value is 75 in the range [0, 100]". Given the same state, the format string "The current value is %2v" results in the text "The current value is 75.00".

The default format string is "%P %%", which (again, given the preceding state) will result in the text "75 %" (here, the %P is replaced with the percentage, and the %% results in a literal % in the generated text).

Now that we know what format strings are and how to create them, how does one replace the default string? To do so, call gtk_progress_set_format_string():

```
void
gtk_progress_set_format_string(GtkProgress *progress,
        const gchar *format);
```

The argument progress is an instance of the GtkProgress-derived class. The argument format is a NULL-terminated ASCII C string, as previously described.

You can generate a copy of the text that would be created for a given value by calling gtk_progress_get_text_from_value():

```
gchar *
gtk_progress_get_text_from_value(GtkProgress *progress, gfloat value);
```

The second argument, value, should be a value in the range supported by the progress widget's adjustment object. Given the default format string and an adjustment object with a range of [0, 1000], passing a value of 100 should return the string "10 %". When you are done with the string that is returned, you can release it by calling g_free(). Note that calling gtk_progress_get_text_from_value() does not change the value of the progress widget adjustment object.

You can get a copy of the text string that corresponds to current state of the progress widget adjustment object by calling gtk_progress_get_current_text():

```
gchar *
gtk_progress_get_current_text(GtkProgress *progress);
```

The returned string can be disposed of by passing it to g_free() when it is no longer needed.

If you want the GtkProgress-derived widget to display text, you must enable it by calling gtk_progress_set_show_text():

```
void
gtk_progress_set_show_text(GtkProgress *progress, gint show_text);
```

Pass FALSE as the show_text argument to disable the showing of text, or pass TRUE to enable it.

The final function provided by GtkProgress, related to text, is gtk_progress_set_text_alignment():

```
void
gtk_progress_set_text_alignment(GtkProgress *progress, gfloat x_align,
        gfloat y_align);
```

Default values for x_align and y_align are 0.5. Acceptable values fall in the range [0.0, 1.0]. With defaults, the text will be centered inside the progress widget. Values other than the default will shift the origin of the text left to right or top to bottom, depending on the values specified by the application. Most applications will use the default values and never call this function.

Value and Percentage

A progress widget is most commonly used to represent the state of some application task that occurs over time. Consider an application that is downloading a file from a server on behalf of the user. In this case, a progress widget might be used to convey to the user the amount of data that has been received so far, as a percentage of the total size of the file. It is up to your application to update a progress widget so that it correctly represents the state of the operation being performed. Several functions provided by GtkProgress allow you to set and get the value of the progress widget, either as an explicit value, or as a percentage of the total range of values that the progress bar is capable of representing. To set the current value of the progress widget as a percentage, call gtk_progress_set_percentage():

```
void
gtk_progress_set_percentage(GtkProgress *progress, gfloat percentage);
```

The argument percentage is in the range of [0.0, 100.0]. To get the current percentage of the progress widget, call gtk_progress_get_current_percentage():

```
gfloat
gtk_progress_get_current_percentage(GtkProgress *progress);
```

The return value is a gfloat, also in the range [0.0, 100.0]. To set and get the current value of the progress widget explicitly, use gtk_progress_set_value() and gtk_progress_get_value(), respectively:

```
void
gtk_progress_set_value(GtkProgress *progress, gfloat value);

gfloat
gtk_progress_get_value(GtkProgress *progress);
```

Finally, you can determine what percentage is represented by a given value by calling gtk_progress_get_percentage_from_value():

```
gfloat
gtk_progress_get_percentage_from_value(GtkProgress *progress,
        gfloat value);
```

The argument value is any value in the range accepted by the progress widget. The function return value is in the range of [0.0, 100.0].

Activity Mode

All progress-derived widgets can support an activity mode. In the context of GtkProgressBar, this activity mode affects how the progress bar renders itself. To set the activity mode, call gtk_progress_set_activity_mode():

```
void
gtk_progress_set_activity_mode(GtkProgress *progress,
        guint activity_mode);
```

The argument progress is an instance of a GtkProgress-derived widget. The argument activity_mode can be set to either FALSE or TRUE. In the case of GtkProgressBar, passing the default value of FALSE causes the progress bar to display percentage information to the user. If set to TRUE, activity mode will be enabled, and percentage information will not be conveyed. Instead, a bar within the activity area of the widget will be continually moved from left to right and back to indicate that activity is occurring.

You would enable activity mode when you need to show progress but are unable to provide accurate percentage or value information about the activity that is occurring. An example of such an activity would be a mail client attempting to connect to a mail server. The amount of time needed to connect to the server cannot be known, so you cannot accurately report the completion percentage of the task. In this case, you would want to set activity_mode to TRUE. An example of a task that is measurable would be the compilation of a project that consists of, say, 24 files. In this case, you would set the range of the progress widget adjustment object so that lower is 0, upper is 24, and the initial value is 0. As each file in the project is processed by the compiler, the value attribute of the progress widget would be incremented by 1. The progress widget, as a result, would display the correct percentage as the compilation of the files in the project progresses. In the next section, I discuss the GtkProgressBar widget. In that section, I will present a sample program that exercises some of the functions provided by GtkProgress.

GtkProgressBar

Class Name

```
GtkProgressBar
```

Parent Class Name

```
GtkProgress
```

Macros

Widget type macro: `GTK_TYPE_PROGRESS_BAR`

Object to widget cast macro: `GTK_PROGRESS_BAR(obj)`

Widget type check macro: `GTK_IS_PROGRESS_BAR(obj)`

Supported Arguments

Prefix: `GtkProgessBar::`

Table 15.9 GtkProgressBar Arguments

Name	*Type*	*Permissions*
adjustment	GTK_TYPE_ADJUSTMENT	GTK_ARG_READWRITE | GTK_ARG_CONSTRUCT
orientation	GTK_TYPE_PROGRESS_BAR_ ORIENTATION	GTK_ARG_READWRITE
bar_style	GTK_TYPE_PROGRESS_BAR_STYLE	GTK_ARG_READWRITE
activity_step	GTK_TYPE_UINT	GTK_ARG_READWRITE
activity_blocks	GTK_TYPE_UINT	GTK_ARG_READWRITE
discrete_blocks	GTK_TYPE_UINT	GTK_ARG_READWRITE

Application-Level API Synopsis

Retrieve the constant GTK_TYPE_PROGRESS_BAR at runtime:

```
GtkType
gtk_progress_bar_get_type(void);
```

Create a new instance of GtkProgressBar:

```
GtkWidget *
gtk_progress_bar_new(void);
```

Create a new instance of GtkProgressBar with a specified adjustment object:

```
GtkWidget *
gtk_progress_bar_new_with_adjustment(GtkAdjustment *adjustment);
```

Set the progress bar style (GTK_PROGRESS_CONTINUOUS or GTK_PROGRESS_DISCRETE):

```
void
gtk_progress_bar_set_bar_style(GtkProgressBar *pbar,
        GtkProgressBarStyle style);
```

Set the number of discrete blocks displayed by the progress bar:

```
void
gtk_progress_bar_set_discrete_blocks(GtkProgressBar *pbar,
        guint blocks);
```

Set the progress bar activity step (see text):

```
void
gtk_progress_bar_set_activity_step(GtkProgressBar *pbar,
        guint step);
```

Set the number of activity blocks displayed by the progress bar:

```
void
gtk_progress_bar_set_activity_blocks(GtkProgressBar *pbar,
        guint blocks);
```

Application-Level API Synopsis (Continued)

Set the progress bar orientation to GTK_PROGRESS_LEFT_TO_RIGHT, GTK_PROGRESS_RIGHT_TO_LEFT, GTK_PROGRESS_BOTTOM_TO_TOP, or GTK_PROGRESS_TOP_TO_BOTTOM:

```
void
gtk_progress_bar_set_orientation(GtkProgressBar *pbar,
        GtkProgressBarOrientation orientation);
```

Class Description

GtkProgressBar is a child class that inherits functionality from GtkProgress. To use GtkProgressBar, you must be familiar with several of the functions that the GtkProgress API provides. For this reason, I suggest that you read the preceding section on GtkProgress before reading this section. I will, at the end of this section, present a small application that will illustrate how both of these classes are typically used together.

GtkProgressBar implements progress bars that are similar to the ones illustrated in Figures 15.1 and 15.2. These figures illustrate the two types of progress bars supported by GtkProgressBar. The first type (see Figure 15.1) is used to indicate what I refer to as start-to-finish progress, as well as the occurrence of an activity. You use a progress bar of this type whenever you know the extent of an activity and can measure its progress as it is being performed. For example, you might be writing a program designed to connect to a server and download a file. If you know the size of the file being downloaded, you can use a start-to-finish progress bar to show activity as the download is performed, as well as to report during that time how much of the file has actually been downloaded.

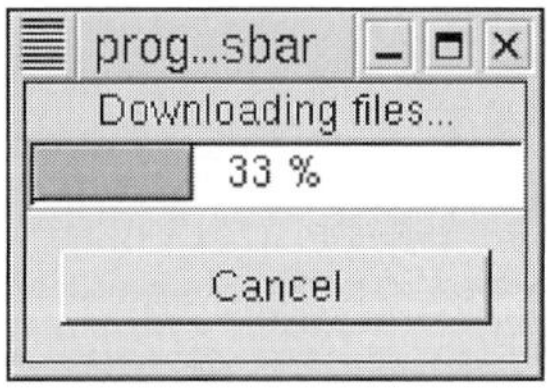

Figure 15.1 Start-To-Finish Progress Bar

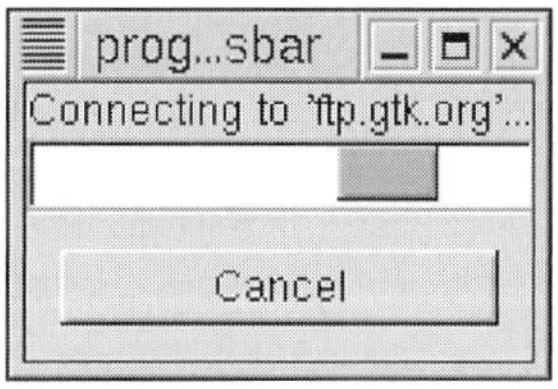

Figure 15.2 Activity Progress Bar

The second type of progress bar (see Figure 15.2) is used when you need to indicate activity but are unable to determine the extent of the activity and/or how far along the activity has progressed from start to finish during the time the activity is occurring. An example of an activity that is well suited to this type of progress bar is connecting to a server such as the one I described in the previous paragraph. Usually, an application will be unable to determine exactly how long it will take for it to connect to a server. In a case such as this, an application might use an activity progress bar. Because an activity progress bar updates itself continuously, the user will know that work is being performed by the application and, perhaps more importantly, that the program has not crashed or become hung while doing it.

Creating Progress Bar Widgets

Now that we know what progress bars are, let's take a look at the functions exposed by the progress bar API. To create a new instance of GtkProgressBar, call gtk_progress_bar_new():

```
GtkWidget *
gtk_progress_bar_new(void);
```

The return value is an instance of GtkWidget. For functions in GtkProgressBar that require an instance of GtkProgressBar, use the GTK_PROGRESS_BAR macro. For example:

```
GtkWidget *w;

w = gtk_progress_bar_new();
gtk_progress_bar_set_activity_step( GTK_PROGRESS_BAR(w), 10);
```

Similarly, if you need to call a GtkProgress function, use the GTK_PROGRESS macro to cast a GtkWidget instance to an instance of GtkProgress.

By calling gtk_progress_bar_new(), an adjustment object will automatically be created for use by the progress bar widget. If you want to provide an adjustment object of your own, you can do so by calling gtk_progress_bar_new_with_adjustment() and passing the adjustment object as an argument:

```
GtkWidget *
gtk_progress_bar_new_with_adjustment(GtkAdjustment *adjustment);
```

Setting the Progress Bar Style

A progress bar can have one of two styles. To change the style, you can call gtk_progress_bar_set_bar_style():

```
void
gtk_progress_bar_set_bar_style(GtkProgressBar *pbar,
        GtkProgressBarStyle style);
```

GtkProgressBar supports two distinct update styles. The first of these styles, GTK_PROGRESS_CONTINUOUS, is the default style. This style tells the progress bar to update immediately as changes are made to the progress widget value or percentage. The progress bar will render as illustrated in Figure 15.1 as a single, continuous bar. The other style, GTK_PROGRESS_DISCRETE, tells the progress bar to update itself at discrete points in time, such as at 10%, 20%, and so forth. The progress bar is rendered to reflect the update interval chosen by the application (the default interval is 10), as shown in Figure 15.3. The bar style is only valid when the progress bar is operating in start-to-finish mode, and it is ignored in activity mode.

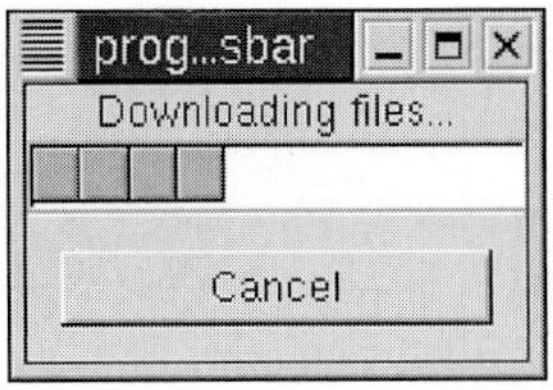

Figure 15.3 Start-To-Finish Progress Bar, Discrete Blocks

You can change the update interval of a GTK_PROGRESS_DISCRETE-style progress bar widget by calling gtk_progress_bar_set_discrete_blocks():

```
void
gtk_progress_bar_set_discrete_blocks(GtkProgressBar *pbar,
        guint blocks);
```

The default number of blocks, as previously mentioned, is 10. To determine at which point blocks will be added to the progress bar with a range of [n, m] and p blocks, use the following equation: (m – n) / p. For example, if the progress bar range is [0, 100] and the number of blocks is set to 20, then 3 blocks will be displayed when the value of the progress bar is set to a value in the range [15, 19].

Controlling the Speed of an Activity Progress Bar

An activity mode progress bar can have a couple of its attributes modified as well. The first of these attributes, the step attribute, determines how rapidly the progress bar moves from left to right and back and can be set by calling gtk_progress_bar_set_activity_step():

```
void
gtk_progress_bar_set_activity_step(GtkProgressBar *pbar, guint step);
```

The argument step is an unsigned integer. However, the widget interprets it internally as a signed value, so make sure you pass a non-negative value (values less than zero appear to cause undefined behavior). Setting the activity step to zero causes the progress bar to stop movement or pause. Values above zero result in increased movement from either end of the progress bar widget. My experience shows that there is little benefit to setting the progress bar step to values greater than about 20 or 30. The default value of 3 is suitable for most applications.

Setting the Bar Size of an Activity Progress Bar

The other attribute you can change is the number of activity blocks displayed by an activity mode progress bar. In reality, what is being set here is the size of the bar that moves back and forth. Meaningful values are in the range of [2, 20] and must be greater than 1; otherwise, Gtk+ will clip the value to 2. To change the number of activity blocks displayed by the progress bar, you can call gtk_progress_bar_set_activity_blocks():

```
void
gtk_progress_bar_set_activity_blocks(GtkProgressBar *pbar,
        guint blocks);
```

Setting the Progress Bar Orientation

The final function supported by GtkProgressBar is used to set the orientation of the progress bar to one of four values: GTK_PROGRESS_LEFT_TO_RIGHT, GTK_PROGRESS_RIGHT_TO_LEFT, GTK_PROGRESS_BOTTOM_TO_TOP, or GTK_PROGRESS_TOP_TO_BOTTOM. The function gtk_progress_bar_set_orientation() accepts a progress bar instance and one of the preceding values:

```
void
gtk_progress_bar_set_orientation(GtkProgressBar *pbar,
        GtkProgressBarOrientation orientation);
```

Most applications will use the default, which is GTK_PROGRESS_LEFT_TO_RIGHT. For the most part, GTK_PROGRESS_LEFT_TO_RIGHT and GTK_PROGRESS_RIGHT_TO_LEFT are identical if the progress bar is executed in activity mode and are used to denote a horizontal progress bar. Similarly, GTK_PROGRESS_BOTTOM_TO_TOP and GTK_PROGRESS_TOP_TO_BOTTOM are identical in activity mode. In start-to-finish mode, GTK_PROGRESS_LEFT_TO_RIGHT indicates a horizontal progress bar that adds blocks from left to right. The other orientations in start-to-finish mode are similarly self-explanatory.

Sample Program

The following is the source code for a sample program that simulates connecting to an ftp server and downloading a set of files (see Figures 15.1 and 15.2):

Listing 15.3 GtkProgressBar Example

```
#include <gtk/gtk.h>
#include <stdlib.h>

// make life easier and make these external

static int timer1, timer2;
static GtkWidget *dloadwin;

#define NUMFILES 25

// generate a random connection time

#define RAND(lower, upper) (int) ((((float) random() / RAND_MAX) * \
    (upper - lower ) ) + lower )

// user canceled the download operation

static void
CancelDownload(GtkWidget *widget, GtkWidget *window)
```

```
{
    gtk_timeout_remove( timer1 );
    gtk_widget_destroy( window );
}

// simulate the completion of a single file download

static gint
DownloadTimeout(gpointer data)
{
    gfloat new_val;
    GtkAdjustment *adj;

    adj = GTK_PROGRESS (data)->adjustment;

    new_val = adj->value + 1;
    if (new_val > adj->upper) {
            CancelDownload( (GtkWidget *) NULL, dloadwin );
            return( FALSE );
    }

    gtk_progress_set_value (GTK_PROGRESS (data), new_val);

    return TRUE;
}

// simulate the download of a set of files

static void
DownloadFile()
{
    GtkWidget *dialog_window, *label, *progress, *button;

    dialog_window = dloadwin = gtk_dialog_new();
    gtk_window_set_modal (GTK_WINDOW(dialog_window),TRUE);

    gtk_window_position(GTK_WINDOW(dialog_window), GTK_WIN_POS_MOUSE);

    label = gtk_label_new( "Downloading files..." );

    gtk_box_pack_start (GTK_BOX (GTK_DIALOG (dialog_window)->vbox),
            label, TRUE, TRUE, 0);

    progress = gtk_progress_bar_new();

    gtk_progress_configure( GTK_PROGRESS(progress), 1.0, 1.0,
            (float) NUMFILES );

    gtk_progress_set_show_text( GTK_PROGRESS(progress), TRUE );

    gtk_box_pack_start (GTK_BOX (GTK_DIALOG (dialog_window)->vbox),
```

```
            progress, TRUE, TRUE, 0);

    button = gtk_button_new_with_label( "Cancel" );

    gtk_signal_connect (GTK_OBJECT (button), "clicked",
            GTK_SIGNAL_FUNC(CancelDownload), dialog_window);

    gtk_box_pack_start(GTK_BOX(GTK_DIALOG(dialog_window)->action_area),
            button, TRUE, TRUE, 0);

    timer1 = gtk_timeout_add(200, DownloadTimeout, progress);

    gtk_widget_show_all (dialog_window);
}

// user hit the "Cancel" button while connecting

static void
CancelConnect(GtkWidget *widget, GtkWidget *window)
{
    gtk_timeout_remove( timer1 );
    gtk_timeout_remove( timer2 );
    gtk_widget_destroy( window );
}

// simulate the connection finishing

static gint
ActivityProgressDone(gpointer data)
{
    GtkWidget *window = (GtkWidget *) data;

    gtk_timeout_remove( timer1 );
    gtk_widget_destroy( window );

    DownloadFile();
    return FALSE;
}

// process an activity mode timeout (simulate the passing of time
// while connecting

static gint
ActivityProgressTimeout(gpointer data)
{
    gfloat new_val;
    GtkAdjustment *adj;

    adj = GTK_PROGRESS (data)->adjustment;

    new_val = adj->value + 1;
```

```
    if (new_val > adj->upper)
            new_val = adj->lower;

    gtk_progress_set_value (GTK_PROGRESS (data), new_val);

    return TRUE;
}

// user hit the "Connect" button in the main dialog

static void
Connect(GtkWidget *widget, GtkEntry *entry)
{
    GtkWidget *dialog_window, *label, *progress, *button;
    char buf[ 128 ];
    int connecttime;

    char *server = gtk_entry_get_text( entry );

    snprintf( buf, sizeof(buf) - 1, "Connecting to '%s'...", server );

    dialog_window = gtk_dialog_new();
    gtk_window_set_modal (GTK_WINDOW(dialog_window),TRUE);

    gtk_window_position(GTK_WINDOW(dialog_window), GTK_WIN_POS_MOUSE);

    label = gtk_label_new( buf );

    gtk_box_pack_start (GTK_BOX (GTK_DIALOG (dialog_window)->vbox),
            label, TRUE, TRUE, 0);

    progress = gtk_progress_bar_new();

    gtk_progress_set_activity_mode( GTK_PROGRESS( progress ), TRUE );

    gtk_progress_configure( GTK_PROGRESS(progress), 1.0, 1.0, 10.0 );

    gtk_box_pack_start (GTK_BOX (GTK_DIALOG (dialog_window)->vbox),
            progress, TRUE, TRUE, 0);

    button = gtk_button_new_with_label( "Cancel" );

    gtk_signal_connect (GTK_OBJECT (button), "clicked",
            GTK_SIGNAL_FUNC(CancelConnect), dialog_window);

    gtk_box_pack_start(GTK_BOX(GTK_DIALOG(dialog_window)->action_area),
            button, TRUE, TRUE, 0);

    timer1 = gtk_timeout_add(100, ActivityProgressTimeout, progress);
    connecttime = RAND(1000, 8000 );
    timer2 = gtk_timeout_add(connecttime, ActivityProgressDone,
```

```
                (gpointer) dialog_window);

        gtk_widget_show_all (dialog_window);
}

main( int argc, char *argv[] )
{
        GtkWidget *dialog_window, *hbox, *button, *label, *entry;

        gtk_init( &argc, &argv );

        dialog_window = gtk_dialog_new();
        gtk_window_position(GTK_WINDOW(dialog_window), GTK_WIN_POS_MOUSE);

        hbox = gtk_hbox_new( FALSE, 5 );
        gtk_box_pack_start (GTK_BOX (GTK_DIALOG (dialog_window)->vbox),
                hbox, TRUE, TRUE, 0);

        label = gtk_label_new( "Server:" );
        entry = gtk_entry_new();
        gtk_entry_set_text( GTK_ENTRY( entry ), "ftp.gtk.org" );

        gtk_box_pack_start (GTK_BOX (hbox), label, TRUE, TRUE, 0);
        gtk_box_pack_start (GTK_BOX (hbox), entry, TRUE, TRUE, 0);

        button = gtk_button_new_with_label( "Connect" );

        gtk_signal_connect (GTK_OBJECT (button), "clicked",
                GTK_SIGNAL_FUNC(Connect), entry);

        gtk_box_pack_start(GTK_BOX(GTK_DIALOG(dialog_window)->action_area),
                button, TRUE, TRUE, 0);

        gtk_widget_show_all (dialog_window);
        gtk_main();
}
```

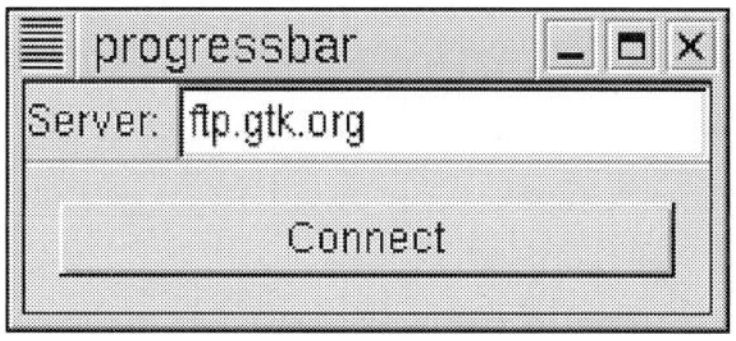

Figure 15.4 Sample Application Dialog

The program is organized as follows. The main() function creates a dialog, as shown in Figure 15.4. When the user clicks the Connect button, the function Connect() is called. Connect() creates a dialog that contains a progress bar and a Cancel button (Figure 15.1). The progress bar is created as follows:

```
153   progress = gtk_progress_bar_new();
154
155   gtk_progress_set_activity_mode( GTK_PROGRESS( progress ), TRUE );
156
157   gtk_progress_configure( GTK_PROGRESS(progress), 1.0, 1.0, 10.0 );
```

On line 153, gtk_progress_bar_new() is called to create the progress bar widget. Then, on line 155, I call gtk_progress_set_activity_mode() to put the progress widget into activity mode. I do this because the progress bar, in this case, is used only to show the passing of time. We are unable to use a start-to-finish progress bar because we have no idea how long the connect operation takes.

On lines 170 through 173, I create two timers. The second of the two timers, timer2, will fire at some random time between 1 and 8 seconds. The timer function called when timer2 expires, ActivityProgressDone(), initiates the simulated ftp download. The first timer, timer1, is fired 10 times a second. The timer function invoked by this timer, ActivityProgressTimeout(), is responsible for updating the progress bar widget to indicate the passage of time as we wait for a connection to the ftp server to be made.

```
170   timer1 = gtk_timeout_add(100, ActivityProgressTimeout, progress);
171   connecttime = RAND(1000, 8000 );
172   timer2 = gtk_timeout_add(connecttime, ActivityProgressDone,
173           (gpointer) dialog_window);
```

Take a look at ActivityProgressTimeout():

```
static gint
ActivityProgressTimeout(gpointer data)
{
   gfloat new_val;
   GtkAdjustment *adj;

   adj = GTK_PROGRESS (data)->adjustment;

   new_val = adj->value + 1;
   if (new_val > adj->upper)
         new_val = adj->lower;

   gtk_progress_set_value (GTK_PROGRESS (data), new_val);

   return TRUE;
}
```

Here we simply increment the progress bar adjustment object by 1, unless the value goes beyond the range of the adjustment object, in which case it is set to the adjustment object's lower attribute. The value of the progress bar is then changed by making a call to gtk_progress_set_value().

Now that we see how an activity mode progress bar is used by this example, we turn to the topic of creating and using a start-to-finish mode progress bar to indicate progress as files are downloaded from the ftp site.

As I mentioned earlier, timer2 will fire when the simulated connection to the ftp server completes. The timer callback function, after tearing down the connection dialog, calls DownloadFile(), which has a structure much like that of Connect(), previously described. DownloadFile() creates a dialog (refer to Figure 15.2) that contains, among other things, a start-to-finish mode progress bar. The code that creates the progress bar is as follows:

```
063     progress = gtk_progress_bar_new();
064
065     gtk_progress_configure( GTK_PROGRESS(progress), 1.0, 1.0,
066             (float) NUMFILES );
067
068     gtk_progress_set_show_text( GTK_PROGRESS(progress), TRUE );
```

On line 065, the range of the progress bar is set to [1, NUMFILES] because we are simulating the download of NUMFILES files. On line 068, I enable display of text in the progress bar widget so that the percentage complete is displayed for the user, as can be seen in Figure 15.2. Finally, on line 081:

```
081     timer1 = gtk_timeout_add(200, DownloadTimeout, progress);
```

I register a Gtk+ timeout to be fired 5 times a second. The timeout function, DownloadTimeout(), increments the adjustment object value by 1 to simulate the downloading of a single file. If we reach NUMFILES, the timer is killed, and the dialog is destroyed by calling CancelDownload() (see line 037). This is the same function that would be invoked if the user were to hit the Cancel button in the download dialog.

GtkTooltips

Class Name

```
GtkTooltips
```

Parent Class Name

```
GtkData
```

Macros

Widget type macro: `GTK_TYPE_TOOLTIPS`

Object to widget cast macro: `GTK_TOOLTIPS(obj)`

Widget type check macro: `GTK_IS_TOOLTIPS(obj)`

Application-Level API Synopsis

Return the constant GTK_TYPE_TOOLTIPS at runtime:
```
GtkType
gtk_tooltips_get_type(void);
```

Create a new instance of GtkTooltips:
```
GtkTooltips *
gtk_tooltips_new(void);
```

Enable tooltip display:
```
void
gtk_tooltips_enable(GtkTooltips *tooltips);
```

Disable tooltip display:
```
void
gtk_tooltips_disable(GtkTooltips *tooltips);
```

Set the delay between mouse-over and tooltip display:
```
void
gtk_tooltips_set_delay(GtkTooltips *tooltips, guint delay);
```

Add/change a tooltip for the specified widget:
```
void
gtk_tooltips_set_tip(GtkTooltips *tooltips, GtkWidget *widget,
        const gchar *tip_text, const gchar *tip_private);
```

Set the tooltip's foreground and background colors:
```
void
gtk_tooltips_set_colors(GtkTooltips *tooltips, GdkColor *background,
        GdkColor *foreground);
```

Class Description

Tooltips are small windows designed to display text (see Figure 15.5). A tooltip window is created with the underlying X window override redirect attribute set to true, which means the window is created without any window manager decorations (close boxes, title bars, menus). A tooltip widget is made visible whenever the user positions the mouse pointer over the widget associated with that tooltip, and the pointer remains inactive (or motionless) for a predefined amount of time (the default time in Gtk+ 1.2 is 500ms).

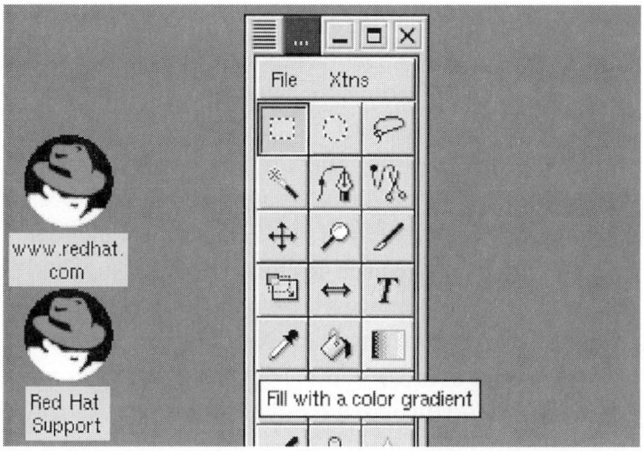

Figure 15.5 The "Fill with a color gradient" Tooltips Window from The GIMP

Using Tooltips

Tooltip windows have two primary uses. The first, and perhaps most common use, is to provide context-sensitive help for application users. (I will refer to this type of tooltip as a "help tooltip" in the remainder of this section.) A help tooltip displays one or two sentences of text telling the user what task will be performed should the widget described by the tooltip become activated (see Figure 15.5). Help tooltips are more effective for application users if they are consistently worded throughout the application and are provided for all widgets of a specific type (e.g., if you provide a help tooltip for one menu item, then help tooltips should be provided for all menu items throughout the application).

Displaying Context-Sensitive Help. Several years ago, Apple Computer devised a help system for the MacOS known as "balloon help." Apple Computer published guidelines for the design of text displayed within balloon help windows. I believe that these guidelines, in the absence of guidelines that may or may not be developed in the future for GNOME or Gtk+, provide a good basis for designing text for the Gtk+ help tooltip windows in your application. The following are some examples of the MacOS guidelines for designing balloon help text:

- The balloon help text for a button must be of the form "To [perform action], click this button" (e.g., the text for an OK button in a dialog might be "To close this dialog and accept your changes, click this button").
- The balloon help text for a menu item must start with a verb and must describe what will happen when the menu item is selected. For example, the Quit menu item in a File menu might display the following help tooltip text: "Quits the application. If there are any unsaved changes in documents that are open when this menu item is selected, you will be given the chance to save them."

When implementing help tooltip windows, it is a good idea to provide the user with a way to enable and disable their display; first-time users of a program will often appreciate help tooltips, but those with experience will often find them to be annoying. GtkTooltips provides functions (described later) that allow an application to enable and disable tooltip windows.

For more information on Apple's Balloon Help Human Interface Guidelines, go to *http://developer.apple.com* and search on "Wording for Specific Balloon Types."

Display Application Data. The second use of tooltip windows is less common but, when used, is often very effective. An application might use a tooltip window to display small amounts of data corresponding to some item displayed in a list or some other container widget. For example, consider a tree widget being used to display the table of contents of an online book. Each entry in the tree widget could have a tooltip that displays a one- or two-line summary of the chapter that the mouse is currently positioned over in the tree. As another example, a list widget might display a set of stock symbols. As the user mouses over a stock symbol in the list, its tooltip window would display the full name of the company associated with the symbol, as well as the current value of the stock and its high and low trading values for the day. In the following text, I refer to this type of tooltip as an application data tooltip.

Tooltips Widgets

A tooltips widget is nothing more than a collection of widget-to-tooltip text mappings. An application can choose to have a single tooltips widget for all of the tooltips that the application supports, or several tooltips widgets to partition the application tooltips into a set of meaningful groups. How these groupings are organized, if at all, is up to you to decide. You might, for example, choose to have one tooltips widget for each dialog, or one tooltips widget for all of the menu items and another tooltips widget for all of the button widgets in the application.

The more your tooltips widgets are organized as groups, the more flexible your application can be in terms of letting the user enable or disable the display of certain types of tooltips used throughout the application. For example, if an application supports both help tooltips and application data tooltips, placing the help tooltips in one tooltips widget and the application data tooltips in another tooltips widget allows your application to give the user the ability to disable the help tooltips without disabling the display of the application data tooltips.

Creating a Tooltips Widget

To create a tooltips widget, call gtk_tooltips_new():

```
GtkTooltips *
gtk_tooltips_new(void);
```

The return value is an instance of GtkTooltips.

Setting the Widget-to-Tooltip Mapping

Now that you have a tooltips widget, you can create a new widget-to-tooltip text mapping and add it to the tooltips collection by calling gtk_tooltips_set_tip():

```
void
gtk_tooltips_set_tip(GtkTooltips *tooltips, GtkWidget *widget,
         const gchar *tip_text, const gchar *tip_private);
```

The argument tooltips is the tooltips widget created by gtk_tooltips_new(), widget is the widget component of the widget-to-tooltip text mapping, tip_text is the text component of the mapping, and tip_private is optional private data that will be stored along with the mapping in the tooltips widget collection and can be used with GtkTipsQuery as I will describe later in this chapter. If you do not use GtkTipsQuery in your application, or if you do not want to support it for this widget, you can set tip_private to NULL.

As previously described, you can add as many tooltip text-to-widget mappings as you desire; simply call gtk_tooltips_set_tip() once for each tooltip you want to add to the tooltips collection. If you want to change the text associated with a specific widget already in the tooltips collection, you can call gtk_tooltips_set_tip() once again with different text; the previous text associated with the widget will be freed by GtkTooltips.

Enabling and Disabling Tooltips

The remaining functions described here apply to all tooltips managed by a tooltips group. To enable the display of tooltips in a tooltip group or collection, call gtk_tooltips_enable():

```
void
gtk_tooltips_enable(GtkTooltips *tooltips);
```

The argument tooltips is the tooltips group being enabled. Similarly, calling gtk_tooltips_disable():

```
void
gtk_tooltips_disable(GtkTooltips *tooltips);
```

will disable the display of tooltip text for all tooltips in a tooltips group. As I mentioned earlier, it is a good idea to provide users with a preference setting or menu item that allows them to show or hide tooltips, especially if the application makes use of a large number of help tooltips.

Setting the Tooltips Delay

To change the amount of time the mouse must be inactive before a tooltip window is displayed, call gtk_tooltips_set_delay():

```
void
gtk_tooltips_set_delay(GtkTooltips *tooltips, guint delay);
```

The argument delay is the value in milliseconds that the mouse must remain motionless before the tooltip window is displayed. The default value for delay is 500 ms, or one-half second (1 second is equal to 1,000 ms).

Changing the Foreground and Background Colors

To set the foreground and background colors used by the tooltips in a tooltips grouping, call gtk_tooltips_set_colors():

```
void
gtk_tooltips_set_colors(GtkTooltips *tooltips, GdkColor *background,
        GdkColor *foreground);
```

The argument colors can be obtained from the style system or from another widget, or they can be allocated by making calls to gdk_color_alloc().

GtkTipsQuery

Class Name

GtkTipsQuery

Parent Class Name

GtkLabel

Macros

Widget type macro: `GTK_TYPE_TIPS_QUERY`

Object to widget cast macro: `GTK_TIPS_QUERY(obj)`

Widget type check macro: `GTK_IS_TIPS_QUERY(obj)`

Supported Arguments

Prefix: `GtkTipsQuery::`

Table 15.10 GtkTipsQuery Arguments

Name	*Type*	*Permissions*
emit_always	GTK_TYPE_BOOL	GTK_ARG_READWRITE
caller	GTK_TYPE_WIDGET	GTK_ARG_READWRITE
label_inactive	GTK_TYPE_STRING	GTK_ARG_WRITABLE
label_no_tip	GTK_TYPE_STRING	GTK_ARG_WRITABLE

Application-Level API Synopsis

Retrieve the constant GTK_TYPE_TIPS_QUERY at runtime:

```
GtkType
gtk_tips_query_get_type(void);
```

Create a new instance of GtkTipsQuery:

```
GtkWidget *
gtk_tips_query_new(void);
```

Enter tooltips query mode:

```
void
gtk_tips_query_start_query(GtkTipsQuery *tips_query);
```

Leave tooltips query mode:

```
void
gtk_tips_query_stop_query(GtkTipsQuery *tips_query);
```

Specify the widget that can be used to trigger leaving tooltips query mode:

```
void
gtk_tips_query_set_caller(GtkTipsQuery *tips_query,
        GtkWidget *caller);
```

Set text to be displayed by widgets that do not have tooltips and by the tips query widget when query mode is not active:

```
void
gtk_tips_query_set_labels(GtkTipsQuery *tips_query,
        const gchar *label_inactive, const gchar *label_no_tip);
```

Class Description

GtkTipsQuery is a relatively simple-to-use widget that can augment a tooltips widget to create a more robust help system for your application. A tips query widget lets the user place an application into a query mode by clicking a button or selecting a menu item (for example) that has been bound to the tips query widget. Once the application is in query mode, the cursor is changed to indicate to the user that the application is in query mode. The user can then click on any widget in the user interface to leave query mode and obtain whatever form of help the application decides to support for the widget that was selected.

Creating an Instance of GtkTipsQuery

The number of functions in the GtkTipsQuery API is small, so we might as well take a look at it now. As you read, you will gain an understanding of when and how to use a tips query widget in your application.

To create an instance of GtkTipsQuery, call gtk_tips_query_new():

```
GtkWidget *
gtk_tips_query_new(void);
```

A widget is returned; use the GTK_TIPS_QUERY macro to coerce this widget to an instance of GtkTipsQuery when calling the functions described in the following sections. The tips query widget must be realized (but not necessarily mapped) for it to function correctly. Being a child of GtkLabel, it will utilize screen real estate if it is added to, say, a box widget and mapped. The idea behind having a visible presence in the user interface is that it gives the application a location to display the tip (private) text (or some other message) as the user mouses over widgets while in query mode. You may or may not want to make use of this aspect of a tips query widget. If you do not want to display the tips query widget, that's okay, but you must ensure that the tips query widget has a parent and that you also realize (but not map) the tips query widget. A widget can be realized by calling gtk_widget_realize(). For example:

```
GtkWidget *w;

gtk_widget_realize( w );
```

The widget_selected Signal

Two signals can be emitted by GtkTipsQuery. The most important of these is the widget_selected signal. It is called when the user clicks on a widget while operating in query mode. The function prototype for the signal function invoked for this signal is as follows:

```
gint (GtkWidget *tips_query, GtkWidget *widget,
        const gchar *tip_text, const gchar *tip_private,
        GdkEventButton *event, gpointer func_data);
```

An impressive number of arguments are passed to this function. Of these, the most important perhaps is tip_private because this can be used as a clue to how the application should handle the signal. As you recall, you can register a text_private string when adding a widget to a tooltip with gtk_tooltips_set_tip(), as explained earlier in this chapter. This string can be anything you want it to be, including text to be displayed in a dialog that you pop up or even the URL to a Web page (either local or remote) containing extensive help facilities. The point is, once you find yourself in the signal function, it is up to you to decide what level of help is provided. You can return TRUE from the widget_selected signal function to indicate that you have handled the signal and that the application can leave query mode. If you return FALSE, the application will remain in query mode until a nontooltips widget, or the widget that put the application into query mode, is clicked on with the mouse. If you choose to return FALSE when handling this signal, be prepared to receive the signal once for the button press and once for the release. To avoid displaying help twice, you should code the signal function to look at the event data passed in and return if the event was a button release. You can do this by adding the code that follows to the top of the widget_selected signal function:

```
if ( event->type == GDK_BUTTON_RELEASE )
        return FALSE;
```

Handling the widget_entered Signal

The other signal, widget_entered, is, like widget_selected, only fired when the application is in query mode. The function prototype for this signal function is similar to the one used for the widget_selected signal:

```
void tips_query_widget_entered(GtkTipsQuery *tips_query,
        GtkWidget *widget, const gchar *tip_text,
        const gchar *tip_private, gpointer *func_data);
```

The only difference is that the widget_selected function passes button event information, whereas the widget_entered function does not.

Generally, a mouse entering the widget is not the best time to be displaying any significant amount of help data. While in query mode, the user may mouse over any number of widgets en route to the widget for which the user has specific help needs. It would not be useful for the application to pop up a dialog for each widget moused over during this process; it would, in fact, be rather distracting. On the other hand, an application might decide to inform the user that help is available for widgets as they are being moused over. One place to do this notification is in the tips query widget if it was realized and mapped by your application. The following widget_entered signal function does just that:

```
static void
tips_query_widget_entered(GtkTipsQuery *tips_query, GtkWidget *widget,
        const gchar *tip_text, const gchar *tip_private, gpointer *func_data)
{
        gtk_label_set_text(GTK_LABEL(tips_query), (tip_private ?
                  "Help is available for this item" :
                  "Help is not available for this item" ) );

        /* don't let GtkTipsQuery reset it's label */

        gtk_signal_emit_stop_by_name(GTK_OBJECT(tips_query), "widget_entered");
}
```

Here I simply reset the text displayed by the tips_query widget to indicate whether the item being moused over has help system support or not. In this example, we presume that the application has registered tooltips for those widgets that support the display of help, and that the tip_private argument passed to gtk_tooltips_set_tip() is used by the help system to determine what help to display and is therefore non-NULL. Widgets displaying tooltips but having no help system support were added with NULL passed as the tip_private argument to gtk_tooltips_set_tip().

Placing a Widget into Query Mode

All that really remains to be discussed is placing the widget into query mode. Query mode will almost always be initiated by the user by selecting a menu item or clicking on a button. Assume that the user clicks on a button labeled Help. To put the application into query mode, we can call gtk_tips_query_start_query() from the button clicked signal function:

```
void
gtk_tips_query_start_query(GtkTipsQuery *tips_query);
```

Or, we can arrange for Gtk+ to call the preceding function directly (e.g., make it the clicked signal function of the button). This last method is the easiest, and most practical, and is done as shown by the following code:

```
GtkTooltips *tips;

gtk_signal_connect_object(GTK_OBJECT(button), "clicked",
GTK_SIGNAL_FUNC(gtk_tips_query_start_query),
         GTK_OBJECT(tipsq));
```

An Example Using GtkTipsQuery

For the most part, the preceding is all you need to know to use a tips query widget. The following sample program puts all of the pieces together, with the exception of how to implement a help system above the tips query facility described here (this is, of course, left to the reader to implement):

```
#include <gtk/gtk.h>

static gint
tips_query_widget_selected(GtkWidget *tips_query, GtkWidget *widget,
    const gchar *tip_text, const gchar *tip_private,
    GdkEventButton *event, gpointer func_data)
{
    if ( tip_private != (char *) NULL )
            DoHelpSystem( tip_private );
    return TRUE;
}
```

The function tips_query_widget_selected(), in the preceding listing, is called whenever the user clicks on a widget (in this example, a button) in query mode. If tip_private is non-NULL, a help system function (not shown here) is called to display help text.

The rest of the program consists of main(), which sets up a dialog containing two button widgets. The first widget, labeled "Button that needs help", is the widget for which tooltip text is registered by the application.

```
013 main( int argc, char *argv[] )
014 {
015     GtkWidget *dialog_window, *button, *tipsq;
016     GtkTooltips *tips;
017
018     gtk_init( &argc, &argv );
019
020     dialog_window = gtk_dialog_new();
021     gtk_window_position(GTK_WINDOW(dialog_window), GTK_WIN_POS_MOUSE);
022
023     button = gtk_button_new_with_label("Button that needs help");
024     gtk_widget_show( button );
025
026     gtk_box_pack_start (GTK_BOX (GTK_DIALOG (dialog_window)->vbox),
027             button, TRUE, TRUE, 0);
028
029     tips = gtk_tooltips_new();
030
031     gtk_tooltips_set_tip(GTK_TOOLTIPS(tips), button,
032             "Click on this button to do something", "help:button1" );
```

Lines 023 through 032 illustrate the creation of the button and show how the tooltips widget (not the tips query widget) is associated with the button. Notice that I set, on line 032, the tip_private text to "help:button1". In this example, I assume that the string passed is meaningful to the help system, which parses it and uses the result to determine what help should be displayed.

On line 034, I create the tips query widget. Then, on lines 036 through 038, I connect the widget_selected signal to the function tips_query_widget_selected() that was previously defined. On line 040, I add the widget to the dialog's vbox, and then on line 042, I realize it by passing it to gtk_widget_realize(). It is important that the tips query widget have a parent before it is realized; Gtk+ will issue errors and behave badly if this is not done. Here is the code I just described:

```
033
034 tipsq = gtk_tips_query_new();
035
036 gtk_signal_connect_object (GTK_OBJECT (tipsq), "widget_selected",
037         GTK_SIGNAL_FUNC(tips_query_widget_selected),
038         GTK_OBJECT(tipsq));
039
040 gtk_box_pack_start (GTK_BOX (GTK_DIALOG (dialog_window)->vbox),
041         tipsq, TRUE, TRUE, 0);
042 gtk_widget_realize( tipsq );
043
```

The rest of main() is straightforward. On lines 044 through 047, a button widget is instantiated and added to the dialog action area. This button, when clicked, places the application into query mode:

```
044       button = gtk_button_new_with_label( "Click to enter query mode!" );
045       gtk_widget_show( button );
046       gtk_box_pack_start(GTK_BOX(GTK_DIALOG(dialog_window)->action_area),
047               button, TRUE, TRUE, 0);
048
```

On line 049, I register the clicked signal function, arranging it to call the GtkTipsQuery function gtk_tips_query_start_query() that was discussed earlier:

```
049       gtk_signal_connect_object (GTK_OBJECT (button), "clicked",
050               GTK_SIGNAL_FUNC(gtk_tips_query_start_query),
051               GTK_OBJECT (tipsq));
052
053       gtk_widget_show(dialog_window);
054       gtk_main();
055   }
```

Leaving Query Mode

As I mentioned at the start of this section, Gtk+ will automatically leave the query mode once the user has clicked on any widget, regardless of whether that widget has a tooltip associated with it or not. You can, if you need to, take the application out of query mode by calling gtk_tips_query_stop_query() and passing it the tips query widget involved:

```
void
gtk_tips_query_stop_query(GtkTipsQuery *tips_query);
```

As we have seen, the button, menu item, or other control that causes the widget to enter query mode will, when clicked, cause the widget to leave query mode and return to normal operation. You can, if you choose, change the widget that will, when clicked, bring the application out of query mode. This can be done by passing the widget to gtk_tips_query_set_caller() anytime prior to entering query mode:

```
void
gtk_tips_query_set_caller(GtkTipsQuery *tips_query,
        GtkWidget *caller);
```

Setting the Text Displayed by Widgets Without Tooltips

The final function I describe sets the text displayed by the tips query widget user interface whenever the user mouses over, in query mode, a widget that does not have a tooltip registered, as well as what is displayed by the tips query widget when the application is not in query mode. This function has no effect if the tips query widget is not made visible in the UI (i.e., it is realized, not mapped). To change these strings, call gtk_tips_query_set_labels():

```
void
gtk_tips_query_set_labels(GtkTipsQuery *tips_query,
        const gchar *label_inactive, const gchar *label_no_tip);
```

The argument label_inactive is the text string that will be displayed by the tips query widget when not in query mode, if visible in the UI. The default is " ", meaning no text will be displayed. The argument label_no_tip is the text displayed for all items that do not have tooltip text when moused over in query mode. The default value of this string is "---No Tip---". You must set both of these arguments to non-NULL values; otherwise, the call will fail.

GtkCombo

Class Name

```
GtkCombo
```

Parent Class Name

```
GtkHBox
```

Macros

Widget type macro: `GTK_TYPE_COMBO`

Object to widget cast macro: `GTK_COMBO(obj)`

Widget type check macro: `GTK_IS_COMBO(obj)`

Application-Level API Synopsis

Retrieve the constant GTK_TYPE_COMBO at runtime:

```
guint
gtk_combo_get_type(void);
```

Create a new instance of GtkCombo:

```
GtkWidget *
gtk_combo_new(void);
```

Force the value in the entry field to match a pop-up list item:

```
void
gtk_combo_set_value_in_list(GtkCombo *combo, gint val,
        gint ok_if_empty);
```

Enable/disable the use of arrow keys to navigate the pop-up list:

```
void
gtk_combo_set_use_arrows(GtkCombo *combo, gint val);
```

Application-Level API Synopsis (Continued)

Control wrapping of arrow keys when used to navigate the pop-up list:

```
void
gtk_combo_set_use_arrows_always(GtkCombo *combo, gint val);
```

Set case sensitivity of pop-up list searches:

```
void
gtk_combo_set_case_sensitive(GtkCombo *combo, gint val);
```

Set the entry field text of a nonlabel widget pop-up list item:

```
void
gtk_combo_set_item_string(GtkCombo *combo, GtkItem *item,
        const gchar * item_value);
```

Set the pop-up list items:

```
void
gtk_combo_set_popdown_strings(GtkCombo *combo, GList * strings);
```

Disable the firing of an activate signal by the entry field:

```
void
gtk_combo_disable_activate(GtkCombo *combo);
```

Class Description

GtkCombo implements the familiar combo widget illustrated in Figures 15.6 and 15.7. A combo widget is a combination of a pop-up list widget and an entry widget. The goal of a combo widget is to obtain a text string from the entry field. The value of the entry field is either text entered into the entry field by the user or a string selected by the user from the pop-up list. An application can force the user to select an item from the list, but the default configuration allows the user to enter arbitrary text into the entry field.

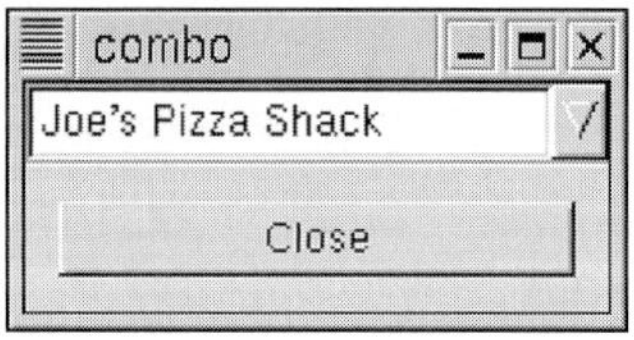

Figure 15.6 Combo Widget

Figure 15.7 Combo Widget Pop-up Menu

For most applications, creating and using a combo widget is a straightforward affair that consists of executing the following steps:

1. Create a combo widget with gtk_combo_new().
2. Add strings to the combo pop-up list with gtk_combo_set_popdown_strings().
3. Set the default value of the combo widget entry field by calling gtk_entry_set_text().
4. When editing has been completed, retrieve the value of the entry field.

Creating a Combo Box Widget

Let's take a look at the two GtkCombo functions previously mentioned and a sample application that makes use of the preceding steps to create a simple combo box in a window and retrieve its value when the user presses an OK button. The code also illustrates how to add strings to the pop-up list based on user input.

To create a combo box widget, call gtk_combo_new():

```
GtkWidget *
gtk_combo_new(void);
```

Like all gtk_*_new() functions, an instance of GtkWidget is returned. For those GtkCombo functions that require an instance of GtkCombo, simply cast the return value to a combo widget instance using the GTK_COMBO macro.

Setting the Combo Box Content

To add strings to the combo pop-up list, call gtk_combo_set_popdown_strings():

```
void
gtk_combo_set_popdown_strings(GtkCombo *combo, GList * strings);
```

The first argument, combo, is an instance of GtkCombo, and the second, strings, is the list of strings that will be displayed in the combo box pop-up list. To create the list of strings, use the Glib g_list functions (see *glib.h*). Perhaps the easiest of these to use is g_list_append(); see the following code for an example. You can call gtk_combo_set_popdown_strings() at any time to change the list of strings displayed by the combo widget pop-up list.

An Example

This sample program (see the following listing and Figures 15.6 and 15.7) illustrates the following:

- How to create an instance of a GtkCombo widget
- How to set the list of strings displayed by the combo widget pop-up list
- How to retrieve the value that was selected or entered by the user
- How to change (add to) the list of strings displayed by the combo pop-up list.

Listing 15.4 GtkCombo Example

```
#include <gtk/gtk.h>

typedef struct cdata {
    GtkWidget *combo;
    GList *cbitems;
} CData;

static void
GetComboEntry(GtkWidget *widget, CData *data)
{
    char *val = (char *) NULL;

    val = gtk_entry_get_text(GTK_ENTRY(GTK_COMBO(data->combo)->entry));
    if ( val )
            printf( "Value entered/selected is %s\n", val );
}

static void
AddComboEntry(GtkWidget *widget, CData *data)
{
    char *buf, *val = (char *) NULL;

    val = gtk_entry_get_text(GTK_ENTRY(GTK_COMBO(data->combo)->entry));
    if ( val != (char *) NULL ) {
            buf = (char *) malloc( strlen( val ) + 1 );
            if ( buf != (char *) NULL ) {
                    strcpy( buf, val );
                    data->cbitems = g_list_append(data->cbitems, buf );
                    gtk_combo_set_popdown_strings(GTK_COMBO(data->combo),
                            data->cbitems);
            }
    }
}

main( int argc, char *argv[] )
{
    GtkWidget *dialog_window, *button;
    CData data;

    data.cbitems = NULL;
    gtk_init( &argc, &argv );

    dialog_window = gtk_dialog_new();
    gtk_window_position (GTK_WINDOW (dialog_window), GTK_WIN_POS_MOUSE);
```

```
045
046     data.combo = gtk_combo_new();
047     data.cbitems = g_list_append(data.cbitems, "Joe's Pizza Shack" );
048     data.cbitems = g_list_append(data.cbitems, "Burgers And Stuff" );
049     data.cbitems = g_list_append(data.cbitems, "Vegetarian Delights" );
050     data.cbitems = g_list_append(data.cbitems, "El Taco Shop" );
051
052     gtk_combo_set_popdown_strings (GTK_COMBO (data.combo), data.cbitems);
053
054     gtk_box_pack_start (GTK_BOX (GTK_DIALOG (dialog_window)->vbox),
055             data.combo, TRUE, TRUE, 0);
056
057     button = gtk_button_new_with_label ("Ok");
058     gtk_signal_connect (GTK_OBJECT (button), "clicked",
059             GTK_SIGNAL_FUNC(GetComboEntry), &data);
060
061     gtk_box_pack_start (GTK_BOX (GTK_DIALOG (dialog_window)->action_area),
062             button, TRUE, TRUE, 0);
063
064     button = gtk_button_new_with_label ("Add");
065     gtk_signal_connect (GTK_OBJECT (button), "clicked",
066             GTK_SIGNAL_FUNC(AddComboEntry), &data);
067
068     gtk_box_pack_start (GTK_BOX (GTK_DIALOG (dialog_window)->action_area),
069             button, TRUE, TRUE, 0);
070
071     gtk_widget_show_all (dialog_window);
072     gtk_main();
073 }
```

Let's start our analysis of this code by taking a look at main(). On lines 003 through 006:

```
003 typedef struct cdata {
004     GtkWidget *combo;
005     GList *cbitems;
006 } CData;
```

I define a new type, CData, that holds a copy of the combo widget and the list of strings that will be displayed by the combo widget pop-up list. On line 040:

```
040     data.cbitems = NULL;
```

I set the string list to NULL because g_list_append() requires the initial list passed in to be NULL. On lines 046 through 052, I instantiate a new combo widget and use g_list_append() to add the names of four fictitious restaurants to the combo pop-up list. When the combo box is displayed, the first item in the list (Joe's Pizza Shack) will be placed in the combo text entry field.

```
046     data.combo = gtk_combo_new();
047     data.cbitems = g_list_append(data.cbitems, "Joe's Pizza Shack" );
048     data.cbitems = g_list_append(data.cbitems, "Burgers And Stuff" );
049     data.cbitems = g_list_append(data.cbitems, "Vegetarian Delights" );
050     data.cbitems = g_list_append(data.cbitems, "El Taco Shop" );
051
052     gtk_combo_set_popdown_strings (GTK_COMBO (data.combo), data.cbitems);
```

Two buttons, one labeled OK, and the other labeled Add, are created. The clicked signal functions for these two buttons are shown on lines 008 through 033. Both of these functions are passed a pointer to the CData structure that was defined by main and that holds references to the strings list and the combo widget. GetComboEntry():

```
008  static void
009  GetComboEntry(GtkWidget *widget, CData *data)
010  {
011      char *val = (char *) NULL;
012
013      val = gtk_entry_get_text(GTK_ENTRY(GTK_COMBO(data->combo)->entry));
014      if ( val )
015              printf( "Value entered/selected is %s\n", val );
016  }
```

calls gtk_entry_get_text() to get the current value of the combo widget entry field and displays it to stdout by calling printf(). AddComboEntry():

```
018  static void
019  AddComboEntry(GtkWidget *widget, CData *data)
020  {
021      char *buf, *val = (char *) NULL;
022
023      val = gtk_entry_get_text(GTK_ENTRY(GTK_COMBO(data->combo)->entry));
024      if ( val != (char *) NULL ) {
025              buf = (char *) malloc( strlen( val ) + 1 );
026              if ( buf != (char *) NULL ) {
027                      strcpy( buf, val );
028                      data->cbitems = g_list_append(data->cbitems, buf );
029                      gtk_combo_set_popdown_strings(GTK_COMBO(data->combo),
030                              data->cbitems);
031              }
032      }
033  }
```

uses get_entry_get_text() to retrieve the current value of the entry field as well. It then appends the text retrieved to the GList stored in the CData structure passed as an argument to the signal function and resets the combo widget pop-up list strings by calling to gtk_combo_set_popdown_strings().

An alternate way of modifying the list would be to add the entry to the end (or start) of the list widget used by GtkCombo to implement the pop-up list. The problem with this method is that it relies on internal knowledge of how the combo box is implemented. On the other hand, GtkCombo does not give an implementation-independent way to extract the value of the entry field; as you saw, we had to use a GtkEntry API function and pass to it an internal combo widget field (entry) to extract the value. With that in mind, we might as well take a look at how to add directly to the list. The following code is a version of the preceding routine, AddComboEntry():

```
018  static void
019  AddComboEntry(GtkWidget *widget, CData *data)
020  {
021     char *buf, *val = (char *) NULL;
022     GtkWidget *item, *label, *hbox;
023
024     val = gtk_entry_get_text(GTK_ENTRY(GTK_COMBO(data->combo)->entry));
025     if ( val != (char *) NULL ) {
026             hbox = gtk_hbox_new (FALSE, 0);
027             gtk_widget_show (hbox);
028             item = gtk_list_item_new();
029             gtk_container_add (GTK_CONTAINER (item), hbox);
030             buf = (char *) malloc( strlen( val ) + 1 );
031             if ( buf != (char *) NULL ) {
032                     strcpy( buf, val );
033                     label = gtk_label_new( buf );
034                     gtk_box_pack_start(GTK_BOX(hbox), label, FALSE,
035                             FALSE, 0);
036                     gtk_combo_set_item_string(GTK_COMBO(data->combo),
037                             GTK_ITEM(item), buf);
038                     gtk_container_add(
039                             GTK_CONTAINER(GTK_COMBO(data->combo)->list),
040                             item);
041                     gtk_widget_show (item);
042             }
043     }
044  }
```

Here, a list item widget is created (line 028), and to that, a horizontal box is added (line 029). The box will hold an instance of GtkLabel (lines 033 through 035) that, in the list, represents the string being added. Before I continue, let me mention a few things. First, I am adding a box to the list item. The reason I do this is to force the label, later added to the hbox, to align itself with the left edge of the hbox and, therefore, the list item. If I were to simply add the label to the item, it would be centered (which would be, in this case, inconsistent with the layout of the items added when I created the combo box back in main()). The other thing to mention, and you may have figured this out already, is that I can add any type of widget to the list using this method. Here, I used an hbox and a label child, but I could have easily added a pixmap or some other widget to the hbox.

Because of this generality, an issue remains. What happens if the user selects this item in the list? The combo widget is not aware of what the list item is composed of and is ill equipped to convert it to a string that can be placed inside the entry widget. Because of this, GtkCombo requires you to associate a text string with the item by calling gtk_combo_set_item_string(), as I have done on line 036. The function gtk_combo_set_item_string():

```
void
gtk_combo_set_item_string(GtkCombo *combo, GtkItem *item,
        const gchar * item_value);
```

accepts a combo widget instance, a list item, and a NULL-terminated C string that will be placed by GtkCombo in the entry widget whenever the user selects the list item from the pop-up list displayed by the combo widget.

Enabling and Disabling Use of Arrow Keys

Now that you know the important stuff, let's finish by taking a look at the remaining functions in the GtkCombo API. The first two functions control if and how the keyboard arrow keys are used to navigate the pop-up list. By default, the up and down arrows can be used to traverse the pop-up list items. Wrapping is not enabled, meaning that if the top item in the list is selected, the up arrow does nothing, and if the bottom item in the list is selected, the down arrow does nothing. You can disable (or re-enable) the use of arrow keys by calling gtk_combo_set_use_arrows():

```
void
gtk_combo_set_use_arrows(GtkCombo *combo, gint val);
```

The argument combo, of course, is an instance of GtkCombo. The argument val should be set to TRUE to enable arrow keys or FALSE to disable them. If you want to enable or disable arrow keys and, when enabling them, toggle the wrapping of arrow keys (e.g., when the top item is selected, pressing the up arrow will cause the last item in the list to become selected), you can make a call to gtk_combo_set_use_arrows_always():

```
void
gtk_combo_set_use_arrows_always(GtkCombo *combo, gint val);
```

The arguments are the same as those passed to gtk_combo_set_use_arrows(); the only difference is the effect this call has on the wrapping of arrow keys. If val is set to TRUE, arrow keys are enabled as well as wrapping. If FALSE, both are disabled. Once you have enabled (or disabled) the wrapping with this call, it persists during subsequent calls to gtk_combo_use_arrows(). This means you can now use gtk_combo_set_use_arrows() to enable or disable the arrow keys without affecting the wrapping attribute.

Forcing Users to Match the Pop-up List Contents During Data Entry

GtkCombo can be placed into a mode such that only text entered by the user in the entry field that equals one of the strings in the pop-up list will be accepted by the combo box. The way this is done is by causing the entry field to grab focus and retain it should the user attempt to move the focus to some other widget, when the entry field contains a text string that is not found by a search of the list of pop-up list strings. To put the combo box in this mode, call gtk_combo_set_value_in_list():

```
void
gtk_combo_set_value_in_list(GtkCombo *combo, gint val,
        gint ok_if_empty);
```

The argument val can be either TRUE or FALSE, depending on what behavior you want to enforce. If val is TRUE and ok_if_empty is also set to TRUE, then an empty string in the entry field will always be considered a match, and a focus change will not be inhibited. If you want to change the case sensitivity of the search performed by the combo widget during this process, you can make a call to gtk_combo_set_case_sensitive():

```
void
gtk_combo_set_case_sensitive(GtkCombo *combo, gint val);
```

val can be either TRUE or FALSE. The default value for a newly create GtkCombo widget is FALSE.

Disabling the Combo Widget Activate Function

The final GtkCombo function, gtk_combo_disable_activate(), can be called to disable the activate function registered by the combo widget entry field:

```
void
gtk_combo_disable_activate(GtkCombo *combo);
```

By default, hitting Enter in the entry field will cause the combo box list to pop up (the entry field will grab focus, if it does not already have it, and a pointer grab will be performed on the pop-up window). If you do not want this behavior to occur, simply call gtk_combo_disable_active() to deactivate it.

GtkStatusbar

Class Name

```
GtkStatusbar
```

Parent Class Name

```
GtkHBox
```

Macros

Widget type macro: `GTK_TYPE_STATUSBAR`

Object to widget cast macro: `GTK_STATUSBAR(obj)`

Widget type check macro: `GTK_IS_STATUSBAR(obj)`

Supported Signals

Table 15.11 Signals

Signal Name	*Condition Causing Signal to Trigger*
text_pushed	Invoked when text is pushed on the stack
text_popped	Invoked when text is popped from the stack

Signal Function Prototypes

```
void
text_pushed(GtkStatusbar *statusbar, guint context_id,
     gchar *text, gpointer user_data);

void
text_popped(GtkStatusbar *statusbar, guint context_id,
     gchar *text, gpointer user_data);
```

Application-Level API Synopsis

Retrieve the constant GTK_TYPE_STATUSBAR at runtime:

```
guint
gtk_statusbar_get_type(void);
```

Create a new instance of GtkStatusbar:

```
GtkWidget *
gtk_statusbar_new(void);
```

Obtain (or create if one doesn't exist) a context ID for the given description text:

```
guint
gtk_statusbar_get_context_id(GtkStatusbar *statusbar, const gchar
         *context_description);
```

Push text onto the statusbar stack specified by the context ID:

```
guint
gtk_statusbar_push(GtkStatusbar *statusbar, guint context_id,
         const gchar *text);
```

Remove the top item from the statusbar stack specified by the context ID:

```
void
gtk_statusbar_pop(GtkStatusbar *statusbar, guint context_id);
```

Application-Level API Synopsis (Continued)

Remove an item from the statusbar stack specified by the context ID:

```
void
gtk_statusbar_remove(GtkStatusbar *statusbar, guint context_id,
        guint message_id);
```

Class Description

A statusbar widget visually resembles an instance of GtkEntry. It is, in fact, nothing more than a frame widget (GtkFrame) that contains a label widget (GtkLabel). The statusbar does not respond to user input, nor can it obtain the input focus. Its job, as far as the user interface is concerned, is to display text in much the same way a label does (using a slightly fancier user interface).

The non-UI portion of a statusbar widget consists of a stack. Each statusbar widget maintains a single stack. Pushing a text string onto the stack causes the text string to be on top of the stack and increases the size of the stack by 1. Popping a text string from the stack removes the topmost item from the stack and reduces the size of the stack by 1. The item immediately below the item popped then becomes the top of the stack.

The only other thing you must know is that the top item of the stack is what is displayed by the statusbar widget UI. Pushing an item on the stack causes that item to be displayed. Popping an item from the stack causes the new top of the stack contents to be displayed.

Probably the more difficult part of GtkStatusbar is deciding when to make use of it. Because a statusbar is, as far as the UI goes, just a frame with a label in it, you can use, instead of a statusbar widget, a frame and a label child and obtain the same visual results. What's more, changing the text of the label widget is easier in this case; you simply call gtk_label_set_text() to change what the label widget is displaying. If, instead, you use an instance of GtkStatusbar, you must do one of the following:

- Pop the current top of the statusbar stack and push a new text string on the stack
- Push a new text string on the stack

In the first case, the size of the stack remains 1 because we pop the stack just before we push a new string. In the second case, the stack grows by 1 each time the status text is pushed. When compared to creating a frame and label on your own, the choices you are provided require either more steps to execute (popping and pushing an entry on a stack plus the work done by the widget to change the label text) or more steps to execute plus a less efficient use of memory (although the inefficiency in terms of memory usage is probably insignificant in most cases).

Because we are dealing with a stack, you can only push and pop items. This is not the most flexible of arrangements, as the following example illustrates. Assume the status bar is being used by an application to display a set of four messages, in order, changing the message displayed once every 10 seconds. You might choose a status bar widget to implement this feature and execute the following steps:

```
1         push "Message 1"
2         wait 10 seconds
3         push "Message 2"
4         wait 10 seconds
...
8         push "Message 4"
```

Our stack, after the above steps have been completed, looks like this:

```
top ->    "Message 4"
          "Message 3"
          "Message 2"
          "Message 1"
```

Let's now see what must be done to cycle back to Message 1 and repeat the process. Two basic strategies come to mind. The simplest of these would be to start the algorithm over again (i.e., push Message 1, wait 10 seconds, push Message 2, and so on). If we adopt this strategy, clearly no advantage would be had by having the messages on the stack; in fact, there would be a penalty in that the size of the stack would grow unbounded, and the amount of code executed to display a status message would be greater than is necessary.

The other strategy would require us to pop items off of the stack. First we would wait 10 seconds. Then we would pop the top three items on the stack and re-enter the algorithm at step 2. Having the items on the stack in this case is a burden because we are required to pop the stack of most of its contents in order to return to the beginning of the list.

Perhaps we want to display the items in reverse order after being pushed onto the stack (i.e., display the messages in the order Message 1, Message 2, Message 3, Message 4, Message 3, Message 2, Message 1, Message 2, and so on). In this case, popping the stack would be the natural way to display the message sequence Message 3, Message 2, Message 1, but if we were to repeat the cycle, we would start again with only one item on the stack, and we would need to push all of the messages, once again, onto the stack.

Regardless of which of the described scenarios you choose, I would argue that it is easier, and more efficient, to store the message text in an array and simply set the value of a label widget that you create yourself whenever you want to change the value it is displaying.

Creating a Statusbar Widget

Let's continue by looking at the GtkStatusbar API. To create a new instance of GtkStatusbar, call gtk_statusbar_new():

```
GtkWidget *
gtk_statusbar_new(void);
```

The returned widget can be added to a box or any other container as needed by the application. Because the statusbar is only displaying text, you should be careful to pack it into the container in such a way that it will be vertically sized by changes in the geometry of its parent container.

Pushing a Status Message onto the Stack

Now that you have a status bar, you can push a text message onto the stack to cause it to be displayed. This is done by calling gtk_statusbar_push():

```
guint
gtk_statusbar_push(GtkStatusbar *statusbar, guint context_id,
        const gchar *text);
```

The first argument, statusbar, is an instance of GtkStatusbar that was created by a call to gtk_statusbar_new(). The argument text is the text string that will be pushed onto the stack and displayed by the statusbar widget upon return. The argument context_id requires a bit of explanation. The stack can be partitioned into multiple contexts. For our example, and in most cases, we really need only a single context. When using a single context, the push operations in our example might have been performed in a manner similar to the following:

```
GtkWidget *w;

gtk_statusbar_push( GTK_STATUSBAR( w ), 1, "Message 1" );
gtk_statusbar_push( GTK_STATUSBAR( w ), 1, "Message 2" );
gtk_statusbar_push( GTK_STATUSBAR( w ), 1, "Message 3" );
gtk_statusbar_push( GTK_STATUSBAR( w ), 1, "Message 4" );
```

You can, however, change the context number, making it unique for each item on the stack if you so desire. There are no rules except that each context ID must be greater than 0 in value. For example, we could have pushed our messages onto the stack with the following code:

```
GtkWidget *w;

gtk_statusbar_push( GTK_STATUSBAR( w ), 1, "Message 1" );
gtk_statusbar_push( GTK_STATUSBAR( w ), 2, "Message 2" );
gtk_statusbar_push( GTK_STATUSBAR( w ), 3, "Message 3" );
gtk_statusbar_push( GTK_STATUSBAR( w ), 1, "Message 4" );
```

In this case, we have three contexts on the stack with the context ids 1, 2, and 3, respectively. The context must be specified when you pop items from the stack using gtk_statusbar_pop(), as I will discuss later.

The value returned by gtk_status_bar_push() is an unsigned integer. This value is a unique ID (unique for all items on the stack, regardless of the number of contexts it stores), assigned to the item that was pushed. You must specify the ID when removing the item from the stack with gtk_statusbar_remove() (see the following discussion).

Handling the text_pushed Signal

Every time an item is pushed onto the stack, GtkStatusbar emits a text_pushed signal. If you have registered one or more signal functions with the statusbar widget to handle this signal, they will be invoked by Gtk+. The function prototype for the text_pushed signal function is as follows:

```
void TextPushedFunction( GtkWidget *w, guint context_id,
    gchar *text );
```

Getting a Context ID

The function gtk_statusbar_get_context_id() allows you to generate a context ID value, given a text string, or to look up the context ID of a string for which a context ID was previously generated.

```
guint
gtk_statusbar_get_context_id(GtkStatusbar *statusbar, const gchar
        *context_description);
```

The argument context_description is a NULL-terminated C string. This function returns a context ID that can be passed to any of the GtkStatusbar functions that require a context ID. You might use this function to map text strings to context IDs if strings are more meaningful to your application than numbers. I don't suspect that this function is used often.

Popping an Item from the Stack

To pop an item from the stack, you call gtk_statusbar_pop():

```
void
gtk_statusbar_pop(GtkStatusbar *statusbar, guint context_id);
```

The argument statusbar is, of course, the status bar widget from which the item is being popped. context_id is used to determine which item is popped from the stack.

Substacks

Each set of items in the stack that shares the same context ID constitutes a substack. For example, if the stack is as follows (the integer value to the left of the text is the context ID):

```
top ->   1 "Message 4"
         3 "Message 3"
         2 "Message 2"
         1 "Message 1"
```

then the following calls:

```
gtk_statusbar_pop( statusbar, 1 );
gtk_statusbar_pop( statusbar, 1 );
```

will pop Message 4 and Message 1 from the stack, leaving the stack as:

```
top ->   3 "Message 3"
         2 "Message 2"
```

If we execute the following:

```
gtk_statusbar_pop( statusbar, 2 );
```

we are left with the following stack:

```
top ->   3 "Message 3"
```

In general, the top of the stack, as far as popping items goes, is defined to be the item closest to the "true" top of the stack that has a matching context ID. To avoid any confusion, you should always set the context ID to a single value (for example, 1), unless the use of different context IDs somehow makes sense for your application (and please e-mail me if you find a reasonable use for this feature, as I am curious to hear about it).

Handling the text_popped Signal

Like pushing an item on the stack, popping an item results in the firing of a signal. In this case, the signal is a text_popped signal. If your application has registered a signal function for this signal, it will be invoked. The signal function prototype is as follows:

```
void TextPoppedFunction( GtkWidget *w, guint context_id,
        gchar *text );
```

The arguments context_id and text identify the item that was popped.

Removing an Arbitrary Item from the Stack

The final function described here allows you to remove an arbitrary item from the stack. The function prototype is as follows:

```
void
gtk_statusbar_remove(GtkStatusbar *statusbar, guint context_id,
        guint message_id);
```

Removing an item from the stack with this function does not cause a text_popped signal to be emitted. The argument context_id identifies the substack from which the item will be removed. The argument message_id is the value identifying the item to be removed, as returned by gtk_statusbar_push() when the item was pushed onto the stack.

Final Thoughts

To summarize, I believe that if you need to display status text in a window, it is probably more efficient (as well as straightforward) for you to create your own statusbar UI. This can be done by creating a GtkLabel widget and adding it to an instance of GtkFrame. You can easily change the message displayed by the label widget with a call to gtk_label_set_text(). However, if, for whatever reason, it makes sense for your application to store the status messages on a stack, then by all means make use of GtkStatusbar.

GtkAccelLabel

Class Name

```
GtkAccelLabel
```

Parent Class Name

```
GtkLabel
```

Macros

Widget type macro: `GTK_TYPE_ACCEL_LABEL`

Object to widget cast macro: `GTK_ACCEL_LABEL(obj)`

Widget type check macro: `GTK_IS_ACCEL_LABEL(obj)`

Supported Arguments

Prefix: `GtkAccelLabel::`

Table 15.12 GtkAccelLabel Arguments

Name	*Type*	*Permission*
accel_widget	GTK_TYPE_WIDGET	GTK_ARG_READWRITE

Application-Level API Synopsis

Retrieve the constant GTK_TYPE_ACCEL_LABEL at runtime:
```
GtkType
gtk_accel_label_get_type(void);
```

Create a new instance of GtkAccelLabel:
```
GtkWidget *
gtk_accel_label_new(const gchar *string);
```

Retrieve the width of the accel label widget in pixels:
```
guint
gtk_accel_label_get_accel_width(GtkAccelLabel *accel_label);
```

Set the widget that will have its accelerators shown by this label:
```
void
gtk_accel_label_set_accel_widget(GtkAccelLabel *accel_label,
        GtkWidget *accel_widget);
```

Recompute the accelerator string and its length:
```
gboolean
gtk_accel_label_refetch(GtkAccelLabel *accel_label);
```

Class Description

GtkAccelLabel is a class used by the Gtk+ menu item classes GtkMenuItem, GtkRadioMenuItem, and GtkCheckMenuItem. An accel label is similar to an instance of GtkLabel, except that an accel label displays accelerator information for the widget to the right of the label text. Primarily designed to be used by widget writers, applications will rarely if ever need to instantiate widgets from this class. Regardless, a short description of the API that the class implements is provided for curious readers (or for widget writers who need the reference material).

Creating an Accel Label Widget

To create an accel label widget, call gtk_accel_label_new():

```
GtkWidget *
gtk_accel_label_new(const gchar *string);
```

The argument string defines the text that will be displayed by the label, not the accelerator text itself. The accelerator text is always added by the widget, which calls gtk_widget_add_accelerator() to do so. When the accelerator for the widget is changed, the accel label widget will be invoked to recompute the string it displays to the right of the menu item label and its size. The function gtk_accel_label_refetch() is the function that performs these functions:

```
gboolean
gtk_accel_label_refetch(GtkAccelLabel *accel_label);
```

It looks up the widget assigned to the accel label, determines what accelerators are supported, and computes the new accelerator label string and its length.

Retrieving the Width of an Accel Label Widget

You can retrieve the width of the accel label widget (and of the padding that exists to its left) in pixels by calling gtk_accel_label_get_accel_width():

```
guint
gtk_accel_label_get_accel_width(GtkAccelLabel *accel_label);
```

Mapping an Accel Label Widget to the Widget It Supports

An important step in the process is telling the accel label widget which widget (e.g., menu item) it supports. This is be done by making a call to gtk_accel_label_set_accel_widget():

```
void
gtk_accel_label_set_accel_widget(GtkAccelLabel *accel_label,
        GtkWidget *accel_widget);
```

Here, accel_label is the accel label widget instance, and accel_widget is the widget that will display the label and that may (or may not) have one or more accelerators associated with it (it is not required for a widget to have an accelerator to be labeled by an instance of GtkAccelLabel).

Readers who are interested in seeing sample code should grep(1) for the string gtk_accel_label in the Gtk+ source code and look at how these functions are used. Files of particular interest are those that implement the various menu item classes (e.g., *gtkmenuitem.c*).

GtkDrawingArea

Class Name

```
GtkDrawingArea
```

Parent Class Name

```
GtkWidget
```

Macros

Widget type macro: `GTK_TYPE_DRAWING_AREA`

Object to widget cast macro: `GTK_DRAWING_AREA(obj)`

Widget type check macro: `GTK_IS_DRAWING_AREA(obj)`

Application-Level API Synopsis

Return the constant GTK_TYPE_DRAWING_AREA at runtime:

```
GtkType
gtk_drawing_area_get_type(void);
```

Create a new instance of GtkDrawingArea:

```
GtkWidget *
gtk_drawing_area_new(void);
```

Set the requisition size of the drawing area and force a resize:

```
void
gtk_drawing_area_size(GtkDrawingArea *darea, gint width,
        gint height);
```

Class Description

GtkDrawingArea is a simple widget that provides nothing more than a window into which an application can draw graphics or plot image data, using functions provided by GDK. One of the main features supporting the drawing of graphics is the solicitation of expose events on the drawing area widget window. This is done on behalf of the application by the drawing area widget when the widget is realized.

Creating a Drawing Area Widget

There are really only two functions that make up the drawing area API. The first of these is no surprise; to create a new drawing area widget, you can call gtk_drawing_area_new():

```
GtkWidget *
gtk_drawing_area_new(void);
```

The widget returned can be added to a container, such as a window or box, by the application.

Setting the Drawing Area Widget Size

Depending on the containment hierarchy of the application, you may find it necessary to set the size of the drawing area widget (as I will do in the following sample program). To set the size of the drawing area widget, call gtk_drawing_area_size():

```
void
gtk_drawing_area_size(GtkDrawingArea *darea, gint width, gint height);
```

The first argument is the drawing area widget of interest. The second and third arguments, width and height, specify the requisition size of the drawing area. Once set, the drawing area widget will initiate a resize request that may or may not be honored, depending on the containment hierarchy of the widget. You can determine the actual size of the drawing area widget, something you need to do if you are scaling image data or graphics to fit the drawing area size. You can determine the size of the drawing area by calling gdk_window_get_geometry(), as in the following example:

```
int width, height;
GtkWidget *w;

w = gtk_drawing_area_new();

...

gdk_window_get_geometry(w->window, NULL, NULL, &width, &height, NULL);
```

The x, y, and depth arguments to gdk_window_get_geometry() can be set to NULL because they are not needed.

Using the Drawing Area Widget

A drawing area widget, as I previously mentioned, is really nothing more than a window to which graphics can be rendered by an application. For example, an application might draw text using gdk_draw_text(), draw lines or arcs using functions such as gdk_draw_line() and gdk_draw_arc(), respectively, or draw pixmaps or images using a function such as gdk_draw_pixmap(). Although I do not completely address in this book how to use GDK to draw text, graphics, or image data (you can refer to *http://developer.gnome.org/doc/API/gdk/index.html* for such reference material), I do present the following sample program that illustrates the important issues you need to know to make effective use of a drawing area widget in your applications.

The sample application is rather straightforward. The application provides a drawing area into which the user can render rectangles (see Figure 15.8). A toolbar at the top of the dialog contains three buttons, each labeled with a pixmap of a different color (red, green, or blue). By clicking on one of the buttons, the user can change the color of rectangles that will be rendered (any previously drawn rectangles retain the color they were given at the time they were drawn). To draw a rectangle, the user positions the mouse over the drawing area widget and presses mouse button 1. A button labeled Clear is placed in the action area of the dialog; clicking on this button will cause all rectangles in the drawing area to be cleared.

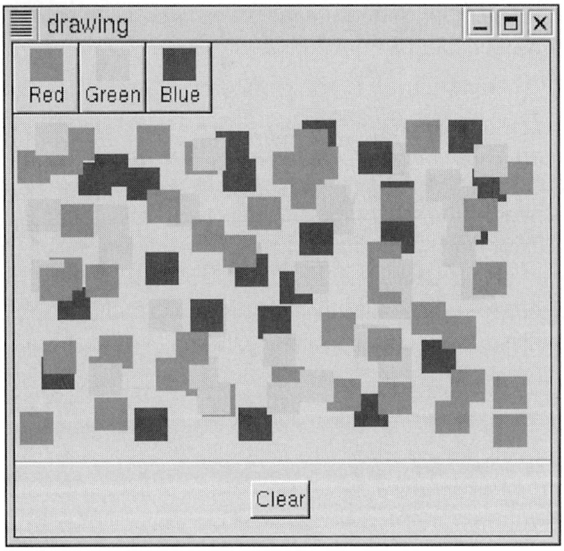

Figure 15.8 GtkDrawingArea Example Screen Shot

A requirement of the application is that it be able to handle expose events. An expose event occurs when an X window is first mapped to the display, as well as any time a region of a mapped window previously obscured by some other window, or offscreen, is brought into view. (Windows that have backing store enabled, when they are run on a server that has backing store enabled, send a minimal amount of expose events.) An expose event is the way in which an application is told by the X server that some, or all, of a window is in need of redrawing.

The code that implements this example is somewhat complex; it is probably the largest sample application presented in this book. However, careful reading of the analysis that follows should greatly increase your understanding of how to use a drawing area widget in an application. I suggest you build and execute the sample code in a debugger such as gdb(1), paying particular attention to how expose events are handled by setting a breakpoint on the expose signal function HandleExpose() and stepping through it a few times.

Listing 15.5 GtkDrawingArea Example (See Figure 15.8)

```
#include <gtk/gtk.h>

#define RED  1
#define GREEN        2
#define BLUE         4

typedef struct piece {
    int x;                      // position of the piece
    int y;
    guint32 time;               // time the piece was added
    unsigned char color;        // its color
} Piece;

typedef struct cleardata {
    GtkWidget *w;
    GList **list;
} ClearData;

static GtkWidget *gRedPmap, *gGreenPmap, *gBluePmap;
static unsigned char gColor = RED;

static GtkWidget*
NewPixmap( char *filename, GdkWindow *window, GdkColor *background )
{
    GtkWidget *wpixmap;
    GdkPixmap *pixmap;
    GdkBitmap *mask;

    pixmap = gdk_pixmap_create_from_xpm( window, &mask, background,
             filename );
    wpixmap = gtk_pixmap_new( pixmap, mask );

    return wpixmap;
}

static void
SetColor( GtkWidget *widget, gpointer arg )
{
    gColor = (unsigned char) arg;
```

```
}

static void
ClearDrawing( GtkWidget *widget, gpointer arg )
{
    ClearData *p = (ClearData *) arg;
    GList **list = p->list;
    GList *tmp_list;

    for (tmp_list = *list; tmp_list; tmp_list = tmp_list->next)
            g_free(tmp_list->data);

    g_list_free(*list);
    *list = (GList *) NULL;

    gdk_window_clear( p->w->window );

}

static int
CompFunc( gconstpointer a, gconstpointer b )
{
    Piece *piece1, *piece2;

    piece1 = (Piece *) a;
    piece2 = (Piece *) b;

    if ( piece1->time < piece2->time )
            return FALSE;
    return TRUE;
}

static gint
ButtonPress( GtkWidget *widget, GdkEventButton *event, gpointer arg )
{
    ClearData *p = (ClearData *) arg;
    GList **items = (GList **) p->list;
    GtkPixmap *pixmap;
    Piece *piece;

    piece = (Piece *) malloc( sizeof( Piece ) );
    piece->color = gColor;
    piece->x = (gint) event->x;
    piece->y = (gint) event->y;
    piece->time = gdk_event_get_time( (GdkEvent *) event );
    *items = g_list_insert_sorted( *items, piece, CompFunc );

    switch ( piece->color ) {
        case RED:
            pixmap = GTK_PIXMAP( gRedPmap );
            break;
```

```
        case GREEN:
             pixmap = GTK_PIXMAP( gGreenPmap );
             break;
        case BLUE:
             pixmap = GTK_PIXMAP( gBluePmap );
             break;
    }

    gdk_draw_pixmap( widget->window, widget->style->black_gc,
             pixmap->pixmap, 0, 0, piece->x, piece->y, -1, -1 );
}

static gint
HandleExpose( GtkWidget *widget, GdkEventExpose *event, gpointer arg )
{
    GList **p = (GList **) arg, *list = (GList *) *p;
    GdkRectangle rect, dest;
    GtkPixmap *pixmap;
    Piece *piece;
    int i;

    for ( i = 0; *p != (GList *) NULL; i++, *p = g_list_next( *p ) ) {
             piece = g_list_nth_data( (GList *) list, i );
             rect.x = piece->x;
             rect.y = piece->y;
             rect.width = rect.height = 20;
             if ( gdk_rectangle_intersect(
                      &rect, &event->area, &dest ) == TRUE ) {
                      switch ( piece->color ) {
                      case RED:
                               pixmap = GTK_PIXMAP( gRedPmap );
                               break;
                      case GREEN:
                               pixmap = GTK_PIXMAP( gGreenPmap );
                               break;
                      case BLUE:
                               pixmap = GTK_PIXMAP( gBluePmap );
                               break;
                      default:
                               continue;
                      }
                      gdk_draw_pixmap( widget->window,
                               widget->style->black_gc,
                               pixmap->pixmap, 0, 0,
                               piece->x, piece->y, -1, -1 );
             }
    }
    *p = list;
}

main( int argc, char *argv[] )
```

```
{
    GtkWidget *dialog, *button, *drawing, *toolbar;
    GList *items = (GList *) NULL;
    ClearData cd;

    gtk_init( &argc, &argv );

    dialog = gtk_dialog_new();
    gtk_window_position( GTK_WINDOW( dialog ), GTK_WIN_POS_MOUSE );
    gtk_widget_show( dialog );

    toolbar = gtk_toolbar_new( GTK_ORIENTATION_HORIZONTAL,
            GTK_TOOLBAR_BOTH );

    gRedPmap = NewPixmap( "red.xpm", dialog->window,
            &dialog->style->bg[GTK_STATE_NORMAL] ),
            gtk_toolbar_append_item( GTK_TOOLBAR( toolbar ), "Red",
            "Draw red square", NULL, gRedPmap,
            (GtkSignalFunc) SetColor, (gpointer) RED );
    gGreenPmap = NewPixmap( "green.xpm", dialog->window,
            &dialog->style->bg[GTK_STATE_NORMAL] ),
            gtk_toolbar_append_item( GTK_TOOLBAR( toolbar ), "Green",
            "Draw green square", NULL, gGreenPmap,
            (GtkSignalFunc) SetColor, (gpointer) GREEN );
    gBluePmap = NewPixmap( "blue.xpm", dialog->window,
            &dialog->style->bg[GTK_STATE_NORMAL] ),
            gtk_toolbar_append_item( GTK_TOOLBAR( toolbar ), "Blue",
            "Draw blue square", NULL, gBluePmap,
            (GtkSignalFunc) SetColor, (gpointer) BLUE );

    gtk_box_pack_start( GTK_BOX( GTK_DIALOG( dialog )->vbox ), toolbar,
            FALSE, TRUE, 0 );

    drawing = gtk_drawing_area_new();
    gtk_drawing_area_size( GTK_DRAWING_AREA( drawing ), 320, 200 );
    gtk_signal_connect( GTK_OBJECT( drawing ), "expose_event",
            GTK_SIGNAL_FUNC( HandleExpose ), &items );
    gtk_widget_set_events( drawing,
            GDK_EXPOSURE_MASK | GDK_BUTTON_PRESS_MASK);
    cd.w = drawing;
    cd.list = &items;
    gtk_signal_connect( GTK_OBJECT( drawing ), "button_press_event",
            GTK_SIGNAL_FUNC( ButtonPress ), &cd );

    gtk_box_pack_start( GTK_BOX( GTK_DIALOG( dialog )->vbox ), drawing,
            TRUE, TRUE, 0 );

    button = gtk_button_new_with_label( "Clear" );
    gtk_box_pack_start( GTK_BOX( GTK_DIALOG( dialog )->action_area ),
            button, TRUE, FALSE, 0 );
    gtk_signal_connect( GTK_OBJECT( button ), "clicked",
```

```
193                 GTK_SIGNAL_FUNC( ClearDrawing ), &cd );
194
195         gtk_widget_show_all( dialog );
196         gtk_main();
197     }
```

Analysis

Let's start by taking a look at main(). The job of main() is to create the application user interface, which consists of a GtkDialog widget. Into the vbox member of the dialog widget a toolbar is packed. This toolbar contains the color-selection buttons. On lines 156, 161, and 166, I call a function named NewPixmap() (see the full listing) that creates an instance of GtkPixmap. These pixmaps not only are used in creating the toolbar buttons, they are also stored in global variables (e.g., gRedPmap) so they can be easily accessed when it is time to draw colored rectangles into the drawing area widget in response to a mouse click event.

On line 175, I create the drawing area widget:

```
175        drawing = gtk_drawing_area_new();
```

On the very next line (line 180) I set its size to 320×200. The dialog widget will size itself to accommodate this request. Note that I pack the drawing area and toolbar widgets into the drawing area vbox so that resizes of the window cause the toolbar to stay anchored at the top of the dialog vbox and the drawing area widget to expand to fill the entire area left over.

```
177        gtk_signal_connect( GTK_OBJECT( drawing ), "expose_event",
178                  GTK_SIGNAL_FUNC( HandleExpose ), &items );
179        gtk_widget_set_events( drawing,
180                  GDK_EXPOSURE_MASK | GDK_BUTTON_PRESS_MASK);
```

On line 177, I set the signal function for the drawing area expose event to HandleExpose(). On line 179, I change the event solicitation for the drawing area widget so that both expose and button press events are sent for the drawing area widget window. The solicitation of expose events is redundant because an expose event is automatically solicited by all drawing area widgets.

On line 181 through 184, I arrange for mouse event signals to be handled by the function ButtonPress(). As client data, I pass a pointer to a structure that contains the drawing area widget and a pointer to a list (I will explain the purpose of this list later in this section):

```
181      cd.w = drawing;
182      cd.list = &items;
183      gtk_signal_connect( GTK_OBJECT( drawing ), "button_press_event",
184              GTK_SIGNAL_FUNC( ButtonPress ), &cd );
```

Finally, on lines 189 through 193, I create a button labeled Clear that, when pressed, clears the display of all rectangles drawn by the user:

```
189    button = gtk_button_new_with_label( "Clear" );
190    gtk_box_pack_start( GTK_BOX( GTK_DIALOG( dialog )->action_area ),
191             button, TRUE, FALSE, 0 );
```

```
192 gtk_signal_connect( GTK_OBJECT( button ), "clicked",
193         GTK_SIGNAL_FUNC( ClearDrawing ), &cd );
```

As you can see on line 193, the "clicked" signal function, ClearDrawing(), is passed a pointer to the same structure that is passed to the ButtonPress() signal function previously mentioned.

Before things get confusing (hopefully you are following this so far), let's take a look at the signal functions in some detail. The first one I will describe is the button_press_event signal function, ButtonPress():

```
072 static gint
073 ButtonPress( GtkWidget *widget, GdkEventButton *event, gpointer arg )
074 {
075    ClearData *p = (ClearData *) arg;
076    GList **items = (GList **) p->list;
077    GtkPixmap *pixmap;
078    Piece *piece;
079
080    piece = (Piece *) malloc( sizeof( Piece ) );
081    piece->color = gColor;
082    piece->x = (gint) event->x;
083    piece->y = (gint) event->y;
084    piece->time = gdk_event_get_time( (GdkEvent *) event );
085    *items = g_list_insert_sorted( *items, piece, CompFunc );
086
087    switch ( piece->color ) {
088         case RED:
089            pixmap = GTK_PIXMAP( gRedPmap );
090            break;
091         case GREEN:
092            pixmap = GTK_PIXMAP( gGreenPmap );
093            break;
094         case BLUE:
095            pixmap = GTK_PIXMAP( gBluePmap );
096            break;
097    }
098
099    gdk_draw_pixmap( widget->window, widget->style->black_gc,
100            pixmap->pixmap, 0, 0, piece->x, piece->y, -1, -1 );
101 }
```

The purpose of ButtonPress() is to plot a rectangle, of the appropriate color, in the drawing area window at the location the user pressed the mouse button. It also adds an entry, sorted by time of button press, to a list that will be traversed if the application receives an expose event for the drawing area widget window. This list contains entries of the following type:

```
007 typedef struct piece {
008    int x; // position of the piece
009    int y;
010    guint32 time; // time the piece was added
```

```
011      unsigned char color; // its color
012   } Piece;
```

The fields x and y record the location of the button press that leads to the drawing of the rectangle corresponding to the list entry. The time of the button press is recorded in the time field, and the color of the rectangle is stored in the field named color. Lines 080 through 085 illustrate how an item is added to the list. The color field comes from a global variable that is set in the clicked callback function of the corresponding toolbar button. Drawing of the rectangle occurs on lines 087 through 100. On line 087, a switch statement is entered; it is within this switch statement that the pixmap data is retrieved from the GtkPixmap instance used to create the toolbar button corresponding to the currently selected color. On line 099, the pixmap is drawn into the drawing area window using gdk_draw_pixmap().

So, now that we know how to draw a rectangle and we know how to build a list that remembers the rectangles that were drawn (position, color, and time), we can look at what happens when an expose event is received. An expose event is described by the following struct:

```
typedef struct _GdkEventExpose GdkEventExpose;

struct _GdkEventExpose
{
  GdkEventType type;
  GdkWindow *window;
  gint8 send_event;
  GdkRectangle area;
  gint count; /* If non-zero, how many more events follow. */
};
```

For an expose event, GdkEventType is always set to GDK_EXPOSE. Window is the window that has been exposed, and area defines the area within the window that was exposed. The area struct has fields named x, y, width, and height. The x and y fields are both window relative (i.e., x = 12, y = 42 refers to the point [12, 42] offset from the origin of the window, not the origin of the screen). Finally, width and height define the size of the area that was exposed. In the sample application, HandleExpose() is the signal function invoked when the an expose event is received for the drawing area widget window:

```
103  static gint
104  HandleExpose( GtkWidget *widget, GdkEventExpose *event, gpointer arg )
105  {
106     GList **p = (GList **) arg, *list = (GList *) *p;
107     GdkRectangle rect, dest;
108     GtkPixmap *pixmap;
109     Piece *piece;
110     int i;
111
112     for ( i = 0; *p != (GList *) NULL; i++, *p = g_list_next( *p ) ) {
113             piece = g_list_nth_data( (GList *) list, i );
114             rect.x = piece->x;
115             rect.y = piece->y;
116             rect.width = rect.height = 20;
```

```
117             if ( gdk_rectangle_intersect(
118                         &rect, &event->area, &dest ) == TRUE ) {
119                         switch ( piece->color ) {
120                         case RED:
121                             pixmap = GTK_PIXMAP( gRedPmap );
122                             break;
123                         case GREEN:
124                             pixmap = GTK_PIXMAP( gGreenPmap );
125                             break;
126                         case BLUE:
127                             pixmap = GTK_PIXMAP( gBluePmap );
128                             break;
129                         default:
130                             continue;
131                         }
132                         gdk_draw_pixmap( widget->window,
133                             widget->style->black_gc,
134                             pixmap->pixmap, 0, 0,
135                             piece->x, piece->y, -1, -1 );
136             }
137     }
138     *p = list;
139 }
```

Your application only needs to redraw the area described by the area struct of the expose event, not the entire window. One could ignore the area field of the expose event completely and redraw the entire window. However, this is seldom done because drawing the entire window almost always increases the amount of time required to process the expose event. Clip regions can be used to minimize the amount of time a complete redraw takes. A clip region tells the X server to draw only pixels falling within the rectangular area(s) described by the clip region and to discard any pixels that fall outside of it. This can reduce the time needed to process an expose event if the cost of drawing each pixel is greater than the time it takes to communicate the clip regions to the X server, combined with the time it takes for the clip regions to be applied.

The solution that the example program takes is to walk the list of rectangles drawn by the user and completely redraw those that intersect the exposed region. I could have combined this strategy with the use of clip regions, and this would be optimal in the case of some clients that render complex graphics. However, I adopted a simpler solution that I expect achieves satisfactory, if not more efficient, results for the type of data being rendered. You should consider the use of clip regions when evaluating an expose event handler strategy (see any good book on Xlib programming for more details). Although not covered in this book, the GDK functions gdk_gc_set_clip_origin(), gdk_gc_set_clip_mask(), and gdk_gc_set_clip_rectangle() correspond to the Xlib functions XSetClipOrigin(), XSetClipMask(), and XSetClipRectangles().

Let's take a look at the expose event handler previously listed. On line 112, I enter a loop that walks the pieces that are on the list. As you recall, each item in this list corresponds to a rectangle drawn into the drawing area widget window by the user. The data field of the list entry is a pointer to a variable of type piece that contains, once again, the location of the rectangle and its color.

```
112 for ( i = 0; *p != (GList *) NULL; i++, *p = g_list_next( *p ) ) {
113         piece = g_list_nth_data( (GList *) list, i );
```

On lines 113 through 116, I set the x, y, width, and height fields of a GdkRectangle struct to describe the location and size of the user-drawn rectangle being processed. On line 117, I call gdk_rectangle_intersect() to determine whether the user-drawn rectangle intersects the area that was exposed:

```
113 piece = g_list_nth_data( (GList *) list, i );
114 rect.x = piece->x;
115 rect.y = piece->y;
116 rect.width = rect.height = 20;
117 if ( gdk_rectangle_intersect(
118             &rect, &event->area, &dest ) == TRUE ) {
```

If the areas do intersect, I draw the user-drawn rectangle using the same algorithm that was used by the mouse button press handler to draw the original rectangle:

```
119                         switch ( piece->color ) {
120                         case RED:
121                                 pixmap = GTK_PIXMAP( gRedPmap );
122                                 break;
123                         case GREEN:
124                                 pixmap = GTK_PIXMAP( gGreenPmap );
125                                 break;
126                         case BLUE:
127                                 pixmap = GTK_PIXMAP( gBluePmap );
128                                 break;
129                         default:
130                                 continue;
131                         }
132                         gdk_draw_pixmap( widget->window,
133                                 widget->style->black_gc,
134                                 pixmap->pixmap, 0, 0,
135                                 piece->x, piece->y, -1, -1 );
```

If I were to adopt clip region support in this example, I would have added it just before line 132. The strategy would be to set the clip rectangle to the region described by the area field of the expose event. After the gdk_draw_pixmap() function has returned, the clip rectangle would need to be reset to NULL. For example:

```
gdk_gc_set_clip_rectangle( widget->style->black_gc, &event->area );
gdk_draw_pixmap( widget->window, ... );
gdk_gc_set_clip_rectangle( widget->style->black_gc, NULL );
```

Once again, I feel that the extra work to specify clip rectangles is not needed by the sample application due to the extra overhead involved and the simplicity of the graphics being drawn. But you should definitely test to see if your application would benefit from the use of clip rectangles.

GtkCalendar

Class Name

```
GtkCalendar
```

Parent Class Name

```
GtkWidget
```

Macros

Widget type macro: `GTK_TYPE_CALENDAR`

Object to widget cast macro: `GTK_CALENDAR(obj)`

Widget type check macro: `GTK_IS_CALENDAR(obj)`

Supported Signals

Table 15.13 Signals

Signal Name	*Condition Causing Signal to Trigger*
month_changed	Month view has changed.
day_selected	The user clicked on a day.
day_selected_double_click	The user double-clicked on a day.
prev_month	Month view has changed to the previous month.
next_month	Month view has changed to the next month.
prev_year	Year view has changed to the previous year.
next_year	Year view has changed to the next year.

Signal Function Prototypes

```
void
month_changed(GtkCalendar *calendar, gpointer user_data);

void
day_selected(GtkCalendar *calendar, gpointer user_data);
```

Signal Function Prototypes (Continued)

```
void
day_selected_double_click(GtkCalendar *calendar, gpointer
user_data);

void
prev_month(GtkCalendar *calendar, gpointer user_data);

void
next_month(GtkCalendar *calendar, gpointer user_data);

void
prev_year(GtkCalendar *calendar, gpointer user_data);

void
next_year(GtkCalendar *calendar, gpointer user_data);
```

Application-Level API Synopsis

Retrieve the constant GTK_TYPE_CALENDAR at runtime:

```
GtkType
gtk_calendar_get_type(void);
```

Create a new instance of GtkCalendar:

```
GtkWidget *
gtk_calendar_new(void);
```

Set the month and year displayed by the calendar:

```
gint
gtk_calendar_select_month(GtkCalendar *calendar, guint month, guint year);
```

Set the day displayed by the calendar:

```
void
gtk_calendar_select_day(GtkCalendar *calendar, guint day);
```

Mark a day number:

```
gint
gtk_calendar_mark_day(GtkCalendar *calendar, guint day);
```

Unmark a day number:

```
gint
gtk_calendar_unmark_day(GtkCalendar *calendar, guint day);
```

Unmark all day number marks:

```
void
gtk_calendar_clear_marks(GtkCalendar *calendar);
```

Application-Level API Synopsis (Continued)

Set calendar widget display options:
```
void
gtk_calendar_display_options(GtkCalendar *calendar,
        GtkCalendarDisplayOptions flags);
```

Retrieve the selected date from the calendar:
```
void
gtk_calendar_get_date(GtkCalendar *calendar,
        guint *year, guint *month, guint *day);
```

Freeze (batch) UI updates to the calendar:
```
void
gtk_calendar_freeze(GtkCalendar *calendar);
```

Unfreeze UI updates to the calendar:
```
void
gtk_calendar_thaw(GtkCalendar *calendar);
```

Class Description

GtkCalendar is a widget that can be used to display a simple calendar within a window or other container. The minimum content displayed by a calendar widget is a month view (see Figure 15.9). The application can set attributes that will cause the widget to render day names, week numbers, or controls that can be used to navigate the calendar on a month-to-month or year-to-year basis in either a forward or a backward direction (see Figure 15.10).

Figure 15.9 Minimal Calendar Display

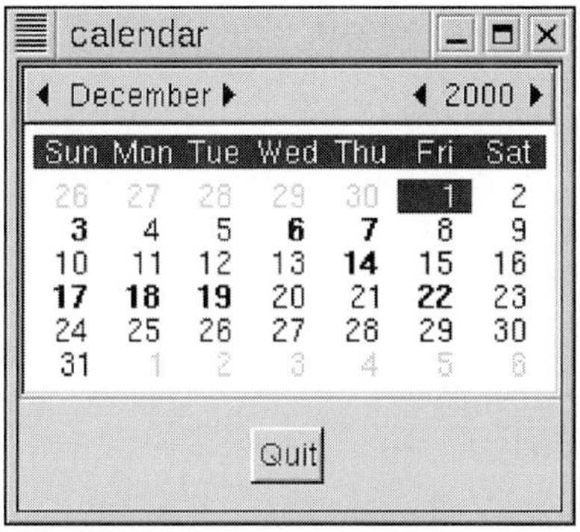

Figure 15.10 Full Calendar Display

An application can arrange to be notified via signals supported by GtkCalendar when the user has changed events such as the month or year or the user has selected a date by positioning the mouse over a date and then clicking or double-clicking mouse button 1. An application can also "mark" and "unmark" days within the currently visible month, as I will describe later. A marked date is drawn in a way that highlights it to the user; no further support for marked dates is provided by the calendar widget.

Creating a Calendar Widget

To create an instance of GtkCalendar, call gtk_calendar_new():

```
GtkWidget *
gtk_calendar_new(void);
```

As is done by nearly every Gtk+ widget creation function, gtk_calendar_new() returns an instance of GtkWidget. The date of the calendar is initialized to the current month and year. The day of the month is always set to 1.

Setting and Retrieving the Date Displayed by the Calendar

Obviously, most applications will need to set the date displayed by the calendar widget, either when the calendar is created and first displayed (if the current month and year is not desired) or in response to some application-defined need (the user requests to view a specific date). To set the month and year displayed by the calendar, call gtk_calendar_select_month():

```
gint
gtk_calendar_select_month(GtkCalendar *calendar, guint month,
        guint year);
```

The argument calendar is an instance of GtkCalendar. The month argument is an unsigned integer value that must be in the range [0, 11]. The year argument, also unsigned, must be greater than or equal to zero in value but can be set to an otherwise arbitrary value.

To set the day displayed by the calendar, call gtk_calendar_select_day():

```
void
gtk_calendar_select_day(GtkCalendar *calendar, guint day);
```

The day argument is a value in the range [1, 31]. If you select a day that is greater than the number of days in the month, this causes the day to be set, but it will not be rendered by the user interface to indicate its selection.

You can retrieve the currently selected date with gtk_calendar_get_date():

```
void
gtk_calendar_get_date(GtkCalendar *calendar,
        guint *year, guint *month, guint *day);
```

The return values specify the year (greater than or equal to zero), the month (1 through 12), and the day (1 through 31) that were selected by the user.

Marking Days

GtkCalendar allows you to mark an arbitrary number of days within a month, up to and including 31, the maximum number of days that a month can have. A marked day is drawn in bold to indicate to the user that it is marked. Marked dates are global in the sense that they persist as the user changes the month and/or year displayed. In some cases, this is good: A user might mark a date (e.g., New Year's Day) and then traverse ahead a few years to see which day of the week it falls on. In other cases, this is bad: An appointment book application might mark all of the days in a given month that contain meetings. Traversing from one month to another requires the application to clear the marks that are not valid for the month and year combination selected by the user.

Other than drawing the days you specify in bold and persisting marked dates as the user traverses the calendar, no support is provided by GtkCalendar except for the functions described in this section. The following sample program illustrates how to use marking in a simple appointment program.

To mark a day number, call gtk_calendar_mark_day():

```
gint
gtk_calendar_mark_day(GtkCalendar *calendar, guint day);
```

If the argument day is not in the range [1, 31], the function returns silently. Otherwise, the specified day will be marked, and the calendar widget will redraw itself so that the marked day is highlighted for the user. To unmark a day, call gtk_calendar_unmark_day():

```
gint
gtk_calendar_unmark_day(GtkCalendar *calendar, guint day);
```

This function takes the same arguments as gtk_calendar_mark_day(). The day specified is unmarked and the calendar is redrawn.

You can unmark all marked dates by passing the calendar widget as an argument to gtk_calendar_clear_marks():

```
void
gtk_calendar_clear_marks(GtkCalendar *calendar);
```

Setting Display Options

Before I present the sample program, let's discuss the remaining functions in the GtkCalendar API.

The first of these functions, gtk_calendar_display_options():

```
void
gtk_calendar_display_options(GtkCalendar *calendar,
        GtkCalendarDisplayOptions flags);
```

allows you to pass a set of flags that control what controls and features of the GtkCalendar widget are displayed. The possible flags are shown in Table 15.14:

Table 15.14 GtkCalendarDisplayOptions Flags

Flag	*Meaning*
GTK_CALENDAR_SHOW_HEADING	Display month and year and controls to change them.
GTK_CALENDAR_SHOW_DAY_NAMES	Show day names.
GTK_CALENDAR_NO_MONTH_CHANGE	If displaying heading, hide controls for changing month and year.
GTK_CALENDAR_SHOW_WEEK_NUMBERS	Show week numbers (1 through 52).
GTK_CALENDAR_WEEK_START_MONDAY	Display week as MTWThFSaSu (default is SuMTWThFSa).

The argument flags are a bitwise OR'ing of the preceding flags. For example, to show the month and year, hide the date traversal controls, and display weeks starting with Monday, you might execute the following code:

```
GtkWidget *cal;

gtk_calendar_display_options( GTK_CALENDAR( cal ),
        GTK_CALENDAR_SHOW_HEADING | GTK_CALENDAR_NO_MONTH_CHANGE |
        GTK_CALENDAR_WEEK_START_MONDAY );
```

GtkCalendar does not supply a function that can be used to retrieve the current flags, but you can get at them via the following code:

```
GtkWidget *cal;
GtkCalendarDisplayOptions flags;

flags = GTK_CALENDAR( cal )->display_flags;
```

Given the preceding, you can clear the GTK_CALENDAR_NO_MONTH_CHANGE flag with the following code:

```
flags &= ~GTK_CALENDAR_NO_MONTH_CHANGE;
gtk_calendar_display_options( GTK_CALENDAR( cal ), flags );
```

Freezing and Thawing the Calendar Display

The two remaining miscellaneous calendar functions, gtk_calendar_freeze() and gtk_calendar_thaw(), are used together in an attempt to reduce visual noise that might occur when a large set of changes is made to the calendar by the application. In my opinion, the only time you would want to wrap calls to the GtkCalendar API with freeze and thaw calls is when setting a number of marks on the currently displaying month. Both of these functions:

```
void
gtk_calendar_freeze(GtkCalendar *calendar);

void
gtk_calendar_thaw(GtkCalendar *calendar);
```

accept an instance of GtkCalendar as an argument. You must ensure that you call gtk_calendar_thaw() after calling gtk_calendar_freeze(); this is the only way to restore proper updates to a frozen calendar widget user interface.

Example Program

The following example is a simple appointment-book application that illustrates the important topics I just described.

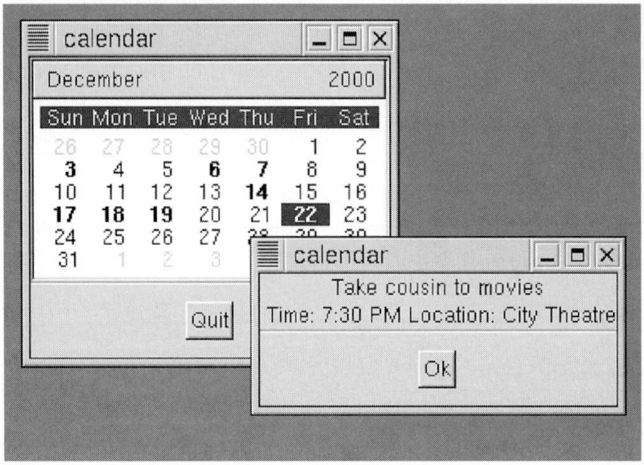

Figure 15.11 GtkCalendar Example Screenshot

Listing 15.6 GtkCalendar Example (See Figure 15.11)

```
#include <gtk/gtk.h>

// an appointment book entry

typedef struct _calentry {
    int day;            // day of the month
    char *timestr;      // time of the appointment
    char *title;        // appointment title
    char *location;     // appointment location
```

```
} CalEntry;

// Appointment book (only 1 month of data here, all hard-coded, for
// simplicity sake

static CalEntry entries[] = {
{ 3, "11:30 AM", "Lunch with Bob", "Joe's Grill"},
{ 6, "5:00 PM", "Pick up Sally at airport", "Airport" },
{ 7, "3:40 PM", "Dentist", "Dr. Jones"},
{ 14, "6:15 PM", "Dinner with team", "TBD"},
{ 17, "9:00 AM", "Golf", "Torrey Pines, North Course"},
{ 18, "1:00 PM", "Sally's flight home", "Airport" },
{ 19, "11:30 AM", "Phone roofer", "N/A"},
{ 22, "7:30 PM", "Take cousin to movies", "City Theatre" }
};

// format and display a message in a modal dialog

void
DisplayMessage( char *title, char *location, char *timestr )
{
    char buf[1024];
    GtkWidget *dialog, *label, *button;

    sprintf( buf, "%s\n Time: %s Location: %s", title, timestr,
             location );

    dialog = gtk_dialog_new();
    gtk_window_position(GTK_WINDOW (dialog), GTK_WIN_POS_MOUSE);
    gtk_window_set_modal(GTK_WINDOW (dialog), TRUE);

    label = gtk_label_new( buf );
    gtk_box_pack_start(GTK_BOX (GTK_DIALOG (dialog)->vbox),
             label, TRUE, TRUE, 0);

    button = gtk_button_new_with_label ("Ok");
    gtk_signal_connect_object(GTK_OBJECT (button), "clicked",
             GTK_SIGNAL_FUNC(gtk_widget_destroy), GTK_OBJECT(dialog));
    gtk_box_pack_start(GTK_BOX (GTK_DIALOG (dialog)->action_area),
             button, FALSE, FALSE, 0);
    gtk_widget_show_all( dialog );
}

// GtkCalendar day_selected signal function. See if the selected day is in
// the appointment book and, if so, display it in a dialog

void
SelectDay (GtkWidget *widget, gpointer data)
{
    guint year, month, day;
    int i;

    // retrieve the selected date

    gtk_calendar_get_date(GTK_CALENDAR(widget), &year, &month, &day);

    // see if it exists in the appointment book, and if it does
```

```
    // display the entry

    for ( i = 0; i < sizeof( entries ) / sizeof( CalEntry ); i++ )
            if ( entries[i].day == day )
                    DisplayMessage( entries[i].title,
                            entries[i].location, entries[i].timestr );
}

main( int argc, char *argv[] )
{
    GtkWidget *button, *calendar, *dialog;
    GtkCalendarDisplayOptions flags;
    int i;

    gtk_init( &argc, &argv );

    dialog = gtk_dialog_new();
    gtk_window_position(GTK_WINDOW (dialog), GTK_WIN_POS_MOUSE);

    // create the calendar widget

    calendar = gtk_calendar_new();

    // retrieve the default flags

    flags = GTK_CALENDAR( calendar )->display_flags;

    // turn off the ability to change the date

    gtk_calendar_display_options( GTK_CALENDAR( calendar ),
            flags | GTK_CALENDAR_NO_MONTH_CHANGE );

    // handle a mouse button 1 press over a day in the calendar

    gtk_signal_connect (GTK_OBJECT (calendar), "day_selected",
            GTK_SIGNAL_FUNC (SelectDay), NULL);

    // mark all days that have an entry in the appointment book

    for ( i = 0; i < sizeof( entries ) / sizeof( CalEntry ); i++ )
            gtk_calendar_mark_day( GTK_CALENDAR(calendar),
                    entries[i].day );

    gtk_box_pack_start(GTK_BOX (GTK_DIALOG (dialog)->vbox),
            calendar, TRUE, TRUE, 0);

    button = gtk_button_new_with_label ("Quit");
    gtk_signal_connect_object(GTK_OBJECT (button), "clicked",
            GTK_SIGNAL_FUNC(gtk_widget_destroy), GTK_OBJECT(dialog));
    gtk_box_pack_start(GTK_BOX (GTK_DIALOG (dialog)->action_area),
            button, FALSE, FALSE, 0);

    gtk_widget_show_all(dialog);
    gtk_main();
}
```

The appointment data in this sample application is hard-coded into an array and is only available for the current month. The program creates a calendar widget and places it in a dialog. Because only data for the current month is provided, I disable the capability for the user to change the month or the year. For each entry in the appointment book array, I mark the day in the month that corresponds to the date of the appointment (for simplicity, only one event per day is stored). A day_selected signal function, SelectDay(), is registered with the calendar widget and is invoked when the user positions the pointer over a day and clicks mouse button 1. The callback retrieves the selected day from the calendar using gtk_calendar_get_date() and then searches the appointment book to see if there is an entry for that day. If so, SelectDay() calls a function that formats the appointment book data and displays it in a dialog.

Summary

In this chapter, we finished coverage of the Gtk+ widget classes by taking a look at some miscellaneous widget classes. A ruler widget (GtkRuler, GtkVRuler, and GtkHRuler) displays a vertical (GtkVRuler) or horizontal (GtkHRuler) ruler in its container. A preview widget (GtkPreview) is capable of displaying color or grayscale image data. A sample program presented in this chapter illustrated how GtkPreview, in conjunction with libtiff, can be used to display TIFF image data.

Progress widgets (GtkProgress and GtkProgressBar) can add significantly to the usability of an application by providing users with visual feedback during tasks that take time to complete. A progress bar widget supports two modes. The first, what I call start-to-finish mode, can be used to convey a percentage-completed status for tasks that take a known amount of time or effort, such as the downloading of a file of a known, fixed size. The second mode, activity mode, can be used to indicate activity of an unknown duration, such as logging in to a server.

A tooltip widget (GtkTooltips) supports the display of context-sensitive help in a small window that is popped up by Gtk+ whenever the user hovers the mouse over a widget for which a tooltip has been registered. A tips query widget (GtkTipsQuery) is a less-often-used widget that provides an alternate way to display context-sensitive help text in an application.

A combo widget (GtkCombo) is a control that allows users to enter data into a text entry field or to select data from a pop-up menu attached to the control. A statusbar (GtkStatusbar) widget is essentially a frame widget that displays a text status message provided by the application. Status messages are stored on a stack; the top of the stack defines the message displayed by the statusbar widget. An accelerator label widget is primarily of interest to widget writers and supports the display of accelerator text in several widgets such as menu items.

Graphics applications can use a drawing-area widget (GtkDrawingArea) as a container for drawings and images. In this chapter, I presented a sample program that illustrated one possible technique for efficiently handling expose events received by a drawing area widget. The final widget discussed in this chapter, GtkCalendar, is useful for applications that need to display a calendar or solicit dates from users. I presented a short sample program that illustrates how an application can mark specific dates in a calendar widget, as well as respond to button presses made by the user upon specific dates that are displayed by the calendar widget.

APPENDIX

GTK+ 1.2 WIDGET HIERARCHY

The following depicts the Gtk+ 1.2 widget hierarchy. The number to the right of a class name specifies the chapter in this book that describes the corresponding widget class. Widget classes not covered in this book are in *italics*.

```
GtkObject  3
 +  GtkWidget  4
 |  +  GtkMisc
 |  |  +  GtkLabel  5
 |  |  |  +  GtkAccelLabel  15
 |  |  |  `  GtkTipsQuery  15
 |  |  +  GtkArrow  8
 |  |  +  GtkImage  8
 |  |  `  GtkPixmap  8
 |  +  GtkContainer  10
 |  |  +  GtkBin
 |  |  |  +  GtkAlignment
 |  |  |  +  GtkFrame  11
 |  |  |  |  `  GtkAspectFrame  11
 |  |  |  +  GtkButton  5
 |  |  |  |  +  GtkToggleButton  5
 |  |  |  |  |  `  GtkCheckButton  5
 |  |  |  |  |  `  GtkRadioButton  5
 |  |  |  |  `  GtkOptionMenu  9
 |  |  |  +  GtkItem
 |  |  |  |  +  GtkMenuItem  9
 |  |  |  |  |  +  GtkCheckMenuItem  9
 |  |  |  |  |  |  `  GtkRadioMenuItem  9
 |  |  |  |  |  `  GtkTearoffMenuItem  9
 |  |  |  |  +  GtkListItem
 |  |  |  |  `  GtkTreeItem  12
 |  |  |  +  GtkWindow  7
```

(Italic in the original: GtkBin, GtkAlignment, GtkItem, GtkListItem.)

```
| | | | + GtkColorSelectionDialog 7
| | | | + GtkDialog 7
| | | | | ` GtkInputDialog
| | | | + GtkDrawWindow
| | | | + GtkFileSelection 7
| | | | + GtkFontSelectionDialog 7
| | | | ` GtkPlug
| | | + GtkEventBox 11
| | | + GtkHandleBox 11
| | | + GtkScrolledWindow 11
| | | ` GtkViewport
| | + GtkBox 10
| | | + GtkButtonBox 10
| | | | + GtkHButtonBox 10
| | | | ` GtkVButtonBox 10
| | | + GtkVBox 10
| | | | + GtkColorSelection 7
| | | | ` GtkGammaCurve
| | | ` GtkHBox 10
| | | + GtkCombo 15
| | | ` GtkStatusbar 15
| | + GtkCList 6
| | | ` GtkCTree 12
| | + GtkFixed 10
| | + GtkNotebook 10
| | | ` GtkFontSelection 7
| | + GtkPaned 11
| | | + GtkHPaned 11
| | | ` GtkVPaned 11
| | + GtkLayout 11
| | + GtkList 6
| | + GtkMenuShell
| | | + GtkMenuBar 9
| | | ` GtkMenu 9
| | + GtkPacker 11
| | + GtkSocket
| | + GtkTable 11
| | + GtkToolbar 11
| | ` GtkTree 12
| + GtkCalendar 15
| + GtkDrawingArea 15
| | ` GtkCurve
| + GtkEditable
| | + GtkEntry 8
| | | ` GtkSpinButton 14
```

```
|  |  `  GtkText  14
|  +  GtkRuler  15
|  |  +  GtkHRuler  15
|  |  `  GtkVRuler  15
|  +  GtkRange  13
|  |  +  GtkScale  13
|  |  |  +  GtkHScale  13
|  |  |  `  GtkVScale  13
|  |  `  GtkScrollbar  13
|  |  +  GtkHScrollbar  13
|  |  `  GtkVScrollbar  13
|  +  GtkSeparator  8
|  |  +  GtkHSeparator  8
|  |  `  GtkVSeparator  8
|  +  GtkPreview  15
|  `  GtkProgress  15
|     `  GtkProgressBar  15
+  GtkData
|  +  GtkAdjustment  13
|  `  GtkTooltips  15
`  GtkItemFactory  9
```

INDEX

D

E

F

G

T

U

V

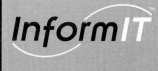